Lecture Notes in Artificial Intellige

T0250650

Subseries of Lecture Notes in Computer Science
Edited by J. Siekmann

Lecture Notes in Computer Science
Edited by G. Goos and J. Hartmanis

H. Boley M. M. Richter (Eds.)

Processing Declarative Knowledge

International Workshop PDK '91
Kaiserslautern, Germany, July 1-3, 1991
Proceedings

Springer-Verlag
Berlin Heidelberg New York
London Paris Tokyo
Hong Kong Barcelona
Budapest

Series Editor

Jörg Siekmann
University of Saarland
German Research Center for Artificial Intelligence (DFKI)
Stuhlsatzenhausweg 3, W-6600 Saarbrücken 11, FRG

Volume Editors

Harold Boley
German Research Center for Artificial Intelligence (DFKI)
Erwin-Schrödinger-Straße, Postfach 2080, W-6700 Kaiserslautern

Michael M. Richter
German Research Center for Artificial Intelligence (DFKI)
and
Computer Science Department, University of Kaiserslautern
Erwin-Schrödinger-Straße, W-6700 Kaiserslautern, FRG

CR Subject Classification (1991): D.1.6, I.2

ISBN 3-540-55033-X Springer-Verlag Berlin Heidelberg New York
ISBN 0-387-55033-X Springer-Verlag New York Berlin Heidelberg

Printed in Germany

Typesetting: Camera ready by author
Printing and binding: Druckhaus Beltz, Hemsbach/Bergstr.
45/3140-543210 - Printed on acid-free paper

Preface

PDK '91 was organized and hosted by the German Research Center for Artificial Intelligence (DFKI) in cooperation with the Association for Logic Programming (ALP) and the Gesellschaft für Informatik e.V. (GI). It aimed at both researchers and developers interested in the processing of declarative knowledge. Knowledge is often represented using definite clauses, rules, constraints, functions, conceptual graphs, and related formalizations. The workshop addressed such high-level representations and their efficient implementation required for declarative knowledge bases.
The workshop was attended by 105 participants and 28 talks were presented. This volume contains 25 submitted papers which appear here after a reviewing process in their final form. We thank the referees, without whose help we would not have been able to accomplish the difficult task of selecting among the many valuable contributions. A large portion of the papers treat representation methods, mainly concept languages. Implementation methods, the other major workshop topic, is mostly concerned with transformation techniques and WAM-like abstract machines. Moreover, there were sessions on semantics, applications, and Prolog extensions.

The intention that PDK be a practice-relevant workshop was reflected by system demonstrations. Twelve implemented knowledge-processing systems were scheduled for presentation, most of which are briefly described in these proceedings. The competition between procedural and declarative paradigms was discussed in a panel session. Revised position statements of panelists appear here in print.
Three invited talks covered important aspects of declarative knowledge processing. They were given by Carlo Zaniolo (MCC, USA) on "Efficient Processing of Declarative Rule-Based Languages for Databases", by Pascal van Hentenryck (Brown University, USA) on "Constraint Logic Programming", and by Andrew Taylor (University of Sydney, AUS) on "High Performance Prolog Implementation through Global Analysis". Carlo Zaniolo made it possible to prepare a written version of his talk for this volume. Two special talks by Chris Moss (Imperial College, GB) and Michel Dorochevsky (ECRC, D) concluded the workshop program with a study of large, real-life Prolog knowledge bases and an investigation of the future of dedicated Prolog hardware.

Kaiserslautern, October 1991 Harold Boley, Michael M. Richter

Program Committee:

Hassan Aït-Kaci, DEC Paris
Hans-Jürgen Appelrath, University of Oldenburg
Woody Bledsoe, University of Texas at Austin
Egon Börger, University of Pisa
Harold Boley, DFKI Kaiserslautern
Maurice Bruynooghe, Catholic University Leuven
Tim Finin, Unisys Paoli
Hervé Gallaire, GSI Paris
Jan Grabowski, Humboldt University Berlin
Alexander Herold, ECRC Munich
Robert Kowalski, Imperial College London
Hans Langmaack, University of Kiel
Jean-Louis Lassez, IBM Yorktown Heights
Michael M. Richter, DFKI Kaiserslautern (Chair)
Erik Sandewall, University of Linköping
John Taylor, Hewlett Packard Bristol
Andrei Voronkov, SINTEL Novosibirsk

Organizing Committee:

Philipp Hanschke, DFKI Kaiserslautern
Knut Hinkelmann, DFKI Kaiserslautern
Manfred Meyer, DFKI Kaiserslautern

Sponsors:

We gratefully acknowledge financial sponsorship by the following institutions:
Daimler Benz AG
Dresdner Bank AG
IBM Deutschland GmbH
Krupp Atlas Elektronik GmbH
Stadtsparkasse Kaiserslautern
Symbolics GmbH

Reviewers:

Jean-Marc Andreoli, ECRC Munich
Marianne Baudinet, Free University Brussels
Eddy Bevers, Catholic University Leuven
Alastair Burt, DFKI Kaiserslautern
David Chan, Hewlett Packard Bristol
Danny DeSchreye, Catholic University Leuven
Kave Eshgi, Hewlett Packard Bristol
Wolfgang Goerigk, University of Kiel
Ramiro Guerreiro, IBM Rio de Janeiro
Philipp Hanschke, DFKI Kaiserslautern
Keith A. Harrison, Hewlett Packard Bristol
Wolfram Heitsch, Humboldt University Berlin
Joxan Jaffar, IBM Yorktown Heights
Hans Jasper, University of Oldenburg
Ho-Fung Leung, Imperial College London
Bern Martens, Catholic University Leuven
John McShane, Hewlett Packard Bristol
Lode Missiaen, Catholic University Leuven
Andreas Nonnengart, University of Kaiserslautern
Peter Päppinghaus, Siemens Munich
Friedemann Simon, University of Kiel
Mark Syrett, Hewlett Packard Bristol
Jiyang Xu, ECRC Munich
Roland Yap, IBM Yorktown Heights

Contents

Invited and Special Talks

Session 1: Concept Languages I

Session 2: Concept Languages II

Session 3: Concept Languages III

Session 4: Semantics

Session 5: Applications

Session 6: PROLOG Extensions

Session 7: Transformation

Efficient Processing of Declarative Rule-Based Languages for Databases *

Carlo Zaniolo

University of California
Los Angeles, CA 90024

Abstract

In recent years, Deductive Databases have progressed from a subject of theoretical interest to an emerging technology area of significant commercial potential. The two main catalysts for progress have been a demand for advanced database applications and a rapid maturation of the enabling technology. Thus, Deductive Databases have now progressed beyond their initial Prolog-oriented beginnings and produced logic-based language, architectures and systems that support a declarative expression of knowledge through rules and their efficient processing on large databases. In this paper, we review the key concepts behind deductive databases, including language constructs, semantics issues, implementation techniques, architectures and prototypes. Then, we discuss key application areas driving the development of this technology, and current research directions in systems and theory.

1 Introduction

Deductive Databases support *queries, reasoning*, and *application development* on databases through a *declarative rule-based* language. The development of this novel technology was motivated by the emergence of a new wave of database applications that are not supported well by the current technology. Examples include:

1. *Computer aided design and manufacturing systems.*
2. *Scientific database applications:* Examples include studies of chemical structures, genomic data, and analysis of satellite data.
3. *Knowledge Mining and Data Dredging:* This require support for browsing and complex ad-hoc queries on large databases [Ts2]. For example, researchers need

*This work was done at MCC, Austin, Texas.

to search through medical histories to validate hypotheses about possible causes of diseases, and airlines want to maximize yields resulting from schedules and fare structures.

In addition to the traditional requirements of databases (such as integrity, sharing and recovery), these new applications demand complex structures, recursively defined objects, high-level languages and rules. For example, a VLSI CAD system typically allows the definitions of "cells," which are designs having other cells as subparts. Operations on such artifacts might expand out the design, say, to create a checkplot. The expansion must be carried on to arbitrary depth, so a recursive logic program is appropriate for defining the operation of cell expansion. These new requirements cannot be supported effectively by commercial database systems, including relational systems exemplified by SQL.

Even more traditional applications suffer from the limited power of current DBMS, where languages such as SQL can only access and modify data in limited ways; thus database applications are now written in a conventional language with intermixed query language calls. But since the non-procedural, set-oriented computational model of SQL is so different from that of procedural languages, and because of incompatible data types, an "impedance mismatch" occurs that hinders application development and causes expensive run-time conversions. This problem is particularly acute in applications such as the Bill-Of-Materials (BOM) dealing with arbitrary structures of unlimited depth [Wahl]. Thus, it has become generally accepted that, for applications at the frontier, we need a single, computationally complete, language that answers the needs previously discussed and serves both as a *query language* and as a *general-purpose application-language*.

Object-oriented systems, where the database is closely integrated with languages such as Smalltalk or C++, address some of the previous requirements, and support useful concepts, such as object-identity and a rich type structure with inheritance of properties from types to their subtypes. However, object-oriented systems lose an important advantage that relational languages have: relational languages are declarative and logic-based. Declarative languages provide the ability to express what one wants, and leave it up to the system the generation of detailed algorithms required to satisfy the request. This ability is essential for ease of use, data independence and code reusability.

Interest in Deductive Databases began in the early seventies with the establishment of the theoretical foundations for the field [GMN]; but experimental activity was then limited to few ground-breaking experiments [Kell]. A new generation of powerful rule-based languages for expert systems applications commanded great attention in the 80's. Among these, Prolog is of particular interest, because it is based on extensions of Horn-clause logic; Horn clauses are a close relative of relational calculus, which provides the semantic underpinning for relational query languages such as SQL. This similarity has led to considerable work at building a deductive database system, either, by extending Prolog with database capabilities or by coupling it with relational DBMSs [CGT]. While these experiments have been successful in producing powerful systems, they have also revealed several problems that stand in the way of complete integration. Some of these problems follow from the general difficulty of marrying DBMSs with programming languages, others are specific to Prolog.

2 Deductive Databases and Prolog

Some of Prolog's limitations, such as the absence of schema and secondary-storage based persistence, can be corrected through suitable extensions; others are so deeply engrained in Prolog's semantics and enabling technology that they are very difficult to overcome. For instance, the cornerstone of Prolog is SLD-resolution according to a left-to-right execution order. This powerful mechanism provides an efficient implementation for Horn-clause logic and an operational semantics to the many non-logic based constructs—such as updates, cuts and meta-level primitives—that were added to the language for expressive power. But the dependence of Prolog, and its enabling technology, on SLD-resolution present serious drawbacks from a database viewpoint:

- Prolog's rigid execution model corresponds to a navigational query execution strategy; thus, it compromises data independence and query optimization that build upon the non-navigational nature of relational query languages.
- In the style of most AI systems, Prolog's update constructs (i.e., assert and retract) are powerful but unruly, inasmuch as they can modify both the data and the program. Furthermore, none of the nine different semantics for updates in Prolog counted so far [Moss], are compatible with that of the relational data model. Indeed, the snapshot-based semantics of relational databases is incompatible with Prolog's execution model, which assumes pipelined execution [KNZ]. Supporting the notion of transactions, which is totally alien to Prolog, compounds these problems.
- The efficiency of Prolog's execution model is predicated upon the use of main memory. Indeed, all current Prolog implementations [WAM] rely on pointers, stacks and full unification algorithms, which are not well-suited to a secondary store-based implementation.

Thus, several research projects aiming to achieve a complete and harmonious integration of logic and databases have rejected Prolog's SLD-based semantics and implementation technology, while retaining Horn clauses with their rule-oriented syntax. This line of research has produced new languages and systems that combine the database functionality and non-procedurality of relational systems, with Prolog's reasoning and symbolic manipulation capability. A new implementation technology was developed for these languages (using extensions of relational DBMSs technology) to ensure their efficient support on, both, main memory and secondary store. Among the several prototypes proposed [Meta,Seta,KiMS], we will base our discussion on the $\mathcal{LDL}$ system [Ceta], due to the level of maturity that it has reached and the author's familiarity with the system. The most distinguished traits of $\mathcal{LDL}$, and similar systems, is as follows:

- Support for all database essentials. There is a clear notion of a (time-varying) database separated from the (time-invariant) rule-based program. The database is described by a schema with unique key constraints declarations, and explicit indexing information. Schemas are thus the vehicle for enforcing constraints and accessing internal relations and external SQL databases. The notions of recovery and database transactions are deeply ingrained in languages such as $\mathcal{LDL}$ [KNZ].
- A semantics that is database-oriented, declarative, and rigorous, as illustrated by the following points:
  1. *Database Orientation:* For instance, a snapshot-based semantics is used for updates in $\mathcal{LDL}$, combined with full support for the concept of database transactions. Other concepts that are derived and extended from relational databases include (a) all-answer solutions (b) duplicate control (c) sets (d) nested relations, and (e) the ability to enforce key constraints and functional dependencies in derived relations (via the `choice` construct).
  2. *Declarative Language:* As discussed in the next section, these systems come closer to implementing the full declarative semantics of Horn clauses, by supporting both forward chaining and backward chaining execution strategies, under automatic system control [UlZa]. Thus, several applications, e.g., those involving non-linear rules or cyclic graphs, are much simpler to write in $\mathcal{LDL}$ than in Prolog [UlZa]. The notion of a query optimizer is also part of these systems, for compatibility with relational systems, better data independence, and enhanced program reusability. Finally, the declarative semantics is extended beyond the Horn clauses to include stratified negation, grouping and non-deterministic pruning (thus eliminating Prolog's cut) [NaTs].
  3. *Rigorous Semantics:* $\mathcal{LDL}$'s formal semantics [NaTs], is the result of a systematic effort to ferret out any ambiguity from both the declarative and the imperative aspects of the language. For instance, in dealing with logical constructs, such as negation and set-grouping, non-stratified programs are disallowed due to the lack a model-theoretic semantics for some of these programs. For imperative constructs, several restrictions are enforced upon programs with updates, such as disallowing updates in disjunctive goals and prohibiting unfailing goals after updates. The objective of these restrictions is to simplify and structure these programs along with their compilation. As a result, $\mathcal{LDL}$ programs with updates must be structured in a precise way—a discipline that requires some learning, but also enhances the value of resulting code as a vehicle for rigorous and complete specifications.
- An implementation technology that is database-oriented, and, in fact, represents an extension to the compiler/optimizer technology of relational systems. Thus

SLD-resolution and unification are respectively replaced with fixpoint computation and matching, which because of their simpler nature can be supported well in secondary as well as in primary storage [Ullm,Ceta]. Furthermore, declarative set-oriented semantics, makes it implementable using an assortment of alternative execution models and strategies— including translation to relational algebra— thus expanding the opportunities for query optimization of relational systems.

We will next review the salient features of deductive database technology, focusing on $\mathcal{LDL}$ as a concrete example.

3 Languages

Constructs for Logic-based languages can be grouped in three main classes, as follows:

1. Horn-clause based constructs
2. Non-monotonic logic-based constructs (such as negation, sets and choice constructs)
3. imperative constructs (such as updates and I/O)

A language such as $\mathcal{LDL}$ shares with Prolog Horn-clause based constructs above, but not the remaining two. There are significant differences even with respect to Horn Clauses, as illustrated by the fact that in deductive databases programs are less dependent on a particular execution model, such as forward-chaining or backward-chaining. A Prolog programmer can only write rules that work with backward chaining; an OPS5 [Forg] programmer can only write rules that work in a forward chaining mode. By contrast, systems such as $\mathcal{LDL}$ [NaTs] and NAIL! [Meta], select the proper inference mode automatically, enabling the user to focus on the logical correctness of the rules rather than on the underlying execution strategy. This point is better illustrated by an example. A methane molecule consists of a carbon atom linked with four hydrogen atoms. An ethane molecule can be constructed by replacing any H of a methane with a carbon with three Hs. Therefore, the respective structures of methane and ethane molecules are as follows:

More complex alkanes can then be obtained inductively, in the same way: i.e., by replacing an H of a simpler alkane by a carbon with three Hs.

We can now define alkanes using Horn clauses. A methane molecule will be represented by a complex term, `carb(h, h, h)`, and an ethane molecule by `carb(h, h, carb(h, h, h))`(thus, we implicitly assume the presence of an additional `h`, the root of our tree). In general, alkane molecules can be inductively defined as follows:

```
all_mol(h, 0, Max).
all_mol(carb(M1, M2, M3), N, Max) ←
                    all_mol(M1, N1, Max),
                    all_mol(M2, N2, Max),
                    all_mol(M3, N3, Max),
                    N= N1+N2+N3+1, N <= Max.
```

In addition to defining alkanes of increasing complexity, these non-linear recursive rules count the carbons in the molecules, ensuring finiteness in their size and number by checking that the tally of carbons never exceeds `Max`.

This alkane definition can be used in different ways. For example, to generate all molecules with no more than four carbons, one can write:

```
?  all_mol(Mol,Cs, 4).
```

To generate all molecules with exactly four carbons one will write:

```
?  all_mol(Mol, 4, 4).
```

Furthermore, if the relation `alk(Name, Str)` associates the names of alkanes with their structure, then the following rule will compute the number of carbons for an alkane given its name (assume that 10000 is a large enough number for all molecules to have a lower carbon complexity).

```
find(Name, Cs) ← alk(Name, Str), all_mol(Str, Cs , 10000).
```

The first two examples can be supported only through a forward chaining computation, which, in turn, translates naturally into the least-fixpoint computation that defines the model-theoretic based semantics of recursive Horn clause programs [NaTs]. The least fixpoint computation amounts to an iterative procedure, where partial results are added to a relation until a steady state is reached.

Therefore, deductive databases support well the first two examples via forward chaining, while Prolog and other backward chaining systems would flounder. In the last example, however, the first argument, `Str`, of `all_mol` is bound to the values generated by the predicate `alk`. Thus a computation such as Prolog's backward chaining, which recursively propagates these bindings, is significantly more efficient than forward chaining. Now, deductive databases solve this problem equally well, by using techniques such as the *Magic Set Method*, or the *Counting Method* that simulate backward chaining through a pair of coupled fixpoint computations [Ullm].

Since fixpoint computations check newly generated values against the set of previous values, cycles are handled automatically. This is a most useful feature since cyclic graphs are often stored in the database; furthermore, derived relations can also be cyclic.

In our alkane example, for instance, there are many equivalent representations for the same alkane. To generate them, equivalence-preserving operations, such as rotation and permutation on the molecules, are used. But, repeated applications of these operations brings back previous structures. In order to detect these cycles in Prolog, programmers frequently use bags to "remember" the previously encountered structures. In deductive databases, there is no need to carry around such a bag since cycles are detected and handled efficiently by the system.

4 Non-Monotonic Constructs

The declarative semantics and programming paradigm of deductive databases extends beyond Horn-clause programming, to include non-monotonic logic-based constructs, such as negation, sets and the `choice` operator [NaTs]. In fact, this line of research has significantly advanced the state-of-the-art on semantics and implementation techniques for non-monotonic logic constructs. For instance, deductive databases support efficiently stratified negation [NaTs], which has a rigorous semantics based on the concept of perfect models [Prz]. While stratified negation is more powerful than negation-by-failure provided by Prolog, many applications require unstratified negation, set grouping operators and aggregates [Wahl]. Research in this area has produced elegant concepts, such as well-founded models [VGRS] and stable models [GeLi], which provide very general declarative semantics for logic programs with negation. But efficient implementations for such semantics remains, in general, an open problem and the the topic of intense research. A solution approach consists in identifying classes of non-monotonic problems for which a declarative formulation is conducive to complexity bounds that are close to those obtainable using procedural programming. An efficient rendering of classical graph algorithms, such as the Dijkstra's minimum spanning tree algorithm, is indeed possible in the deductive database framework [GGZ].

A topic where recent research has solved both the semantic and the computational problems of non-monotonicity is that of non-deterministic pruning operators, such as $\mathcal{LDL}$'s `choice` construct. This construct was introduced in [KrNa], where a semantics based on functional dependency constraints was proposed. For example, if **takes** denotes students taking courses,

```
takes(andy,engl).
takes(ann, math).
takes(mark,engl).
takes(mark,math).
```

then the selection of an arbitrary student for each course can be specified as follows:

```
a_st(St,Crs) ← takes(St,Crs), choice((Crs),(St)).
```

The goal choice((Crs),(St)), in the first rule, specifies that the a_st predicate symbol must associate exactly one student to each course, as per the functional dependency (FD) $Crs \rightarrow St$. This FD establishes a declarative constraint that must hold independent of the particular way in which these rules are processed. This is to be contrasted to how this FD can be enforced in Prolog, assuming that the second argument of a_st, i.e., Crs, is bound:

```
a_st(St,Crs) : -takes(St,Crs),!.
```

But if Crs is free, then, to enforce the same FD, the previous program will have to be rewritten as follows:

```
a_st(St, Crs) :-  takes(_, Crs), as_st1(St, Crs).
a_st1(St, Crs):- takes(St, Crs), ! .
```

Thus, a declarative semantics for pruning constructs improve the reusability and data independence of programs beyond what is possible with operational constructs such as the cut.

There are technical problems with the semantics of choice as formulated in [KrNa] (due to the assumption that constraints are checked after a minimal model is constructed, rather than during the construction of the model itself). These problems have been eliminated by reconducing the semantics of choice to that of negation using stable models [SaZa]. Thus the functional dependency $Crs \rightarrow St$ holds in the model defining the meaning of this program. A program with equivalent meaning can be defined using negation as follows:

```
a_st(St,Crs) ← takes(St,Crs), chosen(Crs,St).
chosen(Crs,St) ← takes(St,Crs),¬diffChoice(Crs,St).
diffChoice(Crs,St) ← chosen(Crs, St̄ ),St ≠ St̄.
takes(andy,engl).
takes(ann, math).
takes(mark,engl).
takes(mark,math).
```

This program with negation has stable model semantics, where the non-determinism is captured by the presence of alternative stable models [SaZa]. This result is significant since it brings together two fundamental non-Horn constructs that have been used in logic programming languages for many years. In the process, our understanding on the nature of negation and non-deterministic pruning is greatly enhanced. Therefore a declarative characterization of the formal semantics of pruning constructs, is possible for both the bottom-up framework of deductive databases, [GPSZ] and for the more traditional top-down framework of traditional logic programming [GGZ]. Furthermore, the semantics with negation is clarified: e.g., a simple explanation is thus provided for the existence of multiple stable models in recursive programs of negation—a situation that was poorly understood by previous researchers. This result also shows that, while the computation of stable models requires, in general, exponential algorithms, there are classes of programs, which do not have total well-founded models, but for which total stable models exist and can be computed efficiently. The re-formulation of `choice` using negation, in fact, suggests that this constructs can simply be implemented by memorizing and checking incrementally previous values, in order to avoid any violation of FD constraints [GPSZ].

5 Architectures

The key implementation problems for Deductive Databases pertain to finding efficient executions for the given set of rules and query. For this purpose, Deductive Database systems perform a global analysis of rules—in contrast to Prolog compilers, which are normally based on local rule analysis. A global analysis is performed at compile time, using suitable representations such as the Rule/Goal graph [Ullm] or the predicate connection graph [Ceta]. Its cornerstone is the notion of bound arguments and free arguments of predicates. For a general idea of this global analysis is performed, consider the following example:

```
usanc(X, Y) <- anc(X,Y), born(Y, usa).

anc(X,Z) <- parent(X,Z).
anc(X,Z) <- parent(X,Y), anc(Y,Z).
```

Thus, the last two rules supply the recursive definition of ancestors (parents of an ancestors are themselves ancestors) and the the first rule choses the ancestors of a given `X` that were born in the USA (lower case is used for constants, and upper case for variables). Then a query such as

```
? usanc(mark, Y).
```

defines the following pattern:

$\mathtt{usanc}^{bf}$

The superscript bf is an *adornment* denoting the fact that the first argument is bound and the second is not.

The global analysis is next applied to determine how the adornments of the query goal can be propagated down to the rest of the rule set. By unifying the query goal with the head of the **usanc** rule, we obtain the adorned rule:

$$\mathtt{usanc}^{bf} < -\mathtt{anc}^{bf}, \mathtt{born}^{bb}.$$

This adornment assumes that the first argument of **born** is bound by the second argument of **anc** according to a sideway information passing principle (SIP) [Ullm]. The next question to arise is whether the recursive goal $\mathtt{anc}^{bf}$ is supportable. The analysis of the **anc** rules yields the following adorned rules (assuming a left-to-right SIP):

$$\mathtt{anc}^{bf} < -\mathtt{parent}^{bf}.$$
$$\mathtt{anc}^{bf} < -\mathtt{parent}^{bf}, \mathtt{anc}^{bf}.$$

The analysis is now complete, since the adornment of the **anc** goal in the tail is the same as that in the head. Assuming that **born** and **parent** are database predicates, the given adornments can easily be implemented through a search taking advantage of the bound first argument in **parent** and both bound arguments in **born**. The recursive predicate **anc** can also be solved efficiently: in fact, a further analysis indicates that the recursive rule is left-linear [Ullm] and that the given adornment can, after some rewriting of the rules, be supported by a single-fixpoint computation [Ullm]. When the recursive predicate cannot be supported through a single fixpoint, other methods are used, including the counting method, and the very general magic set method [Ullm].

Figure 1 describes the architecture of the $\mathcal{LDL}$ system. The first operation to be performed once a query form is given (a query form is a query template with an indication of bound/free arguments) is to propagate constants into recursive rules and to extract the subset of rules relevant to this particular query. By examining alternative goal orderings, execution modes, and methods for supporting recursion the optimizer finds a safe strategy, which minimizes a cost estimate. For rules where all goals refer to database relations, the optimizer behaves like a relational system. The Enhancer's task, is to apply the proper recursive method by rewriting the original rules. A rule rewriting approach is also used to support the idempotence and commutativity properties of set terms. Since recursion is implemented by fixpoint iterations, and only matching is needed at execution time, the abstract target machine and code can be greatly simplified, with respect to that of Prolog [WAM]; thus, it can also be based on simple extensions to relational algebra. For instance, the first (limited) $\mathcal{LDL}$ prototype generated code for an intermediate relational-algebra language for a parallel database machine. The current prototype is based on single-tuple get-next interface designed for both main-memory and secondary store. The single-tuple interface supplies various opportunities for intelligent backtracking and existential variables optimization, exploited by the compiler to obtain good performance from the object code [Meta]. The intermediate object code is actually C, to support portability and a open architecture.

Other experimental systems differ in several ways from the architecture of Figure 1. For instance, NAIL! uses a relational-algebra based intermediate code, and employs *capture rules*, rather than cost-prediction based optimization, to drive the selection of a proper execution strategy [Ceta].

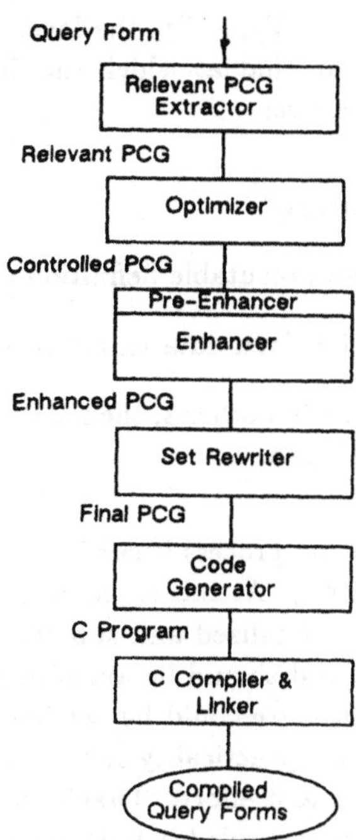

Figure 1. Architecture of the $\mathcal{LDL}$ Compiler

6 Applications

The unique advantages offered by Deductive Databases in several applications areas are well-documented and demonstrated by various pilot applications. These areas range from traditional ones, such as computer-aided manufacturing applications, which presently suffer because of the inability of SQL to support recursive queries and rules, to new scientific applications, such as those connected with the burgeoning areas of molecular biology [Ts1]. Because of space limitations, we will discuss only data dredging and enterprise modeling.

Data Dredging: This term denotes an emerging computational paradigm which supports "knowledge extraction" from, and the "discovery process" on the ever-growing repository of stored data [Ts2]. This usage of databases—in the past primarily associated with the intelligence community— is now becoming pervasive in medicine and science. Data Dredging is also an increasingly common practice of such such business applications as selective marketing and yield-management [Hopp].

The source of the data is typically a large volume of low-level records, collected from measurements and monitoring of empirical processes, intelligence operations and businesses. The problem is how to use this data to verify certain conjectures and to help refine or formulate hypotheses. Typically, the level of abstraction at hypotheses are formulated is much higher than that at which the data was collected. Thus, an iterative approach is needed, as follows:

1. Formulate hypothesis or concept.
2. Translate the concept into an executable definition (e.g., a rule-set and query).
3. Execute the query against the given data and observe the results.
4. If the results fully confirm the hypothesis, then exit; otherwise, modify the initial hypothesis and repeat these steps.

Obviously, the decision to exit the process is subjective and upon the analyst or researcher who is carrying out the study. At this stage he or she may have decided either that the concept is now adequately finalized and substantiated, or that the data does not support the initial conjecture and should be abandoned or tried out with different data. While in principle, this procedure could be carried out using any programming language, the key to the experiment's practicality and timeliness hinges upon the ability to complete it within limited time and effort. Thanks to their ability of quickly formulating very sophisticated queries and ruled-based decisions on large volumes of data, deductive databases are an ideal tool for data dredging. Our experience in developing such applications with $\mathcal{LDL}$ also suggests that its open architecture is important in this process, inasmuch as, for example, a number of low-level, computation intensive tasks (such as filtering and preprocessing) must be used in the high-level, rule-driven discovery process.

Enterprise Modeling: The ability to model the data and the procedures of a business enterprise is key to the successful development of information systems. Some of the advantages of a deductive database environment in this respect were outlined in the introduction; these advantages were confirmed during the one-year field study described in [Aeta]. This study reports on the experience of using the $\mathcal{LDL}$ prototype in conjunction with a structured-design methodology called *POS* (Process, Object and State) [Aeta].

A key idea of the POS methodology is that of using the Entity-Relationship (E-R) framework for modeling both dynamic and static aspects of the enterprise. By using the notions of aggregation and abstraction within the E-R framework, to capture what has traditionally been thought of as derived data, the E-R model can specify most of the processing associated with a specific problem domain. This allows the capture of both data modeling and process modeling within one framework, thus eliminating the need for additional formalisms (such as work-flow diagrams) in the final specifications. Furthermore, when a deductive computing environment is used, both the traditional generalization structures and the less-often-used aggregation structures can be directly encoded in a rule-based description, yielding executable specifications that are well-structured, easy to read and have a formal semantics.

This basic approach was tested in a case study, where a a simplified information system was represented for the automobile registration authority (i.e., Department of Motor Vehicles). This information system involves the modeling of a set of entities (such as manufactures, owners, garages, and motor vehicles of various types) and a set of events or transactions, (such as the registration of various entities and the purchase and destruction of a motor vehicle). Several constraints must be enforced, including uniqueness, existence and cardinality of entities, and restrictions of parties qualified by law to partake in different transaction types. Specific applications to be supported by such an information system include:

- Knowing who is, or was, the registered owner of a vehicle at any time from its construction to its destruction
- Monitoring compliance with certain laws, such as those pertaining to fuel consumption and transfer of ownership

In an informal study, also including a comparison with alternative prototyping frameworks, $\mathcal{LDL}$ proved very effective and desirable, in terms of naturalness of coding, terseness, and readability of the resulting programs. A larger study is now in progress to determine the scalability of these benefits to applications in the large, and to further evaluate the following points:

- Use of $\mathcal{LDL}$ to validate large specifications
- Feasibility of an order of magnitude code compression over 3rd generation languages
- Shift in efforts from coders to requirements specifiers
- An increased scope of data management and decreased scope of application development organizations

7 Future Directions

By enabling the development of several pilot applications, the first generation of deductive database systems has proved the viability of this new technology and demonstrated its practical potential. Yet, this experiences has also revealed the need for several improvements and extensions. For this reason, and to take advantage of more recent technical advances, work is now in progress toward the next generation of deductive database prototypes. For instance, NAIL! has recently undergone a major re-implementation and extension, where a close integration with the procedural world is supported through a procedural shell called Glue [PDR].

The experience with the $\mathcal{LDL}$ prototype has led to the design of the new $\mathcal{LDL}$++ system, which will support the advances in non-monotonic logic previously described, will correct the limitations of the current system and provide support for Abstract Data Types (ADT)s.

For, instance, having found that a better development environment is needed, the $\mathcal{LDL}$++ system will support powerful debugging facilities and fast turnaround on compilation. Furthermore, having realized the benefits of $\mathcal{LDL}$'s system open architecture, the new system will provide transparent interface to several external databases and support (ADT)s. It will thus possible to import classes and methods defined in the external C++ environment and have them behave as first-class $\mathcal{LDL}$++ objects, as to allow the tight integration with external environments. Furthermore, new ADTs can also be defined through the $\mathcal{LDL}$++ module definition mechanism and compiler. Thus $\mathcal{LDL}$++ will combine key ADT features from databases and programming languages.

References

[Aeta] Ackley, D., et al. "System Analysis for Deductive Database Environments: an Enhanced role for Aggregate Entities," *Procs. 9th Int. Conference on Entity-Relationship Approach*, Lausanne, CH, Oct. 8-10, 1990.

[Ceta] Chimenti, D. et al., "The $\mathcal{LDL}$ System Prototype," *IEEE Journal on Data and Knowledge Engineering*, March 1990.

[Hopp] Hopper, D.E., "Rattling SABRE—New Ways to Compete on Information," *Harvard Business Review*, May-June 1990, pp. 118-125.

[CGT] Ceri, S., G. Gottlob and L. Tanca, "Logic Programming and Deductive Databases," Springer-Verlag, 1989.

[DM89] "The Rapid Prototyping Conundrum", DATAMATION, June 1989.

[Forg] Forgy, C. L., Rete: a Fast Algorithm for the Many Pattern/Many Object Patttern Match Problem, *Artificial Intelligence* 19 (1), pp. 17-37, 1982.

[Gane] Gane, C. "Rapid System Development," Prentice Hall, 1989.

[GGZ] Ganguly, S., S. Greco and C. Zaniolo, "Minimum and Maximum Predicates in Logic Programming," Proc. 10th, ACM SIGACT-SIGMOD-SIGART Symposium on Principles of Database Systems, pp. 154-164, 1991.

[GeLi] Gelfond, M., and Lifschitz, V., "The stable model semantics for logic programming", Proc. 5th Int. Conf. and Symp. on Logic Programming, MIT Press, pp. 1070-1080, 1988.

[GPSZ] Giannotti, F., D. Pedreschi, Saccà, D., and Zaniolo, C., "Non-Determinism in Deductive Databases," MCC Technical Report, STP-LD-003-91.

[GMN] Gallaire, H.,J. Minker and J.M. Nicolas,"Logic and Databases: a Deductive Approach," Computer Surveys, Vol. 16, No. 2, 1984.

[Kell] Kellogg, C., "A Practical Amalgam of Knowledge and Data Base Technology" Proc. of AAAI Conference, Pittsburg, Pa., 1982.

[KiMS] Kiernan, G., C. de Maindreville, and E. Simon "Making Deductive Database a Practical Technology: a step forward," Proc. 1990 ACM–SIGMOD Conference on Management of Data, pp. 237-246.

[KNZ] Krishnamurthy, S. Naqvi and Zaniolo, "Database Transactions in $\mathcal{LDL}$", *Proc. Logic Programming North American Conference*, pp. 795-830, MIT Press, 1989.

[KuYo] Kunifji S., H. Yokota, "Prolog and Relational Databases for 5th Generation Computer Systems," in *Advances in Logic and Databases*, Vol. 2, (Gallaire, Minker and Nicolas eds.), Plenum, New York, 1984.

[KrNa] Krishnamurthy, R., and Naqvi, S.A., "Non Deterministic Choice in Datalog", *Proc. 3rd Int. Conf. on Data and Knowledge Bases*, Morgan Kaufmann Pub., Los Altos, pp. 416-424, 1988.

[Meta] Morris, K. et al. "YAWN! (Yet Another Window on NAIL!), Data Engineering, Vol.10, No. 4, pp. 28–44, Dec. 1987.

[Moss] Moss, C., "Cut and Paste—defining the Impure Primitives of Prolog", *Proc. Third Int. Conference on Logic Programming*, London, July 1986, pp. 686-694.

[NaTs] S. A. Naqvi, S. Tsur *"A Logical Language for Data and Knowledge Bases"*, W. H. Freeman, 1989.

[PDR] Phipps, G., M.A., Derr and K. A. Ross, "Glue-Nail: a Deductive Database System," Proc. 1991 ACM–SIGMOD Conference on Management of Data, pp. 308-317 (1991).

[Prz] Przymusinski, T.C., "On the Declarative and Procedural Semantics of Deductive Databases and Logic Programs", in *Foundations of Deductive Databases and Logic Programming*, (Minker, J. ed.), Morgan Kaufman, Los Altos, 1987, pp. 193-216.

[SaZa] Saccà, D., and Zaniolo, C., "Stable models and non determinism in logic programs with negation", Proc. 9th, ACM SIGACT-SIGMOD-SIGART Symposium on Principles of Database Systems, pp. 205-218, 1990.

[Seta] Schmidt, H. et al "Combining Deduction by Certainty with the Power of Magic" *Proc. 1st Int. Conf. on Deductive and O-O Databases*, Dec. 4-6, 1989, Kyoto, Japan.

[Ts1] Tsur S., "Deductive Databases in Action," *ACM SIGMOD-SIGACT Symp. on Principles of Database Systems*, Denver, Colorado, pp. 142-153, 1991.

[Ts2] Tsur S., "Data Dredging," *Data Engineering*, Vol. 13, No. 4, IEEE Computer Society, Dec. 90.

[Ullm] Ullman, J.D., *"Database and Knowledge-Based Systems*, Vols. I and II, Computer Science Press, Rockville, Md., 1989.

[UlZa] Ullman, J. and C. Zaniolo, "Deductive Databases, Achievements and Future Directions," *SIGMOD Record*, pp. 77-83, Vol. 19, No. 4, ACM Press, Dec. 1990.

[VGRS] Van Gelder, A., Ross, K., Schlipf, J.S., "Unfounded Sets and Well-Founded Semantics for General Logic Programs", *ACM SIGMOD-SIGACT Symp. on Principles of Database Systems*, March 1988, pp. 221-230.

[Wahl] Wahl, D., "Bill of Materials in Relational Databases–an analysis of current research and its applications to manufacturing databases," DEC Report 22/2/91.

[WAM] Warren, D.H.D., "An Abstract Prolog Instruction Set," Tech. Note 309, AI Center, Computer Science and Technology Div., SRI, 1983.

[Zani] Zaniolo, C. "Object Identity and Inheritance in Deductive Databases: an Evolutionary Approach," *Proc. 1st Int. Conf. on Deductive and O-O Databases*, Dec. 4-6, 1989, Kyoto, Japan.

Has Dedicated Hardware for Prolog a Future ?

Michel Dorochevsky, Jacques Noyé, Olivier Thibault
European Computer-Industry Research Centre
Parallel and Distributed Systems Group
Arabellastr. 17, D-8000 München 81, FRG

Abstract

Efficiency has always been one of the problems of high-level languages like Prolog. Different solutions have been suggested to speed up the execution of Prolog. One alternative is to build dedicated hardware. Another alternative, using advanced compilation techniques through global analysis, has been taken recently with spectacular results. A third alternative consists of combining hardware and software solutions. This paper discusses the relative merits and shortcomings of the three approaches in the light of the experience gained at ECRC in the KCM (Knowledge Crunching Machine) project, the ultimate question being: "Has dedicated hardware for Prolog a future?".

1 Introduction

Efficiency has always been one of the problems of high-level languages like Prolog. Different solutions have been suggested to speed up the execution of Prolog. One alternative is to build dedicated hardware. This has led, over the past few years, to a significant number of implemented "Prolog machines" [10, 9, 12, 14, 11, 6], including KCM (Knowledge Crunching Machine) [1, 2, 19]. The KCM project, started at ECRC in 1987, built and evaluated a machine that supports Logic Programming at the processor level. Four prototype machines were actually operational in July 1988 and KCM become the first desk-top Prolog machine to reach the 1 MLIPS (Mega Inferences per Second). A small series of pilot machines were subsequently built and distributed in 1990 to various academic sites and research institutes for evaluation purposes and to support the development of large-scale Prolog applications.

Recently, optimising compilers based on static analysis have produced spectacular results. Andrew Taylor reports speeds close to 3 MLips on a state-of-the-art high performance RISC workstation [17]. On the same kind of machine, a 25 MHz MIPS processor, Peter Van Roy claims that his system can run some programs more efficiently than the MIPS C compiler in optimisation mode. The work of Peter Van Roy was combined with the design of the BAM (Berkeley Abstract Machine) processor, a VLSI general purpose processor with extensions to support Prolog.

This paper is an attempt to draw conclusions from the experience gained with KCM. It reviews the benefits and shortcomings of the three main approaches, which consist of emphasizing hardware design, emphasizing software design or combining hardware and software design with the objective of being in a position of answering the question of whether dedicated hardware for Prolog has any future.

The paper is divided into 5 sections. Following this introduction, Section 2 gives an overview of KCM as an example of the *hardware approach.* Section 3 presents PARMA, the compiler of Andrew Taylor, as an example of the *software approach.* Section 4 looks at the combination of both approaches on both the BAM and KCM. Section 5 concludes the paper.

2 KCM: An Example of a Dedicated Hardware Accelerator

In this section we give a short overview of the KCM architecture and summarize the evaluation results available so far [19, 20].

2.1 Overview of KCM

KCM is a single user, single task high-performance back-end processor which, coupled to a UNIX desk-top workstation as shown in Figure 1 , provides a fast and user-friendly Prolog environment catering for both development and execution of significant Prolog applications.

KCM is equipped with its private memory and runs, on top of a small kernel (KCM Kernel [15]), a complete Prolog system (KCM-Sepia [8]). The host computer provides standard UNIX services, mainly I/O and secondary storage.

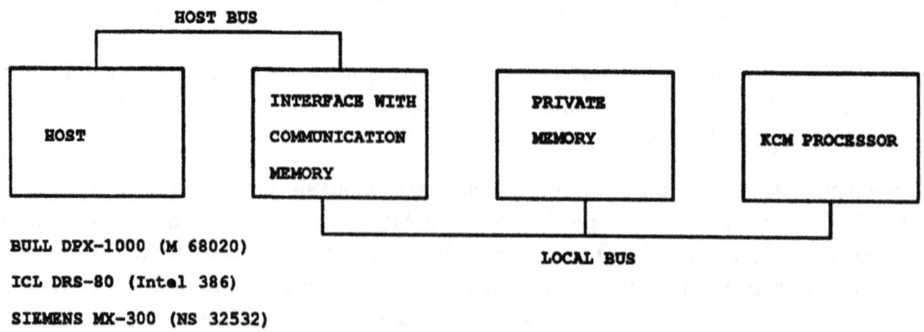

Figure 1: The KCM System

The Instruction Set The instruction set of KCM was designed with two main goals: performance on the one hand, flexibility and extendibility on the other hand. To our knowledge, KCM was the first Prolog machine to really consider the second issue. This led to an instruction set composed of *basic instructions* and *Prolog instructions.*

The higher-level Prolog instructions are very close to the WAM instructions [21]. Through these instructions, the microcode makes it possible to support very efficiently the basic Prolog mechanisms (indexing, unification, continuation, and backtracking).

The lower-level RISC-like instructions constitute a general purpose instruction set which provide the functionality that the standard WAM does not provide but which is necessary for an efficient implementation of the lower-level layers of the system (Prolog runtime, kernel).

As a result, though KCM is dedicated to Prolog, it is not restricted to Prolog and can be seen as a tagged general purpose machine with support for symbolic processing, in particular logic programming.

The CPU The CPU of KCM has the following main characteristics:

- **A 64-bit tagged architecture**: The WAM model of computation assumes tagged data words, i.e. a basic entity constists of a value plus an additional tag field that gives information on its type. A length of 32 bits for each, tag and value was chosen, leading to a word length of 64 bits. This permits the support of full 32-bit integer and floating point arithmetic and leaves space in the tag for various extensions (e.g. coroutining).
- **A Harvard architecture**: The hardware architecture of KCM is based on the Harvard architecture, i.e. it has two separate access paths to the memory system, one for code and one for data.
- **Stack oriented addressing**: KCM supports three addressing modes: direct, pre-address calculation and post-address calculation. All addressing modes allow address computation in a single cycle which is important for all kinds of stack operations.
- **Hardware support for unification and backtracking**: To support unification KCM has a 16-way branch facility in the microcode. This is used to test rapidly the types (tags) of two objects and take the appropriate action. Backtracking is a characteristic of Prolog not found in conventional programming languages that allows program execution to return to the state of computation at a certain point and try other alternative solutions if the previous attempts have failed. The high memory bandwidth of KCM facilitates the saving and restoring of the state of computation in a minimal number of cycles and special hardware support determines at what point of the computation it is necessary to save the state. Using these techniques known as *shallow backtracking* and *delayed choice point creation* much of the saving and restoring overhead is avoided.

- **Microcoded control:** KCM microcoded operations allows the exploitation of micro-parallelism present in the Prolog instructions. Overriding microcode control by hardware allows a rapid change of the execution control flow.
- **64-bit instructions:** The instruction format of KCM is very regular. Most instructions are one word long, which allows for instance the specification of four addresses: two source and two destination registers.
- **A large register file:** 64 registers are available as sources and destinations of all data manipulation instructions. As with RISC processors there are no instructions to directly modify a memory location.

The Memory System The memory system of KCM has also been targeted at the high-speed execution of Prolog. This leads to:

- **Separate data and code caches (8Kx64-bit each):** This reflects the Harvard architecture.
- **Virtual caches:** Both caches are directly connected to the CPU and are accessed using virtual addresses.
- **A Copy-back write policy for the data cache:** Prolog shows a much higher rate of writes to memory than conventional programming languages. Therefore it is important for the data cache to be a copy-back cache which only accesses memory when a cache miss occurs. On the other hand, almost all accesses to the code cache are read operations and therefore it is acceptable to design it as a write-through cache, i.e. each write to the cache will also cause a write to main memory.
- **Data cache split into 8 sections and direct mapped:** The standard WAM uses three stacks and KCM-Sepia uses up to six different stacks. Simulations showed that an associative cache does not greatly improve performance as long as two stacks do not compete for the same cache locations. As a result the data cache of KCM is split into eight sections of 1K x 64 bits. Each of these sections is allocated to a particular memory area and therefore collisions between different stacks are avoided.
- **Support for dereferencing:** Dereferencing of pointer chains, a frequent operation during unification, can be done at the rate of one pointer per cycle.
- **A large main memory of 32 to 256 MBytes.**

Implementation The KCM hardware is implemented using conventional technology (TTL and CMOS) plus two CMOS-ASICs. The processor of the pilot machines has a cycle time of 100 ns (10 MHz). All the boards (CPU, memory, interface) fit in a workstation cabinet.

2.2 Evaluation of KCM

Benefit Analysis of Architectural Features A thorough hardware evaluation of KCM has been made in [19, 20]. This section summarizes the most important results. The evaluation work has been done on a KCM emulator implemented in C running a collection of 22 programs, from benchmarks to small real applications.

Table 1 shows the effects of every hardware feature of KCM taking a *what-if* approach: the performance degradation is quantified on the basis that a specific part of the hardware is removed or changed.

Hardware Feature	Loss
Tagged Architecture	60%
Harvard Architecture	56%
Stack Oriented CPU	53%
Copy-Back Data Cache	50%
Prolog Flags (flag dependent execution)	11%
Trail Operation (pointer comparisons)	7%
Dereferencing (following reference chain)	10%
Unification and Switch (multi-way branch on tag)	23%
Load Term (argument passing)	6%
Choice Point (creation/restoring)	2%
Prolog Support Total	59%

Table 1: Hardware Evaluation of KCM

Removing the facility of the CPU to simultaneously handle tags with value processing and reducing the data paths to 32 bits accounts for a performance loss of 60%. Without a Harvard architecture and the separate access paths to code and data, KCM's speed would decrease by 56%. Omitting to stack support leads to a degradation of 53%. The write policy of the data cache has an important influence (50%) on the performance as well. The number of writes to the data cache is very high, almost equivalent to the number of reads, and even a *write-through* cache with a write buffer would be limited by the bandwidth of the main memory.

The specific Prolog hardware support sums up to a total of 59%. It is interesting to note that the complexity, in term of number of gates for instance, of this Prolog dedicated hardware is very small compared to other architectural features. Hence it has the best performance/cost ratio, but is not sufficient to make a fast machine. It can eventually be added on an already well organised architecture. Such an approach is evaluated in detail in [7]

The effect of the microcode is difficult to quantify and was not part of the evaluation study. One of the premises of the design, part of the CISC philosophy, is that having microcode is a great benefit for a high level language. It allows a reduction in the size of the code and permits complex instructions to utilise efficiently the pipeline and the micro-parallelism available in the machine. A case study in [3] concludes that there is approximatively a factor 3 of difference between execution time on a tagged RISC

	SICSTUS/KCM	
Program	absolute	scaled
nreverse	5.93	14.82
tak	1.34	3.35
qsort	4.51	11.28
serialise	4.05	10.12
queens_8	2.37	5.92
mu	4.26	10.65
zebra	4.86	12.15
deriv	6.36	15.90
crypt	8.33	20.84
query	2.38	5.94
prover	4.58	11.45
poly_10	2.73	6.83
browse	4.14	10.35
reducer	1.81	4.52
boyer	1.28	3.19
nand	3.31	8.27
chat_parser	5.14	12.86

Table 2: KCM versus SICSTUS

architecture and a Prolog CISC architecture when CISC code is expanded into the RISC one. Recent more general studies for non-scientific applications show that the potential for instruction level parallelism is quite important and one can sustain from 2.0 to 5.8 instructions per cycle on a processor that can be reasonably designed today [4].

Performance Table 2 compares the performance of KCM to the performance of SICSTUS (Version 0.6#14), a typical software implementation of Prolog based on a WAM emulator [5]. The figures for SICSTUS are taken from [18]. They were obtained on a MIPS RC3230 desktop workstation, based on a 25MHz R3000 microprocessor. We only considered the subset of the benchmark suite for which we had sources.

The first column of the table gives absolute time ratios between SICSTUS and KCM, which can be understood as the speed-up of KCM over SICSTUS. The second column uses a scaling factor of 2.5 in order to compensate for the difference of cycle time between KCM and the R3000 and abstract from the implementation technology as far as can be. Note that this may slightly advantage KCM since it is unlikely that this scaling factor applies to access to main memory. We believe, however, that considering the size of the benchmarks, the hit ratio of the caches should, in general, be very good and performance should not be influenced much by cache misses.

Considering that the Prolog compiler of KCM is not as polished as the compiler of SICSTUS, the results are fairly good. Basically, the hardware implementation outperforms the software implementation by almost an order of magnitude.

3 PARMA as an Example for a Software Accelerator

Another route, which has been devoted considerable research effort in the past few years, is to make use of more advanced transformation and compilation techniques. The basic research work has mainly revolved around the ideas of *partial evaluation* and *static analysis*. Given an initial goal, partial evaluation consists of transforming a program into a more specialised and efficient version. Static analysis aims at finding useful properties of a program without actual execution. Until very recently most of the work on static analysis and partial evaluation had kept a strong theoritical orientation. This work on partial evaluation and static analysis was accompanied by a significant, more pragmatic, work on basic implementation techniques, notably in the context of WAM-based systems.

This, together with the arrival to maturity of RISC technology, has led to the emergence of optimizing compilers such as PARMA, a Prolog compiler for the MIPS RISC architecture, developed by Andrew Taylor [16, 17, 18]. This section considers PARMA as a successful software accelerator for Prolog and mentions the techniques used and their limitations.

3.1 Performance

Referring to PARMA as a software accelerator for Prolog is justified by Table 3. As before, the figures for PARMA and SICTUS are extracted from [18] and correspond to executing the benchmark programs on a MIPS RC3230. As previously, the figures for KCM are scaled.

Without recourse to static analysis, the performance of PARMA is intermediate between the performance of SICSTUS and KCM. This is already quite impressive. From [18] we conjecture that better shallow determinacy detection and indexing play an important role. For instance, the poor performance of KCM on **tak** is due to the fact that the compiler is not able to recognise the obvious shallow determinacy of a predicate. As discussed below, current limitations of PARMA may also explain some more or less important fraction of the difference. Insufficient insight in the internals of the compiler and the lack of figures on native code compilation of SICSTUS on a RISC machine makes any further discussion hazardous.

With static analysis on, static analysis together with an original representation of variables (aliased free variables are kept in a circular lists and all set to the same value on unification) allows PARMA to transform most unification operations into simple assignments, if not simple register increment. On KCM, unifying a variable (in memory) to a constant in a register or specified in an instruction costs at least 3 cycles, whereas a simple write costs 1 cycle. Therefore it is not surprising that KCM is outperformed by a factor of about 2 on most of the programs. Note the existence of some exceptions like **zebra**, a program whose performance is dominated by calls to general unification.

	SICSTUS/PARMA		PARMA/KCM	
Program	no analysis	analysis	no analysis	analysis
nreverse	4.1	34.0	3.62	0.44
tak	23.0	66.0	0.17	0.06
qsort	7.4	39.0	1.77	0.34
serialise	15.0	30.0	0.76	0.38
queens_8	8.7	29.0	1.18	0.35
mu	7.0	16.0	1.53	0.67
zebra	6.6	10.0	1.75	1.16
deriv	4.4	24.0	3.61	0.66
crypt	17.0	53.0	1.29	0.41
query	8.0	15.0	0.78	0.42
prover	7.5	15.0	1.52	0.76
poly_10	6.2	17.0	1.14	0.42
browse	8.1	18.0	1.28	0.57
reducer	5.5	7.9	0.82	0.57
boyer	3.7	4.1	0.90	0.81
nand	7.9	23.0	1.08	0.37
chat_parser	11.0	19.0	1.26	0.73

Table 3: PARMA versus SICSTUS and KCM

3.2 Limitations of Parma

The brilliant performance obtained by PARMA should not make one forget about the limitations inherent in static analysis as well as the limitations specific to PARMA.

Limitations of static analysis As far as we can see, the main limitations are the following:

1. At first sight, static analysis is not well adapted to program development because it is slow. For instance, analysing the parser of CHAT-80 takes about 37 seconds on a MIPS, whereas the compilation of the whole application only takes 14 seconds on KCM (both the PARMA analyser and the KCM compiler are written in Prolog). Fortunately, according to [18], there is no empirical indication that the average complexity is worse than linear. The slowness of static analysis may actually be alleviated and even circumvented by the use of a good development discipline; performing static analysis on modules of limited size also reduces information loss. One can also imagine doing part of the static analysis incrementally, for instance at edit time. Finally, hardware improvements may also make this concern obsolete.
2. Meta-programming and extra-logical features confound analysis. This topic is extensively covered in [18] and some partial remedies are considered.
3. Some programs escape static analysis because of their inherently dynamic character (e.g. **zebra** and constraint satisfaction problems in general).

Limitations specific to PARMA

1. The most severe limitation is currently the choice of using 32 bit words with 2 bit tags. This is an all pervasive decision which makes it impossible to add new types without drastic changes to the whole system (hence possible efficiency problems with for instance coroutining, constraints,...). This also creates problems in terms of compatibility with external software, e.g. an integer (pointer) passed by an external procedure may not be representable as a Prolog integer (pointer). This may be circumvented by the near availability of 64-bit processors.

2. It is hard to see how garbage collection can live with uninitialised cells. This can be solved by getting rid of this optimisation at the cost of a moderate performance loss.

3. For the time being, PARMA is specific to a given processor. Portability issues may make necessary to give up some optimisations.

4 Combining the Hardware and Software Approach

This section presents the results obtained so far by the BAM project and gives some indication and analysis of the performance to be expected from an optimizing compiler a la PARMA on KCM.

4.1 BAM: Berkeley Abstract Machine

The BAM project [7, 13] took the approach of designing simultaneously a general-purpose microprocessor extended to provide extra support to Prolog and an optimizing Prolog compiler.

The overall architecture of the BAM has quite a number of points in common with KCM:

- A tagged Harvard architecture.
- Support for stack operations (with a register file with two read and two write ports).
- A copy-back data cache. More precisely, the simulation measures of [7] assume a direct mapped data cache with a copy-back policy (the cache is much larger than the cache of KCM, though, which reduces the probability of collisions).

Interestingly, all these points have been determined as being crucial points in our evaluation studies.

The BAM is however radically different from KCM in that it is essentially a RISC architecture. In particular:

	BAM/KCM		BAM/PARMA	
Program	no analysis	analysis	no analysis	analysis
nreverse	13.11	0.43	3.62	0.99
tak	0.17	0.06	1.00	1.01
qsort	4.35	0.34	2.46	1.01
serialise	0.58	0.19	0.76	0.50
queens_8	2.73	0.39	2.32	1.09
mu	2.21	0.54	1.44	0.80
zebra	3.39	1.48	1.93	1.28
deriv	9.10	0.48	2.52	0.73
crypt	2.79	0.29	2.17	0.71
query	0.75	0.31	0.96	0.74
prover	2.35	0.76	1.54	1.00
poly_10	1.72	0.39	1.51	0.94
browse	1.84	0.41	1.44	0.72
reducer	1.37	0.72	1.67	1.26
boyer	1.20	1.01	1.33	1.24
nand	2.19	0.36	2.03	0.97
chat_parser	1.53	0.57	1.21	0.78

Table 4: BAM versus KCM and PARMA

- There is no microcoded control (though "internal opcodes" can be viewed as a very simple form of microcode).
- The number of instructions is about three times less than in KCM.
- The Prolog specific instructions, while being of higher level than typical RISC instructions, are of lower level than the Prolog instructions of KCM.

Software-wise, the optimising compiler of Peter Van Roy, though significantly different in a number of aspects, shows great similarities in approach to PARMA. The design of the Prolog specific instructions have been especially influenced by the design of the optimising compiler.

Table 4, partly extracted from [18] shows the scaled execution time ratios of BAM and KCM, and BAM and PARMA, both with and without static analysis.

Without static analysis, KCM outperforms BAM by a ratio of about 2. This could probably be increased by bringing the compiler of KCM to the same level of sophistication as the compiler of the BAM, especially in terms of indexing and detection of shallow determinacy. The BAM also outperforms PARMA by roughly the same ratio. As expected the performance increases with the level of dedicated hardware.

However, when global analysis is used, the performance of BAM and PARMA is comparable. Both BAM and PARMA outperform KCM by a factor of about 2.

Program	KCM/PARMA
nreverse	1.62
tak	1.50
qsort	1.22

Table 5: Global Analysis on KCM versus PARMA

C1:	
(1)	X4 = [A1-2]
(2)	A1 = [A1+2]
(3)	[A3] = TG
(5)	A3 = TG + 2
(4)	[TG-2] = X4
(4)+(6)	TG = TG + 8
(6)	if (A1 != X5) goto C1

X5 is initialised to nil at the first call.

Table 6: Abstract code for MIPS

4.2 Static Analysis on KCM

The previous results have shown the necessity to improve compilation in order for KCM to remain competitive. Fortunately the existence of the basic instructions makes it possible to apply, at least partially, the techniques developed in PARMA and the BAM compiler.

In order to get some insight on the feasibility of such an approach, three small benchmarks have been optimised by hand and the resulting code run. The results are summarized in Table 5. KCM gets very close to PARMA but is still outperformed.

A closer look at the code generated for the iterative clause of **concatenate/1**, in **nreverse** - see the example of compilation in [18] - is very enlightening. We reproduce in Table 6 an abstract description of the code generated by PARMA and in Table 7 the final result produced by the MIPS assembler [18]. This has to be compared with the abstract description of the code generated for KCM in Table 8 and the final result produced by the KCM assembler in Table 9. The abstract description relies on the WAM terminology [21]. Ai are registers used for argument passing, Xi, registers used to store temporary values, with Ai and Xi corresponding to the same register, the different name simply reflects different usage. TG is a special register holding the top of the Global Stack. We have added between square brackets the number of cycles taken by each instruction. The numbers in round brackets make it easier to relate one figure to the other.

The code generated by PARMA take 7 instructions and therefore 7 cycles whereas the code generated by KCM take 8 instructions and 12 cycles:

- TG is assigned a list tag by PARMA. KCM requires one instruction (1 cycle) to

```
C1:
(1)      lw      v1, -2(a0)     [1]
(2)      lw      a0, 2(a0)      [1]
(3)      sw      s4, 0(a2)      [1]
(5)      addi    a2, s4, 2      [1]
(4+6)    addi    s4, s4, 8      [1]
(7)      bne     a0, v0, C1     [1]
(4)      sw      v1, -10(s4)    [1]
```

Table 7: Binary code for MIPS

```
C1:
(1)      X4 = [A1]
(2)      A1 = [A1+1]
(3)      [A3] = (list, TG)
(4)      [TG+] = X4
(5)      A3 = (ref, TG)
(6)      [TG+] = (ref, 'L3')
(7)      if (A1 != []) goto C1
```

Table 8: Abstract code for KCM

```
C1
(1)      lda       r3, rVOID, r0, 0                 [2]
(2)      lda       r0, rVOID, r0, 1                 [2]
(3)      addi      rSCRATCH, TG, [GZONE, LST, 0]    [1]
(3)      stb       rSCRATCH, rVOID, r2, 0           [1]
(4)      stb       r3, TG, TG, 1                    [1]
(5)      addi      r2, TG, [GZONE, REF, 0]          [1]
(6)      pushstm   VAR:$'L3'                        [1]
(7)      swlst     r0, $'[]', C2, C1, fail          [3]
```

Table 9: Binary code for KCM

create a list pointer from TG (3). The trick used by PARMA could actually be used by KCM (apart from the compiler, only initialisation code would have to be changed).

- PARMA saves 1 cycle by not initialising L3 (6). On KCM, this is actually mandatory in order to allow for garbage collection.
- KCM does not require a specific instruction to update the top of the global stack, post-increment addressing is used instead together with an ad-hoc instruction to deal with immediate values (6).
- KCM loses 2 cycles through the lack of pipelining of memory access in read mode. On the MIPS, the two delay slots of one cycle can be filled. In KCM, this is only possible at the microcode level.
- KCM loses 2 cycles because of the lack of efficient branch on condition. An alternative coding would replace the high-level instruction *switch_on_list* by two low-level instructions, a substraction and a jump on condition. This would correspond to the instruction *branch_if_not_equal* that can be found in the MIPS code (with X5 also initialised to nil). This would however costs 5 cycles instead of the 1 cycle of the MIPS *bne* instruction. There are two points here. The first point is that conditional branches on KCM consist of separate compare and branch instructions (this property is shared by the BAM). The second point is that, again, the delay slots due to the code pipeline break cannot be filled, at the macrocode level, by KCM. Moreover the delay slot of a branch is 3 cycles, whereas there is no delay if the execution continues in sequence. It would be possible to reduce this delay to 2 cycles by changing the microcode. This would however add a delay slot of one cycle when the execution proceeds in sequence, which would penalise some other parts of the execution (e.g. tests for exception after ALU and FPU instructions).

In spite of the simplicity of the example, our experience of Prolog compilation suggests that the above comments are actually pervasive and lead us to extrapolate that KCM, as it stands, is outperformed by the MIPS R3000 when using static analysis. It should be noted that the cost of the delay slots was discussed during the design of KCM but was considered not to be significant. This conclusion is invalidated by the introduction of global analysis. This may not be the only one.

5 Conclusion

Logic Programming is in its infancy. Concepts, languages, and implementations techniques are evolving very quickly. This tends to make hardware development rapidly obsolete and favors software approaches. Also, the introduction of global analysis techniques has created a breakthrough which, in spite of some limitations and uncertainties on its gain when applied to a full system, has considerably bridged the gap which existed so far between software and hardware implementations.

It is very likely, however, that a growing base of users, the availability of free silicon and advances in the methodology and tools for computer design will keep hardware support for Logic Programming attractive. Undoubtedly, future work in this area will better combine hardware and software technologies. The current trends also suggest a focus on Prolog support within general purpose processors.

The ideal, truly general purpose (vs. dedicated to C) processor, mixing RISC and CISC technologies, is still to come.

Acknowledgements

We would like to thank Mike Reeve for his helpful comments on drafts of this paper.

References

[1] H. Benker, J.-M. Beacco, S. Bescos, M. Dorochevsky, T. Jeffré, A. Pöhlmann, J. Noyé, B. Poterie, A. Sexton, J.-C. Syre, O. Thibault, and G. Watzlawik. KCM: A Knowledge Crunching Machine. In *Proceedings of the 16th Annual International Symposium on Computer Architecture*, pages 186–194. IEEE, June 1989.

[2] H. Benker, M. Dorochevsky, J. Noyé, and A. Sexton. A Knowledge Crunching System. In *Proceedings of the 11th ITG/GI-Conference — Architecture of Computing Systems*, pages 9–21, Munich, March 1990.

[3] Gaetano Borriello, Andrew R. Cherenson, Peter B. Danzig, and Michael N. Nelson. RISC versus CISCs for Prolog: A Case Study. In ACM, editor, *Proceedings ASPLOS II*, pages 136–145, October 1987.

[4] Michael Butler, Tse-Yu Yeh, Yale Patt, Mitch Alsup, Hunter Scales, and Michael Shebanow. Single Instruction Stream Parallelism Is Greater than Two. In IEEE/ACM, editor, *Proceedings of the 18th Annual International Symposium on Computer Architecture*, pages 276–286, May 1991.

[5] M. Carlsson and J. Widen. *SICStus Prolog Users Manual.* SICS, October 1988.

[6] Tep Dobry. A coprocessor for ai; lisp, prolog and data bases. In *Spring Compcon 87*, pages 396–402. IEEE, February 1897.

[7] Bruce K. Holmer, Barton Sano, Michael Carlton, Peter Van Roy, Ralph Haygood, William R. Bush, and Alvin M. Despain. Fast Prolog with an Extended General Purpose Architecture. In *Proceedings of the 17th Annual International Symposium on Computer Architecture*, pages 282–291. IEEE/ACM, May 1990.

[8] KCM-Sepia. KCM-Sepia 2.0 User Manual. Technical report, ECRC, May 1990.

[9] A. Konagaya, Shinichi Habata, Atsushi Atarashi, and Minoru Yokota. Performance Evaluation of a Sequential Inference Machine CHI. In *Proceedings of the North American Conference on Logic Programming*, pages 1165–1179, October 1989.

[10] K. Kurosawa, S. Yamaguchi, S. Abe, and T. Bandoh. Instruction Architecture for a High Performance Integrated Prolog Processor IPP. In A. Kowalski and A. Bowen, editors, *Proceedings of the 5th International Conference and Symposium on Logic Programming*, pages 1507–1530. Hitachi Research Laboratories, August 1988.

[11] Hiroshi Nakashima and Katsuto Nakajima. Hardware Architecture of the Sequential Inference Machine: PSI-II. In *Proceedings of the International Symposium on Logic Programming*, pages 104–113. IEEE, September 1987.

[12] A. Pudner. DLM - A Powerful AI Computer for Embedded Expert Systems. In R.P. van de Riet, editor, *Frontiers in Computing*, pages 187 – 201, December 1987.

[13] Peter Van Roy. *Can Logic Programming Execute as Fast as Imperative Programming.* PhD thesis, University of California, Berkeley, December 1990.

[14] Kazuo Seo and Takashi Yokota. Design and Fabrication of Pegasus Prolog Processor. In *Proceedings of the VLSI 89 International Conference*, pages 265–284. IFIP, August 1989.

[15] Alan P. Sexton. The KCM Operating System Interface Manual. Technical Report DPS-95, ECRC, December 1990.

[16] Andrew Taylor. Removal of Dereferencing and Trailing in Prolog Compilation. In Giorgio Levi and Maurizio Martelli, editors, *Proceedings of the International Conference on Logic Programming*, pages 48–60, June 1989.

[17] Andrew Taylor. LIPS on a MIPS — Results from a Prolog Compiler for a RISC. In David H. D. Warren and Peter Szeredi, editors, *Proceedings of the International Conference on Logic Programming*, pages 48–60, June 1990.

[18] Andrew Taylor. *High Performance Prolog Implementation.* PhD thesis, University of Sydney, Basser Department of Computer Science, Sydney, Australia, June 1991.

[19] O. Thibault. Hardware Evaluation of KCM. In *Proceedings of Tools for Artificial Intelligence*, pages 209–217. IEEE, November 1990.

[20] O. Thibault. *Design and Evaluation of a Symbolic Processor.* PhD thesis, Université Paul Sabatier, Toulouse III, Toulouse, France, Mai 1991.

[21] David D.H. Warren. An Abstract Prolog Instruction Set. Technical Note TN-309, SRI, October 1983.

Commercial Applications of Large Prolog Knowledge Bases

Chris Moss
Imperial College, London University
currently at
Centre de Recherche Public- Centre Universitaire, Luxembourg

Abstract

This paper describes a number of the high quality application programs that have been delivered to customers around the world using different versions of Prolog. These include systems which create legal documents, assembly instructions for jet aircraft, and work schedules in hospitals; and systems which help service engineers with telephone faults, interpret chromosomal abnormalities, and diagnose faults in electronic circuits. Each combines various forms of knowledge base with the procedures to apply them in a particular area. Different approaches are used in order to achieve the necessary efficiency, but a common factor appears to be a marked increase in both productivity when creating the application and in the adaptability of the finished product.

1 Introduction

There is a common misconception that Prolog and other declarative knowledge systems are only used for "prototyping" and that for serious work one needs to reimplement the whole program in C or some other "efficient" language. The aim of this paper is to show that this is not the case and that people are delivering finished products using Prolog for a wide variety of purposes world-wide. The paper considers nine delivered and operating programs which have been developed using five different Prolog systems in six countries. Though little more than a thumb-nail sketch, it suggests that it is worth studying more seriously the productivity gains that can be achieved in practice using these techniques in order to provide a partial solution to the much talked-about "software crisis".

It may also be questioned whether Prolog is indeed a "declarative" or procedural knowledge system. We take it for granted that there is a continuum in this area and that it is the use of the tools that determines the product, rather than their potential limits.

These reports are adapted from a wider study undertaken for the British government on the commercial use of Prolog[1]. It was by no means obvious that all of the projects could be described as "Knowledge Bases". However, it was found to be a suitable title for a surprising proportion of them. Many incorporate an identifiable "knowledge subsystem" and in most of the cases the ease of encoding a substantial body of knowledge was a major factor in choosing Prolog as the programming language.

Nevertheless, to describe all commercial Prolog programs as knowledge bases is stretching the notion too far. Our first example—Slot—is deliberately chosen as a counter-example. It is essentially a process control program, although it certainly incorporates various forms of knowledge. A program cannot be described as a knowledge base just because it incorporates directly identifiable knowledge any more than it can be described as an expert system just because it incorporates an expert's understanding.

Much of the information in this paper is derived from descriptions produced by manufacturers of Prolog systems. The author has not yet been able to visit the companies involved or obtain the independent assessment of clients or users. Thus these descriptions are dependent on the good faith of intermediaries.

2.1 An Airport Management System

One of the crucial aspect of controlling an airport is the planning of flight arrivals and departures. Although the volume of data is much less than that involved in, say, passenger bookings, the design considerations are much more complex. The task of efficient traffic coordination is very complex in major airports when historical precedence, IATA regulations and local procedures have to be observed. SLOT is an airport management system which automates many aspects of this task. The consultancy division of the Danish PDC company developed the system using PDC Prolog[2] for Scandinavian Airlines (SAS) and has installed it at several major European airline companies.

The system provides planning of flight arrivals and departures for optimal utilization of airport capacity, automatic evaluation of traffic load compared to local air traffic capacity regulations. The consequence of this is reduced administration costs through automatic processing of IATA standard telex messages from airline companies requesting the use of the airport and schedule validation.

SLOT has communication facilities for data exchange with main-frame computers and for immediate update of local and external databases. It requires the use of a 386 based PC workstation with 8MB RAM using OS/2, VGA or EGA monitor and an OS/2 compatible network. It has an advanced graphic user interface, which gives the operators full overview of the air traffic situation .

The first version took one person-year to develop and extensions for other airlines about the same time, which is a very modest effort for a fully-engineered system of this type. The program is mainly in Prolog with a few C routines to handle low-level tasks. The capacity of the system is sufficient for airlines and the developers estimate it is capable of handling 20,000 movements per day.

PDC Prolog incorporates a type system which is not popular in Prolog circles but probably contributed significantly to the success of this project. It increases the speed of the compiled code by a factor of around 20-50% and helps in the production of error-free code, which may have been important in convincing management of the viability of the product for which reliability is clearly a crucial element.

While it would be hard to describe this program as a knowledge base, the ease with which it can be adapted to differing and changing requirements is undoubtedly an important factor in its acceptability.

2.2 Boeing's Connector Assembly Specification Expert

Some 5,000 packages of electrical connectors go into a typical Boeing jet. To assemble these connectors, workers had to hunt through 20,000 pages of complex cross-referenced specifications to find the most cost-effective and convenient parts, tools and crimping techniques for each custom-made connector. The major requirement at Boeing was to decrease the time needed to produce the assembly instructions for each connector from 42 to 5 minutes, eliminate the long learning process and prevent misinterpretations of specifications. Furthermore, the system had to be easy to modify since changes to process specifications occur daily.

Development of a knowledge-based system to perform the complex preparation of assembly instructions was the solution for Boeing. The Connector Assembly Specification System (CASE) was incrementally built and designed to work in conjunction with existing manuals. The key factor in the application is the system's ability to represent manufacturing process specifications and rules guiding their use. With the expectation that the system would expand to 100,000 rules and several hundred knowledge-based files, CASE was designed so that only documents referenced while building an instruction packet are brought into working memory. This enhances the speed of the system and facilitates updating.

After development of an early prototype system, Boeing realized the need for expanded capacity. Quintus Prolog[3] was chosen because it was fast, flexible and fully supported a declarative programming style, dramatically simplifying the development of automated process specification and rules for their use. The full-scale production version of the system was ported to a DEC MicroVax II with approximately a dozen terminals.

Now, rather than facing a tedious manual task, assemblers type basic information about a connector into a computer and receive a printout of instructions in 5 minutes compared with the average of 42 minutes for manually prepared assembly instructions. The company claims that accuracy has also improved, and new users can learn to use the system in only two hours.

Note that the knowledge base of this system does not include the "real" knowledge—the instructions used by the operators. These are simply held as text. Even then the task is large: 100,000 rules is not an unknown size or beyond the capabilities of many of the high-end Prolog systems around. Yet the increase in productivity in the white-collar sector is impressive and justifies the investment.

2.3 Scrivener — assembling legal documents

Much of its knowledge required by a legal practice is represented as English text and one of the most common demands is to produce various types of documents, such as contracts, wills, incorporation and trust documents. A member of the firm can easily specify how to combine boilerplate with information specific to a particular use.

Scrivener™ is a document assembly program developed by Dianoetic Development Company in Pennsylvania, U.S. To create a document for a user which is compatible with Word Perfect®, Scrivener asks for necessary information to select and combine standardized sentences, paragraphs or other blocks of text, inserting the relevant names and other variable information into the selected text to create a customized document. It therefore reduces the time needed to prepare common forms of document and the possibility of errors in choosing among numerous standardized provisions.

Scrivener can display the model in outline form, with the conditions for including (or excluding) each clause, and provides pull-down menus and other development tools for quick and easy model editing. The user can modify the model while assembling a document and then see the document reassembled with the revised model. The user is only asked necessary and relevant questions when assembling a document and can change any or all answers at any time and then see the document reassembled with the revised answers.

Scrivener uses natural language names for variables and clauses with no artificial numbering or labelling and supports a variety of data types, including text, numbers, dates and multiple choice and a variety of data functions including arithmetic, string manipulation, date arithmetic and financial functions. Dianoetic also offers a library of legal documents in model form, such as incorporation documents, leases, contracts, wills and trusts, for attorneys who wish to purchase and modify prewritten models.

The development time of this project was 6 man-months using an IBM PC and the Arity/Prolog Compiler and Interpreter[4]. The code amounts to 7,500 lines of Prolog and 30 lines of C.

2.4 STAFF — creating work schedules

Many knowledge-based tasks occur in the classic areas of data-processing and therefore a program needs to be able to consult and provide updates to the company database. For example, the requirements for staff shift timetables are often vague, changeable and need the careful balancing of conflicting requirements. Tools written in Cobol do not provide the necessary flexibility and reactivity to combine legal aspects (state law and trade union agreements), staff preferences, payroll data, and the various heuristics required to produce a reasonable compromise.

STAFF is a system for decentralized creation and maintenance of work schedules for larger companies and institutions and written in PDC Prolog[2]. The system works on a PC workstation with optional communication with a central computer system for transfer of payroll data. With STAFF, work schedules are automatically generated and optimized based on skill requirements within departments, available skills, holiday plans and shift preferences. The STAFF planning procedure uses a rule based expert system, which specifies the rules for work schedule generation, based on governing laws, local agreements and planning heuristics. This means that plans are generated with a minimum breach of rules and hence minimum overtime pay.

STAFF provides a local database manager for employee data, accumulated hours, overtime and other data for payroll calculations; a basic plan layout for repetitive shifts and holidays; the automatic generation of full work plan to meet minimum personnel and skill requirements; update of payroll data in the local database and transfer of such data to a central payroll system.

STAFF is in operation in more than 150 institutions, mainly in the hospital sector. It appears to be an ideal planning tool for companies and institutions with modern management structures, where individual preferences are adhered to whenever possible. The first version, for an airline, took approximately 4 person-months to develop, and the hospital version 9 person-months. It is coded entirely in Prolog.

2.5 Infologics Faultfinder System

FaultFinder is a diagnostic tool which combines expert systems and multimedia techniques to enhance the productivity of service engineers. It provides on-line assistance in the form of a knowledge base which helps the service engineer in diagnosis and maintenance. This is backed up by a Knowledge Management System which is used by product specialists in creating and maintaining the knowledge bases. The product is a domain oriented tool, not a general purpose expert system shell. It is an operational system developed by Infologics using LPA-Prolog[5] and is currently used by service engineers at five sites in Sweden to locate and fix faults in the Swedish Telecom service. It is also used by a number of different manufacturers in several European countries.

FaultFinder incorporates both fundamental and heuristic knowledge which Infologics says are both important when troubleshooting technical equipment. Fundamental knowledge is typically that provided by the manufacturers, including design features, test procedures, etc. Heuristic knowledge is based on rule of thumb, usually gained from years of hands-on experience.

FaultFinder knowledge bases can be located at the support centre, in field service or at the repair shop. The support centre is normally the first contact between a customer and the organisation. FaultFinder can be used here to diagnose faults and, if the job is to be handed to a field engineer, pass on information about appropriate spare parts and tools. Repair shops typically have several service engineers maintaining a broad range of products. The company says that FaultFinder will help the engineers to diagnose a broader product range rapidly and accurately: "a novice who uses the knowledge base will therefore have the best expertise available in an integrated knowledge system."

According to Infologics, two separate tests have shown that FaultFinder saves between 45 and 80% of the time used for servicing complex equipment. Cost/benefit analysis performed by key customers has shown that significant savings are made in service organisations when FaultFinder is used.

Hans Becker, product manager at Infologic, believes that storage, manipulation and retrieval of knowledge will be the crucial factor in the service sector. He expects knowledge based systems to play an increasingly important role in helping service organisations to exploit the knowledge needed to support a broad range of products.

2.6 Frenchip: Layout of Integrated circuits

One area in which Prolog is increasingly being used is in VLSI design (see [6,7,8]. The ability to reason symbolically from a description which is very close to a specification has been found to be a powerful tool which, for many designers, has replaced earlier systems in which the size of the code was making maintenance extremely difficult.

Frenchip is a package for synthesizing logic circuits which the French manufacturer Dassault Electronique has used for four years[9]. More than seventy projects have been developed using it, most having 30 to 60 thousand gates, but some more than 100,000. Today Frenchip is used by more than sixty designers who use it for not only general processors but numerical signal processors and bus connectors, etc.

The designer uses a VHDL (Very High-level Definition Language) to construct the project. The design approach is top-down using hierarchical block diagrams. The designer can intervene to modify options or supply parameters in the course of the synthesizing process. The high-level of abstraction of the VHDL models allow the designer to focus on the design and validation of the function and on any aspect which he judges critical. This also leads to increased productivity and control of time and costs. In addition, Frenchip supplies rewriting rules at the same high level to extend the VHDL.

Dassault credits the success of this program to the use of Prolog which enabled it to be programmed rapidly and to take into account the suggestions of the pilot users. Frenchip uses over 60,000 lines of Delphia Prolog[9] and runs on Unix workstation with Xwindows. Because of the enthusiastic reception that Frenchip has received from other designers, Dassault is now marketing it as a product.

2.7 BIS/Estimator System

Project estimating is a notoriously difficult problem which inevitably remains to a significant extent an art. BIS/estimator therefore provides the use of five different estimating methods, which can be divided into two main categories: soft and hard. Each phase of a project can be analysed in detail at different levels. This makes it possible to produce cost estimates for the whole project, the individual phases or any task within a particular phase. The output from the program is a set of reports which include high-level project summaries, estimates at project, phase and task levels and reports which contain the data on which the estimates are based. These estimates can be loaded directly into other systems such as Lotus 1-2-3 or Project Manager Workbench (PMW).

The BIS/Estimator system is a product sold by BIS Applied Systems Ltd. Designed for the project manager, it provides estimates for all phases of development of a data processing application from the initial feasibility study down to the fielding of the implemented system. It is implemented in LPA Prolog Professional[5] on IBM PC's and compatibles and version 5.0 will be soon be available.

Estimator was developed with a mixed language approach using both Prolog and C. The C language was used for low-level input and output such as checking the availability or status of disk drives or files. In a previous version of Estimator, C was also used for running menus, but this has now been replaced by the powerful facilities provided by the Human Computer Interface tool kit provided by LPA which is implemented in Prolog. BIS says that the ability to customize the system in this way was a primary factor in the choice of implementation.

The company has sold the product to a range of users including major manufacturing companies, High Street banks, shops and consultancies. It claims that "the product is appropriate for any company which is developing commercial DP systems."

BIS did seriously consider using C or C++ for this product, but decided on Prolog largely for speed of development. Adrian Stanley, who is doing the major part of the development for the next version, says that "having a programming environment in Prolog makes development a lot quicker than say, in a language like C".

There are two knowledge bases in such a system. One is the built-in set of estimating methods, which cannot be altered by the user. The other is the project experience of the user. The hard estimates allow easy comparisons between the new project and a selection of old projects can provide a useful framework for calibrating the costing of new projects. BIS/Estimator can explain its estimates using heuristic knowledge encoded in rules associated with each task. It also draws expertise from a number of other sources, including statistical knowledge, scheduling, and mathematical techniques such as the Function Point Analysis method.

2.8 Interpreting Chromosomal Abnormalities

ISCN Expert interprets the International Human Cytogenetic Nomenclature, which is the standard notation used to represent human chromosomal abnormalities. These notations, each representing a person's genetic layout, are maintained in a computerized registry for reference and comparison against each other. Inconsistencies may arise, however, because each chromosomal variation can be written in a number of formats and thus be difficult to retrieve from the registry. The expert system allows geneticists to overcome these differences and thus reference and interpret chromosomal abnormalities such as those which result in Down Syndrome, mental retardation or physical disabilities.

ISCN Expert[11] was written in Arity/Prolog[4] version 5.1 for an IBM AT running MS-DOS with 640K RAM and a hard disk. The use of 1 megabyte of total memory is sufficient to avoid any disk paging. Completely summarizing a formula on a 10MHz AT takes between 1 and 10 seconds, depending on its complexity. The program is highly portable and will run with little change on any machine having a Prolog interpreter with Edinburgh syntax. It was developed by Dr. Glen Cooper and Dr. J.M. Friedman and supported by the British Columbia Health Care Research Foundation, together with the Ministry of Advanced Education, Training and Technology of Canada. Glen Cooper & Associates Ltd. (who now market the product) say that the code is very readable and is easily enhanced.

Chromosomal formulae are easily represented symbolically and manipulated using the powerful pattern matching facilities of Prolog. The implementer liked the avoidance of declared data types and the ability to backtrack automatically to previous points in a program if a condition or rule being tested fails. Avoiding declared data types allowed token lists of any type and length to be included in the program without knowing what the user will enter at run time. Another benefit of this is that it allows modification of one part of the code without impacting another since validation of the input notation in this program is distinct from the rules governing formula interpretation and the two portions of the program only communicate by passing a data structure. This means that if the parser is changed by enhancing its treatment of sex chromosomes, for example, most of the rule base will compile properly without recoding. Only those rules that actually mention sex chromosomes and make use of the new information need to be updated.

It is noteworthy that it is the scientists themselves who were comfortable with the programming tool provided. It didn't require an intermediate programmer or "knowledge engineer" to work with a difficult formalism.

2.9 AT&T Graphical Expert System Creation Tool

The Graphical Expert System Creation Tool (GEX-Tool) is an environment for developing large diagnostic expert systems and sold by AT&T for use in electronic assembly plants. To the shop technician, GEX-Tool presents a full colour graphic display of a circuit pack, highlighting suspected components, asking for additional information and suggesting replacements. GEX-Tool handles both single and multiple faults and will trouble-shoot multiple circuit packs simultaneously.

Most expert systems are notoriously slow, but GEX-Tool delivers remarkable performance. Part of the reason for this is that the diagnostic module is written in C, which is generated using proprietary compilation techniques from a Prolog program.

GEX-Tool supports one of the largest, most complex knowledge bases of any industrial expert system and overcomes a primary shortcoming of rule-based diagnostic expert systems—the inability to handle new faults and learn from experience. This is done "off-line" by an expert who can control and check the generated rules.

GEX-Tool consists of four modules of which the first three use Quintus Prolog[3]: automatic rule generation, manual rule editing, rule compilation and a rule exception and operator interface module. The first module takes files describing component and circuit topology together with replacement and testing costs and prepares data for the second module, which allows an engineer to edit and optimize the diagnostic procedures. The third module generates rules in the C language which are then compiled to form the knowledge base used by the shop operator. This cycle can be repeated as often as necessary to deal with changing conditions.

This application shows one way in which different computer tools can each be used to their best advantage. Prolog excels at handling complex rule-based knowledge: in this case megabytes of it. This knowledge is needed to prepare the diagnostic system for use on the shop floor, but the actual diagnosis can be a lot simpler. Hence the translation into a simpler language, one invented, in fact, by the developer.

3 Conclusions

Many of the systems outlined above have been described as "expert systems" but their development pattern seems to be much closer to traditional software engineering. What distinguishes them from other products is the conceptually complex domains in which they operate, the apparent speed with which they have been produced and the ease with which they can be modified. These are virtues which one expects to derive from the knowledge-based approach.

It is commonplace to observe that Prolog programs typically have between one third and one tenth of the number of lines of their equivalents in imperative code. It also appears that the productivity of good Prolog programmers is not very different in terms of the number of lines of code produced per day. This translates into a very significant improvement in development costs which has not yet been measured objectively but is being recognized by developers.

Efficiency is only one constraint on the use of tools: if the level is acceptable then for many purposes it can be forgotten. In most of the above examples, it is evident that the Prolog system gives quite acceptable performance. Where it is not acceptable, one can either adopt a mixed language approach, or use compilation to compile rules into a more efficient language (as in the example of GEX-Tool) to improve the efficiency. This does not apply to all products and increasingly people are seeing declarative methods as one tool among several that are needed.

Finally, it is significant that many of these programs provide help for people working in "knowledge-rich" areas—project estimators, geneticists, lawyers, service engineers—these are professionals whose productivity is hard to improve by more traditional computer techniques. It is their demand that will ultimately determine the market for tools dealing in knowledge.

References

[1] C. Moss [1991] *Logic Programming Applications and Products*. Report for the Central Computer and Telecommunications Agency, H.M. Treasury.

[2] Prolog Development Center, ApS, H.J. Holst Vej 5A, DK-2605 Broendby, Denmark.

[3] Quintus Corporation, 2100 Geng Road, California 94303, U.S.A.

[4] Arity Corporation. 29 Domino Drive, Concord, MA 01742, U.S.A.

[5] Logic Programming Associates. Studio 4, Royal Victoria Patriotic Building, Trinity Road, London SW18 6SX, U.K.

[6] Clocksin, W.F. Logic Programming and Digital Circuit Analysis. Journal of Logic Programming, vol. 4. No. 1. pp59-82, 1987

[7] Jabri, M.A., Brel — A Prolog Knowledge-Based Systems Shell for VLSI CAD. 27th Design Automation Conference. IEEE CS Press, June 1990. pp272-277.

[8] Reintjes, P.B. A Set of Tools for VHDL Design. Proc 8th Int. Conf. on Logic Programming. Cambridge, Mass: The M.I.T. Press. 1991.

[9] Les techniques informatiques avancees et leurs applications. Dassault Electronique. Report NE 485 352. April 1991.

[10] Delphia, 27 ave de la Republique, 38170 Seyssinet, France.

[11] Computers and Biomedical Research 23, 153-164 (1990)

Compiling Conceptual Graphs *

Gerard Ellis
Department of Computer Science
University of Queensland
Brisbane, Queensland 4072 Australia

Abstract

This paper examines storage and retrieval of conceptual graphs using a directed acyclic graph data structure based on the partial order over conceptual graphs. We show how conceptual graphs in this hierarchy can be compiled into instructions which represent specialized cases of the canonical formation rules. Conceptual graphs are compiled as differences between adjacent graphs in the hierarchy. The differences represent the rules used in deriving the graph from the adjacent graphs. Compilation of conceptual graphs is effected in three ways: removal of redundant data, use of simple instructions which ignore redundant checks when performing matching, and by sharing common processing between graphs.

Introduction

Conceptual graphs [1] is an order-sorted logic with intensional descriptions (abstractions) for types, relations, and individuals. The language differs from most concept languages in that the same language for describing concepts is also used for making assertions. Conceptual graphs have a standard mapping into natural language. Conceptual graphs goes beyond first-order logic to allow sentences to be represented that cannot be represented in first-order logic.

John Sowa's conceptual graphs have attracted applications including natural language processing, information retrieval, systems analysis and data modeling, software specification and synthesis, image analysis, planning, and expert systems [2].

Walther [3] showed that an order-sorted logic, which separates a domain into a hierarchy of subdomains, can reduce the possible inferences (useless dead ends) that can

*Part of this work was undertaken while the author was visiting the Department of Computer and Information Sciences, at the University of California, Santa Cruz.

be made, by restricting the domains of functions (ranges) and relations to subdomains (subranges). The use of order-sorted logic reduces the size of the problem: number of clauses, connectives, and variables. Information such as wolves are animals, is recorded in the type signature, rather than as a clause. The domain restrictions in formulas are explicit implications in one-sorted logic. Walther illustrated the utility of order-sorted logic by giving the first mechanical solution to Schubert's Steamroller, a theorem proving challenge problem. This was achieved by reducing the size of the problem and search space using order-sorted logic.

Sowa suggests the inference rules for conceptual graphs allow a proposition to be treated whole, rather than decomposed into many small formulas in clausal form in resolution theorem provers. Decomposition into clausal form increases the difficulty of finding and reassembling the pieces during the proof. Each individual step in a resolution proof is simpler than graph unification, but the number of steps is greatly increased for many small clauses.

We also argue that by abstracting much of the information out of a problem using intensional definitions for concept types (sorts), relation types, and individuals, that a similar reduction in the size of the problem and search space will be achieved.

Davies [4] was the first to give a mechanical solution to Schubert's Steamroller problem using natural deduction rather than refutation as the means of theorem proving. The formulation has 11 axioms and the proof takes 27 steps (c.f. [5]). The main reason for using natural deduction was comprehensibility of formulation and reasoning. The propositions are easy to understand, since there is no need to convert to a normal form. Proof development is easier to follow. Resolution theorem proving employs just one inference rule, whereas natural deduction systems use a set of inference rules which are intended to model the reasoning steps humans use to develop proofs. Both these factors improve the comprehensibility of an expert system's reasoning and help in the construction of natural explanation facilities. It is also easier to identify effective heuristics, because formulas are not written in a clausal form.

The main goal of the authors research is to develop a theorem prover for conceptual graphs, using the unique inference rules of Peirce's Existential Graphs [6]. The use of conceptual graphs will allow powerful explanation facilities due to their standard mapping to natural language. This work is only in its early stages and is not the main topic covered here. It is mentioned to give the framing of the following problem considered in detail.

This paper contributes a method of storing conceptual graphs in a compact form in a data structure representing the partial order over conceptual graphs: the generalization hierarchy. A conceptual graph is represented by the differences between itself and its immediate neighbours in the generalization hierarchy. The differences are instructions which are specialized cases of the canonical formation rules for conceptual graphs.

Section 1 introduces the conceptual graph language and inference rules. Section ?? uses some examples to illustrate conceptual graph inference rules. Section 2 discusses construction of the generalization hierarchy and gives descriptions of instructions which are specialized cases of the canonical formation rules. A query is then examined on a small compiled database.

1 Conceptual Graphs

Conceptual graphs [1] is a system of logic with a standard translation into natural language. Conceptual graphs is an order-sorted version of Charles Sanders Peirce's Existential Graphs (1839-1914) [6] with abstraction. We only consider atomic conceptual graphs here. Atomic conceptual graphs contain no negative contexts nor any lines of identity. That is, they contain no logical connectives nor quantifiers other than the default existential quantifier.

Definition 1.1 *Let s and t be concept or conceptual relation types from the set T, a, b, c, and d be concept variables, r be a conceptual relation variable, i be an individual marker (surrogate) from the set I. Let ψ be a variable over individual markers and conceptual graphs. Let u, v, and w be variables over conceptual graphs. Then the following are* conceptual graphs -

- $c : s$ *(generic concept)*
- $c : s \wedge c = \psi$ *(individual concept when $\psi = i$)*
- $r : t(c_1, \ldots, c_n) \wedge c_1 : s_1 \wedge \ldots \wedge c_n : s_n$ *(a n-ary relation)*
- *a finite, connected, bipartite graph u. The nodes are concepts (generic and individual) or n-ary relations $r : t$, the arcs are represented by concept identifiers $c_1, \ldots, c_n$ occurring in argument positions of n-ary relations.*

There is a linear and a graphical notation for conceptual graphs. A concept $c : s \wedge c = \psi$ is represented by $[s : \psi]$ in the linear form. A binary relation $r : t(c_1, c_2) \wedge c_1 : s_1 \wedge c_2 : s_2$ is represented by $[s_1] \rightarrow (r) \rightarrow [s_2]$ in the linear form. For example the graph u

$$c1 : \text{GIRL} \wedge c1 = \text{Sue} \wedge r1 : \text{AGNT}(c2, c1) \wedge c2 : \text{EAT} \wedge r2 : \text{OBJ}(c2, c3) \wedge c3 : \text{PIE}$$

is represented as

$$[\text{GIRL: Sue}] \leftarrow (\text{AGNT}) \leftarrow [\text{EAT}] \rightarrow (\text{OBJ}) \rightarrow [\text{PIE}]$$

in the linear form. The graph may be informally read as *A girl, Sue, is eating pie".* This states that there is a girl, Sue, and exists an instance of eating, and a pie, where the agent of eating is Sue, and object of that eating is a pie. In the graphical notation boxes replace the square brackets of concepts, and circles replace the parentheses of relations (See Figure 1).

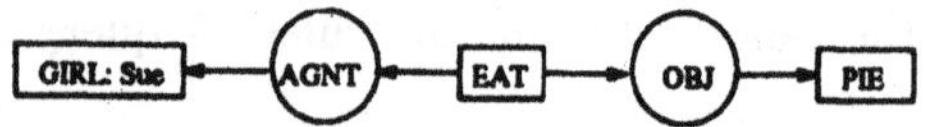

Figure 1: A conceptual graph

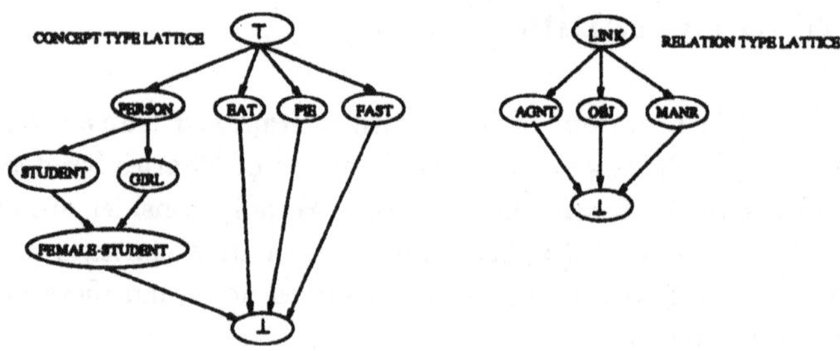

Figure 2: Concept Type and Relation Type Lattices

The direction on the arcs indicates the argument position of each concept attached to the relation. This is suitable for unary and binary relations, but for relations of greater arity the arcs must be labeled with their argument number. All of the examples considered in this paper contain binary relations. An arc pointing from a binary relation to a concept identifies that concept as the second argument. An arc pointing to a binary relation from a concept identifies the concept as the first argument. The particular arrangement of arcs given for the relations (AGNT) and (OBJ) are not iron fast, it is only required that the arcs for a relation are used consistently throughout the database.

The following functions are defined for a conceptual graph u - $type(c) = s$ given $c : s$ is in u; $referent(c) = \psi$ if $c = \psi$ is in u and equal to the generic marker, $*$, otherwise; $type(r) = t$ given $r : t(c_1, \ldots, c_n)$ is in u; and $arc(i, r) = c_i$. In our example $type(c1)$ = GIRL and $referent(c1)$ = Sue; $type(c2)$ = EAT and $referent(c2) = *$; and $type(r1)$ = AGNT, $arc(1, r1) = c2$, and $arc(2, r1) = c1$.

The partial order $\leq$ over the type labels in T, known as the *type hierarchy*, forms a lattice, called the *type lattice*. The type hierarchy makes analytic statements about types - they must be true by intension. The statement GIRL < PERSON is true, because the properties of a person are also associated with a girl. Figure 2 shows the type lattices used in the examples in this paper.

The *minimal common supertype* of a pair of type labels s and t is written $s \cup t$. The *maximal common subtype* is written $s \cap t$. There are two primitive type labels - the *universal type* $\top$, and the *absurd type* $\bot$. For any type label t, $\bot \leq t \leq \top$. The minimal common supertype CAT $\cup$ DOG = CARNIVORE. The maximal common subtype of PET and CAT is PET-CAT. The maximal common subtype CAT $\cap$ DOG = $\bot$, means that it is logically impossible for an entity to be both a dog and a cat.

Definition 1.2 *The* conformity relation :: *relates type labels to individual markers -*

- $type(c) :: referent(c)$.

- $s :: i \wedge s \leq t \supset t :: i$.
- $s :: i \wedge t :: i \supset (s \bigcap t) :: i$.
- $\forall i \in I \; \top :: i \wedge \neg(\bot :: i)$.
- $\forall t \in T \; t :: *$.

The first rule states the referent of a concept must conform to its type label. From our example $type(c1) :: referent(c1)$ or GIRL::Sue means the individual Sue conforms to the type GIRL. The second rule states that if an individual marker conforms to type s, it must also conform to all supertypes of s. Since GIRL::Sue and GIRL < PERSON, then PERSON::Sue. The third rule states that if an individual marker conforms to type s and t, it must also conform to their maximal common subtype. For example, if STUDENT::Sue and GIRL::Sue, then (PERSON $\bigcap$ GIRL) :: Sue. That is, Sue conforms to the type FEMALE-STUDENT, FEMALE-STUDENT::Sue (given Figure 2).

Definition 1.3 *The* projection operator $\pi : v \rightarrow u$ *is defined*
$\forall c \in v \; type(\pi c) \leq type(c) \wedge (c = i \supset \pi c = i)$
$\forall r \in v \; type(\pi r) = type(r) \wedge arc(i, \pi r) = \pi \, arc(i, r), i = 1, \ldots, n.$

Assume we have a graph v

$$d1 : \text{PERSON} \wedge d1 = \text{Sue} \wedge q1 : \text{AGNT}(d2, d1) \wedge d2 : \text{EAT}$$

which is

[PERSON]←(AGNT)←[EAT]

in the linear form. Then the projection $\pi : v \rightarrow u$ is $\{(d1, c1), (q1, r1), (d2, c2)\}$.

Definition 1.4 *An* n-adic abstraction, $\lambda a_1, \ldots a_n u$, *consists of a canonical graph* u *(see below), together with a list of generic concepts* $a_1, \ldots, a_n$ *in* u, *called* formal parameters. *Types can be defined intensionally by* n*-adic abstractions, and individual markers can be defined by aggregations.*

- Concept types. $s =_{def} \lambda a u$.
- Relation types. $t =_{def} \lambda a_1, \ldots, a_n u$.
- Composite Individuals. $t(i) =_{def} u$ *given* $t =_{def} \lambda a v$ *and* $\pi : v \rightarrow u$ *and* $referent(\pi a) = i$.

For example given a concept type, BOOK, is defined by

BOOK = (λx)

[PUBLICATION: $*x$] –
(WRITTEN-BY)→[AUTHOR]
(ENTITLED)→[TITLE]
(PUBLISHED-BY)→[PUBLISHER]
(PUBLISHED-ON)→[YEAR].

Then the individual BOOK, ConceptualStructures, may be defined

BOOK(ConceptualStructures) =

[PUBLICATION: ConceptualStructures] –
(WRITTEN-BY)→[AUTHOR: JohnSowa]
(ENTITLED)→[TITLE: "Conceptual Structures: Information ..."]
(PUBLISHED-BY)→[PUBLISHER: AddisonWesley]
(PUBLISHED-ON)→[YEAR: 1984].

Where JohnSowa and AddisonWesley and the other individuals may also be defined by abstractions.

The relation EATS may be defined

$$\text{EATS} = (\lambda x, y)[\text{ANIMAL: } *x] \leftarrow (\text{AGNT}) \leftarrow [\text{EAT}] \rightarrow (\text{OBJ}) \rightarrow [\text{FOOD: } *y].$$

λ abstractions can be used where their appropriate kind of symbol can be used. Further each abstraction does not necessarily have to have an associated type symbol. Thus unnamed abstractions can occur in concepts and relations without having to create an entry in the type hierarchy.

In the following definition we use the notation $u - \alpha$ to indicate to remove α from the graph u. If α is -

- a. Remove the type of concept a, $a : s$, from u, also the referent, $a = \psi$, if present.
- $a : s$. Remove the type of concept a.
- $a : \psi$. Remove the referent of concept a.
- r. Remove the relation $r : t(a_1, \ldots, a_n)$.
- v. Remove all of the concepts and relations of graph v.

We also use the notation $\{c_1/d_1, \ldots, c_n/d_n\}u$ to mean substitute the concept identifier c_i for the concept identifier d_i in the graph u for all i in parallel.

Definition 1.5 *A* canon $< T, \leq_{T \times T}, I, ::_{T \times I}, B >$ *where B is a finite set of conceptual graphs, called the* canonical basis, *where*

$$\forall u \in B \, \forall c, r \in u \; type(c) \in T \wedge type(r) \in T \wedge (c : i \supset i \in I).$$

The set of canonical graphs *consists of the canonical basis B and any graph w derived from canonical graphs u and v (where u and v may be the same) using one or more of the following canonical formation rules -*

- *copy*(u, w) *– w is a copy of u, renaming all concept and conceptual relation variables.*

- *restrictType*$(u, w) - \exists a \in u\ \exists t\ (t \leq type(a) \wedge t :: referent(a)) \wedge w = (u - a : type(a) + a : t)$.

- *restrictIndividual*$(u, w) - \exists a \in u\ \exists i\ (referent(a) = *) \wedge type(a) :: i \wedge w = (u + (a = i))$.

- *join*$(u, v, w) - \exists c \in u\ \exists d \in v\ type(c) = type(d) \wedge referent(c) = referent(d) \wedge w = (u + \{c/d\}(v - d))$.

- *simplify*$(u, w) - \exists r, r' \in u\ r \neq r' \wedge type(r) = type(r') \wedge (arc(i, r) = arc(i, r'), i = 1, \ldots, n) \wedge w = (u - r')$.

- *conceptContract*$(u, w) - \exists t =_{def} \lambda av\ \pi : v \rightarrow u \wedge type(\pi a) = type(a) \wedge (w = u$ *with concepts and relations in* πv *removed such that the same information can be regained by conceptExpand*(w, u') *where* $u' \supset u$ [1], $\pi a : s$ *is replaced with* $\pi a : \lambda av$ *or equivalently* $\pi a : t$*).*

- *conceptExpand*$(u, w) - \exists c \in u\ type(c) =_{def} \lambda av \wedge w = (u + \{c/a\}(v - a))$.

- *relationContract*$(u, w) - \exists t =_{def} \lambda a_1, \ldots, a_n v\ \pi : v \rightarrow u \wedge distinct(\{\pi a_1, \ldots, \pi a_n\}) \wedge (v' = v - \{a_1, \ldots, a_n\}) \wedge \neg\exists r \in u\ \exists i, j\ (arc(i, r) \in \pi v' \wedge arc(j, r) \in (u - \pi v)) \wedge$
  $w = (u - \pi v' + r : t(\pi a_1, \ldots, \pi a_n)$ *given a new relation variable r).*

- *relationExpand*$(u, w) - \exists r \in u\ r : t(b_1, \ldots, b_n) \wedge t =_{def} \lambda a_1, \ldots, a_n v \wedge$
  $w = (u - r : t(b_1, \ldots, b_n) + \{b_1/a_1, \ldots, b_n/a_n\}(v - \{a_1, \ldots, a_n\}))$.

- *individualExpand*$(u, w) - \exists c \in u\ type(c)(referent(c)) =_{def} v' \wedge$
  $type(c) =_{def} \lambda av \wedge \pi : v \rightarrow v' \wedge w = (u + \{c/a\}(v' - \pi a))$.

We illustrate some of these rules. Figure 3 shows two canonical graphs. The first one may be read ***A girl is eating fast***; and the second, ***A person, Sue, is eating pie***. These are not formal translations of the graphs, but informal verbalizations for discussion of the graphs here.

If the concept [GIRL] in the first graph were restricted to [GIRL: Sue] (by the rule *restrictIndividual*) and the concept of type PERSON in the second graph were restricted to type GIRL (by the rule *restrictType*), then the graphs of Figure 3 would be changed to those in Figure 4. But before doing the restrictions, the conformity relation must be checked to ensure that GIRL :: Sue is true.

[1] See [1] for algorithm.

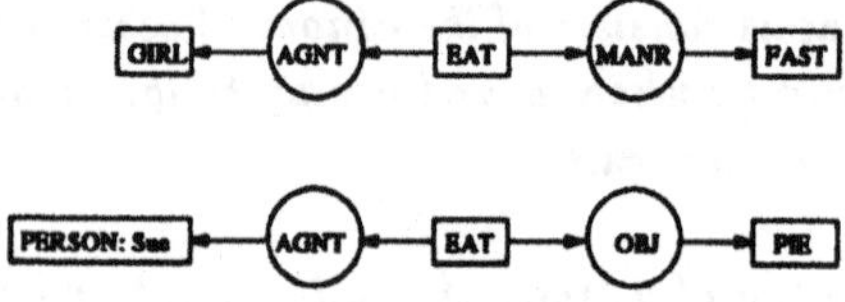

Figure 3: Two canonical graphs

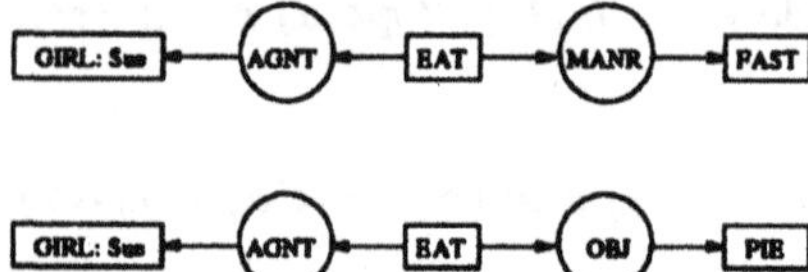

Figure 4: Restriction of two graphs in Figure 3

The two identical pairs of concepts, [GIRL: Sue] and [EAT] , can then be joined to each other using the *join* rule. The result is Figure 5.

In the graph in Figure 5, the two copies of (AGNT) are duplicates. Two conceptual relations of the same type are ***duplicates*** if for each i, the ith arc of one is linked to the same concept as the ith arc of the other. When one of the duplicates is deleted by the ***simplify*** rule, the graph becomes Figure 6, which may be read ***A girl, Sue, is eating pie fast.*** The simplification rule corresponds to the rule of logic that $\mathrm{R}(x,y) \wedge \mathrm{R}(x,y)$ is equivalent to just $\mathrm{R}(x,y)$.

The type QUICK-EATER may be defined as a subtype of PERSON -

QUICK-EATER = (λx) [PERSON: $*x$]←(AGNT)←[EAT]→(MANR)→[FAST].

This states that a quick eater is a person who eats fast. Given the above definition, the graph

[PERSON: Sue]←(AGNT)←[EAT]→(MANR)→[FAST]

can be contracted using the ***conceptContract*** rule to form the graph

[QUICK-EATER: Sue]

read ***A quick eater, Sue.*** It could be expanded using the ***conceptExpand*** rule to regain information from the definition of QUICK-EATER to get the graph

[QUICK-EATER: Sue]←(AGNT)←[EAT]→(MANR)→[FAST]

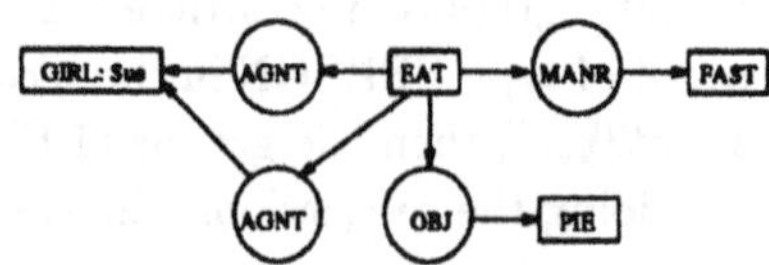

Figure 5: Join of the two graphs in Figure 4

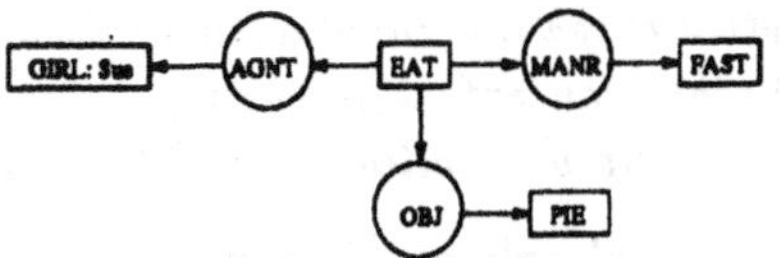

Figure 6: Simplification of Figure 5

Notice that contraction of a concept type followed by expansion does not produce the original graph.

Similarly relation definitions may be contracted or expanded in a graph. By using the *relationContract* rule and the definition given for the EATS relation previously, the graph

[GIRL:Sue]←(AGNT)←[EAT]→(OBJ)→[PIE]

contracts to the form graph

[GIRL:Sue]→(EATS)→[PIE]

By expansion of the definition the original graph is obtained.

The following graph

[BOOK:ConceptualStructures]→(IN)→[LIBRARY: UQ]

read *The book, "Conceptual Structures: Information ...", is in the UQ library* may be expanded using the definition of ConceptualStructures and the *individualExpand* rule

[PUBLICATION: ConceptualStructures] –
(WRITTEN-BY)→[AUTHOR: JohnSowa]
(ENTITLED)→[TITLE: "Conceptual Structures: Information ..."]
(PUBLISHED-BY)→[PUBLISHER: AddisonWesley]
(PUBLISHED-ON)→[YEAR: 1984]
(IN)→[LIBRARY: UQ].

The formation rules are a kind of *graph grammar* for canonical graphs. Besides defining syntax, they also enforce certain semantic constraints. The formation rules make no guarantee about truth or falsity. However, the formation rules are refutation rules. If we assert that the graph

[PERSON]←(AGNT)←[EAT]→(OBJ)→[PIE]

is false, then we can use the formation rules to show that

[GIRL:Sue]←(AGNT)←[EAT]→(OBJ)→[PIE]

is false. That is if a graph can be derived from a false graph, then it must in turn be false. The formation rules are falsity preserving.

Definition 1.6 *If a conceptual graph u is canonically derivable from a conceptual graph v (possibly with the join of other conceptual graphs $w_1, \ldots, w_n$), then u is called a* specialization *of v, written $u \leq v$, and v is called a* generalization *of u.*

Generalization defines a partial ordering of minimal conceptual graphs [2] *called the* generalization hierarchy. *For any conceptual graphs u. and v, the following properties are true -*

- Subgraph. *If v is a subgraph of u, then $u \leq v$.*
- Subtypes. *If u is identical to v except that one or more type labels of v are restricted to subtypes in u, then $u \leq v$.*
- Individuals. *If u is identical to v except that one or more generic concepts of v are restricted to individual concepts of the same type, then $u \leq v$.*
- Top. *The graph* [T] *is a generalization of all other conceptual graphs.*
- Abstractions. $\lambda a_1, \ldots, a_n u \leq \lambda b_1, \ldots, b_n v$ *if* $u \leq v \wedge \pi .: v \rightarrow u \wedge (\pi b_i = a_i, i = 1, \ldots, n)$.

The nodes in the generalization hierarchy are conceptual graphs and the arcs represent the non-transitive ordering between the graphs. In Figure 7 the hierarchy is given for the graphs from the previous examples. The canonical basis in this example would consist of the set of graphs $\{a, b, c\}$. The arc (b, d) indicates:

1. *A girl, Sue, is eating fast* is canonically derivable from *A girl is eating fast.*
2. *A girl, Sue, is eating fast* implies *A girl is eating fast.*
3. *A girl is eating fast* is a generalization of *A girl, Sue, is eating fast.*
4. *A girl, Sue, is eating fast* is a specialization of *A girl is eating fast.*

In the following sections we examine how to use the hierarchy for searching a set of conceptual graphs and how to construct the hierarchy, then show how to store conceptual graphs in the hierarchy in a compact form.

2 Compilation of Conceptual Graphs in the Generalization Hierarchy

One of the central problems of automating conceptual graphs is finding a graph in a large set.

[2]All possible contractions (concept and relation types, individuals) and removal of redundant structures.

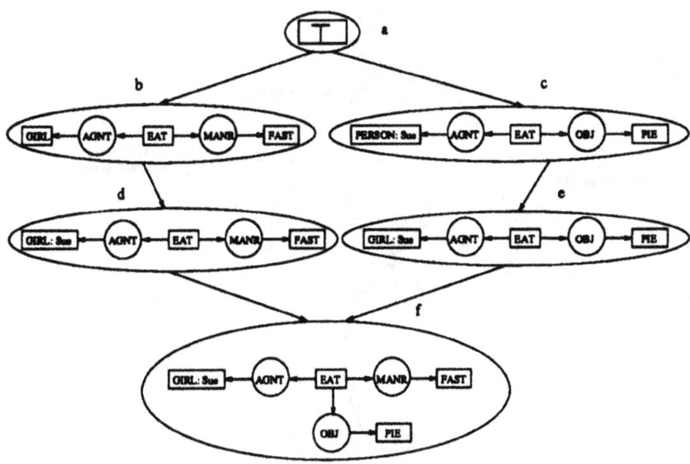

Figure 7: The generalization hierarchy of the graphs in Figures 3, 4, 5 and 6

Our solution for the database is to construct a data structure representing the partial order over conceptual graphs: the generalization hierarchy.

To insert a graph into the hierarchy the sets of immediate generalizations and immediate specializations need to be calculated (see Figure 8[3]). This can be achieved by a two phase breadth-first search. The first phase searches the generalization space until no more closer (specialized) generalizations can be found. These graphs constitute the immediate generalizations. The second phase is a breadth-first search of the intersection of the subhierarchies of the immediate generalizations of u. Search in a subhierarchy discontinues when a specialization is found, that graph is an immediate specialization of u.

Levinson [7] developed algorithms for storing and retrieving chemical graphs in a hierarchy. In more recent work [8] Levinson has proposed hybrid indexing mechanisms for semantic networks.

Garner and Tsui [9] added the idea of storing graphs as the differences between adjacent graphs in the hierarchy. In their method the arcs of the hierarchy are labeled with differences. The differences are data used by an algorithm to reconstruct the graph, which is compared to the query using a general matcher. This method does not use information gathered in constructing matches between generalizations and the query graph. The canonical formation rules are breadth-first in the sense that in general they construct graphs from a number of generalizations.

In our method the graphs are represented as instructions which represent special cases of the canonical formation rules. The instructions are placed in the nodes rather than on the arcs of the hierarchy. They require each of the immediate generalizations to be constructed. This is a matter of course in breadth-first search. The instructions

[3] Fritz Lehmann contributed this diagram.

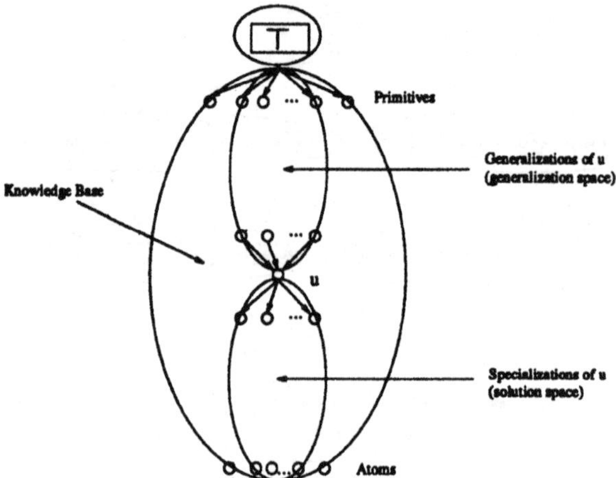

Figure 8: The search space for the graph u in a generalization hierarchy

perform the matching by using mappings of immediate generalizations into the query graph. In this way common computation can be shared through the mappings between generalizations and specializations.

Here we will concentrate on the first phase of breadth-first search: searching the generalization space. In the first phase the aim is to find subgraph morphisms of database graphs in the query. In the second phase the aim is to find subgraph morphisms of the query in the database graphs. In the first phase the database graphs could be thought of as reading from the query graph. In the second phase the database graphs write to the query graph constructing specialized solutions.

Here we give a specialized interpretation of the canonical formation rules based on the mode of operation: read or write. We examine the read mode here. The graphs are reconstructed by the instructions, however here we show the operations that construct the mapping between the database graphs and the query. We examine four specialized cases of the canonical formation rules here.

In the following discussion we use the notation π_v to represent the mapping $\pi : v \rightarrow q$, where q is the query graph.

- *restrictType* $u\ c\ t\ w$ - if $type(\pi_u c) \leq t$ then $\pi_w := \pi_u$ else fail.

  For the database graph w to be a generalization of the query graph q, q must have a subtype of the type of the corresponding concept in u.

- *restrictIndividual* $u\ c\ i\ w$ - if $referent(\pi_u c) = i$ then $\pi_w := \pi_u$ else fail.

  We examine restriction to individual markers, rather than more complex referents such as sets and graphs. These other cases can be handled by other specialized cases of restrict. For $q \leq u$ to be true the query q must have the same individual marker i as the one in the corresponding concept in the database graph u.

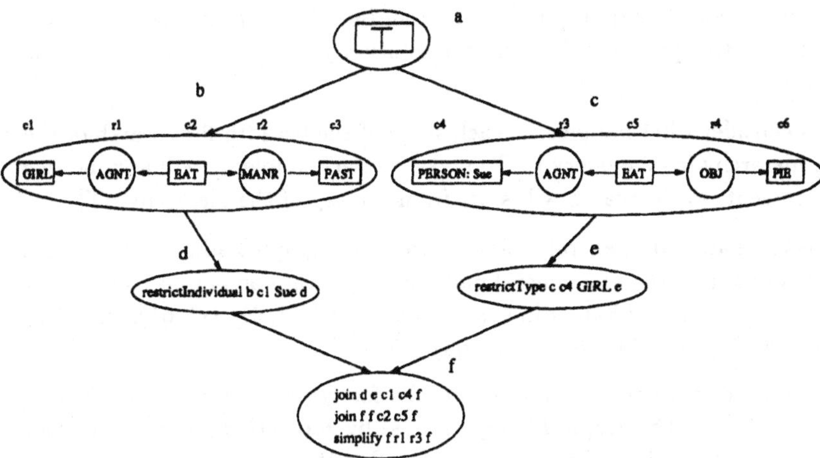

Figure 9: Encoding conceptual graphs in a generalization hierarchy with canonical formation instructions

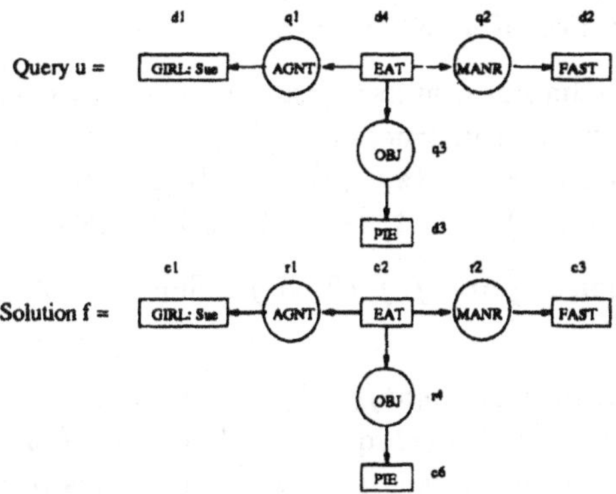

Figure 10: A query u and the solution f for the generalization hierarchy in Figure 9

- *join* $u\ v\ c\ d\ w$ - if $\pi_u c = \pi_v d$ then $\pi_w := \pi_u + (\pi_v - (d, \pi_v d))$ else fail.

  Joining concepts c and d of database graphs u and v respectively in read mode means that c and d must already pointing at the same concept in the query graph q.

- *simplify* $u\ r\ s\ w$ - if $\pi_u r = \pi_u s$ then $\pi_w := \pi_u - (s, \pi_u s)$ else fail.

  Simplifying two duplicate relations in a database graph in read mode means that the two relations must be mapped to the same relation in the query, since the query graph cannot contain duplicates as it is a minimal graph.

In Figure 9 we replace conceptual graphs with instructions. Compare this representation with the generalization hierarchy in Figure 7. We have identified the concepts and relations in the conceptual graphs, so they can be referred to in the instructions. Figure 10 contains the query graph u and the solution f from the generalization hierarchy in Figure 9.

Let us consider what happens in each stage of the breadth-first search of the generalization hierarchy for the query u. To make matters simple we will assume there is no indexing present, so the search will start from the top of the hierarchy [T] .

We first find all of the generalizations of the query graph u adjacent to the graph [T] Let us assume that we use a general matching algorithm on graphs b and c to find the subgraph isomorphisms of b and c in u, such that $\pi_b = \{(\mathrm{c1}, \mathrm{d1}), (\mathrm{r1}, \mathrm{q1}), (\mathrm{c2}, \mathrm{d4}), (\mathrm{r2}, \mathrm{q2}), (\mathrm{c3},$ and $\pi_c = \{(\mathrm{c4}, \mathrm{d1}), (\mathrm{r3}, \mathrm{q1}), (\mathrm{c5}, \mathrm{d4}), (\mathrm{r4}, \mathrm{q3}), (\mathrm{c6}, \mathrm{d3})\}$.

Now we look at b and c's adjacent graphs for generalizations of u. The adjacent graphs are d and e. The graph d is represented by *restrictIndividual* b c1 Sue d. This instructions translates into if $\mathit{referent}(\pi_b \mathrm{c1})$ = Sue then $\pi_d := \pi_b$ else fail. Since π_b c1 = d1 and $\mathit{referent}(\mathrm{d1})$ = Sue, d is a generalization of u and $\pi_d := \pi_b$.

The graph e is represented by *restrictType* c c4 GIRL e. This instruction is implemented as: if $\mathit{type}(\pi_c \mathrm{c4}) \leq$ GIRL then $\pi_e := \pi_c$ else fail. Since π_c c4 = d1 and $\mathit{type}(\mathrm{d1})$ = GIRL, e is a generalization of u, and $\pi_e := \pi_c$.

Now we examine the adjacent graphs of d and e. The only one in this case is f. The graph f is represented by three instructions. The first instruction, *join* d e c1 c4 f, means if π_d c1 = π_e c4 then $\pi_f := \pi_d + (\pi_e - (\mathrm{c4}, \mathrm{d1}))$ else fail. Since π_d c1 = d1 = π_e c4, we calculate $\pi_f = \{(\mathrm{c1}, \mathrm{d1}), (\mathrm{r1}, \mathrm{q1}), (\mathrm{c2}, \mathrm{d4}), (\mathrm{r2}, \mathrm{q2}), (\mathrm{c3}, \mathrm{d2}), (\mathrm{r3}, \mathrm{q1}), (\mathrm{c5}, \mathrm{d4}), (\mathrm{r4}, \mathrm{q3}), (\mathrm{c6}, \mathrm{d3})\}$.

The second instruction is *join* f f c2 c5 f. Since π_f c2 = d4 = π_f c5 we get $\pi_f = \pi_f + (\pi_f - (\mathrm{c5}, \mathrm{d4}))$.

The third instruction in f is *simplify* f r1 r3 f. Since π_f r1 = π_f r3 = q1 we have $\pi_f := \pi_f - (\mathrm{r3}, \mathrm{q1}) = \{(\mathrm{c1}, \mathrm{d1}), (\mathrm{r1}, \mathrm{q1}), (\mathrm{c2}, \mathrm{d4}), (\mathrm{r2}, \mathrm{q2}), (\mathrm{c3}, \mathrm{d2}), (\mathrm{r4}, \mathrm{q3}), (\mathrm{c6}, \mathrm{d3})\}$. Thus f is a generalization of u. In fact $f = u$. Compare this result with the graphs u and f in Figure 10.

Summary

The canonical formation rules distinguish conceptual graphs from other semantic network formalisms. They enforce semantic constraints on the canonical graphs. Algorithms to process them must be developed.

Conceptual graphs are compiled into instructions which are special cases of the canonical formation rules. The instructions operate on immediate generalizations, and construct a mapping between the immediate generalizations and the graph, and hence the query graph during search. Common computation involved in matching database graphs to the query graph is shared through these mappings. Since a specialization implies a generalization, simply constructing the hierarchy compiles static inferences.

Compilation of conceptual graphs is effected in three ways: removal of redundant data, use of simple instructions which ignore redundant checks when performing matching, and by sharing common processing between graphs.

Acknowledgements

I thank Fritz Lehmann, Robert Levinson, Peter Robinson, and John Sowa for discussions on the proceeding topics.

References

[1] John F. Sowa. *Conceptual Structures: Information in Mind and Machine.* Addison-Wesley, Reading, MA, 1984.

[2] John F. Sowa. Conceptual structures bibliography. In Peter Eklund and Laurie Gerholz, editors, *Proceedings of the 5th Annual Conceptual Structures Workshop*, ISBN 91-7870-718-8, Boston&Stockholm, 1990. Linköping University.

[3] Christoph Walther. *A Many-Sorted Calculus Based on Resolution and Paramodulation.* Research Notes in Artificial Intelligence. Morgan Kaufmann, 1987.

[4] Nick J. Davies. Schubert's steamroller in a natural deduction theorem prover. In D. S. Moralee, editor, *Proceedings of Expert Systems 87*, pages 89–102, 1987. Research and Development in Expert Systems IV.

[5] Mark E. Stickel. Schubert's steamroller problem: Formulations and solutions. *Automated Reasoning*, 2(1):89–101, 1986.

[6] Don D. Roberts. *The Existential Graphs of Charles S. Peirce.* Mouton, The Hague, 1973.

[7] Robert A. Levinson. *A Self-Organizing Retrieval System for Graphs.* PhD thesis, University of Texas, May 1985.

[8] Robert A. Levinson. Pattern associativity and the retrieval of semantic networks. *Computers and Mathematics with Applications*, 1991. To appear in the Special Edition on Semantic Networks.

[9] Brian J. Garner and Eric Tsui. A self-organizing dictionary for conceptual structures. In J. F. Gilmore, editor, *Proceedings of the Conference on Applications of Artificial Intelligence*, pages 356–363, 1987. SPIE Proc. 784, 18-20th May, Orlando.

Subsumption in Knowledge Graphs

Mark Willems
Department of Applied Mathematics
University of Twente
P.O. Box 217, 7500 AE Enschede, The Netherlands

Abstract

An important notion for representation formalisms of natural language semantics, is a subsumption hierarchy. Therefore a precise definition of subsumption is necessary. We shall argue that the usual solution of providing an extensional semantics and mapping subsumption onto set-inclusion, is not satisfactory. The problem is that extensions lose track of the structure. A better solution is used for conceptual graphs [13], where derivation rules define generalization.

In this paper we shall introduce knowledge graphs, and give a definition of subsumption, that does keep track of the structure. Moreover, because structural subsumption can be tested with a tractable algorithm, the fundamental tradeoff between expressiveness and complexity of inferences [10] does not occur.

1 Introduction

While applying knowledge graphs [3] to natural language, we have found that subsumption is an important notion. We assume that the semantic content of words is described by graphs, in such a way that the semantic content of a sentence can be computed by joining the graphs of the words. Indeed, if these graphs are part of a well-defined subsumption hierarchy, then the unification or join of two graphs can be defined as a greatest lower bound. This is an elegant application of the compositionality principle.

The notions of subsumption and unification are well-known in artificial intelligence as well as in computational linguistics. Unification of feature terms is the basis of unification grammars [9]. A similar formalism of partially-ordered data type structures was developed by [1]. Terminological knowledge representation languages, like KL-ONE [5], use subsumption to structure a domain of objects. And finally for conceptual graphs [13], the generalization hierarchy is used to define the maximal join of two graphs.

Because of the importance of subsumption, it is necessary to provide a precise definition. The solution of terminological languages is to define an extensional semantics [6], hereby mapping concepts to sets and using set-inclusion for subsumption. As we shall show in Section 3 this is not satisfactory. The problem is that, intuitively, subsumption is a relation between structures, whereas extensions lose track of this structure. The subsumption of conceptual graphs on the other hand, is defined in terms of canonical derivation rules. These rules do keep track of the structure, but the precise definition given in [13] is not correct. In Section 3 we shall provide a correct definition.

Recent research on terminological languages has mainly focused on the complexity of the subsumption test [6, 7, 11]. A fundamental tradeoff exists between the expressiveness of a language and the complexity of its inferences, as pointed out in [10]. In particular, this tradeoff seems to arise for the subsumption test. In Section 4 we shall show that structural subsumption does not have this problem and can have a tractable test.

In order to emphasize the *structure* of descriptions, we shall develop a *graph* formalism that captures some of the basic features of knowledge representation. Subsumption then straightforwardly translates into a kind of subgraph relation. And although determining subgraph isomorphism is an NP-complete problem for arbitrary graphs, knowledge graphs contain extra information in their labels, so the subsumption test is tractable.

2 Knowledge Graphs

In this section we shall define a formalism based on knowledge graphs, see [3]. The special idea of knowledge graphs is that only a few fundamental relations are used. Our formalism will mix elements from conceptual graphs [13] and terminological languages [6]. The former contain concept nodes, role nodes, and numbered arcs to indicate the argument position of a concept towards a role. The latter only contain binary roles, and instead of using a separate type hierarchy, they explicitly represent the construction of types from more primitive types.

Concept nodes in a conceptual graph implicitly distinguish a token and a type label. This label is taken from a separate type hierarchy. Although having a separate hierarchy might be useful for efficient computation, it is not essential for the definition of subsumption. Precisely the same result is achieved by the explicit construction of complex types from primitive types. Therefore knowledge graphs represent a token node, and explicitly connect it to one or more primitive type nodes. The ALI(ke)-relation is used to represent this connection.

Roles are represented as tokens as well, and complex roles can be computed in the same way. In this paper we shall only investigate binary roles, because these are the most common roles in terminological languages. However, roles with more arguments can be considered in a straightforward way. Usually, binary roles are interpreted as properties of an object, which can be filled by some other object. Thus we use two fundamental relations, PAR and EQU, to indicate that a property is PARt of an object and that an object is EQUivalent to some property. An example of a knowledge graph is given in Figure 1.

Unlike conceptual graphs, the distinction between properties and objects is not given by marking the nodes (i.e. boxes versus circles). Rather the position of a token in the

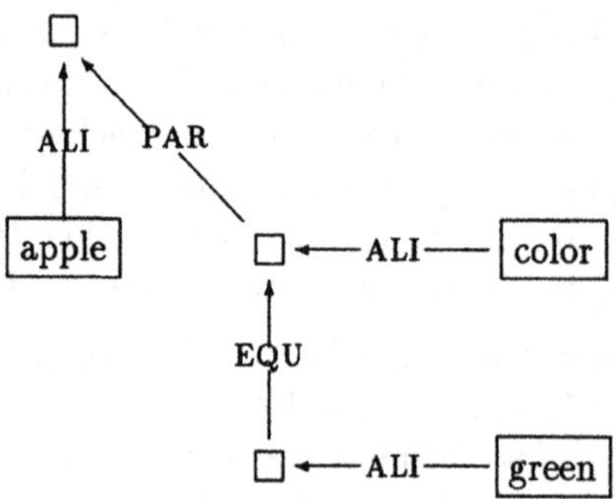

Figure 1: The knowledge graph for "an apple with a green color".

graph results in one or the other interpretation. Therefore we must formulate certain conditions on the form of the graph, which only allow connections between objects and properties or objects and types.

Definition. A *simple knowledge graph* is pair $K = (C, R)$ where C is the set of concepts and R is the set of relations. The function *label* maps the concepts onto their labels. The relations are triples $c_1 \rightarrow r \rightarrow c_2$, where $r \in \{\text{ALI}, \text{PAR}, \text{EQU}\}$.

- A *token* is a concept labeled by the special label "□".
- A *name* is a concept labeled with any string unequal to the token label.
- A *property* is a token with an out-going PAR-relation or an in-coming EQU-relation.
- An *object* is a token that is not a property.
- An ALI relates a name with a token. A property is related to two objects, by a PAR to one and by an EQUto the other. An object can be related to more properties.

■

Thus a simple knowledge graph is a directed graph. There are two kinds of cycles in directed graphs: undirected and directed cycles. An undirected cycle is a cycle of arcs that do not necessarily point in the same direction; if so the cycle is called directed or a circuit. Descriptions in terminological languages correspond to knowledge graphs without any directed cycles. Furthermore, they are connected and have a single sink called the head.

Definition. An *acyclic knowledge graph* is a simple knowledge graph with no circuits, that is no directed cycles. We also assume it to have only one sink. This concept is called the *head*. ■

There are a number of ways to provide a formal semantics for knowledge graphs. We could try to give a translation to first-order logic as in [13], but the construction of complex roles poses a problem. Therefore we shall give an extensional semantics, common for terminological languages.

An abstract universe of individuals U is assumed, and a concept is associated with the set of individuals it describes. This set is called the *extension* of the concept, and a function $\mathcal{E}$ maps concepts to their extension. One can think of a name as a primitive concept whose extension is fixed, such as type labels (person, event) or role labels (father, speed). The extension of tokens on the other hand is determined by the extension of its neighbors.

In the following we use this definition of composition: $\mathcal{E}[p] \circ \mathcal{E}[q] := \{(i,j) \in U \mid \exists k \in U : (i,k) \in \mathcal{E}[p] \textit{ and } (k,j) \in \mathcal{E}[q]\}$. We shall take the extension of a PAR-EQU-path to be the composition of the properties, where the extension of the property is taken when the arcs point against the direction of the path and the inverse is taken otherwise. So for a path $\pi = x - \text{PAR} - p - \text{EQU} - y \rightarrow \text{EQU} \rightarrow q \rightarrow \text{PAR} \rightarrow z$ the extension $\mathcal{E}[\pi]$ is equal to $\mathcal{E}[p] \circ \mathcal{E}[q]^{-1}$. For a path of length zero we take the extension to be the identity $Id = \{(i,i) \mid i \in U\}$.

Definition. Let $K = (C, R)$ be a simple knowledge graph and U a set of individuals. A function $\mathcal{E} : C \rightarrow 2^U \cup 2^{U^2}$ is an *extension function* for K, if it obeys the following conditions:

- For all names $x \in C$ the extension is either that of an object: $\mathcal{E}[x] \subseteq U$ or that of a relation: $\mathcal{E}[x] \subseteq U^2$. The extensions of names are primitive and the names are unique, so if $\textit{label}(x) = \textit{label}(y)$ then $\mathcal{E}[x] = \mathcal{E}[y]$.

- For all objects $x \in C$, $\mathcal{E}[x]$ is the intersection of the following sets:

  (1) the sets $\mathcal{E}[n]$ for all names n such that $n \rightarrow \text{ALI} \rightarrow x$,

  (2) the sets $\{i \in U \mid \exists j : (i,j) \in \mathcal{E}[p]\}$ for all properties p such that $p \rightarrow \text{PAR} \rightarrow x$,

  (3) the sets $\{j \in U \mid \exists j : (i,j) \in \mathcal{E}[p]\}$ for all properties p such that $x \rightarrow \text{EQU} \rightarrow p$,

  (4) the sets $\{i \in U \mid \forall j \in \mathcal{E}[y] : (i,j) \in \mathcal{E}[\pi_1] \cap \mathcal{E}[\pi_2]\}$ for all pairs of disjoint paths π_1 and π_2 from x to y.

- For all properties $x \in C$, $\mathcal{E}[x]$ is the intersection of the following sets

  (5) the sets $\mathcal{E}[n]$ for all names n such that $n \rightarrow \text{ALI} \rightarrow x$,

  (6) the sets $\{(i,j) \in U^2 \mid i \in \mathcal{E}[o]\}$ for all objects o such that $x \rightarrow \text{PAR} \rightarrow o$,

  (7) the sets $\{(i,j) \in U^2 \mid j \in \mathcal{E}[o]\}$ for all objects o such that $o \rightarrow \text{EQU} \rightarrow x$.

■

The extension of a graph can be found by evaluating these intersections. The fourth condition allows us to have "coreference of attributes" as in [1]: when we have two paths $y \rightarrow \text{EQU} \rightarrow p_n \rightarrow \text{PAR} \rightarrow \cdots \rightarrow \text{EQU} \rightarrow p_1 \rightarrow \text{PAR} \rightarrow x$ and $y \rightarrow \text{EQU} \rightarrow q_n \rightarrow \text{PAR} \rightarrow \cdots \rightarrow \text{EQU} \rightarrow q_1 \rightarrow \text{PAR} \rightarrow x$, then

$\mathcal{E}[x]$ contains all i for which the extensions of the paths "commute", i.e. for all individuals j in $\mathcal{E}[y]$ the pair (i,j) is in both $\mathcal{E}[p_1] \circ \cdots \circ \mathcal{E}[p_n]$ and $\mathcal{E}[q_1] \circ \cdots \circ \mathcal{E}[q_n]$.

For directed cycles the intersections correspond to a fixed-point equation. A cycle $x \rightarrow \text{EQU} \rightarrow p_n \rightarrow \text{PAR} \rightarrow \cdots \rightarrow \text{EQU} \rightarrow p_1 \rightarrow \text{PAR} \rightarrow x$ implies two paths from x to x; the cycle itself and a path of length zero. So by (4) we have $\mathcal{E}[x] \subseteq \{i \in U \mid \forall j \in \mathcal{E}[x] : (i,j) \in \mathcal{E}[p_1] \circ \cdots \circ \mathcal{E}[p_n] \cap Id\}$, which is equal to the fixed-point $\{i \in U \mid (i,i) \in \mathcal{E}[p_1] \circ \cdots \circ \mathcal{E}[p_n]\}$.

Next we consider negation, another important aspect of knowledge representation. There are two different kinds one can distinguish: *exclusion*, indicating inequality of objects, and the more common *complementation*, indicating that a token is anything not in the extension of another token. Conceptual graphs combine the two by means of negative contexts [13].

By introducing a NOT-relation between objects, we shall represent complementation. To keep things a little bit simpler we shall only allow the connection of tokens from two different simple knowledge graphs. This enables us to have an asymmetric interpretation of complementation, that only influences the extension of the token it is pointing to.

Definition. Let $K_1 = (C_1, R_1)$ and $K_2 = (C_2, R_2)$ be two knowledge graphs, each containing objects o_1 and o_2 respectively. Then K_1 *complemented by* K_2 is the graph $K = (C, R)$ where $C = C_1 \cup C_2$ and $R = R_1 \cup R_2 \cup \{o_2 \rightarrow \text{NOT} \rightarrow o_1\}$.

The extension function for this graph is evaluated by the following extra equation added to the definition of extension functions: for all objects x the extension $\mathcal{E}[x]$ is also intersected with the set $U - \mathcal{E}[n]$, for all objects n such that $n \rightarrow \text{NOT} \rightarrow x$. ■

Now we must realize that with complementation we can formulate descriptions that in a way have no meaning. Actually when $\mathcal{E}[o_1] \subseteq \mathcal{E}[o_2]$ in the previous definition, the object o_1 in the resulting graph has an empty extension, for all possible functions. Indeed, whenever we use some form of negation in an extensional semantics, we must keep the notion of consistency in mind. In the next definition and the following sections we shall consider acyclic knowledge graphs. This makes things a little bit clearer, because the head can be seen as a single object that is being described by the graph.

Definition. Let K be an acyclic knowledge graph with head h. We say K is *consistent* if there exists at least one extension function such that $\mathcal{E}[h] \neq \emptyset$. Otherwise we call the knowledge graph *inconsistent*. ■

An example of an inconsistent knowledge graph is given in Figure 2. In this way knowledge graphs contain some of the more common constructors of type-descriptions and feature-structures. For instance from the language $\mathcal{ALCRC}$ of [11]: "intersection" $(C \sqcap D)$ of both concepts and roles, "complementation" $(\neg C)$, "existential role quantification" $(\exists R : C)$, and "coreference of attributes" or "role value map" $(P = Q)$.

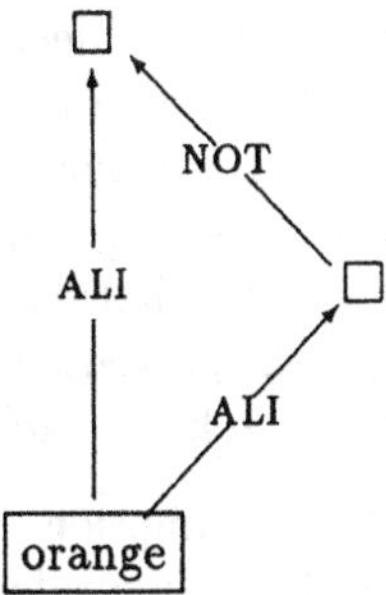

Figure 2: "Something that is an orange as well as not an orange".

3 Subsumption

The usual way to define subsumption in a language with a semantics as given above, would be by set-inclusion of the extensions. Let K_1 and K_2 be two knowledge graphs with heads h_1 and h_2 respectively, we might say K_1 *is subsumed by* K_2, if for any extension function $\mathcal{E}$: $\mathcal{E}[h_1] \subseteq \mathcal{E}[h_2]$.

A formal definition of subsumption can only be accepted, if it correctly captures our intuition. This is that subsumption is an implicit relation between structured types as in [6]:

> "The descriptions themselves implicitly define a taxonomy of subsumption, where type A is subsumed by type B if, *by virtue of their form*, every instance of A is an instance of B. In other words, it can be determined that being an A is implicit in being a B, based only on *the structure of two terms* ..." (italics ours).

Clearly the emphasis is on the structure of descriptions.

The definition by means of extensions, however, is counter-intuitive in the case of an inconsistent knowledge graph. Just because its extension is empty, an inconsistent knowledge graph is subsumed by any other knowledge graph, even though its structure might be completely different. For example, take the inconsistent description of Figure 2, and compare it to the description in Figure 1. In cases like this, subsumption should not be allowed, because it compares incomparable things. (Thou shallt not compare apples and oranges).

This is a problem in logic too, as Barwise and Perry remark in [4], when they criticize the "Frege doctrine". The authors claim that there are logically equivalent sentences, that should not be considered equivalent (like $P \wedge \neg P$ and $Q \wedge \neg Q$). The problem is associated with the fundamental assumption that the reference of a sentence is its truth value. The point is that truth values lose track of the *subject matter*, and so Barwise and Perry define two sentences to be equivalent only if the sentences treat the same subject.

Another reason for keeping track of the subject matter is that we might want to localize the inconsistencies. If an inconsistency arises in a monotonic logic, the whole system collapses. Obviously a logician would say that it has become meaningless, and would forbid inconsistencies alltogether. However they often do arise, and it is sometimes difficult to discover them. We would like queries that do not depend on the inconsistent data to remain unaffected. Relevance logic [2] prevents irrelevant axioms and inconsistencies to affect a proof. One way to do this is to keep track of the structure.

For simple conceptual graphs, subsumption corresponds to generalization, which is defined in terms of four canonical derivation rules: *copy, restrict, join,* and *simplify*, see [13]. Defining subsumption in terms of rules is a way to keep track of the structure. If a graph g_1 is derivable from a graph g_2 by application of these rules, then g_1 is subsumed by g_2. However, care must be taken because contrary to Sowa's claim this does not define a partial order: as a counter example, take the graphs $a \rightarrow r \rightarrow b \leftarrow r \leftarrow a$ and $a \rightarrow r \rightarrow b$. As was shown in [8], these graphs subsume each other, but they are not the same. So the generalization relation is not antisymmetric. A solution is to define an equivalence relation between graphs that generalize each other and consider a partial order on the equivalence classes.

Basically, one graph subsumes another if and only if every concept in the second has a counterpart in the first. For example "a male person" is subsumed by "a person", because the graph "a token x alike *male* and *person*" contains a subgraph "a token y alike *person*". So there must exist a relation (in the mathematical sense) between the nodes, such that every node in the second graph has an image in the first, and if a node is connected to another, then each image is connected to an image in the first graph. The NOT is special in this respect, because it reverses this condition: "something not a person" is subsumed by "something not a male person".

Definition. Let $K_1 = (C_1, R_1)$, and $K_2 = (C_2, R_2)$ be two acyclic knowledge graphs. A relation $\mathbf{S} \subseteq (C_1 \times C_2) \cup (C_2 \times C_1)$, is called a *subsumption relation*, if it obeys the following conditions:

(1) For names $n_1 \in C_1$ and $n_2 \in C_2$, the subsumptions $n_1 \mathbf{S} n_2$ and $n_2 \mathbf{S} n_1$ hold if and only if $label(n_1) = label(n_2)$.

(2) For tokens $x_1 \in C_1$ and $x_2 \in C_2$, the subsumption $x_1 \mathbf{S} x_2$ holds if and only if, for all neighbors $y_2 \dashrightarrow r \dashrightarrow x_2$, there exists a neighbor $y_1 \dashrightarrow r \dashrightarrow x_1$, such that $y_1 \mathbf{S} y_2$ holds in case $r \neq$ NOT. Otherwise $y_2 \mathbf{S} y_1$ must hold.

(3) For the inverse $x_2 \mathbf{S} x_1$, replace C_1 by C_2 and vice versa in (2).

The subsumption relation for graphs is defined in terms of their heads h_1 and h_2 respectively : graph K_1 *is subsumed by* K_2, denoted as $K_1 \leq K_2$, if and only if there exists a subsumption relation $\mathbf{S}$ such that $h_1 \mathbf{S} h_2$. ■

In this way subsumption is a relation between structures, which of course does imply set-inclusion of the extensions. But the important point we would like to make, is that although set-inclusion is a necessary condition for subsumption, it certainly is not a sufficient one.

Regrettably, such a theorem cannot be proven for cyclic knowledge graphs. By our definition the graphs $\square_x$→EQU→$\square$→PAR→$\square$→EQU→$\square$→PAR→$\square_x$ and $\square_x$→EQU→$\square$→PAR→$\square_x$→EQU→$\square_x$→PAR→$\square_x$ subsume each other, but the extensions do not obey set-inclusion. In [1] cyclic structures cause a similar problem for feature-terms.

The important characteristic of a directed cycle in a knowledge graph is that it "repeats itself". If we have a directed cycle like $\square$→EQU→$\square$→PAR→$\square$→EQU→$\square$→PAR→$\square$, we see that it consist of the sequence of arcs →EQU→$\square$→PAR→ twice. However, cycles with this characteristic are not necessarily directed, because we can repeat the sequence →EQU→$\square$→PAR→$\square$—EQU—$\square$—PAR— and obtain an undirected cycle. Therefore we define well-formed knowledge graphs as graphs not containing such "repeating cycles", either directed or undirected.

Definition. A *well-formed* knowledge graphs is a simple knowledge graph, that does not contain cycles consisting of a repeating sequence of arcs.

Theorem 1 *For two well-formed acyclic knowledge graphs K_1 and K_2 with heads h_1 and h_2 respectively, $K_1 \leq K_2$ implies that for any extension function $\mathcal{E}[h_1] \subseteq \mathcal{E}[h_2]$.*

Proof: Suppose that $K_1 \leq K_2$, but that there is an extension function such that $\mathcal{E}[h_1] \not\subseteq \mathcal{E}[h_2]$. There then must be an element $i \in \mathcal{E}[h_1]$, that is not in $\mathcal{E}[h_2]$. Because $\mathcal{E}[h_1]$ is the intersection of its incoming neighbors extensions, we know that all ALI-neighbors of h_1 contain i, that all PAR-neighbors contain a pair (i, j) for some element j, and that all NOT-neighbors do not contain i. For $\mathcal{E}[h_2]$ on the other hand, three cases can occur. Either (a) an ALI-neighbor of h_2 does not contain i, or (b) a PAR-neighbor does not contain any pair (i, j) for some j, or (c) a NOT-neighbor does contain i.

Now because $K_1 \leq K_2$, each ALI-neighbor of h_2 corresponds to an ALI-neighbor of h_1 with the same label, and the extensions must be the same too; (a) cannot occur. For cases (b) and (c) we can repeat the above argument, and conclude that some in-neighbor k_1 does not contain some element, that is contained by its images in the other graph. Again because of the labels, this in-neighbor cannot be an ALI-neighbor.

One reason why k_1 does not contain some individual might be due to a cycle $h_1 \rightarrow \cdots \rightarrow k_1 \leftarrow \cdots \leftarrow h_1$. But if the graph K_1 contains such a cycle, then K_2 contains a cycle $h_2 \rightarrow \cdots \rightarrow k' \leftarrow \cdots \leftarrow x \rightarrow \cdots \rightarrow k'' \leftarrow \cdots \leftarrow h_2$, where k' and k'' are images of k_1 and x of h_1. This cycle is not well-formed unless $k' = k''$ and $x = h_2$, but then the images of k_1 can not contain the aforementioned individual either.

The graphs are acyclic, so repeating the argument down the in-neighbors, we eventually reach a token of K_1 that has only incoming ALI-neighbors. Again each ALI-neighbor corresponds to an ALI-neighbor in K_2, that must have the same label and thus identical extension. We can conclude the final contradiction. It follows that set-inclusion must hold. ■

4 Algorithm

The definition of subsumption given in the previous section, enables us to provide a tractable algorithm. For two arbitrary graphs, the algorithm starts with a relation between the graphs, that contains all pairs obeying the first condition i.e. the labels of names are equal. It then iteratively determines sub-relations by deleting those pairs that do not obey the other conditions.

Algorithm 1 *Given two knowledge graphs* $K_1 = (C_1, R_1)$ *and* $K_2 = (C_2, R_2)$*, determine a relation* $\mathbf{S} \subseteq (C_1 \times C_2) \cup (C_2 \times C_1)$ *such that* $\mathbf{S}$ *is a subsumption relation.*

- *Start with the relation* $\mathbf{S}_0$*, containing all pairs* $(c_1, c_2) \in (C_1 \times C_2) \cup (C_2 \times C_1)$ *such that* $\text{label}(c_1) = \text{label}(c_2)$.
- *Construct* $\mathbf{S}_{n+1}$ *from* $\mathbf{S}_n$ *(for* $n \geq 0$*) by deleting all pairs* $(x_1, x_2) \in \mathbf{S}_n$ *that do not obey conditions (2) and (3) of subsumption: for instance, the pair* (x_1, x_2) *is deleted if there is a neighbor* $y_2 \text{-}r\text{-} x_2$*, but no pair* $(y_1, y_2) \in \mathbf{S}_n$ *such that* $y_1 \text{-}r\text{-} x_1$.
- *Stop with* $\mathbf{S} = \mathbf{S}_n$*, when* $\mathbf{S}_{n+1} = \mathbf{S}_n$ *(for* $n \geq 0$*).* ∎

Note that the algorithm always ends, because there are only a finite number of pairs to delete. It can be executed in time polynomial in the size of the graphs, because in the worst case it deletes all links of **S** one by one, whose number is at most the square of the number of nodes. Furthermore the algorithm is sound and complete.

Theorem 2 *For two knowledge graphs* K_1 *and* K_2 *with heads* h_1 *and* h_2 *respectively,* $K_1 \leq K_2$ *holds, if and only if the result* $\mathbf{S}$ *of Algorithm 1 contains the pair* (h_1, h_2).

Proof: The algorithm is sound because the result obeys the conditions of a subsumption relation. For completeness we suppose $K_1 \leq K_2$. There then exists a subsumption relation **S** that contains (h_1, h_2). By induction we prove that all $\mathbf{S}_n$ in the algorithm contain **S**. First $\mathbf{S}_0$ contains **S**, because the concepts related in the latter must have identical label. Next suppose $\mathbf{S}_n$ contains **S**, then $\mathbf{S}_{n+1}$ must also contain it, because all pairs in **S** obey the link-conditions and will not be deleted. By induction this concludes the proof. ∎

The reason why terminological languages usually do not have a tractable subsumption test is that they translate it to the consistency test. Taking a subsumption like $C \sqsubseteq D$ to be equivalent to consistency of $C \sqcap \neg D$, is a way to lose track of the structure. Determining whether a knowledge graph is consistent is a different question. Moreover testing for consistency is intractable in general.

5 Concluding remarks

Graphs have many advantages over other notations for knowledge representation. First of all they are easier to read, because the notation in terms of concepts and relations is intuitive and close to language. Secondly graphs are more flexible than frame-based languages, because the point of unification between two graphs need not be the head. Note that we could relax the condition formulated in the definition, that acyclic knowledge graphs have a single sink.

Another possibility for graphs is to incorporate roles with an arbitrary number of arguments [12]. Within knowledge graphs it is easy to introduce fundamental arcs labeled by numbers, and get a formalism like conceptual graphs (so instead of -EQU→ and -PAR→, we would have -2→ and -1→ respectively). The semantics of such graphs in terms of an extension function is straightforward, and underlying n-ary relations are n-tuples of individuals.

With an arbitrary number of arguments, there is a problem of determining what a circuit or directed cycle is, because no longer are there only two kinds of arcs i.e. those pointing in and those pointing out of a property. One can solve this by only looking at cycles that repeat the arc numbers (for instance -1-2-1-2- in the binary case); indeed, the repetition of arc numbers is a generalization of a "circuit". A definition of subsumption like the one in this paper can then be given for well-formed knowledge graphs, and there is a tractable algorithm as well.

Concluding, the main advantage of graphs is their transparent structure. It is easy and intuitive to define subsumption as a subgraph relation. In this paper we argued that the extensional semantics of many terminological description languages can not form a sufficient condition for subsumption, because it loses track of the structure. There is no reason to define subsumption in terms of the extensions, if it is a structural relation, intuitively. Moreover, by defining subsumption as a structural relation, a tractable subsumption algorithm is possible.

References

[1] H. Aït-Kaci. An algebraic semantics approach to the effective resolution of type equations. *Theor. Comp. Sc.*, 45:293–351, 1986.

[2] A.R. Anderson and N.D. Belnap. *Entailment: The Logic of Relevance and Necessity.* Princeton University Press, Princeton, 1975.

[3] R. R. Bakker. *Knowledge Graphs: representation and structuring of scientific knowledge.* PhD thesis, University of Twente, Enschede, 1987.

[4] J. Barwise and J. Perry. *Situations and Attitudes.* MIT Press, 1983.

[5] R. J. Brachman. On the epistemological status of semantic networks. In N. V. Findler, editor, *Associative Networks* Representation and Use of Knowledge by Computers, pages 3–50. Academic Press, Inc., 1979.

[6] R. J. Brachman and H. J. Levesque. The tractability of subsumption in frame-based description languages. In *Proceedings of AAAI-84*, pages 34–37. Austin, 1984.

[7] B. Hollunder, W. Nutt, and M. Schmidt-Schauß. Subsumption algorithms for concept description languages. In *Proceedings of 9th European Conference on Artificial Intelligence*, London, 1990. Pitman Publishing.

[8] M.K. Jackman. Inference and the conceptual graph knowledge representation language. In S. Moralee, editor, *Research and development in Expert Systems IV, Proceedings of Expert Systems '87*. Cambridge University Press, 1988.

[9] M. Kay. Parsing in functional unification grammar. In D. Dowty, L. Kartunnen, and A. Zwicky, editors, *Natural Language Parsing*. Cambridge University Press, 1985.

[10] H. J. Levesque and R. J. Brachman. A fundamental tradeoff in knowledge representation and reasoning. In R. J. Brachman and H. J. Levesque, editors, *Readings in Knowledge Representation*, pages 41–70. Morgan Kaufmann Publishers, Inc., 1985.

[11] M. Schmidt-Schauß. Subsumption in KL-ONE is undecidable. In R. Brachman, H. Levesque, and R. Reiter, editors, *Proceedings of First International Conference on Knowledge Representation and Reasoning*. Morgan Kaufmann Publishers, Inc., 1989.

[12] J.G. Schmolze. Terminological knowledge representation systems. In R. Brachman, H. Levesque, and R. Reiter, editors, *Proceedings of First International Conference on Knowledge Representation and Reasoning*. Morgan Kaufmann Publishers, Inc., 1989.

[13] J. F. Sowa. *Conceptual Structures: Information Processing in Mind and Machine*. Addison–Wesley, Reading, 1984.

A Terminological Knowledge Representation System with Complete Inference Algorithms

Franz Baader and Bernhard Hollunder
Deutsches Forschungszentrum für Künstliche Intelligenz (DFKI)
Projektgruppe WINO
Postfach 2080, D-6750 Kaiserslautern, Germany
E-mail: {baader, hollunde}@dfki.uni-kl.de

Abstract

The knowledge representation system KL-ONE first appeared in 1977. Since then many systems based on the idea of KL-ONE have been built. The formal model-theoretic semantics which has been introduced for KL-ONE languages [BL84] provides means for investigating soundness and completeness of inference algorithms. It turned out that almost all implemented KL-ONE systems such as BACK, KL-TWO, LOOM, NIKL, SB-ONE use sound but incomplete algorithms.

Until recently, sound *and* complete algorithms for the basic reasoning facilities in these systems such as consistency checking, subsumption checking (classification) and realization were only known for rather trivial languages. However, in the last two years concept languages (term subsumption languages) have been thoroughly investigated (see for example [SS88, Neb90, HNS90, DLNN91]). As a result of these investigations it is now possible to provide sound and complete algorithms for relatively large concept languages.

In this paper we describe $\mathcal{KRIS}$ which is an implemented prototype of a KL-ONE system where all reasoning facilities are realized by sound and complete algorithms. This system can be used to investigate the behaviour of sound and complete algorithms in practical applications. Hopefully, this may shed a new light on the usefulness of complete algorithms for practical applications, even if their worst case complexity is NP or worse.

$\mathcal{KRIS}$ provides a very expressive concept language, an assertional language, and sound and complete algorithms for reasoning. We have chosen the concept language such that it contains most of the constructs used in KL-ONE systems with the obvious restriction that the interesting inferences such as consistency checking, subsumption checking, and realization are decidable. The assertional language is similar to languages normally used in such systems. The reasoning component of $\mathcal{KRIS}$ depends on sound and complete algorithms for reasoning facilities such as consistency checking, subsumption checking, retrieval, and querying.

1 Introduction and Motivation

In the last decade many knowledge representation systems in the tradition of KL-ONE [BS85] have been built, for example BACK [NvL88, Neb90], CLASSIC [BBMR89], KANDOR [Pat84], KL-TWO [Vil85], KRYPTON [BPGL85], LOOM [MB87], NIKL [KBR86], SB-ONE [Kob89]. A common feature of these systems is the separation of the knowledge into a terminological part and an assertional part. Knowledge about classes of individuals and relationships between these classes is stored in the *TBox*, and knowledge concerning particular individuals can be described in the *ABox*.

The TBox formalism provides a *concept language* (or term subsumption language) for the definition of concepts and roles, where concepts are interpreted as sets of individuals and roles as binary relations between individuals. Starting with primitive concepts and roles the language formalism is used to build up more complex concepts and roles.

For example, assume that `person`, `female`, and `shy` are primitive concepts, and `child` and `female_relative` are primitive roles. Taking the connectives concept conjunction (and), disjunction (or), and negation (not) one can express "persons who are female or not shy" by

(and `person` (or `female` (not `shy`))).

Since concepts are interpreted as sets, concept conjunction can be interpreted as set intersection, concept disjunction as set union, and negation of concepts as set complement. In addition to these operations on sets one can also employ roles for the definition of new concepts. *Value restrictions* can be used for instance to describe "individuals for whom all children are female" by the expression (all `child` `female`). *Number restrictions* allow for instance to describe "individuals having at most three children" by the expression (atmost 3 `child`). Beside the above mentioned constructs there are other well-known concept-forming constructs which are available in $\mathcal{KRIS}$ (see Section 2). An example for a role-forming construct is the conjunction of roles. We can define the role (and `child` `female_relative`), which intuitively yields the role daughter. The concept language presented in the next section also provides functional roles, so-called *attributes*. These attributes are interpreted as partial functions and not as arbitrary binary relations. Natural examples for attributes may be `father` or `first_name`. An *agreement* between two attribute chains for example allows to describe "individuals whose father and grandfather have the same first name" by the expression

(equal (compose `father` `first_name`) (compose `father` `father` `first_name`)).

Interestingly, agreements between attribute chains do not make reasoning in the language undecidable [HN90], whereas agreements between arbitrary role chains cause undecidability [Sch89].

The basic reasoning facilities concerning the TBox are the determination whether a concept denotes nothing, i.e., whether a concept denotes the empty set in every interpretation, and the computation of the subsumption hierarchy. A concept C subsumes (is more general than) a concept D iff in every interpretation the set denoted by C is a superset of the set denoted by D.

The ABox formalism consists of an assertional language which allows the introduction of individuals to express facts about a concrete world. One can state that individuals are instances of concepts, and that pairs of individuals are instances of roles or attributes.

The reasoning facilities concerning both the TBox and the ABox are classified as follows. We need algorithms for inferences such as

- checking the consistency of the represented knowledge,
- given an individual of the ABox, compute the most specific concepts in the TBox this individual is instance of,
- computing all individuals of the ABox that are instances of a given concept.

The formal model-theoretic semantics which has been introduced for KL-ONE languages [BL84] provides means for investigating soundness and completeness of inference algorithms. It turned out that the above mentioned systems use sound but incomplete algorithms. If a sound but incomplete subsumption algorithm detects a subsumption relation, this relation really exists; but if it fails to recognize that a concept subsumes another one, then we do not know anything. A subsumption relation may or may not exist. Thus, the results of the algorithms only partially coincides with what the formal semantics expresses.[1]

Until recently, sound *and* complete algorithms for the above mentioned inferences and for the subsumption problem were only known for rather trivial languages which explains the use of incomplete algorithms in existing KL-ONE systems. Another argument in favour of incomplete algorithms was that for many languages the subsumption problem is at least NP-hard [LB87, Neb88]. Consequently, complete algorithms have to be intractable, whereas incomplete algorithms may still be polynomial. However, one should keep in mind that these complexity results are worst case results. It is not at all clear how complete algorithms may behave for typical knowledge bases.

In [SS88, HNS90, Hol90] it is shown how to devise sound and complete algorithms for the above mentioned inferences in various concept languages. Thus it has become possible to implement a KL-ONE system ($\mathcal{KRIS}$) which provides

- a very expressive concept language,
- powerful reasoning facilities, and
- sound and complete algorithms for these facilities.

The purpose of this paper is as follows. Firstly, we will enumerate the language constructs which are available in $\mathcal{KRIS}$, and will give a formal semantics for their meaning. We have chosen the concept language such that it contains most of the constructs used in KL-ONE systems with the obvious restriction that the interesting inferences such as consistency checking, subsumption checking, and realization are decidable. Of course, taking

[1] But see Patel-Schneider [Pat89] who uses a four-valued semantics to formally describe the behaviour of an algorithm which is incomplete w.r.t. two-valued semantics.

such a large language means that the complexity of the inference algorithms is relatively high. But $\mathcal{KRIS}$ also provides faster algorithms for certain sublanguages.[2] Secondly, we will describe the inference mechanisms provided by $\mathcal{KRIS}$. Then we will explain the principles underlying the reasoning algorithms implemented in $\mathcal{KRIS}$. Finally, we will give an overview of the implemented $\mathcal{KRIS}$ system.

2 Formalisms for Representing Knowledge

In this section we will introduce the formalisms for representing knowledge in $\mathcal{KRIS}$. In Subsection 2.1 the syntax and semantics of the concept language and the terminological axioms are presented. In Subsection 2.2 the assertional language and its semantics are introduced.

2.1 The Concept Language Underlying $\mathcal{KRIS}$

Assume that we have three disjoint alphabets of symbols, called *concept names*, *role names*, and *attribute names*. The special concept name *top* is called *top concept*.

The sets of *concept terms*, *role terms*, and *attribute terms* are inductively defined as follows. Every concept name is a concept term, every role name is a role term, and every attribute name is an attribute term. Now let C, $C_1, \ldots, C_k$ be concept terms, R, $R_1, \ldots, R_l$ be role terms, f, g, $f_1, \ldots, f_m$ be attribute terms already defined, and let n be a nonnegative integer. Then

(and $C_1 \ldots C_k$),	(conjunction)
(or $C_1 \ldots C_k$),	(disjunction)
(not C),	(negation)
(all R C), (all f C),	(value restriction)
(some R C), (some f C),	(exists restriction)
(atleast n R) (atmost n R)	(number restrictions)
(equal f g),	(agreement)
(not-equal f g)	(disagreement)

are concept terms,

(and $R_1 \ldots R_l$)	(role conjunction)

is a role term, and

[2] That coincides with what Ramesh Patil proposed at the Workshop on Term Subsumption Languages in Knowledge Representation: "He therefore strongly opposed any attempt to further restrict the expressiveness of TSL (term subsumption language) systems. Instead, he proposed that such systems be configured on a "pay as you go" basis—if the application uses only a small portion of the expressive power of the TSL, then everything will be fast; if more expressive power is used, then the system may slow down, but still be able to represent and reason with the knowledge given to it." (see [PSOK+90]).

(**and** $f_1 \dots f_m$),	(attribute conjunction)
(**compose** $f_1 \dots f_m$)	(composition)

are attribute terms.

So-called *terminological axioms* are used to introduce names for concept, role, and attribute terms. A finite set of such axioms satisfying certain restrictions is called a terminology (TBox). There are three different ways of introducing new concepts (respectively roles or attributes) into a terminology.

Let A (P, f) be a concept (role, attribute) name, and let C (R, g) be a concept (role, attribute) term. By the terminological axioms

(**defprimconcept** A), (**defprimrole** P), (**defprimattribute** f)

new concept, role, and attribute names are introduced without restricting their interpretation. The terminological axioms

(**defprimconcept** A C), (**defprimrole** P R), (**defprimattribute** f g)

impose necessary conditions on the interpretation of the introduced concept, role, and attribute names. Finally, one can impose necessary and sufficient conditions by the terminological axioms

(**defconcept** A C), (**defrole** P R), (**defattribute** f g).

A *terminology* (*TBox*) $\mathcal{T}$ is a finite set of terminological axioms with the additional restriction that (*i*) every concept, role, and attribute name may appear at most once as a first argument of a terminological axiom in $\mathcal{T}$ (unique definition), and (*ii*) $\mathcal{T}$ must not contain cyclic definitions[3] (acyclicity).

A terminology which describes knowledge about persons and relationships between persons is shown in Figure 1. At first, the attribute `sex` and the concept `male` is introduced. The axioms which define the concepts `female` and `person` can be read as follows: "no individual is both male and female"[4], and "a person has sex male or female." These axioms impose necessary conditions on the interpretation of the introduced concepts. The definition of the concept `parent` impose necessary and sufficient conditions: "an individual is a parent if and only if it is a person and has some child who is a person." The other concepts are also defined according to their intuitive meaning.

We will now give a formal model-theoretic semantics for the concept language and the terminological axioms. An *interpretation* $\mathcal{I}$ consists of a set $\Delta^{\mathcal{I}}$ (the *domain* of $\mathcal{I}$) and a function $\cdot^{\mathcal{I}}$ (the *interpretation function* of $\mathcal{I}$). The interpretation function maps every concept name A to a subset $A^{\mathcal{I}}$ of $\Delta^{\mathcal{I}}$, every role name P to a subset $P^{\mathcal{I}}$ of $\Delta^{\mathcal{I}} \times \Delta^{\mathcal{I}}$, and every attribute name f to a partial function $f^{\mathcal{I}}$ from $\Delta^{\mathcal{I}}$ to $\Delta^{\mathcal{I}}$. With $dom\, f^{\mathcal{I}}$ we

[3]For a discussion of terminological cycles see [Neb88, Baa90a].

[4]It might seem to be more convenient to allow explicit disjointness axioms for expressing such facts. In fact, we could easily provide such axioms at the user interface because they can be simulated by the constructs available in our language [Neb90, Baa90b].

```
(defprimattribute sex)
(defprimconcept male)
(defprimconcept female (not male))
(defprimconcept person (some sex (or male female)))
(defprimrole child)
(defconcept parent (and person (some child person)))
(defconcept mother (and parent (some sex female)))
(defconcept father (and parent (not mother)))
(defconcept grandparent (and parent (some child parent)))
(defconcept parent_with_two_children (and parent (atleast 2 child)))
(defconcept parent_with_sons_only (and parent (all child (some sex male))))
```

Figure 1: A terminology (TBox).

denote the domain of the partial function $f^{\mathcal{I}}$ (i.e., the set of elements of $\Delta^{\mathcal{I}}$ for which $f^{\mathcal{I}}$ is defined).

The interpretation function—which gives an interpretation for concept, role, and attribute names—can be extended to concept, role, and attribute terms as follows. Let C, $C_1, \ldots, C_k$ be concept terms, R, $R_1, \ldots, R_l$ role terms, f, g, $f_1, \ldots, f_m$ attribute terms, and let n be a nonnegative integer. Assume that $C^{\mathcal{I}}$, $C_1^{\mathcal{I}}, \ldots, C_k^{\mathcal{I}}$, $R^{\mathcal{I}}$, $R_1^{\mathcal{I}}, \ldots, R_l^{\mathcal{I}}$, $f^{\mathcal{I}}$, $g^{\mathcal{I}}$, $f_1^{\mathcal{I}}, \ldots, f_m^{\mathcal{I}}$ are already defined. Then

$$
\begin{array}{rcl}
(\textsf{*top*})^{\mathcal{I}} & := & \Delta^{\mathcal{I}} \\
(\textsf{and } C_1 \ldots C_k)^{\mathcal{I}} & := & C_1^{\mathcal{I}} \cap \ldots \cap C_k^{\mathcal{I}} \\
(\textsf{or } C_1 \ldots C_k)^{\mathcal{I}} & := & C_1^{\mathcal{I}} \cup \ldots \cup C_k^{\mathcal{I}} \\
(\textsf{not } C)^{\mathcal{I}} & := & \Delta^{\mathcal{I}} \setminus C^{\mathcal{I}} \\
(\textsf{all } R\ C)^{\mathcal{I}} & := & \{ a \in \Delta^{\mathcal{I}} \mid \forall b : (a,b) \in R^{\mathcal{I}} \Rightarrow b \in C^{\mathcal{I}} \} \\
(\textsf{all } f\ C)^{\mathcal{I}} & := & \{ a \in \Delta^{\mathcal{I}} \mid a \in dom\, f^{\mathcal{I}} \Rightarrow f^{\mathcal{I}}(a) \in C^{\mathcal{I}} \} \\
(\textsf{some } R\ C)^{\mathcal{I}} & := & \{ a \in \Delta^{\mathcal{I}} \mid \exists b : (a,b) \in R^{\mathcal{I}} \wedge b \in C^{\mathcal{I}} \} \\
(\textsf{some } f\ C)^{\mathcal{I}} & := & \{ a \in dom\, f^{\mathcal{I}} \mid f^{\mathcal{I}}(a) \in C^{\mathcal{I}} \} \\
(\textsf{atleast } n\ R)^{\mathcal{I}} & := & \{ a \in \Delta^{\mathcal{I}} \mid |\{ b \in \Delta^{\mathcal{I}} \mid (a,b) \in R^{\mathcal{I}} \}| \geq n \} \\
(\textsf{atmost } n\ R)^{\mathcal{I}} & := & \{ a \in \Delta^{\mathcal{I}} \mid |\{ b \in \Delta^{\mathcal{I}} \mid (a,b) \in R^{\mathcal{I}} \}| \leq n \} \\
(\textsf{equal } f\ g)^{\mathcal{I}} & := & \{ a \in dom\, f^{\mathcal{I}} \cap dom\, g^{\mathcal{I}} \mid f^{\mathcal{I}}(a) = g^{\mathcal{I}}(a) \} \\
(\textsf{not-equal } f\ g)^{\mathcal{I}} & := & \{ a \in dom\, f^{\mathcal{I}} \cap dom\, g^{\mathcal{I}} \mid f^{\mathcal{I}}(a) \neq g^{\mathcal{I}}(a) \} \\
(\textsf{and } R_1 \ldots R_l)^{\mathcal{I}} & := & R_1^{\mathcal{I}} \cap \ldots \cap R_l^{\mathcal{I}} \\
(\textsf{and } f_1 \ldots f_m)^{\mathcal{I}} & := & f_1^{\mathcal{I}} \cap \ldots \cap f_m^{\mathcal{I}} \\
(\textsf{compose } f_1 \ldots f_m)^{\mathcal{I}} & := & f_1^{\mathcal{I}} \circ \ldots \circ f_m^{\mathcal{I}},
\end{array}
$$

where $|X|$ denotes the cardinality of the set X and $\circ$ denotes the composition of functions. The composition should be read from left to right, i.e., $f_1^{\mathcal{I}} \circ \ldots \circ f_m^{\mathcal{I}}$ means that $f_1^{\mathcal{I}}$ is applied first, then $f_2^{\mathcal{I}}$, and so on. Note, that if $f_1^{\mathcal{I}}, \ldots, f_m^{\mathcal{I}}$ are partial functions, then $f_1^{\mathcal{I}} \cap \ldots \cap f_m^{\mathcal{I}}$ and $f_1^{\mathcal{I}} \circ \ldots \circ f_m^{\mathcal{I}}$ are also partial functions.

The semantics of terminological axioms is now defined as follows. An interpretation

$\mathcal{I}$ *satisfies* the terminological axiom

(defprimconcept A C)	iff	$A^{\mathcal{I}} \subseteq C^{\mathcal{I}}$,
(defconcept A C)	iff	$A^{\mathcal{I}} = C^{\mathcal{I}}$,
(defprimrole P R)	iff	$P^{\mathcal{I}} \subseteq R^{\mathcal{I}}$,
(defrole P R)	iff	$P^{\mathcal{I}} = R^{\mathcal{I}}$,
(defprimattribute f g)	iff	$f^{\mathcal{I}} \subseteq g^{\mathcal{I}}$,
(defattribute f g)	iff	$f^{\mathcal{I}} = g^{\mathcal{I}}$,

where A (P, f) is a concept (role, attribute) name, and C (R, g) is a concept (role, attribute) term. Note that the terminological axioms (**defprimconcept** A), (**defprimrole** P), and (**defprimattribute** f) are satisfied in every interpretation by the definition of interpretation. An interpretation $\mathcal{I}$ is a *model* for a TBox $\mathcal{T}$ iff $\mathcal{I}$ satisfies all terminological axioms in $\mathcal{T}$.

2.2 Assertions

The assertional formalism allows to introduce individuals (objects). We can describe a concrete world by stating that individuals are instances of concepts, and that pairs of individuals are instances of roles or attributes.

Assume that we have a further alphabet of symbols, called *individual names*. Names for individuals are introduced by *assertional axioms* which have the form

(**assert-ind** a C), (**assert-ind** a b R), (**assert-ind** a b g),

where a, b are individual names, and C (R, g) is a concept (role, attribute) term. A *world description* (*ABox*) is a finite set of assertional axioms.

Figure 2 shows an example of an ABox. This ABox describes a world in which `Tom` is

```
(assert-ind Tom father)
(assert-ind Tom Peter child)                (assert-ind Tom Harry child)
(assert-ind Mary parent_with_sons_only)
(assert-ind Mary Tom child)                 (assert-ind Mary Chris child)
```

Figure 2: A world description (ABox).

father of `Peter` and `Harry`. Furthermore, `Mary` has only sons; two of them are `Tom` and `Chris`.

Note that an ABox can be considered as a relational database where the arity of each tuple is either one or two. However, in contrast to the closed world semantics which is usually employed in databases, we assume an *open world semantics*, since we want to allow for incomplete knowledge. Thus, we cannot conclude in the above example that `Tom` has exactly two children, since there may exist a world in which `Tom` has some additional children.

The semantics of individual names and assertional axioms is defined as follows. The interpretation function $\cdot^{\mathcal{I}}$ of a TBox interpretation $\mathcal{I}$ can be extended to individual names by mapping them to elements of the domain such that $a^{\mathcal{I}} \neq b^{\mathcal{I}}$ if $a \neq b$. This restriction on the interpretation function ensures that individuals with different names denote different individuals in the world. It is called ***unique name assumption***, which is usually also assumed in the database world.

Let a, b be individual names, and C (R, g) be a concept (role, attribute) term. An interpretation $\mathcal{I}$ *satisfies* the assertional axiom

(assert-ind a C)	iff	$a^{\mathcal{I}} \in C^{\mathcal{I}}$
(assert-ind a b R)	iff	$(a^{\mathcal{I}}, b^{\mathcal{I}}) \in R^{\mathcal{I}}$
(assert-ind a b f)	iff	$f^{\mathcal{I}}(a^{\mathcal{I}}) = b^{\mathcal{I}}$.

The semantics of an ABox together with a TBox is defined as follows. We say that an interpretation $\mathcal{I}$ is a *model* for an ABox $\mathcal{A}$ w.r.t. a TBox $\mathcal{T}$ if $\mathcal{I}$ satisfies all assertional axioms in $\mathcal{A}$ and all terminological axioms in $\mathcal{T}$.

3 Reasoning

In this section we describe the inference mechanisms provided by $\mathcal{KRIS}$. The reasoning component of $\mathcal{KRIS}$ allows one to make knowledge explicit which is only implicitly represented in an ABox and a TBox. For example, from the TBox and ABox given in the previous section one can conclude that `Mary` is a grandparent, though this knowledge is not explicitly stored in the ABox.

An obvious requirement on the represented knowledge is that it should be consistent since everything would be deducible from inconsistent knowledge (from a logical point of view). If, for example, an ABox contains the axioms (assert-ind `Chris mother`) and (assert-ind `Chris father`), then the system should detect this inconsistency.[5] The underlying model-theoretic semantics allows a clear and intuitive definition of consistency. We say that an ABox $\mathcal{A}$ w.r.t. a TBox $\mathcal{T}$ is *consistent* if it has a model. Thus, we have the

Consistency problem of an ABox $\mathcal{A}$ w.r.t. a Tbox $\mathcal{T}$: Does there exist a model for $\mathcal{A}$ w.r.t. $\mathcal{T}$?

In order to devise an algorithm which decides consistency of an ABox w.r.t. a TBox, it is appropriate to reduce this problem to a consistency problem of an ABox w.r.t. the empty TBox, i.e., a TBox that does not contain any terminological axiom. The idea behind the reduction is to enlarge the ABox by the facts expressed in the TBox. More precisely, we apply the following *expansion procedure*.

1. *Elimination of partial definitions in $\mathcal{T}$:* Any partial definition (i.e., a terminological axiom with keyword **defprimconcept**, **defprimrole**, or **defprimattribute** followed by two arguments) occurring in $\mathcal{T}$ is replaced by a complete definition (i.e., a terminological axiom with keyword **defconcept**, **defrole**, or **defattribute**). For example, the partial concept definition

(defprimconcept `female` (not `male`))

[5]However, in general it is not always as easy as in this example to check whether the represented knowledge is consistent.

is replaced by

(defconcept **female** (and (not **male**) **female***))

where the newly introduced concept name **female*** stands for the absent part of the definition of **female**. In a similar way partial role and attribute definitions are replaced by complete definitions. Let $\mathcal{T}'$ be the TBox which is obtained from $\mathcal{T}$ by replacing all partial definitions by complete definitions.
2. *Expansion of* $\mathcal{T}'$*:* Every defined concept, role, and attribute name (i.e., the first argument of a complete definition) which occurs in the defining term of a concept, role, or attribute definition (i.e., in the second argument of a complete definition) is substituted by its defining term. This process is iterated until there remain only undefined concept, role, and attribute names in the second arguments of definitions. This yields a TBox $\mathcal{T}''$.
3. *Expansion of* $\mathcal{A}$*:* Every concept, role, and attribute name occurring in $\mathcal{A}$ which is defined in $\mathcal{T}''$ is substituted by its defining term in $\mathcal{T}''$.

This transformation has the nice property that it is consistency preserving. That means that an ABox $\mathcal{A}$ w.r.t. a TBox $\mathcal{T}$ is consistent if and only if the ABox which is obtained from $\mathcal{A}$ and $\mathcal{T}$ by applying the expansion procedure is consistent. Thus the above defined consistency problem can be reduced to the

Consistency problem of an ABox $\mathcal{A}$: Does there exist a model for $\mathcal{A}$?

Beside an algorithm for checking the consistency of an ABox $\mathcal{KRIS}$ provides algorithms for the basic reasoning facilities such as subsumption and instantiation. Let A, B be defined concepts in a TBox $\mathcal{T}$. We say that *A subsumes B in $\mathcal{T}$* iff for every model $\mathcal{I}$ of $\mathcal{T}$ we have $A^\mathcal{I} \supseteq B^\mathcal{I}$. Thus, given a TBox $\mathcal{T}$ and two defined concepts A, B we have the

Subsumption problem w.r.t. a TBox $\mathcal{T}$: Does A subsume B in $\mathcal{T}$?

The subsumption problem w.r.t. a TBox $\mathcal{T}$ can be reduced to the subsumption problem of concept terms. For two concept terms C, D we say that *C subsumes D* if and only if $C^\mathcal{I} \supseteq D^\mathcal{I}$ in every interpretation $\mathcal{I}$. Let $\mathcal{T}''$ be the TBox which is obtained from $\mathcal{T}$ by applying the first two steps of the expansion procedure. Assume that C and D are the definitions of the defined concepts A and B in $\mathcal{T}''$. Then A subsumes B in $\mathcal{T}$ if and only if the concept term C subsumes the concept term D. Thus the subsumption problem w.r.t. a TBox $\mathcal{T}$ can be reduced to the

Subsumption problem: Does a concept term C subsume a concept term D ?

The subsumption problem in concept languages has been thoroughly investigated in [SS88, HNS90, DLNN91]. In these papers, subsumption algorithms for various concept languages and sublanguages are given and their computational complexity is discussed. In fact, the papers do not directly describe subsumption algorithms but algorithms for a closely related problem—the so-called *satisfiability problem* of concepts. These algorithms check whether a given concept term C is satisfiable, i.e., whether there exists an interpretation $\mathcal{I}$ such that $C^\mathcal{I} \neq \emptyset$. Since C subsumes D if and only if (and D (not C)) is not satisfiable, satisfiability algorithms can also be used to decide subsumption.

An algorithm for instantiation decides whether an assertional axiom is deducible from the represented knowledge. More formally, let α be an assertional axiom. We say that an ABox $\mathcal{A}$ w.r.t. a TBox $\mathcal{T}$ *implies* α iff all models of $\mathcal{A}$ w.r.t. $\mathcal{T}$ satisfy α, written $\mathcal{A}, \mathcal{T} \models \alpha$. Thus we define the

Instantiation problem: Is α implied by $\mathcal{A}$ and $\mathcal{T}$?

If α is of the form (**assert-ind** a b R) or (**assert-ind** a b f), then it is relatively easy to solve the instantiation problem since the concept language contains only few constructs for building complex role or attribute terms. If α is of the form (**assert-ind** a C), the instantiation problem can be reduced to the consistency problem as follows:

$\mathcal{A}, \mathcal{T} \models$ (**assert-ind** a C) iff $\mathcal{A} \cup \{$(**assert-ind** a (**not** C))$\}$ is not consistent w.r.t. $\mathcal{T}$.

In [Hol90], a sound and complete algorithm for the consistency and instantiation problem for a sublanguage of the language defined in Section 2 is described.

$\mathcal{KRIS}$ also provides the user with algorithms which find out certain relationships between the defined concepts, roles, attributes, and individuals. These algorithms are based on the algorithms for subsumption and instantiation. Assume that $\mathcal{T}$ is a TBox and $\mathcal{A}$ is an ABox.

The *subsumption hierarchy* is the preordering of the concept names in $\mathcal{T}$ w.r.t. the subsumption relation. The so-called *classifier* has to solve the

Classification problem: Compute the subsumption hierarchy.

Given an individual in $\mathcal{A}$, one wants to know the set of concept names in $\mathcal{T}$ which describe it most accurately. To be more formal, let a be an individual occurring in $\mathcal{A}$. The set of *most specialized concepts* for a is a set $\{A_1, \ldots, A_n\}$ of concept names occurring in $\mathcal{T}$ such that

1. $\mathcal{A}, \mathcal{T} \models$ (**assert-ind** a A_i) for every i, $1 \leq i \leq n$,
2. for every i, $1 \leq i \leq n$, there does not exist a concept name A in $\mathcal{T}$ such that $\mathcal{A}, \mathcal{T} \models$ (**assert-ind** a A), A_i subsumes A, and A and A_i are different names, and
3. for every concept name A in $\mathcal{T}$ such that $\mathcal{A}, \mathcal{T} \models$ (**assert-ind** a A), there exists an A_i such that A subsumes A_i.

The first condition means that each A_i is in fact a description of a. The second condition guarantees that the set contains only the minimal descriptions w.r.t. the subsumption relation, and the third condition means that we do not omit any nonredundant description. Thus, to describe an individual most accurately we need an algorithm for the

Realization problem: Compute for an individual in $\mathcal{A}$ the set of most specialized concepts in $\mathcal{T}$.

Conversely, one may want to know the individuals of $\mathcal{A}$ which are instances of a given concept term. Let C be a concept term. The set *INST*(C) contains all the individuals $a_1, \ldots, a_n$ of $\mathcal{A}$ such that $\mathcal{A}, \mathcal{T} \models$ (**assert-ind** a_i C) holds. Thus we also have the

Retrieval problem: Compute for a given concept term C the set *INST*(C).

4 The Basic Reasoning Algorithms

In this section we will explain the principles underlying the reasoning algorithms implemented in $\mathcal{KRIS}$. To this purpose, we restrict our attention to the concept language $\mathcal{ALC}$ of Schmidt-Schauß and Smolka [SS88] which allows one to use concept names, role names, and the concept forming constructs conjunction, disjunction, negation, value restriction and exists restriction. The language $\mathcal{ALC}$ is only a sublanguage of the actual concept language available in our system, but it is large enough to demonstrate the principle problems one has to overcome when devising sound and complete algorithms for terminological KR-systems. Algorithms for various other concept languages can e.g. be found in [DLNN91, HB91, HNS90].

In the previous section we have shown that it is enough to have algorithms which test for satisfiability of concept terms and for consistency of ABoxes since all the other introduced reasoning problems can be reduced to these two problems. We will first illustrate by an example how satisfiability can be checked for concept terms of $\mathcal{ALC}$. We will then describe an algorithm which is more appropriate for an implementation than the original one given in [SS88]. Finally, it will be explained how the ideas underlying the satisfiability algorithm can be generalized to consistency checking for ABoxes.

4.1 An Example for the Satisfiability Test for $\mathcal{ALC}$

Assume that C is a concept term of $\mathcal{ALC}$ which has to be checked for satisfiability. In a first step we can push all negations as far as possible into the term using the fact that the terms (not (not D)) and D, (not (and D E) and (or (not D) (not E)), (not (or D E) and (and (not D) (not E)), (not (all R D)) and (some R (not D)), as well as (not (some R D)) and (all R (not D)) are equivalent, that is, they denote the same set in every interpretation. We end up with a term C' in negation normal form where negation is only applied to concept names.

Example 4.1 Let A, B be concept names, and let R be a role name. Assume that we want to know whether (and (some R A) (some R B)) is subsumed by (some R (and A B)). That means that we have to check whether the term

$$C := (\text{and } (\text{some } R\ A)\ (\text{some } R\ B)\ (\text{not } (\text{some } R\ (\text{and } A\ B))))$$

is not satisfiable. The negation normal form of C is the term

$$C' := (\text{and } (\text{some } R\ A)\ (\text{some } R\ B)\ (\text{all } R\ (\text{or } (\text{not } A)\ (\text{not } B)))).$$

In a second step we try to construct a finite interpretation $\mathcal{I}$ such that $C'^{\mathcal{I}} \neq \emptyset$. That means that there has to exist an individual in $\Delta^{\mathcal{I}}$ which is an element of $C'^{\mathcal{I}}$. Thus the algorithm generates such an individual b, and imposes the constraint $b \in C'^{\mathcal{I}}$ on it. In the example, this means that b has to satisfy the following constraints: $b \in (\text{some } R\ A)^{\mathcal{I}}$, $b \in (\text{some } R\ B)^{\mathcal{I}}$, and $b \in (\text{all } R\ (\text{or } (\text{not } A)\ (\text{not } B)))^{\mathcal{I}}$.

From $b \in (\text{some } R\ A)^{\mathcal{I}}$ we can deduce that there has to exist an individual c such that $(b, c) \in R^{\mathcal{I}}$ and $c \in A^{\mathcal{I}}$. Analogously, $b \in (\text{some } R\ B)^{\mathcal{I}}$ implies the existence of an individual d with $(b,d) \in R^{\mathcal{I}}$ and $d \in B^{\mathcal{I}}$. We should not assume that $c = d$ since this would possibly impose too many constraints on the individuals newly introduced to satisfy the exists restrictions on b. Thus the algorithm introduces for any exists restriction a new individual as role-successor, and this individual has to satisfy the constraints expressed by the restriction.

Since b also has to satisfy the value restriction (all R (or (not A) (not B))), and c, d were introduced as $R^{\mathcal{I}}$-successors of b, we also get the constraints $c \in$ (or (not A) (not B))$^{\mathcal{I}}$, and $d \in$ (or (not A) (not B))$^{\mathcal{I}}$. Now c has to satisfy the constraints $c \in A^{\mathcal{I}}$ and $c \in$ (or (not A) (not B))$^{\mathcal{I}}$, whereas d has to satisfy the constraints $d \in B^{\mathcal{I}}$ and $d \in$ (or (not A) (not B))$^{\mathcal{I}}$. Thus the algorithm uses value restrictions in interaction with already defined role relationships to impose new constraints on individuals.

Now $c \in$ (or (not A) (not B))$^{\mathcal{I}}$ means that $c \in$ (not A)$^{\mathcal{I}}$ or $c \in$ (not B)$^{\mathcal{I}}$, and we have to choose one of these possibilities. If we assume $c \in$ (not A)$^{\mathcal{I}}$, this clashes with the other constraint $c \in A^{\mathcal{I}}$. Thus we have to choose $c \in$ (not B)$^{\mathcal{I}}$. Analogously, we have to choose $d \in$ (not A)$^{\mathcal{I}}$ in order to satisfy the constraint $d \in$ (or (not A) (not B))$^{\mathcal{I}}$ without creating a contradiction to $d \in B^{\mathcal{I}}$. Thus, for disjunctive constraints, the algorithm tries both possibilities in successive attempts. It has to backtrack if it reaches a contradiction, i.e., if the same individual has to satisfy conflicting constraints.

In the example, we have now satisfied all the constraints without getting a contradiction. This shows that C' is satisfiable, and thus (and (some R A) (some R B)) is not subsumed by (some R (and A B)). We have generated an interpretation $\mathcal{I}$ as witness for this fact: $\Delta^{\mathcal{I}} = \{b,c,d\}$; $R^{\mathcal{I}} := \{(b,c),(b,d)\}$; $A^{\mathcal{I}} := \{c\}$ and $B^{\mathcal{I}} := \{d\}$. For this interpretation, $b \in C'^{\mathcal{I}}$. That means that $b \in$ (and (some R A) (some R B))$^{\mathcal{I}}$, but $b \notin$ (some R (and A B))$^{\mathcal{I}}$.

Termination of the algorithm is ensured by the fact that the newly introduced constraints are always smaller than the constraints which enforced their introduction.

4.2 A Rule-Based and a Functional Algorithm for Satisfiability

In this subsection, we will first give a more formal description of the algorithm sketched in the previous section. We will then show how this rule-based algorithm can be modified to a functional algorithm which is more appropriate for implementation purposes.

Let C_0 be a concept term of $\mathcal{ALC}$. Without loss of generality we assume that C_0 is in negation normal form. In principle, the algorithm starts with the set $S_0 := \{b_0 \in C_0^{\mathcal{I}}\}$ of constraints, and transforms it with the help of certain rules until one of the following two situations occurs: *(i)* the obtained set of constraints is "obviously contradictory", or *(ii)* the obtained set of constraints is "complete", i.e., one can apply no more rules. In the second case, the complete set of constraints describes an interpretation $\mathcal{I}$ with $C_0^{\mathcal{I}} \neq \emptyset$. For the language $\mathcal{ALC}$, a set of constraints is obviously contradictory iff it contains conflicting constraints of the form $c \in A^{\mathcal{I}}$, $c \in$ (not A)$^{\mathcal{I}}$ for some individual c and concept name A. Please note that such contradictions can only occur between two constraints imposed on the same individual c.

Because of the presence of disjunction in our language, a given set of constraints must sometimes be transformed into two different new sets. For that reason, we will work with sets $\mathcal{M}$ of sets of constraints rather than with a single set of constraints. If we want to test C_0 for satisfiability, we start with the singleton set $\mathcal{M}_0 := \{\{b_0 \in C_0^{\mathcal{I}}\}\}$.

Let $\mathcal{M}$ be a finite set of sets of constraints, and let S be an element of $\mathcal{M}$. The following rules will replace S by a set S' or by two sets S' and S'':

1. *The conjunction rule.* Assume that $c \in (\textsf{and}\ C_1\ C_2)^{\mathcal{I}}$ is in S, and $c \in C_1^{\mathcal{I}}$ or $c \in C_2^{\mathcal{I}}$ is not in S. The set of constaints S' is obtained from S by adding $c \in C_1^{\mathcal{I}}$ and $c \in C_2^{\mathcal{I}}$ to S.

2. *The disjunction rule.* Assume that $c \in (\textsf{or}\ C_1\ C_2)^{\mathcal{I}}$ is in S, and neither $c \in C_1^{\mathcal{I}}$ nor $c \in C_2^{\mathcal{I}}$ is in S. The set of constraints S' is obtained from S by adding $c \in C_1^{\mathcal{I}}$ to S, and the set of constraints S'' is obtained from S by adding $c \in C_2^{\mathcal{I}}$ to S.

3. *The exists restriction rule.* Assume that $c \in (\textsf{some}\ R\ D)^{\mathcal{I}}$ is in S, and there is no individual e such that $(c, e) \in R^{\mathcal{I}}, e \in D^{\mathcal{I}}$ are in S. Then we create a new individual d, and add the constraints $(c, d) \in R^{\mathcal{I}}, d \in D^{\mathcal{I}}$ to S.

4. *The value restriction rule.* Assume that $c \in (\textsf{all}\ R\ D)^{\mathcal{I}}$ and $(c, d) \in R^{\mathcal{I}}$ are in S, and that $d \in D^{\mathcal{I}}$ is not in S. Then the set of constraints S' is obtained from S by adding $d \in D^{\mathcal{I}}$.

It can be shown that there cannot be an infinite chain of sets $\mathcal{M}_0, \mathcal{M}_1, \mathcal{M}_2, \ldots$ where each $\mathcal{M}_{i+1}$ is obtained from $\mathcal{M}_i$ by application of one of the above defined rules. Thus if we start with a set $\mathcal{M}_0 = \{\{b_0 \in C_0^{\mathcal{I}}\}\}$, and apply rules as long as possible, we finally end up with a complete set M_r, i.e., a set to which no more rules are applicable. Now C_0 is satisfiable iff there exists a set of constraints in $\mathcal{M}_r$ which is not obviously contradictory.

Please note that this fact is independent of the order in which the rules have been applied. By using appropriate strategies, one may get optimized versions of the algorithm. We shall now sketch how an algorithm can be derived which no longer depends on an explicit representation of individuals and role relationships between individuals. Until now, such an explicit representation is necessary for the following two reasons. First, we need the individual names to detect which constraints are obviously contradictory. Second, the explicit representation of role relationships is necessary to show for what other individuals d a constraint of the form $c \in (\textsf{all}\ R\ D)^{\mathcal{I}}$ yields a new constraint $d \in D^{\mathcal{I}}$.

In order to explain the ideas underlying our optimized algorithm, we first analyse from which sources constraints for a given individual c may come. On the one hand, application of a conjunction or disjunction rule to a constraint on c itself may yield a new constraint on c. On the other hand, a constraint on c may come from an other individual b when the exists or value restriction rule is applied to b. Please note that in this case c is a role successor of b for some role R, and that there can be at most one such individual b for a given c. There is one exception to this second case. The individual b_0 we start with does not have a role predecessor, but it has the original constraint $b_0 \in C_0^{\mathcal{I}}$.

Assume that we start with the original constraint $b_0 \in C_0^{\mathcal{I}}$. By applying the conjunction and disjunction rule to the constraints on b_0 as long as possible, we obtain all possible

```
sat(C) =
    if A ∈ C and (not A) ∈ C for some concept name A
      then false
    else if (and C1 C2) ∈ C
      then sat(C \ {(and C1 C2)} ∪ {C1, C2})
    else if (or C1 C2) ∈ C
      then sat((C \ {(or C1 C2)}) ∪ {C1}) or sat((C \ {(or C1 C2)}) ∪ {C2})
    else if for all (some R C) ∈ C
              sat({C} ∪ {D | (all R D) ∈ C})
         then true
         else false
```

Figure 3: A functional algorithm deciding satisfiability of $\mathcal{ALC}$-concepts. A concept term C in negation normal form is satisfiable if and only if the call *sat*($\{C\}$) returns *true*.

constraints on b_0. This means that we can now detect all possible obvious contradictions caused by constraints on b_0. Since all exists restrictions for b_0 are already present, we know how many new individuals we have to introduce as role successors of b_0, and since all the value restrictions on b_0 are already present, we also know exactly which constraints are propagated from b_0 to these successors. Obviously, if we have the exists restriction $b_0 \in (\textsf{some}\ R\ D)^{\mathcal{I}}$, and $b_0 \in (\textsf{all}\ R\ E_1)^{\mathcal{I}}, \ldots, b_0 \in (\textsf{all}\ R\ E_k)^{\mathcal{I}}$ are all the value restrictions imposed on b_0 w.r.t. the role R, then the individual c which is created because of this exists restriction has to satisfy the constraints $c \in D^{\mathcal{I}}, c \in E_1^{\mathcal{I}}, \ldots, c \in E_k^{\mathcal{I}}$.

After imposing these constraints on c, all the constraints coming from its unique role predecessor b_0 are already present in the actual constraint system. In this case, one can forget the role relationship between b_0 and c because it no longer yields new constraints on c. Since there is no more interaction between constraints on c and constraints on other individuals, one can test the satisfiability of the constraints on c independently from all the other constraints in our system. This means that we may now continue with c in place of b_0, i.e., first apply conjunction and disjunction rules to the constraints on c as long as possible, etc.

This has to be done independently for all the exists restrictions on b_0. Since we now consider only one individual at a time we need no longer explicitly introduce names for the individuals, and we have already pointed out that one can forget about the role relationships. It is now enough to memorize the concept constraints currently imposed on the actual individual by the corresponding set of concept terms. Obviously, if the conjunction rule (resp. disjunction rule) has been applied for a concept term (and C_1 C_2) (resp. (or C_1 C_2)) of this set, thus adding the terms C_1 and C_2 (resp. C_1 or C_2) to the current set, we can remove the original term from the set.

A functional algorithm which is based on these ideas is presented in Figure 3. Please note that the algorithm, which is described in a Lisp-like notation, can very easily be implemented.

4.3 An Algorithm for Checking the Consistency of an ABox

In this subsection, an algorithm for solving the consistency problem of an ABox will be sketched with the help of an example. As for the satisfiability algorithm, the idea behind this consistency algorithm is that it tries to construct a model for a given ABox. One can view the consistency problem of an ABox as a generalization of the satisfiability problem of concept terms. In fact, suppose that the ABox $\mathcal{A}$ contains the axioms (assert-ind a C_1), ..., (assert-ind a C_n). If $\mathcal{A}$ is consistent, then the concept term (and $C_1 \ldots C_n$) is obviously satisfiable. Thus, a simple-minded idea for a consistency checking algorithm could be: Check for every individual a occurring in the ABox whether the conjunction of all concept terms C_i with (assert-ind a C_i) $\in \mathcal{A}$ is satisfiable. The following example, however, shows that this naive algorithm may fail to detect that an ABox is inconsistent.

Suppose the ABox

$$\mathcal{A} = \{(\text{assert-ind } \texttt{Tim Tom child}), (\text{assert-ind } \texttt{Tom Human})\}$$

is given, and we are interested in whether the fact (assert-ind `Tim` (some `child Human`)) is implied by $\mathcal{A}$. As mentioned in the previous section this instantiation problem can be reduced to the test whether

$$\mathcal{A}' = \mathcal{A} \cup \{(\text{assert-ind } \texttt{Tim} (\text{all } \texttt{child} (\text{not } \texttt{Human})))\}$$

is inconsistent.[6] The naive consistency algorithm from above checks whether the concept terms `Human` (coming from the individual `Tom`) and (all `child` (not `Human`)) (coming from `Tim`) are satisfiable. Since both concept terms are satisfiable it concludes that $\mathcal{A}'$ is consistent. However, it is easy to see that $\mathcal{A}'$ is inconsistent.

The reason why this simple algorithm does not detect the inconsistency is that it ignores role relationships occurring in the ABox. The interaction of role relationships with value restrictions may enforce that individuals of the ABox are instances of additional concepts. Thus, to overcome this problem, we modify our simple algorithm as follows. In a *preprocessing step* we enlarge a given ABox by axioms implied by the interaction of role relationships with value restrictions. If an ABox contains the axioms (assert-ind a b R) and (assert-ind a (all R C)), then the axiom (assert-ind b C) has to be added. This is one of the rules applied in the preprocessing step. However, this rule alone is not sufficient. If (assert-ind a b R) and (assert-ind a (and ... (all R C)...)) are in an ABox, we also have to enlarge the ABox by the axioms (assert-ind b C). Thus we also have to decompose conjunctive and, for similar reasons, disjunctive concept terms occurring in the ABox. This yields the two other rules for the preprocessing step. The preprocessing is finished if applications of the three rules do not add new axioms to the current ABox. As a consequence, role relationships in the ABox thus obtained can be ignored because they no longer carry any additional information. Now, in a second step we can use the simple consistency algorithm mentioned before. This yields a correct and complete algorithm for deciding consistency of an ABox of $\mathcal{ALC}$.

[6] Note that (all `child` (not `Human`)) is the negation normal form of (not (some `child Human`)).

As an example, let us apply this consistency algorithm to the ABox $\mathcal{A}'$ from above. The preprocessing step returns the ABox

$$\mathcal{A}'' = \mathcal{A}' \cup \{(\texttt{assert-ind Tom (not Human)})\}.$$

In the second step we collect for each individual occurring in $\mathcal{A}''$ its concept constraints, and apply a satisfiability algorithm to their conjunction. Thus, to check whether $\mathcal{A}''$ (and hence $\mathcal{A}'$) is consistent we check whether the concept terms (and Human (not Human)) (coming from the individual Tom) and (all child (not Human)) (coming from Tim) are satisfiable. Since the first concept term is obviously not satisfiable, we now correctly conclude that $\mathcal{A}'$ is inconsistent.

5 $\mathcal{KRIS}$: the Overall Structure

In this section we give a short description of $\mathcal{KRIS}$. The representation component offers the formalisms presented in Section 2: a very expressive concept language and an assertional language which is similar to the languages used in most KL-ONE systems. The reasoning component of $\mathcal{KRIS}$ provides sound and complete algorithms which solve the problems mentioned in the previous section.

$\mathcal{KRIS}$ is implemented in Common Lisp on a Symbolics Lisp machine. The main menu of $\mathcal{KRIS}$ is shown in Figure 4.

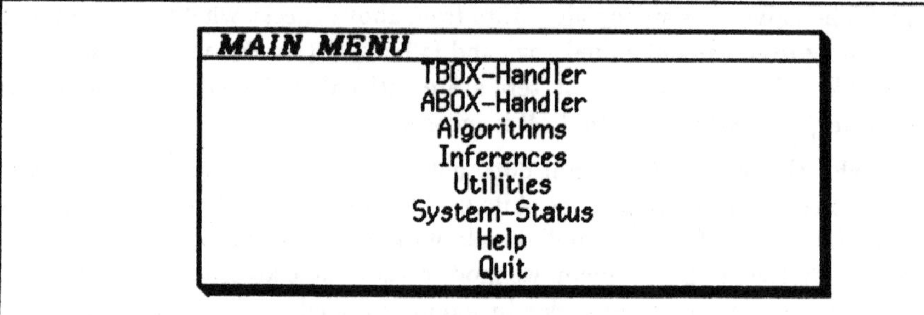

Figure 4: $\mathcal{KRIS}$ main menu.

Clicking one of the menu items causes $\mathcal{KRIS}$ to generate submenus. They allow the following operations.

- The *TBox-Handler* organizes the treatment of terminologies. That means, it can be used to create, load, edit, and delete TBoxes.
- Similarly, the *ABox-Handler* manages ABoxes.
- The item *Algorithms* allows to choose an appropriate algorithm. We have implemented several algorithms for the inferences which are based on different datastructures. Furthermore, for some sublanguages of the concept language presented in Section 2 we have implemented optimized algorithms.

- We can start a chosen algorithm using *Inferences*. $\mathcal{KRIS}$ provides algorithms which solve the consistency problem, the subsumption problem, the instantiation problem, the classification problem, the realization problem, and the retrieval problem.
- *Utilities* provides possibilities to measure the run-time of algorithms.
- *Help* and *System-Status* give more informations about the system.

$\mathcal{KRIS}$ can be used as follows. First of all, the user has to edit the terminological and assertional knowledge of the domain of interest using *TBox-Handler* and *ABox-Handler*. Assume that the TBox of Figure 1 and the ABox of Figure 2 have been edited, and hence are known to $\mathcal{KRIS}$. The consistency algorithm will find out that the represented knowledge is consistent. That means, there exists a model for the ABox w.r.t. the TBox. The classification algorithm computes the subsumption hierarchy as shown in Figure 5.

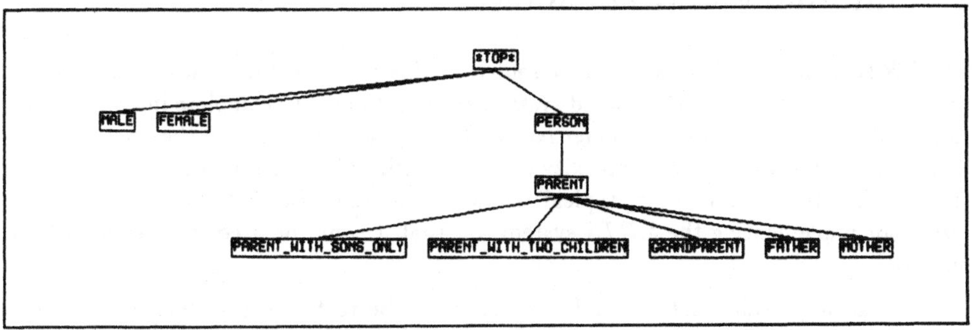

Figure 5: The subsumption hierarchy of the TBox given in Figure 1.

One can use the instantiation algorithm to get the most accurate information about an individual. For example, the algorithm will detect the following relationships:

individual	most specialized concepts
Tom	father, parent_with_two_children
Mary	parent_with_two_children, grandparent, parent_with_sons_only

The retrieval algorithm computes for a given concept term the individuals of the ABox which are instances of it:

concept term	individuals
grandparent	Mary
parent_with_two_children	Mary, Tom
(some sex male)	Tom, Chris

That means, for instance, (*i*) the fact that Tom and Chris have sex male is implied by the represented knowledge, and (*ii*) for the other individuals in $\mathcal{A}$ this property cannot be concluded.

The user may cause $\mathcal{KRIS}$ to compute for a given TBox and ABox (*i*) the subsumption hierarchy, (*ii*) for every individual in the ABox the most specialized concepts, and (*iii*) for every concept name in the TBox the individuals which are instances of it. After $\mathcal{KRIS}$ has once determined these structures, it is able to access this information efficiently.[7] Note that only a small amount of memory is needed to store this information. Consequently, the subsumption problem and the retrieval problem for concepts defined in the TBox, and the instantiation problem can afterwards be solved very fast by looking into the precomputed structures.

At any time the user may add terminological and assertional axioms to an already existing TBox and ABox. Assume that $\mathcal{KRIS}$ has computed the structures mentioned before. In this case $\mathcal{KRIS}$ gives the user the possibility to update these structures. If a terminological axiom is added, then, for instance, the subsumption hierarchy is enlarged by the inserting concept name defined by the axiom at the appropriate place.

6 Summary and Outlook

The $\mathcal{KRIS}$ system which has been presented in this paper distinguishes itself from all the other implemented KL-ONE based systems in that it employs complete inference algorithms. Nevertheless its concept language is relatively large. Of course, the price one has to pay is that the worst case complexity of the algorithms is worse than NP. But it is not clear whether the behaviour for "typical" knowledge bases is also that bad. An important reason for implementing the $\mathcal{KRIS}$ system was that it could be used to investigate this question.

Thus an important part of our future work will be to test the system with typical applications. In addition, we intent to further extend the system. On the one hand, we want to integrate the possibility to refer to concrete domains (such as integers, real numbers, strings, etc.) in the definition of concepts [BH90]. On the other hand, we will allow further concept forming operators such as qualifying number restrictions [HB91] and role forming operators such as transitive closure of roles [Baa90c] (at least for a sublanguage of the presented concept language); for additional constructs see [BBHH+90].

Another point is that until now the user has to specify which algorithm should be used. In an improved $\mathcal{KRIS}$ version, this system will itself choose the optimal algorithm by inspecting what combination of language constructs are used.

The main objective of our research group WINO—as a part of the larger project AKA (Autonomous Cooperating Agents)—is the investigation of logical foundations of knowledge representation formalisms which can be used for applications in cooperating agent scenarios [BM91]. Thus our long term goals also comprise further extensions of $\mathcal{KRIS}$ such as

- a constrained-based approach for integrating full first order predicate logics with concept languages [BBHNS90, Bür90] which can be used to represent non-taxonomical knowledge,

[7]The idea that some of the important inferences can be computed in advance was already used in the original KL-ONE system. Cf. [BS85] p. 178: "In KL-ONE the network (i.e. the subsumption hierarchy) is computed first from the forms of descriptions, and subsumption questions are always read off from the hierarchy."

- modal-logical approaches for the integration of knowledge concerning time and space.

Acknowledgements. We are grateful to our colleague Werner Nutt for his remarks concerning the implementation. We would like to thank Erich Achilles, Armin Laux, Jörg Peter Mohren, and Gebhard Przyrembel for their implementational work. This research was supported by the German Bundesministerium für Forschung und Technologie under grant ITW 8903 0.

References

[Baa90a] F. Baader. "Terminological Cycles in KL-ONE-based Knowledge Representation Languages." In *Proceedings of the 8th National Conference of the AAAI*, pp. 621-626, Boston, Mas., 1990.

[Baa90b] F. Baader. "A Formal Definition for the Expressive Power of Knowledge Representation Languages." In *Proceedings of the 9th European Conference on Artificial Intelligence*, pp. 53–58, Stockholm, Sweden, 1990.

[Baa90c] F. Baader. "Augmenting Concept Languages by Transitive Closure of Roles: An Alternative to Terminological Cycles." To appear in *Proceedings of IJCAI '91.*

[BBHH+90] F. Baader, H.-J. Bürckert, J. Heinsohn, B. Hollunder, J. Müller, B. Nebel, W. Nutt, H.-J. Profitlich. *Terminological Knowledge Representation: A Proposal for a Terminological Logic.* DFKI Technical Memo TM-90-04, DFKI, Postfach 2080, D-6750 Kaiserslautern, Germany.

[BBHNS90] F. Baader, H.-J. Bürckert, B. Hollunder, W. Nutt, J. H. Siekmann. "Concept Logics" In *Proceedings of the Symposium on Computational Logics*, Brüssel, November 1990.

[BH90] F. Baader, P. Hanschke. "A Schema for Integrating Concrete Domains into Concept Languages." To appear in *Proceedings of IJCAI '91.*

[BBMR89] A. Borgida, R. J. Brachman, D. L. McGuinness, L. A. Resnick. "CLASSIC: A Structural Data Model for Objects." In *Proceedings of the International Conference on Management of Data*, Portland, Oregon, 1989.

[BPGL85] R. J. Brachman, V. Pigman Gilbert, H. J. Levesque. "An essential hybrid reasoning system: knowledge and symbol level accounts in KRYPTON." In *Proceedings of the 9th IJCAI*, pp. 532–539, Los Angeles, Cal., 1985.

[BL84] R. J. Brachmann, H. J. Levesque. "The tractability of subsumption in frame based description languages." In *Proceedings of the 4th National Conference of the AAAI*, pp. 34–37, Austin, Tex., 1984.

[BS85] R. J. Brachman, J. G. Schmolze. "An Overview of the KL-ONE knowledge representation system." *Cognitive Science*, 9(2):171-216, April 1985.

[Bür90] H.-J. Bürckert. "A Resolution Principle for Clauses with Constraints" In *Proceedings of the 10th International Conference on Automated Deduction*, Lecture Notes in Artificial Intelligence, LNAI 449, Springer Verlag, pp. 178-192, 1990.

[BM91] H.-J. Bürckert, J. Müller. "RATMAN: A Rational Agent Testbed for Multi Agent Networks", In *Proceedings of Modeling Autonomous Agents in Multi-Agent Worlds*, Elsevier Publishers, 1991.

[DLNN91] F. Donini, M. Lenzerini, D. Nardi, W. Nutt. "The Complexity of Concept Languages." In J. A. Allan, R. Fikes, E. Sandewall (editors), *Proceedings of the Second International Conference on Principles of Knowledge Representation and Reasoning*, Cambridge, Mas., 1991.

[Hol90] B. Hollunder. "Hybrid Inferences in KL-ONE-based Knowledge Representation Systems." In *Proceedings of the 14th German Workshop on Artificial Intelligence*, pp. 38–47, Eringerfeld, Germany, 1990.

[HB91] B. Hollunder, F. Baader. "Qualifying Number Restrictions in Concept Languages." In J. A. Allan, R. Fikes, E. Sandewall (editors), *Proceedings of the Second International Conference on Principles of Knowledge Representation and Reasoning*, Cambridge, Mas., 1991.

[HN90] B. Hollunder, W. Nutt. *Subsumption Algorithms for Concept Description Languages.* DFKI Research Report RR-90-04, DFKI, Postfach 2080, D-6750 Kaiserslautern, Germany.

[HNS90] B. Hollunder, W. Nutt, M. Schmidt-Schauß. "Subsumption Algorithms for Concept Description Languages." In *Proceedings of the 9th European Conference on Artificial Intelligence*, pp. 348–353, Stockholm, Sweden, 1990.

[KBR86] T. S. Kaczmarek, R. Bates, G. Robins. "Recent developments in NIKL." In *Proceedings of the 5th National Conference of the AAAI*, pp. 578–587, Philadelphia, Pa., 1986.

[Kob89] A. Kobsa. "The SB-ONE knowledge representation workbanch" In *Preprints of the Workshop on Formal Aspects of Semantic Networks*, Two Harbors, Cal., February 1989.

[LB87] H. J. Levesque, R. J. Brachman. "Expressiveness and tractability in knowledge representation and reasoning." *Computational Intelligence*, 3:78–93, 1987.

[MB87] R. MacGregor, R. Bates. *The Loom Knowledge Representation Language.* Technical Report ISI/RS-87-188, University of Southern California, Information Science Institute, Marina del Rey, Cal., 1987.

[Neb90] B. Nebel. *Reasoning and Revision in Hybrid Representation Systems*, Lecture Notes in Artificial Intelligence, LNAI 422, Springer Verlag, 1990.

[Neb89] B. Nebel. "Terminological Cycles: Semantics and Computational Properties." In *Proceedings of the Workshop on Formal Aspects of Semantic Networks*, Two Harbors, Cal., February 1989.

[Neb88] B. Nebel. "Computational complexity of terminological reasoning in BACK." *Artificial Intelligence*, 34(3):371–383, 1988.

[NvL88] B. Nebel, K. von Luck. "Hybrid Reasoning in BACK." In Z. W. Ras, L. Saitta (editors), *Methodologies for Intelligent Systems*, pp. 260–269, North Holland, Amsterdam, Netherlands, 1988.

[Pat84] P. Patel-Schneider. "Small can be beautiful in knowledge representation." In *Proceedings of the IEEE Workshop on Principles of Knowledge-Based Systems*, pp. 11–16, Denver, Colo., 1984.

[Pat89] P. Patel-Schneider. "A four-valued Semantics for Terminological Logics." *Artificial Intelligence*, 39(2):263-272, 1989.

[PSOK+90] P. Patel-Schneider, B. Owsnicki-Klewe, A. Kobsa, N. Guarino, R. MacGregor, W. S. Mark, D. L. McGuinness, B. Nebel, A. Schmiedel, J. Yen. "Term Subsumption in Knowledge Representation." In *AI Magazine*, 11(2):16-23, 1990. pp. 11–16, Denver, Colo., 1984.

[Sch89] M. Schmidt-Schauß. "Subsumption in KL-ONE is undecidable." In R. J. Brachmann, H. J. Levesque, R. Reiter (editors), *Proceedings of the 1st International Conference on Principles of Knowledge Representation and Reasoning*, pp. 421–431, Toronto, Ont., 1989.

[SS88] M. Schmidt-Schauß, G. Smolka. "Attributive Concept Descriptions with Complements". *Artificial Intelligence*, 47, 1991.

[Vil85] M. B. Vilain. "The restricted language architecture of a hybrid representation system." In R. J. Bachmann, H. J. Levesque, R. Reiter (editors), *Proceedings of the 9th IJCAI*, pp. 547–551, Los Angeles, Cal., 1985.

An Introduction to Dynamic Concept Systems

Herbert Jaeger
Faculty of Technology
University of Bielefeld
4800 Bielefeld 1, Germany

Abstract

A new kind of concept representation and processing formalisms, *dynamic concept systems* (DCS), is introduced. DCS are designed to model context-sensitive and compositionally productive interaction of many concepts in a quasi-continuous fashion, with subsumption, robust classification and metonymy as derivable features. DCS are symbolic throughout but in some respects inspired by complex systems theory. This paper concentrates on the representational aspects of DCS, giving their procedural features a passing glance.

1 Introduction

Here is a choice of desiderata for a concept representation and processing formalism:

(1) **Interaction dynamics**. Concepts are seldom used in isolation but rather in situations comprising a multitude of concepts. They modify each other dynamically, leading to some sort of reasoning history, in which new concepts may appear and from which concepts may disappear.

(2) **Context sensitivity**. The changes of a concept in changing contexts should be mirrored by its representation.

(3) **Robust classification**. There should be a classification procedure which from degraded input provides a concept representation accomodated to the actual context.

(4) **Metonymy**. Switching between concepts along metonymic relations accounts for much of the flexibility and effectiveness of human thinking. A concept representation and processing formalism should be able to detect and exploit such relations.

(5) **Productivity.** The emergence of new concepts is generally to be fostered but has to be constrained by some quality criterion preventing the system from being flooded by junk concepts.

These desiderata emphasize the interactive, context sensitive, and changeable nature of concepts (surveys in [2][5][6]). The following points (6) and (7) express two main concerns of theoretical AI; finally, (8) is a software engineering basic:

(6) **Default reasoning** is a basic phenomenon and should be accounted for.

(7) **Semantics.** There should be some sort of meaning ascribable to every element of the formalism establishing a well-balanced correspondence between operations on the realm of the denotating and the realm of the denotated.

(8) **Additive extendability.** It should be possible to introduce new concepts and to enrich representations of existing ones without extensive recomputations.

Obviously omitted in this list are features concerning the support of standard logical connectives and quantifiers, deduction, quantitative reasoning, and the like. Yet the selection is actually quite demanding. None of the current "classic" AI techniques for representing and processing conceptual knowledge satisfies most of the list's entries. Connectionist approaches generally come closer but cannot yet cope with (8) and still have considerable difficulties with (7). Thus, a formalism satisfying all of (1) - (8) would be of some value even if it had not much to offer for logico-deductive power.

In this paper I will propose a family of such formalisms. It will be described in detail in my doctoral thesis. In a nutshell, these formalisms, called **dynamic concept systems** (DCS), combine standard ideas of symbolic AI representation formalisms with elementary system theoretic conceptions as they have already made their way into AI via connectionist (and classifier system) approaches. From the latter parentage DCS have inherited their perspective on reasoning as a quasi-continuous process, with concepts modifying one another smoothly. From the symbolic point of view there comes a feeling that even the most basic cognitive strata in the end have to be analyzed into discrete entities with a well-defined functionality.

Intended use of DCS. I hope that DCS can be useful in two ways: first, as a practical construction tool for the design of components for hybrid AI programs, second, as a theoretical framework for the modeling of certain cognitive phenomena. The area where DCS might fruitfully be deployed in AI programs is staked by tasks like

- robust and context sensitive classification,
- associative hypothesis generation e.g. for word sense disambiguation or problem solving in domains which lack concise constraints,
- structuring concept spaces that seem to get mutilated by a predicate logic oriented representation, e.g. intentional and emotional concepts, but also concepts describing sensory impressions, as shapes or sounds,
- assistance for information retrieval in large knowledge bases through context classification.

The last application is the one on which DCS will first be tested at our research group at the University of Bielefeld [11][9].

Scope of this article and overview. DCS are concept representation *and* processing formalisms. This paper focusses on the first aspect, giving the procedural capacities only a glance in passing. It concentrates on conveying the underlying ideas, explicating a baby DCS en route in a semiformal way. In section 2 three basic principles concerning the functioning of conceptual systems, and their realization in DCS, are discussed. In section 3 it will be shown how these principles are formally integrated in a DCS. In section 4 the claims (1) - (8) from above will be revisited, and some shortcomings of DCS be pointed out.

2 Three Guiding Principles

In this section I will discuss three principles concerning the organization of conceptual systems. The first is strongly reminiscent to the principle of compositionality that is central for the physical symbol system paradigm [8][3], the third is intimately related to the logical notion of concept subsumption as exemplified in term subsumption languages [7]. However, I will call these principles by more awkward names in order to avoid certain associations that adhere to the classical labels.

2.1 The Principle of Emergent Conceptual Levels

It is common in AI and cognitive science to describe human or artificial conceptual systems by dividing them into several levels, where entities in a higher level are somehow made up from constituents from lower levels. Here are a few arbitrarily chosen examples:

- In *part-of*-hierarchies more complex entities are assembled from more primitive ones.
- A path down a parse tree transgresses several levels of grammatical description.
- Everyday concepts are interpreted as being composed from more primitive universal semantic constituents, in a highly structured way (e.g., case grammars) or in an associatively "fuzzy" way (e.g., semantic microfeatures [12]).
- In human and computer vision, highly specialized feature detectors feed into more integrative processing modules.

Indeed it seems nearly impossible to model a comprehensive conceptual system without some sort of level architecture. I now will take a closer look at some aspects of this broad conception and comment on the stance taken by DCS.

Topographical Structure of Level Architecture. Level architectures may differ with respect to a variety of structural dimensions:

- **Number of levels.** Just how many levels are modeled by some system depends on very diverse practical and theoretical issues.
- **Branching order.** Descriptive levels need not come in a straight succession. Refinements and abstractions of a description may sometimes follow several entirely different ways, e.g. analyzing a word morphologically vs. analyzing it with respect to its semantic features. This leads to branchings of level succession.
- **Disjointness.** It is a simplifying assumption that two consecutive levels be disjoint. In fact, a realistic reconstruction of a human's conceptual system would almost certainly reveal that adjoining levels are partially interwoven. E.g., the concept `traffic` may naturally be regarded as a situation class, hierarchically superordinated to object concepts like `car`. At the same time, `traffic` may have to be considered a semantic feature of `car`, which locally reverses level order.

A DCS formalism at the current state of the theory describes any number of levels, which are ordered in a chain without branchings and which are disjoint.

Compositionality. There are two ways of looking at higher-level concepts as being composed of lower-level ones.

(1) Composition by explicit definition: lower-level concepts are taken as well-defined building blocks. They are assembled to make a higher-level concept by stating that some equally well-defined relations do hold between them. This definitional version of compositionality is characteristic for the physical symbol system paradigm [8].

(2) Composition by emergence: a concept emerges out of lower-level *processes*. This view is typical for PDP networks and classifier systems. In a broader research context "emergent computation" seems to get established as a methodological paradigm [4].

Both paradigms are integrated in a DCS. Generally, a given level can be described *isolatedly* in a way that looks handsomely declarative. But a level can also be described *with respect to the lower level*. Then higher-level concepts are treated as emergent processes. Both ways of looking at concepts will turn out to be equivalent in DCS.

Influences bottom-up and top-down. Usually there are two directions of control and information flow. *Bottom-up*: data are given as input on lower levels and have to be dealt with on successively higher ones. *Top-down*: goals, hypotheses and other comprehensive directives are instantiated on higher levels and coordinate processing on lower ones. Both directions interact. In the representational subformalism of a DCS there are only bottom-up influences. Each level (save the lowest) is constructively defined on the basis of a lower one. In DCS as a processing formalism, the interactions between several processes within the same level are coordinated in a top-down fashion from the level above. However, these issues will not be treated in this paper.

The concept of concepts. When (re-)constructing an entire intelligent system on many levels, there are quite diverse kinds of entities to be expected on different levels. They may range from low-level single sensor signals to high-level belief sets. Only in some central levels will there be found those entities that we are most used to, entities that represent outside things like flowers and birthday parties, in short: prototypical concepts. DCS theory makes no empirical claims as to what particular sort of entities should be packed into an intelligent system. Rather, DCS proposes a particular view on a particular choice of interactions of entities within and between different layers, be they of any sort you like. Of course many intuitions behind DCS originate in the familiar central region. This heritage is reflected in DCS lingo by calling all entities on all levels "concepts". For the sequel I beg the reader to bear in mind that the DCS notion of concepts aims at encompassing strange entities from distal levels.

An example. I will now introduce the standard example for this article. It depicts small portions from three consecutive conceptual levels in a young child named Little Robin. No assertions about empirical validity are intended. The levels to be depicted will be called L/i-1, L/i and L/i+1. At this point I will just give some examples of the concepts to be found on each level.

L/i contains familiar concepts indeed: `Mom`, `Dad`, `ball`, `garden`, `play`, `eat`, `hungry`, `hot`, `blue`, and the like. L/i+1 contains standard situations in Little Robin's life. These concepts can be rendered by names but in a clumsy way: `going-to-bed-situation`, `evening-meal-setting`, `playing-in-the-garden-scene`. L/i-1 contains more basic sensomotoric and intentional schemata that we usually have no names for at all. Ad-hoc circumscriptions will give us something like `throwing-something-small-forcefully`, `tasting-something-nice`, `wanting-to-see-Mommy` (Fig.1).

level:	contains:
...	...
L/i+1	`going-to-bed-situation`, `evening-meal-setting`,...
L/i	`Mom`, `bed`, `tired`, `blue`...
L/i-1	`tasting-something-nice`, `wanting-to-see-Mommy`,...
...	...

Fig.1 *A small portion of Little Robin's conceptual system*

Summary of 2.1: A DCS aims at describing conceptual systems simultaneously on a sequence of descriptive levels L/1, ..., L/n. Each level is described in a formally similar way. The entities that populate any level are called "concepts" throughout, albeit only in middle levels they will be like the concepts we are most used to. DCS theory is a structural theory and makes no empirical claims concerning the kind of concepts to be found in human conceptual systems or what kind of concepts should best be used in AI systems.

2.2 The Principle of Reversible Contextual Modification

Concepts don't live by themselves. In human-style reasoning, concepts are not just additively loaded together but influence and modify each other in subtle ways. Somehow each concept that is present gets adapted to the actual context of concepts it is surrounded with. Such effects have been demonstrated in many experiments (e.g. [1]).

What exactly is modified when a concept becomes modified? The answer depends on how a concept is represented by a given theoretical approach. Before we go on to explore modification by context in some more detail, a few remarks on possible ways to represent concepts will be helpful. There are at least four, mutually not exclusive, ways how concepts may be represented.

(1) A concept is defined extensionally as a class of objects.

(2) A concept is defined by its properties, essential and/or contingent. This approach often comes in the variant of specifying a superconcept plus differentiating properties.

(3) A higher-level concept is constructed from or emerges from lower-level concepts.
(4) A concept is defined by its position within a topographically structured "concept space".

Approaches (1) and (2) are probably the most widely used. An extensive discussion of problems is provided in [6]. These problems motivated the exclusive use of the less prominent approaches (3) and (4) in DCS theory. Hence I will restrict the discussion of contextual concept modification to (3) and (4).

At this point it is convenient to introduce some DCS notational conventions. Generally, concepts are denoted by capitals X, Y, Z. The fact that X belongs to some level L/i is rendered by the shorthand notation X/i, e.g. `hungry`/i. It is a general convention in DCS notation to indicate for any theoretic entity its belonging to a level L/j by appending "/j" to its notation. This convention will be used in the sequel without further explanation.

Defining a concept X/j in the spirit of (3) in the very simplest form means to regard X/j as a collection of concepts from L/j-1, i.e. X/j = {Y_1/j-1, ..., Y_n/j-1}. Example: `evening-meal-situation`/i+1 = {`Mom`/i, `Dad`/i, `evening`/i, `table`/i, `hungry`/i, `food`/i, `drink`/i}.

If a concept is represented this way, modifying it means to alter the collection of constituent concepts. Example: Little Robin's concept `onion`/i in the context of concepts like `outside`/i, `flower-bed`/i might be represented by `onion`/i = {`presence-of-word-"onion"`/i-1, `plant-bulb-visual-expression`/i-1, `feeling-something-small-and-round`/i-1, `green-plant-stuff-visual-impression`/i-1, `digging-with-hands-in-earth-feeling`/i-1}. In the context of concepts like `kitchen`/i, `kitchen-knife`/i, `cooking`/i it might rather be desirable to have `onion`/i be represented by something like {`presence-of-word-"onion"`/i-1, `plant-bulb-visual-expression`/i-1, `feeling-something-small-and-round`/i-1, `tasting-something-fiery/`i-1, `being-in-kitchen-feeling/`i-1, `being-near-to-Mom/`i-1}.

Sets of this kind, which are used to represent different contextual modifications of a concept and can be interpreted as collections of "constituent" concepts from the next lower level, are called **internal state labels** of a concept. An internal state label is denoted by the capital I, and the fact that some concept X is described by an internal state label I is denoted by I|X.

If different conceptual modifications of X/j are essentially characterized by different sets of concepts from layer L/j-1, the question arises how different these sets can get while still being recognizable as belonging to the same concept X/j. The answer in DCS is that for every concept X/j all these sets essentially share a smallest common subset. In the example from above such a "root" internal state label might be I_0|onion/i = {presence-of-word-"onion"/i-1, plant-bulb-visual-expression/i-1, feeling-something-small-and-round/i-1}.

An internal state label I_1 is said to be a **differentiation** of I_2, if $I_1 \supseteq I_2$ (as sets). By set inclusion the internal state labels of a concept are canonically ordered.

Defining a concept X/j within L/j in the spirit of (4) in the simplest form means to specify the set of those concepts $\{Z_1/j, ..., Z_k/j\}$ that are direct associative neighbors of X/j. However, DCS knows of no globally fixed associative network of concepts which would allow referencing to a concept topographically via its nearest neighbors. Rather, each concept X/j is addressable within L/j via many different such sets of associatively related concepts. In the onion/i example, two such sets might be {bulb/i, fruit/i, biting/i, kitchen/i, cooking/i} and {bulb/i, fruit/i, garden/i, lily-like-blossom/i}. The intuition is to admit a concept set $\{Z_1/j, ..., Z_k/j\}$ as associatively addressing X/j if it "primes" the association of X/j. Such priming sets are called **generating context labels** for X/j. A generating context label is noted down by a capital G . X being described by G is expressed by the notation G|X. Note that a generating context label G|X/j is a set of concepts from the same level j, whereas an internal state label I|X/j is made from concepts from the lower level j-1.

If X/j is represented this way, different contextual modifications of X/j are essentially to be characterized by different generating context labels. A generating context label G_1 is said to be a **differentiation** of G_2 if $G_1 \supseteq G_2$. Again, set inclusion induces an ordering on the generating context labels of X/j.

Now we have introduced in an apparently ad hoc fashion two apparently quite dissimilar ways to characterize different contextual modifications of a given concept X/j. As will be explained in section 3, in a DCS these two ways in fact are closely interrelated: both types of labels can be computed from the same source and thus are essentially interchangeable. This interchangeability of two ways of describing contextual modifications leads to the more comprehensive notion of a **state** of a concept. The states of a concept *are* its contextual modifications and can be *described* by internal state labels and/or generating context labels. A state is noted down by capital S, and X being in state S is written as S|X.

In fact, the situation is even a bit more complex than presented so far. A state of a concept can not only be described by one internal state label and/or by one generating contex label, but by a potentially infinite class of such labels of either kind. As will be shown in section 3, these classes are effectively computable equivalence classes. The ordering induced by set inclusion on single labels (of either kind) carries over to an ordering of the entire equivalence classes, and hence, to an ordering of the states of a concept. As this ordering is derived from set inclusion, it will be denoted by $\leq$. There is a common minimal element of this ordering of states, which is called the **root state**. The root state is noted down conventionally by S_0, and its labels by I_0 resp. G_0. For reasons mainly of formal elegance, this ordering (which may contain multiple direct predecessors) is resolved into a tree ordering (with single predecessors) by introducing duplicate nodes where necessary. This **state tree** of X is denoted by T_X. Each node in the state tree is described by at least one generating context or internal state label.

As will be formalized in section 3, the actual context of a concept may change in time, and so will the concept's state. In particular, any state may get de-differentiated to the root state. Hence, state changes are reversible. This is a crucial difference to the specialization changes treated in the following subsection which motivated this section's heading, "the principle of *reversible* contextual modifications".

Summary of 2.2: A concept X/j comes in contextual modifications, called states, noted down by S|X/j. S|X/j can be characterized by internal state labels, i.e. by sets $\{Y_1/j\text{-}1, ..., Y_n/j\text{-}1\}$ of concepts from the next lower level L/j-1. Alternatively, and equivalently, S|X/j can be characterized by generating context labels, i.e. by sets $\{Z_1/j, ..., Z_k/j\}$ of concepts from the same level L/j. There is a tree ordering called differentiation on the states of X/j, with the root state noted down by S_0|X/j. The appendix "/j" is a general notational convention to indicate that level j is being referred to.

2.3 The Principle of Irreversible Concept Specialization

Within DCS, reasoning is modeled not as a kind of syllogistic switching procedure but rather as a quasi-continuous process, as a "reasoning history" which comprises many concepts on many levels. These concepts interact incessantly, thereby modifying each other's states. These state changes are reversible in the DCS model. But obviously human thinking is an irreversible process. This is answered for in DCS reasoning histories by concept specialization. New concepts can be generated within a reasoning history under certain circumstances. Typically such newcomers are not very specialized at their entrance, but during their lifetime get specialized, e.g. from `car` to `small-car` to `Beetle`. These changes in specialization are treated by DCS theory as irreversible. This irreversibility will supply certain desired "self-organization" phenomena in reasoning histories.

So much for motivation. How, then, are concept specialization relations brought about in a DCS? Concepts in a DCS essentially are represented by their state trees, the nodes S of which are labelled by internal state and/or generating context labels. Assume that concept X specializes Y, written as usual $X \leq Y$. X and Y both are given by their state trees T_X and T_Y. The question is how to express $X \leq Y$ in terms of T_X and T_Y. The answer is as follows. Let the set of states of X and Y be denoted by S(X) and S(Y), respectively. Then, X is a **specialization** of Y, iff there is a tree-order preserving mapping *sub*: $S(X) \rightarrow S(Y)$, where

(1) If $I = \{Y_1, ..., Y_n\}$ is an internal state label at node S in T_X, then there is an internal state label $I' = \{Y_1', ..., Y_n'\}$ at node *sub*(S) in T_Y, where $Y_1 \leq Y_1', ..., Y_n \leq Y_n'$. Shorthand notation: $I|X \leq I'|X$.

(2) If $G = \{Z_1, ..., Z_k\}$ is a generating context label at node S in T_X, then there is a generating context label $G' = \{Z_1', ..., Z_k'\}$ at node *sub*(S) in T_Y, where $Z_1 \leq Z_1', ..., Z_k \leq Z_k'$. Shorthand notation: $G|X \leq G'|X$.

In other words, $X \leq Y$ iff T_X can be projected on T_Y in a label-specializing manner. Note that this projection need not be either surjective or injective, and that the root state of X need not be projected to the root state of Y. However, for the sake of simplicity we will tacitly assume the special case of injectiveness in the sequel. On the other hand, non-surjectiveness is crucial. It introduces a decisive aspect of nonmonotonicitiy. To get a first feeling for this important matter it may be helpful to illustrate a non-surjective projection both by an abstract graph and by an example from Little Robin's world. In figure 2, a surjective and two non-surjective state tree mappings are sketched:

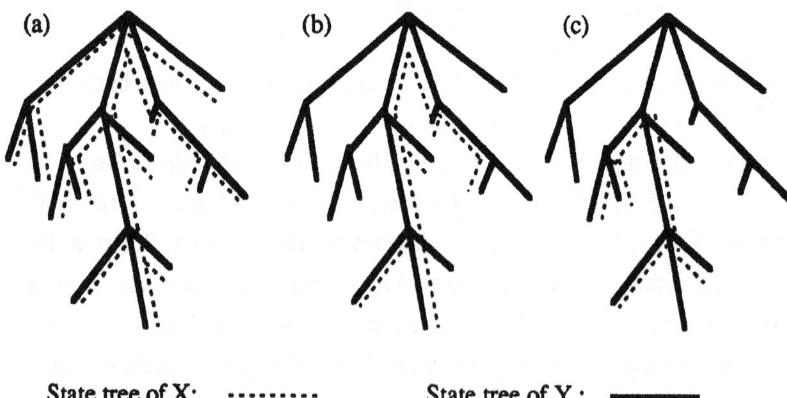

Fig.2 *Projections of the state tree of some concept* X *on the state tree of* Y, *where* $X \leq Y$. *Only (a) is surjective. In (c) the root state of* X *is not mapped to the root state of* Y.

As an example we take X = `icecream` and Y = `sweets`. Figure 3 depicts portions of these concept's state trees. Nodes are labelled frugally by one generating context each.

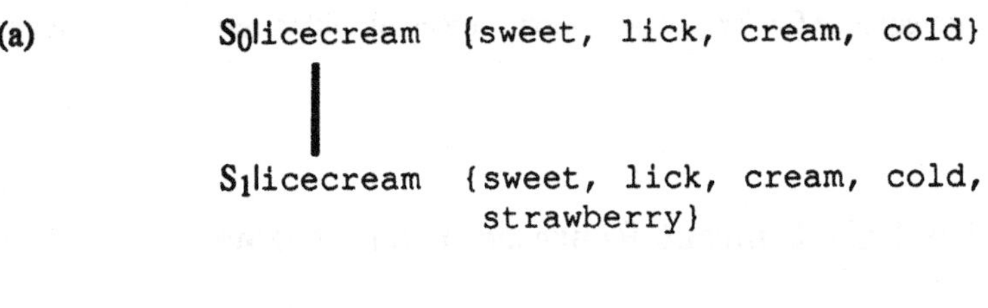

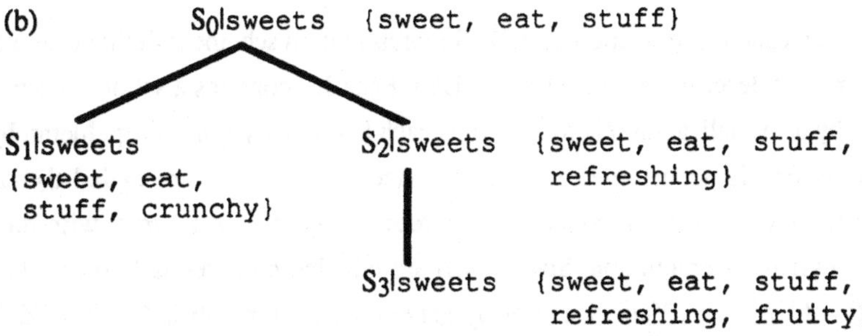

Fig.3 *Portions of state trees of (a)* `icecream` *and (b)* `sweets`. *The state tree projection maps* S_0|`icecream` *on* S_2|`sweets`, S_1|`icecream` *on* S_3|`sweets`. *Condition (2) from the text above is satisfied by virtue of* `sweet` $\le$ `sweet`, `lick` $\le$ `eat`, `cream` $\le$ `stuff`, `cold` $\le$ `refreshing`, `strawberry` $\le$ `fruity`. *This projection is of type (c) in fig.2.*

Some remarks concerning the role of this kind of nonmonotonic concept specialization for "self-organizing" processes in reasoning histories may be of interest here. In reasoning histories, interactions between concepts are (among others) mediated by generating contexts. The fewer generating contexts a concept affords, the fewer interactions are possible. The more specialized a concept's generating contexts are, the more specialized must other concepts be if they are to interact with the first concept. If X $\le$ Y, then X generally has less, and more specialized, generating contexts than Y. In sum, if X $\le$ Y, then X can engage in less, but more specialized, interactions than Y. It has already been mentioned that concepts may develop into more specialized, but not degrade to less specialized concepts. In fact, specialization events are triggered by the presence of suitably specialized generative contexts, whose members in turn may specialize as a consequence of the first event. The overall picture will be the development of co-specializing coherent clusters of concepts.

Summary of 2.3: Within a level L/j, concepts are related to each other by specialization. Specialization is in accordance with concept representation by state trees, in that the state tree T_X of a specialization X of Y can be considered a subtree of T_Y under projection, with labels in T_X being specializations of labels in T_Y. Usually T_X will be a proper subtree of T_Y. This non-monotonicitiy is a prerequisite for "self organization" processes within reasoning histories.

3 Outlines of a DCS Concept Representation Scheme

This is what can be gleaned from section 2: A DCS representation scheme is defined simultaneously on a sequence of descriptive levels L/0, ..., L/m. Each L/j contains a set of concepts X/j which is ordered by a specialization relation $\leq$. Thus each L/j actually is a concept hierarchy (or hetarchy) much as one is accustomed to. These concept hierarchies are called **dynamic concept hierarchies** (DCH). Each concept X/j is represented by a state tree, with the tree ordering $\subseteq$ being called differentiation. States S|X/j are labelled by potentially many internal state labels I|X/j = $\{Y_1/j\text{-}1, ..., Y_n/j\text{-}1\}$ and/or by generating context labels G|X/j = $\{Z_1/j, ..., Z_k/j\}$. In DCH/0 states can only be labelled by generating contexts, because internal state labels are made from concepts from the next lower level, which is not available for DCH/0.

Labels can be stored space-efficiently utilizing inheritance along specialization and differentiation paths:

- If I'|X $\leq$ I|Y, then (as a set) I'|X is nothing else but I|Y with some elements from I|Y specialized. Only the specialized members need to be stored at I'|X, the rest can be inherited. The analogue holds for G'|X $\leq$ G|Y.
- If I'|X differentiates I|X, then (as a set) I'|X $\supseteq$ I|X. Only the difference I'|X-I|X needs to be stored at I'|X, the rest can be inherited. The same holds for G'|X differentiating G|X.

As differentiation and specialization are coupled by state tree projection, both inheritance mechanisms can be coupled for additional effectiveness.

I have indicated in section 2 that internal states and generating contexts were closely interrelated. Also, that internal state labels pertaining to a given state were related to each other by a certain equivalence relation. These issues will now be treated. To this end we must borrow a fragment from the DCS processing formalism.

The DCS processing formalism handles reasoning histories simultaneously on several interacting levels L/j. For our present purpose we may confine ourselves to the simplest case of a reasoning history described on a single level. Such a history is modeled as a succession of "snapshots". These snapshots are called **configurations**, noted down by capital C. A configuration is basically a finite set of concepts in certain states, e.g. $C/j = \{S_1|X_1/j, ..., S_m|X_m/j\}$. In order to govern the succession of configurations to make a reasoning historie $C_0, C_1, C_2, ...$, we make use of **local transformation rules** (LTRs). A LTR is to be applied to a single element of a configuration, i.e. a concept in a certain state, which leads to a transformation of this element. By applying a LTR to an element of C_i, a successor C_{i+1} of C_i is derived. As the choice of elements to be transformed and of rules to be applied is free, succession of configurations is nondeterministic. I like to call reasoning histories "quasi-continuous" because they can be regarded as being driven by many minimal changes. There are many kinds of LTR conceivable. For our baby DCS the following will do:

LTR1 (Differentiation): If $S|X \in C$, and $S' \geq S$, and $G = \{X_1, ..., X_k\}$ is a generating context for $S'|X$, and there are $S_1|X_1, ..., S_k|X_k \in C$, then $S|X$ can be differentiated to $S'|X$.

LTR2 (De-differentiation): If $S'|X \in C$, and $S' \geq S$, and $G = \{X_1, ..., X_k\}$ is a generating context for $S'|X$, and there are $S_1|X_1, ..., S_k|X_k \in C$, then $S'|X$ can be de-differentiated to $S|X$.

LTR3 (Generation): If $G = \{X_1, ..., X_k\}$ is a generating context for $S|X$, and there are $S_1|X_1, ..., S_k|X_k \in C$, then $S|X$ can be added to C.

LTR4 (Deletion): If $S|X \in C$, and $G = \{X_1, ..., X_k\}$ is a generating context for $S|X$, and there are $S_1|X_1, ..., S_k|X_k \in C$, then $S|X$ can be deleted from C.

LTR5 (specialization): If $S|X \in C$, and $S|X' \leq S|X$, and $G = \{X_1, ..., X_k\}$ is a generating context for $S|X$, and $G' = \{X'_1, ..., X'_k\}$ is a generating context for $S|X'$, and $X'_i \leq X_i$ $(i = 1, ..., k)$, and $G'\backslash G := \{X'_i \in G' \mid X'_i \neq X_i\}$, and there are $S_i|X'_i \in C$ for all $X'_i \in G'\backslash G$, then $S|X$ can be specialized to $S|X'$.

Obviously LTR2 and LTR4 are inverse operations to LTR1 and LTR3. Hence, histories constructed by use of LTR1 - LTR4 will be reversible, i.e. "the film run backwards" will also be a valid history. This symmetry is broken by applications of LTR5.

C' directly succeeds C, written $C > C'$, iff C' can be derived from C by application of one of the rules from above. Let >>, the **succession relation**, denote the transitive closure of >. By virtue of >> an equivalence relation on the class of all configurations can be defined. C and C' are said to be **mutually reachable**, written $C <> C'$, iff $C >> C'$ and $C' >> C$.

Equivalence classes with respect to <> may be interpreted as internally structured by >, i.e. within each class > yields a (cyclic) directed graph. Any path along > is a reasoning history, so these equivalence classes may be interpreted as a network of interwoven histories. To put it in suggestive terms: such an equivalence class may be interpreted as a "superposition" (or, the other way round, as a "generator") of cyclic reasoning processes.

Now we have nearly arrived at our goal. The basic idea is to take just such "cyclic reasoning process generators", i.e. <>-equivalence classes, from level L/j-1 as internal states for concepts in DCH/j. More precisely, we demand that for any two internal state labels of a state S|X/j,

$I|X/j = \{Y_1/j\text{-}1, ..., Y_n/j\text{-}1\}$ and $I'|X/j = \{Y'_1/j\text{-}1, ..., Y'_m/j\text{-}1\}$,

there exist configurations

$C/j\text{-}1 = \{S_1|Y_1/j\text{-}1, ..., S_n|Y_n/j\text{-}1\}$ and $C'/j\text{-}1 = \{S'_1|Y'_1/j\text{-}1, ..., S'_m|Y'_m/j\text{-}1\}$

with C/j-1 <> C'/j-1.

One final refinement is to be added. We should not admit every <>-equivalence class as a candidate for an internal state. E.g., {`Dad, ball, play, garden`} seems to be perfect for an internal state of a concept X/i+1 (call it `playing-outside`), whereas {`postman, butter, moon, pink`} is weird. We need some **coherency criterion** to sort out from all <>-equivalence classes those that are sufficiently coherent. There are many coherency criteria conceivable, graded ones and yes-or-no ones. A particular DCS is to a considerable degree characterized by its coherency criterion. As an example I will give a crude yes-or-no criterion:

An <>-equivalence class $(C_i)_{i \in I}$ is **coherent** iff for all $C_i = \{S_1|X_1, ..., S_k|X_k\}$, for all $S_j|X_j \in C_i$ there is a generating context for $S_j|X_j$ within C_i. Furthermore, C_i is not decomposable into two subsets each of which satisfies this condition.

Intuitively, this criterion demands that every constituent of an internal state be associatively supported by other constituents, with these support relations binding the configuration together in an inseparable fashion. Relaxations of this criterion can be obtained by "smearing it over time", e.g. by demanding that for any concept within a particular configuration there is a generating context for this concept in some preceding configuration.

Now here's the recipe for constructing concept states S|X/j+1 from DCH/j: pick a <>-equivalence class $(C_i)_{i \in I}$ from DCH/j, test it for coherency, take any handy subset $(C_k)_{k \in K}$ from $(C_i)_{i \in I}$, strip each $C_k = \{S_1|X_1, ..., S_n|X_n\}$ off its state information to get $I_k = \{X_1, ..., X_n\}$, and take these I_k as internal state labels for S|X/j+1.

As <>-equivalence classes that satisfy the coherency criterion play a constitutional role in DCS theory, they are given an extra name: **resonances**.

Now we possess a toolkit to construct internal states, hence state trees, hence all concepts in DCH/j+1 from a given DCH/j, using only generating context information but not internal state information from DCH/j. The missing link to pull this construction through to DCH/j+2, etc, is a way to obtain generating contexts in DCH/j+1. To this end, let S|X/j+1 be represented by an internal state label I|X/j+1 $= \{Y_1/j, ..., Y_n/j\}$. Then $\{Z_1/j+1, ..., Z_k/j+1\}$ is a generating context label for S|X/j+1 iff there are internal state labels $I_1/j+1, ..., I_k/j+1$ for $S_0|Z_1/j+1, ..., S_0|Z_k/j+1$, such that $I|X/j+1 \subset I_1/j+1 \cap ... \cap I_k/j+1$, with G|X/j+1 minimal with respect to this condition. Intuitively, generating contexts for S|X/j+1 are made by exactly those combinations of concepts whose root resonances in their union furnish the "internal state information" necessary for the resonance of S|X/j+1.

By way of summing up, this is how a DCS concept representation scheme can be constructed:

(1) DCH/0 is given resp. programmed by hand, with only generating context labels but no internal state labels. Construct DCH/j+1 from DCH/j as follows.
(2) Find resonances $(C_i)_{i\in I}$ in DCH/j. Comment: resonances need not be constructed completely. A single >-cycle will do to make most coherency criteria applicable.
(3) Take these resonances as states in DCH/j+1.
(4) Assemble state trees.
(5) Order state trees with respect to specialization.
(6) Strip configurations from resonances off their state information to make internal state labels.
(7) Complete DCH/j+1 by generating context labels.

This construction scheme is incremental. Construction of DCH/j+1 can be started from partially constructed DCH/j, and both sorts of state labels can be added at any level. Fig.4 gives an overall picture of a DCS.

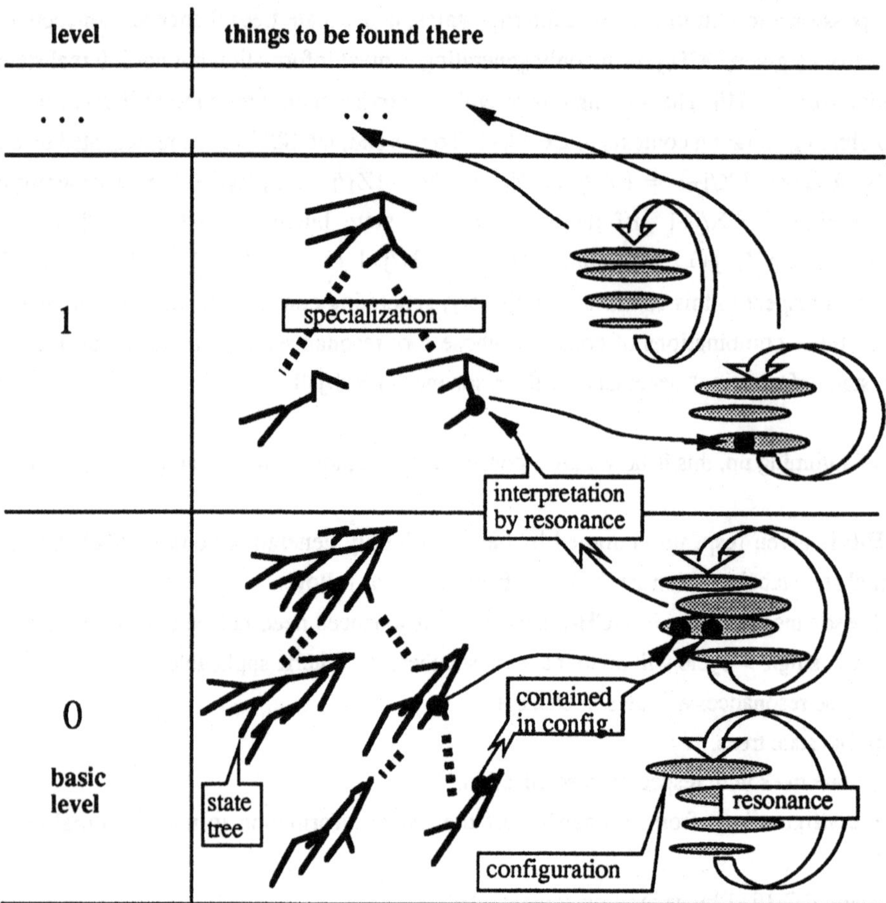

Fig.4 A DCS at a glance

4 Discussion

I have started this article by a collection of eight desiderata for a concept representation and processing formalism and I have claimed DCS to satisfy them. I will now defend these claims.

(1) **Interaction dynamics** could be introduced in this paper only as far as interactions between concepts from one level L/j and within one configuration are concerned. However, the gist of how interaction is treated already shows in this fragment: local transformation rules

(which rely on generating contexts) are applied to concept instances, which leads to a temporal succession of configurations, i.e. a reasoning history.

The procedural part of DCS, which is not a subject of this paper, generalizes these basic ideas to the interaction of concepts from several levels and to the interaction of several configurations. To this end heavy use is made of the internal state idea: essentially, processes on level L/j are coordinated by interpreting them as superpositions of internal states of concepts from L/j+1. This also places the notion of top-down influences in a natural setting.

(2) **Context sensitivity** is built-in.

(3) **Robust classification.** Classification is an ambiguous notion. There are at least two sorts of classifiction tasks, which also may be seen as successive subtasks of a comprehensive classification procedure. First task: given a noisy, incomplete or otherwise degraded input, distil from it a coherent "pattern". Second task: given a cleanly described pattern, transform this description in a way that its placing in some conceptual system becomes evident. The first task is prototypically done by relaxation in recurrent neural networks, the second by KL-ONE-like formalisms. The quality of *robustness* pertains to the first subtask, the term *classification* in a narrow sense belongs to the second subtask.

In the DCS approach, the first task in a simple version can be formulated as follows: given a noisy or only weakly coherent configuration C/j, find a resonance R which contains a configuration C*/j that is a distillate of C/j. The second subtask, then, is to classify R in L/j+1 by finding states to which its configurations can serve as an internal state labels.

The first subtask is done in two iterated steps. First step: develop C/j =: C_0 into a succession $C_0 > C_1 > C_2 > \ldots$, until a cycle $C_i > \ldots C_k > C_i$ is entered, which will necessarily happen if DCH/j is finite. Second step: if this cycle is resonant, exit to the second subtask. Else, delete from the set C_i the concept which is most weakly contextually supported within C_i, or add a concept that strengthens contextual coherency, and return to the first step. This loop will eventually yield a resonant cycle $C_i > \ldots C_k > C_i$. Strip off state information to get internal state label candidates $I_1, \ldots, I_k$.

The second subtask boils down to find within DCH/j+1 states S|X/j+1 which are labelled by I|X/j+1 which can be directly matched to one of $I_1, \ldots, I_k$ via $\leq$ and $\subseteq$. The difficulty is that there may not yet have been generated and stored suitable matching labels within DCH/j+1. In order to match state labels from DCH/j+1 with labels $I_i, \ldots, I_k$, in the worst case it may be necessary to expand the resonant cycle $C_i > \ldots C_k > C_i$ into a complete resonance to get a full coverage of potential matching partners. Depending on the coherency criterion and the LTR's that are used, this expansion may range in complexity from easy to impossible.

(4) **Metonymy.** In each level L/j, with the exception of L/0, two concepts X_1 and X_2 are by definition **metonymes** iff there can be constructed state labels $I_1|X_1$ and $I_1|X_2$ with $I_1|X_1 \cap I_1|X_2 \neq \emptyset$. The greater the overlap is between $I_1|X_1$ and $I_1|X_2$, and the smaller the differences $I_1|X_1 - I_0|X_1$ resp. $I_1|X_2 - I_0|X_2$ are, the stronger the metonymic kinship will be. Looking at set diagrams (fig.5) will help to get a feeling for this definition:

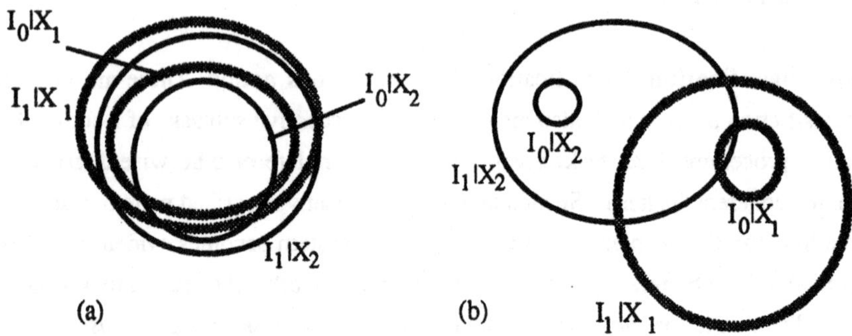

Fig.5 *(a) strong, (b) weak metonymes*

(5) **Productivity** is built-in.

(6) **Default reasoning** in an admittedly confined sense is earned by nonmonotonic projections of state trees. Its particular importance for DCS has been discussed at the end of 2.3.

(7) **Semantics.** In DCS theory the relation between two consecutive levels L/j and L/j+1 is interpreted as semantic, with L/j supplying (intensional) "meanings" for concepts from L/j+1 by way of the resonance interpretation of states. This way of looking at things is really quite natural. For one, there is a direct kinship to the notion of microfeatures, which are unhesitatingly called "*semantic* microfeatures". Also it seems natural to say that L/j+1 *describes* L/j, or more precisely, processes within L/j. But then, what should the terminus "semantic" describe if not description relations?

(8) **Additive extendability** is built-in.

Criticism. Here are the two severe points of criticism. It would be easy to add to the list.

- The practical application of DCS may turn out to be cumbersome e.g. in that the overall behavior of a DCS will respond to details of the basic DCH/0 in an opaque way, or in that when automatically extending DCH/j+1 on the basis of DCH/j, it may be hard to suppress the creation of irrelevant concepts.
- It is completely in the dark whether there is any way leading from concept modeling by DCS to a logical mode of reasoning which is certainly indispensable for most applications.

Related work. DCS has no direct forerunner but has emerged over the years under the influence of ideas imported from disparate fields that I cannot review here. Within AI certain localist connectionist approaches probably lie closest to DCS. In these approaches, there typically is a hetarchy of labelled nodes which represents a composition hetarchy of conceptual entities ranging from microfeatures and morphological particles to phrases and context concepts (a classic is [12]). Networks of this kind are used to model dynamical interactions of conceptual entities within and between different layers of the hetarchy. In a more theoretically minded paper that roughly belongs to the same category [10], the vocabulary used as well as the underlying intuitions about the nature of concepts is very much akin to that of DCS, although mathematical and formal aspects largely differ.

Theoretical applications. DCS formalisms are designed to be directly implementable. But DCS can also be regarded as a theoretical framework for explicitly discussing certain aspects of intelligent systems that cannot yet be easily expressed in other symbolic formalisms, and that yet are only implicity accessible through subsymbolic neural network models. These aspects are centered around context sensitivity, metonymy, and the idea of cognitive processes as quasi-continuous processes. With the aid of DCS as an expressive tool it may be hoped to spell out in more detail than has been possible before testable empirical predictions, e.g. concerning contextually triggered metonymic switches, "specialization drift" of concepts during reasoning processes, or context-driven association priming effects.

Acknowledgements. It is a great pleasure to express my deep gratitude to my mentor and friend Ipke Wachsmuth. In the two years that I have now been with his crew at the University of Bielefeld, he gave me both freedom and guidance in the most productive amalgamation. Only the emotional, scientific and organizational assistance given freely by him and my colleagues Josef Meyer-Fujara and Bärbel Heller have in the end made this work possible.

References

[1] Barsalou, Lawrence W. *The Instability of Graded Structure: Implications for the Nature of Concepts*. In: Neisser, Ulric (ed.): Concepts and Conceptual Development: Ecological and Intellectual Factors in categorization. Cambridge University Press 1987

[2] Chalmers, David J., Robert M. French and Douglas R. Hofstadter. *High-Level Perception, Representation, and Analogy: A Critique of Artificial Intelligence Methodology*. Preprint 1991, submitted to the Journal of Experimental and Theoretical Artificial Intelligence

[3] Fodor, Jerry A. and Zenon W. Pylyshyn. *Connectionism and Cognitive Architecture: A Critical Analysis*. Cognition 28, 1988, 3-71

[4] Forrest, Stephanie. *Emergent Computation: Self-organizing, Collective, and Cooperative Phenomena in Natural and Artificial Computation Networks*. Introduction to the Proceedings of the 9th Annual CNLS Conference. Physica D 42, 1990, 1-11

[5] Goschke, Thomas and Dirk Koppelberg. *Connectionist Representation, Semantic Compositionality, and the Instability of Concept Structure*. Psych. Research 52, 1990, 253-270

[6] Lakoff, George. *Women, Fire, and Dangerous Things*. The Univ. of Chicago Press 1987

[7] Nebel, Bernhard. *Reasoning and Revision in Hybrid Representation Systems*. Springer Lecture Notes in Artificial Intelligence 422, 1990

[8] Newell, Allen. *Physical Symbol Systems*. Cognitive Science 4, 1980, 135-183

[9] Samad, Tariq and Peggy Israel. *A Browser for Large Knowledge Bases Based on a Hybrid Distributed/Local Connectionist Architecture*. IEEE Transactions on Knowledge and Data Engineering, Vol. 3 No. 1, 1991, 89-99

[10] Smolensky, Paul. *Information Processing in Dynamical Systems: Foundations of Harmony Theory*. In: Rumelhart, David E., McClelland, James L. (eds.): Parallel Distributed Processing Vol 1, 1986, 194-281

[11] Wachsmuth, Ipke and Josef Meyer-Fujara. *Addressing the Retrieval Problem in Large Knowledge Bases*. Proceedings of the Computational Intelligence-90 Symposion on Heterogenous Knowledge Representation Systems, Milano, Sept. 1990.

[12] Waltz, David L. and Jordan B. Pollack. *Massively Parallel Parsing: A Strongly Interactive Model of Natural Language Interpretation*. Cognitive Science 9, 1985, 51-74

Querying Concept-based Knowledge Bases

Maurizio Lenzerini, Andrea Schaerf
Dipartimento di Informatica e Sistemistica
Università di Roma "La Sapienza"
via Salaria 113, 00198 Roma, Italia

Abstract

Much of the research on terminological reasoning aims at characterizing concept languages (also called terminological languages) with respect to both expressive power and computational complexity of computing subsumption. On the other hand, little attention has been paid to studying concept languages as query languages, i.e. as a means for extracting information from a concept-based knowledge base. In this paper we address this problem by exploring the possibility of using two different concept languages, one for asserting facts about individual objects, and the other for querying a set of such assertions. Contrary to many negative results on the complexity of terminological reasoning, our work shows that, provided that a limited language is used for the assertions, it is possible to employ a richer query language while keeping the reasoning process tractable. We also show that, on the other hand, there are constructs that make query answering inherently intractable.

1 Introduction

Concept languages (CLs, also called terminological languages) provide a means for expressing knowledge about concepts, i.e. classes of individuals with common properties. A concept is built up of two kinds of symbols, primitive concepts and primitive roles.

These primitives can be combined by various language constructors yielding complex concepts. Different languages are distinguished by the constructors they provide. Concept languages are given a Tarski-style semantics: an interpretation interprets concepts as subsets of a domain and roles as binary relations over the domain.

Much of the research on terminological reasoning aims at characterizing CLs with respect to both expressive power and computational complexity of computing subsumption, i.e. checking if one concept is always a superset of another (see [BL84,Neb88,SS91] and [DHL91,DLN91a])

Other recent work (see [NS89,DLN90,H90]) deals with the problem of using a CL for building what we call a concept-based knowledge base, i.e. a set of assertions about the membership relation between individuals and concepts, and between pairs of individuals and roles.

It is interesting to observe that little attention has been paid to studying CLs as query languages, i.e. as a means for extracting information from a concept-based knowledge base. The existing methods for query answering are generally based on the idea that the system keeps track of a concept taxonomy, where each concept is associated with the set of its instances. When a query Q is entered in the form of a concept, Q is classified with respect to the taxonomy by means of a number of subsumption checks, and the query is answered on the basis of the computed subsumption relation. Moreover, the language used for query formulation is the same as the language used for assertions, and query answering is essentially reduced to subsumption.

Our goal in this paper is to explore the possibility of devising more sophisticated query answering mechanisms, in particular by considering a query language that is more powerful than the assertional language, and by identifying an optimal compromise between expressive power and computational tractability of both the assertional and the query language. Our work has been carried out with the following underlying assumptions:

1. The assertional language is at least as powerful as $\mathcal{FL}^-$ [BL84], which is generally considered as the minimal concept language.

2. A query is formulated in terms of a concept C, with the meaning of asking for the set of all the individuals x such that the knowledge base logically implies that x is an instance of C (see [BBMR89]).

3. Since we want to be able to extract from the knowledge base at least the information that has been asserted, the query language is at least as expressive as the assertional language.

4. The computational complexity of query answering is measured with respect to the size of both the knowledge base and the concept representing the query.

The main result of this paper is to show that one can use a rich CL for query formulation without falling into the computational cliff, provided that a tractable language is used for expressing the knowledge base.

It is worth mentioning that the idea of using a query language richer than the assertional language is not new. For example, relational data bases, which are built up by means of a very limited data definition language, are queried using a full first order language, called relational calculus. Another example is the work by Levesque in [L81], where a first order knowledge base is queried by means of a richer language including a modal operator.

In order to apply this idea in the context of concept-based knowledge bases, we make use of $\mathcal{AL}$ [SS91] for defining the knowledge base, and we define a suitable new language $\mathcal{QL}$ for query formulation. $\mathcal{AL}$ is a tractable language extending $\mathcal{FL}^-$ [BL84] with a constructor for denoting the complement of primitive concepts, whereas $\mathcal{QL}$ extends $\mathcal{AL}$ with role conjunction, roles chaining, collection of individuals, and qualified existential quantification on roles.

Another result of our work is that $\mathcal{QL}$ is almost optimal with respect to the tractability of query answering. In particular, by analyzing the constructs usually considered in terminological languages, we show that, if one aims at retaining tractability, there are inherent limits to the expressive power of the query language.

The paper is organized as follows. In Section 2 we provide some preliminaries on CLs. In Section 3, we deal with the problem of checking subsumption between a concept of $\mathcal{QL}$ and a concept of $\mathcal{AL}$. In Section 4, we make use of the results of Section 3 for devising a polynomial method for answering queries to an $\mathcal{AL}$-knowledge base using $\mathcal{QL}$ as query language. In Section 5 we discuss and motivate the choices of the language used in this work and outline future developments. Finally, conclusions are drawn in Section 6.

2 Preliminaries

In this paper, we consider a family of *concept languages* whose general description can be found in [DLN91a,NS89,SS91].

We are particularly interested in the language $\mathcal{AL}$, where *concepts* (denoted by the letters C and D) are built out by means of the following syntax rule

$$
\begin{array}{lcll}
C, D & \longrightarrow & A \mid & \text{(primitive concept)} \\
 & & \top \mid & \text{(top)} \\
 & & \bot \mid & \text{(bottom)} \\
 & & \neg A \mid & \text{(primitive complement)} \\
 & & C \sqcap D \mid & \text{(intersection)} \\
 & & \forall R.C \mid & \text{(universal quantification)} \\
 & & \exists R & \text{(unqualified existential quantification)}
\end{array}
$$

where R denotes a *role*, that in $\mathcal{AL}$ is always primitive (more general languages provide constructors for roles).

Both $\mathcal{FL}^-$ and $\mathcal{AL}$ provide a restricted form of existential quantification, called *unqualified*: the construct $\exists R$ denotes the set of objects a such that there exists an object b related to a by means of the role R. The existential quantification is unqualified in the sense that no condition is stated to b other than its existence.

An *interpretation* $\mathcal{I} = (\Delta^\mathcal{I}, \cdot^\mathcal{I})$ consists of a set $\Delta^\mathcal{I}$ (the *domain* of $\mathcal{I}$) and a function $\cdot^\mathcal{I}$ (the *interpretation function* of $\mathcal{I}$) that maps every concept to a subset of $\Delta^\mathcal{I}$ and every role to a subset of $\Delta^\mathcal{I} \times \Delta^\mathcal{I}$ such that the following equations are satisfied:

$$
\begin{array}{rcl}
\top^\mathcal{I} & = & \Delta^\mathcal{I} \\
\bot^\mathcal{I} & = & \emptyset
\end{array}
$$

$$\begin{aligned}(C \sqcap D)^{\mathcal{I}} &= C^{\mathcal{I}} \cap D^{\mathcal{I}} \\ (\neg A)^{\mathcal{I}} &= \Delta^{\mathcal{I}} \setminus A^{\mathcal{I}} \\ (\forall R.C)^{\mathcal{I}} &= \{a \in \Delta^{\mathcal{I}} \mid \forall b : (a,b) \in R^{\mathcal{I}} \rightarrow b \in C^{\mathcal{I}}\} \\ (\exists R)^{\mathcal{I}} &= \{a \in \Delta^{\mathcal{I}} \mid \exists b : (a,b) \in R^{\mathcal{I}}\}\end{aligned}$$

An interpretation $\mathcal{I}$ is a *model* for a concept C if $C^{\mathcal{I}}$ is nonempty. A concept is *satisfiable* if it has a model and *unsatisfiable* otherwise. We say that C is *subsumed* by D if $C^{\mathcal{I}} \subseteq D^{\mathcal{I}}$ for every interpretation $\mathcal{I}$, and C is *equivalent* to D if C and D are subsumed by each other.

More general languages are obtained by adding to $\mathcal{AL}$ the following constructors:

- qualified existential quantification, written as $\exists R.C$, and defined by $(\exists R.C)^{\mathcal{I}} = \{a \in \Delta^{\mathcal{I}} \mid \exists b(a,b) \in R^{\mathcal{I}} \wedge b \in C^{\mathcal{I}}\}$. The difference with unqualified existential quantification, is that in this case a condition is specified on object b, namely that it must be an instance of the concept C;
- complement of non-primitive concepts, $(\neg C)^{\mathcal{I}} = \Delta^{\mathcal{I}} \setminus C^{\mathcal{I}}$;
- disjunction of concepts, $(C \sqcup D)^{\mathcal{I}} = C^{\mathcal{I}} \cup D^{\mathcal{I}}$;
- conjunction of roles, $(Q \sqcap R)^{\mathcal{I}} = Q^{\mathcal{I}} \cap R^{\mathcal{I}}$;
- role chaining, $(Q \circ R)^{\mathcal{I}} = \{(a,b) \in \Delta^{\mathcal{I}} \times \Delta^{\mathcal{I}} \mid \exists c \in \Delta^{\mathcal{I}} : (a,c) \in Q^{\mathcal{I}} \wedge (c,b) \in R^{\mathcal{I}}\}$
- collection of individuals (see [BBMR89]), written as $\{a_1, \ldots, a_n\}$, where each a_i is a symbol belonging to a given alphabet $\mathcal{O}$. In order to assign a meaning to such a concept, the interpretation function $\cdot^{\mathcal{I}}$ is extended to individuals in such a way that $a^{\mathcal{I}} \in \Delta^{\mathcal{I}}$ for each individual $a \in \mathcal{O}$ and $a^{\mathcal{I}} \neq b^{\mathcal{I}}$ if $a \neq b$. The semantics of $\{a_1, \ldots, a_n\}$ is then defined by $\{a_1, \ldots, a_n\}^{\mathcal{I}} = \{a_1^{\mathcal{I}}, \ldots, a_n^{\mathcal{I}}\}$.

In [SS91,DLN91a] a calculus for checking concept satisfiability is presented. The calculus operates on constraints of the forms $x{:}\, C$ and xRy, where x, y are variables belonging to an alphabet $\mathcal{V}$, C is a concept and R is a role. Intuitively, $x{:}\, C$ means that the object represented by x is in the interpretation of C, while xRy means that the pair (x,y) is in the interpretation of R.

Let $\mathcal{I}$ be an interpretation. An *$\mathcal{I}$-assignment* α is a function that maps every variable to an element of $\Delta^{\mathcal{I}}$; α *satisfies* $x{:}\, C$ if $\alpha(x) \in C^{\mathcal{I}}$, and α *satisfies* xRy if $(\alpha(x), \alpha(y)) \in R^{\mathcal{I}}$. A *constraint system* S is a finite, nonempty set of constraints. A constraint system S is *satisfiable* if there is an interpretation $\mathcal{I}$ and an $\mathcal{I}$-assignment α such that α satisfies every constraint in S.

It is easy to see that a concept C is satisfiable if and only if the constraint system $\{x{:}\, C\}$ is satisfiable. In order to check C for satisfiability, the calculus starts with the constraint system $S = \{x{:}\, C\}$, adding constraints to S until either a contradiction is generated or an interpretation satisfying C can be obtained from the resulting system.

Constraints are added on the basis of a suitable set of so-called *propagation rules*, whose form depends on the constructs of the language. The propagation rules for the language $\mathcal{AL}$ are the following:

1. $S \rightarrow_{\sqcap} \{x: C_1,\ x: C_2\} \cup S$

   if $x: C_1 \sqcap C_2$ is in S, and $x: C_1$, $x: C_2$ are not both in S

2. $S \rightarrow_{\forall} \{y: C\} \cup S$

   if $x: \forall P.C$ is in S, xPy is in S, and $y: C$ is not in S

3. $S \rightarrow_{T\exists} \{xPy\} \cup S$

   if $x: \exists P$ is in S, y is a new variable and there is no z such that xPz is in S

4. $S \rightarrow_{\bot} \{x: \bot\}$

   if $x: A$ and $x: \neg A$ are in S

A constraint system is *complete* if none of the above completion rules applies to it. A *clash* is a constraint of the form $x: \bot$. We say that S' is a *completion* of S, if S' is complete, and is obtained from S by applying the above completion rules.

In [SS91] it is shown that an $\mathcal{AL}$-concept C is satisfiable if and only the complete constraint system obtained from $\{x: C\}$ by means of the above rules does not contain any clash. Moreover, it is proved that computing the completion of $\{x: C\}$ is a polynomial task. By exploiting the features of the propagation rules, in [DLN91a] it is shown that checking subsumption between two $\mathcal{AL}$-concepts is also a polynomial task.

Concept languages can also be used as *assertional languages*, i.e. to make assertions on individual objects. Let $\mathcal{O}$ be an alphabet of symbols denoting individuals, and $\mathcal{L}$ be a concept language. An $\mathcal{L}$-assertion is a statement of one of the forms:

$$C(a), \quad R(a, b)$$

where C is a concept of $\mathcal{L}$, R is a role of $\mathcal{L}$, and a, b are individuals in $\mathcal{O}$. The meaning of the above assertions is straightforward: if $\mathcal{I} = (\Delta^{\mathcal{I}}, \cdot^{\mathcal{I}})$ is an interpretation, $C(a)$ is satisfied by $\mathcal{I}$ if $a^{\mathcal{I}} \in C^{\mathcal{I}}$, and $R(a, b)$ is satisfied by $\mathcal{I}$ if $(a^{\mathcal{I}}, b^{\mathcal{I}}) \in R^{\mathcal{I}}$.

A set Σ of $\mathcal{L}$-assertions is called an *$\mathcal{L}$-knowledge base*. An interpretation $\mathcal{I}$ is said to be a *model* of Σ if every assertion of Σ is satisfied by $\mathcal{I}$. Σ is said to be *satisfiable* if it admits a model. We say that Σ *logically implies* an assertion α (written $\Sigma \models \alpha$) if α is satisfied by every model of Σ.

Example 1 The knowledge base of fig. 1 represents the *Smith* family: `Male` and `Graduated` are primitive concepts, `CHILD`, `FRIEND` and `WORKSIN` are roles and `john`, `peter`, `mary`, `susan`, `factory` and `bank` are individuals.

It is easy to verify that Σ_{Smith} is satisfiable. Notice also that the addition of the assertion `Graduated(susan)` would make the knowledge base unsatisfiable, because Σ_{Smith} logically implies $\neg$`Graduated(susan)`. □

```
CHILD(john,peter), CHILD(john,mary), CHILD(mary,susan),
FRIEND(peter,susan), WORKSIN(susan,factory), WORKSIN(peter,bank),
Male⊓∀CHILD.∃WORKSIN(john),
Graduated⊓∃CHILD(peter)
∀CHILD.Graduated(peter),
¬Male⊓∀CHILD.¬Graduated(mary)
```

Figure 1: the *Smith* family knowledge base: Σ_{Smith}

```
johnCHILDpeter, johnCHILDmary, maryCHILDsusan,
peterFRIENDsusan, susanWORKSINfactory, peterWORKSINbank,
john:Male⊓∀CHILD.∃WORKSIN,
peter:Graduated⊓∃CHILD,
peter:∀CHILD.Graduated,
mary:¬Male⊓∀CHILD.¬Graduated,

john:Male, john:∀CHILD.∃WORKSIN,   (by →⊓)
peter:Graduated, peter:∃CHILD,   (by →⊓)
mary:∀CHILD.¬Graduated, mary:¬Male,   (by →⊓)
peter:∃WORKSIN, mary:∃WORKSIN ,   (by →∀)
maryWORKSINx,   (by →T∃)
peterCHILDy,   (by →T∃)
susan:¬Graduated,   (by →∀)
y:Graduated,   (by →∀)
```

Figure 2: The completion of Σ_{Smith}

The above propagation rules can be exploited for checking the satisfiability of an $\mathcal{AL}$-knowledge base Σ. The idea is that an $\mathcal{AL}$-knowledge base Σ can be translated into a constraint system, denoted by S_Σ, by replacing every assertion $C(a)$ with $a{:}\,C$, and every assertion $R(a,b)$ with aRb (see [H90]). One can easily verify that, up to variable renaming, only one completion, denoted $COMP_{\mathcal{AL}}(\Sigma)$, can be derived from S_Σ. Notice that the constraints in $COMP_{\mathcal{AL}}(\Sigma)$ regards both individuals in $\mathcal{O}$ and variables in $\mathcal{V}$ (e.g. the application of the $\rightarrow_{T\exists}$-rule to a constraint of the form $a{:}\,\exists R$ results in the new constraint aRx, where $a \in \mathcal{O}$ and $x \in \mathcal{V}$). In the sequel, we use the term *object* as an abstraction for individual and variable.

Example 2 The completion $COMP_{\mathcal{AL}}(\Sigma_{Smith})$ of the knowledge base Σ_{Smith} of example 1 is shown in fig.2 (where x and y are variables). Notice that the addition of the constraint `susan:Graduated` would result in a clash, confirming that $\Sigma_{Smith} \cup$ {`Graduated(susan)`} is unsatisfiable. □

In the sequel, if Z is either a knowledge base or a concept, we write dim_Z to denote the size of Z. Moreover, we use the term *subconcept* of a concept Z to denote any substring of Z that is a concept. For example, the subconcepts of $A \sqcap \forall R.A$, are: $A \sqcap \forall R.A$, A (first occurrence), $\forall R.A$ and A (second occurrence).

Theorem 2.1 *An $\mathcal{AL}$-knowledge base Σ is satisfiable if and only if $COMP_{\mathcal{AL}}(\Sigma)$ is clash-free. Moreover, $COMP_{\mathcal{AL}}(\Sigma)$ can be computed in polynomial time with respect to dim_Σ.*

Proof. For the first part see [H90]. With regard to the complexity, since both the selection and the application of the propagation rules can be clearly done in polynomial time, it is sufficient to show that the completion of Σ contains a number of constraints which is bounded by dim_Σ. Moreover, since the number of constraints is polynomially related to the number of objects, it is sufficient to show that the number of objects in the completion is bounded by dim_Σ. With regard to individuals, their number is obviously bounded by dim_Σ. With regard to variables, they are introduced in $COMP_{\mathcal{AL}}(\Sigma)$ by the constraints of the form $a\colon \exists R$ (where a is either an individual or a variable). The basic observation is that, due to the $\rightarrow_{\mathcal{T}\exists}$-rule, each constraint of the form $a\colon \exists R$ (where a is an object) in $COMP_{\mathcal{AL}}(\Sigma)$ creates at most one new variable z. It follows that the number of variables in $COMP_{\mathcal{AL}}(\Sigma)$ is bounded by the number of individuals times the number of subconcepts of the form $\exists R$ appearing in Σ, and therefore, is bounded by dim_Σ. □

Our use of $\mathcal{AL}$ as assertional language is justified by the above tractability result. Since the simple knowledge base $\{a\colon C\}$ is unsatisfiable if and only if C is unsatisfiable, it follows that the tractability of concept satisfiability for the assertional language is a necessary condition for the tractability of query answering. This observation allows us to rule out several possible extensions of $\mathcal{AL}$ as assertional language, such as $\mathcal{ALU}$, $\mathcal{ALE}$ ($\mathcal{AL}$ + unrestricted existential quantification), and $\mathcal{ALR}$ ($\mathcal{AL}$ + role conjunction) [SS91,DLN91a]. In [LS91b,LS91a] we show that the same holds for the language $\mathcal{ALO}$, obtained from $\mathcal{AL}$ by adding collections of individuals. It is interesting to observe that this result implies that both subsumption and query answering are co-NP-hard in CLASSIC [BBMR89], which is generally assumed to be a tractable concept language.

3 Enriching the language of the subsumer

The goal of this section is to show that, when using a tractable language for the subsumee, it is possible to enrich the language of the subsumer without endangering the tractability of the subsumption problem. To the best of our knowledge, this fact was never noticed before in the research on terminological reasoning. In particular, we study the subsumption problem (is C subsumed by D?) in the hypothesis that the candidate subsumee C is a concept of $\mathcal{AL}$, and the candidate subsumer D is a concept of a richer language, which we call $\mathcal{QL}$.

$\mathcal{QL}$ is an extension of $\mathcal{AL}$ with role conjunction, role chaining, collection of individuals, and qualified existential quantification on roles. Notice that the results reported in

[DLN91a] show that checking subsumption between two $\mathcal{QL}$-concepts is a co-NP-hard problem. The language is defined by the following syntax:

$$\begin{array}{lcl} C, D & \longrightarrow & A \mid \neg A \mid \top \mid \bot \mid \{a_1, \ldots, a_n\} \mid C \sqcap D \mid \forall R.C \mid \exists R.C \\ R, Q & \longrightarrow & P \mid P_1 \sqcap \cdots \sqcap P_m \mid R \circ Q \end{array}$$

where C, D are concepts, R, Q are roles, $P, P_1, \ldots, P_m$ are primitive roles, and $n, m \geq 1$.

Notice that concepts of the form $\{a_1, \ldots, a_n\}$ cannot subsume any $\mathcal{AL}$-concept. Their usefulness will be clear in next section.

A concept C is subsumed by D if and only if $C \sqcap \neg D$ is unsatisfiable, thus we can reduce subsumption between a $\mathcal{QL}$-concept D and an $\mathcal{AL}$-concept C to unsatisfiability of $C \sqcap \neg D$. In order to solve such an unsatisfiability problem, we have devised suitable completion rules for the so called $\mathcal{QL}$-constraint systems, i.e. constraint systems whose constraints have the forms: $x{:}\,C$, $x{:}\,\neg D$, and xRy, where C is an $\mathcal{AL}$-concept, D is a $\mathcal{QL}$-concept, and R is a $\mathcal{QL}$-role.

As a notation, we say that xRy *holds in* a constraint system S if: R is a primitive role P and $xPy \in S$, or R is of the form $P_1 \sqcap \cdots \sqcap P_n$ and $xP_iy \in S$ for $i = 1, \ldots, n$ or R is of the form $R_1 \circ R_2$ and exists z such that xR_1z, zR_2y hold in S.

The set of completion rules for $\mathcal{QL}$-constraint systems is constituted by the rules for $\mathcal{AL}$ presented in Section 2, together with the following rules, that take care of the constructs of $\neg D$.

5. $S \rightarrow_{\neg\sqcap} \{x{:}\,\neg C_i\} \cup S$

   if $x{:}\,\neg(C_1 \sqcap C_2)$ is in S, $i \in \{1, 2\}$, and neither $x{:}\,\neg C_1$ nor $x{:}\,\neg C_2$ is in S

6. $S \rightarrow_{\neg\forall} \{xRy, y{:}\,\neg C\} \cup S$

   if $x{:}\,\neg\forall R.C$ is in S, y is a new variable and there is no variable z such that $xRz, z{:}\,\neg C$ are in S

7. $S \rightarrow_{\circ} \{xR_1z, zR_2y\} \cup S$

   if $x(R_1 \circ R_2)y$ is in S, z is a new variable and there is no variable w such that xR_1w, wR_2y are in S

8. $S \rightarrow_{\mathcal{R}} \{xP_1y, \ldots, xP_ny\} \cup S$

   if $x(P_1 \sqcap \cdots \sqcap P_n)y$ is in S and $xP_1y, \ldots, xP_ny$ are not in S

9. $S \rightarrow_{unify} S[z/y]$

   if xPy, xPz are in S, and $S[y/z]$ is the constraint system obtained from S by replacing the variable z with y

10. $S \rightarrow_{\neg\exists} \{y{:}\,\neg C\} \cup S$

    if $x{:}\,\neg\exists R.C$ is in S, xRy holds in S, and $y{:}\,\neg C$ is not in S.

x:∀CHILD.Graduated⊓∃CHILD⊓¬∃CHILD.Graduated,
x:∀CHILD.Graduated⊓∃CHILD, (by $\rightarrow_{\sqcap}$)
x:¬∃CHILD.Graduated , (by $\rightarrow_{\sqcap}$)
x:∃CHILD, (by $\rightarrow_{\sqcap}$)
x:∀CHILD.Graduated, (by $\rightarrow_{\sqcap}$)
xRy, (by $\rightarrow_{T\exists}$)
y:Graduated, (by $\rightarrow_{\forall}$)
y:¬Graduated, (by $\rightarrow_{\neg\exists}$)
y:⊥ (by $\rightarrow_{\bot}$)

Figure 3: The completion of the $\mathcal{QL}$-constraint system of Example 3

Observe that due to the $\rightarrow_{unify}$-rule, the variables z's created to satisfy constraints of the form $x: \exists P$ are identified with the variables y's created by rules 6 – 8 to satisfy the constraints of the form $x: \neg\forall R.C$. This procedure, that is crucial for efficiency, is made possible by the fact that the existential quantification in $\mathcal{AL}$ is restricted, and hence all the properties imposed on such z's are also imposed on y. It follows that it not necessary to keep track of the z's in the resulting system.

Due to the form of the $\rightarrow_{\neg\sqcap}$-rule, several complete constraint systems can be obtained from $\{x: C \sqcap \neg D\}$. The following theorem establishes soundness and completeness of the above rules. Its proof derives from the above observation about the $\rightarrow_{\neg\forall}$-rule and from the results reported in [SS91].

Theorem 3.1 *Let C be an $\mathcal{AL}$-concept, and let D be a $\mathcal{QL}$-concept. Then $C \sqcap \neg D$ is unsatisfiable if and only if every completion of $\{x: C \sqcap \neg D\}$ contains a clash.*

It is easy to see that, starting from $\{x: C \sqcap \neg D\}$, in a finite number of applications of the rules, all the completions are computed, and easily checked for clash. It follows that the above propagation rules provide an effective procedure to check subsumption between D and C.

Example 3 Consider the problem of checking subsumption between the $\mathcal{QL}$-concept $D =$ ∃CHILD.Graduated and the $\mathcal{AL}$-concept $C =$ ∀CHILD.Graduated ⊓ ∃CHILD. It is easy to verify that C is subsumed by D. The complete constraint system obtained from $x: C \sqcap \neg D$ is shown in fig. 3:

With regard to the computational complexity, we now prove that such a procedure requires polynomial time.

Theorem 3.2 *Let C be an $\mathcal{AL}$-concept, and let D be a $\mathcal{QL}$-concept. Then the set of all the completions of the constraint system $\{x: C \sqcap \neg D\}$ can be computed in polynomial time with respect to $dim_{C \sqcap \neg D}$.*

Proof. Since both the selection and the application of the propagation rules can be done in polynomial time, it is sufficient to show that (*i*) every completion has a size which is polynomially bounded by $dim_{C \sqcap \neg D}$, and that (*ii*) the number of completions obtainable from $x : C \sqcap \neg D$ is bounded by $dim_{C \sqcap \neg D}$. With regard to the point (*i*), it is sufficient to show that the number of variables in any completion S' is bounded by $dim_{C \sqcap \neg D}$. In fact, notice that for each primitive role P and for each variable x, there exists at most one variable y such that xPy is in S'. It follows that the number of variables in S' cannot exceed the number of occurrences of primitive roles appearing in $C \sqcap \neg D$. With regard to the point (*ii*), since for each concept E appearing in D, only one variable x may exist such that $x{:}\neg E$ is in S', it follows that number of complete constraint systems that can be obtained from $\{x{:}\, C \sqcap \neg D\}$ is bounded by the number of occurrences of the symbol $\sqcap$ in D, and therefore is bounded by $dim_{C \sqcap \neg D}$. □

From all the above propositions it follows that checking subsumption between a $\mathcal{QL}$-concept and an $\mathcal{AL}$-concept can be done in polynomial time. This result will be exploited in next section to devise a query answering procedure.

4 Query answering

In this section we propose a query answering method that allows one to pose queries using the language $\mathcal{QL}$ to an $\mathcal{AL}$-knowledge base.

As we said in the introduction, a query has the form of a concept D, and answering a query D posed to the knowledge base Σ means computing the set $\{a \in \mathcal{O} \mid \Sigma \models D(a)\}$. In order to solve this problem, we consider the so-called *instance* problem: given an $\mathcal{AL}$-knowledge base Σ, a $\mathcal{QL}$-concept D, and an individual a, check if $\Sigma \models D(a)$. Since the number of individuals in Σ is finite, it is clear that our method can be directly used for query answering, in particular, by iterating the instance problem for all the individuals in Σ.

Since we aim at the tractability of query answering, we need to impose a certain restriction on the $\mathcal{QL}$-concepts used for formulating the queries. Such restriction is as follows: a $\mathcal{QL}$-concept Q is said to be *safe* if for every subconcept of Q of the form $\exists R.D$ that is not in the scope of a universal quantification, D does not contain any qualified existential quantification (i.e. concept of the form $\exists R.C$, where C is different from $\top$).

The above restriction, that is further discussed in Section 5, allows us to devise a polynomial algorithm for query answering. Throughout this section we assume to deal with queries represented by safe $\mathcal{QL}$-concepts.

Example 4 In order to show the expressive power of our query language, we present some queries that can be formulated using $\mathcal{QL}$. Given the $\mathcal{AL}$-knowledge base Σ_{Smith} of Example 1, consider the following queries:

All the individuals having at least one child that works only in the `factory` and who is `susan` or `peter` or `mary`:

$\exists$CHILD.({susan,peter,mary}$\sqcap\forall$WORKSIN.{factory})

All the individuals having a graduated grandchild:

$\exists$(CHILD$\circ$CHILD).Graduated

Is peter or john a bad father (someone that is not friend of any of his children) ?:

{peter,john}$\sqcap\forall$(CHILD$\sqcap$FRIEND).$\perp$ □

Most of the existing approaches to the instance problem are based on the notion of most specialized concept (MSC). The MSC of an individual a is a representative of the complete set of concepts which a is an instance of. However, a method merely based on the MSC would not work in our case, because of the presence of the qualified existential quantification in $\mathcal{QL}$. For example, in order to answer the query $\Sigma \models \exists P_1 \circ P_2.\{b,d\}(a)$, it is not sufficient to look at the MSC of a, but it is necessary to consider the assertions involving the roles P_1 and P_2 in the knowledge base. For this reason, our method relies on an ad hoc technique that, by navigating through the role assertions, takes into account the whole knowledge about the individuals.

Notice that if an $\mathcal{AL}$-knowledge base Σ is unsatisfiable, then any query to Σ gets a positive answer. As we said in Section 2, checking the satisfiability of Σ can be done in polynomial time by computing the completion of S_Σ.

In the sequel we make use of a function ALL that, given an object a, a $\mathcal{QL}$-role Q of the form $Q = P_1 \sqcap \ldots \sqcap P_n$, and an $\mathcal{AL}$-knowledge base Σ, computes the concept $ALL(a,Q,\Sigma) = C_1 \sqcap \cdots \sqcap C_m$, where $C_1,\ldots,C_m$ are all the concepts appearing in some constraint of the form $a\colon \forall P.C_i$ in $COMP_{\mathcal{AL}}(\Sigma)$ such that $P \in \{P_1,\ldots,P_n\}$. If no such a concept exists, we assume $ALL(a,Q,\Sigma) = \top$. In other words, $ALL(a,Q,\Sigma)$ represents the concept to which every object related to a through Q must belong, according to the assertions in Σ.

Our method heavily relies on the following theorem, which states necessary and sufficient conditions for an assertion to be logically implied by a knowledge base.

Theorem 4.1 *Let Σ be a satisfiable $\mathcal{AL}$-knowledge base, $a,a_1,\ldots,a_n$ be individuals, A be a primitive concept, R be a $\mathcal{QL}$-role, Q be a $\mathcal{QL}$-role of the form $P_1 \sqcap \ldots \sqcap P_m$, and D, D_1, D_2 be $\mathcal{QL}$-concepts. Then the following properties hold:*

1. $\Sigma \models \{a_1,\ldots,a_n\}(a)$ *if and only if* $a \in \{a_1,\ldots,a_n\}$*;*

2. $\Sigma \models A(a)$ *if and only if* $a\colon A \in COMP_{\mathcal{AL}}(\Sigma)$ *and*
$\Sigma \models \neg A(a)$ *if and only if* $a\colon \neg A \in COMP_{\mathcal{AL}}(\Sigma)$*;*

3. $\Sigma \models D_1 \sqcap D_2(a)$ *if and only if* $\Sigma \models D_1(a)$ *and* $\Sigma \models D_2(a)$*;*

4a. $\Sigma \models \forall Q.D(a)$ *if and only if D subsumes* $ALL(a,Q,\Sigma)$*;*

4b. $\Sigma \models \forall(Q \circ R).D(a)$ *if and only if* $\forall R.D$ *subsumes* $ALL(a,Q,\Sigma)$*;*

5. $\Sigma \models \exists R.D(a)$ *if and only if there is a b such that* aRb *holds in* $COMP_{\mathcal{AL}}(\Sigma)$ *and* $\Sigma \models D(b)$

Proof. The proofs of 1, 2 and 3 are straightforward. With regard to 4a, assume that D subsumes $ALL(a, Q, \Sigma)$, and suppose that $\Sigma \not\models \forall Q.D(a)$, i.e. $\Sigma \cup \{\exists Q.\neg D(a)\}$ is satisfiable. This implies that there is a model $\mathcal{I}$ of Σ with an element $d \in \Delta^{\mathcal{I}}$ such that d is related to a by means of Q, and $d \in (\neg D)^{\mathcal{I}}$; but, based on the definition of ALL, it follows that $d \in (ALL(a, Q, \Sigma))^{\mathcal{I}}$, contradicting the hypothesis that $ALL(a, Q, \Sigma)$ is subsumed by D. On the other hand, assume that $\Sigma \models \forall Q.D(a)$, i.e. $\Sigma \cup \{\exists Q.\neg D(a)\}$ is unsatisfiable, implying that $S_\Sigma \cup \{aQz, z\colon \neg D\}$ is unsatisfiable, where z is a new variable. Note that $S_\Sigma \cup \{aQz, z\colon \neg D\}$ is unsatisfiable if and only if $S_\Sigma \cup \{aQz, z\colon \neg D, z\colon ALL(a, Q, \Sigma)\}$ is unsatisfiable. Now, it is possible to verify that, since Σ is satisfiable and z do not appear in Σ, this may happen only because the constraint system $\{z\colon ALL(a, Q, \Sigma), z\colon \neg D\}$ is unsatisfiable, which means that D subsumes $ALL(a, Q, \Sigma)$. Similar arguments can be used for the proof of 4b.

With regard to 5, it is easy to verify that if there is a b such that aRb holds in $COMP_{\mathcal{AL}}(\Sigma)$ and $\Sigma \models D(b)$, then $\Sigma \models \exists R.D(a)$. On the other hand, assume that $\Sigma \models \exists R.D(a)$, and suppose that for no b_i ($i = 1, \ldots, n$) such that aRb_i holds in $COMP_{\mathcal{AL}}(\Sigma)$, $\Sigma \models D(b_i)$. This implies that for each b_i, $\Sigma \cup \{\neg D(b_i)\}$ is satisfiable. Now it is it is possible to prove that there exist n interpretations $M_1, \ldots, M_n$ such that for each $i \in \{1, \ldots, n\}$, M_i is a model of $\Sigma \cup \{\neg D(b_i)\}$, and $M_1 \cup \cdots \cup M_n$ is a model of $\Sigma \cup \{\forall R.\neg D(a)\}$, contradicting the hypothesis that $\Sigma \models \exists R.D(a)$. □

Based on the properties stated in the above theorem, we can directly develop a sound and complete algorithm for query answering. The algorithm, called $ANSWER$ and shown in fig.4. The following theorem states the soundness and the completeness of the algorithm. Moreover, it shows that the time complexity of the algorithm is polynomial.

Theorem 4.2 *Let* Σ *be a satisfiable* $\mathcal{AL}$*-knowledge base, a be an individual, and D be a* $\mathcal{QL}$*-concept. Then* $ANSWER(\Sigma, a, D)$ *terminates, returning true if* $\Sigma \models D(a)$*, and false otherwise. Moreover, it runs in polynomial time with respect to* dim_Σ *and* dim_D*.*

Proof. The correctness of the algorithm easily follows from Theorem 4.1. With respect to termination it is sufficient to observe that in any recursive call of the algorithm the actual parameter corrisponding to D decreases in length. With respect to complexity, notice first of all that the number of recursive calls that are issued during $ANSWER(\Sigma, a, D)$ is linear with respect to dim_D. Moreover both the subsumption check between D and $ALL(a, Q, \Sigma)$, and the check if aRb holds in Σ are polynomial with respect of the size of Σ and D. It follows that any recursive call issued during the execution of $ANSWER(\Sigma, a, D)$ performs a number of operations bounded by the size of D and the size of $COMP_{\mathcal{AL}}(\Sigma)$, which is polynomially related to dim_Σ. □

Algorithm $ANSWER(\Sigma, a, D)$
Input $\mathcal{AL}$-knowledge base Σ, object a, $\mathcal{QL}$-concept D;
Output one value in $\{true, false\}$;
begin
    case D **of**
        $\{a_1, \ldots, a_n\} : ANSWER := a \in \{a_1, \ldots, a_n\}$
        $A : ANSWER := a{:}A \in COMP_{\mathcal{AL}}(\Sigma)$;
        $\neg A : ANSWER := a{:}\neg A \in COMP_{\mathcal{AL}}(\Sigma)$;
        $D_1 \sqcap D_2 : ANSWER := ANSWER(\Sigma, a, D_1) \wedge ANSWER(\Sigma, a, D_2)$;
        $\forall Q.D_1 : ANSWER := D_1$ subsumes $ALL(a, Q, \Sigma)$;
        $\forall(Q \circ R).D_1 : ANSWER := \forall R.D_1$ subsumes $ALL(a, Q, \Sigma)$;
        $\exists R.D_1 : ANSWER := \exists b$ such that (aRb holds in $COMP_{\mathcal{AL}}(\Sigma)$)$\wedge ANSWER(\Sigma, b, D_1)$;
    endcase
end

Figure 4: The algorithm $ANSWER$

5 Limits to the tractability of query answering

In this section we consider some possible extensions of the query language and analyze their effect on the tractability of query answering.

The first observation regards the possibility of using the full power of qualified existential quantification. In [LS91a], we used the full language $\mathcal{QL}$ for query formulation, and we claimed that a polynomial algorithm similar to the one presented in Section 4 was sound and complete for query answering. Unfortunately, while the algorithm is sound, it is in fact not complete if the concept representing the query is not safe. The reason for that is that the proof of point 5 of Theorem 4.1 is no longer valid if we include nested qualified existential quantification in the query language. In fact, we prove in [LS91b] that query answering with full $\mathcal{QL}$ is co-NP-hard.

The second observation is that if C is equivalent to $\top$, then for any knowledge base Σ, it holds that $\Sigma \models C(a)$. It follows that query answering is at least as hard as the so-called ***top-checking*** problem for the query language, i.e. checking whether a concept is equivalent to the universal concept $\top$.

In some language, top-checking is intractable. We show in the following that this is the case already for $\mathcal{FLU}^-$, that is obtained from $\mathcal{FL}^-$ simply by adding disjunction of concepts.

The proof is based on a reduction from the satisfiability problem for a propositional conjunctive normal form (CNF) formula and the top-checking problem in $\mathcal{FLU}^-$.

Let Φ be the following transformation from a propositional CNF formula $\Gamma = \alpha_1 \wedge \cdots \wedge \alpha_m$ to an $\mathcal{FLU}^-$-concept $\Phi(\Gamma)$ (p_i denotes a propositional letter, l_i a literal, and α_i a clause):

$$\begin{aligned}
\Phi(p_i) &= \exists R_{p_i} \\
\Phi(\neg p_i) &= \forall R_{p_i}.A \\
\Phi(l_1 \vee \cdots \vee l_n) &= \Phi(l_1) \sqcap \cdots \sqcap \Phi(l_n) \\
\Phi(\alpha_1 \wedge \cdots \wedge \alpha_m) &= \Phi(\alpha_1) \sqcup \cdots \sqcup \Phi(\alpha_m)
\end{aligned}$$

For example if $\Gamma = (\neg p \vee q) \wedge (\neg q \vee r)$, then the corresponding $\mathcal{FLU}^-$-concept is $\Phi(\Gamma) = (\forall R_p.A \sqcap \exists R_q) \sqcup (\forall R_q.A \sqcap \exists R_r)$.

Theorem 5.1 *A propositional CNF formula Γ is satisfiable if and only if the corresponding $\mathcal{FLU}^-$-concept $\Phi(\Gamma)$ is not equivalent to $\top$.*

Proof. Assume that Γ is satisfiable, and let M be one of its models. Let $\mathcal{I}$ be the interpretation for $\Phi(\Gamma)$ defined as follows:

if $M(p_i) = true$ then $R_{p_i}^{\mathcal{I}} = \emptyset$,

if $M(p_i) = false$ then $R_{p_i}^{\mathcal{I}} = \{(d, d_{p_i})\}$ and $d_{p_i} \notin A^{\mathcal{I}}$.

It follows that for every literal l_k (positive or negative), if $M(l_k) = true$ then $d \notin \Phi(l_i)^{\mathcal{I}}$ and if $M(l_k) = false$ then $d \in \Phi(l_i)^{\mathcal{I}}$. Now, since in every clause α_j of Γ there is a literal whose value in M is true, it follows that in the corresponding concept $\Phi(\alpha_j)$ of $\Phi(\Gamma)$ there is at least one conjunct $\Phi(l_i)$ such that $d \notin \Phi(l_i)^{\mathcal{I}}$. Therefore, for every j we have that $d \notin (\Phi(\alpha_j))^{\mathcal{I}}$ thus $d \notin (\Phi(\Gamma))^{\mathcal{I}}$, and therefore $\Phi(\Gamma)$ is not universal.

On the other hand, assume that $\Phi(\Gamma)$ is not universal, and let $\mathcal{I}$ be an interpretation with an element $d \in \Delta^{\mathcal{I}}$ such that $d \notin (\Phi(\Gamma))^{\mathcal{I}}$. Let M be the truth assignment for Γ defined as follows:

$M(p_i) = true$ if $d \notin (\exists R_{p_i})^{\mathcal{I}}$,

$M(p_i) = false$ if $d \notin (\forall R_{p_i}.A)^{\mathcal{I}}$.

Now, since for each $\alpha_j = (l_1 \vee \cdots \vee l_n)$, $d \notin (\Phi(l_1 \vee \cdots \vee l_n))^{\mathcal{I}}$, it follows that either there exists h such that $l_h = p_i$ and $d \notin (\exists R_{p_i})^{\mathcal{I}}$, or there exists k such that $l_k = \neg p_i$ and $d \notin (\forall R_{p_i}.A)^{\mathcal{I}}$. Therefore, the clause α_j is satisfied by M. Since this holds for every clause of Γ, we can conclude that Γ is satisfiable. □

Theorem 5.2 *Query answering using $\mathcal{FLU}^-$ as query language is co-NP-hard, independently of the assertional language.*

Proof. Since the reduction Φ is clearly polynomial with respect to the size of Γ, the previous theorem shows that top-checking in $\mathcal{FLU}^-$ is co-NP-hard. The thesis follows from the fact that query answering is at least as hard as top-checking in the query language. □

Notice that the transformation Φ does not exploit the full power of $\mathcal{FLU}^-$, in fact the $\sqcup$ construct is used only at the upper level of the query. Indeed, the above theorem shows that answering queries of the form $C_1 \sqcup \cdots \sqcup C_n$, where each C_i is an $\mathcal{FL}^-$-concept, is co-NP-hard, independently of the assertional language.

The above result allows us to derive the intractability of several other concept languages as query languages. For example, the co-NP-hardness clearly extends to both $\mathcal{ALU}$, which is an extension of $\mathcal{AL}$ with disjunction of concepts, and $\mathcal{ALC}$, which extends $\mathcal{FL}^-$ with full negation (see [SS91]).

An analogous result can be achieved for the language $\mathcal{FL}$ [BL84]. To see why, notice that in $\mathcal{FL}$ a concept of the form $\forall(R : C).D$[1] is equivalent to $\top$ if and only if C is subsumed by D. It follows that top-checking in $\mathcal{FL}$ is at least as hard as subsumption, which is a co-NP-hard problem.

We have considered several constructs usually studied in terminological reasoning, namely, full qualified existential quantification, disjunction, full negation, and role restriction. We have seen that none of them can be used in the query language without sacrifycing tractability. This analysis does not cover the set of all the constructs usually considered for concept languages. For example, inverse roles and number restrictions (see [NS89]) have not been taken into account. This issue will be addressed in future work.

6 Conclusion

We have shown that it is possible to use a rich language for querying a concept-based knowledge base while keeping the deduction process still tractable. It is interesting to observe that this is one of the few "positive" results in the recent research on terminological reasoning, after a number of intractability results on reasoning about concepts.

In the future, we aim at addressing several open problems related to the use of concept languages as query languages. First of all, we aim at investigating the possible extensions of $\mathcal{QL}$ which have been discussed in Section 5. Moreover, we want to consider the case where the knowledge base includes a so-called terminology, i.e. an intensional part expressed in terms of concept definitions.

Second, we aim at improving the efficiency of our method for query answering; in fact, the goal of our work was to show that the problem is tractable, but several optimization of the algorithm are needed in order to cope with sizable knowledge bases. In particular, we think that a substantial improvement of the performance of the method can be gained by using the notion of most specialized concept (see [DLN90]) and by employing suitable techniques from the theory of query optimization in the relational data model.

Finally, we aim at considering more complex queries, such as queries constituted

[1] The $R : C$ construct has the following semantics: $(R : C)^{\mathcal{I}} = \{(a, b) \in \Delta^{\mathcal{I}} \times \Delta^{\mathcal{I}} \mid (a, b) \in R^{\mathcal{I}} \wedge b \in C^{\mathcal{I}}\}$.

by a set of atomic assertions, or queries asking information regarding the intensional knowledge associated to the individuals.

References

[BBMR89] A. Borgida, R. J. Brachman, D. L. McGuinness, L. A. Resnick. "CLASSIC: A Structural Data Model for Objects." *Proceeding of ACM SIGMOD-89*, 1989.

[BL84] R. J. Brachman, H. J. Levesque. "The Tractability of Subsumption in Frame-based Description Languages." *Proceedings of the 4th National Conference of the AAAI*, 1984.

[DHL91] F. Donini, B. Hollunder, M. Lenzerini, A. Marchetti Spaccamela, D. Nardi, W. Nutt. "The Complexity of Existential Quantification in Terminological Reasoning", DFKI-Report, DFKI, Postfach 2080, D-6750 Kaiserslautern, West Germany. Submitted for publication, 1991.

[DLN90] F. Donini, M. Lenzerini, D. Nardi, "An Efficient Method for Hybrid Deduction", *Proceedings of European Conference on Artificial Intelligence, ECAI*, 1990.

[DLN91a] F. Donini, M. Lenzerini, D. Nardi, W. Nutt. "The Complexity of Concept Languages." *Proceedings of the 2nd International Conference on Knowledge Representation and Reasoning, KR*, 1991.

[DLN91b] F. Donini, M. Lenzerini, D. Nardi, W. Nutt. "Tractable Concept Languages." *Proceedings of the 12th International Joint Conference on Artificial Intelligence, IJCAI*, 1991.

[H90] B. Hollunder, "Hybrid Inference in KL-ONE-based Knowledge Representation Systems." *German National Conference on Artificial Intelligence*, 1990.

[LS91a] M. Lenzerini, A. Schaerf. "Concept Languages as Query Languages." *Proceedings of the 9th National Conference of the American Association for Artificial Intelligence, AAAI*, 1991.

[LS91b] M. Lenzerini, A. Schaerf. "Concept Languages as Query Languages." *Technical Report*, Dipartimento di Informatica e Sistemistica, Università di Roma "La Sapienza".

[L81] H. J. Levesque. "The Interaction with Incomplete Knowledge Bases: a Formal Treatment." *Proceedings of 7th International Joint Conference on Artificial Intelligence, IJCAI*, 1981.

[Neb88] B. Nebel. "Computational Complexity of Terminological Reasoning in BACK." *Artificial Intelligence*, **34**(3):371–383, 1988.

[NS89] B. Nebel, G. Smolka. "Representation and Reasoning with Attributive Descriptions." IWBS Report 81, IBM Deutschland, Stuttgart, W. Germany, 1989.

[SS91] M. Schmidt-Schauß, G. Smolka. "Attributive Concept Descriptions with Unions and Complements." *Artificial Intelligence*, **48**(1):1–26, 1991.

Subsumption Computation in an Object-Oriented Data Model*

A. Artale, F. Cesarini, G. Soda
Dipartimento di Sistemi e Informatica - Università di Firenze
via S. Marta, 3 - 50139 Firenze - Italy
E-mail: Giovanni@IFIIDG.BITNET

Abstract

This paper deals with furnishing object-oriented database models with a paradigm of taxonomic reasoning, i.e., an inference capability characteristic of the knowledge representation systems developed within the KL-ONE family. This particular ability is based on subsumption computation, i.e., on deducing subset relationships among classes from their structural descriptions. We endow a data model developed in an object-oriented database environment with a formal framework for dealing with taxonomic reasoning. In particular, we define the model's intensional and extensional levels, and an interpretation function specifying their way of interacting; a subsumption algorithm is given and its soundness, completeness, and polynomial complexity are proven.

1 Introduction

In this paper, we examine a way of introducing some inference techniques typical of Knowledge Representation Systems in object-oriented data models, and we especially deal with taxonomic reasoning. This capability is present in the object-based knowledge representation models [19] that derive from the ideas expressed in KL-ONE [8]. The structure of the objects is described by means of a suitable language, and an external denotational semantics gives meaning to the terms used in the descriptions; the set of the objects whose structure conforms to a description is the object class defined by the description. Classes can be **defined** or **primitive**; the description of a primitive class specifies the conditions necessary for an object to belong to that class, while necessary and sufficient conditions are specified in

*This research was partially supported by CNR in the framework of "Progetto Finalizzato Sistemi Informatici e Calcolo Parallelo" - Sottoprogetto 5: "Sistemi Evoluti per Basi di Dati Obiettivo LOGIDATA+".

the case of a definite class. Deductive reasoning about object definitions is performed by means of subsumption and classification. **Subsumption** determines whether or not a class is subclass of another one on the basis of their descriptions; the concept of defined class is fundamental in such derivations, because it allows us to deal with descriptions able to express the extension associated with a class in a complete way. **Classification** puts class descriptions into a taxonomy by means of determining all the subsumers and subsumees of each class. In this environment, particular attention is given to studying relationships between the expressive power of the model definition language and the complexity of the related algorithms [7, 13, 14, 15, 17, 18] in order to obtain tractable systems.

On the other hand, some features commonly present in semantic and object-oriented database models [1, 3, 11, 12] refer to the possibility of dealing with objects of a structured type (i.e., objects with a complex structure) and managing ISA relationships (i.e., subset relationships among classes); furthermore, ISA relationships can only be stated among classes with type descriptions refining each other. These database systems could benefit by taxonomic reasoning in a number of applications. In conceptual schema design [5, 10], it can be used for finding all the ISA relationships that exist because of the way the classes are defined, whether or not there are any explicit statements present. It is then possible to control the whole schema's consistency and remove all cycles and empty classes from it. Schema minimality can also be assured by maintaining only direct links. At an extensional level, instances can be recognized and classified directly by the system. Furthermore, the use of taxonomic reasoning in query answering [4, 6] makes it possible to: 1) deduce relationships that are not mentioned in the query formulated by the user; 2) answer at both an extensional and intensional level; 3) optimize query execution.

As we previously mentioned, taxonomic reasoning strongly relies on the concept of defined class that is not usually present in object-oriented systems; as a matter of fact, the type description of a class only specifies necessary conditions, and therefore ISA relationships must be explicitly stated. From this point of view, we can say that object-oriented database models only consider primitive classes, while object-based knowledge representation systems have greater flexibility because they give a well-founded basis for managing both primitive and defined classes. In our study, we propose to introduce this feature in the object-oriented database field. If classes can be stated to be primitive or defined, then taxonomic reasoning can be usefully used for all the above mentioned purposes, at both an intensional and extensional level.

Some data models, such as CLASSIC [6] and CANDIDE [4], are developed directly in a Knowledge Representation System context, and, therefore, intrinsically possess this feature. On the contrary, in our study we consider a data model developed in an object-oriented data base environment, and endow it with the requirements for taxonomic reasoning. In particular, we consider the LOGIDATA+ data model [3] and give a formal framework for dealing with defined classes. The data model we consider was developed in the framework of a national project on advanced systems for databases. The LOGIDATA+ project aims at defining a deductive database system that extends the abilities of current database systems. The LOGIDATA+ data model is able to handle complex structures and represent ISA relationships between classes; its deductive ability is committed to its logical component, while an object-oriented component is used for structuring data at a static level. From this point of view, this model presents many advanced features (such as a variety of type constructors and the fact that it is both value- and object-based) that are also present in other recent models; see, for example, the last version of O_2 [12]. The introduction of taxonomic reasoning in LOGIDATA+ provides for a deductive capability that is limited with respect to some logical languages but that provides a well-founded inferential service with computational tractability that can be exploited for all the above mentioned features.

In our formalization, we deal with the LOGIDATA+'s features directly involved in subsumption computation and modify some definitions in order to fit our purpose; we call LOGIDATA* the data model object of our investigation.

In section 2, the LOGIDATA* model is illustrated; type and refinement definitions are given in section 2.1; in section 2.2, the intensional level is formally presented by means of a syntax for describing classes; in section 2.3, a description is given of the instance type managed by the system that is both object-based and value-based; the interpretation function defined in section 2.4 specifies the way the intensional and extensional levels interact. The subsumption algorithm is defined in section 3 in accordance with the semantic formalism previously introduced. Section 4 shows the soundness and completeness of the subsumption algorithm, and its polynomial complexity is discussed in section 5. We make our concluding remarks in section 6.

2 The LOGIDATA* model

The LOGIDATA* model substantially derives from LOGIDATA+; as a matter of fact, it is an adjustment of it in order to fit taxonomic reasoning.

The main structures of LOGIDATA+ are the following: *Functions*, *Relations* and *Classes*. The *classes* denote sets of *Objects*, each of which is identified by an *Object Identifier* (OID). The *functions* are used for defining relations among various classes, or among classes and their attributes, in order to associate procedures with classes and manipulate complex objects. *Relations* are tuples of values that may have a nested structure. Both tuples in relations and objects in classes can have complex structures obtained by repeatedly using the *tuple*, *set*, *sequence* and *multiset* constructors applied to both objects and values. Furthermore, *type names* are provided to simplify user statements. A complete description of the model can be found in [3].

In LOGIDATA*, we only deal with classes because we want to investigate the relationships existing between them, and the type system is based exclusively on set and tuple type constructors, because they are the most widely used, see, for example, O_2 [11, 12] and IFO [1]. The framework of our study refers to definite classes, i.e., classes whose type descriptor defines the necessary and sufficient conditions for an object value to belong to the class.

2.1 Schemata

We assume the existence of predefined and disjoint base types (such as string, integer, etc.). Let **B** be a countable set of base type names, **L** a countable set of labels, **C** a countable set of class names and **T** a countable set of type names; **B**, **C**, and **T** are pairwise disjoint sets. We have the following definition of type descriptor, or, briefly, type:

def: type

- -each base type name $\in$ **B** is a type;
- -each class name $\in$ **C** is a type;
- -each type name $\in$ **T** is a type;
- -if t is a type, then $\{t\}$ is also a type called **set-type;**
- -if $t_1 .... t_k$, with $k \geq 0$, are types and $l_1 .... l_k$ are distinct labels, then $(l_1 : t_1 ..... l_k : t_k)$ is also a type, called **tuple-type.** ♦

Let TYP() be a function from **T**$\cup$**C** to the set of type descriptors; this function associates to each type or class name a type that describes its structure. TYP() is such that for each symbol S$\in$**T**$\cup$**C**, TYP(S) is a tuple or set type descriptor.

A partial order among types is introduced according to the following refinement definition:

def: refinement among types

Type t is a **refinement** of type t', $t \leq t'$, if and only if:

R1.	$t \in \mathbf{T} \cup \mathbf{C} \cup \mathbf{B}$ and $t = t'$;
R2a.	$t \in \mathbf{T}$ and $TYP(t) \leq t'$;
R2b.	$t' \in \mathbf{T}$ and $t \leq TYP(t')$;
R2c.	$t, t' \in \mathbf{T}$ and $TYP(t) \leq TYP(t')$;
R3.	$t, t' \in \mathbf{C}$ and $TYP(t) \leq TYP(t')$;
R4.	$t = (l_1 : t_1 ..... l_k : t_k ...... l_{k+p} : t_{k+p})$, $t' = (l_1 : t'_1 .... l_k : t'_k)$ with $k \geq 0$, $p \geq 0$, and $t_i \leq t'_i$, for $i = 1, ..., k$;
R5.	$t = \{t_1\}$ and $t' = \{t'_1\}$, with $t_1 \leq t'_1$. ♦

Let **ISA** be a partial order among classes that satisfies the following requirement: if C1ISAC2, then TYP(C1)$\leq$TYP(C2). The **ISA** relationship represents a user-given inheritance hierarchy; C1**ISA**C2 is intended to mean that each object belonging to class C1 also belongs to class C2, i.e., class C1 is a subclass of C2.

Now we can give the definition of a LOGIDATA* schema:

def: LOGIDATA* schema

A LOGIDATA* schema is a four-tuple S=(**T**,**C**,TYP,**ISA**) where **T**, **C**, TYP and **ISA** are defined as above. ♦

With respect to other object oriented models, for example, O_2 [11, 12] and LOGIDATA+ [3] itself, the crucial point of the above refinement definition is R3. Point R3, together with the Interpretation definition given in sect. 2.4, allows us to characterize **ISA** relationships completely from a syntactical point of view, as will be shown in the following sections; this

```
<declaration> := <type-declaration> | <class-declaration>
<type-declaration> := TYPE <identifier> = <type-constructor>
<class-declaration> := CLASS <identifier> [ISA <class-id>+] : <type-id> |
          CLASS <identifier> [ISA <class-id>+] :<type-constructor>
<type-constructor> := <tuple-type> | <set-type>
<type> := <type-constructor> | <class-id> | <type-id> | <basic-type>
<tuple-type> := TUPLE <component>* END
<component> := <label> : <type>
<set-type> := SET OF <type>
<basic-type> := string | int | ......
<label> := <identifier>
<class-id> := <identifier>
<type-id> := <identifier>
```

<type-declaration> and <class-declaration> can't be defined recursively. "*" indicates zero or more ripetitions, "+" indicates one or more repetitions. Items enclosed in "[ ]" are optional.

Figure 1: LOGIDATA* syntax

means that user-defined **ISA** are merely short-hand notations for exploiting inheritance. On the contrary, object-oriented data models that consider user-defined **ISA** the only basis for a class hierarchy follow a different approach. LOGIDATA+ substitutes our point R3 with the requirement that an **ISA** be declared between the two classes; in O_2, a requirement analogous to our point R3 is only used for defining "all possible inheritance relationships which can occurr between database classes following their types" [12], i.e., in the framework of a type system and not for computing **ISA** relationships among classes.

2.2 Schema Definition Language

A LOGIDATA* schema can be defined by means of the syntax illustrated in figure 1. We note that we don't take any recursive definitions into account, in accordance with the approach usually used by the KRMs we refer to [16]. As far as <basic-type> is concerned, the actual base types depend on the implementation used.

The **ISA** clause allows the user to express *inheritance. Multiple inheritance* is allowed in the case of tuple-type classes, with some restrictions assuring type compatibility (see section 2.2.1 and 2.2.2); analogous restrictions could be introduced directly in the formal definition of the model [3].

We show some type and class definitions:
TYPE Date: **TUPLE** day:int month:int year:int **END**
CLASS Employee: **TUPLE** name:string birth_date:Date emp_code:string salary:int **END**
CLASS Project: **TUPLE** proj_code:string description:string **END**
CLASS Prj_team: **SET OF** Employee

CLASS Research_prj **ISA** Project: **TUPLE** associated_units: **SET OF** string **END**
CLASS Prj_leader **ISA** Employee: **TUPLE** specialization:string prj:Project budget:**TUPLE** prj_amount:int **END END**
CLASS Rsch_leader **ISA** Prj_leader: **TUPLE** prj:Research_prj **END**
CLASS Prj_manager **ISA** Employee: **TUPLE** secretary: Employee manages:Prj_team
budget:**TUPLE** prj_amount:int external_amount:int **END END**
CLASS Supervisor **ISA** Prj_leader Prj_manager: **TUPLE** budget:
TUPLE prj_amount:int external_amount:int budget_plan:int **END END**

We introduce an auxiliary function tp() for simplifying the following definitions. The input of **tp()** is a Class-name C or a Type-name T and the output is one of the following two strings: "tuple-type" or "set-type", according to the C or T description. In particular, given the descriptions:

CLASS C **ISA** C_1......C_n:<type>
TYPE T = <type>

function tp() takes the non-terminal symbol <type> into account; if <type> is a <type-id>, the description of <type-id> is examined.

2.2.1 Correct descriptions

The class descriptions using the **ISA** clause must verify some constraints in order for the type of the subclass elements to be compatible with the superclass type. We give the following definition of a *correct type description*, seen from a syntactical point of view.

def: correct type description

- t = B_i, with $B_i \in \mathbf{B}$ (t = <basic-type>):
  the description of t is correct.
- t = **TUPLE** l_1:t_1.......l_n:t_n **END**:
  the description of t is correct if $l_i \neq l_j$ $\forall i,j=1,.....,n$ with $i \neq j$ and each t_i is a correct type description.
- t = **SET OF** t':
  the description of t is correct if t' is a correct type description.
- **TYPE** t : t' (t = <type-id>):
  the description of t is correct if t' is a correct type description.
- **CLASS** C **ISA** C_1......C_n :<type> (C=<class-id>, <type>=<type-id>/<type-constructor>):
  the description of class C is correct if $tp(C_i) = tp(C)$ $\forall i=1,...,n$, and
  1) if tp(C) = "set-type"
  the description of <type> must be correct; furthermore, <type> must be a refinement of each C_i's type descriptor: <type>=TYP(C) $\leq$ TYP(C_i), $\forall i=1,.....n$;
  2) if tp(C) = "tuple-type"
  the description of <type> must be correct. Furthermore, for labels appearing in some C_i belonging to the **ISA** clause and in <type>, the type associated with such labels in <type> must be a refinement of the type associated with the omologous labels in C_i. Moreover, if the same label appears in more than one C_i with different types, then it must explicitly appear in <type> with a type that is the refinement of all the previous ones. ♦

For example, the definition of Rsch_leader is correct because the prj label appears in both Prj_leader and the tuple type associated with Rsch_leader, and Rsch_project ≤ Project. The definition of Supervisor shows an example of multiple inheritance; the budget label is present in Supervisor with a type that refines both types appearing in Prj_leader and Prj_manager, respectively.

In the following, we assume that each type is described in a correct way; furthermore, a set of type descriptions is a **schema definition** only if all the type and class names appearing in a type description are defined in a previous type- or class-declaration.

2.2.2 Function TYP() evaluation

Given a schema by means of the schema definition language, function TYP( ) can be evaluated by considering the class and type definitions. We distinguish the following cases:

1) In the case of a type name, TYP() associates the type descriptor defined by the expansion of the non-terminal symbol <type-constructor> appearing in the corresponding declaration with the type identifier;

2) In the case of a class name C such that tp(C)="set-type", TYP() associates the type descriptor defined by the expansion of the non-terminal symbol (<type-id> or <type-constructor>) appearing in the corresponding declaration with C;

3) In the case of a class name C such that tp(C)="tuple-type",

3.1) if the ISA clause is not present, TYP() associates the type descriptor defined by the expansion of the non-terminal symbol (<type-id> or <type-constructor>) appearing in the corresponding declaration with C;

3.2) if the ISA clause is present (**CLASS C ISA** C_1.....C_n: **TUPLE** l_1:t_1......l_k:t_k **END** or **CLASS C ISA** C_1.....C_n: T, with T <type-id> such that tp(T)="tuple-type"), then TYP(C) is a tuple-type with all the labels that appear in the superclass descriptions and in the tuple-type that describes the class. If the same label appears in the tuple-type that describes the class and in one or more superclass descriptions, then TYP(C) presents the label as it is defined in the tuple-type describing the class.

From the above definitions, it is clear that multiple inheritance is only allowed in a framework of "re-definition", and re-definition is subjected to some type refinement constraints; a similar approach also appears in O_2 [12].

We show some results obtained by the function TYP evaluation:

TYP(Date) = **TUPLE** day:int month:int year:int **END**

TYP(Rsch_leader) = **TUPLE** name:string birth_date:Date emp_code:string salary:int specialization:string prj:Research_prj budget:**TUPLE** prj_amount:int **END END**

TYP(Supervisor) = **TUPLE** name:string birth_date:Date emp_code:string salary:int prj:Project manages:Prj_team secretary:Employee budget:**TUPLE** prj_amount:int external_amount:int budget_plan:int **END END**

2.3 VALUES

While the type is the basic element of the intensional level of the Knowledge-Base, the basic element of the extensional level is the **value**.

Let D_i be the set of values associated with the base type name $\mathbf{B_i} \in \mathbf{B}$. Let **D** be $D=D_1\cup......\cup D_n$, $n\geq1$. Each element $v \in \mathbf{D}$ is a *basic value.* A particular B_i is *Nil*, whose only element is the *nil* value. We assume that sets D_i are pairwise disjoint.

Let **O** be a countable set of symbols called **object identifiers**; o is a generic object identifier.

def: value
The set Ω of *values* is:

$$\Omega = \mathbf{D} \cup \mathbf{O} \cup \mathbf{VT} \cup \mathbf{VS} \cup \{\text{nil}\} \qquad \text{where}$$

- **VT** is the set of **tuple-values**: $\mathbf{VT} = \{ v_t \mid v_t \text{ is a mapping, } v_t\text{:}\mathbf{L} \rightarrow \Omega\}$.
  We denote with $[l_1\text{:}v_1.........l_k\text{:}v_k]$ the total mapping defined on $\{l_1,........,l_k\}$ such that $v_t(l_i) = v_i \in \Omega$, $\forall i=1,.....,k$.
- **VS** is the set of **set-values**: $\mathbf{VS} = \{ v_s \mid v_s \subseteq \Omega\}$.
  A set-value is denoted by $\{v_1,......,v_k\}$, with $v_i \in \Omega$, $\forall i=1,....,k$. The symbol $\{\}$ denotes the empty set and {nil} the set whose elements are undefined. ♦

Since the objects are usually considered to be pairs of identifiers and values, we assume the existence of a function that assigns a value to an object identifier:
def: value assignment
value assignment is a total mapping, denoted by δ, that associates a value with each object-identifier: $\delta : \mathbf{O} \rightarrow \Omega$. ♦

In the following, whenever a set $\mathbf{V} \subseteq \Omega$ is considered, we assume that **V** is associated with a suitable value assignment; we call such a couple domain:
def: domain
A *domain* Σ is a couple $\Sigma = (\mathbf{V},\delta)$ such that $\mathbf{V} \subseteq \Omega$ and δ is a value assignment that associates a value $v \in \mathbf{V}$ with each $o \in \mathbf{V}$. ♦

Note: Both δ and v_t are defined as total mapping by assuming that 1) $\delta(o)$ = nil in the case that an object is created but is not assigned to any class because nothing is known about its properties; 2) $v_t(l)$ = nil for labels with an undefined value. The *nil* element makes it possible to treat uncomplete knowledge.

2.4 Interpretation

Assuming that the type descriptions are correct, we associate a *semantic* which regulates the relationship between the intensional and extensional level of the model with the LOGIDATA* syntax.

def: interpretation

Given a LOGIDATA* schema S, let Σ be a domain and I a function defined from type definitions in S to P(V)[1] (I: {type} $\rightarrow$ P(V)); I is an *interpretation function* of S over Σ if and only if:

1. If type = basic-type
$I(B_i) \equiv D_i, \forall B_i \in \mathbf{B}$

2. If type = tuple-type
I(tuple-type) = I(**TUPLE** l_1:t_1.............l_k:t_k **END**) =
$=\{v_t \in \mathbf{VT} \mid v_t$ is defined *atleast* on $\{l_1,...,l_k\}$ and $v_t(l_i) \in I(t_i) \cup \{nil\}\ \forall i=1,......,k\}$

3. If type = set-type
I(set-type) = I(**SET OF** t) = $\{v_s \in \mathbf{VS} \mid v_s \subseteq I(t) \cup \{nil\}\}$

4. If type = class-id
I(C) = I(**CLASS** C **ISA** C_1..................C_n : type) =
I(**CLASS** C : TYP(C)) = $\{o \in \mathbf{O} \mid \delta(o) \in I(TYP(C))\}$

5. If type = type-id
I(type-id) = I(**TYPE** type-id : type) = I(type). ♦

This semantics allows us to consider the ISA relationship as an inclusion between classes; as a matter of fact, the following theorem holds:

theorem: semantic coherence

If C is the class **CLASS** C **ISA** C_1.........C_n : <type>
and, therefore, $I(C) \subseteq I(C_1) \cap .... \cap I(C_n)$,
then I(**CLASS** C : TYP(C)) $\subseteq I(C_1) \cap .... \cap I(C_n)$.

Proof

The theorem is proven on the basis of function TYP(), interpretation definition, and refinement soundness by examining the different definitions that can be given of class C [2]. ♦

We note that each value can have more than one type [9]: when a value is of type τ, then it is of type τ', too, in the case that τ refines τ'. The interpretation of a tuple type strictly agrees with Cardelli's approach; a tuple is a subtype of another one if it is more fully defined. For example, if we have:

TUPLE name:string bdate:string **END**

TUPLE name:string bdate:string roles: **SET OF** string **END**

the latter tuple is a subtype of the former because it possesses the roles attribute besides name and bdate.

We show now an instance of the schema reported in section 2.2.

O = {#John,#Anne,#Al,#Marvin,#Roland,#Elain,#Robert,#LOGICDB,#OODB,#prj_team_1}

δ(#LOGICDB) = [prj_code:DB156 description:deductive_database]
δ(#OODB) = [prj_code:DB157 description:object-oriented_database
associated_units:{FI_univ, BO_CNR}]
δ(#John) = [name:John birth_date:[day:nil month:nil year:1963] emp_code:I17646
salary:1200]

---

[1] P(X) denotes the powerset of X.

δ(#Anne) = [name:Anne birth_date:[day:22 month:11 year:1964] emp_code:I76009 salary:1200]
δ(#Elain) = [name:Elain birth_date:[day:15 month:12 year:1967] emp_code:I76010 salary:1200]
δ(#Al) = [name:Al birth_date:[day:25 month:7 year:1964] emp_code:I76010 salary:2000 specialization:computer_science prj:#LOGICDB budget:[prj_amount:1500]]
δ(#prj_team_1) = {#John, #Al}
δ(#Marvin) = [name:Marvin birth_date:[day:17 month:2 year:1951] emp_code:I28032 salary:3000 secretary:#Anne manages:#prj_team_1 budget:[prj_amount:1500 external_amount:500]]
δ(#Roland) = [name:Roland birth_date:[day:2 month:6 year:1947] emp_code:I302 salary:4000 specialization:economics secretary:#Elain prj:#LOGICDB manages:#prj_team_1 budget:[prj_amount:1500 external_amount:500 budget_plan:3000]]
δ(#Robert) = [name:Robert birth_date:[day:7 month:5 year:1954] emp_code:I205 salary:2000 specialization:computer_science prj:#OODB budget:[prj_amount:1000]]

I(Project) = {#LOGICDB, #OODB}
I(Rsch_project) = {#OODB}
I(Employee) = {#John, #Anne, #Al, #Marvin, #Roland, #Elain, #Robert}
I(Prj_leader) = {#Al, #Roland, #Robert}
I(Prj_manager) = {#Marvin, #Roland}
I(Supervisor) = {#Roland}
I(Rsch_leader) = {#Robert}
I(Prj_team) = {#prj_team_1}

3 Computation of ISA relationships

In object-oriented data models, all the **ISA** relationships between classes must usually be stated by the user; the classes are considered to be primitive since the system is not able to deduce them automatically. Let us consider the following declarations:

CLASS Person : **TUPLE** name:string bdate:string **END**
CLASS Player : **TUPLE** name:string bdate:string roles: **SET OF** string **END**

If Player **ISA** Person is not explicitly stated, the system cannot deduce it even if the type of Player is a subtype of Person. The **ISA** relationship is not implied by the class structure; the user is responsible for the whole hierarchical organization.

The introduction of the Interpretation function allows us to formalize the concept of subsumption between classes and define an algorithm for its computation. In our framework, subsumption is equivalent to the **ISA** relationship because our interpretation function is totally based on necessary and sufficient structural characteristics: an object belongs to a class if and only if its structure satisfies the *structural conditions* imposed by the class description.

def: subsumption
Given classes C1 and C2, C2 *subsumes* C1 if and only if for each domain Σ and for each

ISA(C1,C2):

I1. If C1 = C2, then ISA(C1,C2) = TRUE <u>End.</u>
I2. Analysis of the clause **ISA** C_{11}......C_{1n} possibly present in the declaration of C1: if $\exists$i such that C_{1i} = C2 , i=1,...,n, then ISA(C1,C2) = TRUE <u>End.</u>
I3. If tp(C1) $\neq$ tp(C2), then ISA(C1,C2) = FALSE <u>End.</u>
I4. ISA(C1,C2) = TRUE if and only if REF(TYP(C1),TYP(C2)) = TRUE

(a): ISA Algorithm

REF(t,t') = TRUE if and only if:

R1. t $\in$ **T** $\cup$ **C** $\cup$ **B** and t = t' <u>End.</u>
R2a. t $\in$ **T** and REF(TYP(t),t')=TRUE <u>End.</u>
R2b. t' $\in$ **T** and REF(t,TYP(t'))=TRUE <u>End.</u>
R2c. t,t' $\in$ **T** and REF(TYP(t),TYP(t'))=TRUE <u>End.</u>
R3. t,t' $\in$ **C** and REF(TYP(t),TYP(t')) = TRUE <u>End.</u>
R4. $t=(l_1:t_1.....l_m:t_m)$, $t'=(l'_1:t'_1....l'_k:t'_k)$ with k,m$\geq$0 and m$\geq$k $\Rightarrow$ $\forall$ l'_i it must exists l_j such that $l'_i = l_j$ and REF(t_j,t'_i)=TRUE, for i=1,...,k and j=1,....,m <u>End.</u>
R5. t = $\{t_1\}$ and t' = $\{t'_1\}$, and REF(t_1,t'_1)=TRUE <u>End.</u>

(b): Refinement Algorithm

Figure 2: (a) ISA algorithm (b) Refinement algorithm

interpretation function I defined over Σ, I(C1) $\subseteq$ I(C2) holds. ♦

The above definition characterizes subsumption *semantically*; the following theorem, based on refinement, characterizes it *syntactically*.

theorem
Given classes C1 and C2, C2 *subsumes* C1 if and only if TYP(C1) refines TYP(C2).

Proof
In section 4, we show that the theorem is in accordance with the above subsumption definition. ♦

In accordance with this theorem, we define a subsumption algorithm that states whether or not C2 subsumes C1 on the basis of their descriptions; in other words, the algorithm deduces implicit **ISA** relationships. The algorithm, called **ISA algorithm** (illustrated in figure 2), is such that ISA(C1,C2)=TRUE if and only if TYP(C1)$\leq$TYP(C2).

The **ISA** algorithm operates on two classes; it performs some preliminary checks and then calls the **REF** algorithm that determines whether or not a type is the refinement of another one. The REF algorithm is the kernel of the process deducing implicit **ISA** relationships, and is based on the refinement definition given in section 2.1.

In particular, point R4 points out that the refinement between two tuple-types is independent of the label ordering. Point R2, subdivided into the R2a, R2b, and R2c cases, points out that *type-names* are only symbols associated with descriptions; therefore, it is necessary to expand them.

For example, in the case of
TYPE human: **TUPLE** name:string birth_date:string **END**
TYPE employer: **TUPLE** name:string birth_date:string emp:string **END**
CLASS Person: human
CLASS Married **ISA** Person: **TUPLE** married_with:Person **END**
CLASS Father **ISA** Person: **TUPLE** son:human **END**
CLASS Happy-Father **ISA** Person: **TUPLE** son:employer daughter:Married **END**
we have **ISA**(Happy-Father,Father) = TRUE .

4 Soundness and completeness

In this section, we only outline the steps performed for proving that the ISA algorithm is sound and complete. In particular, we illustrate the proof schema by referring to classes with tuple types explicitly given; the complete proofs can be found in [2]. Since cyclic references are not considered, it is possible to use the induction principle in the proofs.

The first theorem, proven by induction, shows the relationship existing between refinement and type semantics.

theorem: refinement soundness

Let t and t' be two types; if $t \le t'$, then for each domain Σ and for each interpretation function I over Σ: $I(t) \subseteq I(t')$.

Proof

We can examine the different cases arising from the nature of t and t':

a. $t \in$ **T** $\cup$ **B** $\cup$ **C** and t = t', then $I(t) \equiv I(t')$.

b. t = **TUPLE** l_1:t_1.........l_m:t_m **END** and t'= **TUPLE** l'_1:t'_1.........l'_k:t'_k **END** with t defined on *at least* all the labels appearing in t' and such that $\forall l'_i$, i=1,....,n, $\exists l_j$ for which $l'_i = l_j$ and $t_j \le t'_i$. Therefore, by induction, $I(t_j) \subseteq I(t'_i)$ and, because of point 2 of the interpretation function: $I(t) \subseteq I(t')$.

c. t = **SET OF** t_1, t' = **SET OF** t'_1 and $t_1 \le t'_1$: by induction $I(t_1) \subseteq I(t'_1)$; therefore, due to point 3 of the interpretation definition, $I(t) \subseteq I(t')$.

d. t and t' $\in$ **C** and TYP(t)$\le$TYP(t'), with TYP(t) and TYP(t') tuple-type or set-type. Due to points b. and c., I(TYP(t)) $\subseteq$I(TYP(t')); then, due to point 1 of the interpretation definition, $I(t) \subseteq I(t')$.

e. t and/or t' $\in$ **T**; assuming t_1=TYP(t) and/or t_1'=TYP(t'), we have $t_1 \le t_1'$, with t_1 and t_1' tuple-type or set-type. Due to points b. and c., $I(t_1) \subseteq I(t_1')$; then, for point 5 of the interpretation definition, $I(t) \equiv I(t_1)$ and $I(t') \equiv I(t'_1)$; therefore, $I(t) \subseteq I(t')$. ♦

At this point, it is easy to prove that the ISA algorithm is sound:

theorem: soundness of the ISA algorithm

Let C1 and C2 be two classes; if ISA(C1,C2)=TRUE, then $\forall\Sigma$ and $\forall$ Interpretation function I over Σ: $I(C1) \subseteq I(C2)$. ♦

The completeness of the REF algorithm and, consequently, of the ISA algorithm can be proven on the basis of the following two lemmas. The first lemma allows us to construct an interpretation function over a domain Σ in such a way that a particular value v_1 is in the interpretation of each tuple-type except for a few particular exceptions.

lemma 1

Let **L** be a set of labels, $l^o \in$ **L**; t a generic type; **V** a set of values. Moreover, let I be an interpretation function over $\Sigma=(\mathbf{V},\delta)$; v_1 and $v^o \in$ **V** such that:

- $v^o \in I(t)$
- v_1 is a tuple-value
- $v_1(l_i) = nil \ \forall l_i \in L$, for $l_i \neq l^o$
- $v_1(l^o) = v^o$.

Then, for every tuple-type x=**TUPLE** l_1:t_1 .... l_k:t_k **END**
if x *doesn't* contain l^o:u, with u such that REF(t,u)=FALSE, then $v_1 \in I(x)$.

Proof

There are two cases.

Case 1

The l^o label is not present in x.
Due to our construction, v_1 is surely defined over all the labels appearing in x: $v_1(l_i) \in I(t_i) \cup \{nil\} \ \forall i=1,...,k$. Then, for point 2 of the interpretation definition, $v_1 \in I(x)$.

Case 2

The l^o label is present in x:

x = **TUPLE** l_1:t_1 ..... l^o:s ..... l_k:t_k **END**

with s a general type such that $t \leq s$.
It is enough to prove that $v_1(l^o) \in I(s)$. Due to our construction, $v_1(l^o) \in I(t)$; but we have $I(t) \subseteq I(s)$ because $t \leq s$, then $v_1(l^o) \in I(s)$. Therefore, $v_1 \in I(x)$. ♦

lemma 2

For every type t, it is possible to define a domain $\Sigma=(\mathbf{V},\delta)$, an Interpretation function I, and an element $v \in$ **V** such that $v \notin I(t)$ ($v \neq nil$).

Proof

According to the type of t, we have various cases to examine. For example,

Case 1

$t = B_i \in$ **B** (t is a base type).
Let $D_i \cup D_j \subset$ **V** with $i \neq j$, $d_j \in D_j$. Since $I(t) = I(B_i) = D_i$, then $d_j \notin I(t)$.

Case 2

t = **TUPLE** l_1:t_1 .... l_k:t_k **END** (t is a tuple-type).
By induction, there are I^*, V^* and v^* such that $v^* \notin I^*(t_k)$. Let v_0 be a tuple-value defined over $\{l_1,.....,l_k\}$ with $v_0(l_k)=v^*$; $V = V^* \cup \{v_0\}$ (with $v_0 \neq v^*$); $I(s) \subseteq I^*(s) \cup \{v_0\}$ for every s. Then $v_0(l_k)=v^* \notin I(t_k)$; indeed, for the interpretation definition, $v_0 \notin I(t)$. ♦

Now we can prove the completeness of the refinement algorithm.

theorem: completeness of the REF algorithm

Let x and y be two types; if $I(x) \subseteq I(y)$, for every domain Σ and for every interpretation function I over Σ, then REF(x,y)=TRUE.

Proof

We prove that if REF(x,y)=FALSE, it is always possible to find a domain Σ and an

interpretation function I over Σ such that: $I(x) \not\subseteq I(y)$.
All the cases in which algorithm REF fails are examined, and a suitable Interpretation function is defined. ♦

It is now easy to prove that the ISA algorithm is complete.
theorem: completeness of the ISA algorithm
Given two classes C1 and C2, if $I(C1) \subseteq I(C2)$, for every domain Σ and for every interpretation function I over Σ, then ISA(C1,C2)=TRUE.

5 Computational complexity

As far as the complexity of ISA(C1,C2) is concerned, we can refer to the same considerations made in [15] about the intractability of terminological reasoning. As a matter of fact, ISA(C1,C2) performs subsequent expansions (except when points I1 and I2 of the ISA algorithm are satisfied) of both classes until it is possible to calculate ISA($\hat{C}1$,$\hat{C}2$), with $\hat{C}1$ and $\hat{C}2$ being *completely expanded classes.*

def: flat-type
A type t is a *flat-type* if has one of these structures:

1. $t=B_i$, with B_i base type;
2. t=**TUPLE** l_1:t_1............l_m:t_m **END** and t_i is a flat-type $\forall i=1,....,m$;
3. t=**SET OF** t_1 and t_1 is a flat-type. ♦

def: completely expanded class (c.e.c.)
A Class $\hat{C}$ is a *completely expanded class* if it has the following structure:

CLASS $\hat{C}$: <type-constructor>

where <type-constructor> is a flat-type. ♦

In other words, $\hat{C}$ is a completely expanded class if TYP($\hat{C}$) doesn't contain any type-names or class-names: every name is replaced by its description. We note that the transformation from C into $\hat{C}$ is possible in a finite numbers of steps because our language doesn't contain any recursive definitions (acyclic terminology).

The execution of ISA($\hat{C}1$,$\hat{C}2$) deals with expressions $\hat{C}$ of size $O(m^n)$, where m is the size of C [15], as the following example shows.
Let B_0 be a base type and:

CLASS C_1 : **TUPLE** l:B_0 l':B_0 **END**
CLASS C_2 : **TUPLE** l:C_1 l':C_1 **END**
....
CLASS C_n : **TUPLE** l:C_{n-1} l':C_{n-1} **END**

In this case the size of $\hat{C}_n$ is $O(2^n)$. This kind of complexity is common to models dealing with names; for example, Abiteboul and Hull [1] use a similar example for noting that the time complexity of the algorithm that assigns a derived type in IFO is exponential in the size of the schema.

Now we show that the subsumption between completely expanded classes is tractable.

def: depth of a flat-type

We indicate by d(t) the depth of a generic flat-type:

1. If t is a basic-type, then d(t)=0;

2. If t=**TUPLE** l_1:t_1........l_m:t_m **END**, then d(t)=1+max(d(t_i), with i=1,.....,m);

3. If t=**SET OF** t_1, then d(t)=1+d(t_1). ♦

def: size of a type

Let t be a flat-type and $\hat{C}$ a c.e.c.; then:

1. If t is a basic-type, then $|t|$=d(t)=0;

2. If t = **TUPLE** l_1:t_1..........l_m:t_m **END**, then $|t|=\sum_{i=1}^{m}(1+|t_i|)$;

3. If t = **SET OF** t_1, then $|t|=1+|t_1|$;

4. If t = $\hat{C}$, then $|\hat{C}|\equiv|$<type-descriptor>$|$. ♦

theorem: subsumption between completely expanded class is tractable

ISA($\hat{C}1$,$\hat{C}2$) runs in $O(|\hat{C}1|\times|\hat{C}2|)$ time.

Proof

Since ISA($\hat{C}1$,$\hat{C}2$)=TRUE if and only if REF(TYP($\hat{C}1$),TYP($\hat{C}2$))=TRUE, we prove that REF(TYP($\hat{C}1$),TYP($\hat{C}2$)) runs in $O(|\hat{C}1|\times|\hat{C}2|)$ time. We outline the proof referred to tuple types:

CLASS $\hat{C}1$: **TUPLE** l_1:t_1..........l_n:t_n **END**

CLASS $\hat{C}2$: **TUPLE** l_1':t_1'.........l_m':t_m' **END**

By induction on the depth of t_i' in $\hat{C}2$:

a. If d(t_i')=0 $\forall t_i$' in $\hat{C}2$ ($|\hat{C}2|$=m), then for each label l_i' the REF(TYP($\hat{C}1$),TYP($\hat{C}2$)) procedure must scan all the l_j appearing in $\hat{C}1$, looking for an equal factor; this is done in $O(|\hat{C}1|\times|\hat{C}2|)$ steps.

b. Let us assume that this is true for max({d(t'$_i$)})=k-1, then d(TYP($\hat{C}2$))=k.

c. Suppose max({d(t_i')$|$ t_i' is in $\hat{C}2$ for i=1,......,m})=k; then, for each label l_i' in $\hat{C}2$ we must find the corresponding l_j in $\hat{C}1$ (at most, in $|\hat{C}1|$ steps) and then recursively call REF(t_j,t_i'), with d(t'$_i$)≤k. By induction, this can be done in roughly $|t_i'|\times|t_j|\leq|t_i'|\times|\hat{C}1|$ steps. Therefore, the total effort for the m labels is:

$$\sum_{i=1}^{m}(|\hat{C}1|+|t_i'|\times|\hat{C}1|) = |\hat{C}1|\times\sum_{i=1}^{m}(1+|t_i'|) = |\hat{C}1|\times|\hat{C}2|.$$

6 Concluding Remarks

This study deals with introducing the automatic computation of ISA relationships into an object-oriented database model (in this case we use the LOGIDATA+ model) and in order to achieve this, we introduce the concept of defined classes as they appear in KRMs, and of subsumption computation. A suitable denotational semantics for the schema definition language is defined; we then define a subsumption algorithm and prove its soundness and completeness; we also prove that the algorithm is polynomial in the size of completely expanded class descriptions, while the expansion in the worst case can be exponential. By means of the subsumption algorithm we define, it is possible to classify classes, i.e., to build the ISA hierarchy that exists as a result of the class definitions. A prototype of a classifier is implemented in C-PROLOG under the MS/DOS operating system; it accepts some class definitions in accordance with the syntax described in section 2.2 and builds a proper taxonomy. Each new class is inserted into the taxonomy by determining its correct position and by rearranging the hierarchy in order to maintain only direct links.

Our study is carried out within a formal framework that could be considered a basis for further investigation. First of all, we are adjusting the model by introducing the possibility of dealing with both defined and primitive classes in a unique formal framework. Furthermore, it is possible to add some other features to LOGIDATA*, in order to obtain a more expressive data language and still maintain the subsumption computation and the associated taxonomic reasoning.

Some features usually present in KRMs that could be usefully introduced into LOGIDATA* refer to limiting the cardinality of the set of values associated with an attribute. For example, it is possible to state that the value of the PERSON's CHILD attribute is a set of at least two and at most four instances of BOY. The cardinality restrictions make it possible to implicitly define disjoint classes; for example, SINGLE, MARRIED and POLYGAMOUS subclasses of PERSON could be defined by restricting the cardinality of a SPOUSE attribute to zero, one and greater than one, respectively. In this case, classification is able to control disjointness between definitions and its propagation through the taxonomy [10]. As far as application on a schema definition level is concerned, the system can refuse contradictory classes, violating disjointness or, in general, cardinality constraints.

References

[1] S.Abiteboul, R.Hull. *IFO: A Formal Semantic Database Model.* ACM Transactions on Database Systems, vol.12, n.4, 1987.

[2] A.Artale, F.Cesarini, G.Soda. *Computation of ISA relationships in LOGIDATA+.* Rapporto tecnico LOGIDATA+ n.5/47, 1990.

[3] P.Atzeni, L.Tanca. *The LOGIDATA+ model and Language.* Workshop "Information Systems 90", Kiev, Oct. 1990, to appear in Lecture Notes in Computer Science, Springer-Verlag.

[4] H.W.Beck, S.K.Gala, S.B.Navathe. *Classification as a query processing technique in the CANDIDE semantic data model.* Fifth IEEE International Conference on Data Engineering, Los Angeles, 1989.

[5] S.Bergamaschi, C.Sartori, P.Tiberio. *On Taxonomic Reasoning in Conceptual Design.* Rapporto Tecnico CIOC CNR n.68, Bologna, 1990.

[6] A.Borgida, R.J.Brachman, D.L.MacGuinness, L.A.Resnick. *CLASSIC: a structural data model for objects.* Proceedings of the 1989 ACM SIGMOD International Conference on Management of Data, Portland, Oreg., June 1989.

[7] R.J.Brachman, H.J.Lévesque. *The tractability of subsumption in Frame-Based description languages*. AAAI National Conference on Artificial Intelligence, Austin, Texas, 1984.

[8] R.J.Brachman, J.G.Schmolze. *An overview of the KL-ONE knowledge representation system*. Cognitve science, 9, 1985.

[9] L.Cardelli. *A Semantic of Multiple Inheritance*. Semantics of Data Type, Lecture Notes in Computer science, Vol. 173, Springer Verlag, 1984.

[10] L.M.L.Delcambre, K.C.Davis. *Automatic Validation of Object-Oriented Database Structures*. proc. of int. conf. Data Engineering, 1989.

[11] C.Lécluse, P.Richard, F.Velez. *O_2, an Object-Orieted Data Model*. Proceedings ACM SIGMOD, 1988.

[12] C.Lecluse, P.Richard. *Modeling Complex Structures in Object-Oriented Databases*, proc. of PODS89, 1989.

[13] H.J.Lévesque, R.J.Brachman. *Expressiveness and tractability in knowledge representation and reasoning*. Computational Intelligence, 3:78-93, 1987.

[14] B.Nebel. *Computational complexity of terminological resoning in BACK*. Artificial Intelligence, 34(3):371-383, April 1988.

[15] B.Nebel. *Terminological reasoning is inherently intractable*. IWBS Report 82, September 1989.

[16] B.Nebel. *On terminological cycles*. Preprints of the Workshop on Formal Aspect of Semantic Networks, Two Harbors, Cal., February 1989.

[17] B.Nebel. *Reasoning and Revision in Hybrid Representation Systems*. Lecture Notes in Artificial Intelligence, n. 422, Springer-Verlag, 1990.

[18] P.F.Patel-Schneider. *Undecidability of subsumption in NIKL*. Artificial Intelligence, 39:263-272, 1989.

[19] P.F.Patel-Schneider. *Practical, Object-Based Knowledge Representation for Knowledge-Based Systems*. Information Systems, vol.15, n.1, 1990.

A Concise Presentation of ITL[1]

Nicola Guarino
National Research Council
Institute for Systems Dynamics and Bioengineering (LADSEB-CNR),
Corso Stati Uniti 4, I-35020 Padova, Italy
guarino@ladseb.pd.cnr.it

Abstract

ITL (Intensional Terminological Language) is a Prolog-based language derived from our previous work on DRL. Like LOGIN, it improves the expressive adequacy of Prolog by the introduction of a separate theory, which represents the sortal structure of the domain. This theory is linked to the object theory by a simple form of order-sorted unification. Differently from LOGIN, however, ITL sorts are not complex structures similar to KL-ONE concepts. The reason is that ITL is not based on generic descriptions: roles (we call them attributes) are represented as independent concepts, which contribute to the structure of more complex concepts through separate statements expressing necessary conditions, sufficient conditions or structural constraints. The result is a fine-grained terminological language, whose syntax resembles in some way OMEGA. Yet, differently from OMEGA, this language does not have the full power of first order logic. It has however an intensional semantics, which we consider as an important characteristic of terminological knowledge. In this paper we briefly discuss the rationale behind ITL, and present its major characteristics.

1 Introduction

ITL (Intensional Terminological Language) is a Prolog-based language derived from our previous work on DRL [11-12]. Like LOGIN [1] and – in some sense – LLILOG [25], it improves the expressive adequacy of Prolog by the introduction of a separate theory, which represents the sortal structure of the domain. This theory is linked to the object theory by a simple form of order-sorted unification. Differently from Login, however, ITL sorts are not complex structures similar to KL-ONE concepts [5]. The reason is that ITL is not based on generic descriptions: roles (we call them attributes) are represented as independent concepts, which contribute to the structure of more complex concepts through separate statements expressing necessary conditions, sufficient conditions or structural constraints. The result is a fine-grained terminological language, whose syntax resembles in some way OMEGA [2]. Yet, differently from OMEGA, this language does not have the full power of first order logic. It has however an intensional semantics, which we consider as an important feature of terminological knowledge. In this paper we briefly discuss the rationale behind ITL, and present its major characteristics. The

[1] This is an extended and revised version of a paper with the same title appeared on *ACM SIGART Bulletin, Special Issue on Implemented Knowledge Representation and Reasoning Systems*, vol. 2, no. 3, june 1991.

general ideas which have motivated the development of ITL are discussed in [14] and [15]. A preliminary formal account of the language is reported in section 7.

2. Desiderata

2.1 Expressive adequacy

- Ontological adequacy. In our opinion, *ontological adequacy* is a notion stronger than epistemological adequacy, as it is defined in [4]. That is, an ontologically adequate language has not only to account for the analytical relationships between concepts which exist in virtue of concept structures, but it must also be able to express knowledge about the single constituents of a concept. As discussed in [14], the basic requirements of an ontological adequate language are the following:
  - *Fine granularity:* the syntax of the language must have enough granularity to express knowledge in terms of ontological relations. Among other things, it is a first prerequisite for large scale knowledge integration (see [18], pp. 17-20).
  - *Intensionality:* while referring to constituents of concepts, it is very important to distinguish between intensional and extensional contexts. Moreover, another desirable aspect of intensionality is the absence of a-priori commitments about existence [17].
  - *Enforced semantics:* formal semantics of current knowledge representation languages usually accounts for a set of models which is *much larger* than the models we are interested in, i.e. real world models. As a consequence, the possibility to state something which is reasonable for the system but not reasonable in the real world is very high. What we need, instead, is a semantics which is *not neutral with respect to some basic ontological assumptions*.
- Incomplete knowledge. Besides ontological adequacy, a crucial requirement for our system is the possibility to express *partial terminological knowledge,* whereas most of current terminological languages are limited to either subsumption relationships between primitive concepts or complete concept definitions.

2.2 Cognitive adequacy

- Cognitive correspondence: according to [28], we want not only to be able to *express* the knowledge relevant to us, but also to reflect in some way its cognitive structure. As much as possible, we would like to exploit a simple english-like syntax in order to achieve this kind of correspondence.
- Economy and uniformity: we want to keep to the minimum the number of conceptual primitives employed by the system, avoiding the use of different primitives for conceptually similar entities (as it happens – in our opinion – for concepts and roles; see [28,19,20]). In this

respect, ITL is a *strongly uniform* system: most of the syntactic constructs introduced in recent KL-ONE-based languages can be easily emulated within the same uniform formalism.

- *Coherence*: for instance, we want the meaning of a slot to be the same independently of the frame where it is defined.
- *Discipline*: we want to *enforce* the development of ontologically well-founded KBs, exploiting linguistic considerations in order to encourage the use of simple, meaningful *names*.

2.3 Inferential adequacy

Inferential adequacy has not been the main issue in the development of ITL. Since the beginning of the work on DRL, what we had in mind was the basic inferential and retrieval capabilities of a Prolog interpreter, extended with a mechanism for reasoning about terminological knowledge, more or less in the spirit of LOGIN. This means that both negation and "reasoning by case" are excluded from our desiderata related to the inferential adequacy.

Concerning tractability, we have tried to be conscious of the main (negative) results regarding terminological logics, avoiding at the same time to sacrifice expressive power simply because of *worst case* intractability. Therefore we have decided to limit the language only where we had the feeling of getting into troubles even for reasonably common situations, concentrating ourselves on *efficient* algorithms for dealing with frequent queries.

3 Ontological assumptions

3.1 Knowledge objects

If we use logic to represent knowledge, we have first to decide the nature of our domain, i.e., the basic kinds of objects which may appear as arguments of logical relations. Since intensionality is among our desiderata, we cannot limit ourselves to so-called "individuals", as in the standard Tarskian framework. Therefore, the basic entities of ITL are the following[1]:

- *Concepts*, which may be *atomic concepts* (like *person* or *john*) or *derived concepts*, such as *boolean concepts* (*animal and thinking_being*), *attribute-concepts* (*phone of john*), or *compound concepts* (*good-grade*).
- *Classes*, intended as generic collections of concepts, and represented as Prolog lists (e.g., *[john, bob]*).

3.2 Kinds of knowledge

Various *relationships* may hold among concepts and classes. We distinguish *taxonomic* rela-

[1] Throughout the paper, we use italics to refer to ITL terms as well as to suggest attention to the reader. ITL expressions will be quoted in case of ambiguity.

tionships from other relationships. This distinction originates different *kinds of knowledge*.

- *Terminological knowledge*. In our opinion [13] terminological knowledge is *specialized knowledge* about *taxonomic relationships* between the domain objects of a logical theory. They include what are usually called the ***subsumption*** (***isA***) and the ***membership*** (*instanceOf*) relationships. In our case, the domain objects are concepts and classes, as sketched above. Terminological knowledge is represented within the Terminological Knowledge Base (TKB), which is the analogous of Frisch's sort theory [10].

- *Relational knowledge*. It is *general knowledge* about *arbitrary*, non-taxonomic relationships among domain objects. While expressing these relationships, we may refer to objects directly, by their name, or *indirectly*, by referring to the concepts of which they are instances. It is natural, in this case, to introduce sorted variables. Relational knowledge is represented within the Relational Knowledge Base (RKB), which is an order-sorted theory akin to Frisch's object theory.

Notice that no a-priori distinction is made between concepts and individuals. A concept may be *seen* as an individual if it participates to a membership relationship: a good example may be *teacher*, which may be a subconcept of *person* as well as an instance of *job*. What is provided by the language is not an a-priori distinction between the two types of entities, but a syntactical tool to distinguish between the two basic relationships. Within this framework, we may conventionally call *individuals* those objects which are instances of something but do not have instances on their own. No assumption is made about the number instances of a concept.

4 The ITL kernel

4.1 Terminological knowledge.

The two taxonomic relationships described above are represented in ITL by means of the same basic construct: *qualification*. A qualification is a form of *predication* expressing the fact that an object shares the properties inherent to a given concept. What is important is that this concept is not itself a predicate as usual, but appears as an argument of a two-place predicate analogous to the copula of natural language. We adopt for this predicate the symbol *"is a"*. Typical qualifications are those expressed by statements like *john is a student* or *any student is a person*. The first statement qualifies a *specific object* as a *student* (and is therefore a *specific predication*), while the second one qualifies a *generic object* as a *person* (and is therefore a *generic predication*). Generic objects are formed by a specific object preceded by a determiner, which can be the universal determiner *any* or the existential determiner *a*. The latter is however not considered in the present paper.

The syntax sketched above is remarkably different from the simple one used for instance in [10], where the sort theory is a first order predicate calculus with sort symbols acting as monadic predicate symbols, and resembles instead the syntax used in more powerful systems like OMEGA [2]. It has a number of non-standard features, which allow for a high granularity and a good cognitive adequacy. First, it is possible to quantify over concepts while keeping a first order syntax. Moreover, the presence of the determiner *any* makes it possible to distinguish between a membership and a subsumption relationship while using the same predicate symbol. In this way we reflect the homogeneity of the cognitive structure of natural language statements: we can state *any student is a person* homogeneously to *john is a student,* and ask *any student is a X* homogeneously to *X is a person:*

any student is a person.
john is a student.

:- *k(any student is a X).*
X=person.
:- *k(X is a person).*
X=any student;
X=john.

As we can see, queries are formulated by putting an ITL proposition as the argument of the meta-predicate *k*. Notice that two distinct queries (*isA* and *instanceOf*) are usually needed to get the two answers of the second query above.

Classes, introduced in section 3.1, are an important element of terminological knowledge. The reason for their introduction is that we want to be able to refer to collections of objects without being obliged to give them a name, i.e. conceptualize them. We want for instance to say that a certain task has been accomplished by John and Mary *together*, while each of them *contributed* to its accomplishment; another example may be the concise representation of a mutual symmetric relation between the members of a class, as in the statement *John, Mary and Bob are brothers* [26]. Classes are represented as Prolog lists[1], and may appear wherever a concept appears. For instance, we can state that *any [john, bob, mark] is a student,* or *any grade is a [a, b, c, d, f]*. Concepts can be associated to the classes which represent their extension by the *extensional equivalence predicate* ":=". For instance – referring to the example 2 below – with *good-grade := [a,b]* we state that the extension of the concept *grade* is completely known, while with *good-grade and bad-grade := []* we state that the intersection between the two extensions is empty. In this way we have therefore a means to distinguish between complete and incomplete knowledge about the extension of concepts.

Accordingly to our ontological assumptions, we can finally notice that – like OMEGA – ITL is an *amalgamated* language. This means that it allows one to state, within the same theory, that a concept is an instance of a meta-concept, and so on. For instance, we can state that *teacher is a job* and *[john, bob, mark] is a group* as well as *any teacher is a person* and *any [john, bob, mark] is a student.*

[1] In order to denote sets, they are rendered insensitive to permutation and duplication of elements by means of internal conversion into canonical form.

4.2 Relational knowledge

Qualification and extensional equivalence are the only predicates that appear within the TKB, which is limited to taxonomic knowledge. Generic relational knowledge is represented within the RKB, and takes the form of a set of arbitrary Prolog clauses, whose variables can be restricted to be instances of concepts appearing in the TKB. We represent these variables (which we call *qualified variables*) by preceding their name with that of a concept, followed by the colon operator. Examples of qualified variables are therefore *person:X*, or *[a,b,c]:Y*. The link between RKB and TKB is realized by order-sorted unification, within what Frisch [10] called substitutional approach to hybrid systems. In order to keep the order-sorted unification algorithm simple and efficient, qualified variables are not allowed to occur within arbitrary Prolog terms. The two examples below will make clearer the interaction between TKB and RKB.

Example 1: bikes (adapted from [9])

any bicycle is an ecologic_vehicle.[1]
any [b1,b2,b3,b4,b5,b6,b7,b8,b9,b10,b11,b12] is a bicycle.

has(bicycle:_, pedals).
owns(alan, b15).

:- k((has(ecologic_vehicle:X, pedals), owns(alan, X))).
X = b15.

The first two clauses represent the TKB, and the second two the RKB. The first subgoal od the query succeeds by unifying *ecologic_vehicle:X* with *bicycle:Y*, due to the first clause of the TKB. The unification result is *X=bicycle:Y*. It unifies with *b15* in the second clause of the RKB, by giving as a final result *X=b15*. Notice that, if we had used ordinary Prolog, the system upon failing to show *owns(alan, b1)* would have tried each bicycle individually.

Example 2: grades (adapted from [1])

any student is a person.
any [peter, mary] is a student.
any grade is a thing.
any good-grade is a good-thing.
good-grade := [a, b].
bad-grade := [c, d, f].

likes(peter, mary).
likes(person:_, good-thing:_).
got(peter, c).
got(mary, a).

---

[1] Just for syntactic sugar, we substitute sometimes *an* to *a*, and *the* to *any*. Notice however that the cardinality implication of *the* is not taken into account.

happy(person:X) if likes(X, Y), got(X, Y).
happy(person:X) if likes(X, Y), happy(Y).

:- k(a is a X).
X=good-grade;
X=grade;
X=good-thing;
X=thing.

:- k(likes(peter, grade:X)).
X=(good-thing and grade):_;
X=good-grade:_;
X=a;
X=b.

:- k(happy(X)).
X=mary;
X=peter.

Notice the use of compound concepts, formed by the Prolog standard operator "-". A built-in ITL axiom (A5, sect. 7) states that *any X-Y is a Y,* and therefore, as we can see by the first query, a good grade is also a grade and (being a good thing) a thing. The second query shows the effect of the unification of *grade:X* with *good-thing:_*, which makes it clear that the sort structure allows for what Cohn [7] calls *anonymous sorts*. In this way it can be showed that a unique most general unifier always exists.

5 Attributes in ITL

5.1 Roles, slots and attributes

The formalism presented in the previous section lacks the possibility of *structuring* terminological knowledge in ways different from the subsumption relationship between concepts. In particular, it lacks the possibility of expressing knowledge about the *components* of a concept. *Roles* have been introduced for this purpose within terminological languages, with the semantics of arbitrary binary relationships. We have argued elsewhere [15] that i) the term "role" is improper, since – according to the natural interpretation of the term – a concept like *bachelor* can be a role without being a component of anything, and ii) roles cannot have the semantics of arbitrary binary relations, since otherwise they lose their epistemological function, and behave exactly like slots. The counterpart of roles in ITL are *attributes*. As discussed in the cited paper, a necessary condition for attributes to be concept components is that they must be concepts themselves: ITL terms like *father* or *color* are both attributes *and* concepts, and an *ad-hoc* semantics interprets them as concepts with an associated binary relation.

By considering attributes as concepts, we satisfy our *desideratum* of uniformity, improving at the same time the *naming discipline*. For instance, commonly used slot names like *childOf*, *hasPart* or *children* cannot be considered as attributes, and, if possible, they have to be substituted with *father, part, child*. If it is not possible, it is a sign that the related information has to be considered as relational knowledge.

5.2 Attributes and values

Being a concept, an attribute represents a set of potential conceptual components of an object. For instance, the extension of *child* is the set of all possible children of somebody. Now, if the attribute *child* is defined for a given object *john, child of john* is still a concept, whose extension consists of the actual children of John. In ITL we say that it is an *attribute-concept*. Attribute-concepts (discussed in more detail in [14]) are a generalization of KL-ONE *RoleSets*, and are somewhat similar to *Qua Concepts* [8] proposed some time ago for KL-ONE systems, and subsequently abandoned.

The first consequence of this choice is *uniformity:* value attribution reduces to an "Instance-Of" relationship, while value restriction reduces to an "Is-A". In the first case we can state for instance that *bob is a child of john*, and in the second that *any child of john is a student*. Moreover, the introduction of the extensional equivalence predicate gives us complete freedom to distinguish between complete and incomplete knowledge about attribute values, and to express "role value maps" between attributes:

child of john := [bob].
child of john := [anne, bob]. (complete knowledge)
child of john := [].

bob is a child of john.
any child of john is a male.
any child of john is a [peter, bob, mark]. (incomplete knowledge)
any child of john is a child of mary.
child of john := child of mary.

We have seen that in ITL attributes are concepts, and also attribute-concepts are concepts. But what is the relationship between the two? It is natural to observe that, if *child* is a concept, then each instance of *child of john* must be a child. That is, the following *Attribute Consistency Postulate* holds: *any X of Y is an X*. Its fundamental consequence is *semantic coherence*, which appears among our desiderata.

5.3 Kinds of attribute-concepts

Attribute-concepts would be too poor if limited to attributes of *individuals*, as in the examples above. Due to the "amalgamated" nature of our language, we must however be careful when dealing with attribute-concepts related to specific objects like concepts or classes, since we have to distinguish a reference to the object as itself from a reference to its instances. We solve the ambiguity by the use of ITL determiners, which mark the second type of reference. Since we have two different determiners, we have to introduce three different kinds of attribute-concepts: one for specific references and two for the two kinds of generic references. They are presented below by using as an example the attribute *number*, which denotes the number of instances of a concept. Their formal semantics is given in Def. 7.10.

a) Attribute-concepts related to specific objects.

number of [[a], [b, c]] := [2].

b) Attribute-concepts related to generic objects.

We distinguish two cases:

b1) Union of all possible sets of attribute values. [1]

number of a [[a], [b, c]] := [1, 2].

b2) Intersection of all possible sets of attribute values.

number of any [[a], [b,c]] := [].
number of any [[a], [b], [c]] := [1].

To look at a more concrete example, let us consider the attribute-concept *phone of any cnr-employee:* supposing that CNR has just one common phone number (i.e., operator's number), the extension of this concept will be exactly that number, while the extension of *phone of a cnr-employee* will include also the office and home number(s) of each employee.

Being concepts, attribute-concepts themselves can have attributes. In this way it is possible to represent some of the "modalities" usually connected to RoleSets in a homogeneous way. For instance, if we represent with *[M..N]* the class of all integer numbers between *M* and *N* (included), the *number* attribute introduced above can be used to express number restriction:

number of car of john := [1].
the number of car of john is a [1..3].

Moreover, chains of attributes can be formed:

color of the car of john := [red].
number of car of an employee of cnr := [221].

Finally, the meta-attribute *attr* is used to state that an attribute is *defined* for a given object. For instance, in the previous example *color is an attr of the car of john* is supposed to hold due to the (omitted) declaration *color is an attr of any car*. For the sake of conciseness, attribute declarations will be omitted in the examples appearing in the present paper.

---

[1] Attribute-concepts of this kind correspond to KL-ONE Generic RoleSets.

5.4 Non-unit clauses, implicit subsumption and realization.

KL-ONE-like definitions can be expressed in ITL as a set of independent necessary or sufficient conditions: the former are represented as unit clauses, while the latter as non-unit clauses. This set of clauses is rather a *description* (in the sense of KRL [3] or OWL [21]) than a *definition:* it is not required to be complete, while it can allow for multiple, independent sufficient and/or necessary conditions. Within non-unit clauses a qualified variable (preceded, for readability purposes, by the determiner *a*) is used to represent the potential instances of the concept to be defined, which have to satisfy the condition(s) expressed in the body (see 4 and 7 in the example below):

Example 3: implicit subsumption (adapted from [24]):

(1) *any parent is a person.*
(2) *any parent_of_doctors is a parent.*
(3) *any child of a parent_of_doctors is a doctor.*
(4) *a person:X is a parent_of_doctors if any child of X is a doctor.*
(5) *any parent_of_lawyer_doctors is a parent.*
(6) *any child of a parent_of_lawyer_doctors is a lawyer and doctor.*
(7) *a person:X is a parent_of_lawyer_doctors if any child of X is a lawyer and doctor.*
(8) *:- k(any parent_of_lawyer_doctors is a parent_of_doctors).*
yes

The implicit subsumption relationship expressed by (8) is computed at preprocessing time in the following way. The only sufficient condition for *parent_of_doctors* is given by (4). The subgraph of the explicit *isA* relationship below *person* is explored looking for its most general subconcepts which satisfy the condition. *parent_of_lawyer_doctors* belongs to this subgraph because of (5) and (1), and satisfies the condition because of (6) and rule R4 (sect. 7.3.2).

Let us present now a more involved example, which shows the use of number restrictions and answers a query regarding the so-called "realization" of an individual. Notice the use of parentheses in place of attributes, which is necessary to distinguish the cardinality of, say, the set of leaders of some modern-team from the number of leader of a given modern-team (see sect. 7).

Example 4: realization (from [23]).

any man is a human.
any woman is a human.
man and woman := [].

any team is a set.
any element of a team is a human.
the (number of element) of a team is a [2..].
any leader of X is an element of X.

any leader is a human.
a set:S is a team if
any element of S is a human,
the (number of element) of S is a [2..].

the (number of element) of a small-team is a [..5].
a team:T is a small-team if the (number of element) of T is a [..5].

the (number of element) of a modern-team is a [..4].
the (number of leader) of a modern-team is a [1..].
any leader of a modern-team is a woman.
a team:T is a modern-team if
the (number of element) of T is a [..4],
the (number of leader) of T is a [1..],
any leader of T is a woman.

teamA is a team.
element of teamA := [mary, dick, john].
mary is a woman.
any [dick, john] is a man.
leader of teamA := [mary].

:- *k(teamA is a X).*
X=modern-team;
X=small-team;
X=team;
X=set.

Notice that even if the fact that *mary is a woman* were not given, *teamA* would still be a *small-team* since any of its elements is a human; in order to prove this, the fact that *any leader is a human* is crucial, but it cannot be expressed within current systems because *leader* would be a role and *human* a concept. As a final consideration regarding the way ITL deals with attributes, notice that attribute-concepts allow to express very simple definitions without resorting to sets of necessary/sufficient conditions. We can write for instance

grandparent of X := parent of a parent of X.

6 The practical value of intensionality

The use of determiners like *any* and *a* underlines the intended intensional semantics of the language: we can state that *any unicorn is a horse* without caring for the fact that, if no unicorn exists, its (empty) *extension* is also subsumed by the extension of any other concept (in other words, we do not want to infer *any unicorn is a cow*, or whatever else). Therefore, no a priori existential commitment is required, differently from what happens with current order-sorted approaches.

However, the practical value of intensionality is not bound to the absence of existential commitments, but to the possibility to distinguish between intensional and extensional references to *fine-grained* objects. For instance, there is an abundant literature on the need of intensional references for the representation of opaque contexts within verbs expressing propositional attitudes like "know". A classical, but still hard example for most logic-based formalisms is the following [22]:

Example 5: Mike's telephone number

phone of mike := [845251].
phone of mike := phone of mary.

knows(pat, phone of mike).
dials(pat, (phone of mike):_).

In the last statement, the second argument refers to a order-sorted variable, which is restricted to be an instance of the attribute-concept *phone of mike*. It is therefore an extensional reference, while that in the preceding statement is an intensional one. It is easy to see that *dials(pat, (phone of mary):_)* and *dials(pat, 845251)* follow, while *knows(pat, phone of mary)* does not.

However, we would like to stress that the practical need for intensionality is not limited to sophisticated linguistic applications, but plays a fundamental role for the representation of common-sense knowledge regarding change, causation and functional descriptions. Consider for instance the following examples:

replaced(keyboard of the macintosh of john).
repaired((keyboard of the macintosh of john):_).

increased(temperature of liquid#3).
controls(thermostat#21, temperature of liquid#3).
measures(instrument#47, temperature of liquid#3).

supports(shaft#14, load of structure#11).

causes(decrease of quantity of oil, increase of temperature of engine).

Notice that some of the intensionality problems present in the example above may be circumvented by using ad-hoc names like *increased_temperature* or *oil_lack*. The point is that this choice would *increase granularity*, making the task of large scale knowledge integration almost impossible, and sacrificing at the same time cognitive transparency.

7 A formal account of the TKB

The reason of this section is simply to give an unambiguous interpretation to the terminological expressions used in the paper. We shall limit ourselves to language used in the TKB, which will be called ITL$^-$. A detailed discussion of the formal properties of ITL will be given elsewhere [16]. The peculiarities of the semantics of attributes have been discussed, in isolation from the rest of the language, in [15].

7.1 Syntax.

Since the symbols used to form terms are not simply constants or variables, but can be constructed by using operators, we give first the definition of the alphabet and the rules to construct the basic *language objects*, then the rules to form *terms* by allowing variables within language objects, and finally the rules to write *formulas* by putting together terms, predicate symbols and logical connectives.

Definition 7.1. The *alphabet* of ITL$^-$ consists of the following disjoint sets of symbols:

(a) a set V of *variables;*
(b) a set C$^-$ of *atomic concepts*, which includes at least the special element **attr**;
(c) a set {**a**, **any**, **and**, **of**, ':', '-'} of term-forming operators. **of** and **and** are right-associative infix operators, while **any** and **a** (called *determiners*) are prefix operators. The relative binding is the following: '-' > **and** > **of** = **any** = **a** = ':'.
(d) a set P = {**is**, **:=**} of terminological predicate symbols, respectively called *qualification* and *extensional equivalence* predicates;
(e) the punctuation symbols ',', '(', ')', '[', ']'.
(f) a set {',', **if**} of connectives.

Definition 7.2. The set O of *language objects*, the set C of *concepts*, the set K of *classes*, and the set S=C∪K of *specific objects* are defined according to the following grammar, where symbols of the alphabet are in boldface and the sets of symbols defined above appear in italics.

<object>::= <specific_object> | <generic_object>.
<specific_object>::= <concept> | <class>.
<generic_object>::= <determiner>, <specific_object>.
<determiner>::= **any** | **a**.
<concept>::= <simple_concept> | <boolean_concept> | <compound_concept>.
<class>::= <simple_class> | <boolean_class>.
<simple_concept>::= *atomic_concept* | <attr_concept>.
<boolean_concept>::= <concept>, **and**, <concept>.
<compound_concept>::= *atomic_concept*, '-', <concept>.
<simple_class>::= '[', ']' | '[', <specific_objects>, ']'.
<boolean_class>::= <class>, **and**, <class>.
<attr_concept>::= *atomic_concept*, **of**,<specific_object> |
<attr_descr>, **of**, <generic_object>.

<specific_objects>::= <specific_object> | <specific_object>, ',', <specific_object>.
<attr_descr>::= *atomic_concept* | '(', *atomic_concept*, **of**, *atomic_concept*, ')'.

Definition 7.3. A *term* of ITL$^-$ is defined according to the following grammar (which refers to previous definitions):

<term>::= *variable* | <specific_term> | <generic_term>.
<specific_term>::= <specific_object> | <attr_conc_term>.
<generic_term>::= <determiner>, <specific_term_or_var>.
<attr_conc_term>::= *atomic_concept*, **of**, <specific_term> |
<attr_descr>, **of**, <generic_term>.
<specific_term_or_var>::= <specific_term> | *variable.*

Notice that the use of variables within terms is very restricted: boolean terms and classes cannot contain variables, in order to make possible their construction by starting only from atomic objects, avoiding in this way the risk of paradoxes. Moreover, variables cannot take the place of attribute descriptors within an attribute-concept term.

Definition 7.4. A *terminological theory* T is a collection of formulas of ITL$^-$. A *formula* of ITL$^-$ is defined as follows:

<itl_formula>::= <atomic_formula> | <non_atomic_formula>.
<atomic_formula>::= <qualification> | <ext_equivalence>.
<non_atomic_formula>::= **a**, <concept>, ':', *variable*, **is**, **a**, <concept>, **if**, <conditions>.
<qualification>::= <specific_term_or_var>, **is**, **a**, <specific_term_or_var> |
any <specific_term_or_var>, **is**, **a**, <specific_term_or_var> .
<ext_equivalence>::= <specific_term_or_var>, **:=**, <specific_term_or_var>.
<conditions>::= <atomic_formula> | <atomic_formula>, ',', <conditions>.

As we can see, non-atomic formulas are extremely limited, since they are designed to capture sufficient conditions only.

7.2 Semantics

The purpose of the non-standard semantics outlined below is to capture the ontological assumptions mentioned in sect. 3. The basic idea is that generic predication is not interpreted extensionally as set inclusion, but intensionally as a relation given a-priori in the interpretation structure. Analogously, specific predication is not simply the consequence of the extensional interpretation of concepts, but it is given a-priori, too. We have therefore two independent relations whithin the interpretation structure, called respectively *analytical subsumption* and *specific predication,* denoted by $\leq$ and ε. A further element of novelty is the relation ρ, which gives the relational interpretation of attributes, and is discussed in greater detail in [15].

Notation. In the following, sets of language objects are denoted with A, C, ..., while sets of domain elements with $\mathcal{B}$, $\mathcal{U}$; metavariables ranging over the domain of discourse with x, y, z;

metavariables ranging over language objects with a for atomic concepts, c for concepts, k for classes, s for specific objects, and x for arbitrary objects; metavariables ranging over (sub)terms with small Greek letters (α and β for specific terms, η for attribute descriptions, ξ for variables, τ for arbitrary terms); metavariables ranging over formulas or set of formulas with capital Greek letters.

Definition 7.5. An *interpretation* of a terminological language ITL^{-} is an ordered tuple I = $<\mathcal{B}, \leq, \varepsilon, \delta, \rho>$, where:

a) $\mathcal{B}$ is a non-empty set called the *intensional base of discourse*. The *universe of discourse* $\mathcal{U}$ is defined in terms of $\mathcal{B}$ as $\mathcal{U} = \mathcal{B} \cup \mathcal{X}$, where $\mathcal{X}$ is called the *extensional base of discourse* and is given as:

$$\mathcal{X} = \bigcup_{j>0} \mathcal{X}_j ,$$

with $\mathcal{X}_1 = 2^{\mathcal{B}}$ and $\mathcal{X}_j = \mathcal{X}_{j-1} \cup 2^{\mathcal{X}_{j-1}}$ for $j > 1$. The elements of $\mathcal{B}$ are called *entities*, while the elements of $\mathcal{X}$ are *sets*.

b) $\leq$ is a partial order on $\mathcal{B}$, such that $\Sigma = <\mathcal{B}, \leq>$ is a complete lattice. We adopt the symbols $\sqcup$ and $\sqcap$ for the join and meet operations on Σ. We denote with the symbol $\perp$ the least element of $\mathcal{B}$.

c) ε is a relation on $\mathcal{U} \times \mathcal{B}$ such that, for any $x \,\varepsilon\, y$ with $y \leq z$, $x \,\varepsilon\, z$.

d) δ is a total function from S into $\mathcal{U}$ called *denotation function*, such that:

d1. $\forall c \in C, \delta(c) \in \mathcal{B}$;

d2. $\forall k \in K, \delta(k) \in \mathcal{X}$;

d3. $\delta([]) = \{\}$; notice that $\{\} \neq \perp$, since $\{\} \in \mathcal{X}$ while $\perp \in \mathcal{B}$.

d4. $\forall s_1,...,s_n \in S, \delta([s_1,...,s_n]) = \{\delta(s_1),...,\delta(s_n)\}$.

d5. $\forall c_1,c_2 \in C, \delta(c_1$ **and** $c_2) = \delta(c_1) \sqcap \delta(c_2)$.

d6. $\forall k_1,k_2 \in K, \delta(k_1$ **and** $k_2) = \delta(k_1) \cap \delta(k_2)$.

e) ρ is a total function from C^{-} into $2^{\mathcal{U} \times \mathcal{U}}$ called *relational interpretation function*, such that, if $<x, y> \in \rho(a)$, then $<x, \delta(a)> \in \rho(\mathbf{attr})$.

Definition 7.6. Given a terminological language ITL^{-} and an interpretation **I**, an atomic concept $a \in C^{-}$ is called an *attribute* in **I** iff there exists an $x \in \mathcal{U}$ such that $<x, \delta(a)> \in \rho(\mathbf{attr})$.

Definition 7.7. The *extension* of a concept $c \in C$ in **I** is denoted with $\chi(c)$ and is given by the set $\{x \in \mathcal{B}.\ x \,\varepsilon\, \delta(c)\}$. A concept c and its denotation $\delta(c)$ are called *abstract* in I iff $\chi(c) = \{\}$. Notice that, for any $c \in C$, $\chi(c) \in \mathcal{X}$.

Definition 7.8. ε^* is a relation on $\mathcal{U}\times\mathcal{U}$ which takes into account, besides specific predication, the membership relations involving elements of $\mathcal{X}$, and is defined as follows. For any $<x,y>\in \mathcal{U}\times \mathcal{U}$, $x\varepsilon^* y$ iff one of the following cases holds:

1. $<x,y>\in \mathcal{U}\times \mathcal{B}$ and $x\varepsilon\, y$
2. $<x,y>\in \mathcal{U}\times \mathcal{X}$ and $x\in y$

We read $x\varepsilon\, y$ as "x is an instance of y", $x\in y$ as "x is an element of y", and $x\varepsilon^* y$ as "x is a y".

Definition 7.9. $\leq^*$ is a relation on $\mathcal{U}\times\mathcal{U}$ which takes into account, besides analytical subsumption, the set inclusion relations between elements of $\mathcal{X}$ and the extensional subsumption between elements of $\mathcal{B}$, and is defined as follows. For any $<x,y>\in \mathcal{U}\times \mathcal{U}$, $x\leq^* y$ iff one of the following cases holds:

1. $<x,y>\in \mathcal{B}\times \mathcal{B}$, $x\neq \perp$, and $x\leq y$
2. $<x,y>\in \mathcal{B}\times \mathcal{X}$, x is not abstract, and, for any $z\,\varepsilon\, x$, $z\in y$
3. $<x,y>\in \mathcal{X}\times \mathcal{B}$, $x\neq \{\}$, and, for any $z\in x$, $z\,\varepsilon\, y$
4. $<x,y>\in \mathcal{X}\times \mathcal{X}$ and $x\subseteq y$.

Definition 7.10. A *natural interpretation* of a terminological language ITL is a tuple N = $<\mathcal{B}, \leq, \varepsilon, \delta, \rho>$ which is an interpretation according to Definition 7.5, and satisfies the following further constraints on δ and ρ:

1. If $<x,y>\in\rho(c)$, then $y\,\varepsilon\,\delta(c)$.
2. $\mathcal{X}$(**a of** s) = $\{y.\ <\delta(s),y>\in\rho(a)\}$.
3. δ(**a of** s) = $\perp$ iff $<\delta(s),\delta(a)>\notin\rho(\mathbf{attr})$.
4. $\delta((a_1$ **of** $a_2)$ **of** s$)=\delta(a_1$ **of** a_2 **of** s).
5. $\delta(\eta$ **of a** s) = $\bigsqcup_{\delta(x)\varepsilon^*\delta(s)}\delta(\eta$ **of** x).
6. $\delta(\eta$ **of any** s) = $\bigsqcap_{\delta(x)\varepsilon^*\delta(s)}\delta(\eta$ **of** x).

Definition 7.11. Given a natural interpretation N of ITL, a *ground* atomic formula ϕ of ITL' is *satisfied* by N (written N |= ϕ) iff it satisfies the following rules:

1. N |= s_1 **is a** s_2 iff $\delta(s_1)\ \varepsilon^*\ \delta(s_2)$
2. N |= **any** s_1 **is a** s_2 iff $\delta(s_1) \leq^* \delta(s_2)$
3. N |= s_1 := s_2 iff either:
   - $\delta(s_1) \leq^* \delta(s_2)$ and $\delta(s_2) \leq^* \delta(s_1)$
   - there exist no x such that $x\ \varepsilon^*\ \delta(s_1)$, nor any y such that $y\ \varepsilon^*\ \delta(s_2)$. That is, s_1 and s_2 are either abstract concepts or empty classes.

For the sake of brevity, the satisfaction conditions for non-ground formulas are not given here.

7.3 Axiomatization.

7.3.1 Axioms.

A1. **any α is a α.** *(ISA reflexivity)*

A2. **any [] is a k.** *(empty class)*

A3. **any a of τ is a a.** *(attribute consistency)*

A4. **any (a_1 of a_2) of τ is a a_1.** *(consistency of composite attributes)*

A5. **any α-β is a β.** *(compound concepts consistency)*

7.3.2 Inference rules.

R1. $$\frac{\text{a } \alpha{:}\xi \text{ is a } \beta \text{ if } \Gamma \quad \Gamma[\xi/\tau] \quad \tau \text{ is a } \alpha}{\tau \text{ is a } \beta}$$ *(modus ponens)*

R2. $$\frac{\phi(\alpha \text{ and } \beta)}{\phi(\beta \text{ and } \alpha)}$$ *(AND commutativity)*

R3. $$\frac{\phi(\alpha \text{ and } (\beta \text{ and } \gamma))}{\phi((\alpha \text{ and } \beta) \text{ and } \gamma)}$$ *(AND associativity)*

R4. $$\begin{array}{c} \tau \text{ is a } \alpha \quad \tau \text{ is a } \beta \\ \hline\hline \tau \text{ is a } \alpha \text{ and } \beta \end{array}$$ if α and β are homogeneous[1] *(AND distributivity)*

R5. $$\frac{\phi(k)}{\phi(k')}$$, where k' is a permutation of k. *(class permutation)*

R6. $$\frac{\phi(k_1 \text{ and } k_2)}{\phi(k)}$$, where $k = k_1 \cap k_2$ *(class intersection)*

R7. $$\begin{array}{c} \alpha_1 \text{ is a } \alpha \quad \ldots \quad \alpha_n \text{ is a } \alpha \\ \hline\hline \text{any } [\alpha_1, \ldots, \alpha_n] \text{ is a } \alpha \end{array}$$ *(class subsumption)*

R8. $$\frac{\tau \text{ is a } \alpha \quad \text{any } \alpha \text{ is a } \beta}{\tau \text{ is a } \beta}$$ *(ISA transitivity)*

R9. $$\frac{\tau \text{ is a } \alpha}{\text{any } \eta \text{ of any } \alpha \text{ is a } \eta \text{ of } \tau}$$ *(referent specialization for attributes)*

R10. $$\frac{\text{any } \alpha \text{ is a } \beta}{\text{any } \eta \text{ of any } \alpha \text{ is a } \eta \text{ of a } \beta}$$ *(referent generalization for attributes)*

R11. $$\frac{\text{any } \alpha \text{ is a } \beta}{\text{any } \eta \text{ of a } \alpha \text{ is a } \eta \text{ of a } \beta}$$ *(attribute-concepts generalization)*

R12. $$\frac{\alpha \text{ is a } \beta}{\text{any } \eta \text{ of } \alpha \text{ is a } \eta \text{ of a } \beta}$$ *(attribute-concepts generalization)*

---

[1] That is, they are both either concepts or classes

R13. $\dfrac{\textbf{any } \alpha \textbf{ is a } \beta \quad \beta := [\,]}{\alpha := [\,]}$ *(inheritance of empty extension)*

R14. $\dfrac{\textbf{any } \alpha \textbf{ is a } \beta \quad \textbf{any } \beta \textbf{ is a } \alpha}{\alpha := \beta}$ (double line) if $\alpha, \beta \neq [\,]$ *(extensional equivalence)*

Example 7.1 Consider the following ITL theory:

(1) *any horse is an animal.*
(2) *any horned_animal is an animal.*
(3) *any cow is a horned_animal.*
(4) *horse and horned_animal := [].*
(5) *any unicorn is a horse and horned_animal.*

It is easy to show that the formalism outlined above allows us to draw the following valid inferences:

(6) *unicorn := [].* (5), (4), R13
(7) *any unicorn is a horse.* (5), R4
(8) *any [] is a [horse].* A2

while the following are not valid:

(9) *any unicorn is a cow.*
(10) *any unicorn is a [].*
(11) *any [] is a horse.*

Note first that (10) cannot be satisfied because of point 2 of Def. 7.11 and point 2 of Def. 7.9. As it is required for soundness, it cannot be derived from (6) because of the proviso on R14. In a similar way, (11) cannot be satisfied because of point 3 of Def. 7.9, nor can it be derived from (6) and (7) by using R14, because of its proviso.

8 Implementation notes

DRL, a precursor of ITL, has been implemented two years ago on Apple Macintosh™ under LPA MacProlog™ [11]. With various simplifications, it is currently being used by two Italian companies for applications regarding natural language understanding and conceptual analysis. A preliminary version of ITL has been implemented exploiting part of the code of DRL. The major reimplementation effort has regarded the use of an efficient data structure for the computation of the transitive closure of the subsumption relationship and for the order-sorted unification algorithm. This data structure is a generalization of what mentioned in [27], and allows to represent a node of a tangled taxonomy as a Prolog term, in such a way that sorted unification reduces to Robinson unification.

Acknowledgements

This research has been made in the framework of a special National project on Hybrid Systems, supported by the "Progetto Finalizzato Informatica e Calcolo Parallelo" of the Italian National Research Council. I am indebted to Pierdaniele Giaretta and Dario Maguolo for their precious suggestions regarding the formal semantics, and to Carlo Chiopris and Alberto Moscatelli for their substantial contribution to the algorithms used in the implementation. I would also thank, together with a couple of anonymous referees, Claudio Sossai and Nino Trainito for their insightful comments to preliminary versions of this work.

Bibliography

[1] Ait-Kaci, H. and Nasr, R. 1986. LOGIN: a logic programming language with built-in inheritance. *Journal of Logic Programming*, no. 3.

[2] Attardi, G. and Simi, M., 1986. A description-oriented logic for building knowledge bases. *Proc. of IEEE*, no. 10.

[3] Bobrow, D. G and Winograd, T., 1977. An Overview of KRL, a Knowledge Representation Language. *Cognitive Science* 1/77

[4] Brachman, R. J. 1979. On the epistemological status of semantic networks. In N. Findler (ed.), *Associative networks: representation and use of knowledge by computers*, Academic Press.

[5] Brachman, R. J., and Schmolze, J. G. 1985. An Overview of the KL-ONE Knowledge Representation System. *Cognitive Science* 9: 171-216.

[6] Brachman, R. J., Levesque, H. J., Reiter, R. (eds.) 1989. *1st Int. Conf. on Principles of Knowledge Representation and Reasoning*. Kaufmann.

[7] Cohn, A. G. 1987. A more expressive formulation of many sorted logic. *J. of Automated Reasoning*, vol. 3, no. 2.

[8] Freeman, M. W. 1982. The qua link. In J. G. Schmolze and R. J. Brachman (eds.), *Proc. of the 1981 KL-ONE Workshop*, pagg. 54-64, Jackson, New Hampshire, June 1982. BBN.

[9] Frisch, A. M. 1985. An investigation into inference with restricted quantification and a taxonomic representation. *SIGART Newsletter*, January.

[10] Frisch, A. M. 1989. A General Framework for Sorted Deduction: Fundamental Results on Hybrid Reasoning. In [6].

[11] Guarino, N. 1988. DRL: terminologic and relational knowledge in Prolog. In Y. Kodratoff (ed.), *Proc. of 8th European Conference on Artificial Intelligence (ECAI-88)*, Muenchen, August 1-5, 1988. Pitman.

[12] Guarino, N. 1988. Attributes and extensional equivalence in DRL. In B. Radig and L. Saitta (eds.), Proc. of the 3rd International Symposium on Methodologies for Intelligent Systems (ISMIS-88), Torino, October 12-15, 1988. North Holland.

[13] Guarino, N. 1989. Nature and structure of terminological knowledge: the DRL approach. *Proc. of the 1st Conf. of the Italian Association for Artificial Intelligence (AI*IA)*, Trento.

[14] Guarino, N. 1990. *What's in a Role: towards an Ontological Foundation for Terminological Logics*. Italian National Research Council, LADSEB-CNR Int. Rep. 06/90, June 1990.

[15] Guarino, N. 1991. Concepts, Attributes, and Arbitrary Relations: Some Linguistic and Ontological Criteria for Structuring Knowledge Bases. To appear on *Data and Knowledge Engineering*.

[16] Guarino, N. 1991. *A Formal Account of ITL*. In preparation.

[17] Hirst, G. 1989. Ontological assumptions in knowledge representation. In [6].

[18] Lenat, D. B., and Guha, R. V. 1990. *Building Large Knowledge-Based Systems: Representation and Inference in the Cyc Project*. Addison-Wesley

[19] Maida, A. 1984. Processing Entailments and Accessing Facts in a Uniform Frame System. *Proc. of AAAI-84*.

[20] Maida, A. 1987. *Frame theory*, in S. Shapiro (ed.), *Encyclopedia of Artificial Intelligence*. John Wyley.

[21] Martin, W. A. 1979. Descriptions and the Specializations of Concepts. In Winston & Brown (ed.), *AI: an MIT perspective*, MIT Press.

[22] McCarthy 1979. First order theories of individual concepts and propositions. In Machine Intelligence 9, Ellis Horwood.

[23] Nebel, B. 1990. *Reasoning and Revision in Hybrid Representation Systems*. Lecture Notes in Artificial Intelligence, vol. 422, Springer Verlag.

[24] Patel-Schneider, P. F. 1987. A hybrid, decidable, logic-based knowledge representation system. *Computational Intelligence* 3, pp. 64-77.

[25] Pletat, U., von Luck, K. 1990. Knowledge Representation in LILOG. In K. H. Bläsius, U. Hedstück and C. R. Rollinger (eds.), *Sorts and Types in Artificial Intelligence*, Lecture Notes in Artificial Intelligence, vol. 418, Springer Verlag.

[26] Shapiro, S.A. 1986. Symmetric relations, intensional individuals, and variable binding. *Proc. of the IEEE*, no. 10.

[27] Schmitt, P.H., Wernecke, W. 1990. Tableau Calculus for Order Sorted Logic. In K. H. Bläsius, U. Hedtstück, C.-R. Rollinger (eds.), *Sorts and Types in Artificial Intelligence*, Lecture Notes in Artificial Intelligence, vol. 418, Springer Verlag.

[28] Wilensky, R. 1987. Some problems and proposals for knowledge representation. University of California, Berkeley, Rep. UCB/CSD 87/351.

Distributed Disjunctions for LIFE

Rolf Backofen
DFKI GmbH
Saarbrücken

Lutz Euler
Universität Hamburg
Fachbereich Informatik — NatS

Günther Görz
Universität Erlangen-Nürnberg
Informatik 8 — KI

Abstract

PC-Life, a dialect of the LIFE language designed by Aït-Kaci, extends the original design by some features, the most important of which are distributed disjunctions. LIFE integrates the functional and the logic-oriented programming styles, and feature types supporting inheritance. This language is well suited for knowledge representation, in particular for applications in computational linguistics.

Keywords: Knowledge representation, AI software, inferences, natural language processing

1 Introduction

Aït-Kaci designed "LIFE" [4, 5], a language developed in an attempt to integrate the three most important programming styles: functional, logic-oriented and object-oriented programming. The functional programming style is defined by deterministic computations and first-classness of functional expressions of any order. A logic-oriented language like Prolog contains constructor terms upon which a unification operation is defined and uses a resolution-based theorem prover. The object-oriented style allows a hierarchy of classes containing objects to be specified. The properties of these objects can be inherited along the hierarchy. The most interesting new ideas in LIFE are the conception of feature types and the treatment of function evaluation in a logic-oriented programming language.

The concept of type in LIFE represents the core of a knowledge representation language upon which further concepts are imposed which serve as building blocks for the rest of this programming language. It is particularly well suited for application in computational linguistics because it offers such obvious advantages as that the same formalism can be used from syntactic processing up to semantics and pragmatics. It permits simultaneous accounting for constraints in different linguistic abstraction levels.

The main goal of the development of PC-LIFE (cf. Backofen, Euler, Görz [7, 8, 11]) was to explore the difficulties that occur in designing a language which combines the programming styles mentioned. PC-SCHEME was chosen as the implementation language for its simplicity and versatility in dealing with complex control structures. This lead to some minor differences to Aït-Kaci's LIFE: Firstly, it was natural to use a LISP-like syntax and user interface as opposed to LIFE's Prolog-like toplevel. Secondly, the functional part of the language is more like SCHEME than like any other "pure" functional language (e. g. ML [16]). This concerns questions of whether functions are of fixed arity, whether automatic currying is possible, whether arguments are passed by pattern matching, etc. The most important differences to Aït-Kaci's design of LIFE are that PC-Life contains closed types, atoms and atomic types. With respect to disjunctions it has a considerably larger expressive power because Aït-Kaci's LIFE admits only type disjunctions.

2 Outline of the Language Design

A program in PC-Life consists of the definition of a type hierarchy and definitions of functions and relations. These are loaded into an interpreter which in turn evaluates functional expressions interactively.

The data types of PC-Life consist of the types in the type hierarchy and of feature terms. The type hierarchy is a partial order on the elementary types on the SCHEME system (`number`, `string`, ...), which are called "atomic types", arbitrary user-defined types, a least element $\perp$ and a greatest element $\top$. The "values" of the SCHEME system (e. g. `42`, `"Deep Thought"`) are called "atomic values" and are also part of the type hierarchy. Atomic types are the only elements of the hierarchy that can semantically[1] be represented as the union of other types, also called *disjunctive types*.

A feature term can be regarded as an extension of first-order constructor terms with variable arity and fields labelled by name instead of position. It consists of a type entry, which is a type symbol, and any number of attributes or features, which are pairs of an attribute name and an attribute value which in turn is a feature term (subterm). Any subterm (including the outermost term) can be labelled with a variable. Use of the same variable at different places expresses a coreference constraint between corresponding subterms.

Any number of functional expressions are admitted at any place where a variable can occur. They may contain references to any variables in the feature term and in this way express functional constraints between subterms.

"Closed types" are a special kind of types which are used to model constructor terms of fixed arity: A feature term of closed type may have only attributes whose names are taken from a fixed list defined with the type.

The structured types of SCHEME lead to a special problem, in particular `pair` whose values are cons cells. Although it was tempting to use these as built-in constructors and to admit any feature term as part of these structures, this turned out to be impossible because the implementation of any feature term must contain extra information for internal management (eg to allow undoing of unification effects in the case of backtracking). So only atomic types and values are admitted as components of structured SCHEME types. Should the user need lists of feature terms, the only solution is to define a closed type `cons` with the attributes `head` and `tail`.

An important extension of the concept of feature terms is the introduction of disjunctions because they allow ambiguous information to be expressed. Therefore, at any place where a feature term can occur a set of feature terms is also admitted.

Integrating functions with types requires that functions may have feature terms as arguments and value, and also that feature terms may contain functional constraints between subterms. To provide full expressive power, functions may pass their arguments by pattern matching. Values

[1] In a set-theoretic semantics, cf. section 4.1

are derived by a unification operation on the actual and formal parameters that does not modify the former ones.

The integration of relations is described in detail in [6]. PC-Life uses a functional top-level where the function **prove**, which takes the application of a relation as its argument, is provided to use the relational part. Calling **prove** starts a resolution prover on this relation which yields the solutions one by one.

A second way in which relations may be used is that the user specifies the partial order of types in the type hierarchy by entering "$<$"-relations of types. In addition, it is possible to define a type as being a feature term of another type which obeys further relational restrictions. If a feature term of such a type is used in a unification it has to be *expanded*, ie, the definition of the type is unified with its feature term and the relational restrictions are added to the list of goals that remain to be proven.

An important advantage of integration is the treatment of evaluation of functional expressions which occur inside feature terms. They must be evaluated when a feature term is defined or unified to check whether the functional constraints are met. To cope with the problem that arguments of function applications may not be sufficiently specified to allow evaluation Aït-Kaci proposed the concept of *residuation*: Evaluation is interrupted and delayed until the arguments that caused the break are sufficiently specified. If disjunctions are used an evaluation may even be restarted several times from the same point with different argument values.

With respect to residuation we can differentiate between three classes of functions in PC-Life :

1. *System functions*, ie, functions of the underlying SCHEME system. They require that all of their arguments are atomic values and residuate on all other feature terms.
2. *Normal functions* accept all values as arguments and pass them using lambda binding. They cannot cause residuation.
3. *Pattern matching* functions residuate if an argument is not sufficiently specified to decide whether it is subsumed by the corresponding pattern.

3 Representation of the Type Hierarchy

Unification and the subsumption test for feature terms are important operations in PC-Life. These operations require calculation of the infimum (glb) of types or checking for "$\leq$"-relations in the type hierarchy. Straightforward implementations of the latter operations require exponential time (in the size of the type hierarchy). In [3] Aït-Kaci describes a coding approach that allows a much more efficient execution of these operations. The basic idea is to embed the partial order of types into a Boolean lattice which is implemented by bitvectors and the mentioned operations are implemented as bitwise logical operations. A coding function maps each type onto its bitvector which can be precomputed in polynomial time and its value for each type can be stored as the code of this type.

Aït-Kaci describes three related coding methods that preserve existent glbs. We have corrected and implemented the algorithm for "compact encoding" which results in an embedding with the following properties:

- The size of the code bitvectors lies between $\log_2 N$ (where N is the number of types) in case the hierarchy is already a Boolean lattice and $N-1$ in the worst case. The important case of the hierarchy being a binary tree leads to a code size of $N/2$.

- At least one lub is preserved, namely $\top$. Only in the case that the hierarchy is a boolean lattice all lubs are preserved. (This last property must hold for all embeddings that preserve glbs.)

Aït-Kaci suggested that type disjunction and negation can be implemented using this encoding, namely by implementing a lub operation by bitwise *or* and negation by bitwise *not*. However, considering the mentioned restrictions on the use of lub operations this results in incorrect semantics.

4 Feature terms with distributed disjunctions

4.1 The ψ-term calculus

Feature terms consist of a type entry, features and coreference constraints. A string of features is called a *path* or an *address*. Formally a feature term is a triple $\langle \Delta, \psi, \tau \rangle$ with Δ as the *prefix-closed* set of all addresses, a type function $\psi : \Delta \to \mathcal{T}$, which assigns a type to each address, and a tag function τ which associates a variable with each address. A feature term is called *inconsistent* iff its denotation is the empty set in all interpretations.

Feature terms come with a set-theoretic semantics which is described in detail in Aït-Kaci [2][2]. Feature terms can be understood as expressions of an attributive representation language that is basically an instance of feature logic. Features are interpreted as partial functions whereas in languages of the KL-ONE family they generalize to roles. It has been shown (cf. [14]) that this leads to undecidability of subsumption.

Feature terms defined so far allow too much redundancy, e.g., one can get equivalent feature terms by consistent variable renaming. Therefore Aït-Kaci introduced abstract objects, ψ-terms, as representatives for equivalence classes of feature terms which denote the same set of objects in every interpretation. In ψ-terms coreferences are expressed by a coreference relation $\mathcal{K}$. Two addresses are coreferent iff they are assigned the same variable. Therefore, a ψ-term is a triple $\langle \Delta, \psi, \mathcal{K} \rangle$ with a *right-invariant* coreference relation. A ψ-term must be *referentially consistent* which means that any address of a coreference class of $\mathcal{K}$ carries the same subterm. A ψ-term is consistent iff $\bot \notin \mathbf{Im}(\psi)$.

The *subsumption order* is a partial order defined on the set of ψ-terms. A ψ-term t_1 is subsumed by a term t_2 ($t_1 \sqsubseteq t_2$) iff in any interpretation $[t_1]^{\mathbf{I}}$ is a subset of $[t_2]^{\mathbf{I}}$. The subsumption relation can be calculated easily using the following syntactic conditions:

$$t_1 \sqsubseteq t_2 \iff (\Delta_2 \subseteq \Delta_1) \wedge (\mathcal{K}_2 \subseteq \mathcal{K}_1) \wedge \forall a \in \Delta_2 : [\psi_1(a) \leq \psi_2(a)].$$

The basic operation on ψ-terms is *unification*. The unification of two ψ-terms t_1 and t_2 combines the information contained in both terms yielding a term $t = t_1 \sqcap t_2$ with $[t]^{\mathbf{I}} = [t_1]^{\mathbf{I}} \cap [t_2]^{\mathbf{I}}$. Syntactically, unification is the process of computing the glb of the terms t_1 and t_2. The most difficult part of this computation is to determine the resulting coreference relation $\mathcal{K}$.

[2] A similar system is introduced in Smolka [15] and Nebel and Smolka [14].

The resulting term domain Δ is simply the union of all equivalence classes of $\mathcal{K}$, and the type of an address $a \in \Delta$ is the glb of all types of all addresses in $a/\mathcal{K}$ in both terms.

Because t is the glb of t_1 and t_2, $\mathcal{K}$ must be the smallest coreference relation containing $\mathcal{K}_1$ and $\mathcal{K}_2$. This is the right-invariant completion of

$$\mathcal{K}' = \bigcup_{n \in \mathbb{N}} (\mathcal{K}_1 \circ \mathcal{K}_2)^n$$

Taking the transitive closure $\mathcal{K}'$ of the composition of $\mathcal{K}_1$ and $\mathcal{K}_2$ means to join all equivalence classes of $\mathcal{K}_1$ and $\mathcal{K}_2$ which have an address in common.

ψ-terms are represented as structures built up of nodes. A node is a data structure with three entries: a type entry, a subnode entry which is a list of pairs consisting of features and corresponding values, and a coreference entry. The unification algorithm presented by Aït-Kaci in [6] descends recursively through both ψ-term structures. Nodes with the same address in both structures are merged by dereferencing them to a new node carrying the joined information. Dereferencing uses the coreference entry. Unification fails if $\perp$ results as a type entry for some node.

4.2 Including disjunctions

The unification of terms corresponds semantically to their intersection. To express the union of ψ-terms we introduce *disjunctions* which are sets of ψ-terms. The unification of disjunctions of ψ-terms is achieved by unifying all possible combinations of ψ-terms from both disjuncts.

Because of the problem of global coreferences, disjunctions cannot be simply admitted as feature values. Global coreferences are generated during unification if a coreference in one term involves an address which is not in the scope of the disjunctions actually looked up in the other term. For example, the coreference between l_1 and l_2 is global in the unification of

$$\begin{array}{l} top(l_1 \Rightarrow X \\ \quad\;\; l_2 \Rightarrow X) \end{array} \sqcap \; top(l_1 \Rightarrow \{+;-\}) \, . \tag{1}$$

The straightforward result of the unification

$$\begin{array}{l} top(l_1 \Rightarrow X : \{+;-\} \\ \quad\;\; l_2 \Rightarrow X : \{+;-\}) \end{array}$$

is incorrect, since it contains the term $top(l_1 \Rightarrow + \, , \, l_2 \Rightarrow -)$ as one possible extension, which is contradictory to the first unificand (see also Eisele and Dörre [10]). One possible solution is to expand the disjunction to the greatest common prefix of all addresses of a global coreference (cf. [10]). Because we want distinct ψ-terms to be able to share identical subterm this method cannot be employed. Instead we decided to use ***distributed disjunctions***. The fundamental idea behind distributed disjunctions is that the problem of global coreferences can be solved by naming disjunctions. So the result of (1) can be calculated in a straightforward manner because now both disjunctions occurring carry the same symbol. It only has to be guaranteed that in later unifications the same alternative of a named disjunction is chosen wherever the disjunction symbol occurs.

Because disjunctions can be nested, not only the pair consisting of a disjunction symbol and the number of the resp. alternative has to be remembered, but a whole set of those pairs. This leads to the notion of *context*. A context *con* is a set of pairs $\langle disj.symbol, alt.number\rangle$ satisfying the following condition: For any disjunction symbol d if there is a pair $\langle d,a\rangle \in con$ then there is no pair $\langle d,b\rangle \in con$ with $a \neq b$. Every node in a disjunctive ψ-term structure has a unique context which can be defined inductively:

- every subnode of a node n has the same context as n;
- every alternative of a disjunction named with d has a context which is extended by $\langle d, alt.number\rangle$.

We define a partial order on contexts and the compatibility of contexts:

- A context con_1 is *smaller* than a context con_2 iff $con_1 \subseteq con_2$.
- con_1 is *compatible* with con_2 iff $con_1 \cup con_2$ is a context.
  iff there is no disjunction symbol d with $\langle d,a\rangle \in con_1$, $\langle d,b\rangle \in con_2$ and $a \neq b$.

The fact that each node has a unique context can be translated into the formal definition of ψ-terms by associating a context to each address in the term domain. A disjunctive term domain is a family of domains $[\Delta_{con}]_{con \in \mathbf{Kon}}$ indexed by contexts, where **Kon** is the set of all possible contexts, and a family of type functions and coreference relations on these term domains. A disjunctive ψ-term, which we call a δ-term, therefore is a triple $\langle[\Delta_{con}],[\psi_{con}],[\mathcal{K}_{con}]\rangle$. The conditions a ψ-term has to satisfy must be slightly modified for δ-terms :

- $[\Delta_{con}]$ must be *weakly prefix-closed*: Every prefix of an address $a \in \Delta_{con}$ must be contained by a term domain $\Delta_{con'}$ with a smaller context con'. This can be motivated using the following example:

  In the term $top(l_1 \Rightarrow \{_{d_1} top\ (l_2 \Rightarrow t_1)\ ;\ t_2\})$ the address $l_1.l_2$ is an element of $\Delta_{\{\langle d_1,1\rangle\}}$. The prefixes ϵ and l_1 are of course in a term domain with smaller context.

- $[\mathcal{K}_{con}]$ has to obey *strong right-invariance*: For every context *con* the coreference relation $\mathcal{K}_{con}$ has to be right-invariant and any coreference of $\mathcal{K}_{con}$ has to be continued right-invariantly to all contexts con' with $con \subseteq con'$:

$$[a \in \Delta_{con} \wedge \langle a,b\rangle \in \mathcal{K}_{con}] \Rightarrow$$
$$\forall con', \forall v : [con \subseteq con' \wedge av \in \Delta_{con'} \Rightarrow \langle av, bv\rangle \in \mathcal{K}_{con'}]$$

  For example, the coreference $\langle l_1, l_2\rangle$ in the term

$$top(l_1 \Rightarrow X : \{_{d_1} top(l_3 \Rightarrow t_1)\ ;\ t_2\}$$
$$l_2 \Rightarrow X)$$

  must influence all coreference relations in all other contexts, eg $\langle l_1.l_3, l_2.l_3\rangle \in \mathcal{K}_{\{\langle d_1,1\rangle\}}$.

- There are additional conditions for $[\Delta_{con}]$ and $[\psi_{con}]$ which have more technical reasons and are left out here for simplicity.

As in the ψ-term calculus, the unification of δ-terms has primarily to compute the resulting family of coreference relations. This again is done by composition of coreference relations of the involved δ-terms. But this time the contexts by which the relations are indexed have to be considered, so that a composition sequence has the form

$$\mathcal{K}^1_{con_{i_1}} \Box \mathcal{K}^2_{con_{j_1}} \Box \cdots \Box \mathcal{K}^1_{con_{i_n}} \Box \mathcal{K}^2_{con_{j_n}}$$

As already mentioned, the object of naming disjunctions was to use the same alternative wherever the disjunction symbol occurs. The contexts of coreference relations within any sequence must be pairwise compatible. The sequence itself has a context *con* which is simply the union of all used contexts. A coreference relation $\mathcal{K}_{con}$ of the resulting δ-term is the union of all sequences with context *con*.

There are two kinds of disjunctions that can occur in δ-terms. ***Value disjunctions*** occur if disjunctions are allowed as feature values. A simple variant of these are disjunctions of atomic values. ***Attribute disjunctions*** constitute the second kind, as in the term

$$t = top(\quad a \Rightarrow + \quad \{_{d_1}\ b \Rightarrow -,\ c \Rightarrow +\ \}).$$

Our formalism supports both value and attribute disjunctions. Although the current implementation of the δ-term unification algorithm handles only value disjunctions, it can easily be extended to attribute disjunctions. In this case the management of the set of all defined features for every node — which is required to process closed types — is more complicated.

A δ-term is represented by a structure which is built up of δ-term nodes. A δ-term node is either a ψ-term node or a named disjunction whose list of alternatives consists of δ-term nodes internally. For possibly nested disjunctions the notion of ***disjunction tree*** is introduced. An alternative in a disjunction tree is a non-disjunction which can be reached by traversing the tree. The context of an alternative a relative to its root disjunction r is defined as $relcon(a, r) = con(a) \backslash con(r)$. It describes the path from r to the alternative a.

The unification algorithm for δ-terms is an extension of the unification algorithm for ψ-terms (see Aït-Kaci [6]). Again both δ-term structures are passed through all possible paths and all nodes reached under the same address are merged. ψ-term nodes are unified as before. In order to unify two disjunction trees, the algorithm determines all alternatives of the first tree together with their relative context. Every alternative is then unified with all alternatives of the second disjunction tree whose relative contexts are compatible to its relative context. In addition, every alternative a of both disjunction trees is bound to a disjunction tree b_a containing all results of unifications involving a. Therefore every alternative of b_a is an element $a \sqcap a'$ with an appropriate alternative a'. The relative context of $a \sqcap a'$ is $relcon(a \sqcap a', a) = con(a') \backslash con(a)$, so that the equation $con(a \sqcap a') = con(a) \cup con(a')$ holds.

Although contexts are only partially ordered by set inclusion, a disjunction tree defines a total ordering on the relative contexts of its nodes. The unification algorithm processes all alternatives in ascending order. This also holds for every alternative of a binding tree b_a. So we can build up the binding tree successively: At the first unification involving the alternative a b_a is built up to the relative context of $a \sqcap a'$. During all further unifications b_a is always extended at the leaves (see also Fig. 1).

Determining consistency is somewhat more costly for δ-terms than for ψ-term structures. A ψ-term node is inconsistent if its type entry is $\bot$ or if there exists a subterm which is inconsistent.

$$\{_{d_1} t_1; t_2\} \sqcap \{_{d_2} \{_{d_3} \{_{d_1} t'_1; t'_2\}; t'_3\}; t'_4\}$$

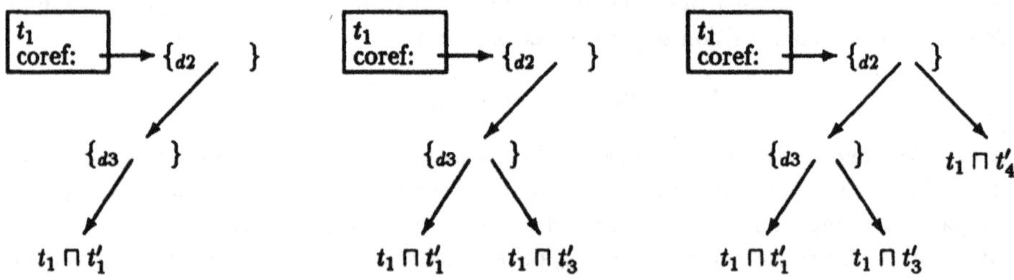

Figure 1: This example shows the successive construction of b_{t_1}. The nodes $t_1 \sqcap t'_i$ are also elements of $b_{ti'}$, eg t'_1 is bound to $t_1 \sqcap t'_1$ thus completing the merging of t_1 and t'_1 in context $\{\langle d_1, 1\rangle; \langle d_2, 1\rangle; \langle d_3, 1\rangle\}$.

A disjunction is inconsistent if all alternatives are inconsistent. Because disjunctions may be distributed, there may be inconsistencies which cannot be detected locally. For example the following term is inconsistent:

$$\begin{aligned} top(l_1 \Rightarrow & \ \{_{d_1} \bot; \{_{d_2} \bot; t_1\}\} \\ l_2 \Rightarrow & \ \{_{d_2} t_2; \{_{d_1} t_3; \bot\}\}) \end{aligned}$$

Therefore all inconsistent contexts must be stored globally.

A detailed description of the δ-term-calculus is given in [8]. Similar systems using distributed disjunctions can be found in Dörre and Eisele [9], and in Maxwell and Kaplan [13].

We see two advantages of our approach compared to Dörre and Eisele's: (1) Their formalism does not treat attribute disjunctions. (2) In our system the unification of disjunctions is defined more abstractly, in that the method of finding appropriate disjunction alternatives is left unspecified, whereas in their system it is not expressed separately but is part of the rewriting rules.

Maxwell and Kaplan provide a general method to extend feature systems into systems with named disjunctions. Every part of the resulting feature structure carries its own context, and rewriting rules used by the original system are translated into a contexted version which rewrites both the context and this part. Because there is no explicit representation of the relation between a context and its corresponding feature structures, the following inefficiencies arise: During unification of feature structures parts are unified although they carry incompatible contexts, and when components with the same context are rewritten a new context is calculated unnecessarily. Therefore, efficient unification algorithms for non-disjunctive feature structures cannot be used.

A remark on negation

The implementation of PC-Life allows only negation of atomic values. For the treatment of negated complex feature terms, and additionally negation of types, undefined feature entries and inequality constraints (disagreements or negations of path equivalences) are required. The latter will cause problems if used in conjunction with closed types: Because of the interpretation of closed types as constructors two nodes carrying the same closed type are unequal iff they are not dereferenced to the same node *and* if a feature exists for which the corresponding subnodes are unequal. This transfer of inequality constraints to subnodes possibly has to be iterated if nodes with closed terms are nested, therefore producing a lot of conditions that have to be tested during each unification.

5 The Functional and Relational Parts of PC-LIFE

In order to handle argument passing by pattern matching and operations with feature terms, we implemented a new evaluator whose design follows Abelson and Sussman [1, p. 293ff]. Feature terms are implemented as a new datatype that is checked for in places where residuation may occur. An assignment in a functional expression will lead to incorrect results if this expression is evaluated from inside a disjunctive feature term. This happens because the state of execution that is saved in the case of a residuation contains only the continuation and not the binding environments. Hence, in case of multiple execution the same environment will be affected incorrectly. Because of this, side-effects must be avoided in all places where a residuation can occur.

The relational part of the language is an elaboration of PROLOG in which first order terms are replaced by δ-terms. The role of the logical variable is taken by term-nodes. This means that coreferences do not only occur between different addresses of one term but also within different parts of a clause. The bound/unbound effect of logical variables is replaced by a gradual refinement of nodes. The resolution prover we implemented is an extension of the one described by Haynes [12]. Its control structure is based on socalled "upward-failure-continuations": The theorem prover returns a failure continuation which is invoked when backtracking is necessary. Failure continuations are implemented as SCHEME continuations. The theorem prover works with a structure copying technique.

Using Haynes' taxonomy [12, p. 673] integrating the relational into the functional part is an *environment embedding*. This means that both share a common environment, therefore providing efficient information transfer. If an embedding additionally allows the sharing of control contexts, it is called *complete*. Although failure continuations which store a specific control context can be obtained at the functional top-level, our embedding is not yet complete, because an arbitrary invocation of failure continuations can violate Prolog's semantics. But the embedding can be completed by incorporating Haynes' *state-space* model (cf. [12]).

References

[1] Harold Abelson and Gerald Jay Sussmann. *Structure and Interpretation of Computer Programs*. MIT Press, 1985.

[2] Hassan Aït-Kaci. An algebraic semantics approach to the effective resolution of type equations. *Theoretical Computer Science*, 45:293–351, 1986.

[3] Hassan Aït-Kaci et al. Efficient implementation of lattice operations. *ACM Transactions on Programming Languages and Systems*, 11(1):115–146, 1989.

[4] Hassan Aït-Kaci and Patrick Lincoln. LIFE — a natural language for natural language. Technical report, Microelectronics and Computer Technology Corporation, Austin (TX), February 1988.

[5] Hassan Aït-Kaci and Andreas Podelski. Is there a meaning to LIFE? Paper submitted to ICLP-91, November 1990

[6] Hassan Aït-Kaci and Roger Nasr. Login: A logic programming language with built-in inheritance. *The Journal of Logic Programming*, 3:185–215, 1986.

[7] Rolf Backofen and Lutz Euler and Günther Görz. Towards the Integration of Functions, Relations and Types in an AI Programming Language. In *Proceedings of the German Workshop on Artificial Intelligence GWAI-90*, Berlin: Springer, 1990.

[8] Rolf Backofen. Integration von Funktionen, Relationen und Typen beim Sprachentwurf. Teil II: Attributterme und Relationen. Diplomarbeit, Universität Erlangen-Nürnberg, 1989.

[9] Jochen Dörre and Andreas Eisele. Determining consistency of feature terms with distributed disjunctions. In D[ieter] Metzing, editor, *Proc. of the 13th German Workshop on Artificial Intelligence*, volume 216 of *Informatik Fachberichte*, pages 270–279. Springer, Berlin, 1989.

[10] Andreas Eisele and Jochen Dörre. Unification of disjunctive feature descriptions. In *26th Annual Meeting of the Association for Computational Linguistics*, pages 186–194, Buffalo (NY), 1988.

[11] Lutz Euler. Integration von Funktionen, Relationen und Typen beim Sprachentwurf. Teil I: Konzeption, Typhierarchie und Funktionen. Diplomarbeit, Universität Erlangen-Nürnberg, 1989.

[12] Christopher T. Haynes. Logic continuations. *Journal of Logic Programming*, 4:157–176, 1987.

[13] John Maxwell and Ronald Kaplan. An overview of disjunctive constraint satisfaction. In *Proceedings of the International Parsing Workshop 1989*, pages 18–27, 1989.

[14] Bernhard Nebel and Gert Smolka. Representation and reasoning with attributive descriptions. IWBS-Report 81, IBM Deutschland GmbH, Stuttgart, 1989.

[15] Gert Smolka. A feature logic with subsorts. LILOG-Report 33, IBM Deutschland GmbH, Stuttgart, May 1988.

[16] Åke Wikström. *Functional Programming Using Standard ML*. Prentice Hall, London, 1987.

Reasoning with Maximal Time Intervals*

Cristina Ribeiro† *and António Porto*
Departamento de Informática
Universidade Nova de Lisboa
2825 Monte da Caparica
Portugal

Abstract

The ability to deal with partial knowledge is particularly important in a temporal domain. We describe a temporal language that accounts for incompletely specified temporal information about propositions. Temporal terms in the language denote time instants and inequality constraints are used to keep incomplete information about their order. The language is semantically based on the notion of *maximal interval*, the denotation of a proposition being a set of maximal intervals where it holds. The adequacy of maximal intervals for temporal knowledge representation has been justified elsewhere [5]. In a partial KB, abduction on the temporal order is generally needed to answer a query, and the answer is then conditional on the abduced facts. To comply with the intended semantics, an implicit form of temporal consistency has to be enforced, and this presents the main challenge to the design of the inference mechanism. We present here the syntax and declarative semantics of a propositional version of the language of maximal intervals and a first discussion of the problems in designing an inference system adequate to work with this temporal framework. Rather than presenting a complete solution, we discuss several approaches.

Keywords: knowledge representation, temporal reasoning, deductive databases.

1 Introduction

Temporal reasoning is recognized as a fundamental part of a system aimed at the formal treatment of commonsense knowledge. The approaches that have been taken so far consider as basic entities some form of temporally qualified propositions, using either periods or instants as the basic structure for time. The representation of a temporal fact is then the association of a proposition with a temporal extent.

---

*This research was supported by Portuguese JNICT project PEROLA.

†Owns a scholarship from INIC.

In [5] we proposed a scheme based on the idea of characterizing each proposition in terms of the set of disjoint maximal time intervals in which it holds. Informally, an interval for a proposition is qualified as maximal if the proposition holds everywhere in it and for no other interval containing it does this happen. Temporal statements about the world are then viewed as supplying partial information about the elements of those sets. We have also justified this approach and showed the difference in perspective from the temporal frameworks presented by Allen [1], McDermott [4], Shoham [7] and Kowalski [2].

In our language of maximal intervals, *MI* for short, we have a way of talking about single time intervals where propositions hold, but the notion of a set of maximal intervals is associated with each proposition. In natural language, information is not usually expressed in terms of maximal intervals, but we can always transform expressions involving non-maximal intervals into constraints on maximal intervals. So we intend *MI* to be used as an internal language, for which the inference mechanism is designed, and along with it we will consider an external language. Knowledge about an interval expressed in the external language is turned into partial knowledge about a maximal interval. We therefore need an effective way of dealing with incomplete information in the process of obtaining an answer to a temporal query.

We also stress the fact that in *MI* there are no temporal terms corresponding to the sets of disjoint intervals. This contrasts with the proposals in [3], where these sets, called non-convex intervals, are the basic temporal entities. Our sets of disjoint intervals belong to the semantic analysis.

2 The ontology of maximal intervals

We are interested in building a temporal framework that will be suited for general knowledge representation and inferencing. It is important to establish precisely the basic objects in the ontology. We chose to consider time intervals and propositions as basic, and express temporal statements by associating a time interval with a proposition.

Our first approach will be a propositional one, and may be seen as a "factoring" of temporal extent out of propositions. We therefore require that basic propositions have no embedded temporal references. This is where we part from the approaches taken by Allen [1] and Shoham [7], where arbitrary propositions are considered as basic objects. As an example, "running for 20 minutes" is considered a possible basic object in these formalisms, where intervals of validity are associated to such a proposition. The problem then arises of relating several intervals where the same proposition holds. These relations, as noted by Shoham, may get arbitrarily complex. In our formalism, "running" is a basic proposition but not "running for 20 minutes", which would have to be built from the basic one. The advantage of considering only maximal intervals for propositions in a KB is that a minimization of temporal information is achieved, as far as knowledge partiality allows. We also want to be able to express complex temporal propositions, but it seems very hard to handle such a task without having a basic temporal reasoning mechanism.

An extra argument for maximal intervals is that causation, taken in a very broad sense, always involves synchronization between end points of maximal intervals.

3 The *MI* language

KB statements are formulas, written as logical implications. Its form is similar to Horn clauses, the difference being in the implicit quantifications for the temporal variables. We are assuming that variables in the body are universally quantified, but those appearing only in the head have existential quantification.

MI supports only two relations: the total order on time points, $\prec$, used to express temporal constraints, and the relation for, between what we generally call *predications* and the corresponding maximal intervals. All entities are interpreted over an infinite universe of ordered time points. KB statements are formulas, and temporal tokens are split in three groups—constants, variables and mobiles. Variables correspond to universally quantified time points and mobiles to existentially quantified ones. This syntactic distinction will be crucial for the inference mechanism; mobiles are akin to Skolem constants and functions, but we need to distinguish them from the other constants in use. We use mobiles to model time points for which some information exists (for example being the end point of the interval for a fact) but whose precise anchorage is yet unknown. Mobiles are global syntactic entities (much like constants) and may therefore be shared among several statements. Variables as usual are local to clauses. In the following we present the syntax and semantics of the propositional version of *MI*.

3.1 Syntax

We define:

$\mathcal{C}$: the set of constants

$\mathcal{M}$: the set of mobiles

$\mathcal{M}_f$: the set of mobile functions, each equiped with an arity greater than 0

$\mathcal{V}$: the set of variables

$\mathcal{P}$: the set of proposition symbols.

Mobile functions behave as function symbols in a classic language. Here they are restricted to play the role of Skolem functions.

The set of *atomic terms* is defined as $\mathcal{C} \cup \mathcal{V} \cup \mathcal{M}$.

The set of *terms* is recursively defined asfollows:

- Every atomic term is a term
- If $m \in \mathcal{M}_f$ is a mobile function with arity n and $T_1, \ldots T_n$ are terms, $m(T_1, \ldots T_n)$ is a term.

The *atomic formulas* are constraint formulas and predicative formulas.

A *constraint formula* has the form $t_1 \prec t_2$, where t_1 and t_2 are terms.

A *predicative formula* has the form $for(t_1, t_2, p)$ where t_1,t_2 are terms and $p \in \mathcal{P}$.

A *clause* is

$$H \leftarrow B$$

where H, the "head", is an atomic formula and B, the "body", is a (possibly empty) conjunction of atomic formulas

$$B = b_1, \ldots, b_n \ (n \geq 0)$$

Whenever the head is a constraint formula the body is empty and the constraint always involves a mobile.

A *definite clause* is a clause with nonempty head. A *fact* is a definite clause with empty body. A *goal* is a clause with empty head. A KB is a set of definite clauses.

3.2 Semantics

Next we define interpretations and satisfiability.

An interpretation $\mathcal{I}$ is a 6-tuple $\langle \mathcal{T}, \leq, \mathcal{I}_C, \mathcal{I}_M, \mathcal{I}_{M_f}, \mathcal{I}_P \rangle$. $\mathcal{T}$ is the domain for the temporal entities, a set of time points. $\leq$ is a reflexive total order relation on $\mathcal{T}$. To this we associate the non-reflexive total order $<$, defined as follows:

$$\forall_{p_1, p_2 \in \mathcal{T}} \ (p_1 < p_2) \Leftrightarrow (p_1 \leq p_2) \wedge \neg(p_2 \leq p_1)$$

Over $\mathcal{T}$, the set of intervals is defined as

$$\mathcal{S} = \{\langle t_1, t_2 \rangle : t_1, t_2 \in \mathcal{T}, t_1 \leq t_2\}$$

and dually for the end points (beginning and ending) of an interval

$$\forall_{i \in \mathcal{S}} \ i = \langle t_1, t_2 \rangle \Rightarrow \ b(i) = t_1, \ e(i) = t_2$$

We build a set $\mathcal{D}$ whose elements are sets of intervals from $\mathcal{S}$ with the property that no two overlapping intervals belong in the same set. Formally

$$\mathcal{D} = \{s \in \wp(\mathcal{S}) : \forall_{i_1, i_2 \in s} \ i_1 \neq i_2 \Rightarrow i_1 <> i_2\}$$

where $i_1 <> i_2$ is to be read as 'i_1 is disjoint from i_2' and may be defined as

$$\forall i_1, i_2 \in \mathcal{S} \ i_1 <> i_2 \Leftrightarrow (e(i_1) < b(i_2)) \vee (e(i_2) < b(i_1))$$

$\mathcal{I}_C$, $\mathcal{I}_M$, $\mathcal{I}_{M_f}$ and $\mathcal{I}_P$ are total functions of the following kinds:

- $\mathcal{I}_C$: $\mathcal{C} \rightarrow \mathcal{T}$ associates a time point with each constant symbol
- $\mathcal{I}_M$: $\mathcal{M} \rightarrow \mathcal{T}$ associates a time point with each mobile constant
- $\mathcal{I}_{M_f}$: is a function that maps each mobile function m of arity n to a function $\mathcal{T}^n \rightarrow \mathcal{T}$
- $\mathcal{I}_P$: $\mathcal{P} \rightarrow \mathcal{D}$ associates a set of disjoint intervals with each proposition symbol.

This last interpretation function leads to an implicit notion of consistency of intervals for the same predication. In fact, allowing overlapping intervals for the same predication would violate the intention that those intervals be maximal.

A *variable assignment* α is a function $\mathcal{V} \rightarrow \mathcal{T}$. For any given interpretation $\mathcal{I}$ and variable assignment α we define the denotations of arbitrary terms as follows

$$
\begin{array}{lcrl}
c \in \mathcal{C} & \Rightarrow & [\![c]\!]_{\mathcal{I}}^{\alpha} & = \mathcal{I}_{C}(c) \\
m \in \mathcal{M} & \Rightarrow & [\![m]\!]_{\mathcal{I}}^{\alpha} & = \mathcal{I}_{M}(m) \\
m \in \mathcal{M}_f & \Rightarrow & [\![m(T_1, \ldots T_n)]\!]_{\mathcal{I}}^{\alpha} & = \mathcal{I}_{M_f}(m)([\![T_1]\!]_{\mathcal{I}}^{\alpha}, \ldots [\![T_n]\!]_{\mathcal{I}}^{\alpha}) \\
v \in \mathcal{V} & \Rightarrow & [\![v]\!]_{\mathcal{I}}^{\alpha} & = \alpha(v) \\
p \in \mathcal{P} & \Rightarrow & [\![p]\!]_{\mathcal{I}}^{\alpha} & = \mathcal{I}_{P}(p)
\end{array}
$$

Now we define $\mathcal{I} \models_\alpha p$, the satisfiability of a formula p wrt an interpretation $\mathcal{I}$ under a variable assignment α

$$
\begin{array}{lll}
\mathcal{I} \models_\alpha t_1 \prec t_2 & \text{iff} & [\![t_1]\!]_{\mathcal{I}}^{\alpha} \leq [\![t_2]\!]_{\mathcal{I}}^{\alpha} \\
\mathcal{I} \models_\alpha for(t_1, t_2, p) & \text{iff} & \langle [\![t_1]\!]_{\mathcal{I}}^{\alpha}, [\![t_2]\!]_{\mathcal{I}}^{\alpha} \rangle \in [\![p]\!]_{\mathcal{I}}^{\alpha} \\
\mathcal{I} \models_\alpha (p_1, p_2) & \text{iff} & \mathcal{I} \models_\alpha p_1 \text{ and } \mathcal{I} \models_\alpha p_2
\end{array}
$$

Satisfaction is defined only for clauses, as the only (implicitly) quantified formulas, in the usual way:

$\mathcal{I} \models H \leftarrow B$ iff for all variable assignments α, $\mathcal{I} \models_\alpha H$ whenever $\mathcal{I} \models_\alpha B$. As usual, a model for a KB is an interpretation satisfying all of its clauses.

4 Inference

Having described *MI* and the declarative semantics which give it the properties we consider essential for temporal reasoning, we now turn to the design of an inference system where such properties will correspond to built-in mechanisms. We shall not propose here an ultimate solution to the inference system, but present some of the problems that emerge when trying to establish its general scheme.

In the presence of a partial KB, we have to devise mechanisms that will produce informative answers. Considering only the facts that are logical consequences of the KB will lead to very limited answers. The kind of answers we consider are logical implications between a set of conditions and an instance of the query. Logical consequence still holds, from the KB to this implication. It has become common in nonmonotonic reasoning to refer to such conditions as abductions, and although this should not be so [6] we shall also use this terminology.

4.1 Consistency

Consistency of a KB expressed in *MI* means the non-existence of overlapping intervals for the same predication. A partial KB has several models and abducing facts for the $\prec$ relation has the effect of reducing the number of such models. But while inferring the truth of a query we want to be sure that at any time the KB plus the abductions made has at least one model. For each mobile in the KB, there are conditions on $\prec$ that lead to an inconsistent KB. These conditions may not be abduced.

The consistency problem can be illustrated by the following paradigmatic example, with two facts for the same predication:

$$for(1, \alpha, p). \qquad 1 \prec \alpha.$$

$$for(\beta, 3, p). \qquad \beta \prec 3.$$

The problem is that there are values for the mobiles for which no model exists, such as $\alpha = 4$, because of the restriction of non-overlapping intervals for the same predication.

4.2 Approaches

Several approaches to inferencing with maximal intervals have been tried. The most obvious starting point is to use resolution on the KB regarded as a set of Horn clauses. Unification must be specialized as it deals only with temporal variables and must account for constraints on their values and relative order. It is quite easy to get possible intervals for each predication in a goal, but the problem remains of assuring consistency of such intervals with the intended models for the KB. A solution is to launch a "consistency check", expressed as a goal of "non-contradiction". This goal generates all intervals for the same predication in order to prove that the given interval is temporally consistent with all those and thus constitutes a solution. The question posed by this consistency check is that all intervals for a predication have to be found each time we want to validate a single interval. Moreover, as mobiles are shared among predications, behaving as global entities to which constraints are applied, it is not enough to look at the intervals for a given predication in order to enforce temporal consistency. New consistency checks are required for those other propositions having end points changed by the abductions made.

The second approach is a step towards making this inference more efficient, and consists in turning the problem around: if we have to compute all intervals for a predication in order to enforce consistency, then we can just compute them all once and select solutions from the set. Compared to the first approach this one avoids some unnecessary repetition of work, but as before all the burden of assuring consistency of the KB is put on the query evaluation process.

Still another way to look at inference is to consider that the KB must be kept consistent at each update, and the inference for a predication has only to test an "integrity formula" for the KB. At each update some of the work of the consistency checks is performed by deriving the formula. Building this integrity formula amounts to generating all KB facts bottom-up, producing the ordered sets of intervals for each predication (subject to multiple choices due to the partial knowledge about the temporal order) and then expressing the possible combinations of such sets in a logical form. The process of obtaining this integrity formula is hardly incremental, and we can easily see that it does not allow an efficient way to test consistency during a derivation. If we take the example in fig. 1, for instance, the consistency formula for a KB containing only those facts could be written as

$$(\alpha = 3 \wedge \beta = 1) \ \vee \ \alpha < \beta$$

where the disjunction accounts for the choice between two classes of models for the KB: those where there is a single maximal interval for p in $\langle 1, 3\rangle$ and those where at least two intervals for p lay there. We can imagine a KB where clauses for other predications exist and suppose the consistency formula is the same. In the derivation of a goal, the consistency formula has to be tested each time an abduction is made. We have assumed this formula is a static one, and so we are always testing the same formula. By using the static consistency formula no use would be made of the fact that the disjunctions in the formula are exclusive as they correspond to effective choices in the possible models of the KB (and consequently on the ordering of facts in the world). If one choice is made during a derivation, a comittment should be taken towards it, by discarding the alternative disjuncts, in order to avoid unnecessary computation.

The above considerations lead us to conclude that an effective approach to inference with maximal intervals must include two aspects. The first is the compilation of static information in the KB into data structures where temporal consistency of intervals is easily tested. The second is a dynamic mechanism to modify these structures according to the constraints from the goal and the abductions made. This way a balance is established between tasks that can take place during update and those that must be performed in the derivation of an answer. Keeping a global structure for constraints the comittment to the abductions made is implicit, and accounts for enforcing both maximality of intervals and consistence of the $\prec$ relation.

4.3 Some Considerations

When looking at all the problems we have stated one might wonder if complexity in inference is a consequence of adopting maximal intervals or if equivalent problems arise in the temporal formalisations proposed by Allen, McDermott, Shoham or Kowalski. The answer to this brings to light the difference in our approach. All these temporal formalisms are designed to talk about arbitrary propositions, associating them with arbitrary intervals and reasoning about their temporal relationships. Both McDermott and Shoham interpret propositions as sets of time entities, and we have followed the same path. But their sets have no general characterization, and Shoham advocates this temporal classification should be made after the basic temporal framework has been laid. From the considerations made here, it is likely that this classification will account for considerable complexity in an inference system. From the point of view of Shoham's classification process, it is apparent that our basic propositions are a particular case, corresponding to his *liquid* proposition-type. Kowalski's event calculus, although presented as a formalism based on events, has a great concern with obtaining intervals for predicates. In that sense we can compare it to an interval calculus. As intervals are always limited by events, we can also view it as as calculus of maximal intervals. The beginning and end of an interval are associated to transitions of truth values of predicates. But in order to obtain temporal consistency of predicates in the event calculus one must write specific axioms for that purpose, and the execution of such axioms leads to the same kind of difficulties for the inference system.

5 Conclusions and ongoing work

We have addressed here the questions to be dealt with in the design of an inference system for a temporal logic where predications are modelled as sets of intervals. It is clear how to impose consistency declaratively, as we can reason in terms of possible interpretations for the temporal terms. But an inference system has to effectively build an (incomplete) interpretation, and have criteria for determining when the temporal anchorage of a mobile has to be constrained in order to maintain consistency.

One important feature still missing in the propositional language is point arithmetic. We intend to have it soon, and be able to account for the duration of intervals.

References

[1] James Allen. Towards a General Theory of Action and Time. *Artificial Intelligence*, (23):123–154, 1984.

[2] Robert Kowalski and Marek Sergot. A logic-based calculus of events. *New Generation Computing*, 4(1):67–95, 1986.

[3] Peter Ladkin. Time representation: a taxonomy of interval relations. In *Proceedings of the* 5th *National Conference on Artificial Intelligence*, pages 360–366, 1986.

[4] Drew McDermott. A Temporal Logic for Reasoning About Processes and Plans. *Cognitive Science*, (6):101–155, 1982.

[5] António Porto and Cristina Ribeiro. *Maximal Intervals: A Logic of Temporal Information.* Technical Report DI-28, Departamento de Informática, FCT-UNL, 1990.

[6] Marek Sergot. Personal communication, 1991.

[7] Yoav Shoham. *Reasonig about Change.* The MIT Press, 1987.

Nonclassical Models for Logic Programs

Valentinas Kriaučiukas
Institute of Mathematics and Informatics
Lithuanian Academy of Sciences
232600, Vilnius, Akademijos 4
Lithuania

Abstract

We present some results on semantics for logic programs. We interpret logic programs in Kripke models. They connect the area of logic programming and that of nonclassical logics. New connectives are carried over dynamic logic to logic programs, resulting in so-called predicate programs. A wide class of predicate programs is shown to have the same meaning as formulas of dynamic logic with context-free programs. This allows to discuss the known problem of introducing the negation into logic programs in new light.

1 Introduction

Logic programming is one of the most important instruments in knowledge processing. Actually, logic programs are logical formulas which can be executed [Ko]. Logic programming is usually understood as a programming in Prolog, although there are other logic programming languages [AM], too. Prolog programs are sets of special formulas (called Horn clauses) in the first order predicate calculus. The execution or, in other words, operational semantics for these programs is defined via the proof theory [AE], hence their logical meaning and operational semantics are different.

Logic programs appear when we are attempting to describe a logic of a world in which any check of a statement can change the state of the world itself. Any knowledge processing system is such a world, because the statement check (proof or disproof) changes the knowledge, and so changes the state of the system. The denotation of the statement in this world is a binary relation between states. Therefore we give the semantics for statements simply by assigning them binary relations on states. Thus statements are rather programs than assertions, therefore we speak here about programs.

Nonclassical logics are used for the investigation of worlds with dynamic behaviour. Dynamic logic [Ha] is one of such logics. We would like to show here that both logic programming and dynamic logic are very close areas.

In this paper we define predicate programs, i.e. programs which are build on first order predicates and are (as it will be shown below) Prolog-like programs extended by new connectives from the dynamic logic. We give the semantics for predicate programs using Kripke-like models. Dynamic logics also take their semantics in such models. We show that some large class of first-order dynamic logic formulas is included in predicate programs. These formulas are "programs" and "assertions" at the same time. This is a specific situation in logic programming. So, we propose an alternative to proof-theoretic bridge between logic and logic programming. In this case the logic is nonclassical, and declarative and operational meanings of logic programs coincide. Let us mention some immediate consequences of this approach:

- Logic programs may be directly used to describe a knowledge in areas with a dynamic behaviour.

  Example 1.1 Let run(x) be a program defining a behaviour of some finite automata with two states {x=0, x=1}. The automata changes a state after reception of a message with data equal to the value of x. This behaviour can be defined in the style of CCS [Mi] as follows:

  $$\mathtt{run(x)} \equiv \mathtt{mes(y)} \land \mathtt{check(x,y)} \land \mathtt{run(x)},$$
  $$\mathtt{mes(x)} \Rightarrow \mathtt{x} = 0 \lor \mathtt{x} = 1,$$
  $$\mathtt{x} = \mathtt{y} = \mathtt{z} \land \mathtt{check(x,y)} \Rightarrow \mathtt{y} = \mathtt{z} \oplus 1,$$
  $$\mathtt{x} \neq \mathtt{y} = \mathtt{z} \land \mathtt{check(x,y)} \Rightarrow \mathtt{y} = \mathtt{z},$$

  where ⊕ is the symbol of binary summation. All the expressions above are predicate programs but at the same time they can be understood and used as assertions. We use the equality '=' predicate as build-in one. ■

- Some questions in the foundation of logic programming, which do not arise in the proof-theoretic paradigm at all, can be raised and solved.

  Example 1.2 A bounded variable can change its value or not? In predicate programs it can, and the assignment operator can be legally used as one of build-in predicates. Denote it as usually x:=t. The predicate check from the previous example can be defined as follows:

  $$\mathtt{check(x,y)} \equiv (\mathtt{x} = \mathtt{y} \land \mathtt{y} := \mathtt{y} \oplus 1) \lor \underline{\mathtt{skip}}.$$ ■

- It allows one to look in new light at the problem of introducing the negation in logic programs.

- Denotational semantics for logic programs can be described in the same way as the semantics for logical formulas.

- Operational semantics for logic programs can be given by direct construction of AND/OR trees with additional backtracking edges.

- Well elaborated nonclassical logics (dynamic, temporal, etc.) can be used to prove properties of logic programs.

The propositional case of predicate programs was considered in [Kr]. It was shown that the propositional case of the language proposed here captures the propositional μ-calculus.

Our paper is organized as follows. In Section 2 we define the syntax of predicate programs. The semantics is defined in Section 3. In Section 4 we discuss the existence of fixed points for recursive programs. All these investigations are made for an unspecified set of program connectives. In Section 5 some concrete set of program connectives is defined and explained. In the next two sections a connection with dynamic logic and Prolog-like programs is established. In the last section the negation problem is discussed.

Related work. Some similar ideas are used in [Gr], where a dynamic logic was enriched by unification predicate (as procedure) and deductive properties of the given dynamic logic was considered. In fact, the programs in [Gr] are predicate programs build over two interpretated predicates (unification and assignment) using monotone connectives. Models used are based on term algebra (Herbrand interpretation) as in logic programming . We consider the general case with no uninterpreted predicates and a larger set of connectives. We also step from dynamic models used in [Gr] to Kripke models, what make our consideration easier.

2 Syntax of Predicate Programs

Let $\Sigma = \Pi \cup \Phi$ be a finite *signature* of the first order predicate calculus, where Π and Φ are the sets of predicate and function symbols, respectively. The *arity* of each symbol $S \in \Sigma$ is denoted by $\alpha(S)$. Let $\mathcal{V}$ be a countable set of *variables*, $\mathcal{T}(\Phi, \mathcal{V})$ be a set of all *terms* over Φ and $\mathcal{V}$, and $\mathcal{E}(\Phi, \Pi, \mathcal{V})$ be a set of all *atomic formulas* over Π and $\mathcal{T}(\Phi, \mathcal{V})$, i.e. formulas of the form $P(t_1, \ldots, t_{\alpha(P)})$, where $t_1, \ldots, t_{\alpha(P)} \in \mathcal{T}(\Phi, \mathcal{V})$ and $P \in \Pi$. Let $\mathcal{C}_0$, $\mathcal{C}_1$ and $\mathcal{C}_2$ be sets of nullary, unary and binary program connectives [1]. All unary program connectives have a higher priority than the binary ones.

Definition 2.1 *The set of* predicate programs $\mathcal{P}(\Phi, \Omega, \mathcal{V})$, $\Omega \subseteq \Pi$, *includes:*

(i) *all formulas from* $\mathcal{E}(\Phi, \Omega, \mathcal{V})$, *called* atomic programs;

(ii) *all* $P \in \mathcal{C}_0$;

(iii) $P\odot$, *where* $P \in \mathcal{P}(\Phi, \Omega, \mathcal{V})$ *and* $\odot \in \mathcal{C}_1$;

(iv) $(P \otimes Q)$, *where* P *and* $Q \in \mathcal{P}(\Phi, \Omega, \mathcal{V})$ *and* $\otimes \in \mathcal{C}_2$;

(v) *programs of the form*

$$[P | X_1 \equiv Q_1, \ldots, X_n \equiv Q_n], \tag{1}$$

where $X_1, \ldots, X_n$ *are atomic programs from* $\mathcal{E}(\emptyset, \Omega_1, \mathcal{V})$, $\Omega_1 \cap \Omega = \emptyset$, *and* $P, Q_1, \ldots, Q_n$ *are programs from* $\mathcal{P}(\Phi, \Omega_1 \cup \Omega, \mathcal{V})$.

Program 1 is called a *recursive program.* Such a program is used to define recursive predicates $X_1, \ldots, X_n$. The equivalence $X \equiv Q$ in (1) defines the predicate X as Q and is called a *definition* of X. Each $X \in \{X_1, \ldots, X_n\}$ may have only one definition in (1).

[1] It is possible to introduce program connectives an arity bigger than two, but the described case is sufficient for us.

3 Semantics for Predicate Programs

Predicate programs are interpreted in Kripke-style models. Each model may be described by some pair $\langle \mathcal{S}, \mathcal{I} \rangle$, where $\mathcal{S}$ is a set of states and $\mathcal{I}$ is an interpretation of atomic programs as binary relations on $\mathcal{S}$. Arguments in atomic programs are terms, so we begin with defining meaning of terms.

As usually, term values are defined in an algebra where function symbols from Φ are interpreted (*Φ-algebra*). We describe the Φ-algebra by the pair $\langle A, I \rangle$, where A is a set and I is an *interpretation* of symbols from Φ as functions of appropriate arities over A. A *state* over A is a partial function $s : \mathcal{V} \to A$ with a finite domain $dom(s) = \{v | s(v) \text{ is defined}\}$. The *restriction* of any state s to a domain $D \subset dom(s)$ is denoted by $s \downarrow D$. We denote the set of states over A by $\mathcal{S}(A)$.

Example 3.1 In pure Prolog terms take their values in some *free-generated* Φ-algebra $\mathcal{T}(\Phi, \mathcal{X})$, where $\mathcal{X}$ is a set of variables, $\mathcal{X} \cap \mathcal{V} = \emptyset$. In any real Prolog this algebra is many-sorted including integers, reals, strings, etc. But nevertheless this algebra is always a Φ-algebra of terms. In this case, states are substitutions. ■

The terms change their values from state to state in usual manner. We distinguish the case of uninterpreted variable in defining the value of a term t in a state s, setting

$$t[s] = \begin{cases} \text{the value of } t \text{ in } s, & \text{if } \mathcal{V}(t) \subseteq dom(s), \\ \omega, & \text{if } t \in \mathcal{V} \setminus dom(s), \\ \text{undefined}, & \text{otherwise,} \end{cases}$$

where $\mathcal{V}(t)$ is the set of variables of t, and ω denotes an special value, $\omega \notin A$. We use the notation $(\vec{t})[s] = \langle t_1[s], \ldots, t_n[s] \rangle$ for a multiple argument $\vec{t} = \langle t_1, \ldots, t_n \rangle$.

To define the meaning of predicate symbols from Π we slightly extend the notion of Φ-algebras.

Definition 3.2 *A pair $\langle A, I \rangle$ is a* dynamic Σ-model *iff A is a set and I is a mapping defined on the signature Σ such that the pair $\langle A, I \downarrow \Phi \rangle$ is a Φ-algebra and, for every symbol $P \in \Pi$, $I(P)$ is a binary relation over $(\{\omega\} \cup A)^{\alpha(P)}$.*

Intuitively, the mapping I defines the predicates as nondeterministic transformations. As above, the symbol ω stands for unbounded variables. By this definition, a bounded variable can change its value or become free in a new state. This general definition covers deterministic functions and procedures from procedural and functional languages, nondeterministic predicates from logic programming.

Example 3.3 This paradigm includes the usual assignment operator since it is defined as follows:

$$I(`:=') = \{\langle\langle \omega, a \rangle, \langle a, a \rangle\rangle, \langle\langle b, a \rangle, \langle a, a \rangle\rangle | a, b \in A\}.$$

The equality predicate used in the examples in Introduction is simply defined:

$$I(`=') = \{\langle\langle a, a \rangle, \langle a, a \rangle\rangle | a \in A\}.$$

The unification predicate **unif** is more complicated:

$$I(\underline{\text{unif}}) = \{\langle\langle u,t\rangle,\langle z,z\rangle\rangle,\langle\langle\omega,t\rangle,\langle t,t\rangle\rangle,\langle\langle t,\omega\rangle,\langle t,t\rangle\rangle \mid \{u,t,z\} \in \mathcal{T}(\Phi,\mathcal{X})\ \&\ z = mgu(u,v)\} \cup \{\langle\langle\omega,\omega\rangle,\langle\omega,\omega\rangle\rangle\}.$$

■

Now we are ready to describe Kripke models appropriate for our purpose.

Definition 3.4 *A pair $\langle\mathcal{S}(A),\mathcal{I}(I)\rangle$ is a* Kripke model *built on a dynamic Σ-model $\langle A,I\rangle$ if $\mathcal{I}(I)$ is a mapping $\mathcal{E}(\Phi,\Pi,\mathcal{V}) \to 2^{\mathcal{S}(A)\times\mathcal{S}(A)}$ defined by I:*

$$\mathcal{I}(I)(P(\vec{t})) = \{\langle r,s\rangle \mid \{r,s\} \subset \mathcal{S}(A),\ \langle\vec{t}[r],\vec{t}[s]\rangle \in I(P),\ \forall x \notin \mathcal{V}(t)\ s(x) = r(x)\}.$$

The last condition excludes side-effects in program execution since programs change only the values of variables occurring explicitly.

Further, for a given Kripke model $\mathcal{K} = \langle\mathcal{S},\mathcal{I}\rangle$, we interpret program connectives as functions defined in the set $2^{\mathcal{S}\times\mathcal{S}}$ of all binary relations. Let $\oslash_{\mathcal{K}}$ denote an interpretation of a program connective $\oslash$ in the model $\mathcal{K}$. We define the meaning of predicate programs as follows.

Definition 3.5 *The extension of interpretation $\mathcal{I}$ from $\mathcal{E}(\Phi,\Pi,\mathcal{V})$ to $\mathcal{P}(\Phi,\Pi,\mathcal{V})$ is given by:*

(i) $\mathcal{I}(\oslash) = \oslash_{\mathcal{K}}$ *for every nullary program connective* $\oslash \in \mathcal{C}_0$;

(ii) $\mathcal{I}(P\odot) = \mathcal{I}(P)\odot_{\mathcal{K}}$ *for every unary program connective* $\odot \in \mathcal{C}_1$;

(iii) $\mathcal{I}(P \otimes Q) = \mathcal{I}(P) \otimes_{\mathcal{K}} \mathcal{I}(Q)$ *for every binary program connective* $\otimes \in \mathcal{C}_2$;

(iv) $\mathcal{I}([P|X_1 \equiv Q_1,\ldots,X_n \equiv Q_n]) = \begin{cases} \mathcal{I}(P), & \text{if } \forall i\, \mathcal{I}(X_i) = \mathcal{I}(Q_i); \\ \text{undefined}, & \text{otherwise.} \end{cases}$

A recursive program is undefined in a model if the set of definitions of the program has no a solution in the model. Some sufficient conditions for solvability of a system of equations $\{\mathcal{I}(X_i) = \mathcal{I}(Q_i) | 1 \le i \le n\}$ are given in the next section.

4 Fixed Points for Recursive Programs

We would like to prove here the possibility to solve the system of equations defined by a recursive program. Let the set of definitions

$$\{X_1 \equiv Q_1,\ldots,X_n \equiv Q_n\} \tag{2}$$

be given. Let also $\Delta \subset \Pi$ denote the set of predicate symbols (called *defined* symbols) occurring in $X_1,\ldots,X_n$, and let $\langle A,I\rangle$ be a dynamic Σ-model. Let denote

$$\Im(I) = \{J | dom(J) = \Delta \text{ and } \langle A, J \cup I{\downarrow}(\Sigma\setminus\Delta)\rangle \text{ is a dynamic } \Sigma\text{-model}\}$$

the set of possible interpretations of defined symbols. The set of definitions (2) *induces* the operator $\mathcal{Q} : \Im(I) \to \Im(I)$ such that

$$\mathcal{Q}(J)(p) = \{\langle\vec{x}[r],\vec{x}[s]\rangle | \langle r,s\rangle \in \mathcal{I}(J)(R)\}$$

for every interpretation $J \in \Im(I)$ and a definition $p(\vec{x}) \equiv R$ from (2).

Below we define sufficient conditions for the existence of a fixed point for this operator $\mathcal{Q}$. We formulate the conditions in terms of the signs of occurrences of the defined predicate symbols. First we define the signs of program connectives.

Let A be an partially ordered set and $f : A^m \to A$ be a function. We define the sign $\text{argsign}(i, f) = +1$ if $a < b$ implies

$$f(x_1, \ldots, x_{i-1}, a, x_{i+1}, \ldots, x_m) \leq f(x_1, \ldots, x_{i-1}, b, x_{i+1}, \ldots, x_m)$$

for all $a, b \in A$. The sign is -1 when the same holds with $\leq$ replaced by $\geq$. Otherwise, $\text{argsign}(i, f)$ is undefined (see Assumption 4.1 below).

We can apply this definition to program connectives because binary relations are partially ordered by the inclusion.

Assumption 4.1 *We consider only such a class of Kripke models in which the function 'argsign' is defined for each program connective and is the same for all models. We also suppose that all the program connectives are continuous functions.*

Now we are able to define signs of predicate symbols in programs. We write $+1/-1 \in \text{sign}(p, P)$ if the symbol p has a positive/negative *occurrence* in the program P, namely:

(i) $+1 \in \text{sign}(p, p(t))$;

(ii) $s \in \text{sign}(p, Q\odot)$, where $\odot \in \mathcal{C}_1$, iff $\exists r \in \text{sign}(p, P)\ s = r \cdot \text{argsign}(1, \odot)$;

(iii) $s \in \text{sign}(p, (Q_1 \otimes Q_2)$, where $\otimes \in \mathcal{C}_2$, iff $\exists r \in \text{sign}(p, Q_i)\ s = r \cdot \text{argsign}(i, \otimes)$.

For us global structure of dependency relations in the set of definitions (2) is important. To formulate briefly our restriction we use some graph theory notions.

A graph $\langle \Delta, E_{+1} \cup E_{-1} \rangle$, where $E_s = \{\langle p, q \rangle | (p(\vec{x}) \equiv Q) \in (2)\ \&\ s \in \text{sign}(q, Q)\}$ is called the *dependence graph* of definitions (2). Edges from E_{+1} (in E_{-1}) are called *positive* (*negative*, respectively).

Assumption 4.2 *The class $\mathcal{P}(\Phi, \Pi, \mathcal{V})$ includes only such recursive programs for which the dependence graph of definitions has an even number of negative edges in every cycle.*

The next theorem claims that by the latter assumption all definitions in a recursive program can be interpreted correctly.

Theorem 4.3 *If the set of definitions $\mathcal{D} = \{X_1 \equiv Q_1, \ldots, X_n \equiv Q_n\}$ satisfies Assumption 4.2 and Δ is the set of predicate symbols defined in $\mathcal{D}$ then for every dynamic model $\langle A, I \rangle$ there exists a dynamic model $\langle A, J \rangle$, where $J{\downarrow}\Sigma \setminus \Delta = I{\downarrow}\Sigma \setminus \Delta$ and J is a fixed point of the operator $\mathcal{Q}$ induced by $\mathcal{D}$, i.e. $J = \mathcal{Q}(J)$.*

Proof. Let $G = \langle \Delta, E_{+1} \cup E_{-1} \rangle$ be the dependence graph of the set $\mathcal{D}$. The set Δ can be divided in two parts Δ_{+1} and Δ_{-1} so that $\Delta = \Delta_{+1} \cup \Delta_{-1}$ and for every $q \in \Delta$ and $p \in \Delta_r$ if $\langle p, q \rangle$ or $\langle q, p \rangle$ belongs to E_s, then $q \in \Delta_{sr}$. Since the graph G does not contain a cycle having an odd number of negative edges, Δ_{-1} and Δ_{+1} can be selected so that $\Delta_{+1} \cap \Delta_{-1} = \emptyset$. Now let

$$\{J_i | \forall i > 0 \; J_i = \mathcal{Q}(J_{i-1})\} \tag{3}$$

be an infinite sequence of interpretations of Δ such that $J_i(q) \subseteq J_{i+1}(q)$ for every $q \in \Delta_{+1}$ and $J_{i+1}(q) \subseteq J_i(q)$ for $q \in \Delta_{-1}$. It is clear that such a sequence has the limit J, where

$$J(q) = \begin{cases} \bigcup\limits_{i=0}^{\infty} J_i(q), & \text{if } q \in \Delta_{+1}, \\ \bigcap\limits_{i=0}^{\infty} J_i(q), & \text{if } q \in \Delta_{-1}. \end{cases}$$

As it follows from the continuity of connectives this limit is a fixed point of the operator $\mathcal{Q}$. To prove the existence of such a sequence it is sufficient to prove the existence of the first two members only. Then, the correctness of the rest of the sequence follows from the monotonicity of program connectives (Assumption 4.1).

Let $Y_1 \equiv R_1, \ldots, Y_k \equiv R_k$ be a set of definitions obtained from $\mathcal{D}$ by deleting all definitions containing a symbol from Δ_{+1} on the left-hand side and by replacing every atomic program $p(\vec{t})$, where $p \in \Delta_{+1}$, by <u>**fail**</u> (see below) in the remaining definitions. The operator $\mathcal{R}$ induced by this set of definitions is monotone because the dependence graph does not contain negative edges at all (the set of vertices of this graph is the set Δ_{-1}). Denote by J_0 the least fixed point of this operator, so $J_0 = \mathcal{R}(J_0)$. We extend J_0 to the whole set Δ by stating $J_0(p) = \emptyset$ for $p \in \Delta_{+1}$.

Let $J_1 = \mathcal{Q}(J_0)$. We must check that $J_i(q) \subseteq J_{i+1}(q)$ for every $q \in \Delta_{+1}$ and $J_{i+1}(q) \subseteq J_i(q)$ for $q \in \Delta_{-1}$. To do this, note that $J_1(p) \subseteq \emptyset = J_0(p)$ for every $p \in \Delta_{+1}$. As far as $J_0(\underline{\mathtt{fail}}) = \emptyset$, we have that

$$J_1 \downarrow \Delta_{-1} = (\mathcal{Q}(J_0)) \downarrow \Delta_{-1} = \mathcal{R}(J_0 \downarrow \Delta_{-1}) = J_0 \downarrow \Delta_{-1},$$

and thus $J_1(p) = J_0(p)$ for $p \in \Delta_{-1}$. Hence J_0 and J are the first two members of sequence (3), and we are done. ■

It is not clear how to define an operational semantics for recursive programs equivalent to the denotational semantics constructed in this proof. The short proof of existence is the unique advantage of this denotational semantics. Really, proof claims only the existence of such semantics, but not define it uniquely. Few determinations are possible in the future work on operational semantics

5 Connectives

The set of connectives used in predicate programs depends on a model of computation for which these programs are written. We suppose that an evaluation of programs is consecutive. This implies that each time only one state is reached. Let $\mathcal{K} = \langle \mathcal{S}, \mathcal{I} \rangle$ be a Kripke model and P be a program, and s be a state. We denote by $\mathcal{I}(P)_s$ the set of edges (i.e. state pairs) $\{\langle s, r \rangle | \langle s, r \rangle \in \mathcal{I}(P)\}$ outgoing from s. The consecutive evaluation of the program P generates some linear order in $\mathcal{I}(P)_s$. The presence of this order is essential in the definition of the Prolog connective "cut". More details of the execution of predicate programs are not used here.

We consider two nullary program connectives $\underline{\texttt{fail}}$ and $\underline{\texttt{skip}}$, two binary connectives '$\wedge$' and '$\vee$' from Prolog, the Prolog cut '!', a new unary connective '#', and two binary connectives '$\Rightarrow$' and '&' from dynamic logic.

Definition 5.1 *Let $\mathcal{K} = \langle \mathcal{S}, I\rangle$ be a Kripke model, then let us define:*

(i) $\underline{\texttt{fail}}_{\mathcal{K}} = \emptyset$;

(ii) $\underline{\texttt{skip}}_{\mathcal{K}} = \{\langle v, v\rangle | v \in \mathcal{S}\}$;

(iii) $\wedge_{\mathcal{K}}$ *is the composition of relations;*

(iv) $\vee_{\mathcal{K}}$ *is the union of relations;*

(v) $\mathcal{I}(P!) = \{\langle s, r\rangle | \langle s, r\rangle$ *is first in the set* $\mathcal{I}(P)_s\}$;

(vi) $\mathcal{I}(P\#) = \{\langle v, v\rangle | \mathcal{I}(P)_v \neq \emptyset\}$;

(vii) $\mathcal{I}(P \,\&\, Q) = \mathcal{I}(P\#) \cap \mathcal{I}(Q\#)$;

(viii) $\mathcal{I}(P \Rightarrow Q) = \{\langle v, v\rangle | \forall r(\langle v, r\rangle \in \mathcal{I}(P) \Rightarrow \mathcal{I}(Q)_r \neq \emptyset)\}$.

It is easy to see that argsign $\equiv +1$ for all the defined program connectives, excluding the connective '$\Rightarrow$', for which argsign$(1, \Rightarrow) = -1$ and argsign$(2, \Rightarrow) = +1$.

This is all we need to consider predicate programs as an extension of Prolog programs.

Example 5.2 The extensions of Pascal-like programs can also be considered within this frame. Operators $\underline{\texttt{while}}$ and $\underline{\texttt{if then else}}$ are defined as follows:

$$
\begin{aligned}
(P\ \underline{\texttt{while}}\ Q) &\equiv. \ Q \wedge P \wedge (P\ \underline{\texttt{while}}\ Q) \vee \underline{\texttt{skip}}, \\
(\underline{\texttt{if}}\, P\ \underline{\texttt{then}}\ Q\ \underline{\texttt{else}}\ R) &\equiv \ (P! \wedge Q) \vee (P \Rightarrow \underline{\texttt{fail}}) \wedge R.
\end{aligned}
$$

These connectives definitions look like predicate definitions and can be used in the same way. However, the connectives are second order predicates. It would be interesting to build some "predicate" calculus of predicates like the λ-calculus of computable functions as the theoretical background for higher order logic programs. ■

We recall from [Kr] some equivalences relating program connectives. They become logical tautologies if one changes all the signs '$\not\equiv$' to '$\equiv$'; program connectives '$\wedge$' and '&' - to the conjunction; $\underline{\texttt{skip}}$ and $\underline{\texttt{fail}}$ - to logical constants $\underline{\texttt{true}}$ and $\underline{\texttt{false}}$:

Lemma 5.3 ([Kr]) *For any predicate programs P and Q the following equivalences hold:*

(i) $\underline{\texttt{skip}} \Rightarrow P \equiv (P \Rightarrow \underline{\texttt{fail}}) \Rightarrow \underline{\texttt{fail}} \equiv \underline{\texttt{skip}} \wedge P \equiv P \,\&\, P \not\equiv$
$P \equiv P \,\&\, \underline{\texttt{skip}} \equiv \underline{\texttt{skip}} \,\&\, P \equiv P \vee P \equiv \underline{\texttt{fail}} \vee P \not\equiv P \wedge P$;

(ii) $P \Rightarrow P \not\equiv \underline{\texttt{skip}} \equiv \underline{\texttt{fail}} \Rightarrow P \equiv P \Rightarrow \underline{\texttt{skip}} \not\equiv \underline{\texttt{skip}} \vee P$;

(iii) $P \Rightarrow Q \equiv P \Rightarrow \underline{\texttt{skip}} \Rightarrow Q$;

(iv) $P \,\&\, Q \equiv Q \,\&\, P \equiv (\underline{\texttt{skip}} \Rightarrow P) \wedge (\underline{\texttt{skip}} \Rightarrow Q)$;

(v) $\underline{\texttt{fail}} \equiv \underline{\texttt{skip}} \Rightarrow \underline{\texttt{fail}} \equiv \underline{\texttt{fail}} \,\&\, P \equiv P \,\&\, \underline{\texttt{fail}}$.

6 Connection with Dynamic Logic

Programs and formulas are considered as different objects in most logics of programs. We have only programs in our language, but the point is that some of them, such as $P\#$ or $P \Rightarrow Q$, can be interpreted as assertions. The language of dynamic logic [Ha] with the so-called context-free programs (CFDL) is nearest to that of predicate programs. I don't know a better way to show the relation between predicate programs and CFDL than to give some formal translation rules of quantifier-free formulas of CFDL to predicates programs.

We use the same notations as in Sections 2 and 3. Divide the set of predicate symbols in two parts $\Pi = \Pi_1 \cup \Pi_2$. Predicates from Π_1 are used for building atomic formulas; predicates from Π_2 are used as nonterminals in context-free definitions of programs.

Definition 6.1 *The sets $\mathcal{F}$ and $\mathcal{P}$ of* formulas *and* programs *of CFDL are defined as follows:*

(i) $\underline{\mathtt{skip}} \in \mathcal{F}$, $\underline{\mathtt{fail}} \in \mathcal{F}$, $\mathcal{E}(\Phi, \Pi_1, \mathcal{V}) \subset \mathcal{F}$;

(ii) $\neg A \in \mathcal{F}$, $(A \vee B) \in \mathcal{F}$ *and* $(A \,\&\, B) \in \mathcal{F}$ *iff* $A \in \mathcal{F}$ *and* $B \in \mathcal{F}$;

(iii) $\exists x A \in \mathcal{F}$, $\forall x A \in \mathcal{F}$, $A? \in \mathcal{P}$, $\langle P \rangle A \in \mathcal{F}$, $[P]A \in \mathcal{F}$ *iff* $A \in \mathcal{F}$, $P \in \mathcal{P}$, $x \in \mathcal{V}$;

(iv) $(x := t) \in \mathcal{P}$ *iff* $x \in \mathcal{V}$ *and* $t \in \mathcal{T}(\Phi, \mathcal{V})$;

(v) $(PQ) \in \mathcal{P}$, $(P \cup Q) \in \mathcal{P}$ *iff* $P \in \mathcal{P}$ *and* $Q \in \mathcal{P}$;

(vi) $[P | X_1 \equiv Q_1, \ldots, X_n \equiv Q_n] \in \mathcal{P}$ *iff* $X_1, \ldots, X_n \in \mathcal{E}(\emptyset, \Pi_2, \mathcal{V})$, $P, Q_1, \ldots, Q_n \in \mathcal{P}$.

Let $\langle A, I \rangle$ be a $\langle \Phi, \Pi_1 \rangle$-model, i.e. $\langle A, I \downarrow \Phi \rangle$ is some Φ-algebra and $I(P) \subseteq A^{\alpha(P)}$ for every $P \in \Pi_1$. The Kripke model for CFDL built from $\langle A, I \rangle$ is the triple $\langle \mathcal{S}, \mathcal{J}, \rho \rangle$ consisting of the set $\mathcal{S}$ of states over A, the *satisfaction function* for formulas $\mathcal{J} : \mathcal{F} \to 2^{\mathcal{J}}$ and the *meaning function* for programs $\rho : \mathcal{F} \to 2^{\mathcal{S} \times \mathcal{S}}$.

Definition 6.2 *The satisfaction function $\mathcal{J}$ and the meaning function ρ are defined simultaneously as follows:*

(i) $\mathcal{J}(\underline{\mathtt{skip}}) = \mathcal{S}$, $\mathcal{J}(\underline{\mathtt{fail}}) = \emptyset$, $\mathcal{J}(P(\vec{t})) = \{s | \vec{t}[s] \in I(P)\}$;

(ii) $\mathcal{J}(\neg A) = \mathcal{S} \setminus \mathcal{J}(A)$, $\mathcal{J}(A \vee B) = \mathcal{J}(A) \cup \mathcal{J}(B)$ *and* $\mathcal{J}(A \,\&\, B) = \mathcal{J}(A) \cap \mathcal{J}(B)$;

(iii) $\mathcal{J}(\exists x A) = \{s | \exists r \in \mathcal{S}(r \in \mathcal{J}(A) \,\&\, \forall v \neq x\ s(v) = r(v) \,\&\, x \in dom(r))\}$,

$\mathcal{J}(\forall x A) = \{s | \forall r \in \mathcal{S}(\forall v \neq x(s(v) = r(v) \,\&\, x \in dom(r)) \Rightarrow r \in \mathcal{J}(A))\}$,

$\rho(A?) = \{\langle s, s \rangle | s \in \mathcal{J}(A)\}$,

$\mathcal{J}(\langle P \rangle A) = \{s | \exists r(\langle s, r \rangle \in \rho(P) \,\&\, r \in \mathcal{J}(A))\}$,

$\mathcal{J}([P]A) = \{s | \forall r(\langle s, r \rangle \in \rho(P) \Rightarrow r \in \mathcal{J}(A))\}$;

(iv) $\rho(x := t) = \{\langle s, r \rangle | \forall v \neq x\ s(v) = r(v) \,\&\, r(x) = t[s]\}$;

(v) $\rho(PQ) = \rho(P)\rho(Q)$, $\rho(P \cup Q) = \rho(P) \cup \rho(Q)$;

(vi) $\rho([P | X_1 \equiv Q_1, \ldots, X_n \equiv Q_n]) = \min\{\rho(P) | \rho(X_i) = \rho(Q_i), 1 \leq i \leq n\}$.

Let $\Re \subset \mathcal{F} \cup \mathcal{P}$ be the subset of quantifier-free formulas and programs and τ denote the *translation function* $\Re \to \mathcal{P}(\Phi, \Pi, \mathcal{V})$ defined as follows:

$$\begin{array}{ll} \tau(\neg A) = (\tau(A) \Rightarrow \underline{\texttt{fail}}), & \tau(A \,\&\, B) = \tau(A) \,\&\, \tau(B), \\ \tau(A \vee B) = \tau(A) \vee \tau(B), & \tau(A?) = \tau(A), \\ \tau(\langle P \rangle A) = \tau(P) \wedge \tau(A), & \tau([P]A) = \tau(P) \Rightarrow \tau(A), \\ \tau(P \cup Q) = \tau(P) \vee \tau(Q), & \tau(PQ) = \tau(P) \wedge \tau(Q), \\ \multicolumn{2}{l}{\tau([P|X_1 \equiv Q_1, \ldots, X_n \equiv Q_n]) = [\tau(P)|\tau(X_1) \equiv \tau(Q_1), \ldots, \tau(X_n) \equiv \tau(Q_n)],} \\ \multicolumn{2}{l}{\text{and } \tau(A) = A \text{ in any other case.}} \end{array} \tag{4}$$

Note that the assignment operator is regarded as one of build-in predicates and is not translated (the last case above).

Theorem 6.3 *For every Kripke model for CFDL $\langle \mathcal{S}, \mathcal{J}, \rho \rangle$ there exists a Kripke model $\langle \mathcal{S}, \mathcal{I} \rangle$ for predicate programs such that*

(i) $\mathcal{I}(\tau(A)\#) = \rho(A?)$ *for any formula* $A \in \Re$, *and*

(ii) $\mathcal{I}(\tau(P)) = \rho(P)$ *for any program* $P \in \Re$.

The converse holds for every Kripke model for predicate programs in which the assignment operator is correctly defined.

Proof by induction on the length of formulas and programs.

7 Connection with Logic Programming

Our language uses a larger set of connectives than that of (pure) Prolog. We are unable to formally present a theorem about the inclusion of Prolog programs in predicate programs. Formal machinery of existing descriptions of denotational semantics of Prolog requires too large amount. We can only present some informal considerations.

As was noted in the example in Section 3 in pure Prolog terms take their values in some *free-generated* Φ-algebra $\mathcal{T}(\Phi, \mathcal{X})$, where $\mathcal{X}$ is a set of variables, $\mathcal{X} \cap \mathcal{V} = \emptyset$. Predicates in Prolog are built-in and defined ones. All built-in predicates act according to Definition 3.2. Built-in predicates include the unification predicate $\underline{\texttt{unif}}(\texttt{x}, \texttt{y})$. Let us show how to rewrite a Prolog program as predicate program.

Any Prolog program consists of clauses having one of the following forms:

$$:-\texttt{C}_1 \wedge \cdots \wedge \texttt{C}_m, \qquad \texttt{A} :- \texttt{B}_1 \wedge \cdots \wedge \texttt{B}_n, \qquad \texttt{A} :-.$$

In the first step we eliminate all compound terms from left-hand sides of clauses. That is we replace a clause $\texttt{P}(\texttt{t}_1, \ldots, \texttt{t}_j) :- \texttt{R}$ by the clause

$$\texttt{P}(\texttt{x}_1, \ldots, \texttt{x}_j) :- \underline{\texttt{unif}}(\texttt{x}_1, \texttt{t}_1) \wedge \cdots \wedge \underline{\texttt{unif}}(\texttt{x}_j, \texttt{t}_j) \wedge \texttt{R},$$

where all $\texttt{x}_1, \ldots, \texttt{x}_j \in \mathcal{V}$ are new different variables.

In the second step we change any string "$: -\texttt{G}\wedge!$" (beginning with "$: -$" and ending with "$\wedge!$"), where G is a formula, by the string "$: -(\texttt{G})!$".

If after these steps some clauses of the form "$\mathtt{A} : -$" remain, we replace them by "$\mathtt{A} : -\underline{\mathtt{skip}}$".

Now, let $\{\mathtt{A} : -\mathtt{F}_1, \ldots, \mathtt{A} : -\mathtt{F}_k\}$ be the set of all clauses having the same predicate symbol in left-hand side. Here we assume without lost of generality that these left-hand sides are identical (we achieve this by renaming the variables). Change this set by the definition $\mathtt{A} \equiv \mathtt{F}_1 \vee \cdots \vee \mathtt{F}_k$. Let $\mathcal{D}$ be the set of all definitions given in such way. The final predicate program takes the form $[\mathtt{H}_1 \vee \cdots \vee \mathtt{H}_i | \mathcal{D}]$, where $\{: -\mathtt{H}_1, \ldots, : -\mathtt{H}_i\}$ is the set of clauses with empty left-hand side.

The connectives '$\Rightarrow$' and '$\#$' are not used in this program, so predicate programs extend the pure Prolog programs. However, in most real Prolog's the program $\underline{\mathtt{not}}(\mathtt{P} \wedge \mathtt{Q})$ can be considered as some analogue of the program $(\mathtt{P} \Rightarrow \mathtt{Q})$. The connective '$\#$' (unbinding test) can be modelled with database operations. Hence, predicate programs do not extend practical Prolog language. But the introduced nonclassical models and the relation with the dynamic logic open new possibilities for the investigation of real logic programs. An example of such a kind of analysis is in the next section.

8 About the negation

The Horn-clause language is a sublanguage of the classical first-order predicate language. Great efforts were made to introduce other logical connectives into Prolog, particularly, the negation. The connection described above between dynamic logic and predicate programs shed some light on this question.

It is clear that the negation can be always introduced in a sublanguage consisting of translated formulas of the dynamic logic. However, one cannot extend the negation to whole set of predicate programs. Indeed, it follows from (4) that the following equivalences must be valid:

$$\begin{array}{lll} \neg\underline{\mathtt{skip}} \equiv \underline{\mathtt{fail}}, & \neg(P \Rightarrow Q) \equiv (P \wedge \neg Q), & \neg(P \,\&\, Q) \equiv (\neg P \vee \neg Q) \\ \neg\underline{\mathtt{fail}} \equiv \underline{\mathtt{skip}}, & \neg(P \wedge Q) \equiv (P \Rightarrow \neg Q), & \neg(P \vee Q) \equiv (\neg P \,\&\, \neg Q). \end{array} \tag{5}$$

From Lemma 5.3 we conclude

$$\begin{array}{rcl} \underline{\mathtt{skip}} \wedge P \Rightarrow \underline{\mathtt{fail}} & \equiv & P \Rightarrow \underline{\mathtt{fail}}, \\ \neg(\underline{\mathtt{skip}} \wedge P \Rightarrow \underline{\mathtt{fail}}) \equiv (\underline{\mathtt{skip}} \Rightarrow P) & \not\equiv & P \equiv \neg(P \Rightarrow \underline{\mathtt{fail}}). \end{array} \tag{6}$$

This means that any negation can not be "purely" logical, because it can not preserve equivalence between programs. However, if we add to (5) the rule

$$\neg R \equiv (R \Rightarrow \underline{\mathtt{fail}}), \tag{7}$$

applied to atomic programs R without defined predicate symbols only, we can speak about the negation $\neg F$ of an arbitrary program F. These transformations not define the negation uniquely, as it follows from (6). Nevertheless, it corresponds better to the intuitive meaning of the negated program $\neg F$ than the "negation as failure" defined directly by (7) and currently used in logic programming. Moreover, the equivalence

$$(R \Rightarrow \underline{\mathtt{fail}}) \Rightarrow \underline{\mathtt{fail}} \equiv R \tag{8}$$

is not true in general. However, it can be assumed as an axiom for all build-in predicates R, laws (5) can be extended for all connectives (with a pure formal introduction of additional dual connectives), and in this way the "transformational" semantics could be built for the negation which satisfy the double negation law for each predicate program.

Conclusions

We have defined a language connecting logic programming and nonclassical logic. This connection is established via certain nonclassical models. This made some questions of logic programming more clear. Moreover, it allows one to use nonclassical logic to prove the properties of logic programs. It also allows one to specify knowledge about a dynamic world directly in a logic programming language. This makes the pair ⟨*logic programs, nonclassical logic*⟩ a powerful basis to developing practical tools for the specification and verification of dynamic systems. This also opens new possibilities to investigate the behaviour of real Prolog programs.

Acknowlegment. The author express his gratitude to Jan Grabowski for his notes and suggestions.

References

[Kr] Kriaučiukas V. *Dynamic logics in a form of logic programs.* Math.Logics and Appl. Vilnius, 1990. No. 6. P. 67-76. (in Russian)

[Ha] Harel D. *First-order dynamic logic.* Lect.Notes Comp.Sci. Springer, 1979. V. 68.

[Ko] Kowalski R.A. *Predicate logic as a programming language.* Proc. IFIP'74, Stockholm. North-Holland, 1974. P. 500-506.

[AM] Abadi A., Manna Z. *Temporal logic programming.* J. Symbolic Computation. 1989. V. 8, No. 2. P. 277-295.

[AE] Apt K.R., van Emden M.H. *Contributions to the theory of logic programming.* J. ACM. 1982. V. 29, No. 3. P. 841-862.

[Mi] Milner R. *A calculus for communicating systems.* Lect.Notes Comp.Sci. Springer, 1980. V. 92.

[Gr] Grabowski J. *Unificational dynamic logic.* Elektron. Inf.verarb.Kybern. EIK. 1986. V. 22, No. 5/6. P. 325-338.

Logical Operational Semantics of Parlog
Part I: And-Parallelism *

Egon Börger
Dip. di Informatica
C.so Italia 40
I-56100 PISA
boerger@dipisa.di.unipi.it

Elvinia Riccobene
Dip. di Matematica
V.le Andrea Doria 6
I-95125 CATANIA
riccobene@mathct.cineca.it

Abstract

We provide a complete mathematical semantics for the parallel logic programming language PARLOG.This semantics is abstract but nevertheless simple and supports the intuitive operational understanding of programs. It is based on Gurevich's notion of *Evolving Algebras* ([8]) and is obtained adapting ideas from the OCCAM formalization in [11] and from the *Evolving Algebras* semantics of full PROLOG in [1]. The first part gives an explicit formalization of the AND-Parallelism in PARLOG, leaving the (orthogonal) OR-Parallelism abstract. Thereby our description can be easily modified for other parallel logic programming languages, too.

In a sequel to this paper the OR-Parallelism is also made explicit by a natural extension of the PARLOG Algebras developed here and the correctness of this extension will be proved.

1 Evolving Algebras

Due to space limitation we skip the introduction and refer instead to [8] and [1] for a general motivation. Gurevich's notion of **Evolving Algebras** is adapted from [8] as follows: *an* **Evolving Algebra** *is a pair* (A, T) *consisting of a (finite), many-sorted, partial, first-order algebra* A *of some finite signature and a finite set* T *of transition rules of the same signature.*

A **computation** *of* A *is a (finite or infinite) sequence* $s_0, s_1, \cdots, s_k, s_{k+1}, \cdots$, *where*

*Part of this work was done when the first author was guest scientist at the Scientific Center of IBM Germany GmbH in Heidelberg, on sabbatical from University of Pisa, and when the second author from July 1990 till November 1990 worked at the Institut für Logik, Komplexität und Deduktionssysteme of University of Karlsruhe (Germany). The second author has been partially supported by "Progetto Finalizzato Sistemi Informatici e Calcolo Parallelo" of CNR, under Grant n.90.00671.69.

$s_0 = A$ *and each* s_{k+1} *is obtained from* s_k *by applying one or more* transition rules.

All the other basic definitions and conventions for *evolving algebras* - in particular for form and meaning of **transition rules** - are taken unchanged from [1] and [3] and due to space limitation are not repeated here.

Remark: A Parlog computation is non-deterministic and so will be the Parlog system of transition rules. Moreover a Parlog computation may involve a concurrent computation of more than one processes. This implies that the transition from a current algebra A_{s_k} to the subsequent algebra $A_{s_{k+1}}$ will be realized applying simultaneously more than one rule (one for each process which works in parallell with others). We will only use non-conflicting rules. For more complete references on related work on the *evolving algebras* approach see [3].

As in [1] we assume the usual list operators to be present without further mentioning. In particular we write:
$f^*(d_1,\cdots,d_n) = (f(d_1),\cdots,f(d_n))$ for $f : D \to T$ and $f^* : D^* \to T^*$;
$List = [head|tail]$ and $List = [proj(1, List),\cdots, proj(length(List), List)]$,
with the *projection* function $proj$: **Index × D* → D**, and length function *length*.

In addition we will use the following functions for term decomposition:
if *op* is an associative term building operator (like "," ,"&", ".", ";") and *t* a *term*, $[op]$-*decomp*(t) denotes the sequence $[t_1,\cdots,t_n]$ of immediate components of *t* w.r.t. *op*, i.e. such that $t \equiv t_1\ op \cdots op\ t_n$ and $\forall i : t_i \not\equiv op(a,b)$. $[op]$-*decomp* comes with its inverse function $[op]$-*comp*.

If $t \equiv t_1\ op \cdots op\ t_n$ with immediate components $t_1,\cdots,t_n$, we also write $[op]$-*head*(t) for *head*$([op]$-*decomp*$(t))$ and $[op]$-*tail*(t) for $[op]$-*comp*$(tail([op]$-*decomp*$(t)))$ with the obvious meaning.

2 Parlog Algebra: universes and functions

Due to space limitation we use the Prolog universes and functions from [1] without further mentioning except for possible refinementes.

Goal is the universe of all terms built up from literals by "," (parallel conjunction) and "&" (sequential conjunction), the former of higher binding priority than the latter.

We imagine the computation of a query Q w.r.t. a Parlog program P as evolution (dynamic construction and traversal) of a "computation tree". This "tree" is not a static structure defined by P; its form (the number of vertices and edges) and its labeling depend on the given query and its evaluation w.r.t. P. We formalize this "tree structure", each incarnation of which represents the essentials of an instantaneous description of a Parlog computation, by introducing a set **Node** as basic (evolving) universe of Parlog Algebras. **Node** comes equipped with the decorating functions *goal* : **Node → Goal** which associates with a *node* the *goal* to be evaluated during the subcomputation starting from *node* and the evolving tree functions *children* : **Node → Node*** yielding the sequence of children associated with a node

$$children(\mathrm{p}) = [child(1,\mathrm{p}),\cdots, child(length(children(\mathrm{p})),\mathrm{p})].$$

We write $child(i,p)$ for $proj(i, children(p))$ i.e. the i-th child of a node p.

By the function *res* : **Node →** $\{success, failure\}$ we keep control of the *success* or *failure* report for the computation performed by a given node. To keep control of the "tree" extension and traversal we take an idea from the description of OCCAM in [11] to introduce a set of *modes* each of which tells the current phase of the computation associated to the given node. Formally speaking we have a universe

$$\mathbf{Mode} = \{dormant, ready, starting, working, waiting, reporting\}$$

and a function $mode : \mathbf{Node} \rightarrow \mathbf{Mode}$.

A node has *mode*: *ready* when it is ready to receive the control; *starting* when it has received the control; *waiting* when it waits for an answer of (one of) its subcomputations; *reporting* when it reports to its parent node; *dormant* when it becomes inactive.

Each node of **Node** has also a label which can be *and-par*, *and-seq* or *or-par*. The node's label is given in order to encode the type of the computation managed by the node.

If a node is labelled by *and-par*, it coordinates the computation of concurrent (conjunctive) processes; *and-seq*, it performs the computation of sequential (conjunctive) processes; *or-par*, it controls the reduction process associated to the execution of a *call* in the given program.

Formally we have a universe $\mathbf{Tag} = \{and-par, and-seq, or-par\}$ with a function $tag : \mathbf{Node} \rightarrow \mathbf{Tag}$. The following function $\tilde{tag} : \mathbf{Term} \rightarrow \mathbf{Tag}$ associates a label of **Tag** to a term t according to the principal functor of t :

$$\tilde{tag}(t) := \begin{cases} \text{and-par} & \text{if} \quad t \equiv t_1, t_2, \cdots, t_n \\ \text{and-seq} & \text{if} \quad t \equiv t_1 \& t_2 \& \cdots \& t_n \\ \text{or-par} & \text{if} \quad t \in \mathbf{Lit} \end{cases}$$

On universe **Sub** of substitutions we introduce a 0-ary function *sub*, representing the current variable bounds.

In Part II (see [2]) we will see that this *"transparent"* substitution allows for Parlog's *stream-And-Parallelism* where calls can be evaluated concurrently, communicating incrementally through bindings to shared variables. We will then introduce *"non-transparent"* substitutions associated to nodes which allow to bind certain variables - during the unification and guard evaluation process in search of a *candidate clause* - which will become transparent (in *sub*) only after commitment to a particular clause.

3 Transition Rule System of Parlog Algebras

In the following Parlog *Transition Rules* the variable p ranges over the universe **Node**.

In writing down these rules we will make use of simplifying notation, like abbreviating:
for all children s of p : b(s, p) for $\forall s(p = parent(s) \rightarrow b(s,p))$;
for some child s of p : b(s, p) for $\exists i \in \mathbf{Index}(s = child(i,p) \& b(s,p))$.

In **function updates** we write "for all children s of p : $f_0(s) = e_0 \& \ldots \& f_n(s) = e_n$", instead of all **function updates** "$f_0(s) = e_0, \ldots, f_n(s) = e_n$" where s ranges over all the nodes s such that p = parent(s).

3.1 Beginning and end of computations

In our description of a Parlog computation started from a query w.r.t. a given program, we give no rule for the initialization of the "computational tree", but assume the following inizialization of Parlog Algebras. The universe **Node** contains a unique element p (the *root*) and the functions are initialized as follows: database:= "program", sub:= empty, tag(p):= $\tilde{\text{tag}}$("query"), mode(p):= starting, goal(p):= "query". .

On the *root* of the "tree" the *parent* function is undefined. (We may also consider $res(p)$ as undefined in the initial algebra.) When the whole computation has terminated the control comes back to the *root*. Based on our assumption that the *root* is uniquely determined by having no parent, we can formalize the **stop rule** as follows:

```
If mode(p) = reporting & parent(p) = undef
then
      mode(p):= dormant.
```

Giving output could be provided by some **output rule** (which we do not formalize here) using the substitution information coded in *sub*.

3.2 The *and-par* node operation

When an *and-par* node receives the control (i.e. when its mode is *starting*), it creates as many children as there are computations that should be executed in parallel. The [,]-*decomp* function on the goal g associated to the node, provides those new parallel processes $g_i = proj(i, [,]\text{-}decomp(g))$ $for\ i = 1, 2, \cdots, n$. The tag of children nodes is determined by $\tilde{tag}$ on term g_i. The *and-par* node becomes *waiting* and the control passes to each of its children which become *ready*. We have therefore the following **and-par starting rule:**

```
If tag(p) = and-par & mode(p) = starting
then
      Let parlist [,]-decomp(goal(p))
      Create p-subtree of children temp(1),..., temp(length(parlist))
      with mode ready and
            tag(temp(i)):= tãg(proj(i,parlist)),
            goal(temp(i)):= proj(i,parlist)
      end Create
```

where

```
Create p-subtree of child{ren} temp(1),..., temp(l)
{ with tag t, mode m, } { passing g ... and }
      updates
end Create
```

is an abbreviation for the following update:

```
Extend Node by temp(1),..., temp(l) with
      child(i,p):= temp(i),
      {tag(temp(i)):= t,
      mode(temp(i)):= m,}
      {g(temp(i)):= g(p),
       :}
      updates
end Extend,
mode(p):= waiting.
```

Typically we will use goal for g; updates stands for a set of function updates; updates written between { } are optional. Note that - in order to avoid the necessity to distinguish the case of a root labelled with *and-par* but with empty query - we understand the preceding rule as doing nothing in case l=0.

Remark. In our formalization of *and-par* nodes we have to depart from the fully parallel point of view taken in Gurevich and Moss (see [11]) for Occam PAR nodes in one major respect: we do not describe how the children of an *and-par* node become *starting*. How such a node becomes *starting* depends on the implementation. In a fully parallel system all children would have *starting* mode because all of them must work simultaneously. If our machine has fewer processors than (parallel) processes, then one or more processors must work on more than one clause. In this case we have not a parallel run, but concurrent runs which are realized by time sharing or (memory) interleaving.

Each child which has been created by the above rule computes one element of the conjunction. A conjunction succeeds if each of its calls succeeds, and fails if one of its calls fails. Therefore an *and-par* node gives back the control either when all of its children have finished their subcomputation with success - the *and-par* node reports *success* - or when one of them has failed its subcomputation - the *and-par* node reports *failure* to the parent and all siblings' computations of the reporting child are aborted (i.e. set to *dormant*) -. These two cases are formally described by the **and – par success rule** and **and – par failure rule**. We have the **and – par success rule** :

> If tag(p) = and-par & mode(p) = waiting
> & for all children q of p : mode(q) = reporting & res(q) = success
> then
> *report from* p-*subtree with* success.

The abbreviation *"report from* p-*subtree (or -leaf) with* success *(or* failure*)"* stands for the following three function updates:

> mode(p):= reporting,
> res(p):= success *(or* failure*)*,
> for each child s of p: mode(s):= dormant.

The latter update is not there if p is a leaf of the "tree". We include the update for later use for reasons of uniformity.

Once a node has become *dormant*, it will never be used any more in our algebra. This means that the whole "subtree" of a *dormant* node is marked for **garbage collection**.

To abort all children's subcomputations of a *reporting* node p, it is not (always) sufficient to change the mode of p's children to *dormant* because a descendant node s of p may remain active when its parent subcomputation has been killed. It can be proved however that these possibly still active sub-sub-computations will not affect the substitution *sub*. How the computation of a child node of a *dormant* node is aborted depends on the working schedular.

Note also that the *and-par success rule* does not update the associated goals. This is because *and-par* nodes can appear only at the root (if the initial query has form $t_1, \cdots, t_n$) or under an *and-seq* node (which will update its restgoalsequence discarding the goal of its *and-par* child).

The **and – par failure rule** is the same as **and-par success rule** replacing success by failure and all by some.

3.3 The *and-seq* node operation

When a node labeled *and-seq* keeps the control, its *goal* function contains a term of the form $a_1 \& a_2 \cdots \& a_n$, with a_i goals to be executed in the indicated order. In *starting* mode the *and-seq* node creates a child having label according to $\tilde{tag}$ function on [&]-*head*(*goal*(p)) : *or-par* if $a_1 \in$ Lit; *and-par* if $a_1 = b_{1_1}, b_{1_2}, \cdots, b_{1_s}$. Thus we have the following **and – seq starting rule** :

If tag(p) = and-seq & mode(p) = starting & goal $\neq$ nil
then
Let goal [&]-head(goal(p))
Create p-*subtree of child* temp
with tag $\tilde{\text{tag}}$(goal), *mode* starting *and*
goal(temp):= goal
end Create

The remaining *and-seq* node operation can easily be formulated by adapting the rules for *(sub)goal success* and *backtracking* of Börger's (Sequential) Prolog Algebras. Due to lack of space we only list these rules here without further explanations end refer to [1] for comments.

and – seq continuation rule :

If tag(p) = and-seq & mode(p) = waiting
& mode(child(p)) = reporting & res(child(p)) = success
then
mode(p):= starting,
goal(p):= [&]-tail(goal(p)),
mode(child(p)):= dormant.

and – seq success rule :

```
If tag(p) = and-seq & mode(p) = starting & goal(p) = nil
then report from p-subtree with success.
```

The **and – seq failure rule** is similar to **and-par failure rule** replacing par by seq.

3.4 The *or-par* node operation

A node *or-par* performs the reduction process for a *call* of a literal. It consists in the selection of a *candidate clause* (if there is one) among those of the *database* and in the subsequent computation of the selected clause body. In Parlog the notion of *candidate clause* is more complex than in Standard Prolog where only the unification between the clause head and the given literal is required. In Part II (see [2]) we will give rules to compute the following function

$$candidate - clause : \textbf{Clause}^* \times \textbf{Node} \times \textbf{Lit} \rightarrow \textbf{Goal} \times \textbf{Sub} \cup \{nil\}$$

which - for reasons of stepwise refinement - we take here as (abstract) function associating to the given clause sequence and the given literal a copy of the body of the selected (renamed corresponding to the node p) clause and the output substitution of its head and the given literal, i.e. the substitution for the *output variables* of the clause head satisfying the **input matching** and the **guard evaluation** conditions. It yields *nil* if there is no such clause. The **or-par starting rule** has an additional guard for allowedness which serves to avoid simultaneous (possibly conflicting) updates of *sub*. The corresponding integrity constraint is that at each moment at most one p has value $allowed(p) = 1$. Due to lack of space we skip the **or-par success** and **failure rules**.

or – par starting rule

```
Let lit subres(goal(p),sub)
If tag(p) = or-par & mode(p) = starting & is-user-defined(goal(p)) = 1
& candidate-clause(database,p,lit) ≠ nil
& allowed(p) = 1
then
      Let body  proj(1,candidate-clause(database,p,lit)),
         unifier  proj(2,candidate-clause(database,p,lit))
      sub:= join(unifier,sub),
       Create p-subtree of child temp
       with tag tãg(body),mode starting, and
             goal(temp):= body
       end Create
```

The function *join* : $\textbf{Sub}^* \rightarrow \textbf{Sub}$ yields the result of combining a sequence of (consistent) substitutions into one substitution.

4 Conclusion

Using an abstract notion of OR-Parallelism we have given a complete formal semantics of the AND-Parallelism in Parlog. This formalization has been given in such a way that it can be easily adapted to other parallel logic programming languages like Concurrent Prolog or GHC. This will allow to investigate interesting relations between these systems on the basis of the uniform and precise *evolving algebras* framework developed here.

References

[1] E.Börger, 1990 *A Logic Operational Semantics of full Prolog. Part II. Built-in Predicates for Database Manipulations*, MFCS'90 Mathematical Foundation of Computer Science (Ed. B.Rovan), Springer LNCS 452, pp. 1-14.

[2] E.Börger & E.Riccobene, 1991 *Logical Operational Semantics of Parlog. Part II:Or-Parallelism* (submitted).

[3] E.Börger & D.Rosenzweig, 1991, *From Prolog Algebras Towards WAM - A Mathematical Study of Implementation*, CSL'90 4rd Workshop on Computer Science Logic (Eds. E.Börger, H.Kleine Büning, M.M.Richter), Springer LNCS (to appear).

[4] E.Börger & D.Rosenzweig, 1991, *WAM Algebras - A Mathematical Study of Implementation. Part II*,Technical Report, CSE-TR-88-91, pp. 21, Dept. of EECS, University of Michigan, Ann Arbor.

[5] T.Conlon, *Programming in Parlog*, Addison Wesley 1989.

[6] T.Conlon & S.Gregory, *Hands on MacPARLOG 2.0 A User's Guide*, PLP Ltd 1990.

[7] S.Gregory, *Parallel Logic Programming in PARLOG*, Addison Wesley 1989.

[8] Y.Gurevich, 1991, *Dynamic Algebras. A Tutorial Introduction*, EATCS Bulletin 43, February 1991.

[9] Y.Gurevich, 1988, *Logic and Challenge of Computer Science*, Trends in Theoretical Computer Science (Ed. E.Börger), Computer Science Press, pp. 1-57.

[10] Y.Gurevich, 1988, *Algorithms in the World of Bounded Resources.* In: *The Universal Turing Machine - a Half-Century Story* (Ed. R.Herken), Oxford University Press, pp. 407-416.

[11] Y.Gurevich & L.S.Moss, 1990, *Algebraic Operational Semantics and Occam*, CSL'89 3rd Workshop on Computer Science Logic (Eds. E.Börger, H.Kleine Büning, M.M.Richter), Springer LNCS 440, pp. 176-192.

A Tool for Building Connectionist-like Networks Based on Term Unification

Zdravko Markov
Institute of Informatics - Bulgarian Academy of Sciences
Acad.G.Bonchev St. Block 29A, 1113 Sofia, Bulgaria

Abstract

The paper presents a network modeling tool called Net-Clause Language (NCL), integrating some connectionist-like and some symbolic processing features in a unified computational environment. Unlike the other connectionist symbol processing approaches, NCL represents and processes symbols not by implementing them as patterns of activity in a traditional neural network, rather it uses some connectionist ideas to organize symbolic computation in a more flexible way. The paper presents two examples (deductive inference and image processing) which show how the connectionist-like and symbolic features of NCL can benefit each from the other.

1 Introduction

The long standing symbolic versus connectionist debate in AI has proved that none of the approaches taken in isolation could be fruitful. Now it is widely acknowledged that instead of looking for a single universal formalism an AI system should be built out of diverse components, some connectionist and some symbolic. This view is well expressed in [10]: "Our purely numeric connectionist networks are inherently deficient in abilities to reason well; our purely symbolic logical systems are inherently deficient in abilities to represent the all-important heuristic connections between things - the uncertain, approximate, and analogical links that we need for making new hypotheses. The versatility that we need can be found only in larger-scale architectures that can exploit and manage the advantages of several types of representations at the same time." There are several possible ways to use the advantages of both connectionist and symbolic approaches at the same time. One of them is putting together symbolic and connectionist systems with a proper interface between them for solving a particular problem. An instance of this approach is the so called *hybrid model* designed to provide complex reasoning about perceptual similarities, described in [2]. It is a combination of a semantic net and a connectionist network, in which the leaves of the semantic net are connected to the output units of the connectionist network. More generally this approach is viewed as a connectionist implementation of various symbolic data-structures such as frames, parse trees, semantic nets etc. and the corresponding algorithms for their processing. Actually this is the so called *connectionist symbol processing* (*Artificial Intelligence* (46) 1990, No.1,2 presents a collection of papers devoted to this approach) aimed at both achieving better implementation of these formalisms ("implementational connectionism") and getting some new useful properties ("revisionist-symbol processing connectionism"). [3,12,13] are instances of this approach. [13] discuses an implementation of LISP-like structures in a connectionist network in order to show that connectionist networks can exhibits some new properties such as compositionality and distal access. Various ways of mapping part-whole hierarchies into connectionist networks are shown in [3]. A general approach for distributed representation of symbolic structures in connectionist systems is described in [12]. All these approaches represent symbols (symbolic structures) either as individual network units (localist representation) or as patterns of activity of collections of units (distributed representation).

There are also some attempts for connectionist implementation of logic (e.g. in [4] a connectionist implementation of propositional logic is discussed), however they are far from filling the huge gap in representational power between logic and connectionism.

Many of the connectionist symbol processing approaches are motivated by cognitive theories. This is probably one of the reasons why all of the approaches mentioned above consider the connectionist component at the lower (implementational or subsymbolic) level of the system and the symbolic one - at the higher (representational) level. In contrast, the approach described in the present paper is motivated by the need to improve the versatility of the symbolic approach, i.e. it is aimed at *using some connectionist ideas to organize symbol representation and processing in a more flexible way.* Thus its lower level is symbolic and higher level is connectionist-like. (Hereafter we use the term "connectionism" in a broader sense, not as an equivalent of "neural computing".) Therefore following the adopted terminology we could call our approach "symbolic connectionism". It is important to note that although it uses some connectionist ideas, it is *not subsymbolic.* In contrast to the connectionist networks the processing units do not perform simple numeric calculations (e.g. weighted functions), rather they implement complicated symbolic algorithms. Furthermore the network connections propagate complex data structures to supply the processing units. The approach is based on the fundamental connectionist idea that hard problems could be solved by interconnecting many independent processing units in a network. The overall organization of the computational process is borrowed from connectionism - this is *distributed control* and *spreading activation.* All these features are implemented in a network modeling environment called *Net-Clause Language (NCL).*

The Net-Clause language is designed for building *network models without centralized control using term unification as a basic processing mechanism.* (Here by the term "network model" we mean both "representational formalism" and "computational architecture" and later we will show that NCL can be used for both purposes.) The basis of NCL is the network formalism presented in [5], where it was considered as an extension of Prolog. This formalism has been further elaborated mainly in the field of logical reasoning [6,7,8]. In [7] its use for natural language processing is also shown.

The paper is organized as follows. Section 2 introduces briefly the Net-clause language. Section 3 discusses the use of the language for implementation of deductive data-driven inference, underlining its ability for declarative knowledge representation. Section 4 shows an example of using NCL for building a connectionist-like architecture for image processing. A discussion of the basic NCL features in the context of some more general computational paradigms is given in Section 5.

2 The Net-Clause Language

Syntactically the Net-Clause language (NCL) is an extension of the standard Prolog. Its semantics however is aimed at modeling graph like structures (networks), consisting of nodes and links. The nodes specify procedures unifying terms, and the links are channels along which the terms are propagated.

The basic constructors of NCL programs are the *net-clauses*. A net-clause is a sequence of nodes, syntactically represented as structures (complex terms), separated by the delimiter ":". The network links are implicitly defined by shared variables among different nodes in a net-clause. The variables in NCL are called *net-variables.*

The NCL networks are built out of two types of nodes - *free nodes* and *procedural nodes.* The free nodes are structures (in the form of Prolog facts) used to access net-variables, inside and outside the net-clause. The procedural nodes are the active elements in the network. Procedures unifying terms are associated to the procedural nodes. The procedures are activated under certain conditions, defined locally in each node. Thus the control in NCL is *distributed.* It is based on the unification procedure, which is also the basic data processing mechanism in the language. Since there are no explicit control means in the language the control in NCL is *data-driven.* Generally when unifying net-variables two possible results can occur: *binding net-variables to non-variable terms* and *sharing net-variables.* These possibilities define the two control schemes in NCL. Each one of them is specified by a particular type of procedural node. We describe briefly only the first control scheme - *spreading activation*, since the second one (*activation by need*) does not relate to the connectionist features of NCL. It is described elsewhere (e.g. [7]) in the framework of *default reasoning.*

The spreading activation control scheme is defined by procedural nodes written in the following syntax: **node(X_1,...,X_n,M,<procedure>)**. The purpose of the node procedure is to unify terms, particularly to bind variables, which in turn could further propagate both data (terms) and control (activation) among other nodes in the network. The node procedure is also an interface to the Prolog system, which is an environment for NCL, i.e. Prolog built-in procedures and predicates can be called too. **M** is an integer number and its semantics is to define a *threshold*, determining the amount of data required to activate the procedure. X_i, **i=1..n** are net-variables which serve as channels for term propagating. They can be used both as *excitatory links* and as *inhibitory links* for the activation of the procedure. The excitatory links are represented as simple (ordinary) variables and the inhibitory links are represented as negated variables (written as $\tilde{}X_i$). The procedure is activated if the difference between the number of the bound simple variables and the number of the bound negated ones is equal to **M**. When defining a spreading activation node the condition **M>0** is required. This ensures that the procedure can not be activated "by definition", i.e. at least one variable binding is needed for that purpose. Actually binding a simple variable decrements **M**, and binding a negated one increments it, thus the procedure is activated when **M=0**. In such a way **M** can be used also to indicate dynamically the number of bound $\mathbf{X}_i$.

Consider the classical neural network example for the XOR function. The following NCL program implements the XOR function in a *pure connectionist fashion*:

```
input1(X): input2(Y): output(Z):
node(X,~Y,1,X1=on): node(Y,~X,1,Y1=on): node(X1,Y1,1,Z=on).
```

In addition to the input/output variables (X,Y and Z), the variables X1 and Y1 are introduced to represent the hidden layer of the network. The following NCL queries illustrate the work of the program (logical "1" is encoded as a bound net-variable and "0" - as a free one; the answers of the NCL interpreter are given in italics):

<- input1(on), output(Z).
Z= on

<- input1(on), input2(on), output(Z).
Z= _1

The NCL network is shown in Figure 1. It is a direct implementation of the corresponding neural network if we assume that a bound net-variable gives weight of connection **1** and a free one - weight of connection **-1**. Then the spreading activation nodes perform *combining function* **summation** and *threshold function* **unit step** (if the combined inputs are greater than 1, then the output is 1, otherwise - 0).

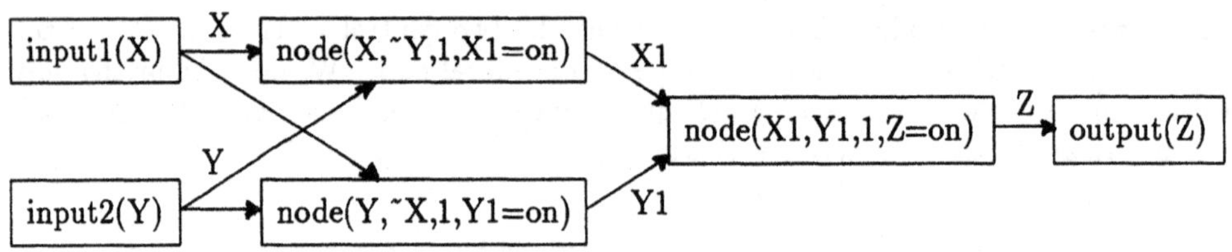

Figure 1. The NCL network for XOR function.

Let us now discuss a "symbolic" example, described also in [5,8]. Consider the problem of polyhedron recognition in the context of Prolog. A polyhedron can be represented as an attributed graph by a list of edges, each one in the following form:

edge(Vertex1,Vertex2,Slope,Length)

Thus an instance of a parallelogram can be represented by the following list:

[edge(1,2,0,20),edge(2,3,30,50),edge(3,4,0,20),edge(4,1,30,50)]

An important feature of this representation is the possibility to define a class of such figures, using variables instead of fixed names or values standing for the vertex names and attributes. Such a class representation is free of any specific geometric properties as size, orientation, etc. The only fact taken into account is the equality or inequality of the attributes, and this is provided by the built-in Prolog unification mechanism. For example the class of parallelograms is represented as follows:

[edge(A,B,S1,L1),edge(B,C,S2,L2),edge(C,D,S1,L1),edge(D,E,S2,L2)]

Using this representation the problem of polyhedron recognition comes to the problem of graph isomorphism. The latter is solved easily (but not efficiently) by a simple recursive predicate in Prolog, checking whether a list is a sublist of another list.

Let us now discuss the NCL solution of the above stated problem. Consider the following net-clause program:

```
/* Free Nodes - Network Inputs */
edge(A,B,S1,L1):
edge(B,C,S2,L1):
edge(C,D,S1,L1):
edge(D,A,S2,L1):
edge(B,E,S2,L2):
edge(E,F,S1,L1):
edge(F,A,S2,L2):
edge(E,G,S3,L3):
edge(G,A,S4,L4):

/* General case of a four-side figure */
node(A,B,E,G,4,fig(four_side_figure)):

/* Hidden node checking perpendicularity */
node(S1,S2,2,perp(S1,S2,P)):

/* Non-perpendicular figures */
node(A,B,E,F,~P,4,fig(parallelogram)):
node(A,B,C,D,~P,4,fig(rhombus)):

/* Perpendicular figures */
node(A,B,E,F,P,5,fig(rectangular)):
node(A,B,C,D,P,5,fig(square)):

/* Free Node - Network Output */
fig(Fig).

/* Prolog procedure calculating perpendicularity */
perp(X,Y,ok):-0 is (X-Y) mod 90,!.
perp(_,_,_).
```

The program describes a network for recognition of planar four-side geometric figures. The figures are represented as collections of edges with parameters. The edges are written as free nodes. The shared variables in these nodes represent the common vertices and the geometric constraints (parallel and same-length edges). The shared variables, grouped in the spreading activation nodes, represent the "part-of" hierarchy. Thus, unifying the free nodes with the nodes of a particular instance of a figure, the bound net-variables activate the corresponding class of figures. The example shows a way of using hidden nodes (an intermediate layer between input and output nodes) in NCL networks. Such node is the node for checking perpendicularity. It is activated when net-variables **S1** and **S2** (representing the slopes of the corresponding edges) are bound. If the condition for perpendicularity is present, then the procedure **perp** binds the net-variable **P**, thus activating the "perpendicular" classes and suppressing the "non-perpendicular" ones (because of the inhibitory link **~P**). The network is activated by specifying the edges of sample figures as net-clause queries. The corresponding class is obtained by free node **fig**. Some examples of the network activation are shown below:

```
<- edge(1,2,0,20),edge(2,3,45,30),edge(3,4,0,20),edge(4,1,45,30),fig(X).
X=parallelogram

yes
<- edge(1,2,0,20),edge(2,3,90,20),edge(3,4,0,20),edge(4,1,90,20),
   fig(square).

yes
<- edge(a,b,0,20),edge(b,c,5,30),edge(c,d,10,40),edge(d,a,50,60),fig(X).
X=four_side_figure
```

When we program the above network we describe how the edges are connected and what constraints they satisfy in order to build a particular class of geometric figures. We do not specify any control component or computational mechanism to describe the recognition task to be performed. So we create our program in a *declarative way.* And this is just enough to make it work. It is important to note that this feature of NCL is due to the data-driven control, i.e. describing the connections between the various data structures in the program (part-of hierarchies, constraints etc.) we actually describe the way these data structures are processed. Hence our program is a *declarative representation* of the problem domain and at the same time it is a *computational architecture* for performing the recognition task for the domain objects.

3 Deduction in NCL

In this section we briefly outline the use of NCL for deductive inference. Deduction is a powerful symbolic method for problem solving. [4] shows an attempt to use connectionist approaches to logic and deduction. However it concerns very limited aspects of logic and reasoning (e.g. only propositional logic). In contrast, our approach provides means to implement a real deductive system, even more elaborated and powerful than traditional logic programming.

The use of NCL for logical inference is based on establishing a correspondence between Horn clauses and Net-clauses [6]. This is also a way of assigning a logical semantics to net-clauses, as it is shown in [8]. In the present paper we consider an extended version of these transformation rules, covering the case of general logic programs (allowing clauses with negated goals). They are defined as follows:

1. Each program clause is translated into a net-clause, where the clause head is represented by a spreading activation node and the clause body - by a collection of free nodes. **X1,...,Xm** are all variables occurring in the literals **A1,...,Ap**. **Y1,...,Yn** are all variables occurring in **B1,...,Bq**.

```
                                         node(X1,...,Xm,m,p(Y1,...,Yn)):
p(Y1,...,Yn) <-- A1,...,Ap    <===>     A1:
                                         ...
                                         Ap.
```

2. The goal clause is represented as a net-clause built out of free nodes, which can share variables, thus introducing means to share variables in the original Horn clause goal.

```
<-- B1,...,Bn    <===>    B1:...Bn.
```

3. The unit clauses are represented as net-clause data (query), which activate the net-clause program.

```
C1 <--
...          <===>     <- C1,...,Cn.
Cn <--
```

The spreading activation scheme implements *data-driven inference (forward chaining)* in Horn clauses. To illustrate this let us discuss an example. Consider the following Horn clause program:

```
1. p(a,b) <--
2. p(c,b) <--
3. p(X,Z) <-- p(X,Y),p(Y,Z)                              (1)
4. p(X,Y) <-- p(Y,X)
5. <-- p(a,c)
```

Applying the above rules this program is transformed into the following net-clause program (the Horn clauses and net-clauses are numbered correspondingly):

```
/* 1,2 */ <- p(a,b),p(c,b).
/* 3 */    node(X,Y,Z,3,p(X,Z)): p(X,Y): p(Y,Z).         (2)
/* 4 */    node(X,Y,2,p(X,Y)): p(Y,X).
/* 5 */    p(a,c):[].
```

Program 1 has clear declarative meaning, however there is no Prolog system, which is able to find a refutation for it. This is because of the fixed computation and search rules used in the practical implementations of the SLD-resolution. Program 2 runs successfully on the net-clause interpreter. It realizes data-driven inference directed from the unit clauses to the goal clause. It is a kind of resolution where the refutation procedure is initiated by the unit clause resolution. In fact the data, which represent the set of unit positive clauses are the input for the resolution process. So, the data-driven inference can be interpreted in terms of *unit resolution*. Furthermore NCL can deal with formulae in a more general form than the standard Logic Programming. From logical point of view a net-clause in general is a conjunction of Horn clauses, where the scope of the universal quantifiers is extended to all Horn clauses represented by a net-clause. Thus a net-clause allows communication links to be established between several Horn clauses through the shared variables. The procedural semantics of NCL can be expressed in terms of *non-clausal resolution*, which is shown in [8].

The following example illustrates the NCL implementation of general logic programs. It shows also a special case (not shown in the transformation rule 1) when positive and negated goals share variables. Then additional variables (**T1, T2**) are introduced to propagate the truth values of the free nodes (the goals in the clause body) to the spreading activation node (the clause head).

```
a(X) :- not b(X), c(X)                  node(T1,~T2,1,a(X)): b(X,T2):c(X,T1).
b(1).                     <===>         <- b(1,true),c(2,true).
c(2).
```

The NCL data-driven inference has also a connectionist-like interpretation. The data-driven rule can be viewed as a threshold element, whose firing indicates the success of the predicate p (see the transformation rule 1). The success of a predicate in terms of NCL data-driven inference means that all its variables are instantiated. So the net-variables **X1,...Xm** are excitatory links whose binding indicate the success of the goals in the clause body. **Y1,...,Yn** are inhibitory links suppressing the success of **p** if some of the negated goals in the body have succeeded (some of **Yi**'s have been bound). Furthermore we can introduce partial success of **p** by using a threshold less than **m**. In this case **p** will succeed even when not all **Ai**'s have succeeded or some **Bi**'s have succeeded. In such a way a logic program (actually the net-clause is a more general form of a first order formula, allowing shared variables among clauses) can be viewed as a localist connectionist network. Each node in this network represents a predicate, and the network links (established dynamically by executing the node procedures) connect the arguments of the complementary literals. The network is activated when some predicates (the data) are set true by binding their variable-arguments. Then these variable bindings are spread into the network eventually binding other variables and setting other predicates true by firing their corresponding procedural nodes. When this process terminates the activated procedural nodes (or the bound by their procedures free nodes) indicate the inferred predicates.

4 Image Processing in NCL

In this section we show how NCL can be used for implementation of a connectionist-like computational architecture based on symbolic processing. Consider the problem of feature detection in an image, represented as a binary pixel array. Our aim is to build a network for recognition of vertical and horizontal lines. These objects are represented as relations between neighboring pixels or domains of pixels grouped in squares 2 by 2 (Figure 2).

P1	P2
P3	P4

```
node(P1, P2, P3, P4, 2, p(P1, P2, P3, P4, U1)).
p(X, _, X, _, 'Vertical line').
p(_, X, _, X, 'Vertical line').
p(X, X, _, _, 'Horizontal line').
p(_, _, X, X, 'Horizontal line').
p(P1, P2, P3, P4, pat(P1, P2, P3, P4)).
```

Figure 2.

The basic processing unit in our model is a spreading activation node activated when at least two of the pixels (sub-domains) of the square are "on" (the corresponding net-variables are bound), i.e. its threshold is 2. The output of the node (net-variable **U1**) is bound by Prolog procedure **p** (Figure 2), defining the properties of the vertical and horizontal lines. The value of **U1** is determined by the contents of the four sub-domains of the square applying the following rules (actually these rules are a declarative representation of our objects):

- If **P1** and **P3** or **P2** and **P4** are both "on" or filled with identical (unifiable) patterns then U1 is bound to "Vertical line" (clauses 1, 2 of **p**);
- If **P1** and **P2** or **P3** and **P4** are both "on" or filled with identical (unifiable) patterns then U1 is bound to "Horizontal line" (clauses 3,4 of **p**);
- If none of the above cases is present then **U1** is bound to **pat(P1,P2,P3,P4)** (the last clause of **p**).

To illustrate the work of our model consider a pixel array 8 by 8. Each square 2 by 2 from the pixel array supplies the four inputs of a spreading activation node from the first layer of the network. The outputs of the first layer nodes are connected in the same way to the inputs of the second layer and so on. Thus we have input pixel array 8 by 8 (free nodes **pix** numbered from 1 to 64), three intermediate layers (16, 4 and 1 node) and an output free node (**out**). A part of the network is shown bellow:

```
/* Inputs */             /* Intermediate layers */                        /* Output */
...                 ...
pix(49,P49):    node(P49,P50,P57,P58,2,p(P49,P50,P57,P58,U13)):    out(O):
pix(50,P50):    ...
pix(57,P57):    node(U9,U10,U13,U14,2,p(U9,U10,U13,U14,W3)):
pix(58,P58):    ...
...             node(W1,W2,W3,W4,2,p(W1,W2,W3,W4,O)):
```

The input image is entered into the network by the following NCL query, binding the corresponding net-variables from the input pixel array:

```
<- pix(4,on),pix(11,on),pix(20,on),pix(27,on),
   pix(36,on),pix(43,on),pix(52,on),pix(59,on),out(X).
X=Vertical line
```

The last goal in the query reads the network output from the output free node out. At the first layer of the network no lines are recognized. So the obtained patterns **pat(_,on,on,_)** are propagated further to the next layer, where the condition for vertical lines is satisfied and the output variables are bound to "Vertical line". The image processed in the example is not a "perfect" line, so the recognition takes place at the second layer of the network, where not pixels but patterns of pixels are processed.

Let us consider some more examples of the network activation, shown in Figure 3.

1. 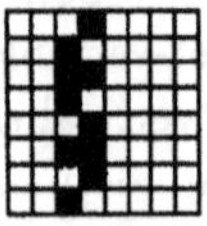 <- on([4, 11, 19, 20, 27, 36, 43, 44, 52, 59]), out(X).
   X=Vertical line

2. 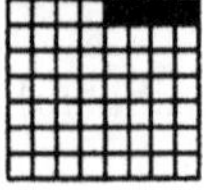 <- on([1, 2, 3, 4, 13, 14, 15, 16]), out(X).
   X=Horizontal line

3. 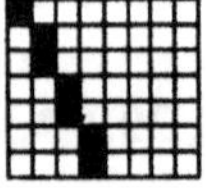 <- on([1, 9, 18, 26, 35, 43, 52, 60]), out(X).
   X=Vertical line

4. 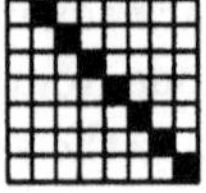 <- on([1, 10, 19, 28, 37, 46, 55, 64]), out(X).
   X=pat(pat(pat(on,_1,_2,on), _3, _4, pat(on,_5,_6,on)), _7, _8,
   pat(pat(on,_9,_10,on), _11, _12, pat(on,_13,_14,on)))

Figure 3.

To simplify the NCL queries, when entering the input image, the following Prolog predicate is used:

```
on([]):-!.
on([X|T]):-pix(X,on),on(T).
```

Example 1 adds some "noise" to the input image, switching on some pixels (19 and 44) and thus making the line "irregular". Despite the noise the same behavior is obtained. This is because the different sub-domains of the "noised" line are unifiable, e.g. **pat(on,on,on,_)** is successfully unified with **pat(_,on,on,_)** by a node from the second layer. Examples 2 and 3 show that slightly rotated lines could be also recognized successfully. The last example illustrates a case when the input image is not recognized as a vertical or horizontal line. Then some pattern in the form of a complex term is obtained at the network output. Though the pattern looks rather complex, it is quite "regular" (self-isomorphic). It is built out of only one sub-term **pat(X,_,_,X)**, where **X** is either "on" or the whole term itself. This regularity is due to the fact that the input image is also regular and self-isomorphic (a diagonal line). The isomorphic part of the obtained pattern (the term **pat(X,_,_,X)**) could be used to modify the node procedure in such a way that later similar patterns could be recognized. This can be done by asserting the following new clause for **p**:

p(X,_,_,X,'Diagonal line').

The modification of the node procedures can be performed automatically. For this purpose we can define a special mode of activation of the network, when all such new patterns (unrecognized objects) are used to modify the procedure **p** (asserting new clauses for **p**). Actually this is an approach to learning form examples.

Using the same unification based processing, more complicated architectures can be implemented (e.g. 3 by 3 object square or overlapping squares) suitable for recognition of more complex objects. For such cases the procedure **p** should be also elaborated to define more complex object features. A hierarchy of objects could be introduced by using names instead of variables for the square sub-domains in the procedure **p**.

The described approach for image processing is suitable for all levels of image processing - from pixels to features and objects. Another advantage is that the objects can be recognized both isolated and as parts of other objects or scenes using the same definition of the node procedure. The latter is a common deficiency of the connectionist network - trained with an isolated object they are unable to recognize it as a part of a scene. In our case, when the object is isolated and fills the whole input layer it is recognized by the output node. When it appears as a component of a scene or as a part of another object, it is recognized by a node at some intermediate layer of the network.

A deficiency of the approach is the large number of nodes required when we use some more elaborated architectures of the network. For example a network using overlapping squares 2 by 2 with 64 input pixels amounts to 204 spreading activation nodes. When the object is a complex one most of these nodes are activated. Furthermore executing the node procedure is quite a time consuming task (unification of compound terms) and in case of sequential implementation the overall efficiency is low. However there is an advantage of this architecture, which allow a parallel implementation. The nodes in each layer work independently and the only synchronization is between the layers. So, the problem could be solved by an implementation of NCL in parallel hardware (this aspect of NCL is discussed in 5.3).

Although the objects are semantically coded as individual nodes the described NCL network is actually a ***distributed*** one due to the following reasons. First, the nodes are not permanently assigned to one meaning (role), rather they comprise the knowledge for all objects recognizable by the network (procedure p) and they are activated when they detect an object locally presented at their inputs. Second, the object description is spread among all active nodes, each one either detecting (successfully matching its four inputs with the parts of a known object) or processing (generating a pattern for the next layers) a sub-part of the object.

5 Discussion

So far we showed that using NCL we can solve various problems in various ways, e.g. connectionist problems in pure connectionist fashion (the XOR function), symbolic problems by symbolic methods (data-driven logical inference) and connectionist problems by connectionist-like architectures based on symbolic processing (the image processing example). Because of this wide range of applicable approaches in the framework of NCL, we called the language *tool for symbolic connectionist processing.* In this section we further discuss the features of NCL and how they relate to some key issues of connectionist and symbolic processing.

5.1 Representational Formalism versus Computational Architecture

Representational and computational aspects of most of the AI languages and tools are separated, i.e. there exist a control component which explicitly specifies the algorithm or computational architecture for knowledge processing. (This actually reflects of the von Neumann's idea of separation of data and control.) Some languages (declarative or specificational ones, e.g. Prolog) offer a built-in computational mechanism, which is implicitly specified by the declarative component of the language used for knowledge representation. In connectionism the things are organized in a reverse way. There is always an explicitly specified computational architecture, and in some cases there could be an implicit representational (symbolic) component and this is the case when we use some of the approaches of connectionist symbol processing.

From the viewpoint of the connection between its representational and computational aspects, NCL occupies the middle between symbolic and connectionist approaches. This is because NCL can be used with equal expressiveness for representation of data structures and for describing computational architectures. Furthermore an NCL network can be viewed at the same time both as a *declarative representation* of the problem domain objects and as a *computational architecture* for processing these objects. This was shown by the geometric figure example (section 2).

5.2 Distributed Processing

Distributed processing is quite a general notion used in many diverse areas, such as Distributed Problem Solving, Distributed AI, Object Programming and Connectionism. Actually there are two aspects of the distributedness - representational and computational. Distributed representation of data means that the data items may not refer directly to some real world entities, and only the whole of the data can be interpreted. Distributed computation is mostly connected with parallelism (though it is a more general notion), since if we have independent processing units it would be more efficient to let them work in parallel. However the real problem is how to split the whole computational process into independent pieces, i.e. how to make the computation distributed. This problem is solved easily only in case of distributed data representation. Actually this is the case in connectionism and that is why it is also called Parallel Distributed Processing (PDP). Another way of viewing distributed computation is as a scheme without centralized control. These are the cases when the work of each processing unit is determined by some local conditions (e.g. receiving messages or data). An example of this approach is data-driven control in case of distributed representation.

Since NCL is a network based formalism (all problems in NCL are represented as networks of nodes) and the control in NCL is decentralized (data-driven), it is clear that in each NCL program, the data and the computational process are split into independent pieces. Hence in NCL, we use distributed representation and distributed computation (and in some cases both of them at the same time, e.g. in the image processing example).

5.3 Parallelism

Parallelism is an inherent feature of connectionist networks (as a part of the PDP paradigm). It is also important in some purely symbolic areas, such as Logic Programming. **PARLOG** [1], **Concurrent Prolog** [11] and **GHC** [14] are typical examples of applying parallel processing approaches in a pure symbolic field. However the main purpose of these works is not integrating symbolic and parallel computation in a consistent way, but rather improving the efficiency of the implementations. To achieve this, additional control means to govern the parallel execution (such as "guards", "read-only" variables etc.) are introduced. However this control language is a departure from logic and from the the nice declarative style of Logic Programming. In this area NCL offers some advantages. Since NCL does not use any control language the deductive inference by NCL (described in section 3) is *purely declarative.* And because of the distributed character of the NCL computation it is also *potentially parallel.* Though NCL is implemented in a purely sequential environment it can simulate parallel execution. Generally the functional behavior of parallelism can be achieved in a sequential computational environment when two properties are present: decentralized control and independence of the computation on the order of the input data for each processing element. While the first condition is an inherent property of NCL, the second one can be achieved by introducing the natural restrictions that the node procedures should not cause side-effects (in Prolog sense). Thus having in hand a distributed computational scheme simulating parallelism, the transition to real parallel processing is merely an implementational step. For this purpose it is necessary to assign a separate process to each procedural node in the NCL network. In this scheme the activation conditions can serve as synchronization conditions for the processes.

5.4 Learning

A way of implementing a learning scheme in NCL was mentioned in section 4. This approach however is not inherently connected with NCL, since it is implemented by a Prolog procedure. There is another more natural way to implement learning in NCL. It is a method coming from NCL symbolic aspects, based on *term generalization.* The basic idea is to replace the net-variables bound during the activation of the network to unifiable terms with shared net-variables. Actually this is a way for automatic creation of network links. It is important to note that this approach is consistent with the basic data-driven paradigm of NCL. Thus the data (terms) in NCL determine both the control schemes and the proper network structure for their processing. The NCL learning based on term generalization has also an interpretation in the framework of *inductive concept learning.* The above mentioned problems concerning the approaches to NCL learning are being currently studied and some results are reported in [9].

References

[1] Gregory, S. *Parallel Logic Programming in PARLOG* (Addison-Wesley, 1987).

[2] Hendler, J. Problem Solving and Reasoning: A Connectionist Perspective. In: *Connectionism in Perspective, R. Pfeifer, Z. Schreter, F. Fogelman-Soulie, L. Steels (Eds.).* North-Holland, Amsterdam, 1989.

[3] Hinton, G.E. Mapping Part-Whole Hierarchies into Connectionist Networks, *Artificial Intelligence* 46 (1990), 47-75.

[4] Kurfess, F and M. Reich. Logic and Reasoning with Neural Models. In: *Connectionism in Perspective, R. Pfeifer, Z. Schreter, F. Fogelman-Soulie, L. Steels (Eds.).* North-Holland, Amsterdam, 1989.

[5] Markov, Z. A framework for network modeling in Prolog, in: *Proceedings of IJCAI-89*, Detroit, U.S.A (1989), 78-83.

[6] Markov, Z. and Ch. Dichev, Logical inference in a network environment, in: *Proceedings of AIMSA'90* (Artificial Intelligence IV, North-Holland, 1990), 169-178.

[7] Markov, Z., L. Sinapova and Ch. Dichev. Default reasoning in a network environment, in: *Proceedings of ECAI-90*, Stockholm, Sweden, August 6-10, 1990, pp.431-436.

[8] Markov, Z. and Ch. Dichev. The Net-Clause Language - A Tool for Data-Driven Inference, In: *Logics in AI, Proceedings of European Workshop JELIA'90*, Amsterdam, The Netherlands, September 1990, pp. 366-385 (Lecture Notes in Computer Science, No.478, Springer-Verlag, 1991).

[9] Markov, Z. An Approach to Data-Driven Learning, in: *Proceedings of the International Workshop on Fundamentals of Artificial Intelligence Research (FAIR'91)*, September 8-12, 1991, Smolenice, Czechoslovakia (to appear in Lecture Notes in Computer Science, Springer-Verlag, 1991).

[10] Minsky, M. Logical versus Analogical or Symbolic versus Connectionist or Neat versus Scruffy, *AI magazine*, Summer 1991, 35-51.

[11] Shapiro, E. Concurrent PROLOG: A Progress Report, in: *Lecture Notes in Computer Science* No. 232 (Springer-Verlag, 1986), 277-313.

[12] Smolensky, P. Tensor Product Variable Binding and the Representation of Symbolic Structures in Connectionist Systems, *Artificial Intelligence* 46 (1990), 159-216.

[13] Touretzky, D.S. BoltzCONS: Dynamic Symbol Structures in a Connectionist Network, *Artificial Intelligence* 46 (1990), 5-46.

[14] Ueda, K. Guarded Horn Clauses, ICOT Technical Report TR-103, 1985.

Providing Declarative Access to a Processing System for Satellite Image Data*

Wolf-Fritz Riekert
Siemens Nixdorf Informationssysteme AG / FAW Ulm
P.O.Box 2060, W-7900 Ulm, Germany
E-Mail: riekert@dulfaw1a.bitnet

Abstract

This paper describes the RESEDA Assistant, a knowledge-based access system to a processing system for satellite data. This system provides declarative access to the functions offered by a commercial data analysis system. That is, instead of requiring users to specify *how* the satellite data should be analyzed, users need only describe *what kind* of target data they are interested in. Descriptions of the data types and methods offered by the underlying data analysis system are represented in a knowledge base and utilized by the system.

1 Introduction

Satellite images of the earth's surface provide a large amount of data that is relevant to the state of the environment. It is possible to analyze the satellite image data by using image-processing systems and spatial information systems [4]. However, making use of these systems is a nontrivial task, because they are very complex and the number of concepts and functions offered is very large. The user interfaces require a procedural interaction style based on commands and macros. This kind of interaction has been found to be very demanding for nonexpert users, such as those from environmental management.

In order to overcome this usability barrier, a knowledge-based access system called the RESEDA Assistant has been developed [2]. This system provides declarative access to the functions offered by a commercial data analysis system, namely the SICAD®-HYGRIS hybrid image-processing system which is a member of the SICAD family of

*This work has been supported by the State of Baden-Württemberg, Germany, and by Siemens Nixdorf Informationssysteme AG, Munich, Germany as part of the environmental research project RESEDA (Remote Sensor Data Analysis) being conducted at the FAW Research Institute for Applied Knowledge Processing in Ulm, Germany.

image-processing and geographic information systems [3]. Instead of having to specify *how* the satellite data are to be analyzed the users only describe *what kind* of target data they are interested in. The user does not need to know whether the desired data is directly available in the database of the image-processing system or whether it has to be computed from existing data (e.g., satellite data, cartographic data, or results from previous analyses) by certain image-processing operators.

The RESEDA Assistant is a planning system [5]. Its main function is to generate so-called *processing plans* from the specifications of the user. A processing plan is a sequence of *computations* that are necessary to derive the desired information from the available data. These computations include applications of image-processing operators, statistical evaluations, manipulations of spatial data, or data management functions offered by a file system. The processing plans generated are displayed on the screen and may be automatically executed. In this context, automatic execution means that the appropriate procedures are called with correct arguments in the correct sequence. Occasionally, these procedures may nonetheless run in interactive mode and require intervention by the user.

Similar to human experts in satellite data analysis, the RESEDA system makes use of two kinds of knowledge:

- knowledge about the various kinds of data to be analyzed and computed in the course of the analysis,
- knowledge about the methods suited to compute certain kinds of data from one another.

This knowledge is sometimes referred to as *meta-information*, since it provides information about information and about methods for processing it.

The knowledge representation technique used in RESEDA is based on PROLOG with some simple object-oriented extensions:

- Knowledge about data is represented in an object-oriented form by using attribute lists. A hierarchy of concepts represents the knowledge about the different data types available.
- Knowledge about methods is represented in clausal form as so-called processing models. PROLOG clauses are being used to describe which kind of data may be computed by a given method and under what circumstances that method is applicable.

2 Meta-information about Data

The main function of the RESEDA Assistant system is to reason about which data may be derived from other data. Therefore a knowledge representation has been developed for the meta-information about the various kinds of data to be handled by the system. Different kinds of geographic data [1] form the most important group among these data. Examples of geographic data are:

- raster images recorded by satellite sensors or derived by image-processing operations;
- geometric and tabular data describing the positions, shapes, and type of spatial objects;
- layers of topographic or thematic maps, converted into a digital format by a raster scanner;
- a digital elevation model;
- results of former analyses.

Other types of data represented in the system include statistics, look-up tables, histograms, and transformation parameters.

In the following discussion, we will focus on geographic data as the most important kind of data. For a geographic data item, the following meta-information can be represented and interpreted by the system:

- the data type (e.g., vegetation image, true color image, land-use classification data);
- the name of the data file used to store the data;
- information about the coordinate system;
- for raster data: window and grid size;
- the processing state: raw, enhanced, calibrated, etc.; and
- a time stamp.

This meta-information is represented in an object-oriented form by the use of *open attribute lists.* Open attribute lists are lists of terms in the form *attribute* = *value*, which end with a variable tail. As an example, the meta-information for a contrast-enhanced vegetation image of the Upper Rhine area geocoded in the Gauss-Krueger coordinate system is represented by the following open attribute list:

```
[ data_type = vegetation_image,
  contrast_enhanced = yes,
  area = 'Upper Rhine',
  projection = gauss_krueger |
  _ ]
```

The variable tail allows for appending additional attribute-value pairs by means of unification. This is done when the RESEDA system infers the values of additional attributes during the consultation. The unification with attribute values is possible using the has/2 predicate:

has (*open-attribute-list*, *attribute* = *value*).

If *attribute* exists in the *open attribute list*, its value is unified with *value*; otherwise, the term *attribute* = *value* is appended to the attribute list. Whole attribute lists may be unified with one another (regardless of the order of their elements) by the recursive use of the has predicate. Additional predicates have been defined for this purpose.

Case-independent information about data items is represented in a hierarchy of data types. Data types are also represented by attribute lists which are anchored as facts in the PROLOG knowledge base. As an example, the data type `landsat_tm_scene` (representing the case-independent properties of a set of satellite data recorded by the TM sensor of the Landsat satellite) is given by the following fact:

```
concept ( landsat_tm_scene,
          [ identifier    = landsat_tm_scene,
            data_type     = data_type,
            superconcepts = [ satellite_scene ],
            init          = [ contrast_enhanced = no,
                              identifier = B,
                              projection = tm(B),
                              gridsize = 30,
                              resampling_period = 16 ] ]).
```

3 Meta-information about Methods

Meta-information about methods is represented by means of so-called *processing models*, which are abstract descriptions of computations. These models are static knowledge-base objects that do not change during a consultation. A model provides meta-information for the use of traditional data-processing methods, and it describes a set of input and output data and an algorithm. The algorithm is represented by a program that contains control structures and calls to the image-processing and GIS subsystems. Processing models are used, for example, to describe how to derive additional geographic data from the images, how to store it in a geographic information system, or how to visualize data by producing maps and images.

Two major types of processing model can be differentiated:

- The first type of processing model is used for 'jumping across the branches' of the data-type hierarchy. That is, the input data and the output data concern different types of data. Computing a vegetation index or performing a land-use classification from sensor data are typical examples of this kind of processing model.
- The second type of processing model is used to change the properties of a single data item. The data type remains the same after the application of this processing model. Performing a histogram equalization (for contrast enhancement) or resampling data onto a different grid are two examples of this kind of processing model.

A clausal form is used to describe which kind of data may be computed by a method and under what circumstances that method is applicable. The clause of the predicate `processing_model` below shows an example of the declarative representation of a method to compute a so-called *vegetation image:*

```
processing_model(tm_vegetation_image, Vegetation_Image) :-
  has_explicitly(Vegetation_Image, data_type = vegetation_image),
  has(Vegetation_Image, projection = P),
  has(Vegetation_Image, gridsize = G),
  has(TM4, data_type = tm_channel),
  has(TM4, channel_nr = 4),
  has(TM5, data_type = tm_channel),
  has(TM5, channel_nr = 5),
  has(TM3, data_type = tm_channel),
  has(TM3, channel_nr = 3),
  inherits_all_but(TM4, Vegetation_Image, [data_type]),
  inherits_all_but(TM5, Vegetation_Image, [data_type]),
  inherits_all_but(TM3, Vegetation_Image, [data_type]),
  requires(Vegetation_Image, [TM4, TM5, TM3]),
  inherits_all_but(Vegetation_Image, TM4, [data_type, channel_nr]).
```

This processing model is applicable if the required data item is of the type `vegetation_image`. The computation requires three instances of input data originating from Landsat TM sensor channels. These required input data items inherit all attributes except the data type from the output image. This representation of processing models allows for recursively planning the computation of the input data.

4 Processing Plans and Computations

Processing plans are dynamic objects that represent the results of a consultation dialog. They may be displayed to the user, translated to a UNIX[1] shell script and executed. Processing plans are trees whose nodes represent data items and computations that are connected to one another in alternating sequence. The root of the tree represents the desired data item that is the final result of the underlying computations, and the leaves of the tree stand for the primary data, used as information sources. The data items that correspond to the interior nodes of the graph serve both as the output of some computation and as the input to at least one other computation. A *computation* is a

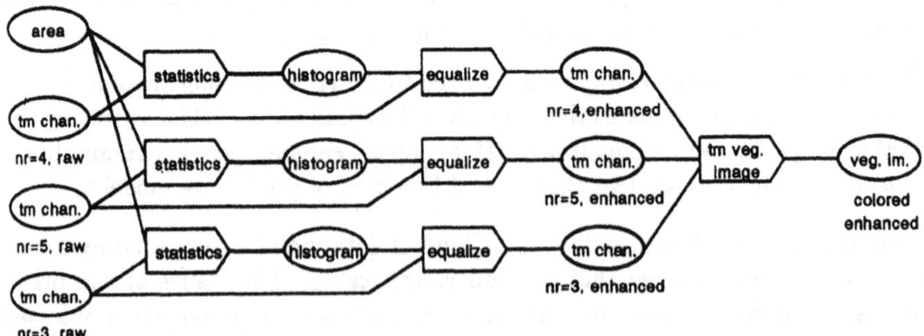

Figure 1: Processing plan for generating a vegetation image.

[1]UNIX® is a registered trademark of UNIX System Laboratories, Inc.

concrete manifestation of some processing model. It computes some data item from other data items. The algorithmic aspect of a computation is represented by an instantiated call of a computer program (including the values of the arguments).

Figure 1 shows a graphic representation of a processing plan. The example given is for the generation of a vegetation image. Data items are encircled by an oval border, whereas computations appear within the shape of an arrow.

5 Implementation of the RESEDA Prototype

The implemented prototype currently supports a subset of typical iconic image-processing algorithms. The underlying data analysis system, which is controlled by the RESEDA Assistant consists of image-processing and spatial analysis components of the SICAD family and of extensions developed in the RESEDA project.

At the beginning of the consultation the user is asked what type of data should be generated. The user may specify a map, an image, or digital data representing geographic information, such as a vegetation map, a true color image, or a data file encoding water-covered areas. Depending on the data type chosen, additional user-definable properties, such as geometric projection, coordinate system, grid size, or contrast enhancement, may be specified as well. The result of this dialog is a partially instantiated attribute list containing all the meta-information that is known about the desired data item.

The global control strategy of the RESEDA expert system is backward-chaining. From the meta-information specified by the user the system tries to activate processing models that are able to compute the desired information from other data. If that data is not present either, the system recursively tries to activate processing models for computing it. The process stops when the system attempts to determine data items that are explicitly labeled as so-called primary data. In that case, the user is asked whether the primary data in question is available. If the user says no, the system backtracks and tries to activate other processing models.

The advantage of the backward-chaining strategy is that the user is asked for available data only if this is actually necessary. Another possible design, namely, not to ask for the available data at all, was rejected since it would have required the implementation of a complete data management system. This was judged to be impractical because of the great number of foreign data sources that can be made available on demand, such as remote sensing data, geographic databases, raster-scanned maps, or even printed maps that can be digitized manually by the user.

The search for processing plans is exhaustive; that is, the search process is iterated until all possible solutions have been found. For this purpose, the system remembers the processing models and the data found during the backward-chaining process. Finally, the set of possible processing plans is displayed to the user.

When the user selects one of the plans presented by the system, the plan will be translated into a UNIX shell script and executed as a batch job. An example of a shell script generated by the system is given below. This shell script implements the processing plan for computing a vegetation image as shown in figure 1.

```
echo 1024 1024 > z.dp.105.idx
count 1024 1024 none < t2pq4r.bld  > z.stat
histequ z.stat t2pq4r.bld  z.dp.105.bld 400 1500 0
echo 1024 1024 > z.dp.107.idx
count 1024 1024 none < t2pq5r.bld  > z.stat
histequ z.stat t2pq5r.bld  z.dp.107.bld 400 1500 0
echo 1024 1024 > z.dp.109.idx
count 1024 1024 none < t2pq3r.bld  > z.stat
histequ z.stat t2pq3r.bld  z.dp.109.bld 400 1500 0
echo 1024 1024 > z.dp.104.idx
T_pseudo 1  z.dp.105.bld z.dp.107.bld z.dp.109.bld  z.dp.104.bld  2
T_display z.dp.104.bld 0 0 400 1024 2
```

6 Conclusions

A knowledge-based access system has been developed to assist a nonexpert user in the analysis of satellite data. The system facilitates the use of traditional data analysis systems. Instead of invoking commands, the user enters descriptions of the information desired.

The knowledge base of the system contains descriptions of the data types and methods offered by the underlying data analysis system. An inference mechanism based on a backward-chaining strategy allows for the efficient interpretation of the declarative information which is both contained in the knowledge base and specified by the user.

References

[1] P.A. Burrough, *Principles of Geographical Information Systems for Land Resources Assessment.* Clarendon Press, Oxford, 1986.

[2] W.-F. Riekert, *"The RESEDA Project: A Knowledge Based Approach to Extracting Environmental Information from Remote Sensor Data"*. In V. Cantoni et al. (eds.), Progress in Image Analysis and Processing. World Scientific, 1990.

[3] SICAD-aktuell, Siemens Computer Aided Design, Kurzinformation, Siemens AG, München, 1988.

[4] P.H. Swain and S.M. Davis (eds.), *Remote Sensing: The Quantitative Approach.* McGraw-Hill, New York, 1978.

[5] R. Wilensky, *Planning and Understanding.* Addison-Wesley, Reading, Massachussetts, 1983.

Declarative functionality descriptions of interactive reasoning modules

Jan Treur

Vrije Universiteit Amsterdam
Department of Mathematics and Computer Science, Artificial Intelligence Group
De Boelelaan 1081a, 1081 HV Amsterdam, The Netherlands, email: treur@cs.vu.nl

Abstract

In this paper a semantical framework is developed that provides a logical description of the functionality of an interactive reasoning module. In particular it can be made more transparent by this framework whether or not the conclusions that may be drawn by a reasoning module fit to the situation that is concerned (soundness and completeness). It will be established that, considered from the viewpoint of functionality, the knowledge in a reasoning module always can be normalized to knowledge in rule format. This shows that the rule format essentially is expressive enough to specify the functionality of a reasoning module. This result gives a justification for the choice that has been made in our framework for design and specification of interacting reasoning modules, DESIRE.

1 Introduction

1.1 A compositional view on reasoning systems

In our view a reasoning system performing a complex reasoning pattern can be designed as an interaction between reasoning modules performing more basic or primitive reasoning processes. The assumption is that these primitive reasoning processes can be described by simple monotonic deduction systems, for instance based on chaining. This *compositional view on reasoning systems* shifts the attention from the study of more sophisticated inference relations and procedures to the patterns of interaction that can be defined between inference processes that are rather simple themselves (cf. [3], [13]). The processing of these interaction patterns can be done by a mechanism for *supervising* or *proof planning at a global level*. One of our main research themes is the development and foundation of formal techniques to support the design and specification of these compositional architectures for reasoning systems. The components or reasoning modules in such a system arise as a result of a functional decomposition of the complex reasoning task into a number of primitive reasoning (sub)tasks. In recent years our compositional view on reasoning systems has been worked out in more detail. We have developed the framework DESIRE (framework for DEsign and Specification of Interacting REasoning modules; see [6]) to design and (formally) specify compositional architectures for reasoning systems. Each of the modules is an interactive reasoning system containing an (often domain-specific) knowledge base. Using DESIRE the whole system is composed of these basic building blocks by using standardized construction principles (described in [15]). The functionality of the resulting system arises from the functionalities of each of the components and the manner in which they are composed. The use of this approach to model different types of dynamic and reflective reasoning patterns is described in [10], [12], [13]. The formal specification language related to DESIRE is supported by syntax-directed editors and an implementation environment including automated implementation generators.

This paper aims both at providing a logical foundation for the interactive reasoning modules used as basic building blocks in DESIRE and at a justification for the chosen format in which knowledge is specified in DESIRE. To obtain a clear and well-defined description of such a compositional architecture, one has to start by defining the (interactive) role of a given interactive module in such an environment: a clear definition is needed of an interactive reasoning module's functionality. Questions concerning soundness, completeness of the whole system or satisfaction of the system's required functionality, can be related to questions concerning the system's compositional structure and questions for the case of a single interactive reasoning module. As a first contribution, this paper only concentrates on the case of a reasoning module and its interactions.

The semantical framework enables us to define what a *declarative functionality description* of a reasoning module is (the input/output possibilities provided by the module). Here the word declarative means that we do not take into account the dynamic aspects of the module: in this paper we are only concerned with what facts *can* be derived in a given situation (information state), and not with *at what time* and in which order specific facts *are* derived. We prove that for any declarative functionality description a knowledge base specification in *rule format* can be found such that the semantic consequence relation (applied to this knowledge base and the additional input facts) satisfies the required functionality. This means that the rule format can be viewed as a kind of standardized or normalized format for the knowledge in the module: knowledge in an interactive reasoning module can always be transformed to knowledge in rule format with the same functionality.

This is a kind of completeness result (which can be compared to [9] and [11]), and gives a justification for the choice we made for the format in which knowledge is specified in DESIRE. Reasoning modules are able to draw partial conclusions if only partial input information is given. Therefore our formal description of the declarative functionality of a module also treats partiality of information, using the strong Kleene partial semantics. We assume some properties that make reasoning modules easy to describe:

- the module can draw (partial) conclusions from partial input information: not for all possible input facts truth values are needed
- the input facts are not changed by the processing of the module; i.e., once a fact has been input as a true fact it remains true during the inference proces (conservatism)
- if a larger set of input facts is given to the module, also the set of derivable facts is larger (monotonicity)

1.2 Interactive reasoning by refining a partial model

Usually a reasoning module is described logically by a static theory **KB** (the knowledge base) which is given beforehand. From this theory conclusions can be derived using some inference mechanism. In case of an interactive reasoning module the information that serves as input facts during the reasoning is viewed as knowledge which is present from the start. In fact one deals with some extended theory $\mathbf{KB}^+$ which additionally contains all information which could be put in from the outside. This seems plain; however, there are some aspects which stay implicit or informal this way.

In fact there is not one theory **KB** but a whole *variety of theories* $\mathbf{KB}^+$ which depend on the situation that can occur in reality, part of which is represented by the input facts that are given to the module. This may be viewed as an implicit parametrization of the knowledge base. How can an explicit logical description of this parametrization be obtained ? Moreover, interactive reasoning modules often have the property that during a session the input facts are added incrementally: for any moment there is only partial input information available. The module draws partial conclusions from this information;. these conclusions may occasionally affect which other input facts are added. For example, in a complex reasoning task like diagnosis these dynamic effects are essential (see [12], [13]). Therefore the knowledge base KB^+ may be dynamic during the reasoning.

It turns out that some parts of the knowledge (the general or situation-independent knowledge) which can be used in the inference process can be described as a *theory* **KB** but other parts (situation-specific knowledge) are better described as a *(partial) model* which represents the actual situation in reality, part of which is represented by the input facts. In reasoning these two kinds of knowledge are combined to obtain a (more detailed) refinement of the partial model.

Therefore essentially we view the reasoning of an interactive reasoning module as *constructing and refining a (partial) model* of the world situation that is concerned. We use partial models as known from logic to represent information states of a reasoning module at a certain moment. Our logical descriptions will be based on partial propositional logic (for a more detailed introduction to partial logic, see [1], [8]). If (many-sorted) predicate logic with a finite number of object names and relation names (and no function names) is used, we can always use a propositional translation of the formulas to fall in the scope of propositional logic.

We consider a description in terms of propositional logic with a non-empty set of *atoms* **A** containing two subsets **S** (possible input atoms) and **H** (possible output atoms). The set of atoms **A** collects all atomic propositions that are used in the reasoning module. The input atoms (sometimes called *observables*) are the atoms for which a truth value may serve as an input to the module. The truth values of output atoms may be wanted by the user or by another module. It is possible that there exist atoms outside these subsets; these *intermediate atoms* can play a role as intermediate results or subgoals in inferences. In the general case they form a subset **I** of **A**, so $A = S \cup I \cup H$. Here **S** and **H** may have a nonempty intersection, although in the examples given below we deal with a disjoint union. From these atoms the set of propositional formulas can be built up by using the logical connectives as usual: $\wedge, \vee, \rightarrow, \neg$. Applications in knowledge bases are often based on a subset of these propositions, namely propositions in *rule format*. These are propositions in implication form where the if-part consists of a conjunction of literals and the then-part consists of one literal (a literal is the basic unit of information we use: it is an atom or the negation of an atom). As a special case of formulas in rule-format, we allow single literals. These are to be interpreted as *general facts* (they may be viewed as rules with an empty condition-part). Examples of propositions in rule-format are the ones in Fig. 1 below. Throughout the paper, without stating this explicitly we assume that $s_i \in S$, $h_i \in H$, et cetera.

rule 1	$s_1 \wedge s_2$	$\rightarrow$	i_1
rule 2	$i_1 \wedge s_3$	$\rightarrow$	h_1
rule 3	$i_1 \wedge \neg s_3$	$\rightarrow$	$\neg h_1$
rule 4	$i_1 \wedge \neg s_3$	$\rightarrow$	h_2

Fig. 1 Example of a knowledge base

To obtain a formal description of the interaction of the reasoning module with the outside world, we will have to give a formal description of all situations the module may get in touch with (for instance, in case of a medical application, all possible patient types). The reasoning is supposed to be about one of these situations; in one session the input information is about a fixed one of them. We define a situation model as a *truth assignment* to the atoms. Some examples of situation models related to the knowledge base of Fig. 1, corresponding to the tuple $< s_1, s_2, s_3, s_4; i_1 ; h_1, h_2 >$, are:

$$M_1 : \; < 1, 1, 1, 0; 1; 1, 0 >$$
$$M_2 : \; < 1, 1, 0, 0; 1; 0, 1 >$$
$$M_3 : \; < 0, 0, 0, 1; 0; 1, 0 >$$

Fig. 2 Some situations models for KB from Fig. 1

Notice that all of these situation models are models of the theory **KB**: for each M every rule of **KB** is true in M.

During a reasoning process at each moment in the system only a part of the information as given by a situation model is available. To represent this partiality we make use of *partial* (situation) *models*: assignments of truth values from {0, 1, u} to each of the atoms. Here the u denotes *undefined* or *unknown*. Notice that the models as defined above (e.g. in Fig. 2) are included here as the truth assignments where to no atom an u is assigned; we distinguish them as the *complete models* among the partial models. The dynamics of the reasoning of a module may be described by representing the subsequent information states by a trace of partial models. Each inference step constructs a new partial model as a refinement of the current partial model by adding to it the derived information. In Fig. 3 we give an example that is related to the knowledge base in Fig. 1; as earlier the tuples of 0, 1, u correspond to $< s_1, s_2, s_3, s_4; i_1 ; h_1, h_2 >$.

N_1 : < 1, 1, 0, u; u; u, u >

inference step 1: rule 1

N_2 : < 1, 1, 0, u; 1; u, u >

inference step 2: rule 3

N_3 : < 1, 1, 0, u; 1; 0, u >

Fig. 3 Reasoning by refining a partial model

Here the concerning world situation that is reasoned about is assumed to be:

$$M = < 1, 1, 0, 0; 1; 0, 1 >$$

We assume that the only initial information we know is about s_1, s_2, s_3; the initial facts $s_1, s_2, \neg s_3$ are observations, done in the world situation. The chain of partial models constructed by this reasoning process is:

$$N_1 \leq N_2 \leq N_3$$

Here $\leq$ is the refinement relation between partial models (i.e. in N_2 more information is known than in N_1, et cetera). Notice that $N_i \leq M$ for each i and that in this example the reasoning is stopped as soon as information is obtained on h_1.

1.3 Overview of the paper

The paper is built up as follows. In Section 2 we define what a domain description is, and especially, in which manner world situations occurring in a domain and partial descriptions of them (information states) can be modelled. We will give some examples and state some properties. In Section 3 we give a formal definition of a declarative functionality description of an interactive reasoning module. Furthermore, we give some results on how well a declarative functionality description fits to (or describes) a given domain description. In Section 4 it is defined what a reasoning module specification is and how well it fits to (or describes) a declarative functionality description and to a domain description. The main result is that the rule format as chosen for DESIRE specifications is expressive enough to cover any reasonable desired functionality of a reasoning module.

The material here continues and extends the line that was put forward in [11]. A difference is that here we treat partiality, and we concentrate on the functionality of a module. Some of the notions introduced below were also included in [7].

2 Domain descriptions

In Section 1 we have sketched how a reasoning module relates to the domain that is concerned, and the specific world situation it is reasoning about. To be able to compare the conclusions drawn by a reasoning module to the facts in this world situation in the domain, a formal framework is needed for describing the domain and the interaction of the reasoning module with it. Therefore we will start by giving more precise definitions that constitute a formal framework to describe a domain. In Sections 3 and 4 the relation between a domain and a reasoning module is defined more formally.

2.1 Describing world situations by complete models

We start by giving the definition of the language elements to describe a domain. In this paper, for convenience we will work only with finite propositional logical languages.

Definition 2.1
A (propositional) ***signature*** Σ is a 3-tuple $<$ **InSig(Σ); IntSig(Σ); OutSig(Σ)** $>$ where **InSig(Σ), IntSig(Σ), OutSig(Σ)** are ordered sets of atom names, respectively called the ***input signature***, the ***internal signature*** and the ***output signature***. The input and output signatures may contain common atom names, but the internal signature is disjoint from them. In this paper all signatures are assumed to be ***finite***. The corresponding sets of literals are denoted by **InLit(Σ), IntLit(Σ), OutLit(Σ)**, while their union is denoted by **Lit(Σ)**. If **M** is a (partial) model based on this signature, then we say **M** is ***of signature*** Σ . The signature Σ' is called a ***subsignature*** of Σ if **InSig(Σ')** $\subset$ **InSig(Σ)**, **IntSig(Σ')** $\subset$ **IntSig(Σ)** and **OutSig(Σ')** $\subset$ **OutSig(Σ)**.

Each of the input, internal and output signatures are viewed as special cases of subsignatures. The following is an example of a signature:

$$< s_1, s_2, s_3, s_4; i_1 ; h_1, h_2 >.$$

We often consider only relations between inputs and outputs; in that case we leave out the internal signature.

Definition 2.2
A ***domain description*** **W** for Σ is a non-empty set of complete truth assignments to the atoms.

In Section 1, Fig. 2, an example of a domain description is shown.

2.2 Describing information states by partial models

During a reasoning process, only a part of the information about a world situation is available to the reasoning system. At any moment the system's information state can be described by a partial model. A (partial) *model* **M** of signature Σ is an assignment of truth values from **{0, 1, u}** to the atoms of Σ. By **M(a)** we will denote the truth value assigned to atom **a**. We call **M** a *complete model* if for all atoms **a** the truth value **M(a)** is not **u**. Let **V** be a non-empty set of partial models of signature Σ. By **P(V)** we denote the set of all partial models that may be refined to a model in **V**. A relevant example is **V = P(W)**, where **W** is a domain description. If **M** is a partial model we denote by **Lit(M)** the set of literals which are true in **M**, and by **InLit(M)** the set of input literals which are true in M. Similarly OutLit(M) denotes the set of output literals which are true in M. The sets of literals InLit(M) and OutLit(M) correspond to the restrictions of the model M to the restricted sets of atoms S and H. These restricted models are called *reducts* (also see [4]) to a subsignature Σ', denoted by $M|\Sigma'$.

Suppose Σ' is a subsignature of Σ and M' is a model of signature Σ'. The *trivial expansion* M of M' to the signature Σ is the model of signature Σ created from M' by assigning a u to any atom outside Σ'. Let M be a model of signature Σ. The model In(M) is defined as the trivial expansion of $M|\Sigma_{in}$ to the signature Σ. This model represents the *input part* (or related *input model*) of M; similarly Out(M) represents the *output part* (or related *output model*) of M. The external source of information that is interacting with the reasoning module can only provide information about the input part of the situation that is concerned. If W is a domain description then the *related set of complete input models* (resp. of *complete output models*) is denoted by In(W) (resp. Out(W)). Any model M of signature Σ with M(a) = u for all atoms a not in InSig(Σ) is called an *input model*. Similarly, M is called an *output model* of signature Σ if M(a) = u for all atoms a not in OutSig(Σ). We will use the symbols P_{in}, P_{out} for non-empty sets of input models, respectively output models. If all these models are complete with respect to InSig(Σ) resp. OutSig(Σ) they may be denoted by respectively W_{in}, W_{out}. Notice that the models In(M) resp. Out(M) are input resp. output models in this sense. If no confusion is expected, we sometimes will leave out the u's; for instance we may identify < 1, 1, 1, 0 > with the input model < 1, 1, 1, 0; u ; u, u >.

By $M \models p$ (to be read as: M *satisfies* p) we denote that the proposition p is true in the model M according to the strong Kleene semantics. The combination tables for truth values according to this approach to partial semantics are given by:

$\neg\varphi$	
1	0
0	1
u	u

$\varphi\wedge\psi$	1	0	u
1	1	0	u
0	0	0	0
u	u	0	u

$\varphi\vee\psi$	1	0	u
1	1	1	1
0	1	0	u
u	1	u	u

$\varphi\rightarrow\psi$	1	0	u
1	1	0	u
0	1	1	1
u	1	u	u

By Λ we denote the *empty* partial model: only u's are assigned. The refinement relation $\leq$ between partial models is defined by $M \leq N$ if for every atom a it holds $M(a) \leq N(a)$ (i.e., point by point), where the partial ordering of truth values is based on unknown < true, unknown < false.

Let V be a non-empty set of partial models. If $M \in P(V)$ then by $M \Vdash_V p$ (to be read as: M *forces* p with respect to V) we denote that for every refinement N of M in V it holds $N \models p$:

$$M \Vdash_V p \Leftrightarrow \forall N \in V\ [M \leq N \Rightarrow N \models p]$$

The *semantic consequence relation* restricted to models in V, denoted by $F \models_V p$ for a set of formulas F is defined by: for all models M' in V with $M' \models F$ it holds $M' \models p$. There is a connection between the forcing relation and the semantic consequence relation restricted to models in V, namely: $M \Vdash_V p$ if and only if $Lit(M) \models_V p$.

We say the members of V *agree* on the atom a if for all $M \in V$ the atom a has the same truth value in M. In the other case we say the members of V *disagree* on a. For a nonempty set V of partial models the *greatest common information state* of V is the partial model N, denoted by gci(V), such that for all $M \in V$ it holds $N \leq M$, and for any N' with the same property it holds $N' \leq N$. One may view this as the maximal information on which all members of V agree. This model gci(V) can be constructed as follows: for any atom a on which all members of V agree, take this truth value, and if the members of V disagree take the truth value u. Notice that, just like the refinement relation, the operation gci is taken point by point.

For any partial model $M \in P(V)$ this gci-construction can be applied to the set of refinements in V of M, i.e. to $V_0 = \{ N \in V \mid M \leq N \}$. The resulting greatest common information state of V_0 is called the *semantic closure* of M with respect to V, and is denoted by $sc_V(M)$. This refinement of M satisfies precisely the literals that are forced by M with respect to V. As an example, the semantic closure of

$$M_0 = < 1, u, u, u; u; u, u >$$

with respect to the domain description W in Fig. 2 is the greatest common information state of the set $\{M_1, M_2\}$; therefore

$$sc_W(M_0) = < 1, 1, u, 0; 1; u, u > .$$

Notice that a semantic closure belongs to $P(V)$ but in general does not belong to V and is not complete, even if all models in V are complete. Some elementary properties of the notions defined here can be found in [14]. We only mention:

Lemma 2.3
Suppose $M, N \in P(V)$.
a) For any literal d it holds
$sc_V(M) \models d \Leftrightarrow M \Vdash_V d$
b) For all partial models $M, N \in P(V)$ it holds:
(i) If $M \leq N \in V$ then $sc_V(M) \leq N$
(ii) $M \leq sc_V(M)$
(iii) $M \leq N \Rightarrow sc_V(M) \leq sc_V(N)$
c) $M \leq sc_V(N) \Rightarrow sc_V(M) \leq sc_V(N)$
and in particular $sc_V(sc_V(M)) = sc_V(M)$
d) If every complete refinement of M is a member of V then $sc_V(M) = M$. In particular this holds for every complete model M in V.

3 Declarative functionality descriptions

After having defined in Section 2 more precisely what a domain description is, we now turn to the properties of a reasoning module related to a given domain. By the declarative functionality of a reasoning module we mean what the module is able to derive, given certain specific input data. In this section, for a given domain description we treat what (declarative) functionality may be required from a reasoning module, in order to cover the domain description. Therefore we define what a declarative functionality description of a reasoning module is in Section 3.1. Furthermore, the notions of soundness and completeness of a declarative functionality description with respect to a given domain description are defined in Section 3.2. In Section 4, in addition it will be treated in what format a module's knowledge base can be specified and when this specification meets the requirement as posed by a declarative functionality description.

3.1 Definitions, constructions and examples

Given a domain description W it may look rather trivial how a reasoning module's functionality should be defined. For a complete input model, the output of the module simply could be prescribed by the model from W that refines the input model. However, there are two complications that require a more detailed analysis. Firstly, there may be no *unique* refinement of the given complete input model in W. So some output literals will have to remain open. Secondly, a reasoning module is expected to give some (partial) answers in the case of an *incomplete input model* as well. Such a partial answer cannot be read directly from one of the complete models in W. Both complications have to do with incomplete information. We will use partial models both for input models and output models to specify these incompletenesses.

In this section we consider the following example of a domain description. The signature of this example is given by $< s_1, s_2; h_1, h_2 >$, and the domain W is given by the following situation models:

M_1 : < 0, 0; 0, 0 >
M_2 : < 0, 1; 0, 1 >
M_3 : < 1, 0; 0, 0 >
M_4 : < 1, 0; 1, 0 >
M_5 : < 1, 1; 1, 1 >

Fig. 4 Example domain

For example, suppose the partial input model < u, 1 > is given. What should the reasoning module conclude about h_1 and h_2 in this case ? If W is inspected it turns out that in W there are two different refinements of (the trivial expansion of) < u, 1 >, namely:

M_2 : < 0, 1; 0, 1 >
M_5 : < 1, 1; 1, 1 >

These two situation models disagree on h_1, but they agree that h_2 is true. From this semantical analysis it follows that the reasoning module may be expected to give as an answer: < u, 1; u, 1 >. This is the greatest common information state of all refinements in W of the given partial input model < u, 1 > , i.e. sc_W(< u, 1 >) which is in this case gci({M_2, M_5}). Using this method we obtain the mapping $\alpha: P_{in} \rightarrow P$ as listed in Fig. 5; here P_{in} = P(In(W)) and P = P(W).

< 0, 0 > → < 0, 0; 0, 0 >
< 0, 1 > → < 0, 1; 0, 1 >
< 0, u > → < 0, u; 0, u >
< 1, 0 > → < 1, 0; u, 0 >
< 1, 1 > → < 1, 1; 1, 1 >
< 1, u > → < 1, u; u, u >
< u, 0 > → < u, 0; u, 0 >
< u, 1 > → < u, 1; u, 1 >
< u, u > → < u, u; u, u >

Fig. 5 Functionality description α for the example domain of Fig. 4

Here any right hand side is obtained by taking the greatest common information state of all refinements in W of the corresponding left hand side (i.e. by taking its semantic closure). It turns out that this construction results in a mapping $\alpha: P_{in} \rightarrow P$ which satisfies a number of nice properties as defined by the following:

Definition 3.1
Suppose a signature Σ is given, a non-empty set of complete input models W_{in} for Σ and a mapping $\alpha: P_{in} \rightarrow P$, where $P_{in} = P(W_{in})$ and P is a set of partial models for Σ.
a) The mapping α is called *conservative* if for all $M \in P_{in}$ it holds: $M \leq \alpha(M)$

b) The mapping α is called *monotonic* if for all $M, N \in P_{in}$ it holds:

$M \leq N \Rightarrow \alpha(M) \leq \alpha(N)$

c) The mapping α is called *self-bounded* if for all $M, N \in P_{in}$ it holds:

$M \leq \alpha(N) \Rightarrow \alpha(M) \leq \alpha(N)$

d) The mapping α is called *well-informed* if for all $M \in P_{in}$ it holds:

$$Out(\alpha(M)) = gci(\{Out(\alpha(N)) \mid N \in W_{in} \ \& \ M \leq N\})$$

As a result of the analysis above, we use these properties to define the notion of a declarative functionality description. Some logical relations between these properties are given in [14]. A declarative functionality description should satisfy some of the properties introduced above to exclude pathological examples. On the other hand the notion should not be too restrictive. The following definition will provide such a notion.

Definition 3.3
Suppose a signature Σ and a non-empty set of complete input models W_{in} for Σ are given. A *declarative functionality description* for Σ is a mapping $\alpha: P_{in} \to P$, where $P_{in} = P(W_{in})$ and P is a set of partial models for Σ, such that α is conservative and self-bounded.

If no confusion is expected, for convenience we often omit the word "declarative". An example of a functionality description is the α as constructed in Fig. 5. This can be stated as the following more general Theorem (which can be derived immediately from Lemma 2.3).

Theorem 3.4
Let a non-empty set of complete input models W_{in} for signature Σ be given and a set V of partial models of signature Σ such that $W_{in} \subset P(V)$. Define the mapping $\alpha: P_{in} \to P$, where $P_{in} = P(W_{in})$ and $P = P(V)$, by $\alpha(M) = sc_V(M)$ for all $M \in P_{in}$. Then α is a declarative functionality description.
In particular this holds if V is a domain description W, and $W_{in} = In(W)$.

In fact, the functionality description $\alpha = sc_W$ additionally satisfies the property of well-informedness. This will also follow from more general results later on (Theorem 3.6 and Proposition 3.7). Definition 3.3 allows more functionality descriptions than that one (see Section 3.2). But there are restrictions as well. For example it is not possible to express a functionality of a module that makes h_1 true if s_1 is unknown (1) and makes h_1 unknown else (2): see Fig. 6.

$$\langle 0 \rangle \to \langle 0; u \rangle$$
$$\langle 1 \rangle \to \langle 1; u \rangle$$
$$\langle u \rangle \to \langle u; 1 \rangle$$

Fig. 6 Not a functionality description

This mapping does not satisfy the monotonicity condition. In fact the conditions of Definition 3.3 imply that it is possible to satisfy the functionality description by an ordinary deduction system.

3.2 Soundness and completeness

Definition 3.3 above does not say anything about how well a functionality description fits to a given domain description. The example as constructed in Section 3.1 covers the concerning domain description, but a slight change may provide a functionality description that does not fit to the domain description. For example, this is the case if the third line in Fig. 5 is changed to $< 0, u > \rightarrow < 0, u; u, u >$. In this section we define additional requirements of soundness and completeness that should be satisfied by a functionality description in order to cover a given domain description.

Definition 3.5
Suppose a domain description is given by signature Σ and non-empty set of situation models W. Let $\alpha: P_{in} \rightarrow P$ be a functionality description, where $P_{in} = P(W_{in})$ and $P = P(W)$.

a) We call α *sound* with respect to W if for all $M \in P_{in}$ and $h \in OutLit(\Sigma)$ it holds
$$\alpha(M) \vdash h \Rightarrow M \Vdash_W h$$

b) We call α *(strongly) complete* with respect to W if for all $M \in P_{in}$ and $h \in OutLit(\Sigma)$
$$M \Vdash_W h \Rightarrow \alpha(M) \vdash h$$

c) We call α *weakly complete (w-complete)* with respect to W if for all $M \in W_{in}$ and $h \in OutLit(\Sigma)$ it holds
$$M \Vdash_W h \Rightarrow \alpha(M) \vdash h$$

d) If both the conditions a) and b) are satisfied we say that α *covers* W. If both the conditions a) and c) are satisfied we say that α *weakly covers (w-covers)* W.

In the more extended report [14] some equivalent formulations of soundness are given. It is easy to verify that the functionality description α as constructed in Fig. 5 in Section 3.1 covers the given domain description. An example where completeness is *not*, whereas w-completeness *is* satisfied is if in the example in Section 3.1 in the lines concerning incomplete input models we replace the output truth values in the right hand side by u. The following theorem shows that, given a domain description, there exists a functionality description that covers it. Its proof can be found in [14].

Theorem 3.6
Suppose a domain description is given by a signature Σ and a non-empty set of situation models W. Let $\alpha: P_{in} \rightarrow P$ be a functionality description, where $P_{in} = P(W_{in})$, $W_{in} = In(W)$ and $P = P(W)$. Then the following hold:

a) The functionality description α is sound with respect to W if and only if
$$Out(\alpha(M)) \leq Out(sc_W(M)) \text{ for all } M \in P_{in}.$$

b) The functionality description α is w-complete with respect to W if and only if
$$Out(\alpha(M)) \geq Out(sc_W(M)) \text{ for all } M \in W_{in}.$$

c) The functionality description α is complete with respect to W if and only if
$$Out(\alpha(M)) \geq Out(sc_W(M)) \text{ for all } M \in P_{in}.$$

d) The functionality description α w-covers W if and only if
$$Out(\alpha(M)) = Out(sc_W(M)) \text{ for all } M \in W_{in}.$$

e) The functionality description α covers W if and only if
$$Out(\alpha(M)) = Out(sc_W(M)) \text{ for all } M \in P_{in}.$$

There exists a functionality description that covers W, namely sc_W.

It turns out that the additional condition of well-informedness is strong enough to make w-completeness equivalent to completeness (see [14]):

Proposition 3.7
Suppose a signature Σ is given with a non-empty set of complete input models W_{in} and P is a set of partial models for Σ. Assume the mapping $\alpha: P_{in} \rightarrow P$, where $P_{in} = P(W_{in})$, is a declarative functionality description for Σ. Moreover, let a domain description W for signature Σ with $In(W) = W_{in}$ be given. Then the following conditions are equivalent:

(i) W is covered by α
(ii) W is w-covered by α and α is well-informed.

From Theorem 3.6 and Proposition 3.7 it follows that in the situation of Theorem 3.4 the functionality description given by $\alpha = sc_W$ is well-informed. A simple example of a functionality description not satisfying well-informedness for signature $< s_1; h_1 >$ is given by the following:

$$< 0 > \rightarrow < 0; 1 >$$
$$< 1 > \rightarrow < 1; 1 >$$
$$< u > \rightarrow < u; u >$$

Fig. 7 Simple example of a not well-informed functionality description

One may raise the question whether or not reasoning modules that satisfy this type of functionality description are desirable. In Section 4 we will return to this issue.

The question may arise whether for any given functionality description α a domain description can be found that is covered by α; this is the reverse situation of Theorem 3.6 above. According to Theorem 3.6e) this question can be formulated equivalently as: given W_{in} and α, does there exist a W such that $Out(\alpha(M)) = Out(sc_W(M))$ for all $M \in P_{in}$. It turns out that any α can be expressed in this way if and only if α is well-informed, as is shown in the extended report [14].

4 Specifications of interactive reasoning modules

The examples of functionality descriptions given in Section 3 are defined by enumerating complete tables for the mappings. However, in practical situations, tables are not an efficient manner of specification. Therefore a more normalized and condensed form of specification is needed. This will be treated in this section. In Section 4.1 we make a choice on the format in which the knowledge base is specified. We will leave the inference relation unspecified. Instead, here we will define a suitable notion of a semantic consequence relation. In principle a choice of a strict format for the knowledge implies a restriction on the expressiveness. However, we will prove in Section 4.3 that for any relevant well-informed functionality description a knowledge base specification in the chosen format is possible such that by the semantic consequence relation the required (declarative) functionality is obtained. This means that any derivability relation that is sound and complete with respect to this semantic consequence relation is able to derive from a given input information state by use of the knowledge base the right conclusions. In another report it will be discussed that also chaining provides a suitable derivability relation.

4.1 Some definitions

By **KB** (the *knowledge base*) we denote the knowledge which may be used by the reasoning module to derive output literals from the available information on inputs. Recall that P_{in} is the non-empty set of all possible partial input models. If $M \in P_{in}$, and c is a conjunction of literals, then by $M \models_{KB} c$ we will denote that c *semantically follows* from the information of M by use of KB, i.e. is a semantic consequence of the theory $Lit(M) \cup KB$. The notions of rule format, semantic consequence and reasoning module specification can be defined formally as follows:

Definition 4.1
Let Σ be a signature and KB a set of propositions for Σ.
a) A proposition in *rule format*, or simply a *rule* is a proposition of one of the following two forms:
(i) d where d is a literal; these rules are sometimes called *general facts*

(ii) $c \rightarrow d$ where c is a conjunction of literals and d is a literal
b) We call KB *consistent* with respect to the input model M if there exists a model N with $M \leq N$ and $N \vdash KB$.
c) If KB is consistent with respect to the input model M then the *semantic consequence* relation $M \vdash_{KB} c$ is defined as: for all models N for Σ with $M \leq N$ and $N \vdash KB$ it holds $N \vdash c$.
d) A *(declarative) reasoning module specification* $< \Sigma, P_{in}, KB >$ consists of a finite signature Σ, a finite non-empty set of rules for this signature KB (knowledge base), and a finite set of input models $P_{in} = P(W_{in})$ where W_{in} is a non-empty set of complete input models for the related input signature.

For a reasoning module specification $< \Sigma, P(W_{in}), KB >$ that is consistent w.r.t. $M \in P_{in}$ we define the *consequence model* $cons_{KB}(M)$ of M as the partial model where all literals that semantically follow are true, and the others are unknown, i.e. for all atoms a it holds

$$cons_{KB}(M)(a) = \begin{cases} 0 & \text{if } M \vdash_{KB} \neg a \\ 1 & \text{if } M \vdash_{KB} a \\ u & \text{else} \end{cases}$$

It is easy to verify that for all $M \in P_{in}$ it holds $M \vdash_{KB} a \Leftrightarrow M \Vdash_{Mod(KB)} a$ and $cons_{KB}(M) = sc_{Mod(KB)}(M)$ where $Mod(KB)$ is the set of all models of KB. The mapping $cons_{KB}$ is a well-informed functionality description, as follows from Theorems 3.4. Therefore we can define:

Definition 4.2
Suppose a signature Σ is given and W_{in} is a non-empty set of input models. Take for P the set of all partial models of signature Σ and $P_{in} = P(W_{in})$. Let a consistent reasoning module specification $< \Sigma, P_{in}, KB >$ be given.
a) We call $cons_{KB}$ *the well-informed functionality description related to* $< \Sigma, P_{in}, KB >$. Sometimes we simply call it the *well-informed functionality description related to (specified by)* KB.
b) We call two reasoning module specifications with the same set of input models P_{in} *equivalent* if they specify the same functionality description.
c) We say a functionality description α is *covered by* the well-informed functionality description related to $< \Sigma, P_{in}, KB >$ if for all $M \in P_{in}$ it holds

$$Out(\alpha(M)) = Out(cons_{KB}(M)).$$

4.2 Soundness and completeness

In this section we give definitions of soundness and completeness of the well-informed functionality description related to a reasoning module specification with respect to a given domain description. In view of Definition 4.2 this can be done very easily:

Definition 4.3
Suppose a signature Σ is given and W_{in} is a non-empty set of input models and W a domain description for Σ and W_{in}. Let a consistent reasoning module specification $< \Sigma, P_{in}, KB >$ be given. The quality of this reasoning module specification with respect to a given domain description can be expressed by respectively *soundness, completeness, w-completeness, covering* with respect to the given domain description of the well-informed functionality description related to the reasoning module specification.

It is easy to verify that the well-informed functionality description related to a reasoning module specification given by **KB** is sound with respect to **W** if and only if every model $M \in W$ is a model of **KB**. Collecting this, together with the connections formulated in Definition 3.5, Theorem 3.6 and Proposition 3.7, more direct statements for these notions can be obtained (see [14]).

In practice, in a reasoning module specification often the set of input models P_{in} is not mentioned. We will interpret this omission as if this set of input models is meant to be the set of all partial models for the input signature (all truth assignments that are theoretically possible). However, in practical domains, often not all theoretically possible input models are used, for instance since there are semantical dependencies between the input atoms. In these cases there may be theoretically possible input models that do not make sense in reality, and especially, there is no (domain) knowledge on what output should be expected for these input models. This means that in such a domain it is *essentially* impossible to prove soundness and completeness, as long as no restriction is put on the set of input models.

On the other hand, in practice it is often unfeasible to enumerate the set of all relevant input models, so in any case *practical* problems can be expected in proving soundness and completeness. What can be done is to collect (during knowledge acquisition) a set of typical, and critical examples of input models, and use this as a representative test set. Another possible approach is, as a part of the knowledge acquisition process, to make all semantic dependencies between input atoms explicit, and use these as constraints to specify P_{in}. This approach has not been tried out yet.

4.3 Existence of reasoning module specifications

In this section we show that for any well-informed functionality description α a reasoning module specification can be found such that its related well-informed functionality description gives the same results as α does, and that this can be done in a minimal sense. To illustrate these issues we return to the example in Section 3.1 of a domain description given by **W** and a well-informed functionality description α, given by Fig. 5. Consider, for example, the third line of the functionality description α in Fig. 5: $< 0, u > \rightarrow < 0, u; 0, u >$. If M is any model in P_{in} refining the left hand side (i.e. $< 0, u > \leq M$), then by monotonicity $< 0, u; 0, u > = \alpha(< 0, u >) \leq \alpha(M)$. Therefore for any $M \in P_{in}$ it holds:

$$\textit{if} < 0, u > \leq M \textit{ then } < 0, u; 0, u > \leq \alpha(M)$$

Since $< 0, u > \leq M$ is equivalent to $M \models \neg s_1$, and $< 0, u; 0, u > \leq \alpha(M)$ is equivalent to $M \models \neg s_1$ and $\alpha(M) \models \neg h_1$, we can restate the above *if-then* rule by the rule $\neg s_1 \rightarrow \neg h_1$. Doing this for all relevant lines of Fig. 5, this results in a knowledge base of 10 rules. By this knowledge base we obtain a reasoning module specification. But this is a very inefficient specification. Sometimes a number of rules are a special case of one rule with less conditions. For instance, it is easy to see that the rule

$$s_2 \rightarrow h_2$$

makes two other rules

$$\neg s_1 \wedge s_2 \rightarrow h_2$$
$$s_1 \wedge s_2 \rightarrow h_2$$

superfluous, since both the complete input models related to the latter rules are refinements of the incomplete input model related to the former rule. This enables us to prune the knowledge base until we obtain a minimal form for it. Here, in our example it can be shown how such a minimization can be done. For example, instead of considering all partial input models $M \in P_{in}$ for which $\alpha(M) \models h_1$, we only take the $M \in P_{in}$ among them that are minimal in P_{in}, i.e. such that there does not exist an $M' \in P_{in}$ with $\alpha(M) \vdash h_1$ such that $M' \leq M$ and $M' \neq M$. Inspecting P_{in}, for each of the four output literals $h_1, \neg h_1, h_2, \neg h_2$ we find one non-trivial minimal element. Using these we obtain the following more concise knowledge base (which is a subset of the knowledge base above): see Fig. 8.

$$\begin{array}{lcl} s_1 \wedge s_2 & \rightarrow & h_1 \\ \neg s_1 & \rightarrow & \neg h_1 \\ \neg s_2 & \rightarrow & \neg h_2 \\ s_2 & \rightarrow & h_2 \end{array}$$

Fig. 8 Minimal knowledge base covering α

By this knowledge base a specification is obtained such that its related well-informed functionality description has the same output models as α (it covers α) and which is minimal in the sense that will be defined below more precisely. We will define this construction more formally such that indeed a minimal specification covering α is obtained.

Definition 4.4
Let a consistent reasoning module specification $< \Sigma, P(W_{in}), KB >$ be given. Then it is called *minimal* if for every rule in KB, and every generalization of it by omitting one of the conditions, replacing the rule by its generalization makes a knowledge base that is not equivalent to KB.

Lemma 4.5
Assume a signature Σ is given, W_{in} is a non-empty set of complete input models and P a set of models for Σ. Assume $\alpha : P_{in} \rightarrow P$ where $P_{in} = P(W_{in})$ is a functionality description. The non-empty set of rules KB_α is constructed as follows. For each output literal h, take

$$T(h) = \{ M \in P_{in} \mid \alpha(M) \vdash h \}$$

and $mT(h)$ the set of minimal (with respect to the refinement relation) elements in $T(h)$. Define KB_α by the following set of rules

$$KB_\alpha = \{ h \mid \Lambda \in mT(h) \} \cup \{ Con(Lit(M)) \rightarrow h \mid M \in mT(h), M \neq \Lambda \}$$

where $Con(..)$ means taking the conjunction of a set of literals.
Then a consistent reasoning module specification $< \Sigma, P_{in}, KB_\alpha >$ is obtained such that for all complete models $M \in W_{in}$ it holds $\alpha(M) \vdash KB_\alpha$.

Theorem 4.6
Assume a signature Σ is given, P_{in} is a non-empty set of partial input models for Σ and $\alpha : P_{in} \rightarrow P$ is a well-informed functionality description. Then the well-informed functionality description related to the consistent reasoning module specification $< \Sigma, P_{in}, KB_\alpha >$ covers α and is minimal.

5 Conclusions

It turns out that our semantical framework may provide adequate logical descriptions for the functionality of an interactive reasoning module. In particular the relation between the conclusions that may be drawn by a module and the situation in reality that is concerned can be made more transparent by our framework. Furthermore, the formal definitions of soundness, completeness and empirical foundedness as given above enable us to establish the (meta-)logical connections between these concepts. As a result it has been established that, considered from the viewpoint of functionality, the knowledge in a reasoning module always can be normalized to knowledge in rule format. This shows that the rule format essentially is expressive enough to specify the functionality of a reasoning module. This result gives a justification for the choice as made in our framework for design and specification of interacting reasoning modules DESIRE.

Acknowledgements

Parts of this research have been supported by SKBS. Earlier drafts of this text have been read and commented upon by Arnoud de Gorter, Pieter van Langen and Izak van Langevelde. This has led to a number of improvements in the text.

References

[1] S. Blamey, Partial Logic, in: D. Gabbay, F. Guenthner (eds.), Handbook of Philosophical Logic, Vol. III, pp.1-70, Reidel, 1986.

[2] B.G. Buchanan, E.H. Shortliffe, Rule-based expert systems, Addison-Wesley, 1985

[3] B. Chandrasekaran, Generic tasks in knowledge-based reasoning: high level building blocks for expert system design, IEEE Expert, Fall 1986

[4] C.C. Chang, H.J. Keisler, Model theory, North Holland, 1973

[5] C.G. Hempel, Philosophy of Science, Prentice-Hall, Englewoods Cliffs, 1966

[6] W. Kowalczyk, J. Treur, On the use of a formalized generic task model in knowledge acquisition, Proc. European Knowledge Acquisition Workshop, EKAW-90, pp. 198-221, 1990

[7] P.H.G. van Langen, J. Treur, Representing world situations and information states by many-sorted partial models, Report PE8904, University of Amsterdam, Expert Systems Section, 1989

[8] T. Langholm, Partiality, Truth and Persistance, CSLI Lecture Notes No. 15, Stanford University, Stanford, 1988.

[9] M. Suwa, A. Garlisle Scott, E.H. Shortliffe, Completeness and consistency in a rule-based system, in: B.G. Buchanan, E.H. Shortliffe, Rule-based expert systems, pp. 159-170, 1985

[10] Y.H. Tan, J. Treur, A bimodular approach to nonmonotonic reasoning, Proc. World Congress on Fundamentals in AI, WOCFAI-91, pp. 461-475, 1991

[11] J. Treur, Completeness and definability in diagnostic expert systems, Proc. European Conference on Artificial Intelligence, ECAI-88, pp. 619-624, 1988

[12] J. Treur, Heuristic reasoning and relative incompleteness, Int. Journal of Approximate Reasoning, to appear, 1992

[13] J. Treur, On the use of reflection principles in modelling complex reasoning, Int. Journal of Intelligent Systems 6 (1991), pp. 277-294

[14] J. Treur, Declarative functionality descriptions of interactive reasoning modules, Report IR-237, Vrije Universiteit, Department of Mathematics and Computer Science, 1990

[15] J. Treur, Interaction types and chemistry of generic task models, Proc. European Knowledge Acquisition Workshop, EKAW-91, 1991

[16] R.W. Weyhrauch, Prolegomena to a theory of mechanized formal reasoning, Artificial Intelligence 13 (1980), pp. 133-170

Appendix: main proofs of Section 4

Proof of Lemma 4.5

Suppose a model $M \in W_{in}$ is given. We will prove that $\alpha(M) \models KB_\alpha$. This also implies consistency. First we treat the general facts in KB_α. Assume $h \in KB_\alpha$ so $\Lambda \in mT(h)$. Therefore $\alpha(\Lambda) \models h$. From monotonicity it follows that $\alpha(M) \models h$. Next we treat a rule that is no general fact, say $Con(Lit(M_0)) \rightarrow h$ with $M_0 \in mT(h)$. Since M is complete, from not $M \models Con(Lit(M_0))$ it follows that $M \models \neg Con(Lit(M_0))$. By the strong Kleene rule for implication in that case the rule is true in M, independent of the truth value of h. By conservatism the same holds for $\alpha(M)$. In the other case $M \models Con(Lit(M_0))$. This implies that $M_0 \leq M$. Therefore, by monotonicity $\alpha(M_0) \leq \alpha(M)$. Now from $M_0 \in mT(h)$ it follows that $\alpha(M_0) \models h$, hence $\alpha(M) \models h$. So also in this case the rule is true in $\alpha(M)$. ∎

Proof of Theorem 4.6

We will prove that the well-informed functionality description of the reasoning module specification with $KB = KB_\alpha$ given in Lemma 4.5 covers α. First we prove that $Out(cons_{KB}(M)) \leq Out(\alpha(M))$ for all $M \in P_{in}$. Let the output literal $h \in OutLit(\Sigma)$ and $M \in P_{in}$ be given with $M \models_{KB} h$. By Lemma 4.5 for every $N \in W_{in}$ with $M \leq N$, $\alpha(N)$ is a model of KB, hence $\alpha(N) \models h$. By well-informedness $\alpha(M) \models h$. Next we prove $Out(cons_{KB}(M)) \geq Out(\alpha(M))$ for all $M \in P_{in}$. Suppose $h \in OutLit(\Sigma)$ and an $M \in P_{in}$ with $\alpha(M) \models h$ are given. We will show that $M \models_{KB} h$. Since $\alpha(M) \models h$ we have $M \in T(h)$. Take a minimal element M' in T(h) with $M' \leq M$. If $M' = \Lambda$, then from $M' \in mT(h)$ it follows $h \in KB$, so $M \models_{KB} h$ and we are done. In the other case that $M' \neq \Lambda$ we have the following rule in KB: $Con(Lit(M')) \rightarrow h$. From $M' \leq M$ it follows that $M \models Con(Lit(M'))$. Therefore for any partial model N with $N \geq M$ and $N \models KB$ it holds $N \models Con(Lit(M'))$. Since $N \models KB$ it holds $N \models Con(Lit(M')) \rightarrow h$. Using the strong Kleene truth value combination table we have $N \models h$. This proves $M \models_{KB} h$. Therefore the well-informed functionality related to the reasoning module specification as constructed covers the given functionality description α. Finally we show it is minimal. Suppose we obtain KB' from KB by leaving out one of the conditions in the condition part of a rule $Con(Lit(M)) \rightarrow h$ with $M \in mT(h) \subset T(d)$ and $M \neq \Lambda$. The resulting condition part corresponds to a partial model $M' \leq M$ with $M' \neq M$. Since M was minimal in T(h), it holds $M' \notin T(h)$; therefore $\alpha(M') \not\models h$, while $M' \models_{KB'} h$. So this knowledge base KB' would not be equivalent to KB. This proves that the constructed KB is minimal. ∎

Rule-Aided Constraint Resolution in LAURE

Yves Caseau

Bellcore, 445 South Street,
Morristown NJ 07962-1910, U.S.A.
e-mail: caseau@bellcore.com

Abstract

This paper presents how deductive rules can be used as heuristics to guide constraint resolution. We describe the LAURE language, which allows the definition of constraints on *order-sorted* finite domains. We propose a semantic for integrating rules and constraints in an object-oriented model. An algorithm for constraint resolution is described, which can be integrated with rule propagation. An illustration of relevance to AI problems is given with examples such as scheduling.

1. Introduction

One of the most difficult areas in AI is the resolution of constraint problems, because of their complexity (NP) and size. Most automatic inference tools, such as deductive languages (PROLOG) or production rule systems (expert system shells), leave the constraint domain apart, because there is no generally good resolution strategy. More recently, a lot of work has been done on constraint resolution as a programming paradigm [CLP] [VH89], but there is little evidence that it could be integrated with more traditional AI work on heuristics and resolution strategies. Here we want to illustrate the benefits of integrating production rules with constraints, both from an expressive power point of view (we can describe more complex problems) but also from an efficiency point of view (the production rules may be used to guide the constraint resolution).

LAURE is an object-oriented knowledge representation language, developed and used for AI applications. We first developed "traditional" deductive capabilities [Ca89], such as deductive and production rules. Because our main concern was efficiency, we based resolution on a compiled strategy, which relies on an object-oriented relational algebra. In order to provide a complete environment for object-oriented logic programming, we found it necessary to introduce explicit global constraints. This paper relates our experiments and our findings to conciliate domain-specific optimizations and a general constraint resolution scheme that is adequate for any constraint on an order-sorted domain.

To successfully integrate various technologies such as deductive rules and constraints into an object-oriented language, we developed yet another model of object-orieted knowledge representation that will be superficially described in the paper. Two advantages are gained from this model. Because this model is very general, it supports a clean integration of set- or relation-based programming techniques, thus enhancing the expressive power and offering a good interface to logic programming. In addition, this model supports the handling of disjunctive information and hypothetical reasoning in a natural and efficient manner.

The paper is organized as follows. Section 2 describes LAURE as a knowledge representation language. We present our extended object-oriented model and show how it supports the previously claimed extensions. Section 3 presents the LAURE logic language, and its application to constraint logic programming. We then study many possible strategies to improve a generic constraint solver with domain-specific knowledge (in order to cross the complexity border). Section 4 provides a semantics for rules and constraints, through an algebraic representation. We then describe an algorithm for solving constraints, through propagation of rules and abstract interpretation of constraints. The last section illustrates our claims with some examples, including a scheduling problem, and concludes with a brief comparison with other similar logic-based systems.

2. Knowledge Representation in LAURE

2.1. MOTIVATIONS

The aim for building yet another object-oriented model of knowledge representation is to have a theoretical framework for a sound and efficient integration of various extensions to what is usually thought as an object-oriented language. This means that we want to deal with objects as a way to encapsulate data and procedures, to use (multiple) inheritance for classification and re-use, to use messages and methods for polymorphism, etc. To this we want to add the following extensions:

- *Sets as a tool for classification.* Classes in an object-oriented language can always be thought of as sets. However, using sets more consistently enhances expressive power two ways: we can use other kinds of sets and get a finer classification; we can attach set properties to classes and obtain automatic classification [BBM89].
- *Explicit relations among objects.* Having a clear representation of relations about objects is, from our point of view, the key to a nice integration with logic programming.
- *Managing disjunctive information.* Many AI applications such as planning or resource allocation deal with incomplete data represented as disjunctions. Disjunctive information must be incorporated in the model for a clean integration with constraint solving (transforms incomplete datainto complete data)
- *Supporting hypothetical reasoning.* We want to be able to make a copy of the current state of the database, modify it with some hypotheses and then return to the previous state if the hypotheses fail. This is needed both by some expert system applications based on decision trees, and by the constraint solver to be truly integrated with the rest of the system.

2.2. AN EXTENDED OBJECT MODEL

The LAURE model [Ca91a] is the abstraction of a semantic network with enumerations and functions. An object has no structure or dimension, it is just a node inside a semantic network; thus, the set of objects is any (possibly infinite) set. The mandatory primitive operations that must be captured (such as integer addition) are seen as a given set of object functions. In our model, objects can be *organized*, and then *described* (using the organization). Organization is based on sets, which are either simple enumerations or other complex objects to which a set value is assigned[1]. Objects are described uniquely through their relationship with one another. These relations can be intensional (the relation is represented by another object, to which a relation value is assigned by the language semantics), or extensional (the graph of the relation is explicitly stored as a collection of tuples). Only binary relations (called slots in LAURE) are carried extensionally in an object-oriented system, yielding to a strong analogy with semantic network [BBM89].

The LAURE system is an instance of this model: it is a collection of tools to build sets and relations on top of objects. Sets and relations are *reified* in the LAURE model, which means that any set or relation (except the very primitive enumerations or slots handled directly by the model) is represented by an object from the language. Our description of the actual LAURE language will be a collection of objects to which we assign a set (relation) value. It also means that we can describe the LAURE actual model into the model itself (thus, into the language). Reflection [MN88] (the ability for the model to be self-described) is the key to extensibility: by extending the afore-mentioned collection of *concept* objects, users often customize the LAURE language to their own needs.

2.3. CLASSES, SETS AND TYPES

2.3.1. Set-based Taxonomy

The taxonomy is described with classes as sets placed in an inclusion lattice. The first task of a LAURE programmer is to set up a taxonomy of his object world, which will help support finer object organization with more complex sets and description through relations. The building unit is the *class* notion, which contains objects with two multi-valued slots: *instance* and *subclass*. As a set, a class is defined as the union of its instances and the recursive value of its subclasses. This is nothing more than giving an intuitive set semantic to class definition. There is a strong dichotomy between the structure and the description, which yields to a simpler mathematical model and an easier integration with logic. Set properties can be added to describe the role of a node (LAURE originality is to take the set analogy more seriously). Each node in the taxonomy can be assigned set properties that the system will ensure throughout schema evolution. Here are some examples:

---

[1] As a consequence, the set of objects is closed under finite enumeration, i.e., any finite subset of objects is an object from this model.

```
[person :: union subset (man woman)]

[boat :: intersection superset (vehicle floating_objects)]

[meta_instruction ::  set_of_classes superset (class)
    powerset_of instruction]
```

The first declaration means that *person* has no local instances, thus is the exact union of its subclasses (any person is either a man or a woman). The second declaration means that *boat* is defined as being exactly the intersection of its two superclasses. Thus, any further definition of a new class that is included both in *vehicle* and *floating_object* will provoke an automatic classification into boat. The interest of classification [BBM89] is both to improve the expressive power (more meaning is caught) and safety (avoid future errors due to poor taxonomy design). Intersection nodes are also used in LAURE to automatically generate a *lattice* structure from any taxonomy (yielding to a set of classes closed by intersection). The last example creates a meta-class (a subset of *class*), defined as the "powerset" of the root class *intersection*. The system will ensure than any class created under *instruction* belongs to this meta-class. This is useful here since resources necessary to the evaluator must be allocated to each set of instructions.

2.3.2. Sets and Types

In addition to enumerations and classes, LAURE permits the definition of other set objects through the selection definition scheme (defining a set from another set and a *selection* predicate). This open-ended capability of defining new sets is used in LAURE to define sets with logic predicates (called queries) such as in the following example:

```
[adult :: query for_all (x person) such_that [age(x) > 18]]
```

Another example is the definition of set-expressions that are used to build the type system. A set expression is a syntactical LAURE object that represents a set built from other LAURE sets and a well-defined mathematical operation. For instance,

```
{person + integer}  is the union of person and integer

{vehicle & floating_object} is the intersection of vehicle and floating
object

{list & {integer set_of}} is the set of lists of integer
```

The type system is an extension of the class system to support fine optimizations in the compiling process [GJ90]. To support constant recognition, an enumeration is a type. Any class is obviously a type, and so is the union or the intersection of two types (to support fine type inference). The powerset of a type is a type to support compiling of set operations, and parameterized types are defined to support truly polymorphic descriptions such as to infer that the result of applying the method *top* to a stack with type `{stack & {range in integer}}` is an integer. Because LAURE uses a type system with inclusion, it supports programming styles varying from strongly-typed (PASCAL) to un-typed (LISP). When types are used tightly, the efficiency of the compiled code for traditional object-oriented programming (creating instances, reading and updating slots, executing methods) is similar to C or C++.

2.4. RELATIONS, RESTRICTIONS AND COMBINATION

2.4.1. Extensional and Intensional Relations

Relations among objects are divided into *properties* and *logic relations*. Because the logic system cannot reason on any program, LAURE makes a clear distinction between the imperative specifications and the logic (declarative) specifications. Relations defined within the LAURE imperative language are called *properties*. They are considered as constant relations by the LAURE logic resolution algorithm. Relations that are defined through logic specifications (rules, constraints, etc.) are called *logic relations*. The principle is to describe what does not change according to logic rules (such as the weight of an object, the method to print it) with the imperative language, and to use logic relations for what will change according to rules or constraints (such as the pressure or the temperature of a physical object).

Properties are described through a collection of *restrictions*, which use the set structure to build a complex definition. Each restriction has a signature (a cartesian product of types), which tells where the restriction is valid. When two restrictions of the same property have conflicting signatures (non-empty intersection), a declaratively specified algorithm reduces each signature and produces a synthetic restriction whose signature is the intersection, called the *combination* of the two restrictions. Thus, each property is well-defined: all restrictions are disjoint and the relation assigned to the property is simply the union of its restrictions. The restriction paradigm allows the combination of different styles to define a complex relation (e.g., the weight of an object can be a slot for some objects and a function for other [composed] objects).

Strictly speaking, there is no inheritance in LAURE. Each restriction decides if it can be applied to a particular tuple of objects. There is no propagation up or down in the taxonomy (descriptions never influence the taxonomy). The expected behavior (a method defined for a class A also applies to the instances of a subclass B) is a natural consequence of the set semantics. "Multiple inheritance" is also implicit here, and inheritance conflicts are solved through restriction combination. Combination is defined through an extensible set of rules based on the type of conflicting restrictions that catches fine discriminating behavior. For instance, the default values of a slot are merged if the conflicting slots are multi-valued, and a random choice and/or a warning is issued otherwise. Another important property is that if the combination operation is commutative and associative, the conflict resolution is purely based on the set semantics, and not on the order in which the taxonomy was built, which is unfortunately the case in most knowledge representation languages.

2.4.2. Logic Relations

Logic relations also combine extensional (pairs) and intensional (rules) definitions. Such a relation can be added between any kinds of objects (such as a relation from strings to integers, which is difficult to describe with a traditional object-oriented language). Each logic relation, which is a binary relation, can be explicitly assigned pairs of objects, such as in the following:

```
[fibonacci :: attribute domain integer -> integer]
[fib(0) is 1] [fib(1) is 1]
```

The distinction between mono-valued and multi-valued relations is important in LAURE. A mono-valued relation R has a functional graph: for each object x, there is at most one object y such that R(x y). Such relations are called *attributes*, whereas *multi_attribute* stands for any binary logic relation. The main feature of logic relations is the ability to define rules or constraints on them, as we shall see in Section 3.

LAURE supports incomplete and disjunctive information for attributes [AKG87] [IV89]. When the "value" of an object for a relation is not known, a set of possible values can be given, either as an explicit enumeration or a complex expression. Here is an example:

```
[father :: attribute domain person -> man]
[father(Paul) is_in {Peter, John}]
[father(John) is_in {person & {eye_color in {Blue}}}]
```

This tells that the father of Paul is either Peter or John, and that the father of John has blue eyes. Attributes can be further defined through the use of constraints, as seen in Section 3. Note that LAURE will actually complain if we further refine our database with a value that is not in the disjunction set.

2.5. HYPOTHESIS AND WORLD MANAGEMENT

As soon as disjunctive information is present, we need a way to try hypotheses, to explore the different states contained in the disjunction. If we consider the previous example, a plausible hypothesis is to try *father(Paul) = Peter*. This new fact may trigger many other consequences throught the use of constraints or production rules. As soon as we use forward chaining (which is sometimes necessary for efficiency reasons), getting back to the initial state (because, for instance, a contradiction occurs) is difficult. This is why a mechanism for hypothetical reasoning must be supported by the model.

In the LAURE model, the set of logic relations is organized into a set of layers, designated by numbers. A world *i* is made of all the information contained in layers less than *i*. To avoid contradictions, sucessive layers are constrained by some monotonicity rules (Section 4), which imposes that multi_attribute can only grow and incomplete attribute can only shrink (thus the world *i+1* contains more information than the world *i*). This structure is somewhat simpler than other constructions of multiple worlds in AI languages, but can be implemented very efficiently [Ca91a], which is the main reason why LAURE is an efficent constraint resolution language and has been used for large applications.

For instance, using the world mechanism, one can answer the question "Would Paul be a cousin of Mark if his father was John?" with the following LAURE code, assuming that *cousin* is defined with an intuitive deductive rule:

```
[do [system world+]          ;; creates a copy of the current state
    [father(Paul) is John]
```

```
[if [Paul % cousins(Mark)]
    ["Paul is a cousin of Mark if his father is John.~%" printf]]
[system world-]]        ;; back to the previous state
```

3. Logic Programming in LAURE

3.1. DEDUCTION AND PRODUCTION RULES

3.1.1. Deductive Rules

Rules and constraints are defined using the LAURE logic language (L_3), which is a first-order logic sub-language with equational extensions, fitted for our object model. This language is used to express conditions among objects, and will be illustrated by some examples. The interest of this language is the existence of an equivalent relational algebra [Ca91a], which describes the possible operations that one can perform in the object database.

A deductive rule in LAURE is made from a condition expressed with L_3, and a conclusion relation. Its intuitive semantics is that any pair of objects that satisfy the condition should be added into the conclusion relation. Rules are used explicitly, and their resolution is made in backward chaining, with a variation on the Query/Subquery algorithm [Vi86] [Ca91a] to deal with recursive rules. For instance, here is a rule computing equivalence connection classes using two base relations *part_of* and *bound* (two objects *x* and *y* are *connected* if there exists a path from *x* to *y* using either the *bound* or *part_of* relation, or their inverses):

```
rule[   if [or   [bound(x y) or part_of(x y)]
                  [connected(y x) or
                     [z exists connected(x z) connected(z y)]]]
        then connected(x y)]
```

Rules may be bound to sets of objects through restrictions of the variables' domains. Inheritance according to the object taxonomy is implicit. This other example defines the *distance* relation, which associates all the lengths of possible physical paths (using pipe objects) to an abstract object [path of x y]. This illustrates the ability to incorporate arithmetic expressions and dynamic creation of objects (object invention [HS88]) inside the logic language L_3.

```
rule[   for_all (x path)(y integer)
        if [z:pipe exists [from(z) = start(x)]
             [or [and [to(z) = end(z)] [y = length(z)]]
                 [y = [length(z) + distance([path of end(z) y])]]]]
        then distance(x y)]
```

3.1.2. Production Rules

Production rules (called axioms in LAURE) are made of an L_3 condition, and a conclusion which can be any LAURE expression. Here the intuitive semantics is that the action will be executed (once) for any pair of objects that satisfy the condition. Thus, axioms are evaluated in forward chaining, like in the RETE algorithm [For82]. Here is an example that detects collisions among particles and calls a method to process the transformation (the condition checks that the distance between the two particles is small enough and the conclusion is a method that will simulate the collision and produce new particles):

```
axiom[  for_all (p1 particle)(p2 particle)
        if [and [[x(p1) - x(p2)] abs] < 10] [[y(p1) - y(p2)] abs] < 10]
        then [p1 collides_with p2]]
```

Integrity constraints are seen as a special case of production rules. Here is the classic database example (an employee shouldn't make more than his manager). Whenever a pair of integers satisfies the condition in the *if* part, then the condition in the then part must be satisfied.

```
constraint[  for_all (x integer) (y integer)
             if [z:employee exists salary(z x) [y = salary(manager(z))]
             check [x < y]]
```

Here is a more complex example that merges logic and procedural programming to compute the average salary of a department. Here the processing is done in a traditional manner (we could have used a method) and we use the production rule only to trigger the computation.

```
axiom[  for_all (d department) (x integer)
        if [p exists [in(p) = d] [salary(p) = x]]
        then [n as count(d)
                [average(d) is [[[average(d) * n] + x] / [n + 1]]]
                [count(d) is [n + 1]]]
```

3.2. CONSTRAINTS

3.2.1. Motivations

Deduction limited to binary logic relations is not enough to capture the wide range of logic programming use. If we consider a very simple example:

team(boss,assistant,secretary,salesman) :-
experienced(boss), young(assistant), versatile(secretary), skilled(salesman)

The predicate *team* is used to group together relevant information for problem solving. In an object-oriented deductive system, there is no structure to welcome the building of a team. We may consider the following "object-oriented" version:

$\exists$ t $\in$ team, boss(t) = w,assistant(t) = x,secretary(t) = y,salesman(t) = z :-
experienced(w), young(x), versatile(y), skilled(z)

This is a logic rule with object invention [HS88] in the conclusion, which is difficult to process. Use of constraints is more natural in the object context to introduce non-deterministic solving. A constraint representation of this example would be:

t $\in$ team $\Rightarrow$ experienced(boss(t)), young(assistant(t)),
versatile(secretary(t)), skilled(salesman(t))

A constraint is the opposite form of a deduction rule. Instead of saying that the system can *deduce* some information if some condition is verified, it says that the system must verify a condition before *choosing* some information. Use of constraints separates the deterministic part from the non-deterministic part in logic programming. Instead of asking for one possible team, the user will create a team and ask the constraint solving system to fill the corresponding attributes in a satisfying manner.

3.2.2. Constraint Definition

A constraint has an *implicit* condition, which binds some *values* (usually some object's attributes) in the converse manner of a rule. A constraint holds on a principal object, which is typed by a *for_all* definition, the values are defined inside the *if* statement and the condition is an L_3 assertion introduced by the keyword *then.* The semantics is that *if* each value is assigned, *then* the condition must hold. Here is an example taken from physics; the "noble gaz laws" says that for such a gaz sample, the equation PV=nRT stands, where P is the pressure, V the volume, T the temperature, R a constant, and n a number that describes the atomic structure of the gaz.

```
constraint[  for_all (x gaz)
             if [P = pressure(x)] [V = volume(x)] [T = temperature(x)]
             then [[P * V] = [n(x) * [R * T]]]]
```

Constraints not only apply to one simple object; through the use of composite objects, they can apply to multiple receivers. If we want to bind two gaz samples by equating their pressure, we may create a class *same_pressure* of binding objects with two slots g1 and g2, such that the existence of such an object x imposes a constraint on $g_1(x)$ and $g_2(x)$:

```
[same_pressure :: class
    with (slot g1 -> gaz) (slot g2 -> gaz)]

constraint[  for_all (X same_pressure)
             if [p1 = pressure(g1(X))] [p2 = pressure(g2(X))]
             then [p1 = p2]]
```

A negative constraint is a formula that specifies some value that cannot be chosen. Here is an example that says that two queens should not be on the same line in the famous gauss problem (how to place 8 queens on a chessboard without conflicts):

```
constraint[  for_all (q queen)(c case)
             if [z:queen exists [line(place(z)) = line(c)]]
             then [place no q c]]
```

3.3. CONSTRAINT RESOLUTION

3.3.1. Modes of Resolution

Constraints are defined on attributes and restrict the value that can be assigned to them. For a complete attribute (an attribute with no disjunctive information), the constraints will only be used as integrity constraints (cf. previously) or as propagation constraints, which would, for instance, change the pressure if the volume of a gaz is modified. This aspect, called dynamic constraint resolution [BMM89] [Fre90], is not covered in this paper. Here we consider constraints over incomplete atttributes. The goal of resolution is to complete those attributes so that each constraint is satisfied.

The principle for constraint resolution in LAURE is, therefore, to describe a set of goals $R_i(x_i)$ such that the value of $R_i(x_i)$ is a disjunctive set, and then to call the resolution algorithm that will choose an object from the set of possible values for each $R_i(x_i)$ such that each constraint that applies to x_i and its attribute R_i is satisfied. There are many modes of resolution, according to the type of exploration, as we shall later see. Here is an example of a constraint query for the gauss problem:

```
;; we look for the place of each queen
   [x all queens  [place(x) to_solve]]

;; we want to count the number of solutions
   [solver search count]
```

3.3.2. Resolution Taxonomy

Constraint resolution thus consists of assigning a value to some attributes for some objects, so that the logic formulae (the *then* assertions) are true. This is a non-deterministic process, since there can be many or no solutions. Constraint resolution is based on the following principle:

- **Stage1:** associate a set of possible values to each goal, starting from its domain and reducing it with various techniques (e.g., CHIP [DSVH87]).
- **Stage2:** choose a goal $R_i(x_i)$, choose a possible value y that doesn't violate any constraint, and assert $R_i(x_i) = y$. Possibly propagate this assertion to reduce other sets of possible values.
- **Stage3:** repeat until all goals are assigned, and backtrack on failure.

This leaves many freedom degrees upon which the efficiency of the resolution will depend.

- *Goal ordering* : some problems (for instance, the n-queens with a large number of queens [VH89]) demand the application of the first-fail principle, which states that the goal with the smallest domain should be tried first; some other problems, such as placement problems, hold a better order derived from the object topology; some others require a "good" order that is known by the user (as a heuristic).
- *Balance between propagation and evaluation*: each constraint can be evaluated lazily just before a value is chosen for a goal, or it can be propagated, so as to maintain the domains for all goals as soon as any hypothetical assignment is made (e.g.,the first-fail principle *requires* some propagation).

3.3.3. Rule-aided Constraint Solving

With all these options and features, LAURE provides a very efficient constraint resolution. However, as the scheduling example will illustrate, there are still many cases where the generic strategy is not optimal. The first option, advocated for instance in CLP(R) [CLP] is to consider a tool-box constraint solver. Although it is elegant, we have found this solution to be impractical with respect to integration with the other LAURE features. Having to write/use a specialized constraint-solver turned out to often be more complex than writing a separated ad hoc program. The second option, traditional to AI, is to use heuristic cost functions, which will help to choose the goal in stage 2, and the value to be tried first. Our experience is that cost functions are eventually necessary for certain classes of problems (including, for instance, those where there is a true cost notion). On the other hand, capturing the intuition behind constraint resolution with cost functions is often difficult.

Let us consider two well-known examples: the queens problems (how to place n queens on a $n \times n$ board) and the pentomino problem (how to tile a 6×10 rectangle with 12 forms of 5 units). In the first case, a good heuristic is to note that if a value belongs to the domain of one unique goal, it must be taken because of the symmetry of the problem. In the second case, a good heuristic suggested by Marc Gilet is to verify that all connected components of the un-tiled rectangle have a cardinal that is a multiple of 5. These two heuristics are difficult to integrate inside the existing constraint solver, and are difficult to describe as a cost function.

Our choice is to use heuristic rules, defined as axioms. A set of axioms can be defined to incrementally maintain some extra information about the system (the inverse choice cardinality in the gauss problem, the connected components in the pentomino problem). This extra information is then used by a constraint, or the axioms can trigger contradictions and modify the domains of possible values. This will be illustrated in the next section. Our claim is that production rules are a more natural framework to express heuristics about the control of constraint resolution.

4. Semantics

4.1. AN ALGEBRAIC FRAMEWORK

The extensional knowledge is represented by a set of binary relation variables. The set of relation variables $R = \{R_1, \ldots R_n\}$ is partitioned into R^1 (attributes) and R^* (multi_attributes), following [KW89]. Each variable from R^* represents a binary relation, organized into sets similar to the implementation in an object-oriented system (for each object x, we store $\{y \mid r(x,y)\}$). A variable from R^1 represents a mono-valued relation. If the value of the relation for an object is not known, we want to represent a set of possible values instead [AKG87]. Therefore, we define a database instance as an assignment from R to ($O \rightarrow$ Powerset(O)).

Definition: *A database instance is a function of* $\mathcal{D} = (\mathcal{R} \rightarrow (O \rightarrow \mathit{Powerset}(O))$.

For each $x \in O$, if $R_i \in R^*$, $d(R_i)(x)$ represents the class of x according to the relation denoted by R_i. If $R_i \in R^1$, $d(R_i)(x)$ represents the set of possible values for $R_i(x)$. If this set has one unique member y, then it means that $R_i(x) = y$.

There is a lattice structure on database instances, derived from the following order:

$$\forall\, d_1, d_2 \in \mathcal{D},\ d_1 < d2 \Leftrightarrow \quad \forall\ \mathcal{R}_i \in \mathcal{R}^*, \forall\, x \in O,\ d_1(\mathcal{R}_i)(x) \subset d_2(\mathcal{R}_i)(x) \wedge$$
$$\forall\ \mathcal{R}_i \in \mathcal{R}^1, \forall\, x \in O,\ d_2(\mathcal{R}_i)(x) \subset d_1(\mathcal{R}_i)(x)$$

The intuitive meaning of this order is that if $d_2 > d_1$, then d_2 contains the knowledge in d_1 plus some additional information. A database instance d usually contains some incomplete information through the value of relations from R^1.

To solve rules and constraints, we use a **relational algebra**, $\mathcal{A}$(R), made from a set of relational variables R and some relational operations. We use classical operations on binary relations [McL81], some other operations are introduced to capture the object functions, and we add the notion of term variable following [Ku85]. Each term T of the algebra represents a binary relation on O for any given database instance, written d(T). A logic assertion and an algebraic term are equivalent if they represent the same relation for every database instance. We have shown that each assertion could be translated into an equivalent algebraic term, and reciprocately [Ca91a].

An important property is that each operation is *monotonic* and can be evaluated on a "set_at_a_time" basis. Moreover, efficient compilation techniques allow us not to physically compute the sets involved in intermediate computations [Ca89]. Differentiation is a *formal* operation in this algebra [Ca91a]. The idea of differentiation is very common. It can be found in the RETE algorithm [Fo82], where it is a tree operation. In a relational database, it is defined by a database computation [BR86]. In this model, we obtain a formal differentiation (on abstract functions instead of database instances), which provides a better implementation of propagation and bottom-up evaluation.

This algebra has another formal property that is very important for constraint resolution. We have developed an *abstract interpretation* [CC77][Ca91b] of the relational calculus to master the computation cost of constraint prediction (Section 3.3). The abstract domain is obtained by replacing the powerset of O by a collection of preferred subsets. When a set does not fit, it is translated into a larger one. The abstract database instance $d^\#$ is defined by induction for each operation of our algebra and its computation has a complexity that does not depend on the database. The interest of abstract interpretation is given by the following theorem:

Theorem[Ca91b]: $\forall\, x \in O, \forall\, t \in \mathcal{A}(\mathcal{R}),\ d^\#(t)(x)$ *is an abstract set which contains* $d(t)(x)$.

4.2. RULES, CONSTRAINTS AND PRODUCTION RULES.

We use the algebra to represent all conditions from the L_3 language. If R_i is multi-valued ($R_i \in R^*$), a rule or axiom $(a(x,y) \Rightarrow R_i(x,y))$ is translated into an algebraic rule $(T \subset R_i)$, where T is equivalent with the L_3 assertion a. If $(T \subset R_i)$ is derived from an *axiom*, it will be evaluated bottom-up, using differentiation; if it is derived from a *rule*, it will be evaluated top-down.

Definition: *A rule is a formula* $(T_i \subset \mathcal{R}_i)$ *where* $T_i \in \mathcal{A}(\mathcal{R})$ *and* $\mathcal{R}_i \in \mathcal{R}^*$.
A database instance d satisfies a rule $(T_i \subset \mathcal{R}_i)$ *if and only if* $d(\mathcal{R}_i) \subset d(T_i)$.

If R_i is mono-valued, too many values could be derived from *a(x,y)*, which would cause a conflict. Therefore, a rule *(a(x,y)* $\Rightarrow$ *R_i(x,y))* is translated into an algebraic constraint, which states that the value $R_i(x)$ must be one of those given by *a(x,y)*[2]. Algebraic constraints are also derived from object constraints (introduced in Section 2.1) by considering each goal $R_i(x)$ and generating a solved-form of the condition T_i, which gives the value of $R_i(x)$ if all other goals are solved. Thus, we represent the constraint with a family of algebraic constraints, which have the converse form of a rule:

Definition: *A (positive) constraint is a formula ($\mathcal{R}_i \subset \mathcal{T}_i$) where $\mathcal{T}_i \in \mathcal{A}(\mathcal{R})$ and $\mathcal{R}_i \in \mathcal{R}^1$.*
A database instance d satisfies a constraint ($\mathcal{R}_i \subset \mathcal{T}_i$) if and only if $d(\mathcal{R}_i) \subset d(\mathcal{T}_i)$.

We now introduce *production rules* to take care of axioms on mono-valued relations and integrity constraints. An algebraic production rule ($T_i \Rightarrow f$) is made with a condition term T_i and a conclusion action f. In the previous case, T_i would be translated from a, and f would be to update $R_i(x)$ to y.

Definition: *A production rule ($\mathcal{T}_i \Rightarrow f$) is made from a term $\mathcal{T} \in \mathcal{A}(\mathcal{R})$ and an action f.*
Its semantics is that f(x,y) is executed each time the database instance changes from d to d' and $(x,y) \in d'(\mathcal{T}_i) \wedge (x,y) \notin d(\mathcal{T}_i)$.

Since we have given no order to production rules, this is a non-deterministic operational semantics (the order in which rules are triggered may be important). In this paper, we only consider three sorts of actions:

- Definite update: $d(R_i)(x) \rightarrow \{y\}$, when the production rule is obtained from an axiom ($a(x,y) \Rightarrow R_i(x,y)$). We shall write them ($T_i \Rightarrow R_i$).
- Condition checking: test if $(x,y) \in d(T')$ and raise a contradiction otherwise. Those production rules are obtained from integrity constraints (Section 2.1). We shall write them ($T_i \Rightarrow T'$)
- Negative constraint: $d(R_i)(x) \rightarrow d(R_i)(x) - \{y\}$. A *negative constraint*, therefore, specifies which value should not be taken for a goal and is implemented as a production rule. We shall write them ($T_i \Rightarrow \neg R_i$).

The semantics of rule resolution is based on a minimal fixpoint [Ta55], as usual:

Theorem: *For any initial database instance d_0, there exists a unique minimal database instance which contains d_0 and satisfies a given set of rules.*

Constraints are more interesting, since we do not simply search for a database that satisfies all constraints (the empty database would do), we look for a complete database instance, which associates one value to each resolution goal (a complete database instance d is such that $|d(R_i)(x)| = 1$ for each R_i in R^1.)

Definition: *A database instance d is a solution for the constraint ($\mathcal{R}_i \subset \mathcal{T}_i$) if and only if d is complete and d satisfies the constraint.*

---

[2] Thus, if there is a unique y for an object x, we get $R_i(x) = y$.

For a given set of constraints, may exist none, one or many incomparable solutions. Looking for one solution (the most common requirement) is a non-deterministic process. However, we can apply each constraint to further refine the set of possible values for each goal, which defines a monotonic transformation. Application of [Ta55] then gives the following result:

Theorem[Ca91b]: *There exists a unique smallest database instance which satisfies all the constraints (it is not necessarily complete). This instance is also included in all the solutions.*

The two previous theorems can be combined and yield to a special database value $\Upsilon(d_0)$, which satisfies all rules and constraints, and which is a good starting point to enumerate all the possible completions and find all possible solutions[3].

4.3. AN ALGORITHM FOR CONSTRAINT RESOLUTION

We shall now describe a resolution algorithm that produces one (possible) solution to a set of constraints, rules and production rules. The first step is to compute an approximation of the fixpoint, using the abstract interpretation. We then start the enumeration of all completions, using the first-fail principle. This algorithm heavily relies on the ability to make copies of the database and return to previously stored states. Fortunately, this is supported efficiently in the LAURE system. Algebraic constraints are divided into two sets: *lazy* constraints are evaluated "at the last moment", whereas *active* constraints are evaluated once in the beginning and maintained by propagation.

The propagation is based on two operations. The function obtained by *differentiation*, $\partial T/\partial R_i(x,y)$, returns the exact set of pairs that appears in d(T) when (x,y) is added in $d(R_i)$[Ca89]. Similarly $\partial^\# T/\partial R_i(x,S)$ returns a set of pairs (x',S') where S' is an abstract interpretation of d(T)(x'), which uses the new value S given to $d(R_i)(x)$. We use an exception handling mechanism described in [Don90], which allows the capture of contradictions raised either by the detection of an empty set of possible values or the violation of an integrity constraint. We may now describe the algorithm (the database instance d, the constraints, rules and production rules are global resources), which solves a list of given goals:

Solve(L): Predict(L) ;
Enumerate(L).

Predict(L)
For each goal $R_i(x_i)$ in L,
For all active constraints $(R_i \subset T_k)$,
If $\neg(d^\#(T_k)(x) \subset d(R_i)(x_i))$
abstract_propagate(R_i,x, $d(R_i)(x_i) \cap d^\#(T_k)(x)$);
For the production rules $(T_k \Rightarrow \neg R_i)$,
$d(R_i)(x_i) \leftarrow d(R_i)(x_i) - d(T_k)(x_i)$;

Enumerate(L)

---

[3] For instance, if $\Upsilon(d_0)(R_i)(x) = \varnothing$ for some R_i, x, we know that there are no solutions.

```
        Choose Ri (xi) in L such that |d(Ri)(xi)| is minimum and more than 2;
        For the lazy constraints (Ri ⊂ Tk), d(Ri)(xi) ← d(Ri)(xi) ∩ d#(Tk)(xi);
        For all values y in d(Ri)(x)
              let d' = copy(d);
              handle contradiction in:
                    propagate(Ri, x, y);
                    if Enumerate(L) = true, returns true;
              d ← d';
        returns false.
abstract_propagate (Ri, x, S)
    if S = Ø, raise(contradiction);
    d(Ri )(x) = S;
    for all active constraints (Rk ⊂ Tk),
          for all (x',S') in (∂#Tk/∂Ri)(x,S),
                abstract_propagate (Rk, x', S')
assert (Ri, x, y)
    if Ri ∈ R*, if y ∉ d(Ri)(x) d(Ri)(x) = d(Ri)(x) ∪ {y}; propagate(Ri, x, y)
    if Ri ∈ R1, if y ∉ d(Ri)(x) raise(contradiction)
                else if d(Ri)(x) ≠ {y}, d(Ri)(x) = {y};
                                          propagate(Ri, x, y);
                                           abstract_propagate (Ri, x, {y})
propagate (Ri, x, y)
    for all rules (Tk⊂ Rk),
          for all (u,v) in ∂Tk /Ri (x,y), assert(Rk, u, v)
    for all production rules (Tk ⇒ f), for all (u,v) in ∂Tk /Ri (x,y),
              if f = Rk   { if d(Rk)(u) ≠ {v} {d(Rk)(u) = {v}; propagate(Rk, u, v);}}
              if f = ¬ Rk {if v ∈ d(Rk)(u), abstract_propagate(Rk, u, d(Rk)(u) - {v})
              if f = Tk   { if (u,v) ∉ d(T'k) raise(contradiction);} .
```

When L is the list of all possible goals, the algorithm is sound and returns one possible solution. With a minor modification, we can use it to build the set of all solutions. We then get the following result (assuming that production rules are deterministic [Ca91b]):

Theorem: *The extended algorithm is sound and complete.*

The proof relies first on the fact that the abstract fixpoint computed by *Predict* is included in $\Upsilon(d_0)$ [Ca91b]. Completeness means that all completions will be tried and results from the semantics of algebraic constraints (the value which we do not try cannot be solutions). Soundness relies on the semantics of differentiation for propagation, and the adequacy [Ca91b] of abstract interpretation: if all sets involved in the abstract interpretation are singletons (which occurs eventually), the result of abstract interpretation is identical to normal evaluation of algebraic terms. We have developed many variations, which allows us, for instance, to apply a discriminating function to each solution or to discard the first-fail principle when the order is determined statically.

5. Application to Advanced Applications

5.1. A SCHEDULING PROBLEM

To illustrate LAURE's behavior, we have chosen a real-life scheduling problem, the building of a five-segment bridge, taken from Bartusch's PhD thesis and reported by P. Van Hentenryck in [VH89]. This problem is made of 46 tasks, with precedence, sharing and domain-specific constraints. Its interest is to be both a representative problem and a well-described one. We first wrote a very simple, declarative LAURE program, with two generic constraints that were instantiated into 150 objects. Each constraint was declared to be used with abstract propagation, and the general algorithm was using the first-fail principle. Here is a sample from this program:

```
;; a precedence is an object which links two tasks
    [precedence :: class
        with (slot t1 -> task) (slot t2 -> task)]

;; the time relation tells when the task starts
    [time :: attribute domain task -> integer]

;; the semantics of precedence is a constraint
    constraint[ for_all (p precedence)
                if [x = time(t1(p))] [y = time(t2(p))]
                then [[x + duration(t1(p))] < y]]

;; a sharing is an object which links two task that shares the same
;; resource
    [sharing :: class
        with (slot t1 -> task) (slot t2 -> task)]

;; its semantics is the disjunction of two precedence
    constraint[ for_all (p precedence)
                if [x = time(t1(p))] [y = time(t2(p))]
                then [or [[x + duration(t1(p))] < y]
                         [[y + duration(t2(p))] < x]]]
```

Our first program performed very poorly, which recalls the limits of pure declarativeness. Following the indications in [VH89], we modified the program by adding an extra attribute (*ordering* on shared tasks) and three extra constraints, so as to take care of mutual exclusion first. It is a well-known strategy that, when each pair of exclusive tasks have been ordered, finding the scheduling is deterministic (through a graph computation of the *atleast* and *atmost* date for each task [VH89]). This second program performed within the range of the original CHIP program, which is nice since LAURE has no specific knowledge about how to solve inequations (such as CHIP). The reason is that abstract interpretation of the scheduling constraint (incremental updates of the abstract domains as soon as any new hypothesis is made) mimic the deterministic computation of the *atleast* and *atmost* date. Each domain is maintained as an interval, whose bounds are updated during the abstract propagation. Here is the LAURE code necessary for this addition:

```
[ordering :: attribute domain sharing -> boolean]

constraint[ for_all (p precedence)
            if  [x = time(t1(p))] [y = time(t2(p))]
            then [if [ordering(p) = t] [[x + duration(t1(p))] < y]
                 else [[y + duration(t2(p))] < x]]]
```

On one hand, this is a strong positive result, since a general technique was able to match a specialized algorithm. This has been also found on some placement problems (automatic layout), where abstract propagation gave very good results. On the other hand, one can say that "Abstract interpretation rediscovered the wheel", since the atleast-atmost algorithm is well-known. Besides, abstract propagation is by no means a very efficient way of implementing this algorithm. To extend LAURE with some knowledge about scheduling problems, we tried several strategies, and eventually found that production rules (axioms) were the most natural way to go. We added a set of four axioms that incrementally compute the two extra attributes *atleast* and *atmost*, kept the ordering of exclusive tasks, and replaced the other constraints by simply choosing eventually the *atleast* date as our final scheduling. Here are some of the production rules that replace the original constraints:

```
[atleast :: attribute domain task -> integer]

;; propagation of atleast over a precedence
   axiom[   for_all (x task) (y integer)
            if [p:precedence exists [x = t2(p)]
                  [y = [atleast(t1(x)) + duration(t1(x))]]
                  [y > atleast(x)]
            then atleast(x)]
```

This third program is fast. It found the optimal solution and its proof of optimality in 4s on a SUN3, whereas CHIP takes 90s and a special-purpose algorithm solved the problem in 43s on a SUN3 (as reported in [VH89]). The efficiency is due to the compiling techniques of LAURE [Ca89], which produce an optimal C-written algorithm from the axioms that are entered declaratively.

5.2. OTHER EXAMPLES

We are now using LAURE to solve a task assignment problem, which offers an interesting combination of complexity (many thousand tasks) and difficulty (the basic problem is a TSP [traveling salesperson] with time constraints). We have used a mixed approach with very few constraints and many production rules, where the control is left to the constraint solver to explore the search tree, but where deductive rules are used to reduce the search space by "intelligent" pruning. The LAURE program has been tested succesfully against an approach based on dynamic programming, and showed an improvement of one order of magnitude. We have also compared our program with some previously developed heuristics and found that a complete exploration (finding the true optimum) lead to a 5% improvement in total work load, which means a lot when many hundreds persons are concerned.

We started to look at applying LAURE to planning problems by taking benchmarks used for inference engines, such as various versions of the "Monkey & banana" problem. We have compared LAURE with a prototype version of a RETE-based [Fo82] inference engine, that generates compiled C code from production rules, and is among the best expert system development environments. We have found LAURE to be between 4-10 times faster on those benchmarks and we plan to continue this promising investigation. We have also used LAURE for an airline database application described in [FSS91]. Here the goal is an efficient computation of a transitive closure of relation that contains over one thousand flights (with obvious circles). This graph is too large to be handled efficiently by PROLOG, whereas LAURE turned out to be 30 times faster than the figures reported in [FSS91] for the LOLA deductive language.

More classical comparisons with either PROLOG or constraint solvers on small well-known problems, such as the 8-queens, may be found in [Ca91c]. However, our recent experience tends to demonstrate that techniques that work well for small problems do not scale up. Our investigations in merging rules with constraints were motivated by a lack of success with pure constraint logic programming over some large problems.

5.3. COMPARISON WITH RELATED WORK

This work bears a lot of similarity with many theoretical approaches to merge object-oriented and logic programming. The best example is the revisited O-logic [KW89], which is also intended as a framework for AI programming. The LAURE model is a strict subset of this more ambitious model, but is able to propose realistic implementation techniques from these restrictions [Ca91a]. This last statement also holds true to other database models ([AK89],[CW89]), which are very ambitious but seem difficult to implement efficiently. Though LAURE shares the same motivations with the work of Aït-Kaci (LOGIN[Ait86] or LIFE[AP90]), which we think is the most impressive contribution to our field, it takes a totally opposite path for this integration. We believe that constraint resolution is the most difficult part of implementing such a hybrid system, so that constraint should be explicit and constraint resolution should be global (all the constraints seen at the same time, by a constraint solver that looks at the whole database).

From a practical perspective, LAURE is close to commercial expert system shells such as ART or pro-Kappa. However, LAURE is a strongly-typed efficient object-oriented language, with a modular compiler, that produces better code for "traditional" object-oriented programming. Our first experiments with production rules showed that LAURE provides a significant improvement on performance. Last, LAURE includes a sophisticated constraint solver, which we think is mandatory in an object-oriented deductive system.

In the family of Constraint Logic Programming languages, LAURE is very different than CLP(R) [CLP], PROLOG-III or other systems intensively based on Horn-Clause resolution, because it uses no logic variables and only deals with global constraints. The LAURE resolution strategy, including the prediction phase (Stage 1) is directly inspired by work performed at the ECRC on the CHIP system [VD86][DSVH87][VH89]. The LAURE constraint solver can be seen as the implementation of CHIP's ideas using an algebraic framework [Ca90], which supports constraint compiling. LAURE also offers a reactive resolution mode that is similar to dynamic constraint solvers [B&al89][Fre90].

6.Conclusion

This paper has raised three issues. First, we argue that constraint solving is implicit in many AI applications when an object-oriented approach is taken, which has been our practical experience. Then we found that domain-specific heuristics are necessary to deal with large constraint problems, for which a generic strategy yields impractical complexity, and that production rules are a natural way to express such heuristics. Eventually, we are confronted with the necessity to provide a complex resolution strategy, which combines constraints, deductive rules, production rules and integrity constraints, and which provides tools for efficient domain prediction. The presented algorithm is a contribution to this task and has been successfully implemented inside LAURE.

Acknowledgements

This work has benefited from many fruitful discussions with Pascal Van Hentenryck and our database research team at Bellcore, including Sam Epstein, Madhur Kholi and Shamim Naqvi. I would also like to thank Drew Adams, Hassan Aït-Kaci, Francois Monnet and Diane Hoffoss for their support and encouragement.

References

[AKG87] S. Abiteboul, P. Kanellakis, G. Grahne. *On the Representation and Querying of Sets of Possible Worlds*. Proc. of ACM SIGMOD, 1987.

[AK89] S. Abiteboul, P. Kanellakis. *Object Identity as a Query Language Primitive*. Proc. ACM Conf. on Management of Data, 1989.

[AP90] H. Ait-Kaci, A. Podelski. *The Meaning of Life*. PRL Research Report, DEC, 1990.

[BBM89] A. Borgida, R. Brachman, D. McGuinness, L.A. Resnick. *CLASSIC: A Structural Data Model for Objects*. ACM SIGMOD International Conference on the Management of Data, Portland, June, 1989.

[BMM89] A. Borning, M. Maher, A. Martindale , M. Wilson. *Constraint Hierarchies and Logic Programming*. Proc. of the Sixth International Logic Programming Conference, Lisbon, June 1989.

[BR86] F. Bancilhon, F. Ramakrishnan. *An Amateur's Introduction to Recursive Query Processing Strategies*. Proceedings ACM SIGMOD Int. Conference on Management of Data, Washington, May 1986.

[Ca89] Y. Caseau. *A Formal System for Producing Demons from Rules*. Proc. of DOOD89, Kyoto 1989.

[Ca91a] Y. Caseau. *A Deductive Object-Oriented Language*. Annals of Mathematics and Artificial Intelligence, Special Issue on Deductive Databases, February 1991.

[Ca91b] Y. Caseau. *Abstract Interpretation of Constraints for Run-Time Optimizations*. To appear in Proc. of the International Logic Programming Symposium, October 1991.

[Ca91c] Y. Caseau. *An Object-Oriented Language for Advanced Applications*. Proc. of TOOLS USA'91, Santa-Barbara, July 1991.

[CLP] N. Heintze, et al.. *Constraint Logic Programming: A Reader*. 4th IEEE Symposium on Logic Programming, San Francisco, 1987.

[CC77] P. Cousot, R. Cousot. *Abstract Interpretation: A Unified Lattice Model for Static Analysis of Programs by Constructions or Approximation of Fixpoints*. Proc. Fourth ACM Symposium of Principles of Programming Languages, 1977.

[DSVH87] M. Dincbas, H. Simonis, P. Van Hentenryck. *Extending Equation Solving and Constraint Handling in Logic Programming*. Colloquium on Resolution of Equation in Algebraic Structures, Austin, May 1987.

[Don90] C. Dony. *Exception Handling and Object-Oriented Programming: Towards a Synthesis*. Proc of OOPSLA'90, Ottawa, 1990.

[Fre90] B. Freeman-Benson. *Kaleidoscope: Mixing Objects, Constraints, and Imperative Programming*. Proc. of OOPLSLA'90, Ottawa, October 1990.

[FSS91] B. Freytag, H. Schütz, G. Specht. *LOLA - A Logic Language for Deductive Databases and its Implementation*. Proc. of DASFAA'91, Tokyo, April 1991.

[Fo82] C.L. Forgy. *RETE: A Fast Algorithm for the Many Pattern/Many Object Pattern Matching Problem*. Artificial Intelligence, no 19, 1982.

[G&al90] M. Ganti, P. Goyal, R. Nassif, P. Sunil. *An Object-Oriented Development Environment*. COMPCON, Feb 1990,.

[GJ90] J. Graver, R. Johnson. *A Type System for Smalltalk*. Proc. of the 17th ACM Symposium on Principles of Programming Languages, San Francisco, 1990.

[HS89] R. Hull, J. Su. *Untyped Sets, Invention, and Computable Queries*. Proceeding of PODS-89, Philadelphia, 1989.

[IV89] T. Imielensky, K. Vadaparty. *Complexity of Querying Databases with OR-Objects*. Proceeding of PODS-89, Philadelphia, 1989.

[KW89] M. Kifer, J. Wu. *A logic for Object-Oriented Logic Programming (Maier's O-Logic Revisited)*. Proceeding of PODS-89, Philadelphia, 1989.

[KL89] M. Kifer, G. Lausen . *F-Logic: A High-Order Language for Reasoning about Objects, Inheritance and Scheme*. ACM SIGMOD Conf. on Management of Data, May 1989.

[Ku85] G. M. Kuper. *The Logical Data Model: A New Approach to Database Logic*. PhD Dissertation, Stanford University, 1985.

[McL81] B.J. MacLennan. *Programming With A Relational Calculus*. Rep n° NPS52-81-013, Naval Postgraduate School, September 1981.

[MN88] P. Maes, D. Nardi. *Meta-level Architecture and Reflection*. Elsevier Science Publication (North Holland), 1988.

[Ta55] A. Tarski. *A Lattice Theoretical Fixpoint Theorem and its Application*. Pacific Journal of Mathematics n° 5, 1955.

[VD86] P. Van Hentenryck, M. Dincbas. *Domains in Logic Programming*. AAAI-86, Philadelphia, Aug. 1986.

[VH89] P. Van Hentenryck. *Constraint Satisfaction in Logic Programming*. The MIT press, Cambridge, 1989.

[Vi86] L. Vieille. *Recursive Axioms in Deductive Databases: The Query/Subquery Approach*. Proc. First Intl. Conference on Expert Database Systems, Charleston, 1986.

Flang : a functional-logic language.

Andrei V.Mantsivoda
Computer Center
Irkutsk State University
Box 26
Irkutsk 664003
U.S.S.R.

Abstract

The functional-logic language Flang is considered in this paper. The ideas of logic programming, functional programming and tools for algebraic computations are unified in it within a single abstract machine. This language is intended for symbolic computations and education.

1 Introduction

The rapid penetration of methods of artificial intelligence into programming entailed considerable increasing of interest to the programming languages used in this field, first of all logic and functional programming languages. One of the interesting problems is to design a programming language unifying features of logic and functional styles. In this paper we consider one of this kind of languages. This is a functional-logic language Flang.

Flang is intended for training students in methods of programming in artificial intelligence, for symbolic data processing and algebraic computations. Flang makes it easy to write programs in functional, logic and mixed styles. The reason is that these two kinds of programming are unified in Flang on some natural basis.

Properties of Flang are

(i) the unified methodology of Flang helps one to write functional and logic (and mixed) programs thinking within a single style;

(ii) Flang programs are natural and easy-to-read (it is also consequence of flexibility of the language);

(iii) Flang supports non-deterministic computations (in the implemented version of Flang *backtracking* and *cut* are used);

(iv) Flang contains special tools (such as constructors with constrains) which are very convenient for use in algebraic computations;

(v) Flang has syntax transformers (such as *oper* and *redef*) which allow to change Flang syntax. We may say that Flang-system supports many languages that have the same semantics but the different syntax descriptions;

Firstly Flang was developed due to pedagogical purposes. Applications of the language to artificial intelligence programming teaching show that students learn the main features and means of Flang very quickly. The experience they get during this process let them turn to using other non-standard languages (*ie* Lisp, Prolog) without difficalties. Besides, specialized algebraic and symbolic computations systems were written in Flang (in group theory, mathematical analysis, *etc*).

The IBM PC Flang interpreter has been implemented. This interpreter version has been succesfully used for education applications. Today the compiler version of Flang is being developed by V.Petukhin and the author. The kernel of compiler now is ready to work. Some important ideas (for example, global analysis of a program and type computations) will enforce the compiler to generate the extremely fast code which for some Flang programs not slower then (Turbo) Pascal programs solving the same task (for instance, some sorting algorithms). But these ideas are the theme of another publication.

2 The main features of Flang.

Functional definitions. At first, we show how to use Flang to write 'purely' functional programs. We use a standard example - the function *factorial*:

```
factorial(0) <= 1;
factorial(x) <= x > 0   x * factorial(x-1);
```

The *factorial* definition consists of two rules. Any rule in Flang has the form:

<head> <= <body>;

The first rule defines *factorial* of 0. The second rule is used when *x>0*. The body of the second rule is a *sequence* of two expressions (terms): *x>0* and *x * factorial(x-1)*. The rule says that the value of *factorial(x)* is equal to the value of this *sequence*.

Let us see how to find the value of a sequence. For this we need a notion of *uncertainty*. Consider the following function:

$$f(x) = \begin{cases} 0 & \text{if } x < 5 \\ x + 1 & \text{if } x > 5 \end{cases}$$

What is the value of *f* when *x* is equal to 5? It is easy to see that in this case *f* is uncertain and we say that the term *f(5)* is equal to *uncertainty*. To denote uncertainty we introduce an atom *fail*. Hence, *f(5) = fail*.

We use the following two laws to find the value of a sequence:

(i) if the value of one of terms in a sequense is equal to fail then the value of a sequence is equal to fail too;

(ii) if all terms in a sequence are certain then its value is equal to the value of the rightmost term.

Let us see how these laws are used to obtain the value of *factorial(1)*. Using the second rule of *factorial* definition we obtain that its value is equal to the value of the sequence

*1 > 0 1 * factorial(1 - 1).*

The first term of the sequence is the relation *more*. To compute *relations* we need two more laws:

(iii) relations in Flang are treated as functions;

(iv) if computation of a relation returns fail then a relation is considered to be false; in any other case it is true.

Since $1 > 0 \neq$ *fail*, the value of the sequence above is equal (by the law (ii)) to the value of *1 * fact(1-1)*, that is, 0.

Logic definitions. Having considered example of purely functional program, let us discuss logic capabilities of Flang. Flang allows to define relations in Prolog-like style. For instance, we can define in Flang the *parent* relation:

parent(Paul John)<=true;

This rule says that the fact "Paul is John's parent" is true. (By the way, Flang permits the shorter Prolog-like representation of this fact:

parent(Paul John);

but we prefer to use the full variant to keep uniformity.) Note that instead of *true* we can use any other atom or number, because in the case of predicates Flang system can distinguish only two variants - certainty and uncertainty. More facts about *parent*:

parent(Paul George)<=true;
parent(George Tom) <=true;
parent(Tom Dic) <=true;

Now we can define the *grandparent* relation:

grandparent(X Y)<=parent(X Z) parent(Z Y);

It is very important that all the laws we formulate above for *factorial* function are valid for *grandparent* relation too. Flang system manipulates these two kinds of definitions in the same way. But in the last case the sign '<=' is understood not as a functional equality, but as '*if*'. Note that in the body of the last rule there is the variable Z which absent in the head of the rule. Besides, the *grandparent* relation sometimes needs non-deterministic computation. The main idea is that Flang system tries to find such a way of the goal computation which leads to a *certain* value. The following laws show how these problems are solved in Flang.

(v) Flang system is able to compute expressions containing uninstantiated variables; during the process of computation these variables may be instantiated by unification;

(vi) if a current path of computation leeds to uncertainty (ie evaluated expression is equal to fail), Flang system backtracks and tries another way of computation.

These laws show also that the current version of Flang possesses the basic features of Prolog (some modification of *cut* is implemented too).

We discussed some functional and logic definitions in Flang. Indeed, in Flang we can write purely functional and purely logic programs. But there is something more in Flang. The definition of a function *ancient* we introduce further will show that we can unify these styles within a single function definition and this capability increases flexibility and expresiveness of the language. But before this we describe data types of Flang.

Data types in Flang. Simple data types of Flang are numbers and atoms. The main data structure of Flang is a term (structural term). Flang manipulates terms like Prolog does. The main distinction is that in Prolog 'computed' terms (predicates) cannot be arguments of other computed or structural terms (*ie* arguments never evaluated). On the other hand, in Flang they may be freely mixed (such examples will be given below). This freedom demands of the Flang system to distinguish functors of structures (constructors) and computed functions. Therefore, any constructor should be declared before use.

In section *Algebraic Computations* we shall show one more important distinction between Flang's and Prolog's data structures: Flang's functors can be defined as non-free constructors (constructors with constrains).

The symbol '.' is the only built-in structural functor in Flang. The expression *x.y* denotes a list with the head *x* and the tail *y*. For example, the list

```
[1 2 3 4 [Paul Tom George] x]
```

is equal to

```
1.2.3.4.(Paul.Tom.George.[]).x.[]
```

where *[]* is the empty list. The function *sum* sums up elements of a list:

```
sum([])<=0;
sum(x.y)<=x+sum(y);
```

The function *append* is defined as follows:

```
append([] x)<=x;
append(x.y z)<=x.append(y z);
```

Note that computed term *append(y z)* in the second rule is the argument of the structural functor '.'.

Functional-logic definitions. Now we are ready to define the function *ancient* we mentioned above. The function *ancient(x y)* returns a list of relatives which are in genealogical tree between ancient *x* and offspring *y*. For example, in the case of relatives we defined above, the expression

```
ancient(Paul Dic)
```

is equal to the list

```
[Paul George Tom Dic].
```

The definition of *ancient* consists of two rules:

```
ancient(x y) <= parent(x y) [x y];
ancient(x y) <= parent(x z) x.ancient(z y);
```

In the second rule the dotted pair *x.ancient(z y)* denotes a list having the head *x* and the tail which returned after computation of *ancient(z y)*. The first rule is used when *x* is a parent of *y* (there are no relatives between them).

The definition of this function is already not Prolog's. But it is not of functional style too, because succesfull computation of this function requires non-deterministic strategy. Non-deterministic functions may have different outputs on the same arguments! - unpardonable sin from the functional standpoint.

3 Algebraic Computations in Flang

Algebraic functions and constructors with constrains. The features of Flang described above are not sufficient to write natural and transparent programs for algebraic computations (such as in Reduce). One more tool of Flang makes this problem much easier. This is the notion of algebraic function (algebraic functions were incorporated to Flang after hot but very fruitful discussions with V.Antimirov and A.Degtyarev). The following example demonstrates the main idea of algebraic function. It is trivial. Let us define the function *f*:

f(0)<=1;

This function has certain value only when its argument is equal to 0:

Goal: *f(0);*	Goal:*f(1);*
Answer: *1*	Answer:*fail*

But if we input

algeb f;

where *algeb* is a special built-in function of Flang declaring *f* as an algebraic function, the situation will be changed:

Goal: *f(0);*	Goal:*f(1);*
Answer: *1*	Answer:*f(1)*

In the second case Flang System tries to apply the rule for *f* to the query *f(1)* . This attempt fails. For usual functions it means that the value of a query is uncertain. But for algebraic functions the situation is different. When Flang fails to reduce some algebraic goal, it leaves the expression alone. More examples:

Goal: *f(1+2);*
Answer: *f(3)*
algeb (+);
algeb (*);

```
Goal:    1+2;                              Answer: 3
Goal:    (a+1)*b;
Answer: (a+1)*b;
(x+y)*z <= x*z + y*z;
Goal:    (a+1)*b;                          Answer: a*b + 1*b;
1*x <= x;
Goal:    (a+1)*b;                          Answer: a*b + b
```

and so on. It is very important that algebraic computations can run, at least, not slower then more cumbersome Prolog's programs of this type because it is not too difficalt to apply the ideas of Warren Abstract Machine [1] to design an appropriate compiler for algebraic programs.

The idea of algebraic computations can be reformulated in the following way. Usually constructors in languages are used to build data structures (the example is dot for lists in Lisp). These constructors are free (we cannot impose any constrain on them). But in Flang the situation is different. For example, we can define the constructor of *ordered* list. We shall use the colon to denote it. Firstly, we declare ':' as right-associative infix operator and as algebraic function (function *oper* below is similar to Prolog's *op*; it is described in the next section):

```
oper : 1 1 7 100;
algeb (:);
```

Now we impose constrain on the constructor by the following rule:

```
x : y : z <= x > y  y : x : z;
```

This is an algebraic specification of ordered list. We can use this rule for sorting (*nil* is new atom for the empty list):

```
Goal:    3:2:1:6:5:4:0:9:nil;
Answer: 0:1:2:3:4:5:6:9:nil
```

This example shows that the idea of non-free constructor makes Flang very powerful language and not less efficient. With the help of non-free constructors, it is sufficient to use for sorting only one simple, transparent rule. The following condition makes this definition correct logically: *any allgebraic expression is reduced by Flang until it does not contain subterms which can be computed (reduced) further*.

The last example is the definition of the function *min* which returns the least element of an ordered list:

```
min(x:y) <= x;
Goal:    min(3:2:1:nil);
Answer: 1
```

Models. The idea of algebraic functions with usual strategies of evaluation (*eg* lazy or eager (strict)) does not always lead to effective computations. Sometimes we need more refined strategies. The notion of model will help us to partially overcome this obstacle. It is easy to explain the idea of the model using the example of computation of 'restricted variant' of disjunctive normal form of a Boolean formula. In our program we should define operators for logical connectives (~, & and *v*) and declare them as algebraic functions. The main part of a program is as follows:

```
~(x & y) <= ~x v ~y;
~(x v y) <= ~x & ~y;
(x v y) & z <= x & z  v  y & z;
x & (y v z) <= x & y  v  x & z;
```

But if we try to compute the expression

```
  F = ~(a &(b v ~(d & e)) &(f v g))
```

we shall get the huge formula. The problem is that Flang system try to compute firstly an innermost and leftmost subformula. But 'intelligent' strategy requires firstly to miniscope negations and only after that to use other rules.

The idea of models is idea to separate the axioms of our program into two groups: first of them consists of rules describing negation (the model for negation NEG) and the second contains distributive laws (the model DIST):

```
  model NEG;
     ~(x & y) <= ~x v ~y;
     ~(x v y) <= ~x & ~y;
  end NEG;
  model DIST
     (x v y) & z <= x & z  v  y & z;
     x & (y v z) <= x & y  v  x & z;
  end DIST;
```

Now the process of computation of F can be as follows: firstly we dip computed formula into the model NEG and all negations are miniscoped, secondly we dip the result of first dive into DIST and distributive laws are applied to this result.

So, the main idea of model is that the computation of the same goal by dipping into different models can lead to different results. The notion of model helps us to refine the strategy of computations in 'purely logical' way.

4 Awxiliary tools of Flang

Declarations of constructors and evaluation control. There is only one predefined *free* constructor in Flang - the dot '.' to construct lists. Any other constructor should be declared. Function *struct* defines functors as free constructors. In the following example we introduce a new unary prefix constructor *s*. With this functor and constant *0* natural numbers are repre- sented: *0*, *s 0* , *s s 0*, *ets* (informally, *s x=x+1)*. Using this representation, let us define addition and multiplication of natural numbers (note that Flang allows to add rules for predefined functions):

```
struct s;
oper s 0 1 2 10;
0 + x <= x;
s x + y <= s (x + y);
0 * x <= 0;
s x * y <= y + x * y;
    Goal:   s s 0 * s s 0
    Answer: s s s s 0.
```

By default, any argument of a Flang's function is evaluated. There are two built-in functions in Flang - *quote* and *qeset* - which intended to control the evaluation process. The role of *quote* is similar to the role of the quote in Lisp. This function suppresses evaluation of its argument:

```
Goal:   1+2        Goal:   quote(1 + 2);
Answer: 3          Answer: 1 + 2
```

(note that *quote* is useful to make *non-free* (algebraic) constructors *free*).

The function *qeset* separates arguments of defined function into two groups. One group consists of arguments which must be evaluated and the second includes arguments which must not. Function *qeset* has two arguments. The first argument is the name of the defined function. The second is the atom which may contain only letters 'e' and 'q'. The length of this atom is equal to the number of arguments of the defined function. If some letter in this atom is 'e' then corresponding (having the same number) argument of the defined function should be evaluated, otherwise the evaluation is forbidden. For example,

```
qeset f eqeq;
```

means that the first and third arguments of function *f* are always evaluated, but the second and fourth arguments are always not. One more example:

```
g(x y)<=[x y];
Goal:    g(1+2, 3+4);
Answer:  [3 7]
```

But if we input

```
qeset g qe;
```

then

```
Goal:    g(1+2, 3+4);
Answer:  [1+2  7]
```

Syntax transformers. Syntax transformers are tools making Flang more flexible and expressive. Any user can choose a syntax variant of Flang which is the most convenient for his or her purposes. Flang includes a few syntax transformers two of which were implemented in the Flang system. They are *redef* and *oper*.

The function *redef* allows to assign to a new atom properties of another atom. For example,

```
redef (+) plus;
```

means that the atom *plus* gets all the properties of '+'. Now a term *2 plus 3* is equal to *5*. A goal

```
redef (<=) :-;
```

gives one a little chance to think in terms of Prolog.

One more syntax transformer is the 5-ary function *oper*. This function defines operators. The idea of *oper* is analogous to Prolog's *op*, but *oper* is more powerful.

Firstly, let us consider how the built-in operator '+' would be defined by *oper*:

```
oper + 1 1 6 30;
```

Arguments of *oper*:

First *(+)* - the atom to be defined as an operator;
Second *(1)* - the number of arguments on the left of the operator;
Third *(1)* - the number of arguments on the right of the operator;
Fourth *(6)* - type of the operator (the number 6 means that '+' is the infix and left-associative operator);
Fifth *(30)* - priority of the operator;

If we want to make '+' be a prefix operator, we should input

```
oper (+) 0 2 2 30;
```

(2 in the fourth argument means that '+' becomes the prefix operator). Now the expression 2+3 should have the form

```
+ 2 3;
```

We can define the function *factorial* using for this standard mathematical denotion:

```
oper ! 1 0 4 10;
0! <= 1;
x! <= x>0  x*(x-1)! ;
```

Oper is able to define operators with variable number of arguments. For this, it is necessary to use the letter *s*:

```
oper sum 0 s 2 40;
```

Now atom *sum* (the definition of the function *sum* see above) is declared as the operator having variable number of arguments on the right:

```
sum 1 2 3 4 5;                              = 15
sum 1 2 3;                                  = 6
```

and even

```
sum;                                        = 0
```

In the conclusion of this section we show how Flang syntax may be converted into Prolog-like syntax:

```
is(x, y)<= x=y;
redef (<=) :-;
oper is 1 1 6 150;
redef (->) !;                 {-> is Flangs's variant of cut}
fact(0, 1) :- !;
fact(X, Y) :- X1 is X-1, fact(X1, Y1), Y is X*Y1;
```

Other means of Flang: higher order functions definitions, disjunction, the cut, imperative computations and assignment, debugging and other built-in functions and relations.

5 FL-calculus

Using FL-calculus which is introduced in this section, we shall define non-deterministic semantics of "pure" Flang. We do not make deep mathematical considerations of Flang's semantics. Only basic ideas are given here.

Definition. Variables and constants are terms. If f is n-ary functional symbol and $\varphi_1, \ldots, \varphi_n$ *are terms or sequences of terms then*

$f(\varphi_1, \ldots, \varphi_n)$ is a term. The sequence of terms is an expression of the form

$t_1 : t_2 : \ldots : t_n$

where t_i are terms.

Informally, the value of the sequence of terms $t_1 : \ldots : t_n$ is equal to the value of t_n if $t_1, \ldots, t_{n-1}$ are certain (not equal to *fail*). Otherwise, the value of this sequence is *fail* too.

Term t is *terminal* if it does not contain subterms which can be computed (reduced) further (this includes a case when term contains algebraic functions which are not defined here explicitly).

Definition. The FL-program is a set of equations (rules) of the form $t=\eta$, where t is a term and η is a sequence of terms.

We use $\Phi[x \leftarrow \psi]$ to denote the expression obtained from Φ by replacing *all* occurences of x in Φ by the sequence or term ψ, and use $\Phi\langle t \leftarrow \psi \rangle$ to denote the expression obtained from Φ by replacing *only one* occurence of the term t in Φ by the term or sequence ψ.

We use FL-calculus to deduce equations of the form $\psi_1 = \psi_2$, where ψ_1 is a term or sequence and ψ_2 is a terminal term.

Let Σ be some FL-program. The *instance* of the rule $t=\eta \in \Sigma$ is any expression obtained from $t=\eta$ by instantiation of some variables in $t=\eta$, *ie* an expression of the form $(t=\eta)[x_1 \leftarrow \psi_1] \ldots [x_n \leftarrow \psi_n]$. Note that an instance may have free variables. Let Ξ be the set of all instances of rules of Σ.

FL-calculus

Axioms: equations of the form $\varphi = \varphi$

Inference rules:

$$\frac{\varphi = \psi}{(\varphi = \psi)[X \leftarrow t]} \qquad \frac{t=\eta \qquad \varphi = \psi}{\varphi = (\psi\langle t \leftarrow \eta \rangle)} \qquad \frac{\varphi = (\psi\langle r \leftarrow t_1 : \ldots : t_i : \ldots : t_n \rangle}{\varphi = (\psi\langle r \leftarrow t_1 : \ldots : t_n \rangle)}$$

where φ, ψ, η are sequences or terms; $t=\eta \in \Xi$; t_i in the third rule is a terminal term, $i<n$.

The first rule is used to instantiate variables in equations (to do substitutions in the implemented Flang interpreter the unification is applied). The second rule applies the instance $t=\eta$ of an equation from the program to the equation $\varphi = \psi$, replacing some occurence of t in ψ by η. The third rule says that t_i $(i<n)$ can be removed from a sequence, if it is terminal.

Easy to show that the scheme of FL-calculus can be projected onto schemes inherent to logic and functional styles of programming, for example, the non-deterministic Prolog scheme. This scheme consists of two rules:

$$\frac{:-t_1,\ldots,\ t_n}{(:-t_1,\ldots,\ t_n)[x\leftarrow t]} \qquad \frac{:-t_1,\ldots t_i\ldots,\ t_n \qquad t_i:-r_1,\ldots,r_k}{:-\ t_1,\ldots r_1,\ldots,r_k,\ldots t_n}$$

where $t_i:-r_1,\ldots,r_k$ is the instance of some fact (when $k=0$) or a rule of the logic program (L-program). The derived objects of this calculus are goals $:-t_1,\ldots,\ t_n$. To prove a goal it is necessary to deduce the empty clause :- from it.

To show that this calculus is a particular case of FL-calculus let us make light syntactic transformations of logic program. Any rule $t:-r_1,\ldots,\ r_k$ is replaced by the equation $t=r_1:\ldots:\ r_k$; any fact t:- is replaced by $t=true$. Now the L-proof of the goal $:-t_1,\ldots,\ t_n$ is easily converted into FL-proof of $t_1:\ldots:\ t_n=true$ from the axiom $t_1:\ldots:t_n = t_1:\ldots:t_n$.

6 Concluding remarks

We regard Flang as more methodological then mathematical work. Fortunately, mathematics is quite simple here. We think it is very important, since a programming language usually is intended to be used by those who maybe were never conserned with pure mathematical problems and do not like to be. We tried not to forget that a good programming language is a thing which is used by thousands of users. Therefore, we kept our mathematical arrogance for other applications. We tried to design the language with very simple 'informal' semantics intended for algebraic and symbolic computations and for education.

Features of Flang cited below distinguish it from some other approaches [2-5]:

(i) It is impossible to separate logic and functional parts in Flang: there is one idea for two styles.

(ii) Flang came from the functional programming. The language is an attempt to answer the question "What is the minimal set of things which should be added to functional programming style to obtain logic programming and 'algebraic computations' features?"

(iii) General semantics of Flang is flexible, easy to understand and permits many differernt concrete strategies of computation - sequentional and concurrent.

(iv) Flang programs can be compiled into very fast code (which sometimes are not slower then Pascal programs). Modification of WAM [1], global analysis and type computations are involved in ompilation.

A relational/functional language RELFUN [6, 7] is based on ideas, some of which are quite similar to main ideas of Flang (*e g*, the idea to use a non-deterministic function). It is very interesting that RELFUN came from logic programming, so Flang and RELFUN are really standing on the border between logic and functional programming styles. Maybe it would be good idea to try to design new language amalgamating best features of RELFUN and Flang. Warren Abstract Machine [1] is used for implementation of both languages. But modification of WAM for implementation of RELFUN [7, 8] and modification for Flang have some important distinctions.

References

1. Warren D.H.D. Implementing Prolog - Compiling predicate logic programs. Technical Report, 39, 40, University of Edinburgh, May 1977.

2. Robinson J.A., Sibert E. The LOGLISP user's manual.- Syracuse Univ., NY, 1981.

3. Bockmayr A. Conditional rewriting and narrowing as theoretical framework for logic-functional programming (A Survay).- Interner Bericht No 10/86, Univ Karlsruhe, 35p., 1986.

4. Goguen J.A., Meseguer J. Equality, types, modules and generics for logic programming.-Proc of the 1985 symp.on logic programming, Boston, MA, 172-184, 1985.

5. Fribourg L. SLOG: a logic programming language interpreter based on clausal superposition and rewriting.-Proc of the 1985 symp.on logic programming, Boston, MA, 172-184.

6. Boley H. RELFUN: A relational/functional integration with valued clauses. SIGPLAN Notices, 21(12), 1986, 87-98.

7. Boley H. A Relational/Functional Language and its Compilation into the WAM. SEKI Report SR-90-05, University of Kaiserslautern., April 1990.

8. Hein H.-G. Adding WAM instructions to support valued clauses for relational/functional integration language RELFUN. Technical Report SWP-90-02, University of Kaiserslautern, December 1989.

Processing functional definitions as declarative knowledge: a reduced bytecode implementation of a functional logic machine

Pierre Bonzon
HEC, University of Lausanne
1015 Lausanne, Switzerland

pbonzon@clsuni51.bitnet

Abstract

Given a logical extension of the Scheme language, we present a bytecode implementation of an abstract machine allowing to process functional definitions in a declarative framework. In contrast to standard Prolog machines, which include specialized instructions to unify terms, the task of building structures and lists relies on the data constructors implementing the functional part of the system. Furthermore, as the different clauses of a logical procedure are explicitely chained from within an object closure, predicate applications follow the same pattern as function applications, i.e. can be controlled by a pair of *apply/return* instructions. These features result in an abstract machine that is very much like a minimally extended *functional machine* coupled with a *unification coprocessor.*

1. Introduction

The integration of logic and functional programming into a unified computational model is a possible solution to the problem of processing functional objects as declarative knowledge. We cannot review here the many proposals that have been made so far (see [5] for a thorough presentation). Let us just mention a particular line of research, which favors the integration of logic programming concepts (such as non-determinism and the logic variable) into traditional functional programming environments. Because of its explicit treatment of functions as first class objects (i.e. lambda closures), the Scheme language, a lexically scoped dialect of Lisp, offers interesting perspectives toward this goal. Recent contributions offering comparable results (such as first class logic variables and relations, abstractions of relations, and so on), include [1] and [9]. Our own proposal, while leaving the user without any control over the evaluation process, allows to define, apply and mix logical procedures (or predicates) in the same way as standard Scheme procedures (or functions). The only language extensions we carry are:

- *logical variables*, prefixed with a question mark (e.g. `?x`), and whose scope is stricly local to the clause in which they appear
- *clause expressions*, analog in their syntax to *lambda expressions*, but introduced with the identifier `clause` and allowing any expression as formal argument.

This research was supported by the Swiss National Research Foundation under Grant 21-27835.89

The following is an example of the kind of integration thus made possible:

```
> (define append (lambda (x y)                                ; function definition
    (cond ((null? x) y)
          (t (cons (car x) (append (cdr x) y))))))
append
> (append '(a) '(b c))                                        ; function application
(a b c)                                                       ; returns a term
> (define appendr (clause ('() ?x ?x)))
appendr                                                       ; predicate definition
> (define appendr (clause ((cons ?a ?x) ?y (cons ?a ?z))
    (appendr ?x ?y ?z)))                                      ; involving two clauses
appendr

> (appendr '(a) '(b c) ?x)                                    ; predicate application
(((a) (b c) (a b c)))                                         ; returns a relation

> (appendr ?x ?y '(a b c))                                    ; predicate application
((() (a b c) (a b c))                                         ; returns a relation
 ((a) (b c) (a b c))
 ((a b) (c) (a b c))
 ((a b c) () (a b c)))
```

This two clauses predicate could also be defined as a one clause predicate without body, but with a function application as formal argument:

```
> (define appendr (clause (?x ?y (append ?x ?y))))
```

This represents a declarative use of a functional object, stating that the third argument in relation *appendr* results from the application of function *append*. With this second definition, the application `(appendr '(a) '(b c) ?x)` would return the same relation as above, provided that the evaluation of arguments proceeds from left to right, interleaved with unification, thus allowing the computation of `(append ?x ?y)` to take place after the unification of `?x` with `'(a)` and of `?y` with `'(b c)` (i.e. at the unification level rather than at the resolvent level). On the other hand, in the application `(appendr ?x ?y '(a b c))`, function `append` would try to access unbound variables, which is an error condition. This unfortunate event, which could have been prevented by *narrowing* [5] the arguments, follows our deliberate decision to avoid costly operational semantics. Other examples of functional definitions in declarative contexts can be found in [2], which proposes a model of reflective objects allowing both objective and reflective computations.

As illustrated above, it is an essential part of the model that actual arguments are evaluated at run time, interleaved with unification. In this regard, we differ from Ruf and Weise (whose combinations are strictly applicative-order), and thus achieve a tighter integration. On the negative side, this prevents the use of standard Prolog abstract instruction sets and techniques for compiling clauses, and led us to look for a novel abstract machine.

2. Related work

Recent efforts have already culminated in the definition of *extended abstract machines* to support both the functional and logic programming paradigms. The WINTER architecture [7] was design to support both Prolog-like and Miranda-like programming styles. While its functional component is based on the graph reduction machine TIM [6], its logic part closely follows the classical WAM architecture [10] of Prolog machines, resulting in an extended *combined* instruction set. As such, the WINTER architecture is a typical exemple of a

Complex Instruction Set Computer, or CISC, embodying a *balanced combination* of the two base paradigms. K-WAM [3] is an example of an extended, highly specialized WAM machine, which was designed to work on *transformed* programs. It thus could be depicted as an example of a CISC architecture biased towards the logic paradigm and embodying a *partial integration* of the two base models. At the other end of the spectrum, the SWIFT architecture [4] embodies a set of simple, fast and rather low level instructions, such that an individual WAM or TIM instruction would typically take many SWIFT instructions to encode. Such an architecture, which is not targeted at any particular computational model, could be described as an example of a RISC architecture, to be used to *emulate* specific machines or combinations of machines.

3. An abstract machine for SchemeLog

3.1 General architecture

This machine's architecture, biased towards the functional paradigm, was designed to embody the *complete integration*, as defined in [1], of the two base models. It essentially incorporates basic features found in either the P-machine [11] or the SECD machine [8], extended to deal with the logic variable and the problem of dereferencing, and with clauses and the problem of non-determinism.

This machine has *five* stores, i.e.
- an execution stack ***S***
- a lexical environment ***E***
- a control (code or program store) ***C***
- a binding trail ***T***
- a data heap ***H***

and thus could be depicted as the *SECTH* machine. As in the P-machine, it has a *program register **P*** pointing to a location in C, and lexical adresses for variables are pairs of numbers indicating the static level difference and the relative displacement within a data segment in *E*. It therefore has a *base address* register ***BA*** pointing to a data segment in *E* and acting as entry point to the *static link chain*, and a separate *base control* register ***BC*** pointing to a control block (or activation record) in S and acting as entry point to the *dynamic link chain*. Apart from the usual *top of stack*, *top of environment*, *top of control*, *top of trail* and *top of heap* registers $S_{top}, E_{top}, C_{top}, T_{top}$ and H_{top}, the machine has also a *backtrack* register ***BK*** pointing to a control block in *S*.

3.2 Data objects

Data formats mimic a tagged architecture. They all include an appropriate *tag* field and allow to represent:

- *numbers*
- *indices*, refering to symbols entered in a global symbol table
- *cons pairs*, holding two addresses in *H*, refering to the head and the tail of a list
- *variable closures*, holding a displacement and a base address in *E*
- *function closures*, comprising the function's cardinality, its code address in *C* and its environment (or base) address in *E*
- *predicate closures*, comprising the predicate's cardinality, its first clause code address in *C*, an address in *H* linking to another predicate closure refering to the predicate's second clause (linking itself to its third clause, and so on), and the first clause environment address in E

3.3 Instruction set

The format of instructions ***<op l a>*** is P-standard, i.e. comprises

- an *operation* code *op*
- an *index* code *l* (e.g. a table index or a level difference)
- an *address a* (e.g. a displacement or an absolute addres)

From the P-machine instruction set, we borrow:

- *loading* and *storing* instructions (i.e. *LIT*, *LOD* and *STO*)
- *control* and *allocation* intructions (i.e. *JMP*, *JPC* and *INT*)
- an extended set *OPR* of *primitive operators* (including *CAR*, *CDR*, *CONS*,...).

From the SECD machine we borrow:

- extended *closure* instructions (i.e. *LDF*, *LDP* and *LDV*)
- extended *apply* instructions (i.e. *APP* and *APD*)
- extended *return* instructions (i.e. *RTF*, *RTS*, *RTP*, *RTA*, *RTQ*, *RTD* and *RTE*)

Finally, from any Prolog machine, we borrow a *unify* instruction (i.e. *UNF*).

To complete the instruction set, there is a *MOV* instruction *moving* data within S, and a peculiar *jump if defined* instruction *JPD*, for implementing global variables, which, according to SchemeLog semantics, evaluate to logical variables when unbound. We also ought to mention that lists are constructed in a non-structure-sharing manner into heap cells, and that a form of *leazy dereferencing* has been adopted, with *CAR* and *CDR* returning dereferenced variables, while allowing *CONS* to operate on uninstantiated logical variables.

3.4 Operational semantics

Much of the complexity of an abstract machine for SchemeLog comes from the dynamic type of applications, which cannot be resolved at compile time. In short, actual delayed arguments of *function applications*, together with the address of the function's own definition environment (as part of the *static link chain*), are transfered to a fresh data segment in *E* (corresponding to the function's local environment), where arguments will subsequently be forced. In *predicates applications*, delayed arguments are moved beyond the current control block in S, awaiting their interleaved forcing and unification with formal arguments. Futhermore, procedures of either type (i.e. functional or logical) can be applied in one of two *modes*. When it appears in a clause body (i.e. in *search* mode), an application either simply succeeds or forces backtracking. When it appears in a clause head or function body (i.e. in *result* mode), an application always return a value, which can be either a single value (possibly depicting failure), or a list of instantiated arguments. Upon exit from a procedure, this application's result will be at the top of S.

A first view at the bytecode interpreter can be given as follows:

```
repeat
 C[P] -> (op,l,a);
 P+1 -> P
 case op of

 LIT:  push(S,constant(l,a))                          load literal

 LOD:  push(S,dereference(E[base(l)+a]))              load variable value

 MOV:  push(S,S[BC+a])                                move

 LDF:  push(S,function(l,a,BA))                       load function closure
```

```
LDP:  push(S,predicate(l,a,0,BA))                    load predicate closure

LDV:  if E[BA+a]="undefined"                          load logic variable value
      then variable(a,BA) -> E[BA+a];
      push(S,dereference(E[BA+a]))

STO:  if S[S_top].tag=predicate                       store value
      and E[base(l)+a].tag=predicate
      then (push(H,S[S_top]); link(E[base(l)+a],H_top))
      else S[S_top] -> E[base(l)+a];
      pop(S)

INT:  for i=1..a do push(E,"undefined")               allocate local variables

JMP:  a -> P                                          unconditional jump

JPC:  if S[S_top]="false" then a -> P;                jump if false
      pop(S)

JPD:  if  S[S_top]="undefined"                        jump if defined
      then  pop(S)
      else  a -> P

OPR:  apply(l)                                        apply primitive operator
                                                      (on arguments on top of S)

APP:  case S[S_top].tag of
function:  pop(S,(card,code,env));                    apply function
           push(E,env);                               (expects the top item of S
           E_top -> BA;                                to hold a function closure
           for i=card..1 do pop(S,E[E_top+i]);         and the next items to be
           E_top+card -> E_top;                        function closures standing
           push(S,"undefined");                        for delayed arguments)
           push(S,(BA,BC,P,l));
           S_top -> BC;
           code -> P

predicate:   pop(S,(card,code,next,env));             apply predicate
             push(E,env);                             (expects the top of S to hold
             E_top -> BA;                              a predicate closure
             for i=card..1 do pop(S,arg_i);            and the next items to be
             push(S,"empty");                          function closures standing
             "undefined" -> adr;                       for delayed arguments)
             push(S,(BA,BC,P,l,BK,T_top,next,card,adr));
             S_top -> BC;
             for i=1..card do push(S,arg_i);
             if l="result" then generate;
             if next>0
             then BC -> BK
             else if l="result" then 0 -> BK;
             code -> P

variable:  if l="result"                              apply variable
           then "false" -> S[S_top]                   (undefined predicate)
           else backtrack
```

APD:	*pop(S,(env,code));* *env -> BA;* *push(S,"undefined");* *push(S,(BA,BC,P));* S_{top} *-> BC;* *code -> P*	force delayed value
UNF:	*pop(S,x);* *pop(S,y);* ***if not*** *unify(x,y)* ***then*** *backtrack*	unify terms
RTF:	***if*** *S[BC].l="search"* ***and*** *S[*S_{top}*]="false"* ***then*** *backtrack* ***else*** *(S[*S_{top}*] -> S[BC-1];* *BC-1 ->* S_{top}*;* *S[BC].P -> P;* *S[BC].BC -> BC;* *S[BC].BA -> BA)*	return from function (in either one of two modes)
RTP:	***if*** *S[BC].l="result"* ***then*** *S[BC].adr -> P* ***else*** *(S[BC].P -> P;* *S[BC].BC -> BC;* *S[BC].BA -> BA)*	return from predicate (in either one of two modes)
RTD:	*S[*S_{top}*] -> S[BC-1];* *BC-1 ->* S_{top}*;* *S[BC].P -> P;* *S[BC].BC -> BC;* *S[BC].BA -> BA*	return from forcing
RTS:	***if*** *S[*S_{top}*]="false"* ***then*** *backtrack*	return from search mode
RTA:	*append(S[*S_{top}*-1],list(instance(S[*S_{top}*])));* *pop(S)*	return argument
RTQ:	*append(S[BC-1],list(S[*S_{top}*]));* *backtrack*	return query argument list
RTE:	*instantiate(S[*S_{top}*]);* *0 -> P*	return to readevalloop

until *P=0*

Most of the auxiliary functions and procedures (such as *push*, *pop*, *dereference*, and so on) used above have obvious meanings. Less common ones can be briefly described as follows:

base(l): returns the base address *l* links down the static chain starting at BA

link(x,adr): links clause at heap address *adr* with predicate closure *x*

unify(x,y): attemps to unify terms *x* and *y*; along the way, possibly binds free variables in *x* or *y*, and pushes these variables on *T*

backtrack: if *BK >0*, forces backtracking to control block at address *BK* (i.e. *BK -> BC*) and try next clause (i.e. *H[S[BC].next].code -> P*), else returns to the nearest control block with *l="result"*; in any case, restore variables that were initially free on entry to that block (i.e. that have been pushed on *T* beyond *S[BC].*T_{top})

generate: pushes code on *C* for appending, to the result list in *S[BC-1]*, a new instantiated list of the query arguments in *S[BC+1], S[BC+2]...*; stores this code's address in *S[BC].adr*

4. Summary and conclusions

We have described an abstract machine based on the *P* and SECD architecture, with the only instruction borrowed from a WAM (i.e. the *unify* instruction) acting merely as a coprocessor, that offers the same degree of integration that has been previously achieved via a metacircular evaluator. At this point, both a bytecode emulator and a compiler have been implemented as PASCAL modules of approximately 500 lines each. No attention has been paid yet to issues such as *code* and *memory optimization, garbage collection*, and the like. We anticipate that much work still has to be done before a suitable implementation could be truly benchmarked.

5. References

[1] Bonzon, P., A Metacircular Evaluator for a Logical Extension of Scheme, Lisp and Symbolic Computation, 2,3 (1990)

[2] Bonzon,. P., Reflection in objects: towards a uniform architecture, Internal Report HEC (Feb. 1991)

[3] Bosco, P., Cecchi, C. and Moiso, C., An Extension of WAM for K-LEAF: a WAM-based compilation of conditional narrowing, Proc. 6th Intl. Conf. on Logic Programming, MIT Press (1989)

[4] Chu, D., and McCabe, F., SWIFT - a New Symbolic Processor, Proc. 5th Intl. Conf. and Symp. on Logic Programming, MIT Press (1988)

[5] De Groot, D. and Lindstrom, G. (eds), *Logic Programming / Functions, Relations and Equations*, Prentice Hall (1986)

[6] Fairbarn, J., and Wray, S., TIM: a Simple, Lazy Abstract Machine to Execute Supercombinators, Proc. Functional Languages and Computer Architecture Conference (1987)

[7] Jamsek, D., Greene, K., Chin, S.-H. and Humenn, P., WINTER: WAMS in TIM Expression Reduction, Proc. North Amer. Conf. on Logic Programming, MIT Press (1989)

[8] Landin, P., The Mechanical Evaluation of Expressions, Computer Journal, 6,4 (1964)

[9] Ruf, E., and Weise, D., LogScheme: Integrating Logic Programming into Scheme, Lisp and Symbolic Computation, 3,3 (1990)

[10] Warren, D.H.D., An abstract Prolog Instruction Set, Technical Note 309, SRI International (1983)

[11] Wirth, N., *Algorithms + Data Structures = Programs*, Prentice-Hall (1976)

Appendix: compiled code for the introductory examples, where ["expr"] denotes a closure.

```
>(DEFINE APPEND(LAMBDA(X Y)
  (COND((NULL X)Y)
       (T(CONS(CAR X)(APPEND(CDR X)Y))))))
 0:JMP 0 34         (DEFINE
 1:INT 0 0          (LAMBDA
 2:LOD 0 0          [X]
 3:APD 0 0          "FORCE"
 4:STO 0 0          -> X
 5:LOD 0 1          [Y]
 6:APD 0 0          "FORCE"
 7:STO 0 1          -> Y
 8:JMP 0 10         (COND ..
 9:JMP 0 33               ..)
10:LOD 0 0          X
11:OPR 9 0          (NULL X)
12:JPC 0 15         "JUMP TO 15 IF FALSE"
13:LOD 0 1          Y
14:JMP 0 9          "EXIT"
15:LIT 2 1          T
16:JPC 0 32         "JUMP TO 32 IF FALSE"
17:LOD 0 0          X
18:OPR 5 0          (CAR X)
19:JMP 0 23         "DELAY"
20:LOD 0 0          X
21:OPR 6 0          (CDR X)
22:RTD 0 0          "RETURN FROM DELAY"
23:LDF 0 20         [(CDR X)]
24:JMP 0 27         "DELAY"
25:LOD 0 1          Y
26:RTD 0 0          "RETURN FROM DELAY"
27:LDF 0 25         [Y]
28:LOD 1 0          APPEND
29:APP 0 0          (APPEND ...)
30:OPR 7 0          (CONS ...)
31:JMP 0 9          "EXIT"
32:LIT 2 0          NIL
33:RTF 0 0          "RETURN FROM FUNCTION"
34:LDF 2 1          [(LAMBDA ...)]
35:STO 0 0          -> APPEND
36:LIT 2 13         'APPEND
37:RTE 0 0          END
APPEND

>(DEFINE APPENDR(CLAUSE(?X ?Y(APPEND ?X ?Y))))
38:JMP 0 62         (DEFINE
39:INT 0 2          (CLAUSE
40:MOV 0 9          ["ARG1"]
41:APD 0 0          "FORCE"
42:LDV 0 0          ?X
43:UNF 0 0          "UNIFY"
44:MOV 0 10         ["ARG2"]
45:APD 0 0          "FORCE"
46:LDV 0 1          ?Y
47:UNF 0 0          "UNIFY"
```

```
48:MOV 0 11         ["ARG3"]
49:APD 0 0          "FORCE"
50:JMP 0 53         "DELAY"
51:LOD 0 0          ?X
52:RTD 0 0          "RETURN FROM DELAY"
53:LDF 0 51         [?X]
54:JMP 0 57         "DELAY"
55:LOD 0 1          ?Y
56:RTD 0 0          "RETURN FROM DELAY"
57:LDF 0 55         [?Y]
58:LOD 1 0          APPEND
59:APP 0 0          (APPEND ..)
60:UNF 0 0          "UNIFY"
61:RTP 0 0          "RETURN FROM PREDICATE"
62:LDP 3 39         [(CLAUSE ..)]
63:STO 0 1          -> APPENDR
64:LIT 2 16         'APPENDR
65:RTE 0 0          END
APPENDR

>(APPENDR '(A) '(B C) ?Z)
66:JMP 0 71         DELAY
67:LIT 2 19         'A
68:LIT 2 0          NIL
69:OPR 7 0          '(A)
70:RTD 0 0          "RETURN FROM DELAY"
71:LDF 0 67         ['(A)]
72:JMP 0 79         "DELAY"
73:LIT 2 20         'B
74:LIT 2 21         'C
75:LIT 2 0          NIL
76:OPR 7 0          '(C)
77:OPR 7 0          '(B C)
78:RTD 0 0          "RETURN FROM DELAY"
79:LDF 0 73         ['(B C)]
80:JMP 0 83         "DELAY"
81:LDV 0 2          ?Z
82:RTD 0 0          "RETURN FROM DELAY"
83:LDF 0 81         [?Z]
84:LOD 0 1          APPENDR
85:APP 0 0          (APPENDR ...)
86:RTE 0 0          END
87:LIT 2 0          NIL
88:MOV 0 9          ["ARG1"]
89:APD 0 0          "FORCE"
90 RTA 0 0          '("ARG2")
91:MOV 0 10         ["ARG2"]
92:APD 0 0          "FORCE"
93:RTA 0 0          '("ARG1" "ARG2")
94:MOV 0 11         ["ARG3"]
95:APD 0 0          "FORCE"
96:RTA 0 0          '("ARG1" "ARG2" "ARG3")
97:RTQ 0 0          "RETURN FROM QUERY"
 (((A) (B C) (A B C)))
```

N.B. Lines 87 to 97 have been generated at runtime by the interpretation of *generate*.

Reducing Scheduling Overheads for Concurrent Logic Programs

Andy King and Paul Soper
Department of Electronics and Computer Science,
University of Southampton, Southampton, S09 5NH, UK.

Abstract

Strictness analysis is crucial for the efficient implementation of the lazy functional languages. A related technique for the concurrent logic languages (CLLs) called schedule analysis is presented which divides at compile-time a CLL program into threads of totally ordered atoms, whose relative ordering is determined at run-time. The technique enables the enqueuing and dequeuing of processes to be reduced, synchronisation tests to be partially removed, introduces the possibility of using unboxed arguments, and permits variables to be migrated from a heap to a stack to affect a form of compile-time garbage collection. The implementation is outlined and some preliminary results are given.

1 Introduction

Traub [1] has proposed dependence analysis as a technique for reducing the run-time overheads of the lenient functional languages. The analysis presented in this paper arose because the lenient functional languages and the concurrent logic languages (CLLs), as described in [2], share similar synchronisation mechanisms. Based on this observation a reinterpretation and reformulation of dependence analysis, called schedule analysis, has been developed for the (CLLs).

Schedule analysis is concerned with deducing at compile-time a partial schedule of processes, or equivalently the guard and body atoms of a clause, which is consistent with the program behaviour. Program termination characteristics are affected if an atom which instantiates a shared variable is ordered after an atom that matches on that variable. In order to avoid this an ordering of the atoms has to be determined which does not contradict any data dependence. In general the processes cannot be totally ordered and thus the analysis leads to a division into threads of totally ordered processes. In this way the work required of the run-time scheduler is reduced to ordering threads.

An additional motivation for schedule analysis is that it allows a number of important optimisations. These are surveyed in section 2. The role of schedule analysis in uniprocessor and multiprocessor implementations of the CLLs is also discussed. Section 3 explains how dependencies between atoms can identify pairs of atoms which must be allocated to different threads. Finally theorem 1, a safety result, states the conditions under which atoms can be partitioned into threads and ordered within a thread whilst preserving the behaviour of the program. The final procedure can be used with existing compile-time analysis techniques. In section 4 we outline our implementation are give some preliminary results. Section 5 presents the concluding discussion.

2 Motivation

In addition to reducing enqueuing and dequeuing of processes by a scheduler, schedule analysis permits several useful optimisations to be applied within a thread. The optimisations all depend on the existence of a total ordering of atoms within a thread.

Gregory [3] uses the sequential and parallel conjuncts of kernel Parlog to express ordered guard and body atoms to enable matching and unification to be partially replaced with assignment and assignment to be partially removed. Synchronisation instructions (which correspond to `DATA/1` atoms in kernel Parlog), if repeated within a sequential conjunct, can also be removed. Crammond [4] explains how variables which are shared between ordered atoms can be allocated to the environments of a stack rather than a heap. Dividing the atoms of a clause into threads of totally ordered atoms extends the scope of these optimisations. Furthermore synchronisation instructions can be removed if producer atoms are ordered before the consumer atoms within the same thread.

Boxing analysis plays a role in realising the speedup of strictness analysis, and also appears to be useful in schedule analysis. Boxing analysis determines whether an argument of a predicate has to be boxed (tagged and referenced indirectly by a pointer) or can be unboxed (is of known type and can be placed in a machine register to be referenced directly without a pointer). Unboxed arguments can often be used if a producer atom is ordered before the consumer atoms within the same thread. Moreover if each clause of a predicate definition synchronises on an argument then it is possible to move the synchronisation instruction to immediately before the invoking atom in the parent clause. In many cases the synchronisation instruction can then be shown to be redundant.

In a multiprocessor implementation there is a tradeoff between scheduling at compile-time and scheduling at run-time. Schedule analysis permits useful optimisations to be applied within a thread but also limits parallelism. Thus schedule analysis should be applied only when parallelism is inappropriate. Parallelism is always inappropriate for a uniprocessor, and can often be inappropriate for a multiprocessor. To give an efficient and balanced untilisation of a multiprocessor a CLL program may be divided into grains, the constituent processes of a grain being executed on a single processor. The division of a CLL program into grains can be performed either manually by the programmer annotating code, or automatically by the compiler applying granularity analysis [5]. Since overheads still occur within a grain, because parallelism has to be emulated, schedule analysis can then be applied to a grain to reduce these overheads.

3 Outline of schedule analysis

In this section we briefly outline the main points of schedule analysis without formal definitions or proofs. A detailed account of the method can be found in [6]. Schedule analysis is based on overestimating the relevances associated with sharing, variable producers and variable consumers. These are assumed to be already derived, for instance by the abstract interpretation techniques reported by King and Soper [7] and Codish, Dams and Yardeni [8].

A relevance relation is constructed by overestimating the atoms which produce a variable and overestimating the atoms which consume the variable. A relevance is included for each such producer to consumer dependence. In the following we use the notation $(p \in)\ P_W$ for the set of predicate symbol occurrences in the program W, with a typical element p, and $(v \in)\ V$ for the set of program variables, with typical element v. For brevity we refer to the atom with predicate symbol p and also the clause defining p by the same symbol p. To describe the procedure for construction the relevance relation a producer map $\mathcal{P} : P_W \rightarrow 2^V$ and a consumer map $\mathcal{C} : P_W \rightarrow 2^V$ are introduced such that: $v \in \mathcal{P}(p)$ if p can affect v; and $v \in \mathcal{C}(p)$ if v can affect p. Specifically $v \notin \mathcal{P}(p)$ if v can be shown to be completely matched or ignored by p and $v \notin \mathcal{C}(p)$ if v can be shown to be completely instantiated or ignored by p. Sharing is encapsulated by the mappings $\mathcal{S} : P_W \rightarrow 2^{\mathbb{N}} \times \mathbb{N}$ and $\mathcal{V} : P_W \times \mathbb{N} \rightarrow 2^V$ which respectively indicate which arguments of an atom can share, and identify the variables in an argument of an atom. More exactly $\langle m, n\rangle \in \mathcal{S}(p)$ if the terms of the mth and nth arguments of the atom p can share, and $v \in \mathcal{V}(p, n)$ if the variable v is part of the nth argument of p. A relevance relation on the set of body atoms Q_p for the clause p can be constructed in terms of $\mathcal{P}$, $\mathcal{C}$, $\mathcal{S}$ and $\mathcal{V}$.

Definition 1 *The relevance relation δ_p is defined by: $\langle q, q'\rangle \in \delta_p$ if and only if*

1. *$\langle m, m'\rangle \in \mathcal{S}(p')$ and $v \in \mathcal{V}(p, m)$ and $v' \in \mathcal{V}(p, m')$ and $v \in \mathcal{P}(q)$ and $v' \in \mathcal{C}(q')$ and $q \neq q'$ or*
2. *$v \in \mathcal{P}(q)$ and $v \in \mathcal{C}(q')$ and $q \neq q'$.*

Note that since δ_p is defined edge-wise it is not necessarily transitive. Although producers and consumers are intuitively connected with relevance, the connection for sharing is indirect are arises through the potential for feedback which can introduce additional relevances into the relevance relation. This is explained in [6].

The δ_p relation summarises the behaviour of clause p independently of the initial query and it can be used to partition the atoms of Q_p into threads of totally ordered atoms. Threads are formed by identifying pairs of atoms which must be allocated to different threads. Pairs of atoms are related in just four ways according to the categories of figure 1 (where δ_p^+ denotes the transitive closure of δ_p). For category one, either q always precedes q' or q sometimes precedes q', so that for both cases q can be ordered before q' within the same thread. Category two is the symmetric variant of category one. For category three the atoms q and q' can be arbitrarily ordered because neither

Category	*Characteristic*	*Order*
1	$\langle q, q' \rangle \in \delta_p^+$ and $\langle q', q \rangle \notin \delta_p^+$	q precedes q'.
2	$\langle q', q \rangle \in \delta_p^+$ and $\langle q, q' \rangle \notin \delta_p^+$	q' precedes q.
3	$\langle q, q' \rangle \notin \delta_p^+$ and $\langle q', q \rangle \notin \delta_p^+$	neither q precedes q' nor q' precedes q.
4	$\langle q, q' \rangle \in \delta_p^+$ and $\langle q', q \rangle \in \delta_p^+$	either q precedes q' or q' precedes q, or q and q' coroutine.

Figure 1: Categorising atom pairs.

q precedes q' nor q' precedes q. Category four either identifies coroutining activity, or different sequences for which q precedes q' in one sequence and q' precedes q in another sequence. In either case the atoms q and q' must be assigned to different threads and the ordering resolved at run-time. Of these four categories only category four corresponds to pairs of atoms that must be allocated to different threads. This is encapsulated as the relation σ_p on Q_p called the separation relation.

Definition 2 *σ_p on Q_p is defined by: $\langle q, q' \rangle \in \sigma_p$ if and only if $\langle q, q' \rangle \in \delta_p^+$ and $\langle q', q \rangle \in \delta_p^+$.*

Atoms which are related by σ_p must be allocated to different threads.

Definition 3 *$\{Q_p^1, \ldots, Q_p^t\}$ is a partition of Q_p such that $q \in Q_p^i$ and $q' \in Q_p^j$ with $i \neq j$ if $\langle q, q' \rangle \in \sigma_p$. o_p^i is a total ordering on Q_p^i such that if $\langle q, q' \rangle \in o_p^i$ then $\langle q', q \rangle \notin \delta_p^+$.*

Q_p^i expresses the constituent atoms of a thread, o_p^i expresses the ordering of atoms within a thread, and t expresses the number of threads. Each o_p^i is chosen not to contradict δ_p.

It is possible for $\{o_p^1, \ldots, o_p^t\}$ to describe a division into threads which affects the behaviour of the clause p. The problem stems from the sequential nature of threads. Collectively $\{o_p^1, \ldots, o_p^t\}$ can introduce extra non-trivial cycles into δ_p. This is because the totally ordered threads induce extra dependencies between atoms. It is as if these extra dependencies are included in another relevance relation which is a superset of the original relevance relation. The superset relevance relation can require a different division into threads. In this case the original partition is inappropriate and can potentially affect program behaviour. The observation that the partition can affect termination if the threads collectively introduce extra non-trivial cycles into the relevance relation motivates the following safety result.

Definition 4 *τ_p on Q_p is defined by $\tau_p = \cup_{i=1,\ldots,t} o_p^i$.*

Definition 5 *An interleave ι_p of $\{o_p^1, \ldots, o_p^t\}$ is a total relation on Q_p such that $\tau_p \subseteq \iota_p$ and if $\langle q, q' \rangle \in \iota_p$ then $\langle q', q \rangle \notin \tau_p$.*

	Data	Get_Const and Get_List	Bind	Unify	Minus and Plus	Less
nfib/2	**1/441**	89/89	**0/264**	177/177	352/353	
nrev/2	**31/496**	91/91		466/466		
sieve/2	473/473	258/258		**247/275**	28/28	51/51

Figure 2: Preliminary schedule analysis results.

Theorem 1 *If $\tau_p \cup \delta_p^+$ has no more non-trivial cycles than δ_p^+ then there exists an interleave ι_p of $\{o_p^1, \ldots, o_p^t\}$ such that for all initial queries ι_p does not contradict any data dependence on Q_p.*

An interleave expresses how the body atoms of a clause can be ordered by scheduling threads. In other words definition 5 states that the ordering of atoms in an interleave must not contradict the ordering of atoms in a thread. Theorem 1 is a safety result in the sense that if τ_p adds no extra non-trivial cycles to δ_p^+ then for all initial queries the threads can always be scheduled so as to resolve all data dependencies. Specifically theorem 1 describes a procedure for safely partitioning the atoms of a clause into threads of totally ordered atoms in such a way that termination characteristics are preserved.

4 Implementation and Preliminary Results

Schedule analysis has been implemented and integrated into an existing FParlog86 compiler. δ_p^+ is calculated as the fixed-point of the Boolean adjacency matrix for δ_p [9]. The problem of finding an optimal partition of Q_p, one which minimises the number of threads t, is NP-complete [10]. Therefore, instead, a good partition is found in polynomial-time by a sequential colouring algorithm [11]. Each o_p^i is formed by topologically sorting the relation induced by δ_p^+ on Q_p^i. The number of non-trivial cycles in δ_p^+ and $\tau_p \cup \delta_p^+$ is counted by a backtracking algorithm [12]. The prototype schedule analysis module has been coded in 350 lines of FParlog86, and typically equates to 10% of execution time of the compiler (excluding the generation of mode information by abstract interpretation). Some preliminary results obtained with the prototype implementation are given in figure 2.

Figure 2 lists the instruction count for three benchmark programs: **nfib/2** which counts the number of reductions required to calculate the tenth number in the Fibonacci sequence; **nrev/2** which computes the naive reverse of a thirty element list; and **sieve/2** which finds the first ten prime numbers by a sieve-based method. The instruction counts are presented in the form c/c^* where c and c^* are the instruction counts obtained with/without applying schedule analysis. Note how the synchronisation, binding and unifying instructions can often be removed. Observe too that because **sieve/2** uses significant amounts of corouting few instructions can be removed from the program.

5 Discussion

A compilation technique called schedule analysis has been presented which divides a program into threads, whose relative ordering is determined at run-time. The analysis has been developed in a formal framework within which safety conditions are established. A practical procedure for constructing threads, which satisfies the safety conditions, is also presented. Schedule analysis plays a more central role than just another intermediate stage of compilation, since it enables the enqueuing and dequeuing of processes to be reduced, binding checks and variable tagging to be partially removed, and variables migrated from a heap to a stack to effect a form of compile-time garbage collection. Since the lenient functional languages are similar in a number of ways to the CLLs the benefits ensuing from dependence analysis suggest that schedule analysis is likely to be worthwhile even for microprocessors equipped with microcoded scheduling support.

Some of the benefits of schedule analysis are linked with replacing bounded-depth scheduling with depth-first scheduling. The scheduling of guard and body atoms is said to be and-fair [2] if any atom capable of being evaluated will eventually be evaluated. And-fairness is only guaranteed by depth-first scheduling if the branch of the SLD-tree emanating from each atom is bounded and can be extended without indefinite suspension. Although the compile-time detection of bounded SLD-tree branches is in general undecidable. Francez [13], Ullman and Van Gelder [14], Walther [15], Apt *et al.* [16], Bezem [17], Van Gelder [18], Plümer [19] and Wang [20] have shown that the termination of logic programs can be usefully detected at compile-time. It has been assumed in this work that an important class of clauses can be identified for which the constituent atoms can be depth-first scheduled without compromising and-fairness or for which depth-first is preferred on the grounds of efficiency [21].

Acknowledgments

We would like to thank Ken Traub whose dependence analysis motivated much of this work and Hugh Glaser and Pieter Hartel for helpful discussions.

References

[1] Traub, K.R. (1989). "Compiling as Partitioning: A New Approach to Compiling Non-strict Functional Languages", *in Proceedings of the Fourth International Conference on Functional Programming*, pp. 75–88. ACM Press.

[2] Shapiro, E.Y. (1989). "The Family of Concurrent Logic Programming Languages", *Journal of ACM Computing Surveys*, 21 (3): 413–510.

[3] Gregory, S. (1987). *Parallel Logic Programming in Parlog, The Language and its Implementation.* Addison-Wesley.

[4] Crammond, J.A. (1988). *Implementation of Committed-Choice Logic Languages on Shared Memory Multiprocessors.* PhD thesis, Heriot-Watt University, Edinburgh.

[5] King, A. and P. Soper (1990). "Granularity Analysis of Concurrent Logic Programs", *in The Fifth International Symposium on Computer and Information Sciences*, Nevsehir, Cappadocia, Turkey.

[6] King, A. and P. Soper (1990). "Schedule Analysis of Concurrent Logic Programs", Technical Report 90-22, Department of Electronics and Computer Science, Southampton University, Southampton, S09 5NH.

[7] King, A. and P. Soper (1991). "A Semantic Approach to Producer and Consumer Analysis", *International Conference on Logic Programming Workshop on Concurrent Logic Programming*, Paris, France.

[8] Codish, M., D. Dams, and E. Yardeni (1990). "Derivation and Safety of an Abstract Unification Algorithm for Groundness and Aliasing Analysis", Technical Report CS90-28, Department of Computer Science, Weizmann Institute of Science, Rehovot 76100, Isreal.

[9] Carré, B. (1979). *Graphs and Networks.* Clarendon Press, Oxford.

[10] Karp, R.M. (1972). *Complexity of Computer Computations*, chapter Reducibility among Combinatorial Problems, pp. 85–103. Plenum Press.

[11] D.W. Matula, G. Marble and J.D. Isaacson (1972). *Graph theory and computing*, chapter Graph colouring algorithms, pp. 109–122. Academic Press, London. Edited by R.C. Read.

[12] Tiernan, J.C. (1970). "An efficient search algorithm to find the elementary ciccuits of a graph", *Communications of the ACM*, 13: 722–726.

[13] Francez, N., O. Grumberg, S. Katz, and A. Pnueli (1985). "Proving Termination of Logic Programs", *in Proceedings of Logics of Programs Conference*, pp. 89–105, Brooklyn, NY. Springer-Verlag.

[14] Ullman, J.D. and A. Van Gelder (1988). "Top-down Termination of Logical Rules", *Journal of the ACM*, 35 (2): 345–373.

[15] Walther, C. (1988). *Automated Termination Proofs.* PhD thesis, University of Karlsruhe.

[16] Apt, K.R., R.N. Bol, and J.W. Klop (1989). "On the safe termination of Prolog programs", *in Proceedings of the Sixth International Conference on Logic Programming*, pp. 353–368, Lisboa, Portugal. MIT Press.

[17] Bezem, M. (1989). "Characterizing Termination of Logic Programs with Level Mappings", *in Proceedings of the North American Conference on Logic Programming*, pp. 69–80, Case Western Reserve University, Cleveland, Ohio.

[18] Gelder, A. Van (1990). "Deriving Constraints Among Argument Sizes in Logic Programs", *in Proceedings of the Ninth ACM Symposium on Principles of Database Systems*, Nashville, Tennessee.

[19] Plumer, L. (1990). "Termination Proofs for Logic Programs based on Predicate Inequalities", *in Proceedings of the Seventh International Conference on Logic Programming*, Jerusalem, Isreal.

[20] Wang, B. and R. K. Shyamasundar (1990). "Towards a Characterisation of the Termination of Logic Programs", *in The Second International Workshop on Programming Language Implementation and Logic Programming*, pp. 204–221, Linkoping, Sweden. Springer-Verlag.

[21] Sato, M., H. Shimizu, A. Matsumoto, K. Rokusawa, and A. Goto (1987). "KL1 Execution Model for PIM Cluster with Shared Memory", *in Proceedings of the Fourth International Conference*, pp. 338–355.

A General Framework for Knowledge Compilation

Henry Kautz and Bart Selman
AI Principles Research Department
AT&T Bell Laboratories
Murray Hill, NJ 07974 USA
{kautz, selman}@research.att.com

Abstract

Computational efficiency is a central concern in the design of knowledge representation systems. In order to obtain efficient systems it has been suggested that one should limit the form of the statements in the knowledge base or use an incomplete inference mechanism. The former approach is often too restrictive for practical applications, whereas the latter leads to uncertainty about exactly what can and cannot be inferred from the knowledge base. We present a third alternative, in which knowledge given in a general representation language is translated (compiled) into a tractable form — allowing for efficient subsequent query answering.

We show how propositional logical theories can be compiled into Horn theories that approximate the original information. The approximations bound the original theory from below and above in terms of logical strength. The procedures are extended to other tractable languages (for example, binary clauses) and to the first-order case. Finally, we demonstrate the generality of our approach by compiling concept descriptions in a general frame-based language into a tractable form.

1 Introduction

A striking feature of commonsense reasoning is that it is *fast.* People can quickly and effortlessly perform such tasks as planning a trip, interpreting a story, or answering a question without relying solely on memory. Levesque [89] gives the example of the question, "Could a crocodile run a steeplechase?" You can answer the question immediately, even though you have never thought about it before! The "logicist" approach to artificial intelligence represents commonsense knowledge by logical formulas, and views reasoning as a kind of formal theorem-proving. This accounts for the flexibility of commonsense reasoning, but not its speed. In both theory and practice the complexity of theorem-proving with general logical theories is very high—exponential or worse.

One way to make the logicist approach more computationally attractive is to restrict the expressive power of the representation language, so that fast, special-purpose inference algorithms can be employed. But this usually renders the language too limited for practical application [6], and leaves unanswered the question of what to do with information that *cannot* be represented in the restricted form.

This paper describes an approach to efficient symbolic inference called *knowledge compilation*, which overcomes these objections. We allow the knowledge base to be specified in a general, unrestricted representation language. The system then computes *approximations* to the knowledge base in a restricted and efficient language. We show how the approximations can be used to speed up inference *without* giving up correctness or completeness: computational costs are simply shifted from "run time" question-answering to the "off-line" compilation process.

The paper begins with an example of approximating general propositional theories by Horn theories. Next we describe the general knowledge compilation framework, and examine a number of other knowledge compilation systems, including ones involving generalizations of Horn clauses, first-order theories, logic programs, and terminological logics.

2 Compiling Propositional Theories

This section briefly introduces the knowledge compilation approach using the concrete example of approximating general propositional theories by Horn theories. This form of knowledge compilation was first introduced in [14]. That paper gives a much more detailed account; the reader who is familiar with it can proceed to the next section.

2.1 Definitions

We assume a standard propositional language, and use p, q, r, and s to denote propositional letters and x, y, and z to denote literals (a *literal* is either a propositional letter, called a positive literal, or its negation, called a negative literal). A *clause* is a disjunction of literals, and can be represented by the set of literals it contains. A clause is *Horn* if and only if it contains at most one positive literal; a set of such clauses is called a *Horn theory.* Formulas are given in conjunctive normal form (a conjunction of disjuncts), so they can be represented by a set of clauses.

In general, determining whether a given formula (the *query*) follows from a set of formulas in a knowledge base is intractable (provided $P \neq NP$) [3]. However, when the knowledge base contains only Horn clauses the problem can be solved in linear time [5]. We therefore take as the goal of our knowledge compilation process the translation of an arbitrary set of clauses into a logically equivalent set of Horn clauses. Since an exact translation is often not possible, we use two sets of Horn clauses to approximate the original theory. The basic idea is to bound the set of models (satisfying truth assignments) of the original theory from below and from above by Horn theories. In the following definition, $\mathcal{M}(\Sigma)$ denotes the set of satisfying truth assignments of the theory Σ.

Definition: Horn lower-bound and Horn upper-bound
Let Σ be a set of clauses. The sets Σ_{lb} and Σ_{ub} of Horn clauses are respectively a Horn lower-bound and a Horn upper-bound of Σ iff

$$\mathcal{M}(\Sigma_{lb}) \subseteq \mathcal{M}(\Sigma) \subseteq \mathcal{M}(\Sigma_{ub})$$

or, equivalently,

$$\Sigma_{lb} \models \Sigma \models \Sigma_{ub}$$

Note that the bounds are defined in terms of models. The reader is cautioned not to associate "lower" with "logically weaker": The *lower* bound has fewer models than the original theory, and is thus logically *stronger* than (*i.e.*, implies) the original theory; whereas the *upper* bound has more models and is thus logically *weaker* than (*i.e.*, is implied by) the original theory.

Instead of simply using any pair of bounds to characterize the initial theory, we wish to use the best possible ones: a *greatest* Horn lower-bound and a *least* Horn upper-bound.

Definition: Greatest Horn lower-bound (GLB)
Let Σ be a set of clauses. The set Σ_{glb} of Horn clauses is a greatest Horn lower-bound of Σ iff $\Sigma_{glb} \models \Sigma$ and there is no set Σ' of Horn clauses such that $\Sigma_{glb} \models \Sigma' \models \Sigma$ and $\Sigma \not\models \Sigma'$.

Definition: Least Horn upper-bound (LUB)
Let Σ be a set of clauses. The set Σ_{lub} of Horn clauses is a least Horn upper-bound of Σ iff $\Sigma \models \Sigma_{lub}$ and there is no set Σ' of Horn clauses such that $\Sigma \models \Sigma' \models \Sigma_{lub}$ and $\Sigma' \not\models \Sigma$.

We call these bounds *Horn approximations* of the original theory Σ. The LUB is unique (up to logical equivalence) because the conjunction of any two upper bounds is another, possibly smaller upper-bound.

Example: Consider the non-Horn theory $\Sigma = (\neg p \vee r) \wedge (\neg q \vee r) \wedge (p \vee q)$. $p \wedge q \wedge r$ is an example of a Horn lower-bound; both $p \wedge r$ and $q \wedge r$ are GLBs; $(\neg p \vee r) \wedge (\neg q \vee r)$ is an example of a Horn upper-bound; and r is the LUB. The reader can verify these bounds by noting that

$$(p \wedge q \wedge r) \models (p \wedge r) \models \Sigma \models r \models ((\neg p \vee r) \wedge (\neg q \vee r))$$

Moreover, there is no Horn theory Σ' different from $p \wedge r$ such that $(p \wedge r) \models \Sigma' \models \Sigma$. Similar properties hold of the other GLB and of the LUB.

2.2 Using Bounds for Fast Inference

Let us now consider how these approximations can be used to improve the efficiency of a knowledge representation system. Suppose a knowledge base (KB) contains the set of clauses Σ, and we want to determine whether the formula α is implied by the KB. The system can proceed as follows. First, it tries to obtain an answer quickly by using the Horn approximations. If $\Sigma_{\text{lub}} \models \alpha$ then it returns "yes, logically follows" or if $\Sigma_{\text{glb}} \not\models \alpha$ then it returns "no, does not logically follow." So far, the procedure takes only time linear in the length of the approximations. (We assume that the lengths of the Horn approximations are roughly the same as that of the original theory; we return to this issue below.) In case no answer is obtained, the system could simply return "don't know," or it could decide to spend more time and use a general inference procedure to determine the answer directly from the original theory.[1] Thus the system can answer certain queries in linear time, resulting in a improvement in its overall response time. Exactly how many queries can be handled directly by the Horn approximations depends on how well the bounds characterize the original theory. Note that we give up neither soundness nor completeness, because we can always fall back to the original theory.

To make this discussion more concrete, consider the following interpretation of the propositional letters in the previous example:

$p \equiv$ Sally is a doctor
$q \equiv$ Sally is a lawyer
$r \equiv$ Sally is rich
$s \equiv$ Sally is a vegetarian

The theory Σ can be understood as asserting that if Sally is a doctor, then she is rich; if Sally is a lawyer, then she is rich; and Sally is a doctor or a lawyer. The LUB asserts that Sally is rich (r), and suppose the system generates the GLB that asserts that Sally is a rich doctor ($p \wedge r$). Now, the query "Does it follow that Sally is rich?" can immediately be answered "yes" because r is implied by the LUB. The query "Does it follow that Sally is a doctor?" is answered "don't know" because a is not implied by the LUB; the fact that it follows from the GLB is not relevant. Finally, the query "Does it follow that Sally is a vegetarian?" is answered "no", because s is not implied by the GLB.

Note these questions can all be answered in time linear in the size of the upper and lower bounds; thus, even if Σ were expanded to contain many more complex domains axioms the queries could still be answered efficiently. Furthermore, the GLB is always no larger than the original theory Σ itself. However, one can construct theories which have an exponentially larger least Horn upper-bound. We are currently investigating the question of whether it is always possible to generate a compact encoding of the LUB (one polynomial in the size of Σ) by introducing new propositional letters.

The system as described does not make any closed world assumptions; for example, it does not conclude "Sally is not a vegetarian." There may be a connection, however, between knowledge compilation and closed world reasoning, in that the logical closure of a theory is a lower bound of the theory.[2]

---

[1] The general inference procedure could still use the approximations to prune its search space.

[2] This observation is due to Mukesh Dalal and David Etherington.

```
GLB Algorithm
Input: a set of clauses Σ = {C1, C2, ..., Cn}.
Output: a greatest Horn lower-bound of Σ.
begin
    L := the lexicographically first Horn-
         strengthening of Σ
    loop
        L' := lexicographically next Horn-
              strengthening of Σ
        if none exists then exit
        if L |= L' then L := L'
    end loop
    remove subsumed clauses from L
    return L
end
```

Figure 1: Algorithm for generating a greatest Horn lower-bound.

2.3 Computing Horn Approximations

We now turn to the problem of generating Horn approximations. As shown in [14], there does not exist a polynomial time procedure for generating such approximations (provided P≠NP). Computing the Horn approximations is therefore treated as a compilation process in which the computational cost is amortized over the total set of subsequent queries to the KB. Since the approximations may be needed for query answering before the compilation process finishes, it is desirable to employ procedures that can output lower- and upper-bounds as intermediate results, generating better and better bounds over time. That is, the approximation algorithms should be "anytime" procedures [1].

Central to our algorithm for computing the GLB (Figure 1) is the following notion.

Definition: Horn-strengthening
A Horn clause C_{H} is a Horn-strengthening of a clause $C = \{x_1, \ldots, x_n\}$ iff $C_{\mathrm{H}} \subseteq C$ and there is no Horn clause C'_{H} such that $C_{\mathrm{H}} \subset C'_{\mathrm{H}} \subseteq C$.

The **GLB algorithm** systematically searches through the various possible Horn-strengthenings of the clauses of the original theory, looking for a most general one. This approach is illustrated with the following example.

Example: Consider the theory $(\neg p \vee q) \wedge (p \vee q \vee r)$. The **GLB algorithm** first tries the Horn-strengthening $L = (\neg p \vee q) \wedge p$, and then $L' = (\neg p \vee q) \wedge q$. Since $L \models L'$, L is set to L', and the algorithm proceeds. (L is used to store best bound obtained so far.) Since the last Horn strengthening $(\neg p \vee q) \wedge r$ is not an improvement, the algorithm returns q as a GLB (the clause $(\neg p \vee q)$ is removed because it is subsumed by q).

Note that the **GLB algorithm** is indeed an anytime algorithm: L represents some lower-

LUB Algorithm
Input: a set of clauses $\Sigma = \Sigma_H \cup \Sigma_N$, where
Σ_H is a set of Horn clauses, and Σ_N is a
set of non-Horn clauses.
Output: a least Horn upper-bound of Σ.

```
begin
    loop
        try to choose clause C0 ∈ ΣH ∪ ΣN and
            C1 ∈ ΣN, such that C2 = Resolve(C0, C1)
            is not subsumed by any clause in ΣH ∪ ΣN
        if no such choice is possible then exit loop
        if C2 is Horn then
            delete from ΣH and ΣN any clauses
                    subsumed by C2
            ΣH := ΣH ∪ {C2}
        else
            delete from ΣN any clauses subsumed by C2
            ΣN := ΣN ∪ {C2}
        end if
    end loop
    return ΣH
end
```

Figure 2: Algorithm for generating a least Horn upper-bound.

bound whenever the algorithm is interrupted.

The **LUB algorithm** shown in Figure 2 exploits that fact that the LUB is logically equivalent to the set of Horn resolvents of the theory. Since even a Horn theory can have exponentially many resolvents (all Horn), it is very inefficient to simply generate all resolvents of the original theory while collecting the Horn ones. It sufficient, however, to resolve only pairs of clauses containing at least one non-Horn clause [15].

3 General Framework

Computing Horn approximations is just one kind of knowledge compilation. This section defines a general framework for approximating a knowledge base. The next section presents a number of different instances of this general framework.

A *knowledge compilation system* is a tuple $\langle \mathcal{L}, \models, \mathcal{L}_S, \mathcal{L}_T, \mathcal{L}_Q, f_L, f_U \rangle$ containing the following components:

$\mathcal{L}$ is a formal language. We identify a language with the set of all its sentences.

$\models$ is a consequence relation over sets of sentences in $\mathcal{L}$. In most of the examples we will study $\models$ has its usual meaning of logical entailment, but the framework allows $\models$ to represent other relationships, such as subsumption.

$\mathcal{L}_S$ is the "source" sublanguage of $\mathcal{L}$, used to express a general knowledge base.

$\mathcal{L}_T$ is the "target" sublanguage of $\mathcal{L}$, used to express approximations to the general knowledge base. It should be easier in some sense (analytically or empirically) to determine if a query is a consequence of a set of sentences in $\mathcal{L}_T$ than of a set sentences in $\mathcal{L}_S$.

$\mathcal{L}_Q$ is the "query" sublanguage of $\mathcal{L}$.

f_L is a function mapping a theory to a (potentially infinite) sequence of (better and better) lower-bounds (defined analogously to the Horn case). Ideally the last element of the sequence is the greatest lower-bound (GLB).

f_U is a function mapping a theory to a (potentially infinite) sequence of (better and better) upper-bounds (again, defined analogously to the Horn case). Ideally the last element of the sequence is the least upper-bound (LUB).

Suppose a knowledge compilation system is presented a query $\alpha \in \mathcal{L}_Q$ after performing i compilation steps on the source theory Σ. Let Σ_{lb} be the *i-th* element of $f_L(\Sigma)$ (or the last element if i is greater than the length of $f_L(\Sigma)$), and Σ_{ub} be the *i-th* (or similarly the last) element of $f_U(\Sigma)$. As described earlier, if $\Sigma_{lb} \not\models \alpha$ then the system answers "no", if $\Sigma_{ub} \models \alpha$ then the system answers "yes", and otherwise it answers "unknown". A definite answer of "yes" or "no" always agrees with the answer to the question "does $\Sigma \models \alpha$?", even if the lower (upper) bound is not the greatest (least) bound.

The case of knowledge compilation using propositional Horn clauses fits into this framework as follows: $\mathcal{L}$ is propositional logic, $\models$ is propositional entailment, $\mathcal{L}_S$ is the set of clauses, $\mathcal{L}_T$ is the set of Horn clauses, and $\mathcal{L}_Q$ contains two kinds of formulas: (1) conjunctions of clauses (CNF); and (2) disjunctions of conjunctions of literals (DNF), where each disjunct contains at most one negative literal. (In this case the query language is strictly more expressive than either $\mathcal{L}_T$ or $\mathcal{L}_S$. The negation of such queries, however, is equivalent to a set of Horn clauses of the same size as the original query, so the linear time algorithm for satisfiability of Horn clauses can be used for query answering.) f_L is given by the sequence of candidate Horn-strengthenings of Σ, as in the previous section, where the last element of the sequence is in fact the GLB. Similarly, f_L is the sequence of larger and larger sets of Horn resolvants where the last such set is the LUB.

4 Other Instances of Knowledge Compilation

4.1 Restricted Clausal Forms

An entire class of knowledge compilation systems can be realized by generalizing the algorithms for the propositional Horn case. The idea of a Horn-strengthening is generalized as follows:

Definition: θ-strengthening

Let θ be a particular set of clauses. A clause in that set is called a θ-clause. A clause C_T is a θ-strengthening of a clause C iff $C_T \subseteq C$ and there is no θ-clause C'_T such that $C_T \subset C'_T \subseteq C$. A θ-strengthening of a set of clauses is a set of θ-strengthenings of each clause.

A knowledge compilation system is created by letting the source language $\mathcal{L}_S$ be the set of arbitrary clauses, and the target language $\mathcal{L}_T$ be such a clause set θ. Suppose such a θ is closed under resolution (*i.e.*, the resolvents of two θ-clauses is a θ-clause). Then the completeness theorem for resolution [10] tells us that *any* (non-tautologous) clause C entailed by a set of θ-clauses Σ must be subsumed by a clause C' which has a resolution proof from Σ; and therefore C' is a θ-clause itself. In other words, Σ entails a θ-strengthening of C. Further suppose that any clause in the source language has a θ-strengthening. Then the GLB in terms of θ-clauses of a theory Σ can be computed by searching for a (local) maximum in the space of θ-strengthenings of Σ. This proves the following theorem:

Theorem 1 *Let Σ be any set of clauses and θ a set of clauses such that (i) the resolvant of any two clauses in θ is also in θ, and (ii) any clause in Σ is subsumed by some clause in θ. Then Σ_{glb} is a greatest lower-bound in terms of θ-clauses iff Σ_{glb} is equivalent to a θ-strengthening of Σ, and there is no θ-strengthening Σ'_{glb} such that $\Sigma_{\text{glb}} \models \Sigma'_{\text{glb}}$ and $\Sigma'_{\text{glb}} \not\models \Sigma_{\text{glb}}$.*

Horn, reverse Horn (clauses containing at most one *negative* literal), and clauses containing two or fewer literals are examples of tractable classes of propositional clauses that meet the conditions of this theorem.

Recall that the Horn LUB of a theory is equivalent to the set of all its Horn resolvants. This is due to the resolution completeness theorem and the fact that propositional Horn clauses are closed under *subsumption*. The latter condition is necessary because one could otherwise imagine cases where resolution only yielded non-Horn clauses which subsumed the entailed Horn clauses. Thus the generalized computation of the Horn LUB is based on the following theorem:

Theorem 2 *Let Σ be any set of clauses and θ a set of clauses such that if $C \in \theta$ and C' subsumes C, then $C' \in \theta$. Then Σ_{lub} is the least upper-bound in terms of θ-clauses of Σ iff Σ_{lub} is equivalent to the set of θ resolvants of Σ.*

As we noted before, it is not actually necessary to compute *all* the θ resolvants of Σ, but only a subset logically equivalent to the entire set, as in the Horn case. All of the classes of restricted clauses mentioned above meet the condition of being closed under subsumption.

Another interesting class which satisfies theorems 1 and 2 consists of clauses *not* containing a given set of propositional letters. (The θ-strengthening of the clause p, where p is a prohibited letter, is the empty clause — that is, false.) While such a class may not have better worst-case complexity than the unrestricted language, it may be empirically desirable to "compile away" certain propositions. Subramanian and Genesereth [16] present a formal system for inferring that certain propositions are *irrelevant* to the computation of a given class of queries. Given this sense of what is irrelevant, knowledge compilation can then be used as way to remove the irrelevant information and simplify the theory.

The class of clauses not containing a given set of letters has the following special property, which follows from Craig's Interpolation Lemma [4]: The LUB is just as good as the original theory for answering queries not containing the prohibited letters. Formally:

Theorem 3 *Let Σ be a set of clauses and both θ and $\mathcal{L}_Q$ sets of clauses not containing a given set of propositional letters. Suppose $\alpha \in \mathcal{L}_Q$, and Σ_{lub} is the the least upper-bound in terms of θ-clauses of Σ. Then $\Sigma \models \alpha$ iff $\Sigma_{\text{lub}} \models \alpha$.*

Example: Let the set of propositions be instantiations of the two-place predicates F and R over a given set of individuals $\{a, b, c\}$. We interpret F as meaning "father of", and R as meaning "related to". The following axiom schema capture the usual relationship between these predicates, where the variables x, y, and z are instantiated over the given set of individuals:

$$F(x,y) \supset R(x,y)$$
$$R(x,y) \wedge R(y,z) \supset R(x,z)$$
$$R(x,y) \supset R(y,x)$$

Suppose Σ consists of these axioms together with a set of facts about specific father-of relationships: $\{F(a,b), F(b,c) \vee F(a,c)\}$. If it were known that queries would concern only the related-to predicate, it would be useful to compute the LUB that prohibits the letter F. This yields a theory (equivalent to) the last two axiom schema (transitivity and reflexivity) together with the the facts $\{R(a,b), R(b,c)\}$.

4.2 First-Order Theories

A further natural extension of restricted clausal forms is to first-order languages. In the first-order case, the worst-case complexity of the general and restricted languages are the same. For example, satisfiability for first-order clauses and first-order Horn clauses is equally undecidable.[3] None the less, the restricted language may have better average-case complexity for a particular domain. In this section we will examine the issues that arise in a straightforward extension of restricted clausal knowledge compilation systems to the first-order case.

We have seen how the greatest-lower bound of a theory Σ can be computed by searching through the space of $\mathcal{L}_T$-strengthenings of Σ. In order to decide if a candidate strengthening Σ'_{lb} is a better lower-bound than the current strengthening Σ_{lb}, the algorithm must

[3]A ***first-order clause*** is a sentence in prenex form containing only universal quantifiers, whose matrix is a disjunction of (first-order) literals. A ***first-order Horn clause*** is a first-order clause containing at most one positive literal.

check if $\Sigma_{lb} \models \Sigma'_{lb}$. In the first-order case this test is not recursive, so the simple search procedure could become "stuck" at Σ_{lb}, even if it is not the greatest lower-bound.

Fortunately, it is not difficult to avoid this problem. The computation steps to determine $\Sigma_{lb} \models \Sigma'_{lb}$ should be interleaved with the generation and test of the lexicographically next candidate $\mathcal{L}_T$-strengthening Σ''_{lb}. If the test $\Sigma_{lb} \models \Sigma''_{lb}$ returns "true", the computation for $\Sigma_{lb} \models \Sigma'_{lb}$ can be abandoned. Similarly the computation for $\Sigma_{lb} \models \Sigma''_{lb}$ can be interleaved with the generation and test of the following candidate strengthening, and so forth. With this modification the generalized **GLB algorithm** is correct for any knowledge compilation system where $\mathcal{L}_S$ consists of first-order clauses, and $\mathcal{L}_T$ is a class of first-order clauses which satisfies the conditions of Theorem 1.

The basic **LUB algorithm** need not be modified for first-order target languages that are closed under subsumption. Theorems 2 and 3 thus hold true for first-order as well as for propositional clauses, where "propositional letter" is understood to mean "predicate". While the classes based on restricting the length of the clauses (or the predicates contained in the clauses) are close, the first-order Horn and reverse Horn classes are *not*. For example, the non-Horn clause $\forall x, y \,.\, P(x, b) \vee P(a, y)$ properly subsumes the Horn clause $P(a, b)$. Therefore the LUB in the first-order Horn case must also incorporate Horn clauses that are subsumed by non-Horn resolvants, as stated in the following theorem.

Theorem 4 *A set of first-order clauses Σ_{lub} is the least Horn upper-bound of a set of first-order clauses Σ iff Σ_{lub} is equivalent to the set of Horn clauses subsumed by resolvants of Σ.*

Similar conditions apply to the reverse Horn case. In [15] we present an algorithm for generating the LUB based on theorem 4.

Finally, we note that the query language $\mathcal{L}_Q$ should be such that the negation of a query falls in $\mathcal{L}_T$. Thus, in general, the queries will be existentially-quantified sentences whose matrix is a subset of DNF. For example, in the Horn case, each disjunct contains at most one negative literal; in the binary clause case, each disjunct contains at most two literals; and so on.

4.3 Definite Clauses and Logic Programs

A *definite clause* is a clause containing exactly one positive literal. Languages based on definite clauses can be efficiently implemented and have found widespread practical applications. For example, function-free first-order definite clauses form the basis of the database language "datalog" [17], and general first-order definite clauses form the basis of the programming language Prolog. (In both cases, non-logical operators such as "cut" and "failure to prove" extend the logical basis.)

It is not possible, in general, to find a definite clause lower-bound of a general theory. For example, there is no definite clause lower-bound for the theory $\{\neg p\}$.

Least upper-bounds do exist, as they do for *any* source and target languages — because the empty set is a trivial upper-bound, and the least upper-bound is equivalent to the union of all upper-bounds. However, definite clauses are not closed under subsumption; for example, the non-definite clause $\neg p$ subsumes the definite clause $\neg p \vee q$. Therefore the original **LUB algorithm** is not sufficient. A version of theorem 4 *does* hold, where "Horn" is replaced by "definite clause", and can be used as the basis for an algorithm (for both the propositional and first-order cases). For example, the definite clause LUB of $\{\neg p\}$ is the set of all (binary) definite clauses subsumed by $\neg p$, *i.e.*, $\{\neg p \vee q,\ \neg p \vee r,\ \neg p \vee s,\ \ldots\}$. In effect, $\neg p$ is approximated by "p implies anything," since the LUB is equivalent to $\{p \supset q,\ p \supset r,\ p \supset s,\ \ldots\}$.

Both lower and upper bounds do exist when the source language as well as the target language consists of definite clauses. Some recent research on the analysis of Prolog programs (for use in, for example, optimization and program specification) can be viewed as a kind of knowledge compilation. For example, [9] describes how to construct a *recursive* (*i.e.*, decidable) approximation to a potentially non-recursive logic program. Their method is based on modifying each predicate by relaxing the relationship between the arguments to the predicate. For example, if a logic program computes (entails) $\{P(a,b) \wedge P(c,d)\}$, the approximation computes (entails) $\{P(a,b) \wedge P(c,d) \wedge P(a,d) \wedge P(c,b)\}$. Thus their method computes a lower-bound of the theory (but not in general the greatest lower-bound).

4.4 Terminological Reasoning

We now consider frame-based knowledge representation languages as studied in [12] (see also [13]).

Levesque and Brachman consider a language $\mathcal{FL}$ in which one can describe structured concepts in terms of other concepts, either complex or primitive. For example, if we wished to describe people whose male friends are all doctors with some specialty, we could use the concept:

```
(person with every male friend is a (doctor with a specialty)).
```

This concept is captured in $\mathcal{FL}$ by

```
(AND person
     (ALL (RESTR friend male)
          (AND doctor
               (SOME specialty)))),
```

which contains all the constructs (the capitalized terms) used in the language. Levesque and Brachman consider the complexity of determining whether one concept *subsumes* another. For example, the concept

```
(person with every male friend is a doctor)
```

subsumes the one given above. Note that this can be determined without really knowing anything about the various concepts used in these descriptions. Now, their central technical result is that determining subsumption in $\mathcal{FL}$ is intractable, but that removing the RESTR construct leads to polynomial time computable subsumption. The restricted language is called $\mathcal{FL}^-$.

So for efficient subsumption, one can use the language $\mathcal{FL}^-$. But this language may not be sufficiently expressive for practical applications. Knowledge compilation provides again an alternative. In this case the idea is to take a concept description in the language $\mathcal{FL}$ and to approximate it using two concept descriptions in $\mathcal{FL}^-$: a best lower-bound, *i.e.*, the most general more specific concept in $\mathcal{FL}^-$, and a best upper-bound, *i.e*, the most specific more general (subsuming) concept in $\mathcal{FL}^-$.

As an example consider the first concept given above. It is not difficult to see that the concepts `person` and

```
(AND person
     (ALL friend
          (AND doctor
               (SOME specialty))))
```

in $\mathcal{FL}^-$ are examples of, respectively, an upper-bound and a lower-bound in $\mathcal{FL}^-$. (These are also the best bounds in this case.) The system can store such bounds with the original concept description, and use them to try to determine quickly whether the newly given concept subsumes it or is subsumed by it.

More formally, we are dealing with the knowledge compilation system $\langle \mathcal{FL}, \Rightarrow, \mathcal{FL}, \mathcal{FL}^-, \mathcal{FL}, f_{\rm L}, f_{\rm U} \rangle$, in which $\Rightarrow$ stands for "is subsumed by." We are currently working on anytime compilation algorithms for computing the functions $f_{\rm L}$ and $f_{\rm U}$. (Note that queries are assumed to be in $\mathcal{FL}$. We conjecture that the subsumption relation between a concept given in $\mathcal{FL}$ and one in $\mathcal{FL}^-$ (*i.e.*, one of bounds) can be determined efficiently.)

So far, we have treated our knowledge base as containing only a single concept description. In general, a KB will of course contain a hierarchy of concepts [2]. In that case, we simply store bounds with each concept. When given a concept, the system can use those bounds in determining the appropriate place of the new concept in the hierarchy.

5 Conclusions

We introduced the notion of knowledge compilation. The central idea behind knowledge compilation is to translate (compile) declarative knowledge into a more efficient form. A unique advantage of our approach is the use of both lower and upper bounds can speed reasoning without giving up correctness or completeness.

We discussed various concrete examples of our approach. In particular, we showed how the procedures for compiling propositional theories into Horn theories [14] can be generalized to apply to other tractable classes of clauses. Those classes were characterized using various closure conditions. The classes containing reverse-Horn clauses, clauses with two or fewer literals, or clauses not containing a certain set of "irrelevant letters" are examples of classes that satisfy the closure conditions. We also showed how to modify our approach to handle the first-order case. Finally, we discussed the compilation of concept descriptions given in a terminological representation languages. This example showed that our knowledge compilation approach appears suited for dealing with a large variety of knowledge representations language — not only traditional logics.

Currently we are working on empirical evaluation of our knowledge compilation approach. The domain under study is a small part of Forbus's qualitative process theory [7]. Qualitative axiomatizations of the physical world can be used to reason about everyday activities such as boiling water, rolling balls, or perhaps even the steeplechasing crocodile mentioned in the introduction. We hope to automatically convert the original non-Horn axiomization of qualitative process theory into Horn approximations; in essence, automating part of the work that Forbus performed when implementing his theory using the ATMS [8].

References

[1] Mark Boddy and Thomas Dean. Solving time dependent planning problems. Technical report, Department of Computer Science, Brown University, 1988.

[2] Ronald J. Brachman, Deborah L. McGuinness, Peter F. Patel-Schneider, Lori Alperin Resnick, and Alexander Borgida. Living with classic: When and how to use a kl-one-like language. In J. Sowa, editor, *Formal Aspects of Semantic Networks*. Morgan Kaufmann, 1990.

[3] S. A. Cook. The complexity of theorem-proving procedures. In *Proceedings of the 3rd Annual ACM Symposium on the Theory of Computing*, pages 151–158, 1971.

[4] W. Craig. Three uses of the herbrand-gentzen theorem in relating model theory and proof theory. *Journal of Symbolic Logic*, 22, 1955.

[5] William F. Dowling and Jean H. Gallier. Linear time algorithms for testing the satisfiability of propositional horn formula. *Journal of Logic Programming*, 3:267–284, 1984.

[6] J. Doyle and R. Patil. Two theses of knowledge representation: Language restrictions, taxonomic classification, and the utility of representation services. *Artificial Intelligence*, 48(3):261–298, 1991.

[7] K.D. Forbus. Qualitative process theory. *Artificial Intelligence*, 24:85–168, 1984.

[8] Kenneth D. Forbus. The qualitative process engine. In Deaniel S. Weld and Johan de Kleer, editors, *Readings in Qualitative Reasoning About Physical Systems*, pages 220–235. Morgan Kaufmann, Los Altos, CA, 1990.

[9] Nevin Heintze and Joxan Jaffar. A finite presentation theorem for approximating logic programs. In *Proceedings of POPL-90*, page 197, 1990.

[10] R. C. T. Lee. *A Completeness Theorem and a Computer Program for Finding Theorems Derivable From Given Axioms.* PhD thesis, University of California at Berkeley, Berkeley, CA, 1967.

[11] Hector J. Levesque. Logic and the complexity of reasoning. Technical Report KRR-TR-89-2, Department of Computer Science, University of Toronto, Toronto, Ontario, Canada, Jan 1989.

[12] H.J. Levesque and R.J. Brachman. A fundamental tradeoff in knowledge representation and reasoning (revised version). In R.J. Brachman and H.J. Levesque, editors, *Readings in Knowledge Representation*, pages 41–70. Morgan Kaufmann, Los Altos, CA, 1985.

[13] P. Patel-Schneider, B. Owsnicki-Klewe, A. Kobsa, N. Guarino, R. MacGregor, W.S. Mark, D.L. McGuinness, B. Nebel, A. Schmiedel, and J. Yen. Term subsumption languages in knowledge representation. *AI Magazine*, 11(2):16–23, 1990.

[14] Bart Selman and Henry Kautz. Knowledge compilation using horn approximations. In *Proceedings of AAAI-91*, Anaheim, CA, 1991.

[15] Bart Selman and Henry Kautz. Methods of knowledge compilation. In Preparation, 1991.

[16] Devika Subramanian and Michael R. Genesereth. The relevance of irrelevance. In *Proceedings of IJCAI-87*, volume 1, page 416, 1987.

[17] Jeffrey D. Ullman. *Principles of Database and Knowledge-Base Systems, Volume I.* Computer Science Press, Rockville, MD, 88.

Data-driven Transformation of Meta-interpreters: A Sketch

Yannis Cosmadopoulos, Marek Sergot and Richard W. Southwick
Logic Programming Group,
Imperial College, London
yac@doc.ic.ac.uk

Abstract

We discuss a transformation method for compiling away meta-interpreters. Our technique is data-driven — references to object data are resolved away. The transformed program can be directly executed, exhibiting considerable savings in execution time and space usage. The method lends itself naturally to incremental compilation for a large subset of meta-interpreters.

1 Introduction

The use of meta-interpreters is a powerful technique in logic programming. Meta-interpreters are used to add functionality to a program without needing to modify the object language that is being interpreted. This separation of knowledge and control is an important programming technique, as it improves clarity and ease of maintenance.

Meta-interpreters can be used to implement layers of control (specialized search strategies, etc.), and to add other facilities (*e.g.* debugging tools and traces). Meta-interpreters are also useful in expert system construction (Hammond and Sergot [3], Sterling and Beer [10]), where they provide user interfaces, explanation, and other facilities necessary for system design.

The main problem with meta-interpreters is that adding a layer of evaluation produces a system that runs an order of magnitude more slowly. In this paper, we present a technique for achieving the benefits of meta-interpretation (a clean representation) without suffering the disadvantages. We describe a source-to-source transformation that "blends" meta-level information into an object-level program at compile time, producing a program that can be directly executed.

2 Program Transformation

This transformation is employed in the following manner: an object program is written in a declarative fashion. The transformer specializes the meta-interpreter to the object program. The resulting program has a behaviour indistinguishable to that of the original meta-interpreter acting on the object program.

To illustrate this blending process we shall use an interpreter that records the execution trace, which is useful for debugging or explanation (Figure 1). User interaction is handled through a query-the-user mechanism (Sergot [8]), whereby the user is asked to supply any missing information.

```
solve([], []) ←
solve([Goal|Rest], [ProofGoal|ProofRest]) ←
      solveOne(Goal, ProofGoal),
      solve(Rest, ProofRest)

solveOne(Goal, clause(Goal, ProofBody)) ←
      rule(Goal, Body),
      solve(Body, ProofBody)
solveOne(Goal, user(Goal)) ←
      askable(Goal),
      query_user(Goal)
```

Figure 1: A Meta-interpreter

Figure 2 is a simple database defining family relationships. The relations **mother** and **father** have been declared **askable**, indicating that they are to be furnished by the user. We make the assumption that the object level rules are represented in the form **rule(Head, Body)** for use by the meta-interpreter.

```
ancestor(X, Y) ← parent(X, Z), ancestor(Z, Y)
ancestor(X, Y) ← parent(X, Y)

parent(X, Y) ← mother(X, Y)
parent(X, Y) ← father(X, Y)
```

Figure 2: A family relationship database

Now consider how the functionality of the meta-interpreter of Figure 1 may be blended into this program. An extra argument to hold the execution trace is added to the head of each clause. Predicates which have been declared **askable** have new predicates generated for them.

Because the transformed program can be executed directly, this method yields a significant increase in speed of execution, at the expense of added complexity. The resulting transformed program is equivalent to the meta-interpreter acting on the untransformed

```
ancestor(X, Y, clause(ancestor(X, Y) [ParentTrace, AncestorTrace])) ←
    parent(X, Z, ParentTrace),
    ancestor(Z, Y, AncestorTrace)

mother(X, Y, user(mother(X, Y))) ← query_user(mother(X, Y))
```

Figure 3: Examples of blended clauses

database. The nature of the transformation is transparent to the user, though user queries need to be transformed to take into account any added arguments.

3 Producing the Transformer

A transformer for the meta-interpreter of Figure 1 yielding a program of the form of Figure 3 could be written by inspection (Cosmadopoulos and Southwick [1]). Here we illustrate a method of generating such a transformer automatically from the meta-interpreter.

Problems of mixing object and meta levels (such as the naming of object level variables at the meta-level) do not concern us. While a meta-interpreter may be intended to denote a provability relation over an object-level program, for our purposes it is to be considered simply as a program which manipulates data. We are only concerned with making meta-interpreters efficient, not justifying their correctness. In order to reduce confusion, however, we will continue to refer to the program as a "meta-interpreter", and the data as the "object-level program".

We require a transformation that preserves equivalence on queries provable through the meta-interpreter, not those directly on the data/object-level. Given a meta-interpreter (program) P, and object-level (data) D, our transformation produces a new program P_d such that

$$P(D) \vdash G \iff P_d \vdash G.$$

A large subset of meta-interpreters (including that of Figure 1) possess a common structure that allows the production of a generic transformer that applies to that class. For those that are not, it is always possible to specify the transformations to be applied. Finally, we note that the transformer is a program whose data is the meta-interpreter. Self-application of the transformer yields a new transformer specialized to that particular meta-interpreter.

Data Absorption

The major step in our transformation is to resolve every reference to the data in the meta-interpreter against the data definitions. This transformation is bottom-up and data-driven — the program is specialised to a given data set. This can be seen as a form of macro-processing (Kowalski [5]).

A major beneficial effect of this data-driven approach is that it lends itself naturally to incremental compilation, in that the transformation operates on single object program clauses. It allows for the compilation of entire programs, or of individual clauses.

The transformer will generate a number of new clauses, often but not always one new clause for every clause in the object program. The meta-interpreter clauses used in the resolution steps can be discarded and replaced by these new clauses. In addition, since we are only interested in preserving answer equivalence with respect to meta-interpreter goals, we can discard the object level program, so that the resultant program contains no references to the data.

As an example let us consider the effect of 'blending'

```
rule(ancestor(X, Y) [parent(X, Z), ancestor(Z, Y)])
```

with our meta-interpreter.

Resolving away data references (rule predicates) yields the new clauses

```
solveOne(ancestor(X, Y), clause(ancestor(X, Y), ProofBody)) ←
    solve([parent(X, Z), ancestor(Z, Y)], ProofBody)
```

Additionally, we resolve away the reference to askable in solveOne.

```
solveOne(mother(X, Y), user(mother(X, Y))) ← query_user(mother(X, Y))
```

Further Transformations

Further transformations may be applied to this program, their suitability dictated by the form of the meta-interpreter. Typically meta-interpreters consist of predicates designed to walk over the structure of a conjunctive goal (solve), selecting literals which are then passed on to predicates dealing with individual cases (solveOne). In such a case a simple transformation is to apply a sequence of resolution steps to eliminate all solve references in solveOne clauses. Resolving away references to solve yields the complete translated program.

```
solveOne(ancestor(X, Y), clause(ancestor(X, Y), [PA, PB])) ←
    solveOne(parent(X, Z), PA),
    solveOne(ancestor(Z, Y), PB)
solveOne(ancestor(X, Y), clause(ancestor(X, Y), [PA])) ←
    solveOne(parent(X, Y), PA)
solveOne(parent(X, Y), clause(parent(X, Y), [PA])) ← solveOne(mother(X, Y), PA)
solveOne(parent(X, Y), clause(parent(X, Y), [PA])) ← solveOne(father(X, Y), PA)
solveOne(mother(X, Y), user(mother(X, Y))) ← query_user(mother(X, Y))
solveOne(father(X, Y), user(father(X, Y))) ← query_user(father(X, Y))
```

User queries are properly treated as headless clauses, and the same transformation applied. Using the example transformation of the preceding section, a conjunctive query is transformed to a conjunction of solveOne predicates. The user query ?- solve([a, b]) would be transformed to the query ?- solveOne(a), solveOne(b). In the above example, note that the elimination of references to solve in solveOne, coupled with the ability to transform user queries, allows us to discard the definition of solve.

Predicate Renaming

The transformed program above, while significantly faster than an equivalent meta-interpreter, suffers from a major drawback. It consists entirely of a single predicate solveOne. In a practical system, with hundreds of object-level clauses, this could cause indexing problems.

To overcome this difficulty we apply a renaming transformation. For each functor symbol F corresponding to an object level predicate, we introduce a new predicate symbol F* defined as

$$F^*(\underline{X}, Args) \leftrightarrow solveOne(F(\underline{X}), Args)$$

This would allow us to rewrite the program as

```
ancestor*(X, Y, clause(ancestor(X, Y), [PA, PB])) ←
      parent*(X, Z, PA)
      ancestor*(Z, Y, PB)
ancestor*(X, Y, clause(ancestor(X, Y), [P])) ← parent*(X, Y, P)
parent*(X, Y, clause(parent(X, Y), [PA])) ← mother*(X, Y, PA)
parent*(X, Y, clause(parent(X, Y), [PA])) ← father*(X, Y, PA)
mother*(X, Y, user(mother(X, Y))) ← query_user(mother(X, Y))
father*(X, Y, user(father(X, Y))) ← query_user(father(X, Y))
```

The transformed program no longer contains any references to the meta-level predicates, nor indeed to those of the object level program. This program could be executed directly by a theorem prover such as Prolog, taking full advantage of compilation and optimisation techniques.

4 Generation of the Compiler

The previous section sketched the kind of transformations that are performed in compiling an object-level program for a given interpreter. Here we describe the general procedure for generating a compiler to perform these transformations.

In general, to write a compiler for a program, we need to specify the transformation steps we require it to perform. It is always possible to apply the *absorption* step (the bottom up resolution), but further transformations depend on the form of the meta-interpreter. Further transformations are most obvious where the meta-interpreter is 'Prolog-like' – if it works backwards from a goal and employs a depth-first search strategy. In this case, partial evaluation may be used to eliminate the recursive components of the meta-interpreter. Variations in the computation rule (selection of goals) are relatively easy to cope with.

For other kinds of meta-interpreter, such as the forward-reasoning Prolog meta-interpreter described by Yamamoto and Tanaka [12], it is not always so easy to devise further transformations after the absorption step.

Once these transformation steps are specified, we have the transformer (or compiler) for the interpreter. The transformer is itself a meta-interpreter whose object-level data is the original interpreter. Thus this transformer can be specialized to optimize its performance, using the techniques described in this paper. A general transformer, able to compile a large class of meta-interpreters, can thus be specialized to generate an efficient compiler for any given interpreter of this class.

Schematically, we construct a transformer T which takes as inputs a meta-interpreter P and a object program D, and generates a new program P_d. Specialization of T yields a new transformer T^* which takes as input D only, giving P_d. Note that after specialization, the interpreter P can be discarded.

5 Partial Evaluation

Partial evaluation (Komorowski [4]) has been proposed as a technique for dealing with the problem of removing unnecessary layers of interpretation, and has been applied to meta-interpreters (Takeuchi and Furukawa [11], Sterling and Beer [10]). The process of partial evaluation can be seen as 'running' a program with a partially instantiated query. All non-evaluable predicates are collected, comprising the conditions for the success of the original query. Special features are necessary to deal with the impure aspects of partially evaluating full Prolog (see *e.g.* Lakhotia and Sterling [6], Sahlin [7]).

Our transformation makes use of the folding and unfolding operations that are the basis for partial evaluation. The fundamental difference is that our transformation is driven by the object-level data, rather than by specializing to a query. Every data reference in the meta-interpreter is resolved against the object data. This *bottom-up* transformation specializes the program to a particular *data set* — the object-level program. Partial evaluation, operating top-down, specializes a program to a particular *query*.

In contrast to our data-driven approach which compiles clauses individually, partial evaluation does not lend itself naturally to incremental compilation. Changes to the object-level program invalidate previous results of partial evaluation, and require its re-evaluation from scratch. Considerable additional work is required to achieve incrementality in partial evaluation (as for example in Fujita and Furukawa [2]).

6 Evaluation of the Transformer

To evaluate the performance of the described transformation, a series of tests were performed, using the well-known "naive reverse" program as a benchmark.

We timed direct execution of the program, and the 'vanilla' meta-interpreter. The transformed program for the vanilla meta-interpreter is isomorphic to the untransformed program. Figure 4 shows the results with bracketed figures indicating time spent garbage collecting.

length	100	200	300	400	500
direct (ms)	116	300	550	950	1400
vanilla (ms)	6733	33150 (6950)	76683 (18067)	133217 (29350)	207084 (45251)

Figure 4: Timing results (seconds in compiled Quintus Prolog)

Before garbage collection is invoked, the blended program is 60 times as fast as the meta-interpreter. In addition, meta-interpreters impose a hidden speed overhead — their higher space requirements cause invocation of the garbage collector at an earlier stage than for direct execution, leading to further deterioration in performance.

7 Summary and Acknowledgements

The high overhead incurred through the use of meta-interpreters can be avoided by applying a program that blends the functionality of the meta-interpreter with an object program, producing a new program that is answer-equivalent. This blending transformer can be produced automatically from a meta-interpreter by a series of transformations, the primary aim of which is to eliminate references to object data. Due to the bottom-up nature of the transformation, the technique is suitable for incremental compilation.

This approach has been implemented. We have a general compiler generator which deals with a large class of common interpreters (and other programs). This generator has been used in practice to generate compilers for meta-interpreters implementing query the user, reason maintenance, communication with external packages and other facilities. These compilers are being used in FOCUS, an ESPRIT project concerned with building intelligent front ends, and in the expert system shell Σkilaki (Sergot and Cosmadopoulos [9]). Evaluation figures show that up to two order of magnitude speed-up can be gained.

The work described in this paper was funded in part by ESPRIT project 2620: FOCUS. The authors would like to thank Tony Kakas, for his discussions and comments.

References

[1] Y. Cosmadopoulos and R. W. Southwick. Using meta-level information for expert system control: A 'blending' transformer approach. In N. Shadbolt, editor, *Research*

and Development in Expert Systems VI, pages 54–65. Cambridge University Press, 1989.

[2] H. Fujita and K. Furukawa. A self-applicable partial evaluator and its use in incremental compilation. Technical Report TM-367, ICOT, Tokyo, Japan, 1987.

[3] P. Hammond and M. J. Sergot. A PROLOG shell for logic based expert systems. In *Proceedings of the Third BCS Expert Systems Conference*, Cambridge, 1983.

[4] J. Komorowski. *A Specification of an Abstract Prolog Machine and its Application to Partial Evaluation.* PhD thesis, Linköping University, 1982.

[5] R. A. Kowalski. *Logic for Problem Solving.* North Holland, Amsterdam, 1979.

[6] A. Lakhotia and L. Sterling. ProMiX: A prolog partial evaluation system. In L. I. Sterling, editor, *The Practice of Prolog*, pages 137–179. MIT Press, 1990.

[7] D. Sahlin. *An Automatic Partial Evaluator for Full Prolog.* PhD thesis, Swdish Institute of Computer Science, Stockholm, 1991.

[8] M. J. Sergot. A query-the user facility for logic programming. In P. Degano and E. Sandewall, editors, *Integrated Interactive Computer Systems*, pages 27–41. North Holland, 1983.

[9] M. J. Sergot and Y. Cosmadopoulos. The logic programming system σkilaki: Design and implementation. Technical report, Logic Programming Group, Imperial College, London, 1991.

[10] L. Sterling and R. D. Beer. Meta-interpreters for expert system construction. Technical report, Case Western Reserve University, Cleveland, Ohio, USA, 1985.

[11] A. Takeuchi and K. Furukawa. Partial evaluation of Prolog programs and its application to meta programming. Technical Report TR-126, ICOT, Tokyo, Japan, 1985.

[12] A. Yamamoto and H. Tanaka. Translating production rules into a forward reasoning Prolog program. *New Generation Computing*, 4(1):97–105, 1986.

Improving the efficiency of constraint logic programming languages by deriving specialized versions*

M. Bruynooghe, V. Dumortier and G. Janssens**

Department of Computer Science, K.U.Leuven
Celestijnenlaan 200A, B-3001 Heverlee

Abstract

Extending logic programming to constraint logic programming has substantially broadened the range of problems solvable in a declarative style. However experiments with the Prolog III system showed that the generality of the constraint solving often incurs a heavy performance penalty for the - often occurring - special cases in which the problem has a simple algorithmic solution. This paper investigates - in the context of Prolog III - the feasibility of automatically extracting specialized versions. This is illustrated on some examples. Extraction of the specialized version is based on a transformation technique "compiling control" which was originally devised for transforming logic programs requiring a special computation rule into Prolog programs.

1. Introduction

Typical for logic programs is that, at least in principle, a predicate can be queried in different ways. So, generated code has to be general enough to cope with different kinds of data flow. The price to be paid for this generality is a performance penalty. The most important step in closing the performance gap with imperative languages has been the design of the WAM [10], but, for some programs, a substantial difference remains. To further close the gap, some authors have proposed to generate different versions - corresponding to different patterns of usage - for the same predicate [1,8,11], e.g. one version of append for concatenating and another for splitting lists.

The introduction of constraint logic programming [3,9] has broadened the range of problems solvable in a declarative style, but if general constraint solving is always applied it also aggravates the performance gap. For a problem having a clean expression in Prolog, the difference in efficiency between its Prolog III [4] program and its Prolog version running on a finetuned implementation can be substantial. Again, a way out

* Work accomplished with support from ESPRIT project PRINCE (CEC), National Funds for Scientific Research (Belgium), DPWB project RFO-AI-02 (Belgium)

** Email: {maurice, veroniek, gerda}@cs.kuleuven.ac.be

seems to be to generate different versions for the same procedure and to select - preferably at compile time - the appropriate version. Such a course has also been taken by Alan Borning in his constraint solving work [6].

In this paper the problems associated with automatic generation of specialized versions are studied for some Prolog III programs. The extraction of a specialized version is based on a transformation technique "compiling control" [2,5] which we have developed to transform logic programs requiring a special computation rule into Prolog programs.

2. Examples

In this section we consider some Prolog III programs together with a description of the class of intended queries - given by their instantiation pattern. For each argument one of the following abstractions is given : X_i^v denotes a free variable, X_i^g a ground term, X_i^a any term and $f(X_1, \ldots, X_n)$ a term with f/n as functor with X_i as abstraction of its ith argument. For each program and each instantiation pattern for the query, there exists an optimal or target program, which avoids the invocation of the general constraint solving techniques as much as possible or, in other words, which is as close to ordinary Prolog as possible. For example, in case of numerical constraints, simple arithmetic evaluation and assignment may suffice, thus completely eliminating the use of the constraint solver. During the execution of a Prolog III program constraints are stepwise added to the set of constraints and they are dealt with by the corresponding constraint solver, which is considered as a black box. However, compile-time analysis can often reveal when a particular constraint will be activated and how the dataflow inside it will be. In such cases, it is preferable to avoid activation of the general constraint solver. Instead, an ordinary Prolog call can be inserted at the appropriate place and directly be executed when activated by the standard left to right computation rule.

In the sequel, such a compile-time analysis is performed by constructing and analysing a so called symbolic trace; the specialised version is then obtained by synthesizing either a Prolog III or ordinary Prolog program from the trace. The symbolic trace is basically an abstraction of an incomplete SLD-tree. Abstraction in the sense that concrete arguments are replaced by their abstractions as explained above. The idea is explained in [2] and formally developed in [5]. The extension towards CLP means that a node (state) not only consists of a conjunction of abstracted subgoals but also of a conjunction of abstracted constraints (the latter enclosed by { }). The computation rule is defined as follows:

—Selection of a constraint has priority over the selection of an ordinary subgoal. However, a constraint may only be selected as soon as it has become sufficiently instantiated. E.g., the numerical constraint $X > Y$ is selected if the values of X and Y are known; the constraint $X = Y - Z$ is selected as soon as the value of at least two variables is known and it is then transformed into the appropriate call of is/2.

—If no constraint is sufficiently instantiated, the leftmost ordinary subgoal is selected.

—If no subgoals are left and the constraint set is not empty, the constraint set has to be dealt with by the general constraint solving algorithm of Prolog III.

2.1 EXAMPLE: Length of a list

*Original program**

```
length([], 0).
length([H | T], N):- length(T, NT) { N > 0, NT = N - 1 }.
```

We consider two classes of queries with the following instantiation patterns : *length*(L^v,N^g) to construct a list of variables of a given length and *length*(L^g,N^v) to compute the length of a given list. Note that the first class can easily be generalized to *length*(L^a,N^g) in order to include *length*(L^g,N^g). For each class of queries we first give the target program and then we investigate the transformation process.

2.1.1 *length*(L^v,N^g)

Target program

In this case general numerical constraint solving, which calls upon the simplex method, can be completely eliminated : the aimed specialization has a clean expression in Prolog:

```
length([], 0).
length([H | T], N):- N > 0, NT is N - 1, length(T, NT).
```

Symbolic trace

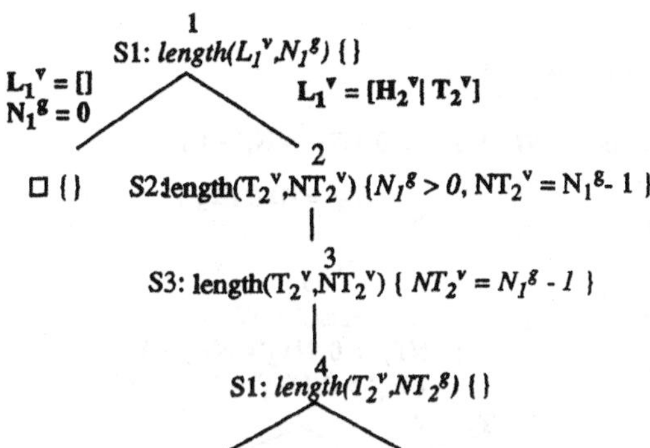

Fig. 1: Symbolic trace tree of length(L^v,N^g). The selected subgoal or constraint is printed in italic

The construction of the symbolic trace tree is illustrated in Fig. 1. State 1 shows the abstraction of the query, i.e. the goal *length*(L_1^v,N_1^g). Using the first clause, the unifications $L_1^v = []$ and $N_1^g = 0$ are performed. The first one causes L_1 to become ground. The arc of the trace tree is labelled with these unifications. The derived state is the empty goal □. Use of the second clause causes a unification $L_1^v = [H_2^v | T_2^v]$ and yields the state labelled S2. In this state, the constraint $N_1^g > 0$ is selected and state S3 is derived.

Now, the constraint $NT_2^v = N_1^g - 1$ is selected. Its activation instantiates NT_2^v, making it ground (NT_2^g) in the next state. This state is actually a renaming of the starting state. It is useless to continue (the trace tree could be folded into a graph) since one would only repeat the same pattern.

* We do not use the original Prolog III syntax but the more familiar Edinburgh variant; typical for Prolog III are the constraints enclosed by { }.

Synthesis

The key is to replace the constraints by appropriate subgoals, i.e. the constraint $N_1^g > 0$ by the subgoal $N_1^g > 0$ and $NT_2^v = N_1^g - 1$ by NT_2^v is $N_1^g - 1$. One can then apply the synthesis technique described in [2] and [5]. This yields the following (meta)program:

```
S1(length([],0)).
S1(length([H | T],N)):- N > 0, NT is N - 1, S1(length(T,NT)).
```

Applying a simple transformation - eliminating the superfluous functors as described in [7] - would yield a renaming of the target program.

2.1.2 *length(L^g,N^v)*

Target program

Again, we want to obtain an ordinary Prolog program in which general numeric constraint solving is no longer performed.

```
length([], 0).
length([H | T], N):- length(T, NT), N is NT + 1 /*, N > 0 */.
```

Note that the test N > 0 will automatically be fulfilled. However, elimination of redundant constraints is not straightforward; its discussion, as well as the derivation of a version with accumulating parameters, is beyond the scope of this paper.

Symbolic trace

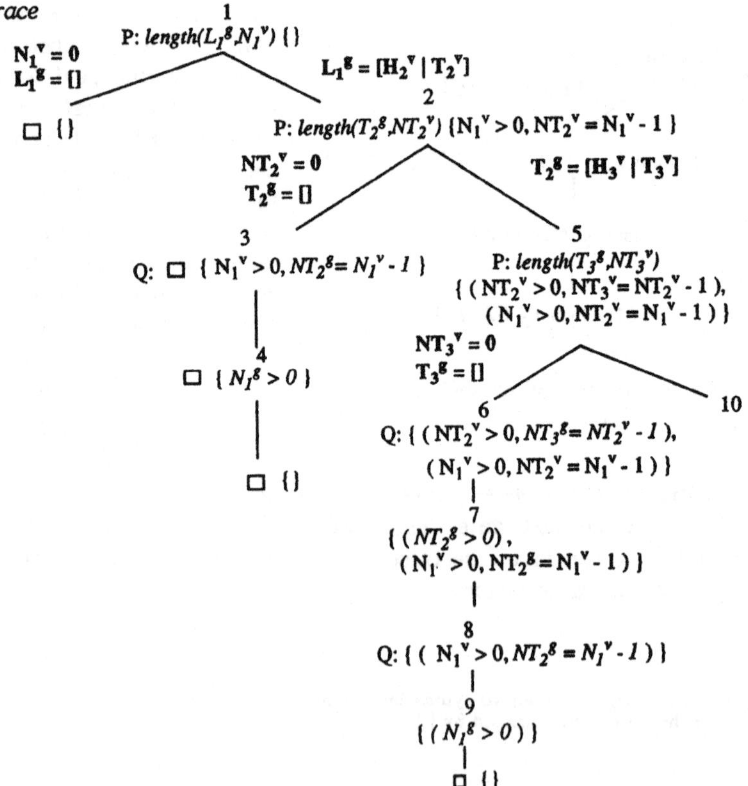

Fig. 2: Symbolic trace tree of length(L^g,N^v)

The symbolic trace tree constructed for the abstract call pattern *length*(L^g_1,N^v_1) is shown in Fig. 2. The numerical constraints are delayed until they are of the form $N^g_i > 0$ and $NT^g_{i+1} = N^v_i - 1$ respectively.

States 1, 2, 5 and 10 are all states having one goal length(T^g_i,NT^v_i) and zero or more times the group of constraints { $NT^v_i > 0$, $NT^v_{i+1} = NT^v_i - 1$ }. Such states, although not renamings of each other, are easily recognized in an automatic way [5] Consequently, is is not necessary to construct the symbolic trace beyond state 10.

Synthesis

Again, the basis of the synthesis is to replace constraints by ordinary subgoals, i.e. the constraint $NT^g_i > 0$ by the subgoal $NT^g_i > 0$ and the constraint $NT^g_{i+1} = NT^v_i - 1$ by NT^v_i is $NT^g_{i+1} + 1$. Applying the synthesis of [2,5] yields the following program:

```
I(length(L,N)):-  P(length(L,N), []).

/* P - Q transitions */
P(length([],0), Cs):-  Q(Cs).
/* P - P transitions */
P(length([H|T],N), Cs):-  P(length(T,NT), [N>0, NT=N-1 | Cs]).

/* Q - □ transitions */
Q([]).
/* Q - Q transitions */
Q([N > 0, NT = N - 1 | Cs]):-  N is NT + 1, N > 0, Q(Cs).
```

This program is tail-recursive but has the drawback that the list of constraints to be processed is carried around (the operations to be performed after completing the recursive predicate P are stacked). A slight improvement could be to stack only the variables NT_i; the constraints can then be reconstructed within the Q predicate.

However, a more important optimization turns up when analyzing the symbolic trace: instead of recursively activating constraints within the Q predicate, they can be shifted back to their original context (where they were created). In fact, this corresponds to replacing the constraints in the original program by ordinary subgoals and by then simply reordering these goals. The second clause is then rewritten as length([H|T],N):- length(T,NT), N is NT + 1, N > 0 . This corresponds exactly to the target program.

2.1.3 Discussion

In these two examples, we notice that constraints are generated, selected and executed according to a very regular pattern. This allows to replace them by ordinary subgoals and to insert these at the right place to be activated by the standard computation rule of Prolog. In general, the synthesized program explicitly manipulates the constraint set. Often however - as in both cases above - the explicit storage and selection of constraints can be eliminated, when constraints can be activated within their original scope; this corresponds to finding an adequate ordering of the subgoals.
We expect that these observations hold for many simple predicates. We envision it is worthwhile to consider the development of libraries of specialized versions of such basic predicates. When used in conventional ways (to be detected at compile-time when possible) a very fast version (in fact faster than in nowadays commercial Prolog

systems as more information, i.e. mode information, is available) should be selected; when used in irregular ways, the general purpose Prolog III version can be selected.

2.2 EXAMPLE: Permutation sort of a Prolog III list

Original program

```
sort(L, S) :- ord(S), perm(L,S) { L :: N , S :: N}.

perm(<>,<>).
perm(<X>.Y, <U>.V) :- del( U, <X>.Y, W), perm(W, V).

del(X, <X>.Y, Y).
del(X, <Y>.U, <Y>.V):- del(X,U,V).

ord(<>).
ord(<X>.<>).
ord(<X,Y>.T):- ord( <Y>.T) { X =< Y }.
```

This Prolog III program deviates from ordinary Prolog programs in two respects. Firstly, instead of ordinary Prolog lists, it uses so called tuples [4]. < > denotes the empty tuple, $<X_1,...,X_n>$ with n > 0 denotes an n-element tuple and . denotes tuple concatenation. Secondly, the constraint X :: N denotes that X is a N-element tuple. The program has a typical Prolog III style : first, the whole system of $\leqslant$ constraints is created; next, perm is executed and a $\leqslant$ constraint is activated as soon as possible and forces backtracking in case of failure.

Target program (for the pattern sort(L^g,S^v))

```
sort(L,S):-
        compute_length(L,N), construct_tuple(S,N), permord(L,S).
permord(<>,<>).
permord(<X>.Y, <U>.V) :-
        delete(U, <X>.Y, W), po(W,U,V).
po(<>,_, <>).
po(<X>.Y, Uprev, <U>.V) :-
        delete(U, <X>.Y, W), Uprev =< U,
        po(W,U,V).
```

The generation of the output list by perm and the generation of the tests by ord are synchronized in such a way that the $\leqslant$ constraint can be executed as a testing subgoal. Due to the special internal representation of tuples, it is desirable to have the subgoals *compute_length(L,N)*, computing the length of tuple L, and *construct_tuple(S,N)*, constructing a tuple of length N, although they are strictly speaking redundant.

Symbolic trace

The symbolic trace is developed in Fig. 3. First, the constraint L_1^g :: N_1^v is selected. It translates into the subgoal *compute_length*(L_1^g,N_1^v); its effect is to bind N_1^v. Next, the constraint S_1^v :: N_1^g is selected; it translates into the subgoal *construct_tuple*(S_1^v,N_1^g) and the effect is to create an n-place tuple which is abstracted as $<E_1^v,...,E_n^v>$ $(n \geqslant 0)$. Then, *ord*($<E_1^v,...,E_n^v>$) is selected. This results in creating the set of constraints {

$E_1^v \leqslant E_2^v,\dots,E_{n-1}^v \leqslant E_n^v$ } (details omitted). Next, the perm subgoal is tackled. After two delete steps (details of delete are omitted), a constraint is selected. From then on, we have a regular interchange between a delete step and the selection of a constraint (S states).

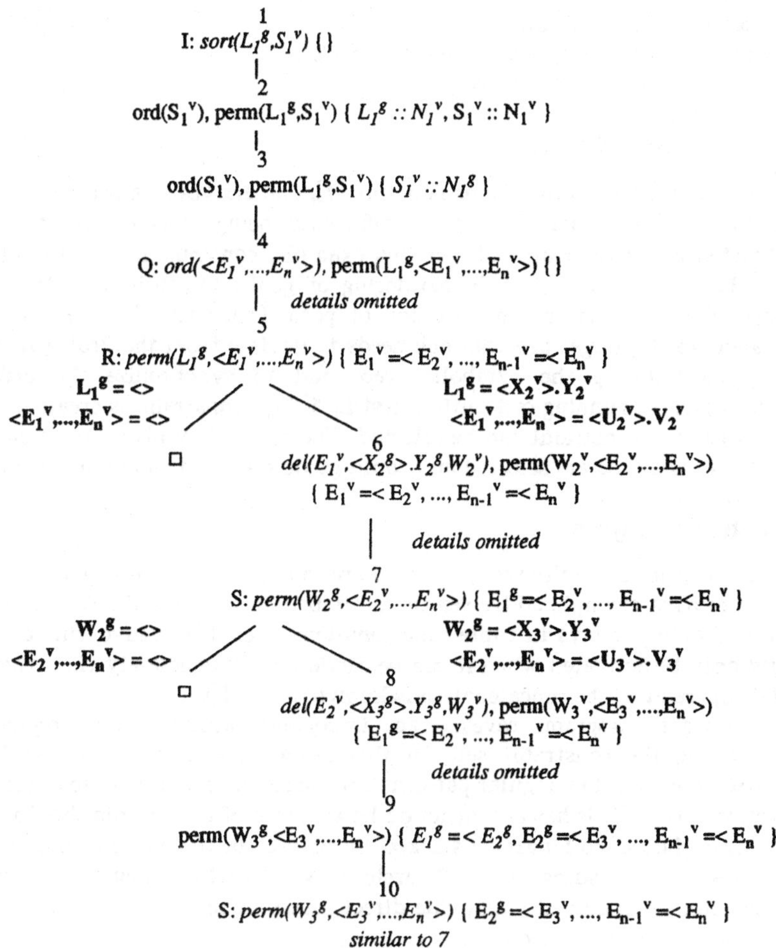

1
$I: sort(L_1^g,S_1^v)\ \{\}$
2
$ord(S_1^v), perm(L_1^g,S_1^v)\ \{ L_1^g :: N_1^v, S_1^v :: N_1^v \}$
3
$ord(S_1^v), perm(L_1^g,S_1^v)\ \{ S_1^v :: N_1^g \}$
4
$Q: ord(<E_1^v,\dots,E_n^v>), perm(L_1^g,<E_1^v,\dots,E_n^v>)\ \{\}$
details omitted
5
$R: perm(L_1^g,<E_1^v,\dots,E_n^v>)\ \{ E_1^v =< E_2^v, \dots, E_{n-1}^v =< E_n^v \}$
$L_1^g = <>$
$<E_1^v,\dots,E_n^v> = <>$
$L_1^g = <X_2^v>.Y_2^v$
$<E_1^v,\dots,E_n^v> = <U_2^v>.V_2^v$
□
6
$del(E_1^v,<X_2^g>.Y_2^g,W_2^v), perm(W_2^v,<E_2^v,\dots,E_n^v>)$
$\{ E_1^v =< E_2^v, \dots, E_{n-1}^v =< E_n^v \}$
details omitted
7
$S: perm(W_2^g,<E_2^v,\dots,E_n^v>)\ \{ E_1^g =< E_2^v, \dots, E_{n-1}^v =< E_n^v \}$
$W_2^g = <>$
$<E_2^v,\dots,E_n^v> = <>$
$W_2^g = <X_3^v>.Y_3^v$
$<E_2^v,\dots,E_n^v> = <U_3^v>.V_3^v$
□
8
$del(E_2^v,<X_3^g>.Y_3^g,W_3^v), perm(W_3^v,<E_3^v,\dots,E_n^v>)$
$\{ E_1^g =< E_2^v, \dots, E_{n-1}^v =< E_n^v \}$
details omitted
9
$perm(W_3^g,<E_3^v,\dots,E_n^v>)\ \{ E_1^g =< E_2^g, E_2^g =< E_3^v, \dots, E_{n-1}^v =< E_n^v \}$
10
$S: perm(W_3^g,<E_3^v,\dots,E_n^v>)\ \{ E_2^g =< E_3^v, \dots, E_{n-1}^v =< E_n^v \}$
similar to 7

Fig. 3: Symbolic trace tree of sort(L^g,S^v).

Synthesis

The standard synthesis of [2,5] yields the program:

```
I(sort(L,S)):-
        compute_length(L :: N), construct_tuple(S :: N),
        Q(ordperm(L,S), <>).
Q(ordperm(<>,<>), Cs):- R(perm(<>,<>), Cs).
Q(ordperm(L,<X>.<>), Cs):- R(perm(L,<X>.<>), Cs).
Q(ordperm(L,<X,Y>.T), Cs):- Q(ordperm(L,<Y>.T), Cs.<X =< Y>).
```

```
R(perm(<>,<>), Cs).
R(perm(<X>.Y,<U>.V), Cs):-
        delete(U, <X>.Y, W),
        S(perm(W,V), Cs).

S(perm(<>,<>), Cs).
S(perm(<X>.Y,<U>.V), <E =< U>.Cs):-
        delete(U, <X>.Y, W),
        E =< U,
        S(perm(W,V), Cs).
```

After cleaning up the superfluous functors [7], one arrives at a program which is quite close to the target one. The main difference being that a list of constraints is constructed and passed around. In this example, constructing the list of constraints cannot be avoided by a simple reordering of goals. Coroutining between constraint generation in ord and the computation of perm is needed. To synthesize a program equivalent to the target program one needs to deviate from the Prolog III computation rule when building the symbolic trace and to synchronize the ord and perm computations i.e. running ord until a first $E_i \leqslant E_{i+1}$ constraint is created, then running perm until that constraint can be selected. The original symbolic trace shows in what order the constraints are selected and could guide the construction of the new one.

2.3 Other examples

Among the other examples we considered are sameleaves and n-queens.
The sameleaves example addresses the optimization of a specific feature of Prolog III, namely avoiding delays in tuple concatenation: a constraint involving a concatenation should only be activated when it can be carried out immediately (i.e. when the size of the left operand of the concatenation is known; cfr. [4]).
The n-queens program reveals an important aspect about representing and manipulating the constraint set. In this example, constraints are still stored and activated according to a regular pattern, but the set-up order is quite different from the activation order. This has an impact on how the set of constraints should be organized: constraints should no longer be stacked linearly as in the above examples, but should be grouped corresponding to the hierarchical way in which they are set up. This more complex storage is needed to provide direct access to the constraints to be activated at some later time during execution.

3. Discussion

Prolog III allows to tackle in a declarative style many problems which are out of the realm of Prolog. However it is no match to finetuned commercial Prolog systems for problems whose algorithmic solution fits the expressiveness of Prolog. This poor performance is inherent to the generality of the applied constraint solvers. To make Prolog III competitive on such algorithmic problems, we believe it is necessary to have multiple specialisation, i.e. different versions of the same procedure.

This paper describes ongoing work concerning the automatic extraction of versions specialised for particular query patterns. Our approach is based on "compiling control", a transformation technique originally developed to transform logic programs requiring a special computation rule into Prolog programs. The proposed method consists of building a symbolic trace, during which constraints are gathered and -when possible- inserted at the appropriate place (to be executed by the standard computation rule). Building the symbolic trace is a form of abstract interpretation. However, besides data abstraction one also has to deal with goal abstraction, i.e. abstracting a set of subgoals or a set of constraints. This still has to be further formalized. Developing the constraint abstraction can be considered as a useful step in the more general context of abstract interpretation of Prolog III (or CLP) programs.

References

[1] M. Bruynooghe, "A practical framework for the abstract interpretation of logic programs" *Journal of Logic Programming*, Vol.10 (2), pp. 91-124 (1991).

[2] M. Bruynooghe, D. De Schreye, and B. Krekels, "Compiling control" *Journal of Logic Programming*, pp. 135-162 (1989).

[3] J. Cohen, "Constraint logic programming languages" *Communications of the ACM*, Vol.30 (7), pp. 52-68 (1990).

[4] A. Colmerauer, "An introduction to Prolog III" *Communications of the ACM*, Vol.30 (7), pp. 69-96 (1990).

[5] D. De Schreye and M. Bruynooghe, "On the transformation of logic programs with instantiation based computation rules" *Journal of Symbolic Computation*, Vol.7, pp. 125-154 (1989).

[6] B. Freeman-Benson, J. Maloney, and A. Borning, "An incremental constraint solver" *Communications of the ACM*, Vol.33 (1), pp. 54-63 (1990).

[7] J. Gallagher and M. Bruynooghe, "Some low-level source transformations for logic programs" pp. 229-244 in *Proceedings of the second workshop on meta-programming in logic*, Leuven, Belgium (1990).

[8] D. Jacobs, A. Langen, and W. Winsborough, "Multiple specialization of logic programs with run-time tests" pp. 717-731 in *Proceedings of the seventh international conference on Logic Programming*, Jeruzalem (1990).

[9] J. Jaffar and J-L. Lassez, "Constraint logic programming" pp. 111-119 in *Proceedings of the Fourteenth ACM symposium of the principles of programming languages*, Munich (1987).

[10] D.H.D. Warren, *An abstract Prolog instruction set*, Technical Report, SRI international, Artificial intelligence center (1983).

[11] W. Winsborough, *Multiple specialisations using minimal-function graph semantics*,, to appear in Journal of Logic Programming (1992).

Parallelizing Prolog on Shared-Memory Multiprocessors

Gao Yaoqing, Wang Dingxing and Qiu Xiaolin
Department of Computer Science and Technology
Tsinghua University, Beijing 100084, P.R.China

Hwang Zhiyi and Hu Shouren
Department of Computer Science
Changsha Institute of Technology
Changsha, Hunan 410073, P.R.China

Abstract

The research goal is to design and evaluate a parallel computer system to execute logic programs in both AND-parallel and OR-parallel. In this paper, we first introduce the OR-forest description. Then we provide a brief overview of the OR-forest-based parallel model RAP/LOP and its parallel abstract machine. We focus on the issues relevant to the parallelization of Prolog at compile-time. The simulation system of the RAP/LOP-PIM has been implemented on the SUN workstation and VAX 11/780.

1 Introduction

Our research goal is to design a high-speed parallel inference machine on shared-memory multiprocessors, for executing logic programs in both AND and OR parallel. In comparison with many other related work [4,7,14,15], the main features of our machine are: (i) The OR-forest description is used to describe the search space of a given problem. It can not only describe OR- and AND- parallelism explicitly, but also avoid a class of redundant computations. (ii) Coarse-grain parallelism is supported by our granularity-based scheduling strategies. (iii) Procedure-level and clause-level analysis at compile-time and dynamic simple run-time checks are used to identify independent goals of the body of a clause. (iv) Several optimization and implementation techniques such as improved indexing mechanism and code space reduction are used to increase the machine's efficiency significantly.

The rest of this paper is organized as follows. First, the OR-forest description is introduced in Section 2. We also give a brief overview of the OR-forest-based model RAP/LOP and its parallel abstract machine. Then we put emphasis on the global compiler to parallelize Prolog in Section 3. Next the experimental results and analysis by software simulation are discussed in

Section 4.

2 An OR-Forest-Based Parallel Model and its Abstract Machine

2.1 RAP/LOP : an OR-Forest-Based Parallel Execution Model

The method of describing the execution of logic programs provides a framework for developing execution modes of logic programs. Different description methods reflect different global views of the execution of logic programs and determine the basic properties of the corresponding execution models. Traditionally, the execution of a logic program can be described by an OR-tree, AND-tree or AND/OR-tree. Here we use a new description method, called the OR-forest description [22].

Definition: OR-forest.

Given a logic program, an initial goal IG, a parallel computation rule PR and a parallel search strategy PS, the execution space of this logic program can be uniquely described as an OR-forest. An OR-forest is a collection of OR-trees with nodes labeled by goals. The nodes in OR-forest are created in following way:

1. One root nodes is created and labeled by the initial goal IG.

2. For any newly created node labeled by a goal G_i, G_i is <-A_1, A_2, ..., A_{l-1}, A_l, A_{l+1}, ..., A_m (m >= 1,1 =< l =< m). If G_i is a *null* goal or a *fail* goal, the node is a *leaf* node. Otherwise, the PR is used to selects mutually independent groups of subgoals G_i'.

(1) If $\#G_i'=1$,i.e., no mutually independent groups of subgoals are discovered (# means "number of"), the node labeled by G_i is a *normal* node and the PR picks out the subgoal A_l from G_i' and the PS selects C_{i+1} from P, which is a set of the clauses with heads that are unifiable with the selected subgoal.

(a) If $\#C_{i+1}=0$, i.e., there is no clause with heads that are unifiable with the selected subgoal A_l, the node labeled by G_i becomes a *leaf* node.

(b) If $\#C_{i+1}>0$ (OR-parallelism), the node labeled by G_i has $\#C_{i+1}$ successors: <- (A_1, A_2, ..., $C_{i+1\ j}$, ..., A_k) θ_j where $C_{i+1\ j}$ is a member of C_{i+1} and θj is the most general unification of A_l and $C_{i+1\ j}$.

(2) If $\#G_i'>1$,i.e., there are $\#G_i'$ mutually independent subgoals, the node labeled by G_i becomes a *seed* node and $\#G_i'$ new *slave* tree are derived with *root* nodes labeled by A_i, $A_i \in G_i'$, respectively (AND-parallelism). Assuming the *slave* tree for A_i contains k_i *leaf* nodes labeled by *null* goals (corresponding to k_i solutions to A_i), let $K=k_1*k_2*...*k_n$.

(a) If K=0, the node labeled by G_i becomes a *leaf* node.

(b) If K>0, the node labeled by G_i has K successors labeled by $(G-G_i')\theta_j$, where θ_j (1 =< j =< K) is one of the cross product solutions.

Consider the following Example 1, its different descriptions are shown in Fig. 1.

```
?-h(X,Y).
h(X,Y):-p(X),q(Y).
p(1). p(2). ... p(m).
q(1). q(2). ... q(m). ... q(n).
```

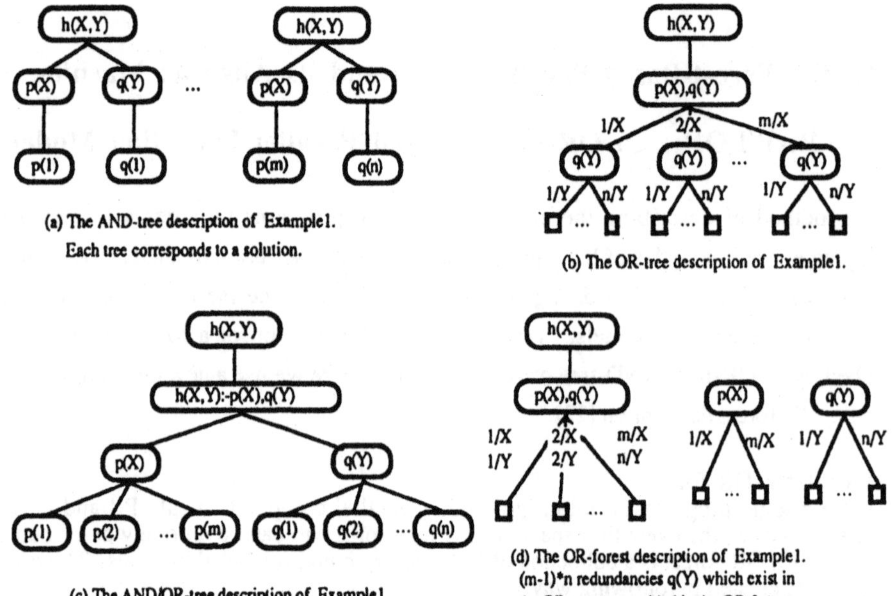

(a) The AND-tree description of Example1. Each tree corresponds to a solution.

(b) The OR-tree description of Example1.

(c) The AND/OR-tree description of Example1.

(d) The OR-forest description of Example1. (m-1)*n redundancies q(Y) which exist in the OR-tree are avoided in the OR-forest.

Fig. 1 The different descriptions of the Example 1.

The merits of the OR-forest description are as follows:

(1) Both AND- and OR-parallelism can be explicitly described instead of only one type of parallelism described in the OR-tree and AND-tree.

(2) Redundancies which exist in the OR-tree description are avoided because the execution of each independent subgoal is described by one separate subtree.

(3) Since the branches of the AND/OR-tree reflect only the static structure of the program, in AND/OR-tree-based execution models the execution of a program is carried out by passing messages among a hierarchy of processes corresponding to nodes of the tree. The communication overhead of OR-forest-based models is less than that of AND/OR-tree-based execution models.

Based on the OR-forest description, we present an implementation-oriented model -- Restricted And-Parallel and Limited Or-Parallel model (RAP/LOP). The OR-forest description is used to describe the search space of a given problem in our model. Computations can be considered as searching an OR-forest by a number of processes. We regard some part of the OR-forest as a process, a node as a process instead. Therefore moderate granularity of parallelism can be exploited flexibly to reduce the overheads of control and management.

An approach of combining dynamic and static detection of AND-parallelism is used [16]. Instead of only clause-level analysis in DeGroot's scheme, We use both procedure-level and clause-level analysis to reduce check overheads at run-time. We predict the properties of a program at compile-time through abstract interpretation. Based on the analysis, the information such as modes is obtained to guide a precompiler to generate conditional-graph-expressions (CGE) of the program. At run-time, simple checks are used to determine whether the goals in the body can be executed in AND-parallel.

OR-parallelism is limited by the number of processors available. When all the processors are busy, every processor runs in some part of the OR-forest and works on the candidate OR branches through backtracking.

The multi-stack memory management scheme is introduced in the model, which reduces the overheads of garbage collection and offers much better locality of reference. Both data coping and data sharing are used in our model.

Reflective computation is introduced in our model. A logic program LP can be viewed as two components: a source code S and control information C (or called knowledge), i.e., LP=<S,C>.

The control information of a program come from: (a) User annotation. That is, users give some information in their programs by their expertise. (b) Static automatic generation. In the precompile phase, the global information such as global model, and granularity is generated by abstract interpretation. (c) Dynamic automatic generation. At run-time, the statistics information, such granularity, frequently-used mode and success branch with high possibility, is collected. The statistical information collected before will guide next execution of the machine. (e) Both static and dynamic automatic generation.

In the initial stage of software development, a programmer can write a non-annotated program (by a naive user), annotated program (by an expert) or combination of both. The program is compiled by the precompiler and compiler. After the code generated by the compiler running several times in a machine, the historical control information is accumulated and is fed back into the precompiler. The precompiler and compiler use the knowledge, generated by static analysis, dynamic statistic or combination of both, to produce executable code which is as time and space efficient as possible (Fig.2).

Multi-processor scheduling is the problem of assigning tasks to processors in a parallel machine to meet some optimal criterions. In our case, the criterions are those: the degree of load balance, the efficiency of executing as necessary computations as possible, and overhead of control and management. In most existing logic programming systems, the simple blind search strategies such as depth-first, breadth-first and etc. are usually used. In our machine, the indexing mechanism is used to prune unnecessary expansions of the search space, and the granularity of parallelism is used to guide the task scheduling.

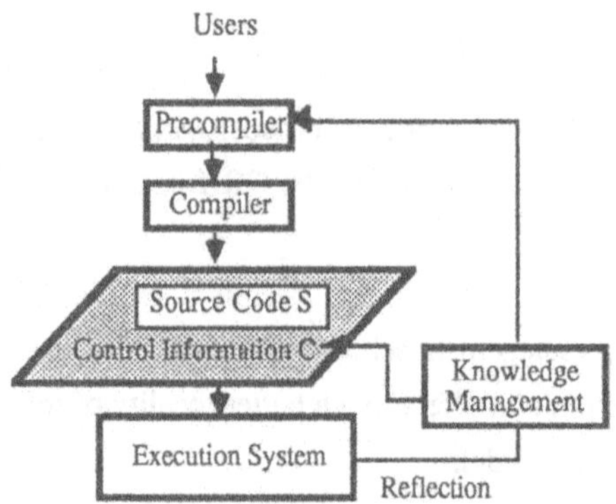

Fig.2 Reflective Architecture

2.2 The Parallel Abstract Machine

Based on the RAP/LOP parallel execution model, we design a parallel abstract machine RAP/LOP-WAM which has four components: the memory space, the data objects, the machine states (Fig.3) and the instruction set.

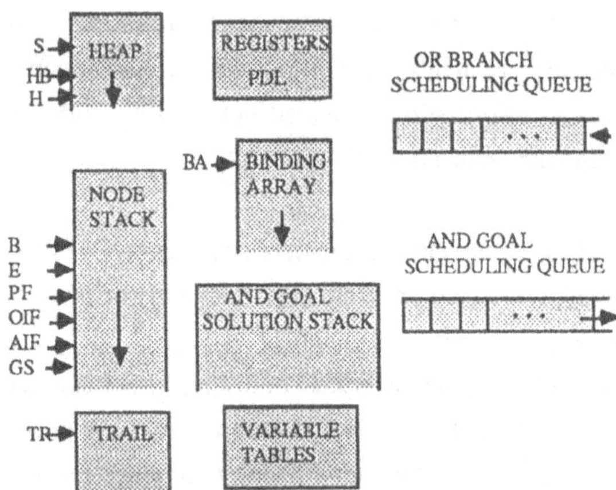

Fig.3 RAP/LOP-WAM processor state

The RAP/LOP-WAM can be viewed as an extension of the WAM [9,25]. In comparison with the WAM, a binding array is added to support multi-bindings of the same variable in OR-parallelism, an OR branch scheduling queue and AND goal stack for process scheduling, and an AND goal solution stack which saves solutions from parallel AND goals in order to avoid redundant computations, in our RAP/LOP-WAM.

Each machine has access to the stack, heap, OR branch scheduling queue, AND goal scheduling stack, AND goal solution stack of other machines.

The instruction set of our RAP/LOP-WAM can be classified into the argument loading, goal calling, unifying, indexing and filtering, variable checking, goal scheduling and some control instructions .

3 Global Parallel Compiler

The compilation process can be divided into two levels: source-to-source (including source-to-CGE) and source-to-instruction level (see Fig. 4).

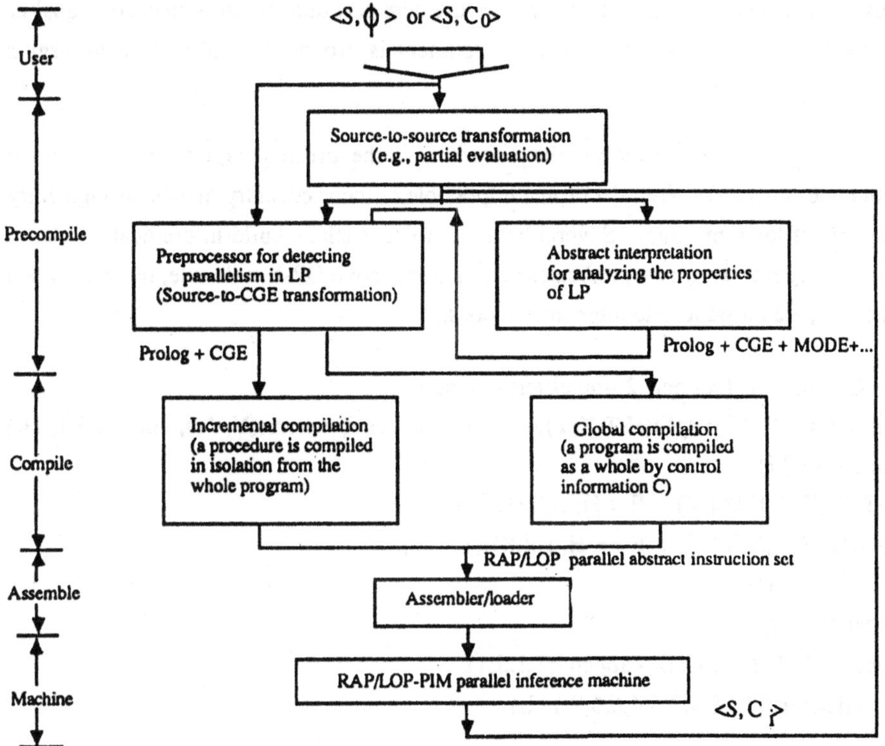

Fig. 4 The outline of the compilation process

3.1 Precompilation

In the precompile-time, we use global analysis to determine the input/output behaviors (modes) which actually occur for each procedure in a program, to detect data-dependencies among the goals in a clause for exploiting AND-Parallelism, and generate granularity information for task scheduling.

3.1.1 Detecting AND-Parallelism

The approach described here consists of three phases: analysis of entry modes; derivation of exit modes; and determination of conditional execution graph expressions.

An entry mode of a clause specifies whether the arguments of the clause head are instantiated after a goal invokes it and unifies with its head; an exit mode of a clause specifies whether the arguments of the clause head are instantiated after the goals of its body are solved. An entry mode of a goal specifies whether its arguments are instantiated before it is about to be executed; an exit mode of a goal specifies whether its arguments are instantiated after it is solved. The mode-inference technique we use here partitions the arguments of a goal into two classes: G means the corresponding argument is ground, and N means the argument is non-ground;

In the first phase, we analyze the procedures in the directed graph from bottom up until the root node is reached. We reject some impossible or incorrect entry modes through entry mode analysis of logic program. Several heuristic rules, such as build-in predicates rule, variable consistency rule, recursive predicates rule, non-recursive OR-bundle rule, recursive OR-bundle rule ,etc., are introduced to infer entry modes.

Consider the Example 2 --quicksort program:

```
quicksort([H|T],S):-split(H,T,X,Y),quicksort(X,X1), quicksort(Y,Y1), append(X1,[H|Y1],S).
quicksort([],[]).
split(H,[E|T],[E|X],Y) :- E < H, split(H,T,X,Y).
split(H,[E|T],X,[E|Y]) :- E >= H, split(H,T,X,Y).
split(H,[],[],[]).
append([],L,L).
append([H|T],L,[H|L1]) :- append(T,L,L1).
?- quicksort([10,8,9,7,5,4,6,3,2,1],L).
```

Based on our analysis, the following possible modes can be derived.
The possible entry modes for quicksort are: GG,GN.
The possible entry modes for split are: GGNN, GGGN, GGNG,GGGG.
append has no entry mode requirement here.

The second phase is derivation of exit modes. We derive the exit mode for every possible entry mode of each procedure.

Algorithm: Exit mode derivation:
Input: a clause C: C^+ :- C^- and its entry mode
Output: an exit mode
Vars: GV: current set of instantiated variables
NV: current set of uninstantiated variables
VS: current set of variables occurring in the clause
S: current subgoal
SG, SN: sets of instantiated and uninstantiated variables of S after S is executed, respectively
SV: variable set of S
i: a pointer

1. initialization.
   i := 1,
   GV := {variables in the clause head's arguments whose entry modes are G}.
   NV := {variables in the clause head's arguments whose entry modes are N}.
   VS := {variables in the clause head}.
2. set S to the ith subgoal of C^-.
3. if S = nil, goto 5.
4. the following steps are done for S.
   i) determine the entry mode of S according to GV, NV and VS.
   ii) compute the exit mode of the entry mode according to the entry/exit mode table of S.
   iii) evaluate SG,SN and SV according to the exit mode of S.
   iv) GV := GV U SG,
   NV := NV U SN,
   VS := VS U SV.
   v) i := i + 1, go to 2.
5. decide the exit mode according to GV, NV and VS.

The final phase is determination of execution graph expressions. For a clause, its different entry modes will lead to different dependence relationships among goals in its body and different AND-parallelism in it. Therefore, We generate the CGE for each entry mode of a clause so that the maximum AND-parallelism may be exploited. The quicksort program can be precompiled into the following CGE:

```
quicksort([H|T],S,GG) :- split(H,T,X,Y,GGNN),
        (PAR|quicksort(X,X1,GN)&quicksort(Y,Y1,GN)), append(X1,[H|Y1],S,GGG).
quicksort([H|T],S,GN) :- split(H,T,X,Y,GGNN),
        (PAR|quicksort(X,X1,GN)&quicksort(Y,Y1,GN)), append(X1,[H|Y1],S,GGN).
quicksort([],[],GG).
quicksort([],[],GN).
split(H,[E|T],[E|X],Y,GGNN) :- (PAR|(E < H,GG),&split(H,T,X,Y,GGNN)).
split(H,[E|T],[E|X],Y,GGGN) :- (PAR|(E < H,GG),&split(H,T,X,Y,GGGN)).
split(H,[E|T],[E|X],Y,GGNG) :- (PAR|(E < H,GG),&split(H,T,X,Y,GGNG)).
split(H,[E|T],[E|X],Y,GGGG) :- (PAR|(E < H,GG),&split(H,T,X,Y,GGGG)).
split(H,[E|T],X,[E|Y],GGNN) :- (PAR|(E >= H,GG)&split(H,T,X,Y,GGNN)).
split(H,[E|T],X,[E|Y],GGGN) :- (PAR|(E >= H,GG)&split(H,T,X,Y,GGGN)).
split(H,[E|T],X,[E|Y],GGNG) :- (PAR|(E >= H,GG)&split(H,T,X,Y,GGNG)).
split(H,[E|T],X,[E|Y],GGGG) :- (PAR|(E >= H,GG)&split(H,T,X,Y,GGGG)).
split(H,[],[],[],GGNN).
split(H,[],[],[],GGGN).
split(H,[],[],[],GGNG).
split(H,[],[],[],GGGG).
```

Note that we must generate a CGE for each possible entry mode of a clause in our approach.

Therefore, the compiled abstract instruction code expands largely with the entry modes' increasing exponentially. According to our experiments, the extended parallel WAM code space compiled from the approach is two to six times the sequential WAM code space. To solve the problem, we adopt a special technique to infer one or two user-Frequently-Used entry Modes (FUM). For the other possibly-used entry modes, we abstract a Default Entry Mode (DEM) from them. In this way, we can ensure the seldom used modes will be dealt with correctly without much loss of parallelism while we can accurately exploit AND-parallelism in most cases.

In this improved scheme, the first phase of analyzing entry modes is divided into two sub-phases: automatic inference of possible entry modes and automatic inference of FUMs. In the first sub-phase, the bottom-up abstract interpretation, whose abstract domain is {G,N}, is used to infer the possible entry modes of user programs, as described above. In the second sub-phase, we adopt the top-down abstract interpretation whose abstract domain is {G,N,?}, ? means that whether the corresponding argument of a goal is ground or not is unknown. At first, we regard the possible entry mode as the FUM of the top procedure and use it to infer the entry modes of procedures the top procedure invokes. We then use these entry modes as their FUMs and continue above process to get the FUM of every procedure. For example, we obtain the FUMs of the quicksort program as follows:

The FUMs of quicksort are GN and GG.
The FUM of split is GGNN.
The FUMs of append are GGN and GGG.

For the other possible entry modes, we can abstract a DEM to represent them:
The DEM of split is G???.
The DEM of append is ???.

We generate a CGE for every FUM and a default CGE for the other possible entry modes. Significant improvements in space efficiency can be achieved using the approach.

3.1.2 Generating Granularity Information

Logic programs offer many opportunities for the exploitation of parallelism. However, some Prolog programs are not likely to be speedup by parallel processing, due to the overheads associated with process creation, scheduling, communication,etc.. In the procedure split of the quicksort program, the tests E<H and E>=H, can typically be executed in one or two machine instructions. Obviously it is not cost-effective to spawn the tests as separate tasks and execute them in parallel. In order to effectively utilize the processing power of multiprocessors.

Prolog programs should be executed in parallel only when benefits are believed to outweigh overheads. Here we present some schemes to determine goal granularity and exploit parallelism efficiently.

Static analysis: At compile-time, the source program is first converted into a cyclic AND/OR hierarchical call graph G=(N,E). Here N is a set of nodes and E is a set of edges. A node in the graph denotes a literal or a clause. There are two kinds of edges in the graph: AND branches and OR branches which occur alternatively.

A procedure's granularity is the sum of the granularities of all of its clauses, and a clause's granularity is the sum of the granularities of the procedures it calls. The database predicates and build-in predicates are one by definition. Granularity estimate for a set of non-recursive predicates is relatively simple. The granularity of a self-recursive clause (as append) is represented by its recursive times. It is difficult to determine the recursive strength of a procedure. Because the work done by a call to a recursive predicate typically depends on the size of its input, e.g., term-size, list-length,etc.. The measure appropriate in a given situation generally be determined by examining the operations used in the program (the list-length is used to represent the recursive times in append). Here we assume that the recursive times of a recursive predicate is approximately equal to the length of its dominant argument. The dominant argument of a recursive procedure is defined as the one which the recursive times of the procedure depend strongly on. Therefore, the recursive times of a predicate can be determined by tracing its dominant argument size at compile-time and by statistics at run-time. The granularities of mutually recursive goals are calculated by cutting a call cycle at the lowest level in the graph and calculating the granularities of the lowest nodes.

Dynamic statistics: In our system, for OR parallelism, we have the consideration: the frequency of process migration increases dramatically near the end of program execution. Therefore, the most effective positions for the OR-parallel nodes tend to be higher up in the search tree. Our scheduling strategy picks tasks from the node nearest to the root of the tree.

The reflective computations are introduced in our system. For AND-parallelism, the scheduling is based on the granularity (an integer) of a parallel AND goal. The granularities are generated through collecting statistical information at run-time. Every time a program is executed, its historical control information is stored into the machine. At run-time, the new control information of an AND goal will be collected into its corresponding environment, such as statistical granularity at the i-th depth. After finishing the execution of a program, the information of each goal will be formed in a list and inserted into the corresponding goal of the program as an extra parameter. In addition to the granularity informatión, we collect the information such as user-frequently-used mode information for compiler to reduce code space in our system.

Hybrid scheme: The compile-time granularity analysis is a conservative estimate of the amount of work performed at run-time. In other hand, it is expensive to determine the granularity information at run-time. Therefore we can use the hybrid scheme which combine the static and dynamic schemes. In the hybrid scheme, the granularities of non-recursive procedures are first computed. Then as much of the granularity analysis for recursive procedures is done at compile-time as possible, but the actual computations of granularities are postponed until run-time. We can hire the techniques similar to [6].

Consider the Example 3:
C1: fib(0,0).
C2: fib(1,1).
C3: fib(M,N) :- M>1, M1 is M-1, M2 is M-2, fib(M1,N1), fib(M2,N2), N is N1+N2.

Its granularity can be computed through the following difference equations:

$$grain_{C1} = 1,$$
$$grain_{C2} = 1,$$
$$grain_{C3} = grain_{fib}(n-1)+grain_{fib}(n-2)+1, \; n>1,$$
$$grain_{fib}(n) = grain_{C1}+grain_{C2}+grain_{C3}$$
$$= grain_{fib}(n-1)+grain_{fib}(n-2)+1$$
$$= 2*grain_{fib}(n-1)+3$$

This yields the solution $grain_{fib}(n)=2^{n+1}-1$ which can be evaluated at run-time, when the size of the dominant argument is known.

3.2 Compilation

3.2.1 Procedure Compilation

A procedure is a set of clauses whose heads have the same predicate and arity. The indexing instructions are introduced to link together the different clauses in a procedure and filter out a subset of those clauses which could potentially match a given procedure. The instructions extends and improves Warren's through the knowledge given by precompilation phase.

An optimization for a class of procedures, called Exclusive-OR (XOR) procedures, can be used. For a XOR subset X of a procedure and given a calling goal, at most one clause in X can match it. An optimization is to find a key by that at most one clause in its XOR subset is unified with a calling goal every time a procedure is called.

Algorithm: A class of XOR procedures are identified.

(1) Let C_1 (C_1^+:- C_1^-) and C_2 (C_2^+:- C_2^-) be two arbitrary clauses of a procedure. The parameters corresponding to mode N and ? are removed from the clause heads C_1^+, C_2^+. If even one pair of the modified clause heads unify, the procedure is not XOR one, and goto (2). Otherwise, the procedure is a XOR one.

(2) The first several arithmetic comparison predicates (build-in predicates) whose arguments are all ground of C_1^- and C_2^- are analyzed to find exclusive build-in predicates(a restricted scheme).

The WAM's switching instructions only examine the first parameter of a procedure. We introduce a modified version of the **switch_on_xxx** family of the instructions which can filter clauses by **Ai** and some other instructions to improve the WAM's indexing mechanism.

switch_on_ground Ai N TABLE: The instruction assumes that Ai is a ground term. It provides hash table access to a group of clauses having a constant, a ground list or structure pointer in Ai.

less Xi Xj Label (greater, equal): If the number contained in Xi is less than that in Xj, control passes to the next instruction; otherwise it jumps to Label.

Consider the CGE of split of the quicksort program generated by the improved precompiler:

```
C1: C11: split(H,[E|T],[E|X],Y,GGNN) :- (PAR|(E < H,GG),&split(H,T,X,Y,GGNN)).
    C12: split(H,[E|T],[E|X],Y,G???) :- (PAR|(E < H,GG),&split(H,T,X,Y,G???)).
C2: C21: split(H,[E|T],X,[E|Y],GGNN) :- (PAR|(E >= H,GG)&split(H,T,X,Y,GGNN)).
    C22: split(H,[E|T],X,[E|Y],G???) :- (PAR|(E >= H,GG)&split(H,T,X,Y,G???)).
C3: C31: split(H,[],[],[],GGNN).
    C32: split(H,[],[],[],G???).
```

They can be compiled into the following code:

```
procedure split/2
switch_on_mode 2 TABLE1
   TABLE1: GGNN: entry1
           G ? ? ? : entry2
entry1: switch_on_ground A2 2 TABLE2
           TABLE2: []  l1
                   ·/2 l2
                   default fail
l1: <C31 code>
l2: get_list A2
    unify_variable X4
    unify_variable X5
    less X4 X1 l22
l21: <C11 code>
l22: <C21 code>
entry2: switch_on_ground A2 2 TABLE3
           TABLE3: []  l3
                   ·/2 l4
                   default fail
l3: <C32 code>
```

```
14: seq_choice 2 TABLE4
     TABLE4: 141
             142
141: <C12 code>
142: <C22 code>
```

For a clause whose head has more than one entry modes, the switch_on_mode N TABLE jumps to the entry corresponding to the input mode of the head of a clause.

3.2.2 Clause Compilation

The clause compilation is a sophisticated process. It has five steps: the clause transformation, variable identification and allocation, intermediate code generation, instruction types determination, and code optimization

The clause transformation step transforms terms of goals into those without embedded lists, structures by introducing intermediate variables, and transforms clauses into ones without nested CGE by introducing dump predicates. The variable identification and allocation classify variables into three types: temporal, permanent and intermediate variables. The intermediate code generation finishes the frame of the instruction sequence of a clause. For every CGE subexpression, it can be compiled into two blocks: one is a sequential block, the other is parallel block. The determination step of instruction types annotates the types (variable, temp_variable, constant, list, structure) of operands of instructions. The final step is code optimization to generate efficient code.

For example, the quicksort procedure can be compiled into the following code form:

```
procedure quicksort/2
switch_on_mode 2 TABLE1    { Jump to the corresponding entry points
   TABLE1:  GG entry1        according to different entry modes }
            GN entry2
entry1: switch_on_ground A1 TABLE2
          TABLE2: [ ]: 10
                  ·/2: 11
                  default fail
10: get_nil X1
    get_nil X2
    Proceed
11: allocate 7             { Allocate the environment for quicksort/2 }
    get_list A1
    unify_variable Y3
    unify_variable Y7
    get_variable Y1 A2
    put_value Y3 A1
    put_value Y7 A2
    put_variable Y6 A3
    put_variable Y5 A4
    call split/4 GGNN
```

```
allocate_pcall 2          { Allocate the parallel frame for parallel AND goals }
allocate_vartable 1       { Create the variable table for parallel AND goals }
  put_value Y6 A1
  put_vt_variable Y4 A2       { Load the arguments of quicksort }
  push_call quicksort/2 GN { Push quicksort into goal stack for scheduling }
allocate_vartable 2
  put_value Y5 A1
  put_vt_variable Y2 A2
  push_call quicksort/2 GN
pop_and_goal                 { Execute parallel AND goals }
and_join                     { Create the cross-product set }
put_value Y4 A1
put_list A2
unify_value Y3
unify_value Y2
put_value Y1 A3
deallocate                  { Deallocate the environment for quicksort}
call append/3 GGG
entry2: (omitted)            { Similar to the code in entry1 }
```

4 Experimental Results and Performance Analysis

In order to validate our model, we have implemented a simulation system of the RAP/LOP-PIM parallel inference machine in the programming language C on VAX11/780 and SUN3 (Fig.5). Lots of benchmarks such as append, reverse, quicksort, 8queen, maze, map_coloring, matrix_multiplication, small_database, etc. have been executed in our system.

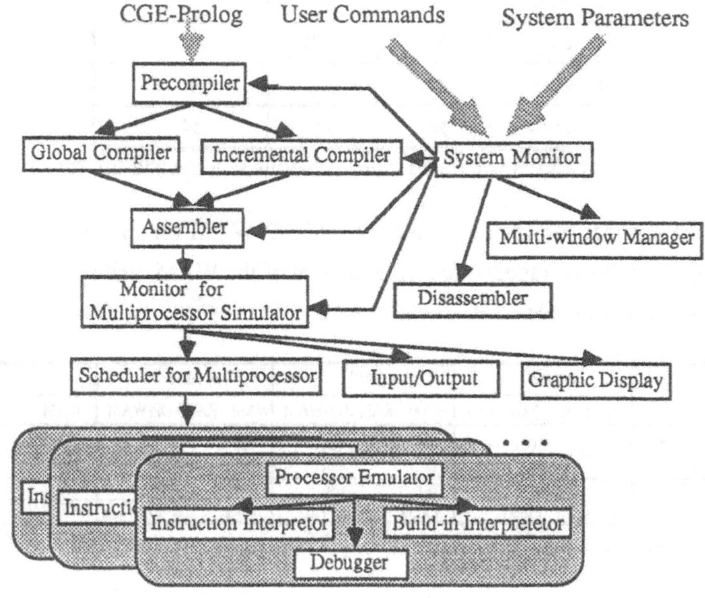

Fig.5 The RAP/LOP-PIM simulation system

In Tab.6, We can know our machine needs much less dynamic overhead than DeGroot's scheme for AND-parallelism.

PROGRAMS	CHECK TYPES	DeGroots	Ours
quicksort	IPAR	38	0
	GPAR	38	0
nqueen	IPAR	72	0
	GPAR	176	0
matrix_ multiplication	IPAR	12	12
	GPAR	12	0
hanoi_tower	IPAR	0	0
	GPAR	31	0
maze	IPAR	0	0
	GPAR	30	0
factorial	IPAR	0	0
	GPAR	19	0
in total	IPAR	122	12
	GPAR	306	0

Tab.6 Number of checks used at run-time

Tab. 7 shows that the improved precompilation scheme reduces the number of the CGEs of a program (excluding its facts). Therefore the space efficiency is increased significantly.

PROGRAMS	num. of clauses	num. of CGEs	num. of CGEs (reduced)
quicksort	4	20	9
nqueen	5	14	8
matrix_ multiplication	6	18	12
hanoi_tower	3	17	5
maze	4	24	16
factorial	2	4	4
in total	24	97	54

Tab. 7 Number of CGEs generated in the previous scheme and improved scheme

Tab.8 is the comparison results of our RAP/LOP-WAM on single processor and the WAM. It shows that on average, compared with that of the WAM, the space overhead of the RAP/LOP-WAM is reasonable.

Examples	reverse20		qsort50		serialize		query	
	WAM	RAP/LOP-WAM	WAM	RAP/LOP-WAM	WAM	RAP/LOP-WAM	WAM	RAP/LOP-WAM
Max. hei. of heap	991	1021	659	904	393	453	23	23
Max. hei. of stack	184	184	3967	3967	1037	2632	120	120
Max. hei. of trail	467	932	381	656	167	402	9	18
Num.of data ref.	11393	13806	15233	17926	9741	14878	275246	281577

Tab.8 Comparison of our RAP/LOP-WAM of single processor and the WAM

We use different scheduling strategies to measure the performance improvement ratio of the system. Here the performance improvement ratio of the system is defined as its speedup. The values were obtained by averaging measured values of all the benchmarks (see Fig.9). The results show that with the number of processors increasing, the performance improvement ratio of the granularity-based scheduling strategies is better than that of the simple blind strategies such as the depth-first and breadth-first ones.

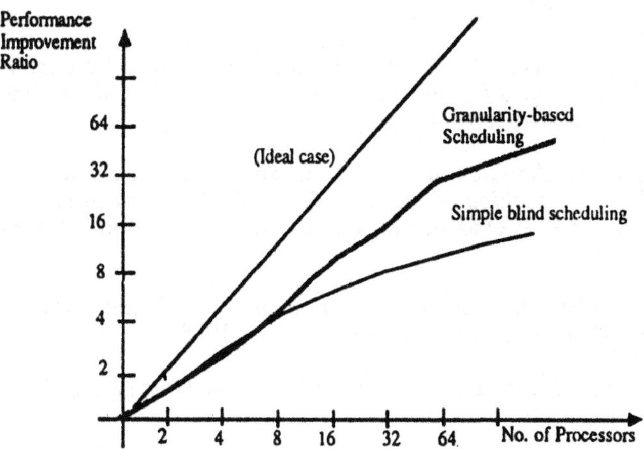

Fig.9 Performance improvement ratio due to granularity-based scheduling

Our experimental results indicate that the substantial speedup (at least an order magnitude) are attainable for logic programs when we choose more than 16 processors. Our next step is to port our simulation system to commercially available shared-memory multiprocessors.

References

[1] Baron, U., de Kergommeaux, J.C., Hailperin, M., Ratcliffe, M., Robert, P., Syre, J.C. and Westphal, H., *"The Parallel ECRC PROLOG System PEPSys: an Overview and Evaluation Results,"* in Proc. of Int'l Conf. on FGCS 1988.

[2] J.-H. Chang, A. M. Despain and D. DeGroot, "*And-parallelism of logic programs based on a static data dependency analysis,*" COMPCON 85, San Francisco, Feb., 1985.

[3] A.Ciepielewski,and S.Haridi, *"Control of Activities in an OR- Parallel Token machine,"* Proc. of logic programming workshop 83, July,1983.

[4] Conery.J.S., *"The AND/OR model for parallel interpretation of Logic Programs,"* Ph.D thesis, Dept. of Infor. and Comp. Sci., UC Irvine, 1983.

[5] S.K. Debray and D.S. Warren, *"Automatic Mode Inference for Prolog Programs,"* Journal of Logic Programming, 207-229, Sept. 1988.

[6] S.K.Debray, Nai-Wei Lin and M.Hermenegildo, *"Task Granularity Analysis in Logic Programs,"* Proc. of the ACM SIGPLAN'90 Conf. on Programming Language Design and Implementation. White Plains, New York, Jun.,1990.

[7] D. DeGroot, *"Restricted And-parallelism,"* Proc. of the Int'l Conf. on FGCS, Tokyo, Nov. 1984.

[8] D. DeGroot, *"A technique for compiling execution graph expressions for restricted And-parallelism in logic programs,"* Proc. of the 1987 Int'l Supercomputing Conf., Athens, Greece, (June 1987).

[9] Gao Yaoqing, *"A RAP/LOP-WAM Parallel Abstract Instruction Set,"* Tech. Report. Changsha Institute of Technology. 1988.

[10] Gao Yaoqing, Sun Chengzheng and Hu Shouren, *"Study of a Parallel Inference Machine for Parallel Execution of Logic Programs,"* Int'l Joint Conf. on Vector and Parallel Processing, Zurich, Switzerland, Nov. 1990.

[11] Gao Yaoqing, Hu Shouren and Sun Chengzheng, *"Design and Implementation of a Parallel Abstract Machine Model RAP/LOP-WAM for Parallel Execution of Logic Programs,"* Proceedings of an International Conference on Information Processing, Tokyo, Japan, Oct. 1990.

[12] Gopal Gupta, *"Compiled And-Or Parallelism on Shared Memory Multiprocessor,"* Logic Programming: Proc. of the North American Conf., 1988.

[13] Gregory S., *"Parallel Programming in PARLOG, the Language and its Implementation."* Addision Wesley, 1987.

[14] B.Hausman, A.Ciepielewski, and S.Haridi, *"OR-parallel Prolog made efficient on shared memory multiprocessors,"* In The 1987 Int'l Symp. on Logic Programming, San Francisco, California, IEEE 1987.

[15] M.V.Hermengildo, *"An Abstract Prolog Machine based Execution Model for Computer Architecture Design and Efficient Implementation of Logic Programs in Parallel,"* Ph.D thesis, The University of Texas at Austin, 1986.

[16] Zhiyi Hwang and Shouren Hu, *"A Compiling Approach for Exploiting And-parallelism in Parallel logic Programming Systems,"* Proc. of the Int'l Conf. on Parallel Architecture and Language, Europe, the Netherlands, 1989.

[17] L.V.Kale, *"Completeness and Full Parallelism of Parallel Logic Programming Schemes."* Proc. Fourth IEEE Symp. on Logic Programming, San Francisco, CA,IEEE,1987.

[18] Lusk,E., Warren, D.H.D, Haridi, S., Butler,R., Calderwood, A., Disz, T., Olson, R., Overbeek, R., Stevens, R., Szerdi, P., Brand, P., Carlsson, M., Cipelewski, A. and Hausman, B., *"The Aurora OR-Parallel PROLOG System,"* in Proc. of Int'l Conf. on FGCS 1988.

[19] Pattie Maes, *"Issues in Computational Reflection,"* Meta-Level Architectures and Reflection, P.Maes, D.Nardi (Editors), Elsevier Science Publishers B.V., 1988.

[20] C.S. Mellish, *"Abstract Interpretation of Prolog Programs,"* In 3rd International Conf. on Logic Programming," Imperial College, Springer-Verlag, July 1986.

[21] K. Muthukumar and M. Hermenegildo, *"The CDG, UDG and MEL Methods for Automatic Compile-time Parallelization of Logic Programs for Independent And-parallelism,"* TR ACA- ST-023-90, MCC, Austin, TX 78759, 1990.

[22] Sun Chengzheng and Tzu Yungui, *"The OR-forest Description for the Execution of*

Programs.," Lec. Notes in Computer Sci., the Proc. of the 3rd Int'l Conf. on Logic Programming. July, 1986.

[23] Sun Chengzheng and Ci Yungui, *"PSOF: A Process Model Based on the OR-forest Description,"* Proc. of the int'l Conf. on Computer and Communication, 1986, Beijing.

[24] E.Tick, *"Compile-Time Granularity Analysis for Parallel Logic Programming Languages,"* Int'l Conf. on FGCS, Tokey, Japan, 1988.

[25] D.H.Warren, *"An Abstract Prolog Instruction Set,"* Tech. Note 309, SRI International, AI Center, Computer Sci. and Technology Division, 1983.

[26] David H. D. Warren, *"The SRI Model for OR-Parallel Execution of Prolog--Abstract Design and Implementation Issues,"* In The 1987 Int'l Symp. on Logic Programming, California, IEEE, 1987.

[27] Yu-Wen Tung and Dan I. Moldovan, *"Detection of And-parallelism in logic programming,"* Proc. of the 1986 Int'l Conf. on Parallel Processing, IEEE, Pennsylvania, 1986, pp. 984-991.

[28] Ueda,K., *"Guarded Horn Clauses,"* Ph.D. Thesis, Information Engineering Course, Faculty of Engineering, University of Tokey, 1986.

Processing Abductive Reasoning via Contextual Logic Programming *

Evelina Lamma and Paola Mello
DEIS, Università di Bologna
Viale Risorgimento 2, 40136 Bologna, Italy

Abstract

Different extensions to logic programming have recently been introduced to deal with abductive reasoning. In this work we address the issue of how to process abductive reasoning in the field of logic programming by following a compilation-based approach. In particular, we describe how an abductive reasoning system can be translated in Contextual Logic Programming, so we can use the efficiency of already existing compile-based implementation for contexts.

1 Introduction

A great deal of interest has recently been devoted to the logical formalization of adbuctive reasoning in different fields. Poole [11] has given a logical foundation of abductive reasoning in the context of diagnostic problem solving. Eshgi and Kowalski [3] discuss an abductive framework in a logic programming setting and its operational semantics, and apply it to implement negation as failure. Kakas and Mancarella [4] declaratively formalize abductive reasoning by using the stable model semantics, while in [2] both a procedural and declarative semantics based on perfect models is discussed for abductive logic programming.

In the meanwhile, some efforts have been made to define how to process abductive reasoning in logic programming by designing efficient implementations. In [12] it is shown how to implement a default reasoning system (embedding abduction) "by compiling its inputs into Horn clauses with negation as failure , thereby allowing direct use advances in logic programming implementation technology".

*This research was partially supported by. C.N.R. "Progetto Finalizzato Sistemi Informatici e Calcolo Parallelo" under grant n. 890004269

In this paper, we further investigate compilation-based implementation techniques to process abductive reasoning in logic programming systems such as those proposed in [3,2,1]. The implementation is strictly related to an operational semantics given in terms of inference rules. An equivalent declarative semantics is given in [1], in terms of admissible Herbrand models.

Since abductive hypotheses are considered as updates to the theory currently in use, the processing of abduction here proposed is an interesting application of Contextual Logic Programming ([10,9]), slightly modified, where units can be *generic* theories. In particular, whenever an atom A is abducted, it is added to the current database of clauses (i.e. the current context) as an instance of a generic theory by using *context extensions*, and integrity constraints are checked by reasoning backward in this new, extended database. Processing abduction via translation in an extended Contextual Logic Programming language (hereinafter called Ctx_Prolog [8]), can take advantage of the efficient, compiled-based implementation of this language [6,7].

2 The Abductive Framework

Recently, abduction has been recognized as a fundamental mode of inference in logic programming, closely related to hypothetical reasoning [3,4,2]. In practice, given a theory T and a formula G, through abduction (in a complementary way with respect to deduction) we find the set of atoms (hypotheses) Ta that have to be assumed to make true G, i.e. such that $T \cup Ta \vdash G$. Operationally, G is derivable in T with the conditional answer Ta. The generation of abductive hypotheses can be restricted by considering integrity constraints. In this way only meaningful answers consistent with the constraints are derived. Both in [3] and [4] integrity constraints are introduced as a set of formulae, IC, to be satisfied by the program P and the set of hypotheses Ta (i.e. $T \cup Ta \vdash IC$). In practice, to perform abductive reasoning, we have to determine a set of abducible atoms. Operationally, during the resolution procedure, whenever an *abducible* atom A is encountered, A is assumed, provided it is consistent to do so. We have different ways for determining abducible atoms (see [2]). Here we adopt predicate specific abduction by associating to each program a set of abducible predicate symbols.

Example 2.1 *The following program P1, inspired to [5], where the set of abducible predicates is { broken_spokes, punctured_tube, leaky_valve }, shows that abduction is a natural way for performing fault diagnosis:*

$wobbly\_wheel \leftarrow flat\_tyre$
$wobbly\_wheel \leftarrow broken\_spokes$
$flat\_tyre \leftarrow punctured\_tube$
$flat\_tyre \leftarrow leaky\_valve$
$tyre\_holds\_air \leftarrow$

Consider the integrity constraint $\leftarrow flat\_tyre, tyre\_holds\_air$.
The possible causes of wobbly_wheel (i.e. its explanations) can be determined by reasoning backward from the goal $\leftarrow wobbly\_wheel$. *In this case, we obtain three conditional*

answers, respectively {broken_spokes}, {punctured_tube} and {leaky_valve}, among which only the first is consistent with the integrity constraint. □

We restrict ourselves to the case of ***variable–free hypotheses*** (as in [3]) in order to avoid the assumption of existentially quantified atomic formulae. As stated in [3], "this is the analogue of restricting the selection of negative subgoals to variable–free literals in negation by failure", and can be accomplished by a safe computation rule.

3 Operational Semantics

In this section we present the operational semantics of the abductive framework discussed above in terms of inference rules (in a sequent–style notation). The implementation "via" Contextual Logic Programming (described in section 4) is largely inspired by these rules.

For the sake of simplicity we assume that integrity checking is done each time an atom is abducted, that abducted atoms are always ground and integrity constraints are only denials as in [3]. Therefore, even if it is generally more efficient to check consistency in an incremental way by reasoning forward from abductive hypotheses (see [3]), we check constraints by reasoning backward from them. The constraints are satisfied if there is no refutation for them. This does not necessitate any extension to the theorem-proving technique used to execute logic programs. In the operational semantics, we have to maintain, at each step, the current set of abducted atoms, to perform integrity checking. Moreover, we have to explicitly represent conditional answers besides answer substitutions. More formally, a (conjunctive) formula $G\vartheta$ is derivable with conditional answer Abd' in program P (with substitution ϑ and the set of abducted atoms Abd) if there exists a proof for $P \cup Abd \vdash_{\vartheta,Abd'} G$. A proof for $P \cup Abd \vdash_{\vartheta,Abd'} G$ is a tree such that the root node is labelled by $P \cup Abd \vdash_{\vartheta,Abd'} G$, the internal nodes are derived by using the inference rules of definition 3.1 and all the leaves are labelled by the empty formula (*true*). In the sequel, let P be a program (i.e. a set of clauses belonging), Δ_P the set of abducible predicate symbols of P, A, A' atoms, G_1, G_2 (conjunctive) formulae, ϑ, γ substitutions, ϵ the empty substitution and Abd, Abd', Abd'' sets of abducibles. Let $mgu(A, A')$ be the most general unifier between A and A'.

Definition 3.1 *(Inference Rules)*

(1) True

$$\frac{}{P \cup Abd \vdash_{\epsilon,\{\}} true}$$

True is always proved with the empty substitution and without any abduction.

(2) Conjunction

$$\frac{P \cup Abd \vdash_{\vartheta,Abd'} G_1; \; P \cup Abd \cup Abd' \vdash_{\gamma,Abd''} (G_2)\vartheta}{P \cup Abd \vdash_{\vartheta\gamma,Abd' \cup Abd''} (G_1, G_2)}$$

To prove a conjunction we separately prove its conjoined formulae. Then we suitably compose the resulting substitutions and abducted atoms. Notice that, since only ground atoms can be abducted, intermediate substitutions determined during the proof for the second conjoined formula (i.e. ϑ) are not applied to already abducted atoms (i.e. Abd').

(3) Atomic Formula

$$\frac{A' \leftarrow G \in P \cup Abd; \vartheta = mgu(A, A');\;\; P \cup Abd \;\vdash_{\gamma, Abd'} (G)\vartheta}{P \cup Abd \;\vdash_{\vartheta\gamma, Abd'}\; A}$$

To prove an atomic formula we find a clause in the program and try to prove its body G. The resulting abducted atoms are those abducted to prove G.

(4) Abducible Formula

$$\frac{A = p(T); p\; \in \Delta_P; P \cup Abd \cup \{A\} \;\vdash_{SLDNF}\; IC}{P \cup Abd \;\vdash_{\epsilon, \{A\}}\; A}$$

When an abducible atom A is encountered, we add it to program P and the current set of abducted atoms Abd, then check the integrity constraints IC in this new set of clauses by using a standard SLDNF resolution. In such a derivation no abduction is performed.

4 Implementation through Contexts

As can be inferred from the operational semantics presented in section 3, when processing abductive reasoning we have to face the dynamic addition of the code corresponding to the abducted atoms. While this issue is not a real problem if we follow an interpretative approach, implementing dynamic addition of new code is not trivial when following a compilation-based approach.

Since abductive hypotheses are considered as updates to the theory currently in use, we take advantage of Contextual Logic Programming ([10,9]) and, in particular, translate logic programs with abduction into the language Ctx_Prolog ([8]), which is based on Contextual Logic Programming. While in logic programming the set of clauses to be used during a proof is statically fixed and cannot be changed, in Contextual Logic Programming this set can be dynamically determined and changed by suitably composing separate theories (called *units*) in *contexts*. More in detail, the context, denoted by a list of unit names, represents the virtual (current) set of clauses used to prove a goal. Contexts can be dynamically built by using the extension operator ($\gg$). In particular, the execution of $u_{N+1} \gg G$ in the current context $C = [u_N, ..., u_i, ..., u_1]$, where u_{N+1} is a unit name and G a goal formula, causes the proof of G to be executed in a new context $C1 = [u_{N+1}, u_N, ..., u_i, ..., u_1]$ obtained by pushing u_{N+1} on top of the previous context (see [9] for the operational semantics).

Example 4.1 *Let us consider the following program:*

unit $u1$:	*unit* $u2$:	*unit* $u3$:
$b(1) \leftarrow$	$a(X) \leftarrow b(X)$	$c(X) \leftarrow a(X)$

The top goal $\leftarrow u1 \gg u2 \gg u3 \gg c(X)$ *is proved, with answer substitution* $\{X/1\}$. *In particular,* $c(X)$ *is proved in the context* $[u3, u2, u1]$, *i.e.* $[u3, u2, u1] \vdash c(X)$, *by "virtually" using the dynamically composed set of clauses:*

$c(X) \leftarrow a(X)$
$b(1) \leftarrow$ □
$a(X) \leftarrow b(X)$

One useful extension of Contextual Logic Programming, present in Ctx_Prolog, concerns the use of *parameters* in units, in order to use "specialized" versions of them. This can be accomplished by using a general term rather than just a constant to refer to a unit, encoding the unit name as the main functor and the parameters as arguments.

To process abductive reasoning, we use parametric units to represent abducible atoms. Each abducible atom with structure p/n is represented by a single, parametric unit of the form:

unit $p(X1, ...Xn)$:
$\$extends(p/n)$
$p(X1, ...Xn) \leftarrow$

where the declaration $\$extends(p/n)$ means that this definition extends (and does not override as happens in the default case) previous definitions in the context. This is necessary since we can have multiple abducted atoms or predicate definitions with the same functor and arity in the context, and all have to be considered for integrity checking. Each abducted atom $p(t_1, ..., t_n)$ corresponds to a specialization of the associated parametric unit, where parameters are bound to the ground terms $t_1,...,t_n$. Whenever an abducible atom $p(t_1, ..., t_n)$ is encountered during the computation, the current context is extended with the corresponding specialized parametric unit. Then, to perform integrity checking, we add to the context the original version of program (P). Integrity constraints are checked in this new, extended database composed of P and all abducted atoms.

Example 4.2 *Let us consider program P1 of example 2.1 and the integrity constraint,* $ic = not(flat\_tyre, tyre\_holds\_air)$. *Through an automatic translation, we can produce a Ctx_Prolog program composed of two units,* pl_abd *and* pl, *which are used, respectively, during abduction and integrity checking.*

unit pl_abd :

wobbly_wheel	$\leftarrow$	*flat_tyre*
wobbly_wheel	$\leftarrow$	*broken_spokes* $\gg$ pl $\gg$ *ic*
flat_tyre	$\leftarrow$	*punctured_tube* $\gg$ pl $\gg$ *ic*
flat_tyre	$\leftarrow$	*leaky_valve* $\gg$ pl $\gg$ *ic*
tyre_holds_air	$\leftarrow$	

unit p1 :
wobbly_wheel ← *flat_tyre*
wobbly_wheel ← *broken_spokes*
flat_tyre ← *punctured_tube*
flat_tyre ← *leaky_valve*
tyre_holds_air ←

Moreover, for instance, the abducible predicate leaky_valve gives origin to the following unit:
unit leaky_valve :
$extends(*leaky_valve*)
leaky_valve ←

The goal ← *wobbly_wheel in P*1 *corresponds to the invocation of the goal:*
← p1*_abd* ≫ *wobbly_wheel*
in the empty context. □

Thanks to the implementation of contexts we choose (see [7] with regard to the ***conservative policy***), when we extend the context with the original program to perform integrity checking, all the bindings for the predicate calls corresponding to abducible predicates can be determined. This avoids a dynamic search along the current context at each call in the original program of some abducible predicate.

The only problem in using contexts for implementing abduction with constraints arises when we add an abducted atom to the context. As can be inferred from the operational semantics defined in section 3, (definition 3.1, rule (2)) abducted atoms are maintained and passed through conjunctions. This is not the case in Contextual Logic Programming. If C is the current context, it will be the same for all conjunctive formulae [10]. To overcome this problem, we introduce two kinds of context extension operators. The temporary context extension ($U \gg G$) performs a context extension with U whose duration is the proof of G. The permanent context extension ($U \ll G$) extends the context with U and does not discard U at the end of the proof for G, but maintains it until the end of the computation. Therefore, from the operational semantics point of view, we consider only context extensions involving units corresponding to abducible atoms as *permanent*.

4.1 The WAM–based Implementation

The Warren Abstract Machine (WAM [13]) is an abstract machine for efficient implementation of the Prolog language, adopted as the basic implementation support by most Prolog compilers. When implementing extensions to Logic Programming, we can follow two implementation methods: the first is based on "naive" translation into standard Prolog code (as in [12]) and then compilation on a standard WAM, while the second is based on a direct compilation on an extended WAM. The main drawback of the first approach (the simpler one) is a great increase in overhead since at run–time more unifications are performed due to additional arguments introduced in each program clause. The main drawback of the second approach (more efficient) is that WAM extensions are sometimes complex and require the implementation of a new emulation environment.

Our approach in processing abductive reasoning can be considered an intermediate one. In fact, abductive logic programs are translated into contextual logic programs by mapping each abduction into a context extension. Contextual Logic Programming implementation, in turn, is based on direct compilation of programs into an intermediate code which is executed on an extended WAM supporting contexts and parametric units. With respect to standard WAM, in the extended machine we have a new data area (called *context stack*) which maintains the dynamic set of clauses representing abducted atoms to be used for integrity checking and to provide the final conditional answer. The context stack grows (allocate_ctx instruction) whenever a temporary/permanent extension $U \gg G$ / $U \ll G$ occurs, and shrinks when G definitely fails or is deterministically solved in the case of temporary extensions (deallocate_ctx instruction). Notice that you can have multiple occurrences of each unit in the context, i.e. multiple instances of the same unit U. This is important since, in our abductive framework, we need to have different *instances* of the same abducible atom, with different substitutions. For this reason, to keep trace of the right substitutions, when extending the context with a parametric unit an appropriate area is allocated to store the actual value of arguments. For details on the implementation of parametric units see [7].

5 Conclusions

This paper shows how to process abductive reasoning taking advantage of extensions of Logic Programming dealing with dynamic knowledge assimilation, such as Contextual Logic Programming. The implementation is based on an operational semantics given in terms of inference rules and is obtained by the translation of abductive logic programs into programs based on Contextual Logic Programming implemented, in turn, on an extended Warren Abstract Machine. This approach turns out to be quite efficient and allows us to integrate abductive reasoning into a framework where dynamic assimilation of knowledge is provided through context extension.

In the future, we plan to follow two complementary directions. The first concerns revision of the implementation on the basis of performance benchmarks made on significant programs, and the definition of tools such a translator of abductive programs into contextual logic programs. The second concerns the application of Truth Maintenance Techniques in order to perform integrity checking more efficiently and withdraw hypotheses non–monotonically whenever some constraint is no longer satisfied.

References

[1] A. Brogi, E. Lamma, P. Mancarella, and P. Mello. Abduction in a multi-theory

framework. In S. Gaglio, editor, *Proceedings 2nd Congress AI*IA*. Lecture Notes on Artificial Intelligence, Springer–Verlag, October 1991, Forthcoming.

[2] W. Chen and D.H. Warren. Abductive logic programming. Technical report, State University of New York at Stony Brook, 1989.

[3] K. Eshgi and R.A. Kowalski. Abduction compared with negation by failure. In G. Levi and M. Martelli, editors, *Proc. Sixth International Conference on Logic Programming*, page 234. The MIT Press, 1989.

[4] A.C. Kakas and P. Mancarella. Generalized stable models: a semantics for abduction. In *Proceedings of 9th European Conference on Artificial Intelligence*. Pitman, 1990.

[5] R.A. Kowalski. Problems and promises of computational logic. In *Proceedings of Symposium on Computational Logic*, pages 1–36. Springer-Verlag, November 1990.

[6] E. Lamma, P. Mello, and A. Natali. The design of an abstract machine for efficient implementation of contexts in logic programming. In G. Levi and M. Martelli, editors, *Proc. Sixth International Conference on Logic Programming*, pages 303–317. The MIT Press, 1989.

[7] E. Lamma, P. Mello, and A. Natali. An extended warren abstract machine for the execution of structured logic programs. *To appear in Journal of Logic Programming*, 1991.

[8] E. Lamma, P. Mello, and G.F. Rossi. Parametric composable modules in a logic programming language. Technical report, Department of Computer Science, University of Udine and DEIS, University of Bologna, 1991.

[9] P. Mello, A. Natali, and C. Ruggieri. Logic programming in a software engineering perspective. In L. Lusk and R.A. Overbeek, editors, *Proc. NACLP*, pages 451–458. The MIT Press, 1989.

[10] L. Monteiro and A. Porto. Contextual logic programming. In G. Levi and M. Martelli, editors, *Proc. Sixth International Conference on Logic Programming*, pages 284–302. The MIT Press, 1989.

[11] D.L. Poole. Representing knowledge for logic–based diagnosis. In *Proc. Int'l Conf. FGCS*, pages 1282–1290, 1988.

[12] D.L. Poole. Compiling a default reasoning system into Prolog. *New Generation Computing*, 9:3–38, 1991.

[13] D.H.D. Warren. An abstract Prolog instruction set. Technical Report TR 309, SRI International, 1983.

Efficient Implementation of Narrowing and Rewriting

*Michael Hanus**
Technische Fakultät, Universität Bielefeld
W-4800 Bielefeld 1, Germany
e-mail: hanus@techfak.uni-bielefeld.de

Abstract

We present an efficient implementation method for a language that amalgamates functional and logic programming styles. The operational semantics of the language consists of resolution to solve predicates and narrowing and rewriting to evaluate functional expressions. The implementation is based on an extension of the Warren Abstract Machine (WAM). This extension causes no overhead for pure logic programs and allows the execution of functional programs by narrowing and rewriting with the same efficiency as their relational equivalents. Moreover, there are many cases where functional programs are more efficiently executed than their relational equivalents.

1 Introduction

During the last years a lot of approaches have been proposed in order to amalgamate functional and logic programming languages [7] [1]. Such integrations have several advantages:

1. Functional and logic programming styles can be used in one language.
2. It extends logic programming by allowing nested expressions, i.e., it is not necessary to flatten complex expressions as in Prolog.
3. It extends functional programming by solving equations between functional expressions.
4. It allows the programmer to specify functional dependencies between data. This information can be used for a more efficient implementation.
5. Large parts of logic programs are functional computations. In an integrated language these parts are defined as functions which can be more efficiently executed than their relational equivalents.

Point 1 is a matter of taste, and point 2 is no real argument since nested expressions can be flattened by a preprocessor [4]. But the last three arguments show that an integration of functional and logic languages yields a proper extension of each of these language types.

*on leave from Fachbereich Informatik, Universität Dortmund, W-4600 Dortmund 50

For instance, consider the following logic program for the addition of natural numbers where numbers are represented as terms constructed by 0 and s:

```
add(0, N, N) ←
add(N, 0, N) ←
add(s(M), N, s(L))  ←  add(M, N, L)
add(N, s(M), s(L))  ←  add(N, M, L)
```

If the literal add(0,0,Z) should be proved, then a backtrack point (also called "choice point" in [33]) must be generated since there are two alternative proofs yielding the result {Z/0} in both cases. The equivalent functional program is

```
0 + N  =  N
N + 0  =  N
s(M) + N  =  s(M + N)
N + s(M)  =  s(N + M)
```

The equation 0 + 0 = Z can be solved in a determinstic way by applying one of the first two equations to the left-hand side. A creation of a backtrack point is unnecessary since "+" is a function which has a unique result. One could argue that a Prolog compiler can also optimize the code for the predicate add but this requires some sort of mode information which is not available if the equation X + Y = s(0) should also be solved (where X and Y are free variables). A genuine integration of functional and logic languages permits such goals and has no fixed modes for the application of functions. In this paper we present such a language together with an implementation which avoids the creation of backtrack points if it is not necessary.

Another advantage of an integrated functional and logic language is the reduction of the search space by functional computations: Fribourg [8] has given examples for terminating functional-logic programs where equivalent Prolog programs do not terminate or need more computation steps. This aspect is also covered by our language and we will discuss this point in more detail in subsequent sections.

A lot of the proposed integrations of functional and logic languages are based on Horn clause logic with equality [31] which offers predicates defined by Horn clauses for logic programming and functions defined by (conditional) equations for functional programming. The declarative semantics is the well-known Horn clause logic [25] with the restriction that the equality predicate is always interpreted as identity. The operational semantics is based on *resolution* for predicates (like in logic languages) and *rewriting* for functions (like in functional languages). Since it is also required to *solve* equations between functional expressions, a new inference rules is added: *narrowing* is a combination of unification and rewriting, i.e., a subterm of the goal is unified with the left-hand side of an equation such that the instantiated subterm can be rewritten with that equation and the unifier is applied to the whole goal. This general strategy has been refined by Hölldobler [19] to the *innermost basic narrowing* strategy where exactly one possible subterm must be narrowed in a computation step. This strategy has the same efficiency as SLD-resolution, but Hölldobler has shown that goals can also be simplified by rewriting before a narrowing step is performed. This loses no solutions and is more efficient than Prolog's computation strategy.

However, the discussion about the better efficiency of functional computations is only relevant if there is a good implementation technique for narrowing and rewriting. Up to now most of the proposed systems are implemented by an interpreter which can not compete with present Prolog implementations based on a compilational approach [33]. Merely [3], [24], [27] and [26] contain approaches to compile (lazy) narrowing rules into code of an abstract machine, but the integration of rewriting is not addressed in these papers. This paper presents an implementation technique for a functional and logic programming language with the following properties:

- The operational semantics of the language is based on resolution, narrowing and rewriting.
- Pure logic programs without functions are compiled in the same way as in Prolog systems based on the Warren Abstract Machine (WAM) [33], i.e., there is no overhead because of the functional part.
- There is a particular technique to deal with occurrences (references to subterms) where the next narrowing or rewrite rule can be applied. Thus functional programs are executed by narrowing and rewriting at least with almost the same efficiency as their relational equivalents by resolution. Moreover, there are large classes of programs where the functional versions are more efficiently executed by narrowing and rewriting than the relational versions by resolution.
- There are no modes for the execution of functions. Similarly to logic programming, functions can be evaluated with ground or non-ground terms at each argument position. However, functions are evaluated by determinstic rewriting if the arguments are ground, and in other cases (non-deterministic) narrowing is applied. This is automatically decided at run time, i.e., user annotations are not necessary to specify where rewriting or narrowing should be applied.

Our implementation is based on an extension of the WAM [33] and therefore we assume familiarity with the basic concepts of this machine. The techniques presented in this paper are based on a previous proposal [12] but have the following basic differences: The current implementation simplifies the goal by rewriting before *each* narrowing step (normalized narrowing) whereas in [12] rewriting is only applied before an entire narrowing derivation is computed. Furthermore, we present new techniques for the management of occurrences which speeds up the execution time up to 30% and saves up to 40% of the heap space because of a delayed copying of function symbols onto the heap.

This paper is organized as follows. In the next section we define the operational semantics implemented by our system. The techniques for the efficient management of occurrences are shown in section 3 and details about our abstract machine are presented in section 4. For the sake of simplicity we introduce the basic implementation techniques only for unconditional equations. The necessary extensions to deal with conditional equations are shown in section 5. Section 6 shows some results of our implementation.

2 The implemented operational semantics

We have mentioned in the introduction that our approach to integrate functional and logic programming languages is based on Horn clause logic with equality (see [31] for details) which extends pure Horn logic by allowing user definitions for the binary predicate "=". Since Horn clause logic with equality interprets this predicate as identity, we can define functions by this feature. For instance, the following clauses define a function **isort** on lists which produces a sorted permutation of the argument list by the insertion sort method (we use the Prolog notation for lists [6] and we assume that the ordering predicates =< and > are defined elsewhere):

```
isort([])      = []
isort([E|L])   = insert(E,isort(L))
insert(E,[])     = [E]
insert(E,[F|L])  = [E,F|L]              ←   E =< F
insert(E,[F|L])  = [F|insert(E,L)]      ←   E > F
```

Clauses for the predicate "=" are also called **conditional equations**. If the condition is empty, we call it also **unconditional equation**. Note that this program is neither a valid K-LEAF program [3] (since the left-hand side of the two conditional equations are identical) nor a valid BABEL program (since the conditions of the two conditional equations are "propositional satisfiable" [28]). But it is allowed in our language since we only require the confluence of the term rewriting relation generated by the (conditional) equations (the **insert** equation system is confluent since "`E =< F` *and* `E > F`" is unsatisfiable).

Our source language ALF ("**A**lgebraic **L**ogic **F**unctional language") consists of Horn clauses for user-defined predicates and equations for user-defined functions (the left-hand sides can also be non-linear in contrast to K-LEAF and BABEL). Furthermore, ALF has a (parametrized) module system and a many-sorted type structure. Since these features have no influence on the execution of ALF-programs, we omit the details here and refer the interested reader to [12] and [15]. An important aspect of the language is the distinction between **constructors** and **functions**. A constructor must not be the outermost symbol of the left-hand side of a conditional equation, i.e., constructor terms are always irreducible. This distinction is specified by the user [12] and necessary for the notion of *innermost occurrences* [8].

The *declarative semantics* of ALF is the well-known Horn clause logic with equality as to be found in [31]. As mentioned in the introduction, the *operational semantics* of ALF is based on resolution for predicates and rewriting and innermost basic narrowing for functions. In order to give a precise definition of the operational semantics, we represent a goal by a skeleton and an environment part [19]: the *skeleton* is a goal composed of terms and literals occurring in the original program, and the *environment* is a substitution which has to be applied to the goal in order to obtain the actual goal. The initial goal G is represented by the pair $< G; id >$ where id is the identity substitution. We define the following inference rules to derive a new goal from a given one (if π is a position in a term t, then t/π denotes the subterm of t at position π and $t[\pi \leftarrow s]$ denotes the term obtained by replacing the subterm t/π by s in t): Let $< L_1, \dots, L_n \; ; \; \sigma >$ be a given goal ($L_1, \dots, L_n$ are the skeleton literals and σ is the environment).

1. If L_1 is an equation $s = t$ and there is a mgu σ' for $\sigma(s)$ and $\sigma(t)$, then the goal

$$< L_2, \dots, L_n \; ; \; \sigma' \circ \sigma >$$

is derived by **reflection.**

2. If L_1 is not an equation and there is a new variant $L \leftarrow C$ of a program clause and σ' is a mgu for $\sigma(L_1)$ and L, then the goal

$$< C, L_2, \ldots, L_n \; ; \; \sigma' \circ \sigma >$$

is derived by **resolution.**

3. Let π be a leftmost-innermost position in the first skeleton literal L_1, i.e., the subterm L_1/π has a defined function symbol at the top and all argument terms consist of variables and constructors (cf. [8]).
   (a) If there is a new variant $l = r \leftarrow C$ of a program clause and $\sigma(L_1/\pi)$ and l are unifiable with mgu σ', then the goal

   $$< C, L_1[\pi \leftarrow r], L_2, \ldots, L_n \; ; \; \sigma' \circ \sigma >$$

   is derived by **innermost basic narrowing.**
   (b) If x is a new variable and σ' is the substitution $\{x \leftarrow \sigma(L_1/\pi)\}$, then the goal

   $$< L_1[\pi \leftarrow x], L_2, \ldots, L_n \; ; \; \sigma' \circ \sigma >$$

   is derived by **innermost reflection** (this corresponds to the elimination of an innermost redex [19]).

4. If π is a non-variable position in L_1, $l = r \leftarrow C$ is a new variant of a program clause and σ' is a substitution with $\sigma(L_1/\pi) = \sigma'(l)$ and the goal $< C \; ; \; \sigma' >$ can be derived to the empty goal without instantiating any variables from $\sigma(L_1)$, then the goal

$$< L_1[\pi \leftarrow \sigma'(r)], L_2, \ldots, L_n \; ; \; \sigma >$$

is derived by **rewriting** (thus rewriting is only applied to the first literal, but this is no restriction since a conjunction like L_1, L_2, L_3 can also be written as an equation $and(L_1, and(L_2, L_3)) = true$).

5. If L_1 is an equation and the two sides have different constructors at the same outermost position (a position not belonging to arguments of functions), then the whole goal is **rejected,** i.e., the proof fails.

The complete operational semantics of ALF is shown in figure 1. The innermost reflection rule must only be applied to *partial* functions, i.e., functions which are not reducible for all ground terms of appropriate sorts [19]. The attribute *basic* of a narrowing step emphasizes that a narrowing step is only applied at an occurrence of the original program and not at occurrences introduced by substitutions [21]. The restriction to basic occurrences is important for an efficient implementation of narrowing and rewriting (see below). The rewriting rule has the disadvantage that terms from the environment part can be moved to the skeleton part, but it has been shown that such terms can be safely moved back to the environment part [30]. Therefore environment terms are never moved to the skeleton part in our implementation.

Start: Apply *rewriting* as long as possible (from innermost to outermost positions).
If the goal is not *rejected* then:

Narrow: If possible, apply the *innermost basic narrowing* rule and go to **Start**.
If possible, apply the *innermost reflection* rule and goto **Narrow**.
If the first literal of the goal is an equation
then: If possible, apply the *reflection* rule and go to **Start**.
else: If possible, apply the *resolution* rule and go to **Start**.
Otherwise: fail (and try an alternative proof)

Figure 1: Operational semantics of ALF

This operational semantics is sound and complete if the term rewriting relation generated by the conditional equations is canonical and the condition and the right-hand side of each conditional equation do not contain *extra-variables* [19]. If these restrictions are not satisfied, it may be possible to transform the program into an equivalent program for which this operational semantics is complete. For instance, Bertling and Ganzinger [2] have proposed a method to transform conditional equations with extra-variables such that narrowing and reflection will be complete. Therefore we allow extra-variables in conditional equations. For instance, our operational semantics is complete for the following set of equations defining quicksort, which can be proved by the CEC completion system [2] (we omit the definition of `=<` and `>`):

```
conc([],L)     = L
conc([E|R],L) = [E|conc(R,L)]

split(E,[])     = ([],[])
split(E,[F|L]) = ([F|L1],L2)  ←  E >  F, split(E,L) = (L1,L2)
split(E,[F|L]) = (L1,[F|L2])  ←  E =< F, split(E,L) = (L1,L2)

qsort([])     = []
qsort([E|L]) = conc(qsort(L1),[E|qsort(L2)])  ←   split(E,L) = (L1,L2)
```

('`,`' is defined as an infix operator for building pairs of lists). Note that this is not a valid K-LEAF or BABEL program since the extra-variables `L1` and `L2` occur in the right-hand side of the defining equations. In order to avoid the extra-variables one has to replace the last equation by

```
qsort([E|L]) = conc(qsort(split1(E,L)),[E|qsort(split2(E,L))])
```

and redefine the split function. This solution is less efficient (because the list `L` must be processed twice) and simplification orderings fail to prove the termination of the rewrite relation [2]. These drawbacks may be accepted, but there are other examples where the use of extra-variables cannot be avoided with simple transformations. The function `last` computes the last element of a given list. It can be explicitly defined or, if conc is defined as above, by the simple conditional equation

```
last(L) = E  ←  conc(L1,[E]) = L
```

In this case `last(L)` is evaluated by searching the right instantiations of `L1` and `E` (note that there is at most one solution if `L` is given). The use of extra-variables gives us the full power of logic programming inside functional programming. Hence ALF allows extra-variables in conditional equations. If such a conditional equation is applied in a rewrite step, only the first solution to the extra-variables is considered. This is sufficient because all equations are required to be confluent.

It is also possible to specify additional equational clauses which are only used for rewriting. For instance, Fribourg [8] has shown that the addition of inductive axioms for rewriting is useful to reduce the search space. In this case the proved goals are valid with respect to the least Herbrand model but may be invalid in the class of all models. Therefore an ALF-program consists of three groups of clauses: relational clauses which define all predicates except "=", conditional equations used for narrowing and conditional equations used for rewriting (Fribourg's SLOG language allows only unconditional equations for rewriting). Usually, all conditional equations in an ALF-program are used for narrowing and rewriting, but the programmer can specify that some equations should only be applied for narrowing or rewriting, respectively. For instance, the inductive axiom `rev(rev(L)) = L` can be used for rewriting to reduce the search space (the function `rev` reverses all elements in a list). To use it as a narrowing rule makes no sense since this would expand the search space.

Similarly to Prolog, the program clauses in ALF are ordered and the different choices for clauses in a computation step are implemented by a backtracking strategy. Note that backtracking is only necessary in the resolution and narrowing rule but not in rewriting since simplification by rewriting produces unique terms independently of the chosen clauses (because of the confluence of the term rewriting relation). Therefore rewriting is a *deterministic* process and the simplification of a goal by rewriting before a narrowing step means that in ALF deterministic computations are performed whenever possible and nondeterministic computations (narrowing/resolution) are only used when it is not avoidable. The Andorra computation model [17] is related to ALF's operational semantics. But in contrast to the Andorra model the rewriting mechanism of ALF yields deterministic computations also when more than one clause matches (see `add` example in section 1) and may delete goals with infinite or nondeterministic computations. E.g., if `X*0 = 0` is a defining equation for the function `*`, then a term like t `* 0` will be simplified to `0`, i.e., the entire subterm t will be deleted. This is important if t contains unevaluated functions with variable arguments.

In order to demonstrate the improved efficiency of this operational semantics in comparison to Prolog's computation strategy, consider the following equations for the concatenation function on lists:

```
conc([],L)    = L
conc([E|R],L) = [E|conc(R,L)]
```

If `a` and `b` are constructors, then the goal

```
conc(conc([a|V],W),Y) = [b|Z]
```

is simplified by rewriting to the goal

```
[a|conc(conc(V,W),Y)] = [b|Z]
```

which is immediately rejected since `a` and `b` are different constructors. The equivalent Prolog goal

```
append([a|V],W,L), append(L,Y,[b|Z])
```

causes an infinite loop for any order of literals and clauses [29]. More details about the advantages of rewriting and rejection in combination with narrowing can be found in [8] and [19].

3 The management of occurrences

In this section we want to show the basic ideas to implement the operational semantics of ALF in an efficient way. Since Prolog's operational semantics is included in our language, we have decided to extend the WAM in order to implement the new aspects of ALF. The resolution and reflection rule can be directly implemented in the WAM since there is no difference to Prolog. The implementation of rejection is also obvious (note the similarity between unification and rejection). Therefore we discuss the implementation of narrowing and rewriting in more detail. For the sake of simplicity we consider only unconditional equations in this section. The necessary extensions to deal with conditional equations are shown in section 5.

The WAM stores terms on the heap. In order to obtain an efficient implementation of narrowing and rewriting, we need a fast access to the subterm where the next narrowing or rewrite rule should be applied. A dynamic search through the argument term of the current literal is too expensive for this purpose. But since we use an innermost basic strategy, all relevant occurrences of subterms can be determined at compile time. For instance, consider the clause

```
fac(s(N))  =  fac(N) * s(N)
```

If this equation is applied to reduce a term of the form `fac(A)`, then we know by the innermost basic strategy that the argument term `A` does not contain any occurrences of functions belonging to the skeleton part. Therefore we replace the term `fac(A)` by the right-hand side `fac(N) * s(N)` (after unifying `A` and `s(N)`) and then we reduce the subterm `fac(N)`. If this subterm is completely reduced to a term `T`, then the term `T * s(N)` is the next term where an equation must be applied.

Hence we introduce a new data structure called **occurrence stack**. An **occurrence** is a reference to a term on the heap. The occurrence stack contains all references to subterms of an argument of the current literal where narrowing and rewrite rules could be applied (in innermost order, i.e., the reference to the innermost term is always the top element). For instance, if `p(f(c(g(X))))` is the current skeleton literal, `f` and `g` are functions and `c` a constructor, then the occurrence stack contains a reference to the subterm `f(c(g(X)))` and a reference to the subterm `g(X)` at the top. Now it is easy to see that the compiler can generate all necessary instructions for the manipulation of the occurrence stack. For instance, the right-hand side of the above equation for `fac` can be translated into

<replace the term at the current occurrence by `fac(N) * s(N)`>
<push a reference to the subterm `fac(N)` onto the occurrence stack>

The right-hand side contains two functions, therefore an additional occurrence must be pushed onto the occurrence stack. If the right-hand side does not contain a function symbol (i.e., only constructors and variables), then an element must be popped from the occurrence stack. For instance, the right-hand side of the clause `fac(0) = s(0)` is translated into

<replace the term at the current occurrence by `s(0)`>
<pop a reference from the occurrence stack>

This has the effect that the computation proceeds at the next innermost occurrence stored on the occurrence stack.

Before a literal is proved by resolution, all arguments must be evaluated by rewriting and narrowing. Therefore the arguments must be stored on the heap and the occurrence stack is initialized with the appropriate references. For instance, the literal `p(f(c(g(X))))` is translated into

<write the term `f(c(g(X)))` onto the heap>
<push reference to the term `f(c(g(X)))` onto the occurrence stack>
<push reference to the term `g(X)` onto the occurrence stack>
<start rewriting and narrowing>

Now a new problem occurs. Rewriting tries to simplify the current argument term by applying rewrite rules from innermost to outermost positions in the term. If a subterm cannot be rewritten, then the next innermost position is tried, i.e., an element is popped from the occurrence stack. This is necessary as the following example shows: If the only equations for `f` and `g` are

```
f(Z) = 0
g(0) = 0
```

then the term `g(X)` cannot be rewritten (only narrowing could be applied), but the term `f(c(g(X)))` can be simplified to `0`.

Hence the rewriting process pops all elements from the occurrence stack and therefore the stack is empty when rewriting is finished and a narrowing rule should be applied. In order to avoid a dynamic search for the appropriate innermost occurrence, we introduce a second stack for storing the deleted occurrences (in [12] all occurrences are stored on one stack and therefore more time is needed to recompute the occurrences in case of successful rewriting). This stack (called **copy occurrence stack**) contains all occurrences if rewriting is finished and the original occurrence stack is empty. Thus the occurrence stack can be reinstalled by a simple block-copy operation. There is only one case where this method cannot be applied (but fortunately this case rarely occurs): If a rewrite rule deletes a subterm because there are variables on the left-hand side which do not occur on the right-hand side (as in the clause `f(Z) = 0`) and the copy occurrence stack is not empty, then some occurrences must be deleted from the copy occurrence stack. Since this is expensive or requires additional information in the data structures, we have implemented a simple solution: In this case the copy occurrence stack is marked as "invalid" which has the consequence that a new occurrence stack for the current argument term is computed before a narrowing rule is applied.

The presented technique for the management of occurrences has the advantage that the next relevant subterm for rewriting or narrowing can be found in constant time and a dynamic search for reducible subterms is not necessary. As a consequence we will see in section 6 that functional programs are executed by rewriting and narrowing with almost the same efficiency as their relational equivalents by resolution.

4 Details of the abstract machine

After discussing the basic ideas of the implementation in the previous section, we can present more details about our abstract machine. The abstract machine for the efficient execution of ALF-programs, called **A-WAM**, is an extension of the WAM. Hence the main data areas of the A-WAM are the *code area* containing the compiled code of the ALF-program, the *local stack* containing environments and backtrack points, the *heap* containing terms constructed at run time, the *trail* containing variables bound during unification, and the *occurrence stack* and the *copy occurrence stack* as described in the last section. In contrast to the WAM, the trail contains also the contents of heap cells which were replaced by an application of a rewrite or narrowing rule, and the terms in the heap have an additional tag indicating whether they belong to the skeleton or environment part of the goal. This is necessary because the basic occurrences must be recomputed in some cases (cf. previous section).

The A-WAM has several additional registers and instructions for the implementation of rewriting and narrowing. A description of these can be found in the appendix. In this section we describe the A-WAM by selected examples.

An equational clause $l = r$ is always translated into the following scheme:

<unify or match the left-hand side l with the current subterm>
<replace the current subterm by the right-hand side r>
<update the occurrence stack (delete or add occurrences)>
<proceed with rewriting/narrowing at new innermost occurrence>

The current subterm is referenced by the top element of the occurrence stack. Therefore this top element is always stored in the particular A-WAM-register `A0`, i.e., the occurrence stack is empty iff `A0` is undefined. Similarly to the WAM, the arguments of a n-ary predicate or function are passed through the argument registers `A1`,...,`An`. Hence the `get`-instructions of the WAM can be used to unify the left-hand side of an equation. If this equation is used as a rewrite rule, then the left-hand side must be *matched* with the current subterm, i.e., variables in the current subterm must not be bound. One possible implementation of this behaviour is the introduction of additional registers `R` and `HR` which point to the local stack and heap, respectively. Before rewriting is called, `R` and `HR` are set to the top of the local stack and the top of the heap, respectively. If a variable is bound to a term in the unification procedure, the WAM-instruction `trail` is called. Now we modify the instruction `trail` such that this instruction causes a `fail` if the variable to be bound is stored in the local stack before address `R` or in the heap before address `HR`. With this small modification we need no additional instructions for matching but can use the given `get`-instructions.

In order to replace the current subterm (pointed by register `A0`) by a new term (the right-hand side of an equation), the A-WAM contains a duplicated set of put-instructions with the suffix _occ which replace the current subterm in the heap by another term. For instance, the instruction **put_const_occ C** writes the constant C on the heap at address A0 and stores the old value at occurrence A0 on the trail, and the instruction **put_struct_occ f/n** puts a new structure on the top of the heap, replaces the heap cell at address A0 by a reference to this new structure and trails the old value at A0.

The A-WAM has three instructions for the manipulation of the occurrence stack: **load_occ R** sets register A0 to the value in register R, **push_occ R** pushes the value in R onto the occurrence stack, and **pop_occ** pops an element from the occurrence stack and stores its value in register A0.

Now we can show the **translation of rewrite rules** (remember that each equation can be used as a rewrite rule as well as a narrowing rule). Consider the two rewrite rules for the function rev:

```
rev([])     = []
rev([E|R])  = conc(rev(R),[E])
```

The first rewrite rule is translated into

```
get_nil A1
put_nil_occ
pop_occ
execute_rewriting A0
```

The first instruction matches the current argument stored in A1 with the constant [] representing the empty list. If this is successful, the second instruction replaces the current subterm by the empty list. Now rewriting must proceed at the next innermost occurrence. Therefore an element is popped from the occurrence stack by the third instruction and the last instruction loads the argument registers with the components of the new current subterm and jumps to the code of the appropriate rewrite rules. The second rewrite rule for rev is translated into

```
get_list A1                 % match A1 with [E|R]
unify_variable X4
unify_variable A1
put_list X3                 % write [E] on the heap
unify_value X4
unify_nil
put_struct_occ conc/2       % replace current subterm by conc(_,[E])
unify_variable X2
unify_value X3
push_occ A0                 % update occurrence stack
load_occ X2
execute_rewriting rev/1     % jump to the rewrite rules for rev/1
```

Note that the subterm rev(R) is not written on the heap because this is the next innermost subterm where a rewrite rule should be applied. Therefore a new unbound variable is stored instead of this subterm and the argument register A1 is set to the value of R (this is different from the implementation presented in [12]). If a rewrite rule can be applied to **rev(R)**, then the variable is overwritten by the right-hand side of the applied rule. Otherwise rewriting must be applied at the next innermost position. Thus the last alternative of the sequence of rewrite rules for **rev** is always the code sequence

```
put_function_occ rev/1
copy_pop_occ
execute_rewriting A0
```

The first instruction puts the structure **rev/1** with the value of argument register **A1** onto the heap at address **A0** if this heap cell contains an unbound variable. The second instruction pops an element from the occurrence stack and pushes it onto the copy occurrence stack (as described in section 3). The last instruction proceeds with rewriting at the new occurrence.

We have also mentioned in section 3 that the copy occurrence stack may become invalid if the rewrite rule deletes a subterm in an argument. Therefore the instruction **invalid_os** must be generated if a rewrite rule is applied where the right-hand side does not contain all variables of the left-hand side. For instance, the rewrite rule **f(Z) = 0** is translated into

```
put_const_occ 0
pop_occ
invalid_os
execute_rewriting A0
```

The instruction **invalid_os** marks the copy occurrence stack as invalid if it is not empty. In this case the occurrence stack must be recomputed before a narrowing rule is applied.

The translation of narrowing rules is similarly to rewrite rules. The only difference is that after an application of a narrowing rule we do not proceed with another narrowing rule but must perform rewriting and rejection first. Hence the narrowing rule **conc([],L) = L** is translated into

```
get_nil A1
put_value_occ A2
pop_occ
call_rewriting A0
rebuild_occ_stack
reject
execute_narrowing A0
```

The instruction **call_rewriting A0** sets the registers **R** and **HR** and jumps to the rewrite code of the function at occurrence **A0**. When the whole term is simplified by rewriting, execution continues with the instruction **rebuild_occ_stack** which moves the copy occurrence stack to the occurrence stack (if it is valid) or recomputes the occurrence stack. **reject** performs the rejection rule if the current literal is an equation, and **execute_narrowing A0** tries to apply a narrowing rule at the occurrence **A0**.

The **indexing scheme** for narrowing rules is similar to the WAM-translation scheme for predicates, i.e., all narrowing rules for a function are connected with a chain of **try_me_else**-, **retry_me_else**- and **trust_me_else_fail**-instructions. Moreover, instructions for indexing on the first argument are generated. For rewrite rules the same

```
conc/2: r_try_me_else b2
        switch_on_term c1a,c1,c2,fail
c1a:    r_try_me_else c2a        % Clause: conc([],L) = L
c1:     get_nil A1
        put_value_occ A2
        pop_occ
        execute_rewriting A0
c2a:    r_trust_me_else_fail     % Clause: conc([E|R],L) = [E|conc(R,L)]
c2:     get_list A1
        unify_variable X4
        unify_variable A1
        put_list_occ
        unify_value X4
        unify_variable X3
        load_occ X3
        execute_rewriting conc/2
b2:     put_function_occ conc/2  % go to next innermost position
        copy_pop_occ
        execute_rewriting A0
```

Figure 2: A-WAM-code of the rewrite rules for conc

scheme is generated, but all indexing instructions are replaced by "rewrite indexing instructions" which are prefixed by `r_`. This is due to the fact that rewriting is a deterministic process and rewrite rules do not change the current literal before the right-hand side is inserted. Therefore the A-WAM contains two registers RFP1 and RFP2 which contains the address of an alternative rewrite rule (*two* registers are necessary because there may exist two backtrack points for one clause due to the indexing scheme [33]). These registers are set by the `r_try...`-instructions instead of creating a backtrack point. The instruction `fail`, which is executed on failure, considers the values of RFP1 and RFP2: If one of these registers is defined (not equal to "fail"), P is set to the last one, otherwise the computation state is reset to the last backtrack point. The instruction `execute_rewriting`, which is always executed at the end of a rewrite rule, sets RFP1 and RFP2 to "fail" which implements the determinstic behaviour of rewriting. The complete translation of the rewrite rules for the function conc is shown in figure 2.

If an argument term of a literal in a goal contains function symbols, then this argument term must be evaluated by rewriting and narrowing before the resolution rule is applied to the literal. Therefore instructions for initializing the occurrence stack and rewriting and narrowing instructions must be inserted in such literals. For instance, the literal `p(fac(s(0)))` in a goal is translated into

```
put_structure s/1, X2     % store argument term  fac(s(0))
unify_constant 0
put_structure fac/1, Y2
```

```
unify_value X2
set_begin_of_term Y2        % store root of argument term
load_occ Y2                 % initialize occurrence stack
call_rewriting A0, 2
rebuild_occ_stack
call_narrowing A0, 2
put_value Y2, A1            % restore argument term
call p/1, 1
```

The first 4 instructions are identical to the WAM-code with the only difference that the root of the argument term is not stored in register `A1` but in the permanent variable `Y2`. This is necessary since argument registers are altered during rewriting and narrowing. The A-WAM has a register `TS` which contains the root of the argument currently evaluated by rewriting and narrowing. This register is used when the occurrence stack must be recomputed after rewriting if the copy occurrence stack has been marked as invalid. Therefore `TS` is initialized by the instruction `set_begin_of_term` with the appropriate value. The second arguments of `call_rewriting` and `call_narrowing` are the number of permanent variables which are still in use in the current environment (similar to the WAM-instruction `call`).

Now we have shown how ALF-programs (with unconditional equations) can be translated into A-WAM-code. Note that the A-WAM-code for functions is very similar to the WAM-code for the equivalent predicate (e.g., compare the code for the functions `conc` and `rev` with the WAM-code for the naive reverse program). Thus functional programs are executed with the same efficiency as their relational equivalents. Moreover, backtrack points are not generated for rewriting and therefore many functional programs are more efficiently executed. Before we present concrete results of our implementation, we will show how conditional equations are implemented in our framework.

5 Conditional equations

Conditional equations causes a new problem since the condition must be proved before the equation could be applied. To prove the condition rewriting and narrowing may be recursively used. Hence the current occurrence stack must be saved before the condition is proved and restored after the proof of the condition. To implement this recursive structure of the narrowing process, the A-WAM contains not only one occurrence stack but a list (or stack) of occurrence stacks. The last element of this list is always the current occurrence stack belonging to the argument term currently evaluated by narrowing or rewriting. Since rewriting may have a recursive structure too, the copy occurrence stack is also a list of stacks where the last element is the current copy occurrence stack.

The A-WAM has two instructions to manipulate the list of occurrence stacks. The instruction `allocate_occ` adds a new (empty) occurrence stack to the list of occurrence stacks. It is used before a condition in a narrowing or rewrite rule will be proved. At the end of the condition the instruction `deallocate_occ` is executed which deletes the last element from the list of occurrence stacks. If a backtrack point has been created during the proof of the condition, then the last occurrence stack is not deleted since it is needed on backtracking. Hence a backtrack point freezes the current occurrence stack (note the similarity to environments and the **allocate/deallocate**-instructions in the WAM).

Consider the conditional equation **f(N) = 0** ← **odd(g(N))**. It is translated as a narrowing rule into the following code:

```
allocate
get_variable X2, A1
allocate_occ                % create a new occ. stack for the condition
put_structure g/1, Y1       % create argument term g(N)
unify_value X2
set_begin_of_term Y1
load_occ Y1
call_rewriting A0, 1        % rewrite argument term g(N)
rebuild_occ_stack
call_narrowing A0, 1        % narrow argument term g(N)
put_value Y1, A1
call odd/1, 1
deallocate_occ              % delete occurrence stack for the condition
put_const_occ 0
deallocate
pop_occ
call_rewriting A0           % proceed with rewriting at next occurrence
rebuild_occ_stack
reject
execute_narrowing A0        % proceed with narrowing
```

The compilation scheme for conditional rewrite rules is a little bit more complicated because it is sufficient to compute *one* solution for the condition (rewriting is a deterministic process). Thus backtrack points generated during the proof of the condition can be safely deleted. The second problem is that the indexing scheme for rewrite rules (**r_try...**-instructions) does not generate backtrack points. Therefore a backtrack point must be created at the beginning of the condition. Hence a conditional rewrite rule of the form $l = r \leftarrow c$ is translated into

```
   allocate
   <get-instructions for l>
   l_try_me_else L,A,N          % create new backtrack point for condition
   allocate_occ                 % create new occurrence stack
   <instructions for condition c>
   deallocate_occ               % delete occurrence stack for condition
   l_trust_me_else fail         % delete backtrack points for condition
   <put..._occ-instructions for r>
   <occurrence-stack-instructions for r>
   deallocate
   invalid_os                   % if necessary
   execute_rewriting A0
L: l_trust_me_else fail         % delete backtrack points for condition
```

```
deallocate
fail                              % try next rewrite rule
```

The instruction `l_try_me_else L,A,N` creates a backtrack point similarly to `try_me_else L,A` (`A` is the number of argument registers to be saved) and stores the address of the last backtrack point in the environment (usually in the permanent variable `Y1`). The additional argument `N` contains the size of the current environment (the WAM accesses the size of the current environment via the continuation pointer `CP` which is not possible in this context). The instruction `l_trust_me_else fail` deletes all backtrack points generated during the proof of the condition, i.e., the pointer to the last backtrack point (WAM-register `B`) is set to `Y1` (the backtrack point before the condition).

6 Results

The current implementation consists of two parts: a compiler written in Prolog which translates ALF-programs into a compact bytecode representing A-WAM-programs, and a bytecode emulator for the A-WAM written in C. The details of the implementation together with a complete formal specification of the A-WAM in the style of [10] can be found in [16]. In this section we present some results of our implementation.

First of all, let us remark that pure logic programs without equations are compiled identical to the WAM, i.e., there is no overhead because of the functional part of our language (only backtrack points are a little bit bigger because of the additional registers of the A-WAM). Although the current implementation is a first prototype and not very fast[1], it is interesting to see the relation between execution times for functional programs and their relational equivalents, because this shows the relationship between our implementation of narrowing and rewriting and the current techniques for logic programming.

The first example is the classical (but controversial) naive reverse benchmark. The relational version is executed by resolution, the functional version by narrowing and rewriting. The following table shows the time for reversing a list of 30 elements in both directions (all benchmarks were executed on a Sun4):

Naive reverse		
Initial goal:	`rev([···]) = L`	`rev(L) = [···]`
Relational "naive reverse":	18 msec	190 msec
Functional "naive reverse":	19 msec	210 msec

The next example demonstrates one advantage of integrating functions into logic programming languages. In the first section we have shown clauses for defining the predicate `add` and the function `+`. We have stated that the functional computation is more efficient than the relational because no backtrack points must be generated for evaluating the function by rewriting. The following table shows that this is true in our implementation

[1]The performance of our current implementation is approximately 38 KLips on a Sun4 for the naive reverse benchmark; for typical logic programming examples with backtracking, like the permutation sort program (see below), our implementation is approximately 6-7 times slower than a commercial Prolog system (Quintus-Prolog 3.0).

(in the implementation natural numbers are represented as terms constructed by s and 0):

Functional vs. relational computations		
Initial goal:	add(100,100,S)	100 + 100 = S
Time used (msec):	16	8
Heap used (bytes):	2412	2420
Local stack used (bytes):	13352	124
Trail used (bytes):	808	0
Occurrence stack used (bytes):	0	0

This table contains the time and space used for computing the first solution to the initial goal. The time and the local stack space shows the advantage of functional computations.

However, our implementation is not restricted to evaluate functions by rewriting, but also narrowing steps are applied if rewriting fails and some variables of the goal must be instantiated in order to proceed with rewriting. Fribourg [8] has shown that the combination of narrowing and rewriting can reduce the search space in comparison to resolution. At the end of section 2 we have presented an example where rewriting cuts down an infinite search space to a finite one. It is also possible that a finite search space can be dramatically reduced by rewriting. For instance, in the "permutation sort" program a list is sorted by enumerating all permutations and checking whether they are sorted. The relational version of the program ([32], p. 55) enumerates *all* permutations whereas in the functional version not all permutations are enumerated since the generation of a permutation is stopped (by rewriting the goal to "fail") if two consecutive elements X and Y have the wrong ordering Y < X (cf. [8], p. 182). Therefore we yield the following execution times in seconds for different lengths of the input list in our system:

Functional vs. relational computations: permutation sort				
Program:	*Initial goal:*	$n = 6$	$n = 8$	$n = 10$
Relational ([32], p. 55)	psort([n,...,1],L)	0.65	37.92	3569.50
Functional ([8], p. 182)	psort([n,...,1]) = L	0.27	1.43	7.43

This is a typical example for the class of "generate-and-test" programs. The rewriting process performs the "test part" of the program: if a portion of the potential solution is generated by narrowing, rewriting immediately tests whether or not this can be a part of the solution. Therefore narrowing and rewriting yield a more efficient control strategy than SLD-resolution for equivalent relational programs. This is achieved in a purely clean and declarative way without any user annotations to control the proof strategy or transformations applied to the source program [5]. A more detailed discussion on this advantage of a functional language based on rewriting and narrowing can be found in [14].

We have also compared our implementation with other implementations of functional languages with pattern matching. The following table contains the results of the naive reverse benchmark for different implementations which we had available.

Naive reverse for a list of 30 elements		
System:	*Machine:*	*Time:*
ALF	Sun4	19 msec
Standard-ML (Edinburgh)	Sun3	54 msec
CAML V 2-6.1	Sun4	28 msec
OBJ3	Sun3	5070 msec
RAP 2.0	Sun4	4800 msec

OBJ3 [23] and RAP [9] are systems for executing equational specifications by rewriting (and narrowing in case of RAP). Since these are based on an interpreter, we can observe the impressive speeding up achieved by our compilational approach. Thus we conjecture that our approach is also more efficient than the implementation technique proposed by Josephson and Dershowitz [22] because they handle unification and control at the interpretive level.

7 Conclusions

We have presented a method to compile a language that amalgamates functional and logic programming styles into code of an abstract machine which can be easily implemented on conventional architectures. The operational semantics of our language is based on resolution for predicates and rewriting and narrowing to evaluate functional expressions. We have shown that narrowing in combination with rewriting is more efficient than resolution for equivalent (flattened) relational programs. This was clear from a theoretical point of view, but our implementation has shown that these advantages can also be used in practical applications.

The integration of functions into logic programming leads to programs which are more readable and easier to understand because functions need not be simulated by predicates and nested functional expressions need not be flattened. Since the programmer can express functional dependencies between data, this information could be used for a better implementation. In our system a functional expression is simplified by rewriting before a narrowing rule is applied. This reduces the search space (without "cuts"!) and avoids the generation of superfluous backtrack points since rewriting is a deterministic process. Thus the non-deterministic narrowing operation is rarely applied.

In some cases the positive effect of rewriting (search space reduction) can also be achieved by analysing a logic program in order to find deterministic computations and inserting "cuts" at appropriate program points. But this analysis may be expensive and do not yield satisfactory results if a predicate is called in different modes: a call with ground terms could have a deterministic computation while a call with non-ground terms may have a non-deterministic computation. Such problems are solved by our implementation in a clean and declarative way: Since rewriting is applied before each narrowing step, a goal is simplified by deterministic rewriting as long as possible depending on the instantiation state of the arguments. A similar behaviour can also be obtained in logic programs by using other control strategies instead of Prolog's fixed left-to-right strategy [29]. But this requires the insertion of control annotations into the program (which may effect completeness because of floundering problems) and the extension of the WAM to deal with such a flexible control strategy. In our declarative solution control annotations are not necessary (see also [8]).

Currently we are working on better methods for code generation which can speed up the rewriting part of the system. At the moment we are using the WAM-instructions for rewriting as shown in this paper, but it is possible to generate particular code for fast pattern matching (see, e.g., [18]). We are also working on the integration of types into the computation process [11] [13] [20] since this allows a further reduction of the search space.

Acknowledgements: The author is grateful to Renate Schäfers for many discussions on the design of the A-WAM and to Andreas Schwab and the members of the project group "PILS" for the implementation of the A-WAM.

References

[1] M. Bellia and G. Levi. The Relation between Logic and Functional Languages: A Survey. *Journal of Logic Programming (3)*, pp. 217–236, 1986.

[2] H. Bertling and H. Ganzinger. Completion-Time Optimization of Rewrite-Time Goal Solving. In *Proc. of the Conference on Rewriting Techniques and Applications*, pp. 45–58. Springer LNCS 355, 1989.

[3] P.G. Bosco, C. Cecchi, and C. Moiso. An extension of WAM for K-LEAF: a WAM-based compilation of conditional narrowing. In *Proc. Sixth International Conference on Logic Programming (Lisboa)*, pp. 318–333. MIT Press, 1989.

[4] P.G. Bosco, E. Giovannetti, and C. Moiso. Refined strategies for semantic unification. In *Proc. of the TAPSOFT '87*, pp. 276–290. Springer LNCS 250, 1987.

[5] M. Bruynooghe, D. De Schreye, and B. Krekels. Compiling Control. *Journal of Logic Programming (6)*, pp. 135–162, 1989.

[6] W.F. Clocksin and C.S. Mellish. *Programming in Prolog.* Springer, third rev. and ext. edition, 1987.

[7] D. DeGroot and G. Lindstrom, editors. *Logic Programming, Functions, Relations, and Equations.* Prentice Hall, 1986.

[8] L. Fribourg. SLOG: A Logic Programming Language Interpreter Based on Clausal Superposition and Rewriting. In *Proc. IEEE Internat. Symposium on Logic Programming*, pp. 172–184, Boston, 1985.

[9] A. Geser and H. Hussmann. Experiences with the RAP system – a specification interpreter combining term rewriting and resolution. In *Proc. of ESOP 86*, pp. 339–350. Springer LNCS 213, 1986.

[10] M. Hanus. Formal Specification of a Prolog Compiler. In *Proc. of the Workshop on Programming Language Implementation and Logic Programming*, pp. 273–282, Orléans, 1988. Springer LNCS 348.

[11] M. Hanus. Polymorphic Higher-Order Programming in Prolog. In *Proc. Sixth International Conference on Logic Programming (Lisboa)*, pp. 382–397. MIT Press, 1989.

[12] M. Hanus. Compiling Logic Programs with Equality. In *Proc. of the 2nd Int. Workshop on Programming Language Implementation and Logic Programming*, pp. 387–401. Springer LNCS 456, 1990.

[13] M. Hanus. A Functional and Logic Language with Polymorphic Types. In *Proc. Int. Symposium on Design and Implementation of Symbolic Computation Systems*, pp. 215–224. Springer LNCS 429, 1990.

[14] M. Hanus. A Declarative Approach to Improve Control in Logic Programming. Univ. Dortmund, 1991.

[15] M. Hanus and A. Schwab. ALF User's Manual. FB Informatik, Univ. Dortmund, 1991.

[16] M. Hanus and A. Schwab. The Implementation of the Functional-Logic Language ALF. FB Informatik, Univ. Dortmund, 1991.

[17] S. Haridi and P. Brand. Andorra Prolog: An Integration of Prolog and Committed Choice Languages. In *Proc. Int. Conf. on Fifth Generation Computer Systems*, pp. 745–754, 1988.

[18] T. Heuillard. Compiling conditional rewriting systems. In *Proc. 1st Int. Workshop on Conditional Term Rewriting Systems*, pp. 111–128. Springer LNCS 308, 1987.

[19] S. Hölldobler. From Paramodulation to Narrowing. In *Proc. 5th Conference on Logic Programming & 5th Symposium on Logic Programming (Seattle)*, pp. 327–342, 1988.

[20] M. Huber and I. Varsek. Extended Prolog with Order-Sorted Resolution. In *Proc. 4th IEEE Internat. Symposium on Logic Programming*, pp. 34–43, San Francisco, 1987.

[21] J.-M. Hullot. Canonical Forms and Unification. In *Proc. 5th Conference on Automated Deduction*, pp. 318–334. Springer LNCS 87, 1980.

[22] A. Josephson and N. Dershowitz. An Implementation of Narrowing. *Journal of Logic Programming (6)*, pp. 57–77, 1989.

[23] C. Kirchner, H. Kirchner, and J. Meseguer. Operational Semantics of OBJ3 (Extended Abstract). In *Proc. of the 15th ICALP*, pp. 287–301. Springer LNCS 317, 1988.

[24] H. Kuchen, R. Loogen, J.J. Moreno-Navarro, and M. Rodríguez-Artalejo. Graph-based Implementation of a Functional Logic Language. In *Proc. ESOP 90*, pp. 271–290. Springer LNCS 432, 1990.

[25] J.W. Lloyd. *Foundations of Logic Programming.* Springer, second, extended edition, 1987.

[26] R. Loogen. From Reduction Machines to Narrowing Machines. In *Proc. of the TAPSOFT '91*, pp. 438–457. Springer LNCS 494, 1991.

[27] J.J. Moreno-Navarro, H. Kuchen, R. Loogen, and M. Rodríguez-Artalejo. Lazy Narrowing in a Graph Machine. In *Proc. Second International Conference on Algebraic and Logic Programming*, pp. 298–317. Springer LNCS 463, 1990.

[28] J.J. Moreno-Navarro and M. Rodríguez-Artalejo. Logic Programming with Functions and Predicates: The Language BABEL. Technical Report DIA/89/3, Universidad Complutense, Madrid, 1989.

[29] L. Naish. *Negation and Control in Prolog.* Springer LNCS 238, 1987.

[30] W. Nutt, P. Rety, and G. Smolka. Basic Narrowing Revisited. SEKI Report SR-87-07, FB Informatik, Univ. Kaiserslautern, 1987.

[31] P. Padawitz. *Computing in Horn Clause Theories*, volume 16 of *EATCS Monographs on Theoretical Computer Science.* Springer, 1988.

[32] L. Sterling and E. Shapiro. *The Art of Prolog.* MIT Press, 1986.

[33] D.H.D. Warren. An Abstract Prolog Instruction Set. Technical Note 309, SRI International, Stanford, 1983.

A Registers of the A-WAM

Name	Function
P	program pointer
CP	continuation program pointer
E	last environment
B	last backtrack point
H	top of heap
TR	top of trail
S	structure pointer
RW	read/write mode for unify instructions
A1, A2, ...	argument registers
X1, X2, ...	temporary variables
R	rewrite pointer (to the local stack)
HR	heap rewrite pointer (to the heap)
OM	top of current occurrence stack
OR	top of current copy occurrence stack
AO	actual occurrence (reference to the current subterm to be evaluated)
TS	term start (root of the current argument term)
OV	Is the current copy occ. stack valid? May be set to false during rewriting.
RFP1, RFP2	rewrite fail pointers (addresses of alternative rewrite rules)

The argument registers and temporary variables are identical to the WAM registers [33].

B New instructions of the A-WAM

In the following we list the new instructions of the A-WAM together with a short explanation in alphabetical order.

`allocate_occ:` This instruction is used before a condition in a narrowing or rewrite rule will be proved. It saves the occurrences in AO and TS onto the occurrence stack and adds a new (empty) current occurrence stack to the list of all occurrence stacks.

`call_narrowing AO,N:` Load the components of the structure at position AO into the argument registers and call the narrowing rules for the function at occurrence AO. N is the number of permanent variables in the current environment.

`call_rewriting R:` This instruction is used to rewrite the current argument term after a narrowing rule has been applied. It starts rewriting at the innermost occurrence R (f/n or AO) and continues with the next instruction (rebuild_occ_stack) if the rewriting process is finished.

`call_rewriting R,N:` This instruction is used to rewrite the current argument term in a literal where N is the number of permanent variables in the current environment. It starts rewriting at the innermost occurrence R (f/n or AO) and continues with the next instruction (rebuild_occ_stack) if the rewriting process is finished.

`copy_pop_occ:` Push AO onto the current copy occurrence stack and execute pop_occ.

`deallocate_occ:` Delete the last element from the list of occurrence stacks and load registers AO and TS from the previous occurrence stack. If a backtrack point has been created after the corresponding **allocate_occ**-instruction, it is not allowed to alter previous elements of the occurrence stack list since only the current occurrence stack has been saved into the backtrack point. In this case **deallocate_occ** creates a copy of the previous occurrence stack and adds this copy to the list of occurrence stacks.

`execute_narrowing AO:` This instruction terminates a narrowing rule. The narrowing rules for the function at occurrence AO are executed if AO is defined, otherwise program pointer P is set to CP.

`execute_rewriting R:` This instruction terminates a rewrite rule. Registers RFP1 and RFP2 are set to "fail" and the rewrite rules for the function `f/n` are executed if R=`f/n`, otherwise (R=AO) the rewrite rules for the function at occurrence AO are executed.

`inner_reflection:` This is the last alternative in a sequence of narrowing rules for a partial function. It implements the innermost reflection rule: The term at the actual occurrence AO is marked as "environment" and the A-WAM-instruction sequence "**pop_occ ; execute_narrowing AO**" is executed.

`invalid_os:` Set register OV to false if the current copy occurrence stack is not empty.

`load_occ R:` Set the actual occurrence register AO to the contents of R.

`l_trust_me_else fail:` Delete all backtrack points generated after the corresponding `l_try_me_else`, i.e., the pointer to the last backtrack point (register B) is set to Y1.

`l_try_me_else L,A,N:` Create a backtrack point and store the address of the last backtrack point in the permanent variable Y1. A is the number of argument registers to be saved and N contains the number of permanent variables in the current environment.

`pop_occ:` Pop an element from the current occurrence stack and store the value in register AO. If the current occurrence stack is empty, set AO to "undefined".

`push_occ R:` Push the contents of R onto the current occurrence stack.

`put_...._occ R:` Substitute the current subterm at address AO by R and store the old value at AO on the trail. Furthermore, `put_struct_occ f/n` puts a new structure `f/n` on the top of the heap and replaces the heap cell at address AO by a reference to this new structure.

`put_function_occ f/n:` Put the structure `f/n` with the values of the argument registers A1,...,An onto the heap at address AO if this heap cell contains an unbound variable. It is used in the last alternative of the rewrite rules for `f/n`.

`rebuild_occ_stack:` Replace the current (empty) occurrence stack by the current copy occurrence stack if OV is true, otherwise by a new occurrence stack for the term at position TS (if the copy occurrence stack is invalid).

`reflection:` This instruction implements the reflection rule. It unifies the two sides of an equation (the current literal) which must be a structure referenced by register TS.

`reject:` If the current literal is an equation (referenced by register TS), then this instruction causes a failure if both sides have different constructors at the same outermost position (a position not belonging to arguments of functions). Otherwise, no action is taken.

`r_try...:` The indexing instructions for rewrite rules are prefixed by `r_`. In contrast to the indexing instructions of the WAM no backtrack point is generated but the address of the alternative clause is stored in RFP1 or RFP2.

`set_begin_of_term R:` Set the term start register TS to the contents of R.

TIM: THE TOULOUSE INFERENCE MACHINE FOR NON–CLASSICAL LOGIC PROGRAMMING

Philippe BALBIANI, *Andreas HERZIG,*
Mamede LIMA MARQUES

Institut de Recherche en Informatique de Toulouse
Université Paul Sabatier
118, route de Narbonne
F-31062 Toulouse cedex – France

abstract

We present an environment for logic programming languages called Toulouse Inference Machine (TIM). Its meta-level architecture permits the user to define how to compute a new goal from a given one. Our aim is to define a frame as general as possible for creating extensions of Prolog and, in particular, to provide a general methodology to implement non–classical logics. There are three basic assumptions on which our frame is built: first, to keep as a base the fundamental logic programming mechanisms that are backward chaining, depth first strategy, backtracking, and unification; second, to parametrize the inference step, and finally, to select clauses "by hand". Applications in logic programming and, in particular, in non-classic logic programming are presented: we specify with a few TIM inference rules various extensions of Prolog by non–classical concepts which have been proposed in the literature.

1 INTRODUCTION

In order to get closer to the human reasoning, computer systems, and in particular logic programming systems, have to deal with various concepts such as time, belief, knowledge, contexts, etc. Prolog is just what is needed to treat the Horn clause fragment of first order logic, but what about non–classical logics? Just suppose we want to represent in Prolog time, knowledge, hypotheses, or two of them at the same time; or to organize our program in modules, to have equational theories, to treat fuzzy predicates or clauses. All those cases need different ways of computing a new goal from an existing one.

Theoretical solutions have been found for each of the enumerated cases, and particular extensions of Prolog have been proposed in this sense in the literature. Examples are [7], [18], Tokio [16], N-PROLOG [17], Context Extension [20], Templog [4], Temporal Prolog [23], and [22].

For all these solutions it is possible to write specific meta–interpreters in Prolog which implement those non–classical systems ([24]). But there are disadvantages of a meta-interpreter e.g. lower speed and compilation notoriously inefficient. If we want to go a step further, and to write proper extensions of Prolog, then the problem is that costs for that are relatively high (because for each case we will lead to write a new extension), and we are bound to specific domains, e.g. we can only do temporal reasoning, but not reasoning about knowledge (and what if we want to add modules?).

Our aim is to define a frame as general as possible for creating extensions of Prolog. Hence, we must provide a general methodology to implement non–classical logics.

There are three basic assumptions on which our frame is built:

1. to keep as a base the *fundamental logic programming mechanisms* that are backward chaining, depth first strategy, backtracking, and unification,
2. *to parametrize the inference step*: it is the user who specifies how to compute the new goal from a given one, and he specifies it in logic programming style.
3. *to select clauses "by hand"*.

Point (2) postulates a more flexible way of computing goals than that of Prolog, where first a clause is selected from the program, then the unification algorithm is applied to the clause and the head of the goal, and possibly a new goal is formed.

Point (3) introduces a further flexibility: the user may select clauses which do not unify exactly with the current goal, but just resemble it in some sense. Even more, if the current goal contains enough information to produce the next goal, or if we just want to simplify a goal or to reorder literals we don't need to select a fact clause at all.

The assumptions (1) and (2) were at base of the development of a meta-level inference system called MOLOG [15], [2], [5], [13], [12]. The Toulouse Inference Machine that is presented in this paper is a revised version of MOLOG realizing assumption (3). It is currently under development at IRIT ([8] and [1]).

The power of an approach based on these three assumptions will be demonstrated in this paper: we specify with a few TIM inference rules various extensions of Prolog by non–classical concepts which have been proposed in the literature ([4], [9], [17] and [20]). Our claim is that TIM furnishes a meaningful and general logic programming paradigm.

2 THE SYNTAX

The base of the language of TIM is that of Prolog. That language can (but need not) be enriched with *context operators* if one wants to mechanize non-classical logics.

Characteristically, non–classical logics possess symbols with a particular behaviour. These symbols are

- either classical connectors with modified semantics (e.g. intuitionist, minimal, relevant, paraconsistent logics)
- or new connectors called context operators (*necessary* and *possible* in modal, *knows* in epistemic, *always* in temporal, *if* in conditional logics).

Example In epistemic logics, the context operators are *knows* and *comp*, and

> *knows(a):P* means that agent *a* knows that *P*
> *comp(a):P* means that it is compatible with *a*'s knowledge that *P*

Hence inference engines for non-classical logics must reckon for the particular behaviour of some given symbols. These properties will be handled by built-in features of the inference engine.

The *conditio sine qua non* for logic programming languages is that they possess an implicational symbol to which a procedural sense can be given. To define a programming language it's less important if this is material implication or not, but it's rather the dynamic aspect of implication which makes the execution of a logic program possible. That is why the TIM language is built around some arrow-like symbol.

TIM syntax is very close to the Edinburgh Prolog syntax, we note:

> `<-` the implication symbol (`:-`)
> `&` the conjunction symbol (`,`)
> `cut` the cut predefined predicate (`!`)

We suppose the usual definition of *terms* and *atomic formulas* of logic programming. Intuitively, *TIM Horn Clauses* are formulas built with the above connectors, such that dropping the context we may get a classical Horn clauses. Now for each logic programming language we suppose a particular set of context operators. This set depends on the logic programming language we want to implement, e.g. in epistemic logic it is {*knows, comp*} and in temporal logic it is {*always, sometimes*}. Formally we define by mutual recursion:

Definition 2. 1 - Contexts

$m(t_1, ..., t_n)$ is a context if m is a context operator $n \geq 0$, and for $1 \leq i \leq n$ every t_i is either a term or a definite clause.

Definition 2. 2 - Goal clauses

?P is a goal clause if P is an atomic formula

?(G & F) is a goal clause if ?G, ?F are goal clauses

?MOD:F are goal clauses if ?F is a goal clause and MOD is a context

Definition 2. 3 - Definite clauses

P is a definite clause if P is an atomic formula

MOD:F is a definite clause if F is a definite clause and MOD is a context

F <- G is a definite clause if F is a definite clause and G is a goal clause

Definition 2. 4 - TIM Horn clause

A TIM Horn clause (or Horn clause for short) is either a goal clause or a definite clause. Note that Horn clauses may contain several implication symbols.

We shall also use the term *Modal Horn clauses* if we are speaking of a modal logic.

Example 1: Epistemic Logics

In epistemic logics, Horn clauses are as follows:

?comp(a):F, ?knows(a):F are goal clauses if ?F is a goal clause and a is an agent

comp(a):F, knows(a):F are definite clauses if F is a definite clause, where a is an agent

An example of a Horn clause is

```
knows(george):(p<-q)  <-  knows(mike):r .
```

As we can see by this example, a recursive definition of Horn clauses is often necessary. Dropping the context we get the clause (p <- q) <- r which is equivalent to the classical Horn clause p <- q & r.

Example 2: Conditional Logics

Modal operators may also have formulas as arguments. Thus to do hypothetical reasoning we use the operator *assume*, where the argument of *assume* is the assumption under which the qualified clause is true:

```
assume(it_rains):road_slippy.
```

means that if we suppose that it rains, the road will be slippy.

3 PROCEDURAL SPECIFICATION

As mentioned above, TIM can be viewed as a meta-program written in Prolog. Just as Prolog, TIM works with backward chaining, depth first strategy and backtracking. In order to give the intuitive idea how TIM works, and in order to avoid describing the existing C and ADA implementations [1] we specify it in Prolog.

Basically, TIM works like usual meta–interpreter [24] calling a predicate `step(G, NG)` which computes the goal `NG` from a given goal `G`.

Various ways to do the inference step can be described by the predicate **step**. The definition of this predicate is the task of the super–user in order to implement 'his' logic programming language. Typically, in accordance with assumptions (2 and (3), of section (1), the definition uses a predicate `select` selecting a clause from the database, and a recursively defined predicate `infer` which states how to infer a new goal from the given goal and the selected clause. Hence we complete the scheme in the following way:

```
step(?G, ?NG) <-
        select-L(?G, C) &
        infer(C, ?G, ?Res)  &
        normal(?Res,?NG).

infer(G, ?G, ?truth) .
infer(C, ?G, ?NG)  <-
        ...  &
        infer(C', ?G',  ?NG') &
        ...

normal(?G, ?NG)  <-
        ...  &
        normal(?G', ?NG') &
        ...
```

where `G'` is a subformula of `G` and `NG'` is a subformula of `NG`. The predicate **select-L** is a TIM system predicate whose role is to select a clause of the database. Generally speaking `select-L(C,G)` chooses a clause C which corresponds in some way to a given goal `G`, depending on the logic programming language $\mathcal{L}$ under concern. There are several possibilities to optimize clause selection (in view of the particular inference rules associated to $\mathcal{L}$), and thus several implementations of that database mechanism. The predicate **normal** is a user-defined predicate which puts formulas in normal form. It is superfluous if we want to implement Prolog, but useful in many other cases, particularly for extended unification.

In order to get familiar with the TIM programming style we show how pure Prolog[1] can be implemented.

[1]To be complete we should also specify the cut predicate. Actually it is not so easy in the frame of this specification. Notwithstanding, cut has been implemented in TIM and can be employed in logic

```
step(?G, ?NG) <-
        select(?G, C) &
        infer(C, ?G, ?NG).

infer(G, ?G, ?truth).
infer(H<-T, ?G, ?T&NG)  <-
        infer(H, ?G, ?NG).
infer(C, ?G&R, ?NG&R)  <-
        infer(C, ?G, ?NG).
```

4 HOW TO SOLVE IT IN TIM

4.1 TEMPORAL LOGICS

A logic programming language able to reason about time close to Templog [4][2] may contain the above rules for pure Prolog, plus

```
infer(always:C, ?always:G, ?always:NG)   <-
        infer(C, ?G, ?NG).
infer(always:C, ?sometimes:G, ?sometimes:NG)   <-
        infer(C, ?G, ?NG).
infer(sometimes:C, ?sometimes:G, ?sometimes:NG) <-
        infer(C, ?G, ?NG).
```

In this case we need the **normal** predicate: From the clause **always:it_rains** and the goal **sometimes:it_rains** the infer predicate furnishes the new goal **?sometimes:-truth**. Now in order to make the goal succeed, one must simplify beforehand the goal **?sometimes:truth** to **?truth**. What we need is

```
normal(G & R,R)  <-  normal(G,truth) & cut.
normal(G & R,NG & R)  <-  cut & normal(G,NG).
normal(G <- H,truth)  <-  normal(G,truth) & cut.
normal(G <- H,NG <- H)  <-  cut & normal(G,NG).
normal(MOD:G, truth) <- normal(G,truth) & cut.
normal(MOD:G, MOD:NG) <- normal(G, NG) & cut.
normal(G,G)  <-  atom(G).
```

programs. Nevertheless (as usual in meta-programming) its procedural semantics is less clear than in Prolog, and it is rather tricky to know what cuts in TIM Horn clauses mean.

[2]In order to implement Templog, it is necessary to define inference rules for a third modal operator *next* (or *tomorrow*). Templog has been implemented in TIM, but for lack of space we cannot present it here.

4.2 PROLOG + HYPOTHETICAL REASONING

Goals may be asked under hypotheses. E.g. the goal $p \leftarrow p$ is admitted[3].

It can read "under hypothesis p, does p hold?" and must succeed (even with an empty database). This implements N-PROLOG [17] [4].

4.2.1 Definition of the inference step

```
step(G&R,NG) :-
        !, step(G,Res),
        normal(Res&R,NG).
step(G,NG) :-
        hselect(G,C),
        infer(C,G,Res),
        normal(Res,NG).
```

"`hselect`" selects a clause with same head.

```
step(G<-H,NG<-H) :- infer(H,G,Res), normal(Res<-H,NG).
```

The infer predicate is essentially that of pure Prolog. The normal predicate is needed to simplify goals of the form $truth \leftarrow H$ to truth.

4.2.2 Example of database

```
p.
q <- p.
r <- q & t.
```

Query-examples:

```
r.   => failure
r<-t.  => success
```

P. J. de la Quintana (see [10]) has extended N-Prolog with modal operators (and thus epistemic operators). This system works with full first order epistemic logic with both included or free domains. In TIM, this amounts basically to put together the implementation of N-Prolog and the definition of epistemic logic (see 4.5)[5].

---

[3] We could have denoted hypothetical goals as well by *assume(H):G* as done in example 2, sections 2, and in the section 5.3

[4] Representing negation $\neg F$ by $falsity \leftarrow F$, it is possible to use negation by inconsistency adding the clause `step(G,falsity) :- atom(G), not(G=falsity)`

[5] This invalidates a criticism in [19], where it has been stated that MOLOG neither supports general formulas nor included and free domains.

4.3 MODULES WITH DYNAMIC IMPORT

Every module name, as `m,m1,m(2)`, etc. is considered to be a context.

The goal `m1:m2:G` succeeds if G can be proved using clauses from the modules `m1` and `m2`.

4.3.1 The inference step

```
step(G&R,NG) :-
        !,step(G,Res),
        normal(Res&R,NG).
step(M:G,NG) :-
        step(G,Res),
        normal(M:Res,NG).
step(G,NG) :-
        mselect(G,C),
        infer(C,G,Res),
        normal(Res,NG).
```

`mselect` selects the clauses which are in the module specified by the context of the goal. The `infer` predicate is that of pure Prolog, plus

```
infer(MOD:C, MOD:G, MOD:NG) :-
        infer(C,G,NG).
infer(C , MOD:G, MOD:NG) :-
        infer(C,G,NG).
```

The `normal` predicate is used to simplify goals of the form `m:truth` to `truth`.

4.3.2 Example of database

```
m1:p.
m2:(q <- p).
```

Query-example:

```
m1:m2:q.    => success
```

4.4 MODULES WITH CONTEXT EXTENSION

Again, module names are considered to be contexts of clauses.

The modules are loaded in left to right order, i.e. with priority to the last module governing the goal predicate. The definitions in a newly loaded module overwrite, those of the modules loaded before (on the other hand, if there is no redefinition of a predicate name, the previous definitions remains valid). This implements the context-extension mechanism of [20]. Every goal and clause head must be in the scope of a modal operator (else it cannot succeed) [6].

4.4.1 Definition of the inference step

Here, the `infer` predicate is that for dynamic import of 4.3, but moreover it succeeds with new goal already when both lied atoms have the same predicate name.

Hence we have

```
infer(G,G,truth) :- !.
infer(A,G,deffail) :-
        functor(A,F,_),
        functor(G,F,_).
```

Nevertheless, the normal predicate is as before (and consequently fails to normalize `deffail`).

```
step(G&R,NG) :- step(G,Res), normal(Res&R,NG).
step(M:G,NG) :- step(G,Res), normal(M:Res,NG).
```

This clause succeeds if the goal atom is defined by a module loaded inside `G`, entailing an inference to `truth` or `deffail`.

```
step(M:G,NG) :- not(step(G,_)), mselect(M:G,C),
        infer(C,M:G,Res), normal(Res,NG).
```

This clause succeeds if the goal atom is not defined by a module inside `G`, and if there is clause `C` of module `M` which can be used for an inference.

4.4.2 Example of database

```
p(a).
m1:p(b).
m2:p(c).
m2:p(X)<-p(X).
m2:(q(X) <- p(X)).
```

[6]To state a cumulative predicate definition (where loading the module `m` does not over-write the definition of `p`, but extends it), add to the database the clause `m:p(x1,...,xn) <- p(x1,...,xn)`.

Query-examples:

```
p(a).  => failure
m1:m2:p(b).  => success
m2:m1:p(c).  => failure
m1:m2:(p(b)&p(c)).  => success
m1:m2:q(b).  => success
m2:m1:q(a).  => failure
```

4.5 EPISTEMIC LOGIC

Here, the context operators are *knows* and *comp*.

4.5.1 Definition of the inference step

```
step(G,NG) :-
        pselect(G,C),
        infer(C,G,Res),
        normal(Res,NG).
```

pselect selects a clause from the database with the same head atoms as the goal head. The **normal** predicate is defined as for modules (section 4.3). The **infer** predicate is as for pure Prolog, plus the following:

```
infer(knows(X):C,comp(X):G,comp(X):NG) :-
        infer(knows(X):C,G,NG).
infer(knows(X):C,comp(X):G,comp(X):NG) :-
        infer(C,comp(X):G,NG).
infer(knows(X):C,knows(X):G,knows(X):NG) :-
        infer(knows(X):C,G,NG).
infer(comp(X):C,comp(X):G,knows(X):NG) :-
        infer(C,comp(X):G,NG).
infer(knows(X):C,G,NG) :-
        infer(C,G,NG).
infer(C,comp(X):G,NG) :-
        infer(C,G,NG).
```

4.5.2 The unavoidable wise men puzzle

The wise men puzzle (version with two wise men): There are two wise men who cannot see the colour of their hats, and know that there is at least one white hat. The goal is to show that after a first questioning where nobody answers, 1 is able to tell the colour of his hat: `?- knows(1):white(1)` should succeed.

1 knows that 2 has a white hat:

(a) `knows(1):white(2).`

1 knows that 2 knows that one of the hats is white (in non-Horn clause form).

$$knows(1) : knows(2) : (white(1) \vee white(2))$$

(b) `knows(1):knows(2):(white(1) <- notwhite(2)).`

1 knows that if his hat is black 2 knows it (in non-Horn clause form):

$$knows(1) : (\neg white(1) \rightarrow knows(2) : \neg white(1))$$

(c) `knows(1):(white(1) <- comp(2):white(1)).`

After the first questioning, 1 knows that 2 does not know the colour of his hat:

$$knows(1) : \neg knows(2) : white(2)$$

(d) `knows(1):comp(2):notwhite(2).`

Now from the goal `knows(1):white(1)` and the database clause (c) one can deduce `knows(1):comp(2):white(1)`, and from that goal and (b) one can deduce `knows(1):comp(2)white(2)`; from which one can deduce truth with clause (d).

4.6 AN INTERACTIVE INFERENCE SYSTEM

A simple example of an interactive inference machine, e.g. for expert systems is often cited in the literature ([9]). It is a backward chaining meta-interpreter which asks the user when facts are lacking. Basically, this mechanism can be defined in TIM as follows.

```
step(?G, ?NG) <-
        select-L(?G, C) &
        infer(C, ?G, ?Res).
step(?G, ?truth) <-
        atomic(?G) &
        not select(?G, C) &
        write('Does ') & write(?G) &
        write('hold ? ') &
        read(yes).
```

The `infer` predicate is the same as for pure Prolog[7].

[7] In a more intelligent approach we put the positive and negative answers in the knowledge base.

4.7 OTHER IMPLEMENTATIONS

Generally, the TIM programmer may create his own set of resolution rules using the rule compiler, and he also may use the already existing set of resolution rules belonging to the theorem prover library (T.P.L.). The T.P.L. contains the well known modal systems as Q, T, S4, S5 (modal operators *nec* and *pos*), epistemic logics as S4(n) (n different modal operators *knows(1),...,knows(n)* and *comp(1),...,comp(n))*. Moreover it contains mechanized modal systems that allow us to do hypothetical reasoning (in intuitionistic logic), to manipulate modules, and to handle uncertain information.

5 TIM AND NON-CLASSICAL DEDUCTION

TIM is particularly suitable to do logic programming with non-classical logics. To every non-classical logic corresponds a (non-classical) logic programming language. Formally, what can be mechanised with TIM are non-classical inference systems axiomatized by (one or more) sequent calculi embedded in one top level sequent calculus. The embedded sequent calculi depend on the non-classical logic under concern.

As for the procedural specification we give a scheme of a non-classical inference mechanism. First we define the top level sequent calculus. It involves sets of definite clauses (noted *S*), goals (noted *?G*, *?G'*), and substitutions.

$$S \vdash ?\mathbf{truth}$$

$$\frac{S \vdash ?G \qquad C, ?G \vdash_1 ?G'(\sigma)}{S \vdash ?G'(\sigma)} \qquad \text{for some clause } C \in S$$

$$\frac{S \vdash ?G \qquad ?G \vdash_2 ?G'(\sigma)}{S \vdash ?G'(\sigma)}$$

The meaning e.g. of the second inference rule is that in the calculus $\vdash$, the goal $\neg G'(\sigma)$ can be proved from a set of clauses S if $\neg G$ can be proved from S in the calculus $\vdash$, and in the calculus $\vdash_1$ $\neg G'(\sigma)$ can be proved from $\neg G$ and some clause C of S.

Hence the embedded sequents establish how to get from a given goal clause, a new goal clause, eventually using a selected definite clause $C \in S$. Definite clauses are noted C, C' and goal clauses are noted $?G$, $?G'$, $?NG$, $?NG'$. The sequents are defined by axioms and inference rules of the following type:

$$C, ?G \vdash_1 ?\mathbf{truth}(\sigma) \qquad \text{if } C, G \text{ are atomic and } \sigma \text{ is a mgu of } C \text{ and } G$$

$$\frac{C, ?G \vdash_1 ?NG(\sigma)}{C', ?G' \vdash_1 ?NG'(\sigma')}$$

$$\frac{?G \vdash_2 ?NG(\sigma)}{?G' \vdash_2 ?NG'(\sigma')}$$

where C', G', NG' are typically (but not necessarily) subformulas of C, G, NG, and σ is more general than σ'. We may also have inference rules of the following type:

$$\frac{C, ?G \vdash_1 ?NG(\sigma)}{?G' \vdash_2 ?NG'(\sigma')}$$ where C is e.g. some subformula of G'.

5.1 PROLOG

Prolog can be defined easily in this framework letting

$C, ?G \vdash_1 ?truth(\sigma)$ if C,G are atomic and σ is the mgu of C and G

$$\frac{C, ?G \vdash_1 ?NG(\sigma)}{C', ?G\&R \vdash_1 ?NG\&R(\sigma)}$$

$$\frac{H, ?G \vdash_1 ?NG(\sigma)}{H <- T, ?G \vdash_1 ?T\&NG(\sigma)}$$

5.2 EPISTEMIC LOGIC

knows(a):p & knows(a):(p -> q) -> knows(a):q

being a theorem of epistemic logic, under TIM the goal **?knows(a):q** should be proven from the set of definite clause.

S = knows(a):p, knows(a):(q <- p)

The toplevel sequent proof is

$$\frac{\dfrac{knows(a){:}p,\ ?knows(a){:}(q <- p) \vdash\ ?truth}{knows(a){:}p,\ ?knows(a){:}(q <- p) \vdash\ ?knows(a){:}p}}{knows(a){:}p,\ ?knows(a){:}(q <- p) \vdash\ ?knows(a){:}q}$$

5.3 CONDITIONAL LOGICS

?assume(A) : (A & B) ⊢ ?assume(A) : B

In order to prove "*A* and *B*, assuming *A*" (i.e. under hypothesis *A)*, we must prove the new goal "*B* assuming *A*", because *A* is true under hypothesis *A*.

TIM inference rules are described by defining the step predicate. Thus, the rules for a given non-classical system are entered as particular parameters for the inference engine.

6 DECLARATIVE SEMANTICS

Just as one can associate a fixpoint semantics to Prolog programs, it is possible to define a fixpoint operator for non-classical programs.

This has been done e.g. in [3] for modal logics Q and S4, and in [20] for a logic for modules.

In the case of classical logic programming, van Emden and Kowalski [25], has defined a fixpoint operator T_P on the complete lattice of subsets of $\mathcal{B}_P$, the Herbrand base of the logic program P considered. This operator has been proved to be continuous, and its least fixpoint is equal to the set of ground atomic consequences of P in predicate logic. In the case of modal logic programming, things are a little bit more complete. A fixpoint semantics is defined within the set of trees $t =< W, R, m >$ where

1. W is a set of nodes
2. R is a binary relation over W such that $\omega R \omega'$ whenever ω' is a child of ω in the tree
3. m is a mapping from W to $2^{\mathcal{B}_P}$

Union and intersection operators have been defined on $\Im$ which is a complete lattice. An operator T_P has been defined on $\Im$, too. Its purpose is to extend van Emden and Kowalski's operator to modal logic programs. To any tree t (which can be considered as a model of modal logic) T_P associates the tree $t' = T_P(t)$ in which every direct consequence of the modal program P and of the formula true in t should be true. It has been shown in [3] that T_P is continuous in the complex lattice $\Im$. Thus it possesses a least fixpoint $T_P \uparrow \omega$ which has been proved to be equivalent to the set of ground modal atomic consequences of P.

7 COMPLETENESS ISSUES

It is possible to define the goal computation rules in an empiric, ad hoc manner without bothering about the properties of the resulting logic: TIM programmers need not be logicians to find well-working rules and write e.g. prototypes of expert systems. But just as Prolog is not merely a high-level programming language, but also its underlying resolution principle furnishes a sound and complete proof procedure for a fragment of first order logic (namely the set of Horn clauses), the rule set TIM uses is a proof procedure for the TIM Horn clause fragment of the corresponding non-classical logic.

If we refer to an existing non-classical logic, soundness and completeness of the inference rules used in TIM are crucial. Just as Prolog employs resolution rules à la Robinson, in the case of TIM it is sufficient to possess a resolution principle for the non-classical logic under consideration in order to mechanize it. We remark that just as Prolog isn't complete with respect to predicate logic semantics, TIM with e.g. the modal inference rules of [14] isn't complete w.r.t. modal semantics. This is due to the depth-first strategy, and changing to breadth-first strategy would achieve completeness in the case of Prolog as well as in the case of TIM.

The only thing to do in order to possess a "modal Prolog" is to run TIM under the resolution rules corresponding to the particular modal logic which is needed. Nevertheless, problems appear concerning the closure of the modal Horn clause fragment under resolution: The resolvent of a fact clause and a goal clause is not necessarily a goal clause. This is connected with the fact that some modal operators (for example the "possible" operator) hide existential quantifiers. And it is well known from classical logic that it is generally difficult to handle (unskolemized) existential quantifiers. An immediate solution to this problem is to restrict the language of modal Horn clauses and to forbid e.g. clauses whose head is governed by a "possible" operator (and like it has been done in [21], [4]. Another possibility would be to admit the whole language as defined above, to make the resolvents of two Horn clauses be a Horn clause (by dropping some subformula), and to admit that the completeness of the resulting rules isn't ensured. A simple solution where the language is closed under resolution and completeness is ensured has been given in [3], where a skolemization like technique for (existential) modal operators has been defined in order to obtain modal Horn clauses closed under resolution.

8 THE IMPLEMENTATIONS

The first implementations of TIM (called MOLOG at that time) have been done in Prolog within *Esprit project p973* on advanced logic programming environments (ALPES) [2], [5], [13], [20], [6], [11]. After a prototype written in LISP [8], there has been implementation of compiled versions in C, following the principles of the WAM [1] (the primitives of the WAM being not sufficient to implement TIM). This work has been continued, and a distributed implementation in ADA is in progress.

Contrarily to Prolog, where the inference rule is unique, in TIM several inference rules may apply to a given goal and select clause. Therefore a particular inference rule chaining mechanism has been worked out [1] in order to overcome the uniform backtracking mechanism of Prolog which makes no difference between programs and meta-programs: in TIM, the super-user can (but is not obliged to) alter the control of the inference process by specifying which inference rule should be tried after the current one in the success case and which one in the failure case.

9 CONCLUSION

We have presented a general framework called TIM within which non-classical inference engines can be implemented.

It is based on three assumptions: to keep the basic control features of Prolog, to parametrize the inference step, and to do clause selection explicitly. We have shown that this permits us to implement uniformly a large class of Prolog extensions.

We have given a variety of examples of applications in the domain of logic programming among which are modules, epistemic, temporal and conditional reasoning and an interactive inference system. We have also shown that it is easy, in TIM, to experiment with different sets of inference rules for these concepts.

ACKNOWLEDGEMENTS

We would like to thank Pierre Bieber and specially Luis Fariñas del Cerro for important suggestions and criticisms.

References

[1] J. M. ALLIOT and J. GARMENDIA. Une implementation en "C" de MOLOG. Rapport D.E.A., Université Paul Sabatier, Toulouse, France, 1988.

[2] R. Arthaud, P. Bieber, L. Fariñas del Cerro, J. Henry, and A. Herzig. Automated modal reasoning. In *Proc. of the Int. Conf. on Information Processing and Management of Uncertainty in Knowledge-Based Systems*, Paris, july 1986.

[3] P. Balbiani, L. Fariñas del Cerro, and A. Herzig. Declarative semantics for modal logics. In *Proc. of the Int. Conf. on Fifth Generation Computer Systems*, Tokyo, 1988.

[4] Marianne Baudinet. *Logic Programming Semantics: Techniques and Applications.* PhD thesis, Stanford University, feb 1989.

[5] P. Bieber, L. Fariñas del Cerro, and A. Herzig. MOLOG - a modal PROLOG. In E. Lusk and R. Overbeek, editors, *Proc. of the 9th Int. Conf. on Automated Deduction*, LNCS 310, pages 487–499, Argonne - USA, may 1988. Springer Verlag.

[6] P. Bieber, L. Fariñas del Cerro, and A. Herzig. A modal logic for modules. draft, 1989.

[7] K. A. Bowen and R. A. Kowalski. Amalgamating language and metalanguage in logic programming. In K. Clark and S. Tarnlund, editors, *Logic Programming*, pages 153–172. Academic Press, 1982.

[8] M. Bricard. Une machine abstraite pour compiler MOLOG. Rapport D.E.A., Université Paul Sabatier - LSI, 1987.

[9] H. Coelho, J. C. Cotta, and L. M. Pereira. *How to solve it in Prolog.* Laboratório Nacional de Engenharia Civil, Lisbon, Portugal, 2nd edition, 1980.

[10] P. J. de la Quintana. Computing quantifiers in predicate modal logics. In *Proceedings of European Conference on Artificial Intelligence*, pages 519–524, München, August 1988.

[11] Esprit project - The Alpes Consortium. *Advanced Logic Programming Environments*, sept 1989. ALPES Final Report.

[12] Esprit Project p973 "ALPES". *MOLOG Technical Report*, may 1987. Esprit Technical Report.

[13] Esprit Project p973 "ALPES". *MOLOG User Manual*, may 1987. Esprit Technical Report.

[14] L. Fariñas del Cerro. A simple deduction method for modal logic. *Information Processing Letters*, 14(2), 1982.

[15] L. Fariñas del Cerro. MOLOG: A system that extends PROLOG with modal logic. *New Generation Computing*, 4:35–50, 1986.

[16] M. Fujita, S. Kono, H. Tanaka, and T. Moto-Oka. Tokio: Logic programming language based on temporal logic and its compilation to prolog. In *Third Int. Conf. on Logic Programming*, pages 695–709, jul 1986.

[17] D. Gabbay and U. Reyle. N-prolog: An extension of prolog with hypothetical implications. *Jounal of Logic Programming*, 1:319–355, 1984.

[18] M. Gallaire and C. Lasserre. Meta-level control for logic programs. In K. Clark and S. Tarnlund, editors, *Logic Programming*, pages 173–188. Academic Press, 1982.

[19] P. Jackson, H. Reichgelt, and F. van Harmelen. *Logic-Based Knowledge Representation*. The MIT Press, USA, 1989.

[20] Luis Monteiro and Antonio Porto. Modules for logic programming based on context extension. In *Int. Conf. on Logic Programming*, 1988.

[21] Mitsuhiro Okada. Mathematical basis of modal logic programming. In *Journés Europènnes Logique et Intelligence Artificielle*. Roscoff, 1988.

[22] Y Sakakibara. Programming in modal logic: An extension of PROLOG based on modal logic. In *Int. Conf. on Logic Programming*, 1987.

[23] Takashi Sakuragawa. Temporal PROLOG. In *RIMS Conf. on software science and engineering*, 1989.

[24] L Sterling and E. Shapiro. *The Art of Prolog*. The MIT Press, USA, 1986.

[25] M. H. van Emden and R. A. Kowalski. The semantics of predicate logic as a programming language. *Journal of the Association for Computing Machinery*, 23(4):733–742, 1976.

Declarative and procedural paradigms – do they really compete? (Panel Outline)*

Harold Boley
Deutsches Forschungszentrum für Künstliche Intelligenz
Universität Kaiserslautern

1 Introduction

Some may be tempted to rephrase the title: are the paradigms still competing or competing again? have they stopped competing? And in the latter case we may add: are they beginning to cooperate? The former procedural/declarative controversy [Win75] has reappeared under various guises, e.g., in discussions about object-oriented/logic programming or knowledge representation. Both research paradigms have developed into large user communities, while the 'logicism' debate following Drew McDermott's "A critique of pure reason" [Lev87] has not yet influenced developers of knowledge-based systems. The present workshop is concerned more with technical issues, including the compilation of declarative knowledge into procedural forms. But now that efficient knowledge-base compilers are being developed, the declarativist position may become relevant for practice ("declarative knowledge can work") and perhaps, reconciled with the proceduralist position ("declarative and procedural knowledge can be combined"). Hopefully the panel had something to say to AI developers puzzled both by epistemological sophistries and expert-system shells.

2 Competition

The term 'declarative' has often been contrasted to two different antonyms for programming and representation languages:

- Computer science distinguishes declarative (high-level) programs, e.g. written in Backus' FP, and **imperative** (low-level) programs, e.g. coded in C.

*Many thanks to the other panelists for the lively discussion and the (revised) position statements. An impression of the only panelist position missing in these proceedings, that of *Hassan Aït-Kaci*, can be found in Cristina Ribeiro's PDK report, printed, e.g., in the Feb. 1992 issue of the ALP Newsletter.

- Artificial intelligence distinguishes declarative (explicit) representations, e.g. written in pure Prolog, and **procedural** (implicit) representations, e.g. codified in full Common Lisp.

Since there is no sharp boundary between programming and representation languages (Lisp, e.g., is ambiguous in this respect), we don't need to keep the two distinctions orthogonal here.

Declarative formalisms have been useful in foundational work, and are slowly spreading into applications. For example, there now exist a number of Prolog knowledge bases for real-life applications [Mos91]. The question is, how pure such Prolog applications are, how declarative they can be now that efficiency is taken care of by refined WAM-compiler technology. Considerable practical advantages of declarative representations can arise from their high level of explicit description: this facilitates the readability, maintenance, and parallelization of knowledge bases, as well as deductive and inductive inferences, including the discovery of new relationships between knowledge items.

However, several nondeclarative formalisms are successful and spreading, too, from the Common Lisp Object System, Smalltalk, and C++ to neural-network software or even hardware. The OOP community, fuelled by iconic 'objects' on graphics workstations, has been performing *veni, vidi, vici*, especially in industry. And a number of expert-system shells have been (manually) rewritten from Lisp to C(++), mainly for efficiency. It might be claimed that formalisms for the real world cannot be (purely) declarative because the real world itself isn't that way (there is state change, side effect, sharing, etc.).

3 Cooperation

Of course, we can try to **combine** declarative and procedural formalisms in order to obtain the best of both approaches. For instance, in an expert system, low-level recognition tasks might be accomplished by a neural net, whereas the high-level interpretation problems could be solved by a logic program. Or, system structuring "in-the-large" may be done using an OOP class hierarchy, while each object "in-the-small" could be a rule, constraint, or taxonomic system. However, the nature of such hybrid declarative/procedural couplings is not quite clear. Where exactly should the boundary lie (e.g., do we have taxonomic hierarchies **within** objects and a separate class hierarchy **between** objects)? Should cooperation be loose (perhaps duplicating compiled knowledge bases) or tight (perhaps enforcing a global control)? How should hybrid knowledge (de)compilation be organized (static translations or run-time interfaces)?

Also, 'pure declarativists' may still hope that even the low-level parts of large real-life systems can eventually be **specified** in a declarative fashion. This would provide a reference level against which to verify, or from which to (automatically) generate, procedural **implementations**. A knowledge-processing laboratory might consist of a refinement hierarchy extending from high-level specifications to low-level implementations, thus permitting both declarative and procedural views of the same knowledge. Moreover, even paradigms that started out procedural may end up declarative. For example, the object-oriented paradigm is currently being reconstructed by Prologish committed-choice languages and by declarative formalisms such as linear logic. Will, sometime in the future, complete neural nets be de/compiled to/from large, purely declarative knowledge bases?

References

[Lev87] Hector Levesque. Taking issue: Guest editor's introduction. *Computational Intelligence*, 3:149–150, 1987.

[Mos91] Chris Moss. Commercial applications of large Prolog knowledge bases. This Volume, 1991.

[Win75] Terry Winograd. Frame representations and the declarative/procedural controversy. In Daniel G. Bobrow and Allan Collins, editors, *Representation and Understanding - Studies in Cognitive Science*, pages 185–210. Academic Press, 1975.

Declarative and Procedural Paradigms - Do they Really Compete? (Panel Position Statement)

Micha Meier
European Computer-Industry Research Centre
Arabellastr. 17, D-8000 Munich 81, Germany
email: micha@ecrc.de

No, they do not. And it is a shame. I will only discuss Prolog, which itself has the most potential among declarative languages. Prolog certainly does not compete with procedural languages, not so because it is suitable for different types of applications as people often say, but simply because it is too inefficient for the competition in applications which are feasible with procedural languages. Thus areas where Prolog can be used are rather limited - rapid prototyping, dynamic problems, constraint logic programming, and perhaps expert systems. Note that I do not even mention compiler writing, because major Prolog vendors have rejected the idea to write their Prolog compilers in Prolog.

1 What is the Problem?

Although the main Prolog problem is efficiency, it has even further consequences: the language has to have impure features to increase efficiency, the programmers write programs in a non-declarative way to make them efficient, and people outside of the logic programming community are reluctant to use Prolog because it is neither efficient nor declarative (and they have heard that it can go into an infinite loop even with a correct declarative program).

Superficially seen, the distinction between Prolog and procedural languages is declarativeness versus efficiency, and we might ask the question "can Prolog have both of them?". However, I think it is more appropriate to start with "why is Prolog neither declarative nor efficient?".

2 What does "Declarative" Mean?

Most Prolog programs are not declarative. Not because they are using nondeclarative features (although they are), but because the programmers must concentrate on the use of proper data structures and on encoding a particular algorithm, rather than just describing the properties of the solution, otherwise the program would not run, or it would be too inefficient. This may still be considered as declarative, however the resulting program implements a particular algorithm and particular data structures, and often it also uses particular features of the underlying Prolog compiler (e.g. indexing on the first argument). Thus efficient Prolog programming enforces a particular programming style which very often is at a very low level of abstraction and it is in fact much closer to the procedural programming, unfortunately without its efficiency.

To conclude, the programmer must encrypt his ideas at a too low level, which makes his programs more difficult to write, debug, maintain and understand, and the system, on the other hand, must decrypt what was the intention of the programmer in order to compile his program efficiently. The difference between current Prolog and true declarative programming seems the same as between assembler and FORTRAN.

3 How Can Program Analysis Help Us?

Current research concentrates on methods of program analysis and transformation which would allow the system to execute the user programs more efficiently. Unfortunately, program analysis can often infer only very simple properties of the underlying program, e.g. types, modes, aliasing, dependency, etc. but to really efficiently process the program it would be necessary to infer the *meaning* of the program or a predicate. For example, when the user wants to obtain a copy of a term, he must write a nontrivial recursive predicate that actually does the copying, using a particular method, depth-first or breadth-first, left-to-right or right-to left. For the compiler it is a fairly complicated task to understand what the meaning of this predicate is, because it must be encoded with all details and this prevents the compiler to generate a more efficient code for it.

4 So What Can We Do?

We have to break this deadlock - the programmers write nondeclarative programs because of efficiency, but this makes them programs more difficult to understand and to execute efficiently. Removing the impure primitives (as e.g. in Gödel [1]) is only a part of the solution, because even then it is not guaranteed that declarative programs will be efficient.

There are basically two ways to go: make the declarative programs easier compilable, i.e. improve the compilation of the low-level programs. This is the approach of e.g. Trilogy or PDC-Prolog and it basically means to introduce some restrictions which bring the declarative programs closer to the procedural ones.

We should take the other way - the users must give up low-level programming, and write programs at the highest possible level of abstraction. Consequently, more work is shifted to the system, and this will actually enable it to process the program efficiently. If the program is abstract enough and it does not rely on particular data types or control, the system has more freedom to select the appropriate processing, than if the program is encoded at a lower level.

For example, it is quite easy to transform recursion in Prolog into iteration which uses destructive assignment at the machine level and which keeps the loop invariants unchanged [2], although it is impossible to program this at the source level. The point is, that here the system optimizes the use of its internal data, namely stack frames, and so it has a precise idea how this data behaves. It is much more difficult to optimize the use of data which the user can manipulate explicitly.

Before including some optimizations into Prolog, we also have to ask "does this cure the disease or only one of its symptoms?". For instance, before trying to optimize a predicate that makes a naive list reversal, we must ask "why should we reverse the list?" and "why use lists at all?".

5 But Declarative Programs Are Inefficient!

Obviously, we have to give up the idea that every declarative solution to a problem is as efficient as another one, even if they are written at the same level of abstraction. For example, finding the minimal element in a list can also be done in a strange way:

```
min_element(List, Min) :-
    permutation(List, [Min|Rest]),
    sorted([Min|Rest]).
```

It makes no sense to try to execute this program more efficiently as it is, however no matter how clumsy this program is, the system can very easily infer what is its intended meaning, and then use a completely different approach.

On the other hand, if the programmer tried to be smart and used a more efficient sorting procedure, the system might not at all be able to deduce that all the program does is to find the minimal element. The system could also try to add a delay declaration to the program and to swap the order of sorted/1 and permutation/2 so that the tests delay and make the generation faster. This would be a half-way solution, exactly like in the case of reversing a list. We must first ask "why to generate the permutations in the first place?".

Prolog compiler writers generally believe that it is possible to compile Prolog as efficiently as procedural languages, however the amount of work to achieve this is tremendous. I argue that this task would become simpler not by programming at a level which is closer to the procedural languages, but the opposite - programming at a more abstract level in a true declarative way. In this way, the analysis of the program yields more information and the system is able to transform the input program into an intermediate form, which is close to procedural languages like the current Prolog programs, but with annotations that are available from the high-level analysis and that allow more efficient processing.

References

[1] P. M. Hill and J. W. Lloyd. The Gödel report (preliminary version). Technical Report TR-91-02, Department of Computer Science, University of Bristol, March 1991.

[2] Micha Meier. Recursion vs. iteration in Prolog. In *Proceedings of the ICLP'91*, pages 157–169, Paris, June 1991.

Do the Declarative and Procedural paradigms compete in Software Engineering?

Chris Moss
Imperial College, London University
currently at
CRP-CU, Luxembourg

First, we need to ask what the declarative and procedural paradigms are competing for. Obviously, in this context the answer is that they are competing as a means of knowledge representation in constructing knowledge bases. But what is the purpose of that knowledge representation?

The first obvious goal for knowledge representation is to act as a basis for constructing computer systems. As programmers, we spend most of our lives reinventing wheels, which is a highly inefficient process. We have to find ways of making the results of our activities accumulate and this goal primarily concerns making our knowledge available in an easily comprehensible fashion.

A second goal arises from the fact that computer technology puts forward new possibilities for people to store and use their general knowledge about the world. At present, this is limited to the several forms of information retrieval and the capture of conventional encyclopaedias on CD-ROM. But there is clearly enormous potential for more "knowledge-based" forms of storage. Currently hypertext is the only real contender in this field, but some forms of semantic, deductive and probably inductive capabilities would make such systems much more powerful. However, I'm not sure whether sufficient experience has yet been gained in this field to address the issues: certainly I don't have that experience.

The third possible goal is that knowledge representation is used to create artificial intelligence. The conventional wisdom says that the basis of our intelligence as human beings is our knowledge and a necessary step on the way to creating artificial intelligence is to represent that knowledge in some way.

I wish to distance myself from this last viewpoint, both as a plausible basis of what intelligence is all about and as the framework in which we are talking about knowledge representation. I do not believe that by giving all our knowledge to some externally programmed automaton we will come anywhere near to creating an intelligent being, even if this first step were possible. Also I do not believe this goal forms a useful context for a discussion of the real issues, though this is not the time (and certainly not the place!) to pursue this argument further (but see [1]).

Thus the core of what I think we should be concerned with is the more prosaic world of software engineering and I will limit my remarks to this topic.

Using knowledge to design programs

There are at least three areas which come within the field of program design, all loosely called specification, and in which knowledge may need representation:

1. Describing the organisation into which the computer system fits. i.e. systems analysis.
2. Describing the constraints on a program and its relationship to the organisation and to the computer system in which it exists.
3. Describing the content or behaviour of the programs.

Conventionally, different representations are used for each of these steps. Dataflow diagrams and structure charts are used for the first; natural language or logic (particularly temporal) for the second, again accompanied by dataflow diagrams; procedural code is used for the third.

I think that the experience of the last few years has shown that declarative representations have great value in all three areas, though they are not completely satisfactory in any of them. For instance it is in the long term desirable to model the basic concepts of an organisation as a resource that can be drawn upon later in generating particular programs. The so-called "4th-generation languages" quickly degenerate into purely procedural code because their knowledge representation techniques are inadequate.

Descriptions and specifications are necessarily incomplete. In part this results from the complexity of what is addressed. It is almost always preferable to spend money making the system do more rather than on ensuring one has a complete description of it. In addition, the boundary between the formal and the informal always exists: how does one prove that one's formal specification is correct? The boundary has to be drawn somewhere and this means that specifications are only one weapon in the armoury that must be employed. Trial and error are unavoidable.

Procedural representations are used primarily in the third area, the program, though also to a limited extent in the simulation of the other two. In this area the two paradigms clearly do compete. Certainly, some people aim to write fully "declarative" programs and to do away altogether with the non-declarative, though the line between the two has been incurably blurred by the invention of logic programming systems. Most of the evils of procedural programs — spaghetti code, programming tricks, and even the assignment statement — can be found in Prolog-built systems. Questions of termination do not go away because of a declarative representation and the multiplicity of modes even makes that issue more difficult in some cases.

So I would suggest that the key question is whether languages whose model and operational semantics coincide (i.e. declarative languages) will in the long term do away with the rest? My guess is that the answer is no. The reason is not that, for example, program transformation techniques will not eventually work, but that by then the scene will have changed so much that the formalisation cannot catch up. For example we will be using some type of network-parallel machines invented only last year. In addition, programs often need to cause real side-effects in the real world, which is in no way declarative.

On the other hand, we will be needing the declarative even more by then, so the declarative and procedural will need to coexist for the foreseeable future.

Object-oriented Logic Programming

The key need is to learn to manage the boundary between the declarative and the procedural rather more effectively. While logic programming is an excellent way of stating the micro-problem, it does not scale up as well as one would like. The most promising candidate for organising the larger scene comes from the object-oriented world. Although this may sound like a total retreat from goals of declarativeness I don't think this is inevitable. The object-oriented paradigm brings together three principles that are necessary for any large system.

The principles are encapsulation, inheritance and concurrency. Encapsulation protects us from the outside world, using abstract datatypes as the fundamental organising principle. Inheritance allows us to reuse code that we designed earlier and even in a different way using dynamic binding. Concurrency frees us from the "flatness" of the declarative system, allowing change to occur in different parts of the system simultaneously.

These principles are well expressed in the new languages being built on top of Prolog, such as Prolog++ from LPA. They need little change to the underlying Prolog system, though they do cause a reorientation in the way programs are written, towards objects and attributes and away from relations.

Up till now, the reasons for introducing object-oriented principles into Prolog seem a little confused: in the object systems introduced to aid practical programming in, for example, a windows environment, they seem simply to be an excuse for introducing the assignment statement. For the theoretician they appear to be a challenge to represent change declaratively. Both of these approaches ignore the problem of scale.

Change, or concurrency, is only one of the three aspects of the object-oriented approach that is non-declarative: the other two, encapsulation and inheritance, are capable of a declarative interpretation, though most proposals do not give much attention to encapsulation. But a purely declarative account of change seems ultimately unsatisfying. It is possible to reason *about* change, but many programs are concerned with actually performing change, either in the real world or the documents they are manipulating.

One possibility is that by introducing concurrency (as in Parlog++ for instance) one can formally do without any non-declarative features and these can be simulated by coroutining on sequential systems. However, in practical systems on sequential machines, assignment is at present necessary, though it is better used to capture the major changes in program state than to code the minor steps. This seems an inevitable consequence of the mode of evaluation of languages based on Prolog, and it remains to be seen whether effective equivalents to true concurrency will be found.

We need to encourage declarativeness at the micro level of the program and to be open to object approach in constructing larger systems. Declarative notions have not yet made much headway in the almost exclusively procedural world of objects. But there is great potential.

---

[1] Chris Moss: Logic, Language and the Quest for Intelligence. Proc. U.K. Logic Programming Conference, Bristol. 1990.

Position Statement
PDK Panel Discussion

Michael M. Richter, Kaiserslautern

We will look on the relation between declarative and procedural languages from a foundational, mathematical and historical point of view. While imperative programs are based on the notion of a procedure (or in terms of classical mathematics "construction") declarative knowledge representation relies in the first place on the notion of truth. The most comprehensive approach to truth in formal languages goes back to a paper of A. Tarski. This is, however, only one half of the story: The notion of "truth" has to be complemented by the notion of "proof". Two theorems by K. Gödel made clear that for first order predicate logic truth and proof are nothing but two sides of the same coin but that this is not the case for arbitrary logics. From the viewpoint of information processing one is certainly more interested in the proof aspect. In order to be informative not every proof can be accepted; when the existence of objects is claimed one needs an explicit construction. This was tacitly assumed in mathematics until the time of Kronecker and was again propagated in intuitionism, in particular by Brouwer. In intuitionistic logic every true statement carries its proof with it. This constructive aspect is underlying declarative knowledge representation, too.
Constructive logic is on the other hand strongly related to recursive function theory (i. e. to procedures) via the notion of realizability.

Our first claim is that every declarative knowledge representation useful for information processing is of intuitionistic character. This is e. g. the case for Horn logic. For general Prolog and various other systems this aspect is not understood equally well. We claim that a good theoretical understanding of such a system needs a clear description of its intuitionistic nature.
Next we claim that we need an insight into the relation between proofs and programs. From this point of view procedures become a kind of semantics for statements. At the very moment one has a proof for a statement one should also be able to construct the procedures involved. In other words, we need to "implement statements by procedures".

We think that there is a strong analogy between the relation of classical and constructive mathematics on the one the one side and declarative and procedural knowledge representation on the other side. Constructive proofs as well as imperative programs provide more insight and information than classical proofs and declarative programs resp.; sometimes this additional information is unnecessary or even unwanted, however. We feel that the intuitionistic view on the notions of statement, proof and recursive function can contribute to the understanding of the declarative and procedural languages. A better insight into these foundational aspects could be a basis for a uniform view on the technical problems which face us presently.

WHAT IS DECLARATIVE PROGRAMMING?

A. A. Voronkov
International Laboratory of Intelligent Systems (SINTEL)
Universitetski Prospekt 4
630090 Novosibirsk 90, USSR

This statement is not a criticism of the declarative style of programming, but tries to understand the phenomenon of declarativity. I wanted to stress that the essence of declarative programming is very vague and unclear and that the usual definitions of 'declarative' as 'logical' or 'non-procedural' seem very controversial. When I spoke with other people during PDK'91 about the essence of declarative programming I discovered some interesting contradictions in some men's opinions: (a) Everybody is speaking about declarative programming but nobody can define more or less clearly what is it. (b) Nobody can define declarative programming but everybody says that they write declarative programs. Most of the people agree that using cuts in Prolog programs goes beyond the declarative style. (c) Everybody insisting on using a declarative style uses cuts in his Prolog programs or writes programs in C which is not a declarative language. (d) Everybody is speaking about some future languages which will be purely declarative, but nobody knows how these languages might look.

From this I infer that declarative programming is some kind of "common belief". Many arguments in defense of declarative programming are like the following: (1) I believe in it and you must also believe; (2) Programming must be declarative; (3) Nobody is allowed to use non-declarative styles; (4) If you do not use a declarative style then you are a hacker; (5) Declarativity is our nice future.

For a man from a communist country all these statements look quite familiar, but I do not want to accuse my opponents for communism, so I shall instead try to raise some of the questions. I can partially agree with (1)-(5) if we shall extend the definition of declarativity far beyond the usual understanding of this word. I shall be very glad if this paper will initiate some discussion about the essence of the declarative approach. When I tried to understand it I could find more questions than answers. And I would like to ask the same questions to the people who know (or pretend to know) what "declarative" might mean in the context of programming. I shall also try to convince the reader that the definition of declarative programming as the opposite of procedural is artificial.

On declarative and procedural semantics of declarative languages or, does non-procedural programming exist?

There are several definitions of the word "declarative"and related words in English language dictionaries. One can summarize the definitions of the word *declare* as *to make clear or plain; to state formally or in explicit terms.*

This definition fits very well in my understanding of what is truly declarative programming. First, the program must be clear in relation to the problem solved by the program. Second, it must also clearly hint the way how the problem is solved from the algorithmical viewpoint. So in my opinion the distinction between declarative and non-declarative is not just the distinction between what to do and how to do it. Logic is very good (sometimes) in describing static parts of the problem. But you should add many procedural features to the logic to describe a dynamic part. So the real Prolog is in one sense more declarative than some pure parts of Prolog.

Let us consider one small (rather static) example to understand whether completely non-procedural programming exists at all. To this end I shall try to write a very declarative specification of a sorting algorithm. I think that everybody agrees that truly declarative specifications must describe new relations in terms of other ones coming down finally to some primitive relations such as $<$ on numbers. It is interesting that under this understanding it is not easy to write the needed specification. But anyhow, let us try. As usual we can define sorting as finding an ordered permutation of the original list:

$$\mathrm{sort}(x,y) := \mathrm{perm}(x,y) \wedge \mathrm{ordered}(y)$$

We can relatively easily describe what is *ordered* if we have as a primitive the relation $x \sqsubseteq y$ (x is a sublist of y) and some other primitives defined on lists and numbers:

$$\mathrm{ordered}(y) := (\forall x \sqsubseteq y)(\mathrm{length}(y) \geq 2 \Rightarrow \mathrm{car}(x) \geq \mathrm{cadr}(x))$$

It is a bit more difficult to define what a permutation is because it is not so easy to define the number of occurrences of an element in a list. But if we have it in the language, then

$$\mathrm{perm}(x,y) := (\forall z)(\forall n)(\mathrm{occurs}(z,x,n) \Leftrightarrow \mathrm{occurs}(z,y,n)).$$

So finally we have a purely declarative specification. Can it be considered as a program? No. There is no hint on the algorithm for finding an ordered permutation.

People experienced in Prolog can immediately say that there is also a very declarative Horn clause program solving the same problem, e.g.

$$\begin{array}{l} \mathrm{sort}([],[]). \\ \mathrm{sort}([X],[X]). \\ \mathrm{sort}([X|Y],Z) : -\mathrm{sort}(Y,U), \mathrm{insert}(X,U,Z). \end{array}$$

But let me ask what does it mean, especially the third clause? It does not describe sort via more primitive relations, but instead it defines sort via sort. I can agree that statements from the program are true on the needed relation, the problem is what relation they define?

Is it the same relation that I wanted to define? *To understand these clauses we have to know either the procedural semantics of Prolog or the least fixed point semantics which is even more complicated.* So we have either a purely declarative specification which cannot be considered as a program or a set of Horn clauses for the understanding of which we need to know the procedural semantics. You can say that there are semantics like Clark's completion which explain the meaning of the program. But it is not true. Even Clark's completion can have non-standard models and it is not so easy to understand. So does pure declarative programming exist? Or is declarative the opposite of procedural? Is a pure Horn clause program with recursion non-procedural?

Can I trust the computer?

There is a common belief that we can delegate to computers the process of making an efficient program from an inefficient (but declarative) one. For example it is assumed that a man can write a specification which implies an algorithm of exponential complexity and the wise computer translates it to a linear complexity algorithm for the same problem. This illusion is usually demonstrated by particular examples of such transformations. If one considers these examples more thoroughly then it is usually clear that to write this linear algorithm from the very beginning was as easy as to write the exponential one.

Suppose, then, that a programmer can choose to write non-efficient but declarative programs leaving efficiency problems to the computer. Suppose even that the computer is extremely clever and can sometimes improve complexity. (It is relevant to remember that the problem whether one program is more efficient than another is undecidable!). What will the experienced programmer do? Is it better to leave efficiency to the computer or to write more efficient programs (even spending much more time for it). In the latter case the programmer will know that his program is linear. In the former he will wake up in the night dreaming that the program caused exhaustive exponential search, running as part of a very important system. Let us now think what is better (even under the assumption that the computer is very clever): (1) To write a linear program; (2) To write an exponential program leaving efficiency to the computer and (a) to test the computer-generated program on 101 inputs and to have nightmares about the 102nd input? or (b) Consider the text of the computer-generated program and to spend 10 days trying to understand that it is correct and really much faster.

The problem here is that the program (even written in logic) has much more information than it states. For example, a program can implicitly contain information about complexity of the algorithm solving the problem. If we leave efficiency problems to a clever compiler then a program which is extremely declarative in the usual understanding of this word does not contain any more information about efficiency (this information is hidden because the final program will be generated by the compiler). Or we can take a more or less procedural program which is not so logical but with clear procedural semantics which gives us an answer about efficiency.

So the question is the following: can we consider as declarative a program which is wittingly inefficient if we know that there is a program (with not so good logical semantics) but which clearly has information about efficiency? And once more the question arises about understanding the declarative program. You need to know procedural semantics to understand a declarative program and you need to know the same to understand a procedural one. But the procedural program can be much more informative than the declarative (in the usual sense) one? So is declarative opposed to procedural? Or should we change our point of view on declarative programming?

Future declarative languages

Let me ask once more: what is a declarative language? Is there any hope that we shall have some completely non-procedural or completely logical languages? The development of Prolog shows that the new Prolog-like languages do not look much more non-procedural or more logical than the ordinary Prolog. Consider three examples.

1. Constraint logic programming languages. They supply very high-level descriptive formalism for some kinds of problems. For these kinds of problems programs in these languages are shorter, have less non-logical features like cuts etc. But if you consider semantics of constraint logic programming languages you discover that now we have two different types of goals with different behaviors. The same relation $<$ on numbers has different semantics depending on the part of clause where it occurs. Is it so logical and so non-procedural? Once more we come to the conclusion that to understand declarative semantics we have to know procedural semantics. I have nothing against including constraint logic programming languages to the list of declarative languages, but what makes them declarative? The logical features, or the non-procedural features, or the more intelligent problem solver or something else?

2. Parallel logic programming languages. Parallel programming is the future and logic programming languages seem more suitable for parallel execution than traditional procedural or functional languages. But the feature making them suitable for parallel programming is their procedural semantics: reductions of goals to subgoals. Many of the new concurrent logic programming languages do not seem more logical or more non-procedural than Prolog. Many of them have no cut operator, and sometimes the order of clauses is not relevant but they have guards and very complicated semantics which made people make errors even in very simple programs published in journal articles. Moreover, in some new languages clause bodies can have even three different parts, which makes them more expressive. If a language can express something substantial but lacks in semantic issues can we say that it is more declarative? And if yes, then what is declarative programming at all?

3. Object-oriented (logic) programming. For many kinds of applications object-oriented programming allows to represent knowledge (static or dynamic) in a form very close to human understanding of the problem. The classical example is object-oriented window interfaces. From this viewpoint object-oriented programming ought to be considered as a declarative formalism. But object-oriented programming has very

bad semantic properties. The descriptions of formal semantics of object-oriented languages are very clumsy and not elegant. Even object-oriented logic programming languages (e.g. Prolog++) have an assignment construction which is needed to describe state changes of an object. And assignment is the consequence of using objects. Thus using more a understandable formalism results in using the assignment. Should we include the assignment in the set of declarative tools under some conditions? It is possible to give other examples where the use of a more or less pure logical language makes programs more complicated. Some people claim that if we describe impure primitives of Prolog like var in the metalevel by means of pure Horn clauses we shall get declarative variants of these primitives. But if we describe var in a different language then the semantics of this primitive is not changed - it is just rewritten in other terms. And encoding of impure Prolog programs by pure constructions in the metalevel does not make programs more understandable. In the same way one can write an interpreter of Basic in Prolog and call programming in Basic declarative.

Procedural and non-procedural human thinking

If we agree that declarative knowledge representation means more understandable or more human knowledge representation then the next question is whether human thinking is procedural or non-procedural. The answer is not so easy. The procedural or algorithmic (and even imperative) way of thinking is as usual for humans as the non-procedural one.

Programs are written for people and by people but they are written on computers, which makes programming very different from e.g. mathematics. It is not clear whether knowledge representation in logic is superior to procedural representations. When I taught Prolog to students who did not know anything about programming I tried to introduce Prolog via logic. One of the first examples was the well known program

$$\text{man(Socrates).}$$
$$\text{mortal(Person)} : -\text{man(Person)}.$$

(This program is extremely declarative, isn't it?) I explained that if you would ask the computer whether Socrates is mortal it says "yes" because this logically follows from the program statements. The students understood that this might be the right answer but their first words were "Yes, this is good what you are saying, but how can the computer know the answer?" They did not understand me until I introduced procedural semantics. The same problem appeared with the first recursive program, describing finding a route in a graph. It was difficult for students to understand that the given program was sufficient for the computer. Everything became clear only after introducing procedural semantics.

Once I had a discussion with my friend who wrote several large applied programs in Prolog. He confessed that he never uses negation in his programs because cut is more understandable. So he thought about semantics of Prolog not in logical terms. So it is not quite clear what gives Prolog its expressive power and makes it more declarative - either logic foundations or built-in search capabilities or the goal-oriented style of programming or something else.

The GCLA II programming language

Martin Aronsson and Lars-Henrik Eriksson
Swedish Institute of Computer Science (SICS)
Box 1263
S-164 28 KISTA, SWEDEN

e-mail: gcla@sics.se

Language description

The GCLA II programming language is based on the work of Lars Hallnäs and Peter Schroeder-Heister on definitions as rules. "GCLA" stands for "Generalised Horn Clause Language", since the language is, in a sense, an extension to pure Prolog.

The difference between the Horn clauses making up Prolog programs and the generalised Horn clauses making up GCLA programs, is that the latter can have hypothetical assumptions in their clause bodies. Hypothetical constructs are syntactically the same as logical implications, but has (in general) a different meaning, depending on the exact contents of the GCLA programs.

Just as Prolog can be seen as an executable form of Horn clause logic, GCLA can be seen as an executable form of the theory of partial inductive definitions, developed by Lars Hallnäs. This theory comprises a proof system with several inference rules, which in GCLA take the place of the SLD-resolution in Prolog. Again, as the Horn clauses of Prolog are special cases of the generalised Horn clauses of GCLA, SLD-resolution is a special case of one of the inference rules of the theory of partial inductive definitions.

As the proof system of partial inductive definitions use sequents, a goal of a GCLA execution is a sequent. Inference rules can be applied either to the conclusion or to any of the assumptions of the sequent.

GCLA retains the basic backtracking left-to-right depth-first search strategy of Prolog. However, as each step of a GCLA program execution permits more choices than a Prolog SLD-resolution step, the risk of combinatorical explosion is very great for any non-trivial use of GCLA. To address this problem, GCLA II programs are divided into two parts: the declarative part, as described above, and a control part that determines the particular search strategy to be used when executing the program.

The control part defines a number of strategies. By examining the current subgoal, a strategy decides which inference rules (or chains of inference rules) are applicable to it, and what strategies should control the continued execution of the resulting subgoals. Strategies have similarities with tactics in LCF-style systems. While strategies cannot change the basic backtracking depth-first search behaviour, they do decide which inference rules should be applied and in what order.

As the control language also consists of generalised Horn clauses, it is possible to give a natural operational semantics of GCLA in the language itself.

Use of GCLA for knowledge-based systems, and programming in general

GCLA was developed with the double purpose of investigating the computational properties of partial inductive definitions and to provide a language suitable for implementation of inference mechanisms for knowledge based systems.

The proof system underlying GCLA is very powerful, and permits the expression of different programming techniques. Apart from the obvious use of GCLA for relational (i.e. Prolog) programming, GCLA can be used for functional programming, object oriented programming and quasi-parallell computations. As all of these are expressed in the same language, they can easily be combined.

By virtue of the hypothetical constructions and the possibility to have assumptions in sequents, GCLA can do hypothetical reasoning in a natural way. The precise form of the inference rules of the proof system are actually determined by the contents of the GCLA program. This means that the both the search strategy and - to an extent - the operation of each execution step, can be defined by the GCLA program. This latter property makes it easy to do basic reasoning in GCLA. By coding a knowledge base into a set of generalised Horn clauses, the GCLA execution mechanism is turned into an inference engine for that knowledge base. Of course, to provide a real reasoning system a substantial amount of additional GCLA programming must be done to manage the reasoning, but the basic steps can be performed directly in the language.

GCLA has been used for the implementation of an small experimental planning system for building construction sites. In cooperation with DFKI, conceptual modelling and terminological reasoning has been attempted using GCLA. Additionally, several toy programs have been written to illustrate how planning, simulation, reasoning etc. techniques can be done using GCLA.

Implementations

GCLA II is implemented in SICStus Prolog using an interpreter. The programming system provides a basic programming environment including a Byrd-style port debugger and facilities for use together with the GNU EMACS editor.

A previous version of the language with much simpler control (GCLA I) was also implemented with a compiler and an abstract machine based on the WAM. A compiler for GCLA II is planned.

The GCLA II implementation and documentation are available from SICS.

Bibliography

Lars Hallnäs, *Partial Inductive Definitions*, In: A. Avron et. al. (eds.), *Workshop on General Logic*, Report ECS-LFCS-88-52. Dept. of Computer Science, Univ. of Edinburgh, 1987. Also published as Research Report SICS R86005C by the Swedish Institute of Computer Science, 1988. A revised version to appear in Theoretical Computer Science 1990.

Lars Hallnäs, Peter Schroeder-Heister: *A Proof-Theoretic Approach to Logic Programming. 1. Clauses as rules*, Journal of Logic and Computation Vol 1, no. 2, 1990.

Martin Aronsson, *GCLA User's Manual*, Internal SICS note, 1991.

Martin Aronsson, Lars-Henrik Eriksson, Anette Gäredal, Lars Hallnäs, Peter Olin, *The programming Language GCLA: A definitional approach to Logic Programming*, New Generation Computing Vol 7, no. 4, 1990.

Martin Aronsson, Lars-Henrik Eriksson, Per Kreuger, Lars Hallnäs, *A Survey of GCLA: A Definitional Approach to Logic Programming*, In: Peter Schroeder-Heister (ed.), *Extensions of Logic Programming*, Springer Lecture Notes in Computer Science 475, 1991.

A brief description of the PROTOS-L system

Christoph Beierle, Gregor Meyer, Heiner Semle
IBM Germany, Scientific Center
Institute for Knowledge Based Systems
P.O. Box 80 08 80
D-7000 Stuttgart 80, Germany
e-mail: BEIERLE at DSØLILOG.BITNET

The PROTOS-L system is an outcome of a research effort within the EUREKA Project PROTOS (Logic Programming Tools for Building Expert Systems, EU 56) aimed at overcoming some of the shortcomings of Prolog. It consists of a logic programming language including various advanced features together with a state-of-the-art implementation approach based on an abstract machine.

The PROTOS-L language

PROTOS-L ([2], [3]) is a logic programming language based on typed Horn clause logic. The type concept which has been derived from TEL ([9]) allows for subtypes as well as for parametric polymorphism. The types lead to better structured programs since they allow to make the data structure of a program explicit. They are exploited at compile time for static consistency checks, so that many programming errors can be detected early in the program development. The type information is also present at runtime through typed unification: Free variables can be constrained to subtypes without binding them to a particular value, thus offering a tool for saving time by reducing the amount of backtracking. Moreover, terms can be tested for subtype membership and types can be compared to each other w.r.t. the type hierarchy.

In addition PROTOS-L offers a module concept with a threefold purpose: First, it provides a means for the structured development of large programs by supporting separate compilation of module interfaces and bodies. Furthermore, it provides a powerful means for the definition of abstract data types: At the level of interfaces the realization of types and operations on this type can be hidden.

In this way, modules also provide both a structured and transparent database access. Through a special kind of module bodies called database bodies an external relational database can be accessed, where this access is transparent at the level of the interface. Moreover, the inference rules in database bodies are interpreted by a deductive database component, combining advantages of relational databases, like efficient set-oriented evaluation, with advantages of the logic programming paradigm, like high-level programming and recursion.

Another highlight of PROTOS-L is the integration of an object-oriented interface to OSF/Motif. Based on this object oriented interface, high-level end-user interfaces can be developed within PROTOS-L. All described features together with an advanced set of built-ins like file handling, array manipulation, string operations, etc. are embedded into PROTOS-L in a completely type safe way.

The PROTOS-L system

The implementation of PROTOS-L is based on the PROTOS inference engine (PIE) which consists of the PROTOS abstract machine PAM – an extension of the WAM ([10]), the database interpreter DBI and the PROTOS window manager PWM (c.f. Figures 1 and 2). The PAM ([8], [4]):

- realizes the necessary polymorphic order-sorted unification required by the type system,

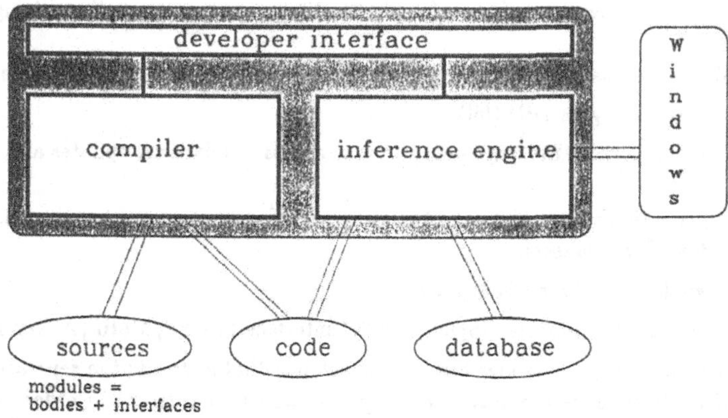

Figure 1: The PROTOS-L System

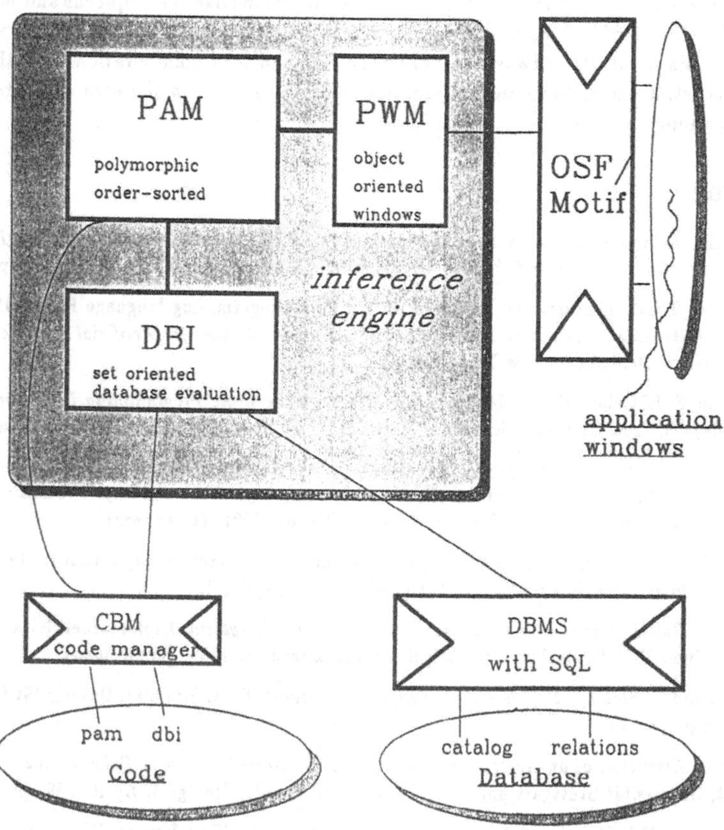

Figure 2: The PROTOS inference engine PIE

- provides a set of type safe built-ins for file handling, array manipulation, string operations, etc., and
- offers a debug modus providing detailed information on its current machine state, etc.

The database inference engine DBI ([6])

- controls the relational DBMS according to read access to relations, updates and transactions, and
- evaluates deduction rules which may be recursive; it is complete and terminating for Datalog (function free Horn clauses).

The PROTOS window manager PWM ([5])

- provides a simple but flexible, object-oriented interface to OSF/Motif (AIX-Windows).

In addition to the PIE, a compiler has been developed that supports the seperate compilation and loading of modules, does the static type checking and type inferene in order to detect type inconsistencies early in the program development, and produces machine code for the PIE.

The PIE has been developed in C under AIX and runs on an IBM PS/2, on IBM RT/PC 6150 coupled with SQL/RT, and on IBM RS/6000 coupled with ORACLE and OSF/Motif. The compiler for PROTOS-L is implemented in TEL ([9], [7]) which runs on Quintus Prolog.

In order to test and demonstrate the features of the PROTOS-L system several applications have been developed ([1]). Besides well-known search problems like the N-queens and map colouring problem, there exist some larger applications like a railway route planning system which uses a database containing all IC railway connections in Germany. In collaboration with the PROTOS partner Hoechst, a knowledge based production planning system in the area of fibers production has been developed.

References

[1] C. Beierle. An overview on planning applications in PROTOS-L. In *Proceedings 13th IMACS World Congress on Computation and Applied Mathematics*, Dublin, Ireland, July 1991. (to appear).

[2] C. Beierle. Types, modules and databases in the logic programming language PROTOS-L. In K. H. Bläsius, U. Hedtstück, and C.-R. Rollinger, editors, *Sorts and Types for Artificial Intelligence*, Springer-Verlag, Berlin, Heidelberg, New York, 1990.

[3] C. Beierle, S. Böttcher, and G. Meyer. *Draft Report of the Logic Programming Language PROTOS-L.* IWBS Report, IBM Germany, Scientific Center, Inst. for Knowledge Based Systems, Stuttgart, 1991.

[4] C. Beierle, G. Meyer, and H. Semle. Extending the Warren Abstract Machine to polymorphic order-sorted resolution. In V. Saraswat and K. Uedo, editors, *Logic Programming: Proceedings of the 1991 International Symposium*, MIT Press, San Diego, October 1991. (to appear).

[5] H. Jasper. A logic-based programming environment for interactive applications. In *Proc. Human Computer Interaction International*, Stuttgart, 1991. (to appear).

[6] G. Meyer. *Rule Evaluation on Databases in the PROTOS-L System.* Diplomarbeit Nr. 630, Universität Stuttgart und IBM Deutschland GmbH, Stuttgart, December 1989. (in German).

[7] W. Nutt and G. Smolka. *Implementing TEL.* SEKI-Report, FB Informatik, Universität Kaiserslautern, 1991. (in preparation).

[8] H. Semle. *Extension of an Abstract Machine for Order-Sorted Prolog to Polymorphism.* Diplomarbeit Nr. 583, Universität Stuttgart und IBM Deutschland GmbH, Stuttgart, April 1989. (in German).

[9] G. Smolka. *TEL (Version 0.9), Report and User Manual.* SEKI-Report SR 87-17, FB Informatik, Universität Kaiserslautern, 1988.

[10] D. Warren. *An Abstract PROLOG Instruction Set.* Technical Report 309, SRI, 1983.

PCPL - PROLOG Constraint Processing Library

Version 2.0

Stefan Fricke, Manfred Hein
Technische Universität Berlin, Fachbereich Informatik
Franklinstr. 28/29, Sekr. FR 6-7, W-1000 Berlin 10, Germany
e-mail: fricke@opal.cs.tu-berlin.de

Overview

PCPL (**PROLOG Constraint Processing Library**) [Fricke, Hein 90], [Fricke 91], [Fricke, Hein, Papaioannou 91] is a library which enables to process efficiently extensional constraints in standard PROLOG. In the field of finite domains, CHIP [VanHentenryck 89] is an impressive demonstration on the power of stating and solving CSPs. We have developed PCPL in order to copy these efficiency and effectiveness in constraint handling for standard PROLOG.

The library is implemented in standard PROLOG and can therefore be integrated in any PROLOG environment. A domain concept [VanHentenryck 86] allows the definition of domain variables with any set of symbolic values. Searching is realized by the looking ahead strategy. Sets of values are propagated throughout the network until the constraint net becomes local consistent. PCPL is an incremental system, therefore constraints can be inserted in the net at any time.

In an application we have proved the feasibility of PCPL for configuration problems. Further examples lead to the experience that PCPL is, in spite of the implementation in standard PROLOG, approximately as efficient as CHIP.

PCPL is available for QUINTUS-PROLOG. Furthermore there is a special version for the KCM (KCM-SEPIA). A version for SEPIA-PROLOG will be realized soon.

Description of PCPL

The library has two components, a compiler for compiling the extensional relations and a constraint executer for stating and solving the constraint net. The compiler's output makes possible a fairly rapid access to sets of tuples at the propagation time. Since the compiler can process any PROLOG goal as input, it is also possible (to a limited extend) to work with intensional relations. For that, an adequate representation is required to use the goal as a generic predicate. After compilation, the compiled relation can be used immediately in a constraint network or can be written into a file for later use.

The interface of the constraint executer consists of predicates for stating the network (adding constraints to it) and for generating solutions. A constraint is generated by binding each row of the corresponding relation to a domain variable. Constraints are connected via shared variables. All operations on a constraint net are performed by simple PROLOG predicates and are backtrackable. This makes it feasible to generate and process different instances of one constraint net. A special equality predicate performs the intensional equality constraint. For instance it can be used for connecting several nets together. Furthermore it is possible to save a constraint net on a file. This enables the user to state and solve the constraint network seperately. Together with the backtrack facility it is possible to distribute the generation of solutions for various constraint solving processes.

Demons can be attached to constraint variables. After restricting the domain of a constraint variable to a single value, all demons connected to that variable are executed. With this facility, processing predicates according to the forward checking strategy (e.g. unequality) is uncomplicated.

The first fail principle is integrated into PCPL as a method for choosing the most constraint variable. The process of generating solutions for the local consistent constraint net is done by successively binding domain variables to single values. For variables with large domains it is useful first to split the search space into several parts using the domain splitting facility and then to proceed the solving process in each disjunct part seperately.

Constraint relaxation can be handled easily by stating relations with an additional colum that holds information about the degree of satisfaction Relaxation of a constraint is then done by restricting the domain of the extra colum.

Implementation

Our main effort was to gain efficiency. The propagation algorithm uses set operations in order to detect the tuples of a constraint relation that became inconsistent in consequence of a domain reduction. So we decided to represent sets of tuples as bit vectors in order to reduce the cost for the set operations to a linear quantity. The compiler converts a relation into a table that allows quick access to all tuples with one value on a specified position.

Constraints are managed as objects manupulating domains and relation entries; propagation is done by message passing. Both domains and constraint relations are realized as dynamic facts. In order to achieve correct backtracking behaviour, these facts are organized in a stack-like manner.

Future research

For the next version, PCPL will be enlarged by a concept for intervals. A new component containing a mechanism for interval propagation will be implemented. It will also embody a simplex-like algorithm in order to deal with systems of linear equations.

References

[VanHentenryck 89] P. Van Hentenryck: Constraint Satisfaction in Logic Programming. The MIT Press 1989.

[VanHentenryck 86] P. Van Hentenryck, M. Dincbas: Domains in Logic Programming. In: AAAI-86 Proceedings, 1986, Seite 759 - 765.

[Fricke, Hein 90] S. Fricke, M. Hein: PCPL-Manual. TU Berlin, 1990

[Fricke 91] S. Fricke: Konzeption eines Constraintsystems auf der Basis von Standard-PROLOG für Konfigurierungsprobleme. Studienarbeit, TU Berlin, 1991.

[Fricke, Hein, Papaioannou 91] S.Fricke, M.Hein, S.Papaioannou: PCPL - eine PROLOG-Bibliothek zur effizienten Verarbeitung von extensionalen Constraints. TU Berlin, 1991.

A mini-description of the ITL system

Nicola Guarino
National Research Council
Institute for Systems Dynamics and Bioengineering (LADSEB-CNR),
Corso Stati Uniti 4, I-35020 Padova, Italy
guarino@ladseb.pd.cnr.it

1 Introduction

In this paper we briefly describe the current implementation of ITL, and present the ways of interaction with the system. A general presentation of the system appears in [1], together with a preliminar formal account of the language.

The system is implemented in LPA MacProlog™ and runs on an Apple Macintosh™ with at least 4 MB of RAM memory. In the current version, the user has access to the whole Prolog environment, and interacts with the system via the standard menus of MacProlog. An extra menu called ITL is provided for ITL-specific operations.

An ITL knowledge base resides on two separate windows, called TKB (Terminological Knowledge Base) and RKB (Relational Knowledge Base). These windows have an associated syntax which is of course different from LPA Prolog: however, they behave exactly like a program window, except that a specialized processor is invoked when they are compiled. In this way, ITL can be easily linked with any Prolog application. ITL windows are created and accessed via the ITL menu.

ITL queries are handled as standard Prolog queries, and are formulated by putting an ITL proposition as the argument of the meta-predicate *k*. TKB and RKB queries are homogeneous to the user.

2 TKB management

The main design choice for the software devoted to TKB management is the optimization of the transitive closure of the explicit subsumption relationship. For this purpose a novel data structure has been designed, which represents a node of the taxonomy as a Prolog term, whose structure reflects the structure of the taxonomy above it. In this way lattice operations on the taxonomy reduce to ordinary Prolog unifications. In the case of trees the principle is very simple, and it has been exploited for instance in [3]: a given node of the tree is represented as an incomplete data structure, consisting of a list whose first elements are the nodes found in the path from the root, and whose tail is a variable. In this way the representation of a node unifies only with the representation of all the nodes of the same branch.

In the case of tangled taxonomies the situation is much more difficult, since every "anomalous node" (i.e., in our terminology, a node with more than one parent) generates a whole "cluster" of nodes which have to unify one each other. An example of the data structure we have designed is given in the figure 1 below. A detailed discussion of the algorithms used for lattice operations is reported elsewhere [2].

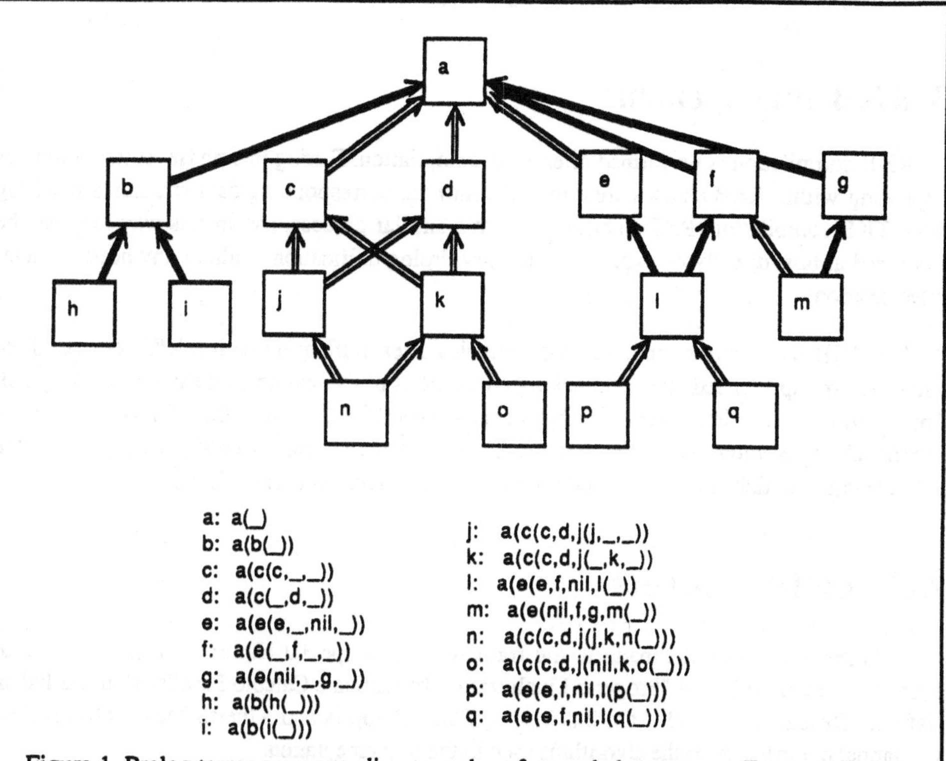

Figure 1. Prolog terms corresponding to nodes of a tangled taxonomy. Functors denote independent subgraphs. Two terms unify iff the corresponding nodes have a glb. For instance, the terms corresponding to nodes *c* and *d* (which both belong to the subgraph denoted with *c*) unify by giving the structure *a(c(c,d,_)),* which corresponds to the anonymous node *c and d.*

The compilation process generates first the data structure for the taxonomy resulting from unit clauses only; after that the implicit IsA links resulting from non-unit clauses are computed, and the whole data structure is updated. This second process corresponds to the classification of those concepts for which sufficient conditions have been defined.

Depending on the free variables appearing in the query, the basic operations related to the TKB are *test, get* and *lookup*. They respectivelly correspond to ITL queries of the form *k(α is a β), k(X is a α)*, and *k(α is a X)*. Notice that, if a free variable appears in a query, its answer substitution is generated by considering only the *explicit* terms appearing in the TKB, and not all the possible terms which satisfy the query. Moreover, trivial answers descending from the reflexivity of the subsumption relationship are not computed. The substitution algorithm is therefore deliberatelly incomplete: for instance, for the query *k(any student is a X), X=student* does not appear among the answers, although *k(any student is a student)* is true.

3 RKB management

RKB compilation is performed after TKB compilation. During this phase, sorted variables appearing within RKB clauses are converted into the corresponding data structures resulting from TKB compilation. RKB queries undergo a similar process, and in this way they can be answered almost directly by exploiting ordinary Prolog unification, without any need of meta-interpretation.

If a RKB query still contains sorted variables after unification with a RKB clause, these variables are "specialized" on backtracking on the basis of the taxonomy described by the TKB. For instance, if the query is *k(likes(person:X,Y))* and the RKB clause is *likes(student:_,goodgrade:_)*, the first answer is *X=student:_* and *Y=goodgrade:_*, and all the possible combinations of students and good grades are given on backtracking.

Acknowledgements

This research has been made in the framework of a special National project on Hybrid Systems, supported by the "Progetto Finalizzato Informatica e Calcolo Parallelo" of the Italian National Research Council. I am indebted to Carlo Chiopris and Alberto Moscatelli for their substantial contribution to the algorithms used in the implementation.

Bibliography

[1] Guarino, N. 1991. A Concise Presentation of ITL. In this volume.

[2] Guarino, N. 1991. Efficient handling of transitive relations in Prolog. In preparation.

[3] Schmitt, P.H., Wernecke, W. 1990. Tableau Calculus for Order Sorted Logic. In K. H. Bläsius, U. Hedtstück, C.-R. Rollinger (eds.), *Sorts and Types in Artificial Intelligence*, Lecture Notes in Artificial Intelligence, vol. 418, Springer Verlag.

TAXON: A Concept Language with Concrete Domains*

Philipp Hanschke[†], *Andreas Abecker*, *Dennis Drollinger*
German Research Center for AI (DFKI)
Kaiserslautern, Germany

1 Introduction

Concept languages based on KL-ONE [Brachman and Schmolze, 1985] are used to represent the taxonomical and conceptual knowledge of a particular problem domain on an abstract logical level. To describe this kind of knowledge, one starts with atomic concepts and roles, and defines new concepts using the operations provided by the language. Concepts can be considered as unary predicates which are interpreted as sets of individuals, and roles as binary predicates which are interpreted as binary relations between individuals. Examples for atomic concepts may be Human and Male, and for roles child. If the logical connective of conjunction "⊓" is present as a language construct, one may describe the concept Man as "humans who are male", and represent it by the expression Human ⊓ Male. Many languages provide quantification over role fillers which allows for example to describe the concept Father by the expression Man ⊓ ∃child.Human.

KL-ONE was first developed for the purpose of natural language processing [Brachman *et al.*, 1979], and some of the existing systems are still mostly used in this context (see e.g., SB-ONE [Kobsa, 1989]). However, its success in this area has also led to applications in other fields (see e.g., MESON [Edelmann and Owsnicki, 1986] which is used for computer configuration tasks, CLASSIC [Borgida *et al.*, 1989] which is e.g. used in the area of CAD/CAM, or K-REP [Mays *et al.*, 1988] which is used in a financial marketing domain).

2 Concrete Domains

A problem with pure KL-ONE languages is that all of the terminological knowledge has to be defined on the abstract logical level. In many applications one would like to be able to refer to predicates over "concrete domains" when defining concepts.

For instance, in a technical application the adequate representation of geometrical concepts requires to relate points in a coordinate system. For that purpose one would e.g. like to have access to real arithmetic. For example a truncated cone on a fixed axis (Truncone, Figure 1) can be characterized by a 4 tuple of real numbers, namely two radii ra, rb and

*Supported by BMFT Research Project ARC-TEC (grant ITW 8902 C4)

†Please, send correspondence to this author; hanschke@dfki.uni-kl.de

two centers ca, cb. These numbers should also satisfy certain side conditions ensuring that they really define a truncated cone and not just a line, a circle, or a point. TAXON uses functional roles (often called features) as an interface to the concrete domain such that these requirements can be formulated using an appropriate predicate. Thus the concept Truncone could be defined as well_truncone(ra, rb, ca, cd), where well_truncone is a 4-place predicate over real numbers and ra, ra, ca, cb are features. This concept can now be spezialized to e.g. a Cylinder (resp. Ring) by Truncone $\sqcap$(ra = rb) (resp. Truncone $\sqcap$(ca = cb)).

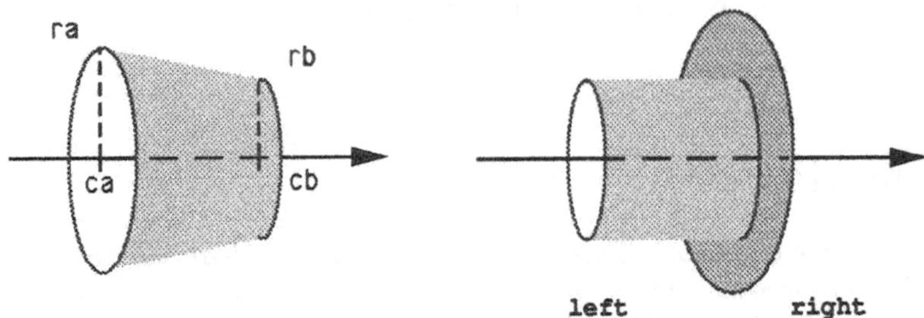

Figure 1: A Truncated Cone Figure 2: Two Connected Truncated Cones

Describing larger, composite geometric entities requires to formulate conditions over chainings of functional roles.

For example, a biconic defined by

$$\exists\text{left.Truncone} \sqcap \exists\text{right.Truncone} \sqcap (\text{left rb} = \text{right ra}) \sqcap (\text{left cb} = \text{right ca})$$

is an ordered pair of two connected Truncones (Figure 2). This concept is formulated using two new features left and right (for the components of the ordered pair) and the equality predicate over real numbers applied to pairs of feature chainings (to express that the truncated cones are connected).

Similar motivations have already led to extensions of KL-ONE in the above mentioned systems MESON, CLASSIC, and K-REP.

In [Baader and Hanschke, 1991] a scheme, based on the ideas mentioned, to extend concept languages by concrete domains is presented. As an instance of this extension scheme, TAXON satisfies the following requirements:

- It has a formal declarative semantics which is very close to the usual semantics employed for concept languages. Actually, if there is no reference to a concrete domain it behaves as the original language.
- The reasoning algorithm of TAXON is generic. One part deals with the abstract conventional portion of the concept language and generates queries to another part that depends on the concrete domain plugged into the system. This second part can be implemented using well-known algorithms of the concrete domain.
- It provides sound and complete reasoning algorithms for the usual inferences that come along with terminological reasoning systems, if the inference algorithm of the concrete domain satisfies reasonable requirements (see [Baader and Hanschke, 1991] for details).

3 Conclusion

TAXON is a prototypical, experimental implementation of the above extension scheme in Common Lisp. It provides a bare ASCII user interface [Abecker and Hanschke, 1991] based on Lisp macros and functions, and is tailored for combination with other reasoning formalisms. The efficiency of the relatively new sound and complete reasoning algorithms for this kind of concept languages has to be improved. For instance, the reuse of already computed subsumption relations in a subsumption test is expected to cause a dramatic speed up. For real world applications, concept languages with their specialized, efficient reasoning algorithms for terminological reasoning have to be combined elegantly with other formalisms covering other classes of knowledge. Rule-based formalisms seem to be well-suited candidates for this kind of combination [Boley *et al.*, 1991; Hanschke, 1991].

References

[Abecker and Hanschke, 1991] A. Abecker and P. Hanschke. TAXON: Instructions for use. Draft, 1991.

[Baader and Hanschke, 1991] F. Baader and P. Hanschke. A scheme for integrating concrete domains into concept languages. In *Proceedings of the* 12th *International Joint Conference on Artificial Intelligence*, 1991. A long version is available as DFKI Research Report RR-91-10.

[Boley *et al.*, 1991] H. Boley, P. Hanschke, K. Hinkelmann, and M. Meyer. Towards a knowledge compilation laboratory. 3rd International Workshop on Data, Expert Knowledge and Decision: Using Knowledge to Transform Data into Information for Decision Support, 1991.

[Borgida *et al.*, 1989] A. Borgida, R. J. Brachman, D. L. McGuinness, and L. A. Resnick. CLASSIC: A structural data model for objects. In *International Conference on Management of Data.* ACM SIGMOD, 1989.

[Brachman and Schmolze, 1985] R. J. Brachman and J. G. Schmolze. An overview of the KL-ONE knowledge representation system. *Cognitive Science*, 9(2):171–216, 1985.

[Brachman *et al.*, 1979] R. J. Brachman, R. J. Bobrow, P. R. Cohen, J. W. Klovstad, B. L. Webber, and W. A. Woods. Research in natural language understanding, annual report. Tech. Rep. No. 4274, Cambrige, MA, 1979. Bolt Beranek and Newman.

[Edelmann and Owsnicki, 1986] J. Edelmann and B. Owsnicki. Data models in knowledge representation systems: a case study. In GWAI-86 *und 2. Östereichische Artificial-Intelligence-Tagung*, volume 124 of *Informatik-Fachberichte*, pages 69–74. Springer, 1986.

[Hanschke, 1991] P. Hanschke. TAXLOG — a logic programming language with deeply-modeled type hierarchies. ARC-TEC DiscussionPaper 91-8, DFKI GmbH, March 1991.

[Kobsa, 1989] A. Kobsa. The SB-ONE knowledge representation workbench. In *Preprints of the Workshop on Formal Aspects of Semantic Networks*, 1989. Two Harbors, Cal.

[Mays *et al.*, 1988] E. Mays, C. Apté, J. Griesmer, and J. Kastner. Experience with K-Rep: an object centered knowledge representation language. In *Proceedings of* IEEE CAIA-88, pages 62–67, 1988.

The ALF System: An Efficient Implementation of a Functional Logic Language

*Michael Hanus**
Technische Fakultät, Universität Bielefeld
W-4800 Bielefeld 1, Germany
e-mail: hanus@techfak.uni-bielefeld.de

ALF (**A***lgebraic* **L***ogic* **F***unctional programming language*) is a language which combines functional and logic programming techniques. The foundation of ALF is Horn clause logic with equality which consists of predicates and Horn clauses for logic programming, and functions and equations for functional programming. Since ALF is a genuine integration of both programming paradigms, any functional expression can be used in a goal literal and arbitrary predicates can occur in conditions of equations. Figure 1 shows an ALF program to sort a list of natural numbers where naturals are represented by the constructors `0` and `s` and lists are defined as in Prolog. This program defines the functions `isort` to sort a list of naturals, `insert` to insert an element in an ordered list, and the predicates `=<` and `>` to compare natural numbers.

The operational semantics of ALF is based on the resolution rule to solve literals and narrowing to evaluate functional expressions. In order to reduce the number of possible narrowing steps, a leftmost-innermost basic narrowing strategy [6] is used which can be efficiently implemented [1]. Furthermore, terms are simplified by rewriting before a narrowing step is applied and also equations are rejected if the two sides have different constructors at the top. Rewriting and rejection can result in a large reduction of the search tree. Therefore this operational semantics is more efficient than Prolog's resolution strategy.

The ALF system is *an efficient implementation of the combination of resolution, narrowing, rewriting and rejection.* Similarly to Prolog, ALF uses a backtracking strategy corresponding to a depth-first search in the derivation tree. ALF programs are compiled into instructions of an abstract machine. The abstract machine is based on the Warren Abstract Machine (WAM [7]) with several extensions to implement narrowing and rewriting [3]. In the current implementation programs of this abstract machine are executed by an emulator written in C.

ALF has also a type and module concept which allows the definition of generic modules [4]. A preprocessor checks the type consistence of the program and combines all needed modules into one flat-ALF program which is compiled into a compact bytecode representing an abstract machine program. The current implementation has the following properties:

- The machine code for pure logic programs without defined functions is identical to

*on leave from Fachbereich Informatik, Universität Dortmund, W-4600 Dortmund 50

```
module isort.

    datatype nat  = { 0 ; s(nat) }.
    datatype list = { '.'(nat,list) ; [] }.

    func isort :  list -> list;
         insert:  nat, list -> list.

    pred =< :  nat, nat infix;
         >  :  nat, nat infix.
rules.
    isort([])     = [].
    isort([E|L]) = insert(E,isort(L)).

    insert(E,[])      = [E].
    insert(E,[F|L]) = [E,F|L]            :- E =< F.
    insert(E,[F|L]) = [F|insert(E,L)] :- E > F.

    0 =< N.
    s(M) =< s(N) :- M =< N.

    s(M) > 0.
    s(M) > s(N) :- M > N.

end isort.

?- isort([3,1,5,4,1,3,2]) = L.
```

Figure 1: ALF program for insertion sort

the code of the original WAM, i.e., for logic programs there is no overhead because of the functional part of the language.

- Functional programs where only ground terms have to be evaluated are executed by deterministic rewriting without any dynamic search for subterms positions where the next rewriting step can be applied. The compiler computes these positions and generates particular machine instructions. Therefore such programs are also efficiently executed.

- In mixed functional and logic programs argument terms are simplified by rewriting before narrowing is applied and therefore function calls with ground arguments are automatically evaluated by rewriting and not by narrowing. This is more efficient because rewriting is a deterministic process. Hence in most practical cases the combined rewriting/narrowing implementation is more efficient than an implementation of narrowing by flattening terms and applying SLD-resolution.

In order to get an impression of the current implementation, the following table contains a comparison of the ALF system with other functional languages.

Naive reverse for a list of 30 elements		
System:	*Machine:*	*Time:*
ALF	Sun4	19 msec
Standard-ML (Edinburgh)	Sun3	54 msec
CAML V 2-6.1	Sun4	28 msec
OBJ3	Sun3	5070 msec

It was mentioned above that rewriting and rejection can reduce the search space. A typical class of programs for this optimization are the so-called "generate-and-test" programs. For instance, permutation sort is a program where a list is sorted by constructing a permutation of the list and checking whether the permuted list is a sorted one. The relational version of this program, which is a pure Prolog program, must enumerate all permutations of a list to sort that list. The equivalent functional version of this program stops the generation of a permutation if two consecutive elements in the permutation have the wrong ordering (due to the rewriting mechanism of ALF). Hence we obtain the following execution times in seconds to sort the list `[`n`,...,2,1]` for different values of n:

Length of the list:	5	6	7	8	9	10
Relational version	0.10	0.65	4.63	37.92	348.70	3569.50
Functional version	0.10	0.27	0.61	1.43	3.28	7.43

More details on this subject can be found in [2].

The current version of the ALF system, which is a first prototype implementation [5], is available on Sun-3 and Sun-4 machines under SunOS 4.0. The preprocessor which checks the types and modules is written in ALF, the compiler is written in Prolog (a Quintus-Prolog and a SB-Prolog version are available) and the emulator of the abstract machine is written in C.

References

[1] M. Hanus. Compiling Logic Programs with Equality. In *Proc. of the 2nd Int. Workshop on Programming Language Implementation and Logic Programming*, pp. 387–401. Springer LNCS 456, 1990.

[2] M. Hanus. A Declarative Approach to Improve Control in Logic Programming. Univ. Dortmund, 1991.

[3] M. Hanus. Efficient Implementation of Narrowing and Rewriting. In *Proc. Int. Workshop on Processing Declarative Knowledge* 1991. This volume.

[4] M. Hanus and A. Schwab. ALF User's Manual. FB Informatik, Univ. Dortmund, 1991.

[5] M. Hanus and A. Schwab. The Implementation of the Functional-Logic Language ALF. FB Informatik, Univ. Dortmund, 1991.

[6] S. Hölldobler. From Paramodulation to Narrowing. In *Proc. 5th Conference on Logic Programming & 5th Symposium on Logic Programming (Seattle)*, pp. 327–342, 1988.

[7] D.H.D. Warren. An Abstract Prolog Instruction Set. Technical Note 309, SRI International, Stanford, 1983.

Transforming Horn Clauses for Forward Reasoning

Knut Hinkelmann, Martin Harm, Thomas Labisch

Deutsches Forschungszentrum für Künstliche Intelligenz (DFKI) GmbH, Postfach 2080, 6750 Kaiserslautern
email: {hinkelma,harm,labisch}@dfki.uni-kl.de

Forward Reasoning Horn Clauses

In principle there are two reasoning directions for Horn clauses. *Top-down* reasoning starts with a query, applying the clauses in backward direction until a fact is reached for every subgoal. The result of backward reasoning is a substitution for the variables of the query. Top-down reasoning can be implemented rather efficiently in the Warren Abstract Machine (WAM, [War83]). *Bottom-up* strategies start with the facts and apply the rules in forward direction.

Although Horn logic itself does not prescribe any inference strategy, a kind of top-down reasoning is mostly used in logic programming, e.g. in Prolog. Most approaches which integrate forward chaining into Prolog use disjoint sets of rules for the two reasoning directions ([Mor81], [Cha87], [Fin89]). We will present an approach to explicitly perform forward reasoning over the same set of Horn clauses that is employed for the usual backward chaining. The original Horn clauses are translated into special clauses for the predicate name *forward*. The translation is obtained by partial evaluation of a meta interpreter for forward reasoning.

Givien an initial fact F, the core of forward reasoning is to apply a clause, which has a premise unifiable with F. A goal `?- forward(F,Concl)` succeeds, if `Concl` can be derived from `F` in one step:

```
forward(Fact,Head) :- clause(Head,Body),
                      unifiable_premise(Fact,Body,Rem_premises),
                      prove_list(Rem_premises),
                      retain(Head).
```

A clause is applied in forward direction if one of its premises is unifiable with the initial fact (`unifiable_premise/3`). The remaining premises are verified by Prolog's SLD-resolution (`prove_list/1`). The conclusion is asserted and can trigger further forward clauses: a call to the *retain* predicate accepts only a *new* conclusion, not subsumed by any previously derived fact.

To increase efficiency of the meta interpreter we partially evaluate (unfold) the clause wrt a logic program. The result of this partial evaluation is a set of forward clauses which, when interpreted in a top-down reasoning system, simulate forward application of the original Horn clauses. For every clause $q(...) \text{ :- } p_1(...),...,p_n(...)$.of the original logic program we get a sequence of forward clauses following this pattern:

$forward(p_1(...),q(...)) \text{ :- } p_2(...),...,p_n(...),\ retain(q(...)).$

$forward(p_2(...),q(...)) \text{ :- } p_1(...),p_3(...),...,p_n(...),\ retain(q(...)).$

...

$forward(p_n(...),q(...)) \text{ :- } p_1(...),p_2(...),...,p_{n-1}(...),\ retain(q(...))$

These forward clauses can also be got by a translation procedure, which is applied to every rule of the original program; facts are not considered. Since we simulate forward reasoning by SLD-resolution (plus assert or retain) significant information has to appear in the head of the forward clause: the first argument of *forward* is the rule's trigger. The second argument of *forward* is the conclusion of the original clause.. Because forward evaluation of a Horn clause can be triggered by a fact unifying any premise of the clause, for every premise $p_1(...),...,p_n(...)$ of the original clause a *forward* clause is generated. This is an important diference to Yamamoto and Tanaka's translation for production rules [Yam86], where only goal-directed forward reasoning is supported.

Various control strategies are available: depth-first enumeration (df-enum/2) of results, breadth-first enumeration (bf-enum/2), and computing the results all at once (bf-all/2).

Example

Horn clause program P:

```
parent(peter, john).
parent(john, joe).
parent(peter, mary).
anc(X,Y) :- parent(X,Y).
anc(X,Y) :- parent(X,Z), anc(Z,Y).
```

Forward clauses P':

```
forward(parent(X,Y),anc(X,Y)).
forward(parent(X,Z),anc(X,Y)) :- anc(Z,Y).
forward(anc(Z,Y),anc(X,Y)) :- parent(X,Z).
```

Goal:

```
?- bf_enum(parent(peter,X),Conclusion).
   X = john, Conclusion = anc(peter,john);
   X = mary, Conslusion = anc(peter,mary);
   X = john, Conclusion = anc(peter,joe);
no
```

Implementation

After source-to-source transformation of a Horn clause program P into a *forward* clause Prolog program P', the clauses of P and P' are compiled into WAM code. Several improvements for *forward* clauses are possible. While values on the local and global stacks may be destroyed on backtracking, derived facts must survive for the whole forward inference chain. Therefore the WAM is extended by a special stack area for derived facts, called *retain stack* or RETAIN. The predicate *retain/1* in a forward clause is compiled into a sequence of WAM operations pushing its argument -- the derived fact -- as a structure onto the retain stack.

```
retain/1:  not_r_subsumed X1       % Test for subsumption
           push_fact_retain X1     % Copying to RETAIN
```

To accept a derived fact, we must be ensure that it is not subsumed by any structure already existing on the stack. A new operation, `not_r_subsumed Xi`, is introduced for this test. The fact referenced by `Xi` is matched against *every* entry on the retain stack. It calls the function `subsumes(x,y)` to test subsumption. Backtracking occurs, if `subsumes` of the derived fact with any previously derived fact succeeds. If subsumption fails no backtracking occurs: the new fact is pushed onto the retain stack by the operation `push_fact_retain Xi`.

The presented forward reasoning approach is an extension of the "hornish" part of RELFUN [Bol90], a relational-functional language, and compiled into the RFM system. Translator, compiler, and partial evaluator are implemented in Common Lisp.

Application

Our forward reasoning approach is applied to generate a work plan for a given workpiece on a lathe turning machine. A first step in production planning is the recognition of those production-specific features which give valuable hints on how the workpiece should be produced. For this feature recognition a data-driven strategy is preferable to a goal-directed one. Instead of enumerating all the possible features and testing whether they can be found in a product model, reasoning starts with (a subset of) the facts describing the workpiece to identify the features present. With this approach only the features inherent in the product model are computed.

Conclusions

Forward reasoning of Horn clause programs is part of a hybrid expert system shell COLAB consisting of a taxonomic and an assertional component [Bol91]. The plain control strategy is induced by the SLD-resolution procedure of logic programming. Forward clauses are selected for execution in a strictly sequential manner. Implementation methods for production systems like Rete algorithm [For82] are not appropriate since premises are proved by backward reasoning in our approach. Nevertheless, besides breadth-first and depth-first strategies, more sophisticated control strategies are conceivable, especially in larger applications, where rules reflect an expert's heuristics. One matter of future research is looking for the appropriate level of rule firing control and its integration into the compiler and the run-time system. It will be influenced by our application of production planning.

Bibliography

[Bol90] Boley H. A Relational/Functional Language and its Compilation into the WAM, SEKI Report SR-90-05, University of Kaiserslautern, 1990.

[Bol91] Boley, H., Hanschke, P., Hinkelmann, K., and Meyer, M. COLAB: A Hybrid Knowledge Compilation Laboratory. 3rd International Workshop on Data, Expert Knowledge and Decisions: Using Knowledge to Transform Data into Information for Decision Support, Schloß Reisensburg, Günzburg, Germany, 1991, forthcoming.

[Cha87] Chan, D., Dufresne, P., and Enders, R. Report on PHOCUS. Technical Report TR-LP-21-02, ECRC, Arabellastraße 17 D8 München 81, April, 1987.

[Fin89] Finin, T., Fritzson, R., and Matuszek, D. Adding Forward Chaining and Truth Maintenance to Prolog. In *Artificial Intelligence Applications Conference*, IEEE, Miami, March 1989, pp. 123-130.

[For82] Forgy, C.L. Rete: A Fast Algorithm for the Many Pattern / Many Object Pattern Match Problem. Artificial Intelligence *19*(1982), pp. 17-37.

[Hin91] Hinkelmann, K. Bidirectional Reasoning of Horn Clause Programs: Transformation and Compilation. Technical Memo TM-91-02, DFKI GmbH, January, 1991.

[Mor81] Morris, P. A Forward Chaining Problem Solver. Logic Programming Newsletter 2(Autumn 1981), pp. 6-7.

[War83] Warren, D.H.D. An Abstract Prolog Instruction Set. Technical Note 309, SRI International, Menlo Park, CA, October, 1983.

[Yam86] Yamamoto, A. and Tanaka, H. Translating Production Rules into a Forward Reasoning Prolog Program. New Generation Computing 4(1986), pp. 97-105.

Implementation of the functional-logic language Flang

A. Mantsivoda, V. Petukhin
Box 26
Computing Center
Irkutsk University
Irkutsk 664003
USSR

1 Language description

Flang [3] is a functional-logic language intended for symbolic data processing and algebraic computationsas as well as for training students in methods of artificial intelligence. Flang makes it easy to write programs in functional, logic and mixed styles. The reason is that these two kinds of programming are unified in Flang on some natural basis.

Flang can be considered as an extension of Prolog, but really it came from the functional style of programming. It is impossible to separate logic and functional parts of Flang: there is one idea for two styles.

Flang contains two main types of functions:

(i) non-deterministic functions;

(ii) algebraic functions.

There is the following distinction between them. When the Flang machine fails to reduce a non-deterministic goal it uses the backtracking procedure, but when the goal is algebraic, the system uses a kind of self-quotation (leaves the goal unreduced).

2 Flang Compiler

The main ideas of compilation of Flang are quite similar to compilation techniques for RELFUN [1, 2].

Compilation of Flang is based on ideas of the Warren Abstract Machine (WAM) [4]. Unfortunately, the 'pure' WAM is not convenient for compiling Flang, since it does not support some important features of the language, e.g. functionality. To overcome these obstacles we use some modification of the WAM (so-called Flang Abstract Machine — FAM). We use also a preprocessor to translate source Flang programs into some normalized form.

The compilation of a Flang program consists of the following steps:

Source Flang program
⇓
Preprocessor
Global Analysis + Type Checking
Compiler to FAM Code
Translator to Native Code of Target Computer + Optimizer
⇓
Executable Code

Some of the main steps of the compilation are global analysis, type checking, local analysis and generation of FAM-code.

Global analysis will contain the following steps:

(i) Analysis of input/output arguments; (ii) Analysis of run-time behavior of registers; (iii) Analysis of choice points, backtracking and tail recursion; (iv) Analysis of dereferencing; (v) Type checking for functions, arguments and variables.

3 Results

A compiler from Flang to the native code of the IBM PC has been implemented in C. The performance of executable code is very high. For example, for some benchmarks the performance of Flang programs is close to corresponding programs written in TurboPascal. On some benchmarks the Flang Compiler generates code which is 8-10 times faster than the code of the Arity/Prolog Compiler (N-Queens problem, some sorting algorithms).

References

[1] Harold Boley. A relational/functional Language and its Compilation into the WAM. SEKI Report SR-90-05, Universität Kaiserslautern, 1990.

[2] Hans-Günther Hein. Adding WAM-instructions to support Valued Clauses for the Relational/Functional Language RELFUN. SEKI Working Paper SWP-90-02, Universität Kaiserslautern, Fachbereich Informatik, December 1989.

[3] A. Mantsivoda. Flang: A Functional-Logic Language. In *Proceedings PDK-91*, Kaiserslautern, Germany, 1991.

[4] David. H. D. Warren. An Abstract Prolog Instruction Set. Technical Note 309, SRI International, Menlo Park, CA, October 1983.

SEPIA 3.0 – An Extensible Prolog System

Micha Meier, Joachim Schimpf
European Computer Industry Research Centre (ECRC)
Arabellastraße 17, D-8000 München 81, FRG
{micha,joachim}@ecrc.de

European Computer-Industry Research Centre, one of the leading institutes in the area of logic programming, announces the release of the SEPIA Prolog system version 3.0. SEPIA, which stands for **Standard ECRC Prolog Integrating Advanced Features**, is a sophisticated Prolog system that has been developed at ECRC with the aim of studying efficient Prolog implementation, integration of new features into Prolog and providing a solid basis for Prolog extensions. Below we list a number of main SEPIA features.

- Fast incremental **compiler** (600 lines/sec.), no interpreter, even the debugger works on compiled code and so the code being debugged is fast. On a set of large benchmark programs SEPIA achieves speed which is at least comparable with professional systems that use the same technology, namely emulating WAM instructions.

- Declarative **coroutining** facility. The fixed left-to-right executing rule can be changed in SEPIA by specifying the conditions when a call has to be suspended, and later woken by the instantiation or binding of a variable. SEPIA provides *delay clauses* to control the suspension, which have the advantage that they are completely compiled, their meaning is declarative, and they can be extended by user-defined predicates. For example, a delay clause

  delay p([_|A], B) if var(A), nonground(B).

  says that a call to **p/2** should be delayed if its first argument is a pair with uninstantiated tail and its second argument is a term which is not ground.

  This primitive is superior to **freeze/2** because it can directly express conditions of the type 'delay p(A, B) if both A and B are variables', or even more complex conditions like the one for logical conjunction

  delay and(Op1, Op2, Res) if
  var(Op1), var(Op2), Op1 \== Op2, Res \== 1.

  The implementation of coroutining is very efficient, based on our experiences with other compiler-based coroutining systems. Non-accessible suspended goals are garbage collected. The extended SEPIA debugger is able to trace suspended and woken goals.

- SEPIA provides built-in **event handling**, both synchronous and asynchronous. The event handlers, which are user-definable procedures, are invoked when an event occurs. An event can be an error as well as an exceptional situation which the user may wish to handle in a special way. Through event handling it is possible to change SEPIA behaviour considerably, e.g. to make it compatible with other Prolog dialects.

  SEPIA can also handle interrupts in a true asynchronous way, i.e. when a signal occurs, the current execution is immediately interrupted and the corresponding interrupt handler is invoked. The event handlers can be traced with the SEPIA debugger.

- SEPIA includes **metaterms** as a generic data type representing an attributed variable, implemented using the coroutining and event mechanisms. Unification of metaterms and their occurrence in built-in predicates raises an event and the result is specified using an user-defined handler.

- **Constructive negation** implemented on top of the coroutining facilities. The constructive negation is a true negation (as compared to negation as failure) because it is able to answer negative queries and construct negative answers using constraints on the input variables. Thus e.g. if city(munich) and city(newyork) is true, the query ?- neg city(X). yields the answer X ~= munich, X ~= newyork.

- Sophisticated predicate-based incremental **module** system, which can be used both to structure the user sources and to restrict the access to some modules when e.g. delivering an application program. Although the module system is predicate-based, operators, recorded terms, global variables and input macros are module-dependent.

- SEPIA now includes the first release of the **high level debugging tool** OPIUM, which e.g. allows the user to write programs that debug other programs, while keeping the efficiency of a compiled program. Beginners to OPIUM can use some of the predefined debugging scenarios which include all functionalities found in other Prolog debuggers.

- Fast incremental **garbage collector**.

- Source **variable names** can be kept during the execution and displayed by the debugger and output predicates.

- String data type with garbage-collectable strings.

- Fast floating-point operations.

- Non-logical **arrays** and global variables used in connection with interrupt handlers, external predicates, graphics, counters etc.

- SEPIA belongs to the Edinburgh family of Prolog dialects, it also contains compatibility libraries for C-Prolog, SICStus and Quintus, which makes it in a high degree compatible with these systems. The SEPIA syntax can be modified to accommodate individual needs.

- Profiling tool to collect statistics about the Prolog execution.
- Stream based I/O.
- There are only very few limits imposed on Prolog data. There is no limit on the number or length of atoms and strings, no limit on the arity of functors, no limit on code size, number of procedures or complexity of clauses so that it can e.g. easily process huge automatically generated Prolog programs.
- SEPIA provides external interface to predicates written in C. It is a lower-level interface which allows to access and modify Prolog data, so that it can be used to integrate various extensions to Prolog. The external predicates can backtrack, delay, call Prolog predicates or be a condition in a delay clause. Structured C data can be mapped on Prolog arrays and global variables. The length of a basic Prolog word is 64 bits so that any external data can be mapped directly on Prolog data. IEEE single floats and 32-bit integers are supported.

  Since a separate word is used for the tag, new types with new tags can be defined and used. A macro facility can be used to convert a source representation of new types into the internal representation with new tags.
- The SEPIA system is accompanied with $\sim$ 1100 pages of documentation and online documentation.

The SEPIA system is being delivered with KEGI which stands for Kernel ECRC Graphic Interface and which is a graphic system that may be used to construct graphic interfaces from Prolog. KEGI consist of three parts, a user programming environment *kegitool*, a 2D graphic package for quick graphic output, and the version 2.5 of PCE, which is an object-oriented graphic system originally developed at the University of Amsterdam, further developed by ICL and ECRC and distributed by ICL. KEGI is running under SunView and X, and programs written for these two systems are source-level compatible.

SEPIA is currently available on the following systems:

1. Sun-3,4/SUNOS 4.0, SunView and X11R4
2. Vax 78*/BSD 4.3
3. Bull DPX-1000 and DPX-2000/SPIX
4. Siemens MX-300 and MX-500/SINIX, X11R3
5. ICL DRS-80/UNIX System V/386 Release 3.2

The binary release of the SEPIA system is available to academic sites for a nominal fee of 300 DM (about $ 200) for any number of machines. For further information and orders please contact the authors or send e-mail to **sepia_request@ecrc.de**.

FIDO: Exploring Finite Domain Consistency Techniques in Logic Programming

*Manfred Meyer**
German Research Center for Artificial Intelligence (DFKI)
P. O. Box 20 80
D-6750 Kaiserslautern
Germany

Jörg Müller & Stefan Schrödl
Computer Science Department
University of Kaiserslautern
P. O. Box 30 49
D-6750 Kaiserslautern
Germany

1 Overview

The inefficiency of standard logic programming languages such as PROLOG for solving combinatorial constrained search problems has led to the design of several constraint logic programming languages combining the declarative aspects of logic programming with the efficiency of constraint-solving techniques. One of these languages is FIDO [9, 8], which extends a usual logic programming language by providing **FI**nite **DO**mains together with efficient consistency techniques such as *forward checking* and *lookahead* [10]. This extension leads to a substantial improvement on efficiency for this class of combinatorial problems and contributes to make constraint logic programming an appropriate tool for expressing and solving constraint satisfaction problems.

In the FIDO laboratory, different approaches towards an integration of finite domain consistency techniques in logic programming are investigated. Starting with the implementation of a *meta-interpreter* for FIDO written in PROLOG (cf. [9]), we subsequently investigated the more sophisticated approach of horizontally compiling FIDO programs into SEPIA [6] by making use of the built-in coroutining mechanism (cf. [8]). This *horizontal compilation* approach made clear that the integration and handling of domain variables is the major issue concerning runtime efficiency and implementation complexity. Therefore, now we have started implementing a *vertical compilation* approach (cf. [3]) compiling finite domain constraints down into a WAM architecture, extending the basic WAM data structures and using a *freeze*-like control scheme. Further developments will include the extension of this approach to dealing with hierarchically structured domains as used in CONTAX, a constraint system currently under development at DFKI as part of the Knowledge Compilation **La**boratory CoLab [1].

---

*The work of the first author is carried out as part of the ARC-TEC project, supported by BMFT under grant ITW 8902 C4. Please, send correspondence to the first author; e-mail: meyer@dfki.uni-kl.de

2 The Meta-Interpretation Approach

When extending PROLOG for handling finite domains by constructing a meta-interpreter, one has to implement one's own meta-unification routine working on an explicit representation of meta-variables. In our approach [9], which is similar to that presented in [5], meta-variables are simply represented as PROLOG terms. Domain-variables can then be implemented by extending the terms representing meta-variables by additional arguments holding the domain, the forward-goals depending on this variable, and pointers to variables and constants which have to be checked for inequality with this domain variable. The domains themselves can be represented using bit vectors or ordered linked-lists. Because of its runtime advantages, we decided to implement a bit vector representation scheme for domains in FIDO.

With this meta-interpretation approach we have been able to run a lot of benchmarks, mostly taken from [10]. These small applications have shown a runtime behaviour of FIDO superior to normal PROLOG execution with backtracking. But, as in general with meta-interpretation, the main disadvantage of this approach remains its lack of efficient runtime performance resulting from the necessity to do a lot of work on the meta-level, which the underlying PROLOG system could do fairly more efficiently.

3 The Horizontal Compilation Approach

Because of the drawbacks of the meta-interpretation approach we went to a next step towards FIDO implementation, which led us to horizontal compilation. The aim of this approach is to build an intermediate step carrying the control regime and the work to be done for domain handling down to lower system layers, finally arriving at the WAM itself. One of the main ideas in doing horizontal compilation for FIDO is to make use of coroutining, which in SEPIA is forced by introducing `delay` declarations. More sophisticated control can be gained without introducing much runtime overhead. The very heart of the horizontal compilation model is a preprocessor compiling ordinary PROLOG programs enhanced by control declarations (e.g. forward checking, lookahead and domain definitions) into a standard PROLOG (SEPIA) program with `delay` declarations, thus performing a source-to-source transformation. This approach is based on ideas presented in [2]. For most applications, lookahead is too inefficient as it produces much overhead. This is the reason why, in the horizontal approach, we directed our attention towards forward checking. Besides a general forward checking algorithm for arbitrary constraints, for some frequently used constraints (such as $\neq =, <$, and $>$), we provide specialized forward checking implementations to optimize access behaviour. A more detailed discussion can be found in [7].

Both the FIDO meta-interpreter and the preprocessor are implemented in SEPIA and are running on SUN4 workstations. First run time results show a significant performance improvement by using horizontal compilation and coroutining: The preprocessed program solves the 16 queens problem about seven times faster than the meta-interpreted program does with the 8 queens problem.

4 The Vertical Compilation Approach

Although the results for FIDO appear quite reasonable for smaller applications, the limitations become rather clear once we try to solve more complex real-life problems.[1] This elucidates the need for a deeper integration of domain handling, domain variable unification and consistency techniques into the PROLOG system, which leads us to a modification of the WAM..

The two major aspects for integrating finite domain constraints in the WAM are a mechanism for the revised control strategies (*forward checking*, *lookahead*) and an extension of the WAM unification algorithm coping with domain unification together with a set of domain-variable specific WAM instructions. At the moment we have started with the design and implementation of the domain unification routine for handling finite domains. By using the WAM compilation scheme presented in [4], it will then be possible to deduce the new WAM instructions by partially evaluating the basic WAM domain-unification routine.

References

[1] H. Boley, P. Hanschke, K. Hinkelmann, and M. Meyer. COLAB: A Hybrid Knowledge Compilation Laboratory. 3rd International Workshop on Data, Expert Knowledge and Decisions: Using Knowledge to Transform Data into Information for Decision Support, September 1991.

[2] D. de Schreye, D. Pollet, J. Ronsyn, and M. Bruynooghe. Implementing Finite–domain Constraint Logic Programming on Top of a PROLOG–System with Delay–mechanism. In N. Jones, editor, *Proc. of ESOP 90*, pages 106–117, 1990.

[3] H.-G. Hein. Consistency Techniques in WAM-based Architectures. Diploma thesis, Universität Kaiserslautern, FB Informatik, Postfach 3049, D-6750 Kaiserslautern, 1991. Forthcoming.

[4] H.-G. Hein and M. Meyer. A WAM Compilation Scheme. In *Proceedings of the 2nd Russian Conference on Logic Programming.* Lecture Notes in AI, Springer-Verlag, Heidelberg, 1991.

[5] Ch. Holzbaur. Realization of Forward Checking in Logic Programming through Extended Unification. Technical Report TR–90–11, Austrian Research Institute for AI, June 1990.

[6] M. Meier, A. Aggoun, D. Chan, P. Dufresne, R. Enders, D.H. de Villeneuve, A. Herold, P. Kay, B. Perez, E. van Rossum, and J. Schimpf. SEPIA – An Extendible Prolog System. In G. Ritter, editor, *Proceedings of the IFIP 11th World Computer Congress*, pages 1127–1132, August 1989.

[7] M. Meyer, H.-G. Hein, and J. Müller. FIDO: Finite Domain Consistency Techniques in Logic Programming. In *Proceedings of the 2nd Russian Conference on Logic Programming.* Lecture Notes in AI, Springer-Verlag, Heidelberg, 1991.

[8] J. Müller. Design and Implementation of a Finite Domain Constraint Logic Programming System based on PROLOG with Coroutining. Diploma thesis, Universität Kaiserslautern, FB Informatik, Postfach 3049, D-6750 Kaiserslautern, 1991. Forthcoming.

[9] S. Schrödl. FIDO: Ein Constraint-Logic-Programming-System mit Finite Domains. ARC-TEC Discussion Paper 91-05, DFKI GmbH, Postfach 2080, D-6750 Kaiserslautern, June 1991.

[10] P. van Hentenryck. *Constraint Satisfaction in Logic Programming.* MIT Press, 1989.

[1] The run time for N queens grows significantly for problems of $N > 50$. The CHIP approach providing a deep integration of domains and consistency techniques into the WAM becomes the more superior the more complex the applications are.

Lecture Notes in Artificial Intelligence (LNAI)

Lecture Notes in Computer Science

Vol. 509: A. Endres, H. Weber (Eds.), Software Development Environments and CASE Technology. Proceedings, 1991. VIII, 286 pages. 1991.

Vol. 510: J. Leach Albert, B. Monien, M. Rodríguez (Eds.), Automata, Languages and Programming. Proceedings, 1991. XII, 763 pages. 1991.

Vol. 511: A. C. F. Colchester, D.J. Hawkes (Eds.), Information Processing in Medical Imaging. Proceedings, 1991. XI, 512 pages. 1991.

Vol. 512: P. America (Ed.), ECOOP '91. European Conference on Object-Oriented Programming. Proceedings, 1991. X, 396 pages. 1991.

Vol. 513: N. M. Mattos, An Approach to Knowledge Base Management. IX, 247 pages. 1991. (Subseries LNAI).

Vol. 514: G. Cohen, P. Charpin (Eds.), EUROCODE '90. Proceedings, 1990. XI, 392 pages. 1991.

Vol. 515: J. P. Martins, M. Reinfrank (Eds.), Truth Maintenance Systems. Proceedings, 1990. VII, 177 pages. 1991. (Subseries LNAI).

Vol. 516: S. Kaplan, M. Okada (Eds.), Conditional and Typed Rewriting Systems. Proceedings, 1990. IX, 461 pages. 1991.

Vol. 517: K. Nökel, Temporally Distributed Symptoms in Technical Diagnosis. IX, 164 pages. 1991. (Subseries LNAI).

Vol. 518: J. G. Williams, Instantiation Theory. VIII, 133 pages. 1991. (Subseries LNAI).

Vol. 519: F. Dehne, J.-R. Sack, N. Santoro (Eds.), Algorithms and Data Structures. Proceedings, 1991. X, 496 pages. 1991.

Vol. 520: A. Tarlecki (Ed.), Mathematical Foundations of Computer Science 1991. Proceedings, 1991. XI, 435 pages. 1991.

Vol. 521: B. Bouchon-Meunier, R. R. Yager, L. A. Zadek (Eds.), Uncertainty in Knowledge-Bases. Proceedings, 1990. X, 609 pages. 1991.

Vol. 522: J. Hertzberg (Ed.), European Workshop on Planning. Proceedings, 1991. VII, 121 pages. 1991. (Subseries LNAI).

Vol. 523: J. Hughes (Ed.), Functional Programming Languages and Computer Architecture. Proceedings, 1991. VIII, 666 pages. 1991.

Vol. 524: G. Rozenberg (Ed.), Advances in Petri Nets 1991. VIII, 572 pages. 1991.

Vol. 525: O. Günther, H.-J. Schek (Eds.), Large Spatial Databases. Proceedings, 1991. XI, 471 pages. 1991.

Vol. 526: T. Ito, A. R. Meyer (Eds.), Theoretical Aspects of Computer Software. Proceedings, 1991. X, 772 pages. 1991.

Vol. 527: J.C.M. Baeten, J. F. Groote (Eds.), CONCUR '91. Proceedings, 1991. VIII, 541 pages. 1991.

Vol. 528: J. Maluszynski, M. Wirsing (Eds.) Programming Language Implementation and Logic Programming. Proceedings, 1991. XI, 433 pages. 1991.

Vol. 529: L. Budach (Ed.) Fundamentals of Computation Theory. Proceedings, 1991. XII, 426 pages. 1991.

Vol. 530: D. H. Pitt, P.-L. Curien, S. Abramsky, A. M. Pitts, A. Poigné, D. E. Rydeheard (Eds.), Category Theory and Computer Science. Proceedings, 1991. VII, 301 pages. 1991.

Vol. 531: E. M. Clarke, R. P. Kurshan (Eds.), Computer-Aided Verification. Proceedings, 1990. VIII, 372 pages. 1991.

Vol. 532: H. Ehrig, H.-J. Kreowski, G. Rozenberg (Eds.), Graph Grammars and Their Application to Computer Science. Proceedings, 1990. X, 703 pages. 1991.

Vol. 533: E. Börger, H. Kleine Büning, M. M. Richter, W. Schönfeld (Eds.), Computer Science Logic. Proceedings, 1990. VIII, 399 pages. 1991.

Vol. 534: H. Ehrig, K. P. Jantke, F. Orejas, H. Reichel (Eds.), Recent Trends in Data Type Specification. Proceedings, 1990. VIII, 379 pages. 1991.

Vol. 535: P. Jorrand, J. Kelemen (Eds.), Fundamentals of Artificial Intelligence Research. Proceedings, 1991. VIII, 255 pages. 1991. (Subseries LNAI).

Vol. 536: J. E. Tomayko, Software Engineering Education. Proceedings, 1991. VIII, 296 pages. 1991.

Vol. 539: H. F. Mattson, T. Mora, T. R. N. Rao (Eds.), Applied Algebra, Algebraic Algorithms and Error-Correcting Codes. Proceedings, 1991. XI, 489 pages. 1991.

Vol. 540: A. Prieto (Ed.), Artificial Neural Networks. Proceedings, 1991. XIII, 476 pages. 1991.

Vol. 541: P. Barahona, L. Moniz Pereira, A. Porto (Eds.), EPIA '91. Proceedings, 1991. VIII, 292 pages. 1991. (Subseries LNAI).

Vol. 542: Z. W. Ras, M. Zemankova (Eds.), Methodologies for Intelligent Systems. Proceedings, 1991. X, 644 pages. 1991. (Subseries LNAI).

Vol. 543: J. Dix, K. P. Jantke, P. H. Schmitt (Eds.), Nonmonotonic and Inductive Logic. Proceedings, 1990. X, 243 pages. 1991. (Subseries LNAI).

Vol. 546: O. Herzog, C.-R. Rollinger (Eds.), Text Understanding in LILOG. XI, 738 pages. 1991. (Subseries LNAI).

Vol. 549: E. Ardizzone, S. Gaglio, F. Sorbello (Eds.), Trends in Artificial Intelligence. Proceedings, 1991. XIV, 479 pages. 1991. (Subseries LNAI).

Vol. 565: J. D. Becker, I. Eisele, F. W. Mündemann (Eds.), Parallelism, Learning, Evolution. Proceedings, 1989. VIII, 525 pages. 1991. (Subseries LNAI).

Vol. 567: H. Boley, M. M. Richter (Eds.), Processing Declarative Kowledge. Proceedings, 1991. XII, 427 pages. 1991. (Subseries LNAI).